MW01401013

WATCHES 2000 INTERNATIONAL

THE ORIGINAL ANNUAL OF THE WORLD'S FINEST WRISTWATCHES

First published in the United States of America in 2000 by

Tourbillon International, LLC.
11 West 25 Street, 8th floor
New York, NY 10010
Tel: +1 (212) 627-7732 - Telefax +1 (212) 627-9093
Web-site: www.tourbillon-watches.com

CHAIRMAN
Joseph Zerbib

CHIEF EXECUTIVE OFFICER & PUBLISHER
Caroline Childers

EDITORIAL DIRECTOR
Maurizio Zinelli

EDITOR-IN-CHIEF
Renata Pescatori

In association with

RIZZOLI
INTERNATIONAL PUBLICATIONS INC.

300 Park Avenue South
New York, NY 10010
John Brancati, VICE PRESIDENT & GENERAL MANAGER, RIZZOLI BOOKSTORES

Distributed by St. Martin's Press

COPYRIGHT©2000 TOURBILLON INTERNATIONAL, LLC.
ALL RIGHTS RESERVED

No part of this publication may be reproduced in any manner whatsoever without prior permission in writing from Tourbillon International, LLC.

ISBN: 0-8478-2309-1

LIBRARY OF CONGRESS CATALOG CARD NUMBER: 00-090587

DISCLAIMER: THE INFORMATION CONTAINED IN WATCHES INTERNATIONAL 2000 HAS BEEN PROVIDED BY THIRD PARTIES. WHILE WE BELIEVE THAT THESE SOURCES ARE RELIABLE, WE ASSUME NO RESPONSIBILTY OR LIABILITY FOR THE ACCURACY OF TECHNICAL DETAILS CONTAINED IN THIS BOOK.

EVERY EFFORT HAS BEEN MADE TO LOCATE THE COPYRIGHT HOLDERS OF MATERIALS IN THIS BOOK. SHOULD THERE BE ANY ERRORS OR OMISSIONS, WE APOLOGIZE AND SHALL BE PLEASED TO MAKE ACKNOWLEDGEMENTS IN FUTURE EDITIONS.

PRINTED IN SINGAPORE

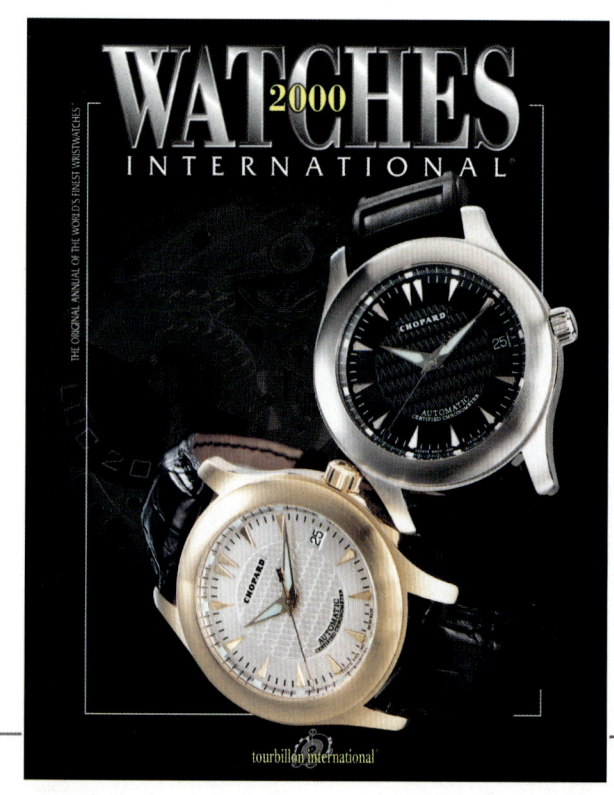

de GRISOGONO®
GENEVE

INSTRUMENTO
Nº UNO

STAINLESS STEEL AUTOMATIC WATCH WITH DUAL TIME ZONE AND OVERSIZED DATE
BLACKENED MOVEMENT AND CROWN SET WITH A NATURAL BLACK DIAMOND

GENEVA - PARIS - LONDON - GSTAAD

(41 22) 317 10 80
www.degrisogono.com

Dear Reader,

After launching so many successful books on luxury timepieces throughout the past decade, I am incredibly enthusiastic about this newest joint venture. As BW Publishing teamed up with Editoriale Tourbillon - publishers of Le Collezioni OROLOGI..., a book that during the past decade has set the standard for watch publications around the world - a thrill went through me.

We were about to embark not just on an adventure into the new millennium together, but also on an adventure into a new era of watch appreciation and devotion. Together, with the backing of internationally renowned Rizzoli and St. Martin's Press, this expert international team now unveils a unique reference annual for watch lovers - WATCHES International 2000.

WATCHES International 2000 offers an intoxicating wealth of information, complete with the rich flavor of heritage and craftsmanship associated with the distinguished art of watchmaking. With 300 full color pages, this fine annual presents not only an historical overview of the world's leading brands, but also a peek inside each brand's hallowed halls to highlights of the latest product innovations. Photographs with unparalleled technical descriptions make this the most complete reference book for watch lovers, collectors, retailers, makers and aficionados of luxury goods in general.

What's more, we are poised on the horizon of an exciting time. The new venture brings together the expertise of an already successful publication and the talents of BW's top-notch consumer writers. This fabulous new publication is now distributed in First and Business class airport lounges and flight sections, in Rizzoli and Barnes & Nobel Bookstores, and via top retail stores and newsstands worldwide.

While we're incredibly proud to present WATCHES International 2000, as we sit on the dawn of a new horizon, we look forward to the opportunity to make Watches International 2001 even more captivating, motivating and inspiring via lifestyle reporting on sectors related to the lives of watch aficionados. We invite you to join us in our venture.

Caroline Childers

The publication in your hands and that you are about to consult, is the result of an idea that has been a reality in Italy over the last ten years. As a matter of fact we originally created a product that would integrate the existing offer of monthly magazines and our publication would be the first annual review in the world, dedicated to high quality watches to be sold to the general public.

In the meantime the rights of the original Italian "OROLOGI meccanici più prestigiosi del mondo" have been transferred to foreign publishers to be translated, published and distributed in other countries. The idea was so smart that some publisher simply copied it in form and contents.

The reason why this happened is that the Italian market is very particular. So much so that for years Swiss watchmakers have used it as a test ground to obtain basic indications of the potential of their medium-high class models. This has allowed specialized publishers to acquire specific know-how in the watchmaking sector.

The joint venture between Editoriale Tourbillon of Rome and BW Publishing of New York results in the establishment of a new publishing company, Tourbillon International.

This is a minor-scale parallel of what is happening in the world of Swiss watchmaking. Here we have recently seen the conglomeration (financial, operational or both) of many names with a more or less declared increase of the potential of the single participants.

The first issue of the international edition - WATCHES International 2000, The Original Annual of the World's Finest Wristwatches - would like to launch the result of our work in the most positive way possible. Our goal is in fact to induce an increasing number of people to consider the culture of watches, especially mechanical ones, so that they can appreciate their value, starting from the mechanism and leading them through an overall and very detailed presentation, in order to give them the possibility to understand and to love these diminutive works of art, that are the object of our passion.

Maurizio Zinelli

EBEL

T H E   A R C H I T E C T S   O F   T I M E

"Sport Classic XL" in steel and gold. Water resistant to 50m. 5 year international warranty.

HARRISON FORD AND HIS SPORT CLASSIC

portrait by Hans Gissinger

WATCHES 2000 INTERNATIONAL

THE ORIGINAL ANNUAL OF THE WORLD'S FINEST WRISTWATCHES

Tourbillon International, LLC.
HEAD OFFICE, ADMINISTRATION, ADVERTISING SALES
11 West 25th Street, 8th floor, New York, NY 10010
Tf. +1 (212) 627-7732 - Fax +1 (212) 627-9093
E-mail: cchilders@bway.net

CHAIRMAN
Joseph Zerbib

CHIEF EXECUTIVE OFFICER & PUBLISHER
Caroline Childers

EDITORIAL DIRECTOR
Maurizio Zinelli

EDITOR-IN-CHIEF
Renata Pescatori

TECHNICAL CONSULTANT
Roland G. Murphy

ASSOCIATE EDITORS
Nicole Coppey, Roberta Naas, Norma Buchanan

DISTRIBUTION
Rizzoli, John Brancati, Vice President & General Manager, Rizzoli Bookstores

WORLDWIDE DISTRIBUTION
St. Martin's Press

EDITORIAL DIVISION, SUSCRIPTIONS & ORDERS
Tourbillon International
Via Pietro Maestri 3, 00191 Rome, Italy
Tf. +39 (06) 3294-976 - Fax +39 (06) 3294-977
E-mail: tourbillon@tourbillon.it

CONTRIBUTING EDITORS
Paolo Gobbi, Barbara Notarangelo, Verena Fisher, Maurizio M. Alessi, Maria Teresa Steri, Donatella Aragozzini, Gabriele Marconi, Alessandro Lodolini, Dante Cortis

TRANSLATIONS
Igino Schraffl, Susan O'Leary

ART DIRECTOR
Franca Vitali - E-mail: graficaeffe@mclink.it

EDP MANAGER
Marco Biancotto

PHOTOGRAPHERS
Corinto Marianelli, Studio Sergio Bortolotti
PHOTOGRAPHS ARCHIVE, PROPERTY OF EDITORIALE TOURBILLON SRL

ART DIRECTOR WEB-SITE
Dimitri Darseyne - E-mail: impact42@yahoo.com

Editorial

Perhaps nothing in life is as influential and all-encompassing as time. Time governs all we do, all we accomplish and all we strive to achieve. As a result, one of the most pervasive, important and inspiring things in our lives is timekeeping.

Over the centuries, timepieces of all sorts have recorded times of athletes in competition, of the breaking of world records, of new ventures. And always, the timepieces made to track such monumental moments in our lives, evolve.

Luxury watchmaking is a practiced art, one handed down from generation to generation. Only in the past few decades have high-technology and computer aided design entered the world of watchmaking - and then only in terms of research and design. High-resolution monitors reveal the expert's ideas for cases and movements, simulate the interaction of the movement pieces, and signal the feasibility of the design. But the most complex and luxurious timepieces are still made by hand at the watchmaker's bench.

In well-lighted watch factories nestled in different regions of Switzerland, the finest master watchmakers toil for hours creating complex movements, fine-tuning precision instruments for sport watches, and working side by side with gem setters - meticulously placing diamonds and other fine gemstones into high-jewelry pieces.

It is the dedication of these master watchmakers, along with the allure of their work, that makes fine watches reign supreme. Watch lovers, aficionados, and collectors abound. These are people for whom watches are an aphrodisiac, something that's "in their blood" - "must-have" items. This is the reason so many watches at auction command record-breaking prices, why waiting lists exist for the most complicated timepieces. What's more, most of these watch lovers crave knowledge about these fine houses that have mastered the art of watchmaking, and about the newest creations and innovations they have developed.

The pages of WATCHES International 2000 pay homage to these fine houses, to the heritage they continue in and the legacies they leave to us. As a veteran journalist with nearly 20 years in the watch industry, I have witnessed the coming and going of many watch-related publications. I believe that WATCHES International 2000 is a winner, and its subsequent annual issues can only shine brighter.

Roberta Naas

Would You Park a Ferrari on the Street?

*Then surely you don't drop
your fine watches into a drawer.*

Serious watch enthusiasts the world over use Scatola del Tempo boxes. With compartments for bracelet or strap watches and rotors to keep automatic watches fully wound–they're the ideal place for fine watch collections.

Single-watch boxes are more than a convenience - they help watches last longer and run more accurately.

Choose from more than two dozen Italian handcrafted leather-and-silk collector boxes.

SCATOLA del TEMPO ®

The World's Finest Time Keepers.

S.C.S. & Co. - Via dei Mille, 17 - I 23891 Barzanò - ITALY - Tel. +39 039 9211481 - Fax +39 039 958970 - www.scatoladeltempo.com

BEDAT & C° N°7 STEEL SET WITH PRINCESS CUT TOURMALINE (LEFT) OR DIAMONDS (RIGHT) FROM US$ 6'950.-

INFORMATION OR CATALOGS AT
BEDAT & C° USA
3501 CALIFORNIA STREET · SUITE 200 · SAN FRANCISCO · CA 94118 · TOLL FREE 1-877-2332826 · WWW.BEDAT.COM

BEDAT & C° HAS CREATED THE A.O.S.C.® QUALITY LABEL IN ORDER TO GUARANTEE THE SWISS QUALITY OF ITS COMPONENTS AND THE HIGH MANUFACTURING STANDARD OF ITS TIMEPIECES. BEDAT & C° GENEVE AND SWISS A.O.S.C.® ARE REGISTERED TRADEMARKS OF BEDAT & BEDAT SA, GENEVA, SWITZERLAND

BEDAT & C°
GENEVE

Summary

Editorials	pag. 6
Master watchmakers	pag. 16

Vincent Calabrese,
Svend Andersen,
Antoine Preziuso,
Kiu Tai Yu,
Philippe Dufour,
Christiaan van der Klaauw,
Cédric Johner

Jewellers' parade	pag. 24

de Grisogono,
Casa Damiani,
Fred

Design & Fashion	pag. 28

Versace

Introduction	pag. 33
Watches collections	pag. 34
Addresses	pag. 298

A. Lange & Söhne	pag. 34
Audemars Piguet	pag. 38
Baume & Mercier	pag. 46
Bedat & Co.	pag. 48
Blancpain	pag. 56
Boucheron	pag. 62
Breguet	pag. 68
Breitling	pag. 72
Bulgari	pag. 80
Cartier	pag. 84
Chaumet	pag. 90
Chopard	pag. 94
Concord	pag. 110
Daniel JeanRichard	pag. 118
Daniel Roth	pag. 124
Ebel	pag. 128
Eberhard	pag. 132
European Company Watch	pag. 142
Franck Muller	pag. 144
Gérald Genta	pag. 152
Girard-Perregaux	pag. 156
Glashütte Original	pag. 174
Hublot	pag. 182
Iwc	pag. 186
Jaeger-Le Coultre	pag. 194
Officine Panerai	pag. 202
Omega	pag. 206
Parmigiani Fleurier	pag. 210
Patek Philippe	pag. 216
Paul Picot	pag. 228
Piaget	pag. 242
Raymond Weil	pag. 248
Roger Dubuis	pag. 250
Rolex	pag. 256
Sdt Scatola Del Tempo	pag. 264
Tag Heuer	pag. 270
Ulysse Nardin	pag. 274
Vacheron Constantin	pag. 280
Van Cleef & Arpels	pag. 286
Zannetti	pag. 290
Zenith	pag. 294

INNER BEAUTY.

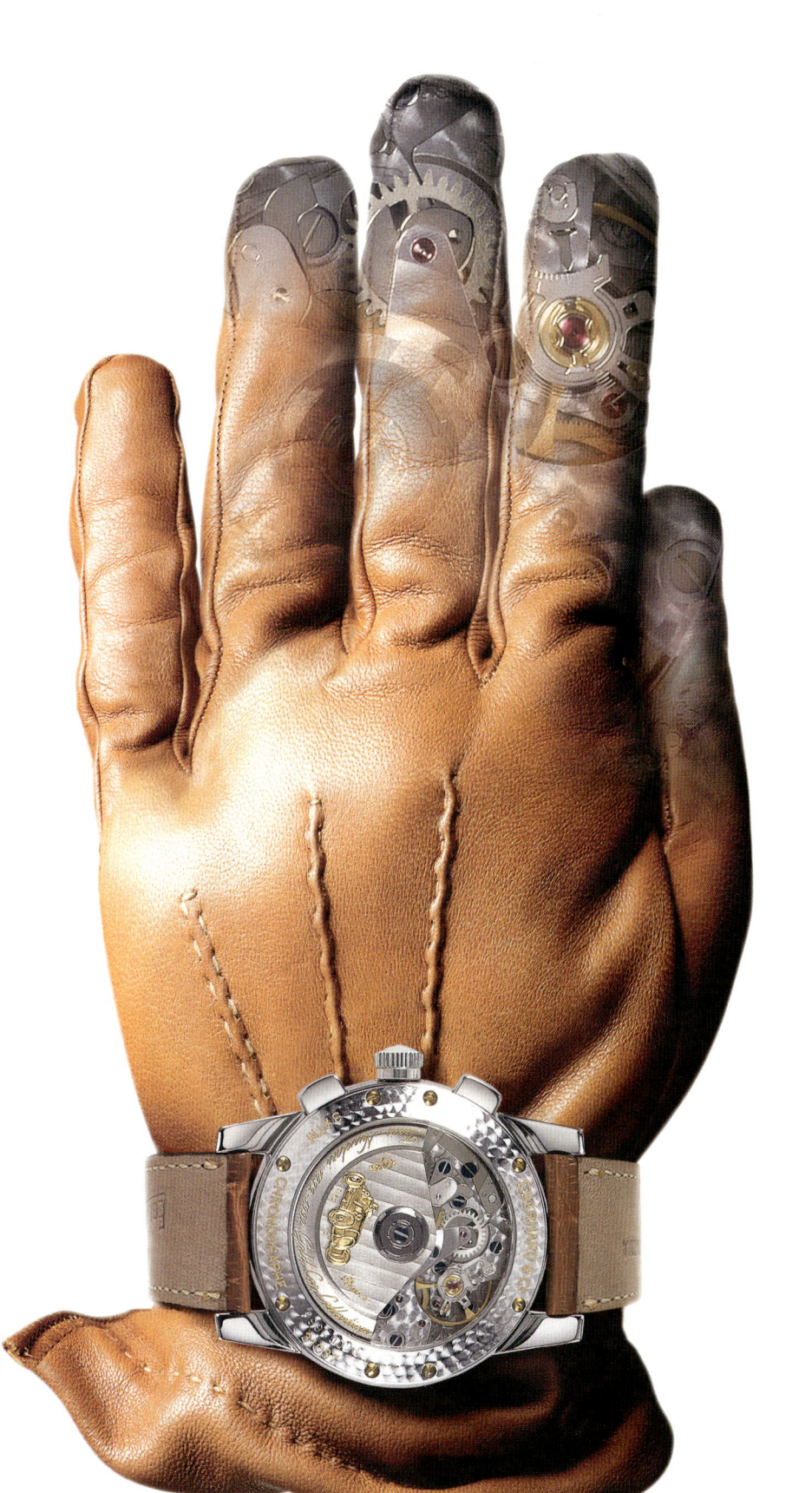

Tazio Nuvolari
Gold Car Collection
Ref. 31037 - Steel - 3 atm.

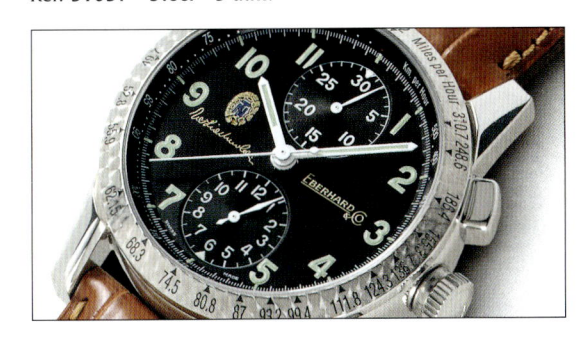

A veritable beauty from top to bottom, the *Tazio Nuvolari Gold Car Collection* is a special edition of that chronograph which Eberhard & Co. has dedicated to the great Tazio Nuvolari. One unusual feature of this extra-special model is its transparent caseback which reveals the magnificent workmanship imparted to its movement with its rotor showing an 18 ct gold replica of the Alfa Romeo which the "Flying Mantuan" used to drive to his legendary victories. Water-resistant down to 3 atm. and made of stainless steel, the *Tazio Nuvolari Gold Car Collection* looks all set to be another best-seller from Eberhard & Co.

EBERHARD&CO

Manufacture Suisse d'Horlogerie depuis 1887

EBERHARD & CO. S.A. - BIENNE - SUISSE

International Trade: ASTOR TIME LTD. - Lugano - Tel. +41 91/993.26.01 - Fax +41 91/993.26.05

www.eberhard-co-watches.ch

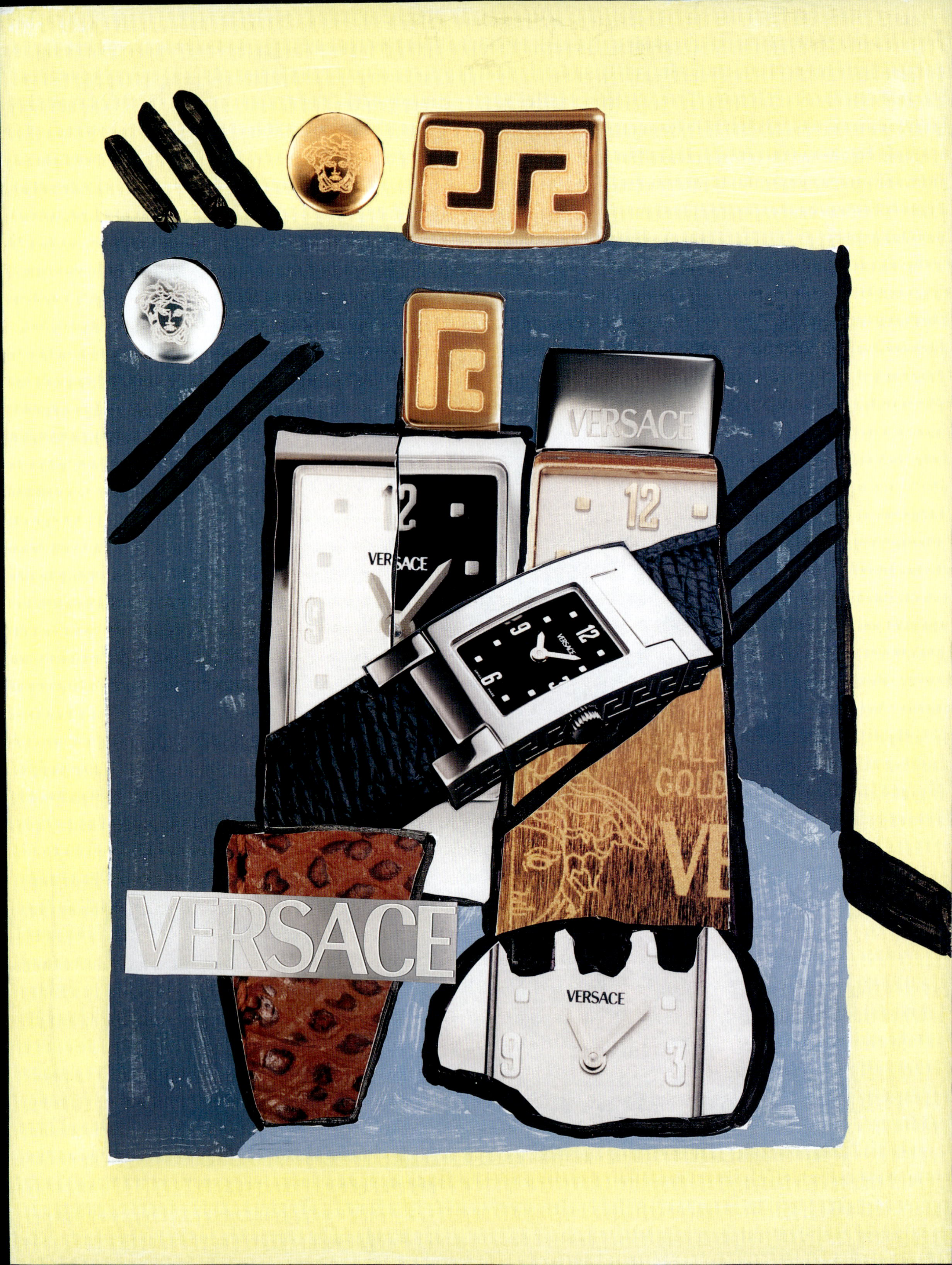
VERSACE
VERSACE
VERSACE
VERSACE

VERSACE

GRECA FOR THE MILLENIUM

It owes its name to the Grecian frieze, the signature so dear to Versace, found on this model and engraved into the gently curving sides of the watch and bracelet. This pattern, revived from antiquity, encircles the wrist in a refined yet deliberately contemporary creation. The rectangular case is perfectly aligned with links forming a semi-rigid band designed to be worn like a bracelet.

For the millennium, Versace made a luminous version of the GRECA model. Colored gemstones such as tourmalines, peridots, tsavorites or diamonds are set in the polished stainless steel of the case and the bracelet. The pink Millenium watch is outstandingly feminine, crafted entirely in rubies, and becomes a brilliant accessory of eye-catching significance for the spring-summer fashion.

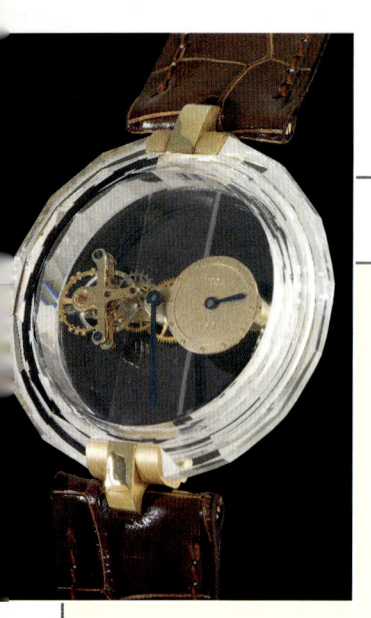

Master watchmakers

Small but significant: this is how we have chosen to open this chapter of our Annual Review. News from the world of fine watchmaking, created by small companies but with a significant impact on the reality in which they operate. We will begin with small, independent, master watchmakers who, in recent years, have been receiving their due recognition. Their stands at the specialized expositions are where curiosity reigns supreme, where marvel is not ignited by gleaming gold but rather by the surprising complications. The AHCI signs (this academy has united some of these master craftsmen under one banner), for example, attract connoisseurs and the curious as well as directors of the important houses. Between one important meeting and another, they do not forget to browse there, secretly hoping to come across something extraordinary, the latest ingenious expression of these small, self-contained entrepreneurs. In all the great Manufactures, each new, fabulous proposal is the child of a creation by a single artist, who has put brain, heart and imagination at the service of his talented, highly trained hands. The Academy of Independent "creators", with its brilliant and cosmopolitan delegation, is always an appreciated presence at watchmaking expositions throughout Europe. It has brought together about fifteen members exhibiting handcrafted creations that are often stupefying for their technical level. Among their tourbillon and jumping functions, minute repeaters or rare and bizarre complications often enriched by just as bizarre decorations, the Academy members do not produce only wristwatches. The photos on these pages represent their most recent production. They also have given thought to the dear old "turnips" that had been in Grandfather's pocket and have produced pieces of great watchmaking, with original pendulum clocks for wall or table and long case watches with chimes.

Vincent Calabrese

His name is the immediate synthesis of what is Italian and Swiss, as are even more so his creations demonstrate aesthetic research and technological mastery. He is one of the two founders of AHCI (the other is Svend Andersen). As an independent watchmaker, he has kept his love for extreme exploration. His "transparent" watches are very famous among the lovers of fine watchmaking for their aligned movements; the Baladin Jumping-Hour with mobile hour and minute aperture. The dial is dominated by formal purity and is the ideal stage for this unusual representation of time. A more classic level, where the art of watchmaking bridles time in conventional spaces, offers Calabrese the idea for a more traditional collection (double time zone, power reserve, weeks or day-night). There is the extraordinary Petra: sapphire crystal case, either wholly transparent or diamond pavé dial. His latest pieces develop some of the artist and mechanical themes he likes best. First of all the Tourbillon Phantom which encloses in a sophisticated sapphire crystal case a small masterpiece of fine mechanics: a tourbillon with gold carriage, regulator display (central minutes, hours at 3, seconds integrated with the tourbillon carriage). Then there is a series of models whose movement follows graphics chosen by the client (a letter or a drawing): here we have Pegasus, ordered by a Japanese client, and where the movement is concealed in the representation of the winged horse. Its golden bridges between two sheets of sapphire crystal enclosed in a gold case represents the union between artist and master watchmaker, The collection Horus has new dials, red for the steel case, white for the gold. It works the same with its small additional zone, provided with an hour hand, which moving clockwise, turns on itself however counter-clockwise to keep the 12 on top and shows the minutes on the flange. The latest innovation is the Internet site www.vincent-calabrese.ch, a window open to the world showing the experiments and innovations of this modern master of fine mechanics.

Noblesse du détail

TECHNICUM

Self-winding chronograph with fly-back second hand, power reserve and complete calendar.

Water-resistant to 50 m. Certified « Chronometer » by C.O.S.C.

Paul Picot
Artisan - Horloger - Suisse

Paul Picot S.A. - 2340 Le Noirmont - Switzerland - Tel. **4132 953 15 31 - Fax **4132 953 10 45 - www.paulpicot.ch - E-mail: paulpicot@bluewin.ch

Master watchmakers

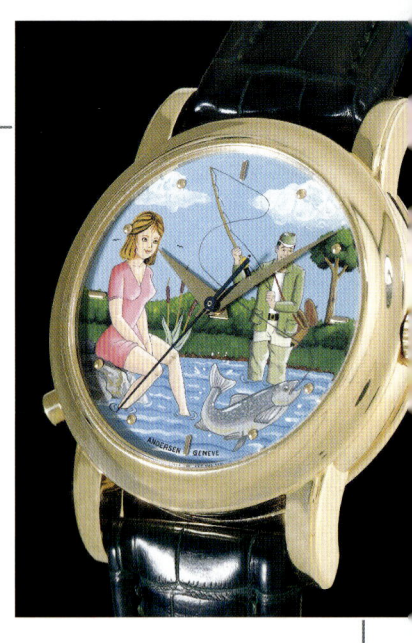

Svend Andersen

Svend Andersen and Vincent Calabrese together founded the Académie Horlogère des Créateurs and worked together at Patek Philippe, which encouraged his passion for complex movements. The smallest calendar in the world and the thinnest GMT are his creations. Andersen's creative energy moves from particular complications (like the Perpetual Secular Calendar or the Alarm) to the purely aesthetic (like Châton or Etrier). Among the Danish master's more particular creations is the erotic watch, discretely hidden on the back of a classic hour and minute: in Eros the automata are operated by pressure on a side pusher and do not mechanically interfere with the working of the watch. Different from the erotic pocket watches which came before it, these are made up of 11 movable elements as opposed to three or four in the others. For the year 2000 Andersen presents a new erotic subject which we could call "sports fishing". This possibility is not new in the world of "libertine" watchmaking, and was used in pocket and table watches in the early XIXth century where a seemingly innocent dial or cover hid scenes that were not vaguely erotic as much as they were comically depressing. The collection "Montre à tact" is also developed and interprets in an exclusively aesthetic key the famous creations of Abraham-Louis Breguet. The new pieces have, besides the usual "secret" display of the hour between the lugs (allowing the watch to be read without turning the dial up) two new gold dials with engine-turned (guilloché) finish, one with traditional hours and minutes and the other with the aperture in the upper part and showing the Empire State Building.

Antoine Preziuso

Antoine Preziuso has an old-fashioned story. He put his first watch together at seven and continued to exercise this curiosity up through the end of his studies (at the Geneva Watchmaking Institute). He worked for the most exclusive Swiss manufactures and finally was able to create his own brand. The great complications have no mystery for him, his pieces show how the old art of watchmaking can easily blend with the newest aesthetic forms. The focal point of his skill is in "rewriting" the great classics, by changing them without betraying their contents and aesthetic values. And this would be evident even without the Geneva Seal. The platinum Traveller Tourbillon is his perfect visiting card: an extraordinary product with double jumping hours for local time and for the second time zone. The dial, in palladium white gold, hand-engraved, shows a bas-relief theme of man, travel, time and a glimpse of Geneva. Preziuso has paid homage to his origins in the wrist version of the clock of the "Torre del Mangia" on the Piazza del Campo in Siena. The marble dial reproduces the original hour and minute markers and hands of the great clock. The small chronograph (diameter 31 mm) with bell-shaped case and knot-shaped lugs is animated by an old Valjoux 69 10''' caliber that can be seen through the back. His most recent collection continues to evolve and is characterized by the elegantly tonneau-curved case. The Hours of Love are part of this collection with automata on the back. The bezel is available hand-engraved and set with diamonds. The Heure du Monde is absolutely new and is available both in gold and in steel, characterized by the indication of two different time zones, one central and one on an additional zone at 6, with the particular aperture at 12 which shows six reference cities chosen by the client. It has an automatic movement by ETA caliber 2004, greatly modified to put the new functions in place. The last proposal among the tonneau is the Olympic Dreams chronograph, in steel or gold with automatic movement caliber 1185 by Frédéric Piguet with hand-engraved 21 kt gold rotor.

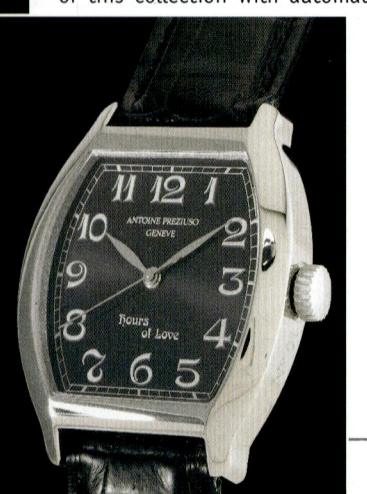

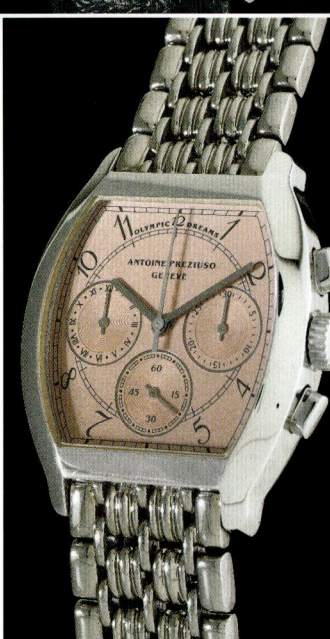

Torus Quantième Perpétuel Model. Gentlemen's automatic wristwatch (diameter 41 mm) with perpetual calendar, moon phases, indication of day, date, month and leap year. See-through back revealing 22 ct red gold oscillating weight. Available in 18 ct yellow gold or platinum. International 10-year guarantee. Swiss hand-made.

PARMIGIANI
FLEURIER

Célébrer le Temps.

For any further information, please contact:

USA *Horological Works* T +1 203 531 32 76 • **Japan** *Europassion SA* T +81 662 45 55 71 • **China/Hong Kong** *Times Concept Intl.* T +852 27 23 30 33 • **Taiwan** *Healthy Develop Trading Co. Ltd* T +886 2 25 79 61 86 • **Singapore** *Yafriro International Pte Ltd.* T +65 734 48 86 • **Middle East** *Startime Middle East Co.* T +971 422 88 850 • **Argentina** *Richard Courbrant* T +5411 43 22 10 38 **Spain** *Pamies Collectors* T +34 977 12 75 14 • **France** *Kronometry* T +33 4 97 06 69 70 • **Germany/Denmark** *Falco-Markenvertrieb* T +49 482 19 28 38 • **Belgium** *Ginotti Jewellers* T +32 32 31 56 92 • **Italy** *Alexander & Paul s.r.l.* T +39 02 551 909 42 • **Switzerland** *Gübelin Jewelry & Watches* T +41 41 429 15 15

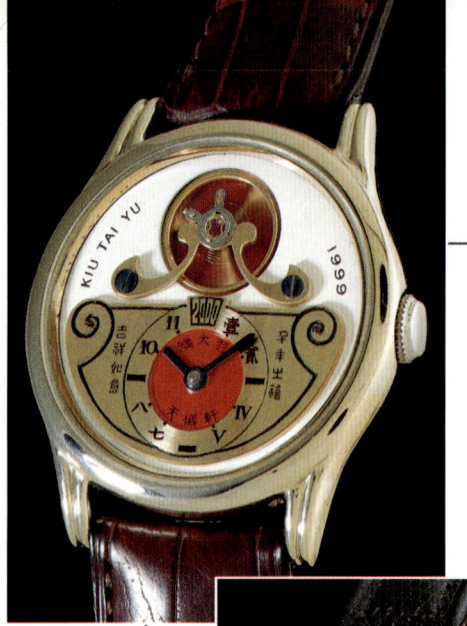

Master watchmakers

Kiu Tai Yu

Each watch by Kiu Tai Yu represents, for those who look at it, a trip into another aesthetics, the Far East aesthetics. Chinese lacquerware and gold, sensual curves and ideograms recreate the formal canons of watchmaking through a cultural diaphragm which is completely different from tradition. His creations, starting from the Tourbillon Flying models, the only example of this mechanism now made for wrist watch, include the Mystery Tourbillon Rectangular, made in pink, yellow and white gold volutes and a rectangular yellow and white gold case, that follows the curve of the wrist, recalls the ancient shapes of the pagoda. Then the Mystery Flying Tourbillon No. 12 (tourbillon at 9 and hour and minute zone at 2) is also full of classic decorative elements from the Chinese tradition cleverly substituting the conventional minute markers of the dial and zones. Tourbillon No. 13 includes all the classical technical themes of this Oriental master watchmaker: visible flying tourbillon carriage and off-center hours. In this particular example, the balance and balance-spring are off-center with respect to the tourbillon carriage and a six marker wheel is mounted on the escapement wheel. The tourbillon seems not to hold mysteries for Kiu Tai Yu, having investigated virtually all the technical solutions allowed by this complication. We must stress that every single piece of this splendid watches, from the case to the dial, to the movement itself, is completely hand-made and produced in single specimens, each incredibly fascinating. The last piece, Tourbillon No. 14, called "Joy of the Millennium", made entirely in platinum, has as its distinctive element the organization of the dial, the big upper bridge that sustains the tourbillon carriage and the hours indicator off-center and in the lower part. This artistically recalls the "delicate" mechanisms of the heavenly clocks, the Chinese astronomical clocks, used more than 1000 years ago.

Philippe Dufour

Philippe Dufour was only 30 when he joined the "brotherhood" of the Independent; he belongs to the very limited number of master watchmakers able to make by themselves all of the fundamental components of a movement. His most prestigious creation is undoubtedly the Grande Sonnerie, awarded the gold medal for the best technical creation at the Basel Show in 1992, queen of the mechanical complications, made entirely in his workshop and only one per year. The one shown in 1999, the sixth to have been made, is characterized by the new hinged bezel which conceals the on/mute selector of the grande and petite sonnerie. In this way the general look of the watches is improved, and only the crown with the minute repeater pusher is external to the gold case. Another constructive detail are the markers applied by a vacuum metalization process on the underside of the crystal, the blued steel hands and the buckle are hand-made. The movement used is a caliber DF 12, hand winding mechanical, completely visible from both in front and behind.

ROGER DUBUIS
horloger genevois

MuchMore

For further information on this and other watches in our collection, please contact:
MANUFACTURE ROGER DUBUIS SA – 12, avenue Industrielle – 1227 Genève
Tel.: +4122-827 49 49 – Fax: +4122-827 49 40

Master watchmakers

Christiaan van der Klaauw

The Dutch watchmaker became famous especially for his astrological-astronomical pieces which in 1997 were an evolution of the zodiac watch. It had two versions - Star Watch and Yin Yang Watch, made with the designers Marco Biancati and Mauve La Fleur. The principle behind this watch is the technical and aesthetic "rewriting" of Renaissance astrolabes, based on the geocentric vision which characterized all the old tower clocks. He also has a weekly calendar; a splendid Chronograph with 24 hours, calendar and moon phases, a beautiful repeater Chrono, a day-date Chronograph and an automatic Chronometer, with date at 6 and finely engraved rotor. Common to his latest creations is the power reserve adapted to the day-date with week indication and to the automatic chronograph. The other technical speciality regards the piece with small seconds and date, and hand-winding movement caliber Unitas finely engraved. The most important specimen presented in 1999, the Planetarium watch based on a caliber 39 Glashütte Original, automatic winding (but it is also available with an ETA caliber 2824-2), has a precious engine turned (guilloché) silver dial that shows the planets and the signs of the zodiac at 12 (the planets are made with little ceramic spheres). The other new example, the Millennium 2000, shows in actual time the position of the sun-moon for 24 hours at 12, with the moon phases at 6. The graphics of the dial are particularly attractive, using enamel colors creatively and tastefully. Its movement, mechanical, hand-winding chronograph of the Venus caliber 175m was greatly refined and modified by the Dutch master.

Special praise should go to those who, in spite of the thousand obstacles raised by bureaucracy and commerce in these times, have "thrown their hearts over the wall" risking their own personal production inspired by passion, taste and particularly efficacious technology, in this world of mechanical watches. These craftsmen keep watchmaking alive in its real significance and fewer headlines in financial papers. We are sure that their example will help recover the healthy spirit of competition that characterized the Eighties.

Cédric Johner

This young designer was trained in the field of fine jewellery and refined his talents working in a great Genevan Maison. Soon the need to be able to express his own creativity urged him to open his workshop, while continuing to work for important names in the region, He is also active in professional training. He has created his own personal collection where the need to have his own mark in the world of fine watchmaking can already be seen in the particular design of the case, a very stylized tonneau that follows the hexagonal dial. His visiting card is a Jumping-hour Charter of Human Rights, and the basic text is engraved on the dial. His most important collection, the Abyss is characterized by the plastic and sinuous form of the tonneau case, completely made by hand from the solid piece. The stylized and original graphics of the dial are unmistakable, the indications are placed gracefully and with a special spatial sense and the large slightly deformed Roman numerals, that seem to be beneath water, are painted on a beautifully guilloché decoration. The Abyss this year has a new perpetual calendar in a slightly smaller case with respect to last years, it has an automatic ETA caliber 2890/A9 movement, the dial in silver-plated and guilloché solid gold for the version with the yellow gold case, or in blue enamel for the one in platinum. Another innovation is the Saltarello, with manual movement Jacques & Baume caliber 1727 (based on an old A. Schild). The large numbers of the minute scale dominate much of the bottom and follow the eyes to the off-center dial, bordered by the minute track. The Regulator is very interesting and has a Jacques & Baume movement, but here it has an automatic caliber 876500, and the 24 Hours that suggests two convincing personalized versions with respect to the traditional time indication. The women's version is automatic and the white gold case and bracelet are completely studded with diamonds (5.90 kt).

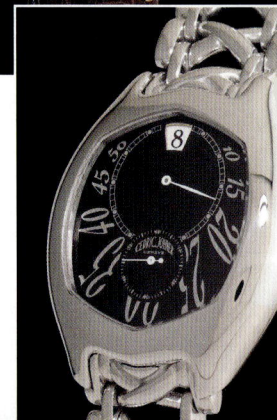

On the other side, the planets meet

Reverso Sun Moon
For those with celestial standards, this Reverso has the elegance to offer both the sun and the moon, and then turns smoothly to reveal its intricate workings through a sapphire crystal on the other side. Complete with power-reserve, this tiny mechanical planet is something of a star performer.

JAEGER-LeCOULTRE

For your free copy of the Manufacture's book of Timepieces contact your local retailer
or Jaeger-LeCoultre, CH-Le Sentier, tel. (+41) 21 845 02 02. www.mjlc.com

Jewellers' parade

Watchmaking is closely linked to the world of elegance - the links are so tight that sometimes it is hard to see who has designed what. Some of the world's greatest jewellers, such as Boucheron, Cartier, Chaumet, Chopard and Van Cleef & Arpels, began designing watches early in the history - as early as the XIXth century; others such as Harry Winston, Tiffany, Bulgari and Fred, introduced their first efforts as recently as 70 years ago. No matter when these great jewellers began designing watches, their product is now known the world over. They create some of the most stunning wearable works of art. The jewellery and the watches take their inspiration one from the other, and the designers at times are inspired by outside elements, such as architecture, nature or even the stones they use in their creations.

de Grisogono

The first "de Grisogono" boutique at number 106 rue du Rhône in Geneva opened in 1993. Fawaz Gruosi is one of the most important jewellers in the world, a genuine couturier of high quality jewellery, who has managed this shop for over twenty years. The name "de Grisogono" is that of an old aristocratic family from Northern Italy, and his homage to his country of origin. A distinctive element of the House are the black diamonds, natural gems that seem opaque but are really translucent or semi-transparent. They are very rare and very difficult to find (they come exclusively from South-Africa and Australia); they need great care while being worth because of their great fragility. Black diamonds are the bases of the most exclusive creation by Fawaz Gruosi who, in his search for perfection and his particular taste for what is new (a temptation few women succeed in ignoring), offers a totally new to conceive jewels and consequently to express one's own femineness. Among his watches is Ice Cube, precious in white gold set with diamonds created for Chopard.

The first watch signed by de Grisogono is "Instrumento N°Uno", a stainless steel model water-resistant to 30 meters, with leather strap and crown set with a natural black diamond cabochon. Mechanical movement with automatic winding and 42-hour power reserve, showing two time-zones and oversized date. A "guilloché" dial enhanced by applied numerals specially designed for de Grisogono.

EUROPEAN COMPANY WATCH

MOD. PANHARD - F11 -

- MONOBLOC STEEL CASE
  HANDMADE FINISHING
  SCREW ON CROWNS

- SWISS AUTOMATIC CHRONOGRAPH

- SAPPHIRE GLASS WITH DOUBLE
  ANTIREFLEX TREATMENT

- MADE IN ITALY

PANHARD

R.C. Time

Via Fatebenefratelli n°30 - Milano - Tel. + 39 - 02 - 65 92 288 - Fax. + 39 - 02 - 65 97 789

Jewellers' parade

Casa Damiani

"Ego", Damiani's watch is the meeting point between the highest expression of the art of jewellery making and that of watchmaking and creates a concentration of fascination, technology and elegance, as the many famous lovers of Damiani jewels desire, representatives of the theater and culture who wished this product of the natural complement of the collections.

Damiani's first watch is called "Ego", it is a women's watch that is strong and harmonious, designed by Jorg Hysek; it is presented in different versions: in steel, gold (white, pink or yellow), with or without diamonds. Its charm and elegance are made evident by the original and typically Damiani design of the case, a precious square curved, water-resistant to 50 meters, and by the dials and hands, protected by an elegant domed sapphire crystal and the crown which is innovative and personalized. The versions in steel are decidedly new with their bracelet that can be worn with bracelets, rings and chokers of the same design, and those with rubber straps, black or colored (yellow, red, orange, turquoise, blue).

Fred

Creative, modern and feminine: these three key words have always described the jewellery created by Fred and guarantee its élite character and stylistic avant-garde. Since 1936 this Parisian jeweller has identified his production with new creations based on the continuing reinvention of the very style of jewellery respecting at the same time the fundamental rules for the greatest elegance and greatest quality. In watchmaking - the newest watches from Fred mimic the House's dramatic style - he has two main collections: the Montre Cat, an original "geometry puzzle" that plays with shapes and light to create a model that is extremely original and feminine, the Montre 36, instead, presented in a rectangular version for the hour and minute version and round for the chronograph, has a more traditional character and the chronograph model adapts itself to the masculine wrist.

La Montgolfier
Double Fuseaux

ZANNETTI

HANDMADE WATCHES

00186 Rome/Italy - Via Monte d'Oro, 19 - Tel. +39/06.68.76.651 - Fax +39/06.68.75.027

Design & Fashion

In the last half of the twentieth century, all kinds of designers grew interested in timepieces. No longer were watches considered simply a functional item; they took on a new dimension as fashion accessories. Among the first to take an interest in creating watches were the great jewelry houses. Some had already begun earlier in the century, while others took to it anew, creating luxurious watches that bespoke their eminent origins. Clothing designers were another important group to recognize the importance of watches for fashion and design. Many savvy fashion designers embraced timepieces as though they had been created explicitly for them - producing watches that mimicked either the designer's logo, clothing styles, fabrics, or overall image. The time and effort that these original designers put into the development and marketing of watches as fashion accessories and elements of style propelled the world of timepieces to new heights. By the close of the twentieth century, nearly two dozen top designers and jewelry houses had achieved the fame in the world of watches.

Versace

Sleek and sophisticated, with inspired touches of boldness and daring. That is the spirit of Versace's new collection of timepieces, presented at the 1999 Basel-Show. The brand was indeed refining its style, passing from the opulent Baroque to a more subtle classicism, offering sober yet clearly identifiable models, proposing pure shapes highlighted by those small differences that make a great name. 
The success achieved last year confirmed the tendency. On the eve of the third millennium, Versace proposes a contemporary style, highly fashionable products, but always original touches: a heritage of the now famous story of one of the greatest designers of our age. Therefore the 2000 collection of watches has been supplemented with three new models that happily complete an already remarkable range of products.
Elegant, modern and sober, intended equally for men and women, "Character by Versace" has a curved case showing clear-cut perpendicular lines; it has a square dial and a micro fiber black strap. The curved sapphire crystal reveals a black dial, a date and luminescent hours and hands.

PERRELET

1777

INVENTOR OF THE AUTOMATIC WATCH

Neuchâtel watchmaker Abraham-Louis Perrelet, invented the automatic movement in 1770.

«RECTANGLE ROYALE»
Automatic watch with double rotor
New Perrelet calibre PR.3H-2000 with date
Stainless steel case
18K white gold upper rotor
Fined brushed dial with powdered hour markers
Anti-glare sapphire crystal
Hand-crafted alligator strap

MONTRES PERRELET   RUE DU TRÉSOR 2   2000 NEUCHÂTEL SWITZERLAND
TEL. +41 32 721 33 43   FAX +41 32 721 35 33
E-MAIL: perrelet@vtx.ch

"Part Pit Bull, all French Charm"
DAVID COLMAN NEW YORK TIMES

"To Frenchway Travel who makes my impossible trips possible — with passion."
BW PUBLISHING

THE FRENCHW

11 WEST 25TH STREET 8TH FL.
TEL: 212 243 3500   FAX: 212 243 3535   TOLL FREE: 800 243 3575

"Best thing that happens to us"
FILIPA FINO HARPERS BAZAAR

"For the people who work around the world and around the clock, Frenchway Travel is a perfect match for us."
ELLIOTT ELBAZ FIRST SECURITY VAN KASPER

"If I've got a girl going from New York to London to Paris to Miami and back to New York, and a day to pull it together, they (Frenchway) can get it — for a great price."
MAY AU BOOKER WITH MEN WOMEN MANAGEMENT

"The only way to go, FRENCHWAY"
STEPHEN BALDWIN

AY TRAVEL INC.

WE DO IT... WITH PASSION

NEW YORK N.Y. 10010
http://www.frenchwaytravel.com

"La Haute Couture Du Voyage"
DIANE VON FURSTENBERG

"The French Mission Impossible"
DAVID BONNOUVRIER DNA MODELS

DANIEL MINK
SWITZERLAND

THE INTRINSIC COLLECTION

- CERTIFIED CHRONOMETER
- GUILLOCHÉ DIAL
- 40 HR POWER RESERVE INDICATOR
- 24 HR SUBDIAL FOR EITHER DUAL OR MILITARY TIME
- SWEEP SECOND HAND & DATE
- WATER RESISTANT TO 100 METERS
- SKELETON CASE BACK
- AVAILABLE ON A STEEL BRACELET OR ALLIGATOR STRAP

The Intrinsic Collection is Available at these authorized retailers

Joseph Edwards
New York, NY
(212) 730-7300

Kenjo
New York, NY
(212) 333-7220

Bergdorf Goodman
The Art of Watchmaking
New York, NY
(212) 339-3381

Stephen Leigh Jewelers
Quincy, MA
(617) 471-4824

Raphael
West End, NJ
(732) 870-9115

Davinci
Miami, FL
(305) 375-0154

Maurice's Jewelers
Miami, FL
(305) 253-0154

State & Company
Chicago, IL
(312) 795-9200

Curtis Miller
Dallas, TX
(214) 741-3333

Unique Design
San Francisco, CA
(415) 863-3384

Paul Thomas Jewelers
Salt Lake City, UT
(801) 363-2123

T.K. Dodrill Jewelers
All Locations
(800) 280-4748

The Montreux Group LC, Sole Distributor of Daniel Mink for North America (212) 481-0205

Introduction

We are dedicating the following chapter to the mechanical watches built by the most prestigious watchmaking Houses. There are many new pieces this year as well and there are proportionately fewer watches that have gone out of production.

Using the catalogue will be simple for the reader because it has been put together with the intention of making it immediately comprehensible both for the photos and for the text. As far as possible, we have respected the full current offer made by each House, and we have prepared a brief profile for each. After this comes the most difficult part of our project: the presentation of the watches themselves, based on a photograph and a technical description. The decision to give preference to mechanical movements is an attempt to underscore how much the centuries of culture, to which the Houses refer, still succeed in expressing that formidable blend of pure watchmaking art and aesthetic research- substance and form - that is the particular boast of Swiss production throughout the world.

Photography

We ourselves have taken the photographs of all the watches and all the movements dedicating particular care to mechanical watchmaking, without overlooking the newest most recent products presented mostly at the main meetings of this sector, the watchmaking exposition of Basel and the salon of quality watchmaking at Geneva, that take place in April each year. In order to make comparisons of one model to another easier, and to have a key to seeing the watches without a more or less favorable presentation, they have been photographed from the same angle and against the same background. We have also maintained the proportions between one watch and another. In some cases a particular name might have a percentage reduction, but the size ratio among the models presented has been maintained.

Technical description

The technical description includes all the information needed to evaluate the quality and compare the products among themselves. It includes a description of: Movement and Functions; Case, Dial and Bracelet; Prices and Other Versions. Movement: when possible we have indicated the base calibre. In this case subsequent specifications attempt to indicate only the differences between that calibre and the execution mounted on the watch of that name; differences that are technical-functional and that instead depend on decoration and finishing. All the other characteristics are those of the base calibre whose technical description will be in the chapter dedicated to movement manufacturers. Some watchmaking Houses are reluctant to name the calibre being used. In these cases, we have attempted a complete description of all its particularities.
Case: we tried to complete as much as possible the information regarding the size of the watches, indicating the diameter (or width and length of the watches with particular shapes) and the height.

Prices

In order to facilitate comparison of the costs of the models of different names, we have published, when possible, the purchase price (including taxes) in Switzerland. This price list is the point of reference for the foreign lists. The price differences that can be found for the same model in various countries, are usually due to reasons that vary from transportation charges to insurance, customs, differing sales taxes (7.5% in Switzerland), to the kind of service offered after sale and the marketing policies followed by branch shops or by local distributors.

Remember that at this time 1,000 Swiss francs (CHF) are worth about $598.00, £379.00, Euro 622.00, Yen 64,000.00
Some companies have preferred to quote their prices in different currencies since their price lists are "constructed" in different ways; yet others have preferred to leave it to the reader to query local distributors (their names and addresses can be obtained by the main offices listed on the last page of this publication) to get the local price list.

A. Lange & Söhne

Emil, second-born of Adolph Lange, managed the House from 1875.

Through all of horology's history watchmakers have been driven by the desire to miniaturize - to compress devices that once required huge amounts of space into areas no larger than an after-dinner mint.

In one of its new watches, the 1815 moonphase (Ref. 231.031), A. Lange & Söhne has performed a giant feat of miniaturization - shrinking a mechanism once found only in huge astronomical clocks into something small enough to fit on your wrist. It's a moonphase indicator that will be accurate for more than 1,000 years without needing adjustment. The device automatically adjusts itself twice a day and will deviate by one day only after 386,435 days (that's 1,058 years). Whereas other moonphase watches assume the moon orbits the earth in 29 days, the 1815 is based on the more precise "synodic" month - 29 days, 12 hours, 44 minutes and 3 seconds. And, while conventional moonphase watches are set to the day, the 1815 model is set to the hour, by means of a lunar calendar which comes with the watch. The mechanism is incorporated in a 26-jewel movement (calibre L943.1) just 3.85 millimeters thick and 27.5 millimeters in diameter. The manual-wind watch has a 21,600-oscillation-per-hour balance and 45-hour power reserve. Underlining the astronomical theme are star-shaped hour markers at 3, 6 and 9 o'clock and a picture of the Big Dipper star constellation, consisting of gold appliques. The watch back is see-through sapphire crystal. The 1815 Moonphase (the "1815" refers to the year the company's founder, Adolph Lange, was born) is being offered in a limited edition of 150 watches in platinum and 250 in pink gold. It is being introduced in honor of the 150th birthday of Adolph Lange's son, Emil, who ran the company for 40 years.

A. Lange & Söhne has also introduced a new chronograph this year: the Datograph (Ref. 403.035). It has three unusual features. The first is a very precise "jumping" 30-minute counter, which springs forward one notch at the exact instant when the center seconds chrono hand passes the 60-second mark. This makes possible unambiguous readings of elapsed time. The watch's second unusual feature is its fly-back mechanism, which enables the wearer to return the chrono hand to zero with a single push of a button, then to restart it instantly by releasing the button. Thirdly, the watch has an unusually large date window for easy reading. The movement (calibre L951.1) has 390 parts, is 7.5 mm thick and 30 mm in diameter. The Datograph's case in platinum has a see-through caseback; the black dial has a tachymeter scale.

The History

1846 - A. Lange develops the so-called "Lathe of Glashütte", (the lathe of Glashütte), where the flywheel takes the place of the bow so that components could be made with greater precision. **1863** - The first Pocket chronograph is presented. **1866** - A watch was built carrying the date, day, month and moon phase. **1874** - A women's model was created only 25 millimeters in diameter. **1891** - The first "perpetual" Pocket watch had a platinum oscillating weight.

The Twenties - After the First World War, the Glashütte watch manufacturing companies formed two large groups in order to face the recession: at the time, 100 billion marks were worth one single American dollar. **1945** - The factory was destroyed by Russian bombing. **1948** - Lange & Söhne was seized by the G.D.R. pro-Soviet government and nationalized. Walter Lange, forced to abandon the country, fled to the West. **1990** - In December, the Lange Uhren GmbH was included in the Dresden registry. The Company was able to use its original name on a new production plant opened on the premises which had belonged to Strasser & Rohde, makers of precision pendulum clocks.

1994 - The modern collection which bound numerous technological innovations to traditional perfection in manual movements, was immediately recognized as being at the highest level of watch production.

1997 - This was a very important year for the Company: it saw the birth of the Langematic, the first watch with Sax-O-Mat movement for automatic winding: the start of a new era for Lange. Its mechanism for regulating the hands is a world class innovation.

1998 - Walter Lange received the award of the Order of the Free State of Saxony from the Prime Minister. A limited commemorative production was made of 100 Lange 1 watches - part of the escape wheel was in gold (the famous "golden pallet lever") as well as the dial - celebrates the construction of a second building for watch production (the original 1500 square meters have become 4000, and there are now 120 people employed by the Company) as well as the opening of the Lange watch-making school. This structure offers nine aprenticeships in the production plant where special attention is dedicated to "historic" watches.

A. LANGE & SÖHNE

LANGEMATIK — REF. 308.021

Movement: mechanical, automatic winding, A. Lange & Söhne caliber 921.4 SAX-O-MAT. Hand-finished and hand-engraved.
Functions: hour, minute, small second, date.
Case: 18 kt yellow gold, three-piece case, polished and brushed finish (Ø 37 mm, thickness 9.7 mm); flat sapphire crystal; rectangular date corrector pusher at 10; gold crown with embossed logo; case back attached by 6 screws displaying the movement through a sapphire crystal. Water-resistant to 3 atm.
Dial: silver, small second zone engine turned (guilloché) with concentric-circle pattern; applied yellow gold bâton markers; 4 luminescent dots on the printed minute track; luminescent yellow gold Alpha hands.
Indications: small second at 6 (with zero set), yellow gold bordered patented big date at 12.
Strap: crocodile leather, hand stitched; yellow gold clasp.
Price: 21'850 CHF.
Also available: (x 1000) with bracelet 34'850; white gold, black dial, leather strap 21'850, bracelet 36'100; platinum, grey dial, leather strap 31'650, bracelet on request.

LANGEMATIK — REF. 301.025

Movement: mechanical, automatic winding, A. Lange & Söhne caliber 921.2 SAX-O-MAT. Hand-finished and hand-engraved.
Functions: hour, minute, small second.
Case: platinum, three-piece case, polished and brushed finish (Ø 37 mm, thickness 8 mm); flat sapphire crystal; platinum crown with embossed logo; case back attached by 6 screws displaying the movement through a sapphire crystal. Water-resistant to 3 atm.
Dial: silver, grey; small second zone engine turned (guilloché) with concentric-circle pattern; applied rhodium-plated gold bâton markers (arabic numeral 12); 4 luminescent dots on the minute track; luminescent rhodium-plated gold Alpha hands.
Indications: small second at 6 (with zero set).
Strap: crocodile leather, hand stitched; platinum clasp.
Price: 25'300 CHF.
Also available: with bracelet (on request); yellow gold, champagne dial, leather strap 16'200, with bracelet 29'200; white gold, black dial, leather strap 16'200, with bracelet 30'450.

SAXONIA — REF. 105.035

Movement: mechanical, manual winding, A. Lange & Söhne, caliber 941.3. Hand-finished and hand-engraved.
Functions: hour, minute, small second, date.
Case: platinum, three-piece case, polished and brushed finish (Ø 34 mm, thickness 9 mm); flat sapphire crystal; rectangular date corrector pusher on case side; platinum crown with embossed logo; case back attached by 6 screws, displaying the movement through a sapphire crystal. Water-resistant to 3 atm.
Dial: silver, black, coloring obtained by a galvanization method; applied rhodium-plated gold lozenge markers on the minute track; rhodium-plated gold Alpha hands.
Indications: small second at 6, big date at 12 bordered in rhodium-plated gold.
Strap: crocodile leather, hand stitched; platinum clasp.
Price: 21'950 CHF.
Also available: with grey dial; with bracelet (on request); yellow gold, silver or champagne dial, leather strap 14'500, bracelet 27'500; white gold, black dial, leather strap 14'500, bracelet 28'750; white gold with baguette diamond bezel 49'750, with brilliant bezel 26'900, with pavé diamonds 59'500; with closed bottom (on request).

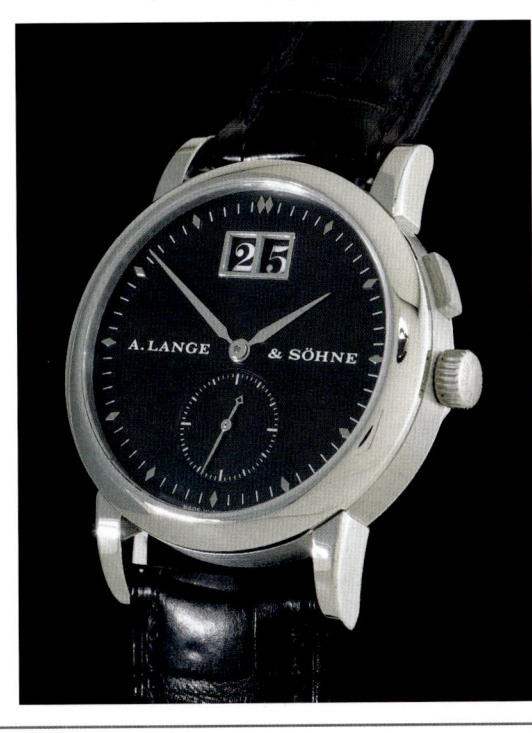

DATOGRAPH — REF. 403.035

Movement: mechanical, manual winding, A. Lange & Söhne, caliber 951.1. Hand-finished and hand-engraved.
Functions: hour, minute, small second, date, chronograph with fly-back feature and 2 counters.
Case: platinum, three-piece case, polished and brushed finish (Ø 39 mm, thickness 10,8 mm); flat sapphire crystal; rectangular pushers; rectangular date corrector pusher at 10; platinum crown with embossed logo; case back attached by 6 screws displaying the movement through a sapphire crystal. Water-resistant to 3 atm.
Dial: silver, black (obtained through galvanization); applied rhodium-plated gold bâton markers and Roman numerals; luminescent rhodium-plated gold Alpha hands, counter hands in rhodium-plated and burnished gold.
Indications: exactly jumping minute counter at 4, small second at 8, big date at 12 (bordered in rhodium-plated gold), center fly-back second counter, minute track with divisions for 1/5 of a second, tachymeter scale.
Strap: crocodile leather, hand stitched; platinum clasp.
Price: 54'200 CHF.

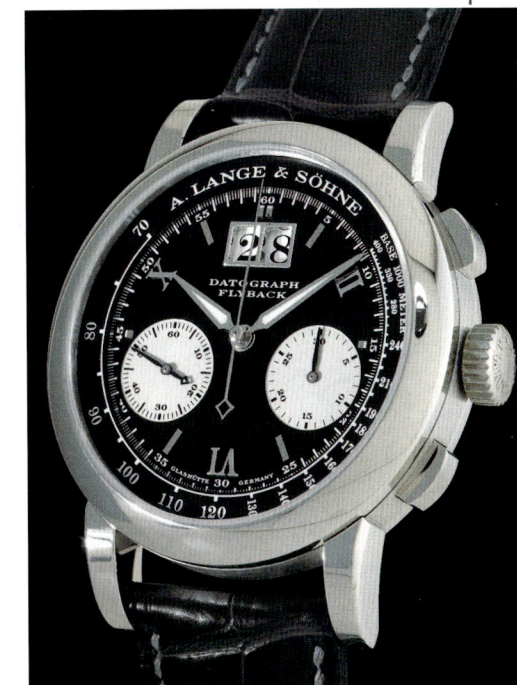

A. LANGE & SÖHNE

LANGE 1 — REF. 101.032

Movement: mechanical, manual winding, A. Lange & Söhne, caliber 901.0. Hand-finished and hand-engraved.
Functions: hour, minute, small second, date, power reserve.
Case: 18 kt red gold, three-piece case, polished and brushed finish (Ø 38,5 mm, thickness 10 mm); flat sapphire crystal; rectangular date corrector pusher on case side; red gold crown with embossed logo; case back attached by 6 screws, displaying the movement through a sapphire crystal. Water-resistant to 3 atm.
Dial: silver.
Indications: off-center hour and minute at 9 on background decorated with concentric-circle pattern; applied pink gold lozenge markers and Roman numerals; black minute track; pink gold Alpha hands; red-gold bordered patented big date at 12 at 1, power reserve at 3, small second between 4 and 5.
Strap: crocodile leather, hand stitched; red gold clasp.
Price: 23'250 CHF.
Also available: black dial; bracelet 36'250; yellow gold, silver or champagne dial, leather strap 23'250, bracelet 36'250; white gold, blue dial, leather strap 23'250, bracelet 37'500; platinum, grey or black dial, leather strap 33'450, bracelet on request; closed bottom (prices on request).

LANGE 1 "LITTLE" — REF. 111.025

Movement: mechanical, manual winding, A. Lange & Söhne, caliber 901.0. Hand-finished and hand-engraved.
Functions: hour, minute, small second, date, power reserve.
Case: platinum, three-piece case, polished and brushed finish (Ø 36 mm, thickness 10 mm); flat sapphire crystal; date corrector on case side; platinum crown with embossed logo; case back attached by 6 screws, displaying the movement through a sapphire crystal. Water-resistant to 3 atm
Dial: silver, black, coloring by galvanization.
Indications: off-center hour and minute at 9 on background decorated with a concentric-circle pattern; applied rhodium-plated gold lozenge markers and Roman numerals; white minute track; rhodium-plated gold Alpha hands; rhodium-plated gold bordered patented big date at 1, power reserve at 3, small second between 4 and 5.
Strap: crocodile leather, hand stitched; platinum clasp.
Price: 30'100 CHF.
Also available: yellow gold, champagne or blue dial; pink gold, silver or black dial (prices on request).

1815 "UP AND DOWN" — REF. 221.025

Movement: mechanical, manual winding, A. Lange & Söhne, caliber 942.1. Hand-finished and hand-engraved.
Functions: hour, minute, small second, power reserve.
Case: platinum, three-piece case, polished and brushed finish (Ø 36 mm, thickness 8 mm); flat sapphire crystal; platinum crown with embossed logo; case back attached by 6 screws, displaying the movement through a sapphire crystal. Water-resistant to 3 atm.
Dial: silver; printed Arabic numerals; printed railway minute track; burnished stainless steel Alpha hands.
Indications: small second (with stopping device) at 4, power reserve at 8.
Strap: crocodile leather, hand stitched; platinum clasp.
Price: 20'700 CHF.
Also available: with bracelet (price on request); yellow gold, silver dial, leather strap 14'950, with bracelet price on request; white gold, blue dial, leather strap or bracelet (prices on request).

1815 — REF. 206.021

Movement: mechanical, manual winding, A. Lange & Söhne, caliber 941.1. Hand-finished and hand-engraved.
Functions: hour, minute, small second.
Case: 18 kt yellow gold, three-piece case, polished and brushed finish (Ø 36 mm, thickness 7.1 mm); flat sapphire crystal; gold crown with embossed logo; case back attached by 6 screws, displaying the movement through a sapphire crystal. Water-resistant to 3 atm.
Dial: silver; printed Arabic numerals; printed railway minute track; burnished stainless steel Alpha hands.
Indications: small second at 6.
Strap: crocodile leather, hand stitched; yellow gold clasp.
Price: 10'600 CHF.
Also available: with bracelet (on request); in platinum, silver dial, leather strap 23'600, with bracelet on request; white gold, blue dial, leather strap or bracelet (prices on request).

A. LANGE & SÖHNE

1815 MOON PHASE — REF. 231.031

Movement: mechanical, manual winding, A. Lange & Söhne, caliber 943.1. Hand-finished and hand-engraved.
Functions: hour, minute, small second, moon phase.
Case: 18 kt red gold, three-piece case, polished and brushed finish (Ø 36 mm, thickness 8 mm); flat sapphire crystal; gold crown with embossed logo; case back attached by 6 screws, displaying the movement through a sapphire crystal. Water-resistant to 3 atm.
Dial: silver, black (coloring obtained by a galvanization method); applied red-gold star shaped and round markers (arabic numeral 12); printed railway minute track; seven gold hemisphere applied so as to make up the pattern of the constellation of the Great Bear; red gold Alpha hands; gold moon phase disc.
Indications: small second (with stopping device) at 4, moon phase at 8.
Strap: crocodile leather, hand stitched; red gold clasp.
Price: 15'500 CHF. Limited edition numbered from 1 to 250 pieces.
Also available: platinum 21'400, 150 pieces (on side).

1815 MOON PHASE — REF. 231.035

Just in the era of electronics, the last creation by the watchmakers of Glashütte is a little triumph of precision mechanics and at the same time a homage to Emil Lange, one among the most famous sons of the Saxon watchmaker dynasty. Second-born of Adolph Lange, the founder of the watch factory, Emil was born 150 years ago and has been managing the family business for over 40 years, first together with his brother Richard and then alone starting from 1887. The 1815 Moon Phase, produced in a limited number of 150 platinum copies and of 250 in red gold, is dedicated to him. Its mechanism exactly reproduces the moon's synodical revolution time equal to 29 days, 12 hours, 44 minutes and 3 seconds, revising the position of the moon twice a day and assuring a divergence of one day with respect to the actual rotation of the moon only after 386.435 days (i.e. 1058 years), of course provided that the watch worked constantly. For its initial adjustment, one must check a table which is furnished together with the watch.
Price: 21'400 CHF.

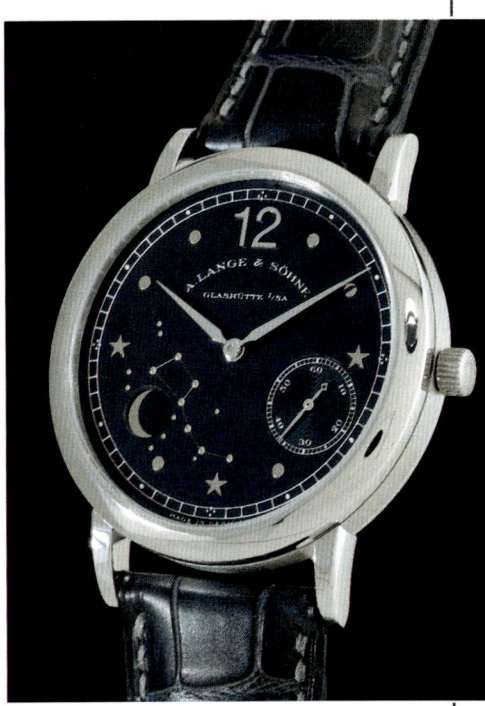

CABARET — REF. 107.027

Movement: mechanical, manual winding, A. Lange & Söhne caliber 931.3. Hand-finished and hand-engraved.
Functions: hour, minute, small second, date.
Case: 18 kt white gold, three-piece rectangular case (dim. 36 mm, width 25.5 mm, thickness 9 mm); curved sapphire crystal; date corrector on case side at 2; white gold crown with embossed logo; case back attached by 6 screws, displaying the movement through a sapphire crystal. Water-resistant to 3 atm.
Dial: silver, blue (coloring obtained by oxidizing vaporization); applied rhodium-plated gold lozenge markers and Roman numerals; rhodium plated gold Alpha hands. **Indications:** small second (with stopping device) at 6, rhodium plated gold bordered patented big date at 12.
Strap: crocodile leather, hand stitched; white gold clasp.
Price: 18'800 CHF.
Also available: with bracelet 32'300; platinum, black dial, leather strap 27'800, bracelet on request; yellow gold, champagne dial, leather strap 18'800, bracelet 30'950; red gold with silver or black dial, leather strap 18'800, bracelet 30'950; closed bottom (on request); white gold with brilliant bezel 35'100, with baguette diamond bezel (on request).

ARKADE — REF. 103.035

Movement: mechanical, manual winding, A. Lange & Söhne caliber 911.4. Hand-finished and hand-engraved.
Functions: hour, minute, small second, date.
Case: platinum, two-piece elliptic case (height 29 mm, width 22 mm, thickness 8,4 mm); flat sapphire crystal; date corrector on case side; platinum crown with embossed logo; case back attached by 4 screws, engraved firm name and individual watch number, displaying the movement through a sapphire crystal. Water-resistant to 3 atm.
Dial: silver, black (coloring by galvanization); applied rhodium-plated gold lozenge markers and Roman numerals; rhodium-plated gold Alpha hands.
Indications: small second at 6, patented big date at 12 (bordered in rhodium-plated gold).
Strap: crocodile leather, hand stitched; platinum clasp.
Price: 23'200 CHF.
Also available: with bracelet (on request); white gold, blue dial, leather strap 18.100, bracelet 33.600; yellow gold, champagne dial, leather strap 18.100, bracelet 32.300; same versions with closed bottom (on request); as jewel-watch (on request).

Audemars Piguet

For lovers and collectors, just a glance at the Audemars Piguet's collection is enough to found throughout the new production all the most appreciate models. To begin with, we have the great virtuosities, pieces of undeniable technical value that have delighted us in recent years with uncommon regularity given the times we are living. It was the idea of creating a special piece that after eight years gave rise to the Tourbillon Minute Repeater Split-second Chronograph Jules Audemars. This piece encloses within the narrow space of a wristwatch not a simple overlying of modules upon a base movement, but rather a homogeneous combination of highly developed mechanisms. An exceptionally pretty chest inlaid by an artisan of the Vallée de Joux, a footed piece with 10 drawers, will hold it. The fifteen collectors to win possession of this piece, for the sum of 425,000 Swiss Francs, will have to wait another seven years for it to be finished, however.

The Royal Oak is greatly loved for its original and distinctive design, and because of its casual, sporting elegance. There are some new models in this collection, including one having a yearly calendar with month and date and that needs no adjustments for 12 months. Produced in a limited number, 450 watches in steel and 50 in gold, it is the end-of-century commemoration watch for the A.P. Foundation. The Royal Oak is on the dial and the rotor. The lady's models supplement the brightly polished version, and the Off-Shore supplements the quartz models at very competitive prices.

There are those who love timeless classics, where fascination for hand crafting somehow blends with the tradition of high precision mechanical movements. The new catalogue presents a re-edition of Canapé just for them: designed in 1940, a man's watch with tourbillon in a limited series of 25 numbered pieces. The movement is sheltered in a curved, pink gold case with a sapphire crystal window back. The lady's watch is an hour and minute, with mechanical

The History

Looking back at its 120 year old history, Audemars Piguet can well acknowledge having created masterpieces which have become points of reference in the limited world of quality watchmaking. The House was founded at Le Brassus in 1875 by Edward Auguste Piguet and Jules-Louis Audemars. Piguet brought into the Company the sum of 10,000 francs, while Audemars' contribution amounted to exactly 18 complicated mechanical movements he himself had built. As frequently happened in those times, the official registration of their name or trademarks took place at a later time, when the masterpieces created at Le Brassus had already become known among connoisseurs. Audemars Piguet's fame reached new heights in 1889, with their triumph at the Paris World's Fair; some of their pieces are now in the British Museum. The Museum at Le Brassus, in the same building where the first workshop had been, recounts the history of the House and the inventions which have made it famous through a precious collection of antique watches, most of which have extremely complicated movements. Audemars Piguet is very active in environmental protection, particularly with regard to protecting forests through the Audemars Piguet Foundation "Time for the Trees", established in 1992 on the 20th Anniversary of the "Royal Oak". Besides this, it also contributes to sports with a sponsorship and communications policy begun in 1985, first with sailing, then golf and soccer - contributing to the enthusiasm for various sports champions which Audemars itself has enjoyed on its own grounds.

1875 - Jules Audemars and Edward Piguet join forces at Le Brassus.
1882 - The trademark and name "Audemars Piguet & Cie" is registered as a company specialized in the production of ultra thin and complicated watches. This was the year of the "Grande Complication" pocket watch (minute repeater, perpetual calendar, moon phases, split seconds chronograph with minute counter).
1889 - Presentation of a "Grande Complication" with Grande sonnerie and petite sonnerie.
1906 - The first wristwatch with minute repeater (at the start of the century an inventory recorded the production of 110 watches with minute repeaters out of the 230 movements then available in the company.
1915 - The smallest minute repeater watch in the world (15.8 mm in diameter)
1925 - Audemars Piguet creates an ultra thin movement for a pocket watch, Calibre 17.5-SVS in two versions: the first (v. 5) 1.55 mm height; the second (v. 6) only 1.32.
1934 - The first Audemars Piguet Skeleton watch
1946 - Audemars Piguet prepares the movement for an ultra thin wristwatch, Calibre 9'''ML, 1.64 mm height.
1967 - Creation of an automatic movement for wristwatches 2.45 mm high; the center rotor is 21 kt. gold.
1970 - At the time the automatic calibre, with date and gold center rotor, was the flattest in the world at 3.05 mm.
1972 - The Le Brassus company entered the world of sports watches with the luxury version, Royal Oak, designed by Gérald Genta.

1978 - An automatic wristwatch was made with automatic rewinding and perpetual calendar, this too was the thinnest in the world.
1982 - "La Montre Philosophique" shows the hour in two time zones with a single hand and a turning bezel.
1986 - The first extra thin wristwatch with an automatic tourbillon movement.
1990 - The Dual Time: automatic rewinding and two time zones, date and power reserve.
1991 - The new automatic tourbillon; the escapement placed at 6 o'clock; the power reserve is also shown.
1992 - The Triple Complication wristwatch, having no fewer than 12 functions it became the star of the Basel Exposition. It was flanked by the precious, rectangular jumping model with minute repeater.
1993 - Presentation of the Royal Oak offshore chronograph, water resistant to 10 atm.
1994 - After three years of work starting from its illustrious pocket model precedent, the Grande Sonnerie appears as a wristwatch model, the first in the world with hour and quarter repeaters.
1995 - For its 120th Anniversary, Audemars presented a commemorative Royal Oak in pink gold with automatic movement, perpetual calendar and 52 week indicator. Only 120 pieces were made. This same year a minute repeater made for the American industrialist, John Shaeffer, in 1907 was reproduced and the Tourbillon Skeleton automatic was also created.
1996 - The Company broadens its horizons with the models Millenary and Carnegie, bringing a taste of modernization to the traditional watchmaking world. Millenary seems the watch of the future, with its original, horizontally set oval case.
1997 - The great innovation is the Royal Oak Chrono with the new automatic caliber 2385. Celebrating the first 25 years of the collection, the first sports tourbillon in steel was produced in a limited edition of 25 pieces. Another limited edition, this time 325 pieces, was made of the Royal Oak Golf Set to honor Nick Faldo, the golf champion.. The Royal Oak mini is the lady's version. There is, finally, a unique example of extraordinary mastery of this art: the pocket model of the Grande Complication which has perpetual calendar, moon phases, split seconds chronograph, minute repeater and is set with 288 diamonds, 98 diamond baguettes, 86 emerald baguettes and 6 cabochon emeralds totalling 47.45 carats.
1998 - The Jules Audemars Minute Repeater Carillon for ladies is the newest "jewel" of the Le Brassus company, the smallest watch with sonnerie on the market. The Jules Audemars case holds the Tourbillon with titanium carriage and automatic movement. The Cambré, with perpetual calendar, is very elegant and somewhat aggressive. 1998 is the year three lines of jewellery were featured in gold and precious stones recalling the collections of the same names: Royal Oak, Carnegie and Charleston.

movement and comes in a jewelled version as well.
Chronographs have not been neglected and those interested can count on the Edouard Piguet model. Besides its rectangular shape and the fine movement used, it can boast of being the most expensive chronograph made by Audemars (21,600 Swiss Francs in white gold or pink gold).
The model on the left - a specific request from italian market - is a traditional manual winding watch, with transparent back, draws strength from its purity of form. It has a round case in white or pink gold, a two level silvered dial protected by a curved crystal, painted hour markers and a simple buckle.

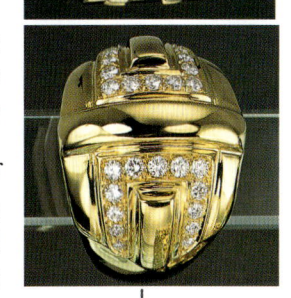

Awaiting next year, which will be the 125th Anniversary of Audemars Piguet (and we can expect some special pieces) the Manufacture has, for the first time, presented a complete matching collection of watches and jewellery. "Promesses" stresses a thoughtful, very modern design of curves and sensual volumes. A rectangular case in yellow or white gold, diamonds, sky-blue, black or white dials for the watch; the jewellery takes the form of two matched sets either entirely in gold or with diamonds and exceptionally large, first quality stones cut precisely to measure, from Blue Topaz, to Citrine, to Garnet - the colors of sky, sun and fire.

AUDEMARS PIGUET

Audemars Piguet's photographs was reduced by 8% with respect to the other pieces.

J. AUDEMARS TOURB. REPEATER RATTRAPANTE   REF. 25923PT.0.0022CR/01

Movement: mechanical, manual winding, with tourbillon and polished and beveled steel cage, A. Piguet, made up by 474 elements. Hand-made and hand-finished; rhodium plated pillar-plate and bridges; beveled and polished steel parts; Côtes de Genève finished bridges, circular-graining finished pillar-plate.
Functions: hour, minute, small second, minute repeater, split-second chronograph with 2 counters. 
Case: platinum, three-piece case, polished and brushed finish (Ø 42,3 mm, thickness 15 mm); curved sapphire crystal; repeater slide on case side; platinum crown with split-second pusher; pushers with case protection; snap-on back displaying the movement through a sapphire crystal. Moisture protection.
Dial: silvered, engine turned (guilloché); aperture on the tourbillon; white gold Roman numerals; printed minute track; white gold leaf style hands.
Indications: minute counter at 3, small second at 6 integrated with the tourbillon carriage, center second and split-second counters.
Strap: crocodile leather; platinum fold-over clasp.
Price: 425'000 CHF. Edition limited to 20 pieces.

JULES AUDEMARS GRANDE SONNERIE CARILLON   REF. 25825OR.0.0002/01

Movement: mechanical, manual winding, Audemars Piguet caliber 2890. Hand-finished (Côtes de Genève and circular graining).
Functions: hour, minute, small second, grande and petite sonnerie, minute repeater.
Case: 18 kt pink gold, three-piece case (Ø 39 mm, thickness 10,26 mm); curved sapphire crystal; slide-contact at 2 to select the grande sonnerie (strikes the hours and the quarters by three timbres), the petite sonnerie (strikes the hours) or the mute position; minute repeater pusher at 10; pink gold crown; case back attached by 5 screws. 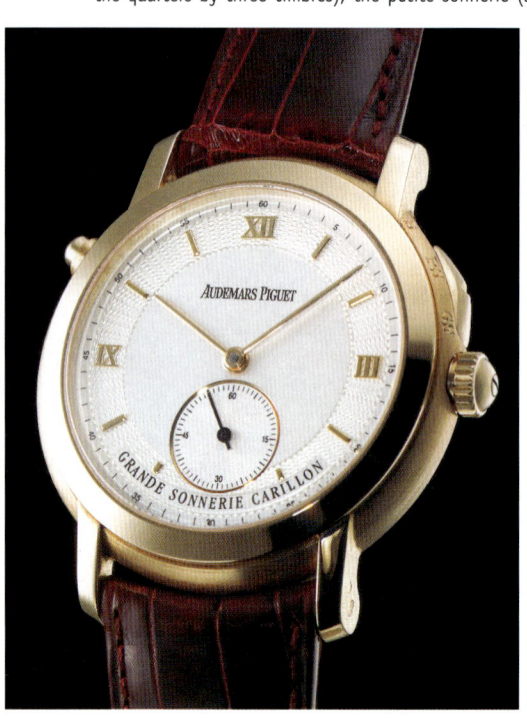
Dial: silvered, engine turned (guilloché); applied pink gold bâton markers and Roman numerals; printed minute track; pink gold bâton hands.
Indications: small second at 6.
Strap: crocodile leather; pink gold clasp.
Price: 350'000 CHF.
Also available: platinum (on request).

JULES AUDEMARS TOURBILLON   REF. 25873OR.0.0002/01

Movement: mechanical, automatic winding, with tourbillon and titanium cage, Audemars Piguet caliber 2875. Hand-finished (Côtes de Genève and circular graining).
Functions: hour, minute, date, power reserve.
Case: 18 kt pink gold, three-piece case, polished and brushed finish (Ø 40 mm, thickness 11,16 mm); drop-shaped lugs; curved sapphire crystal; pink gold crown on case back attached by 6 screws. Moisture protection. 
Dial: silvered, matte finish, aperture on the tourbillon.
Indications: off-center hour and minute; applied pink gold bâton markers and Arabic numerals; pink gold bâton hands; date at 3, power reserve at 9.
Strap: crocodile leather, hand stitched; pink gold clasp.
Price: 108'000 CHF.

JULES AUDEMARS CHRONOGRAPH   REF. 25859BA.0.0001CR/01

Movement: mechanical, automatic winding, Audemars Piguet caliber 2226/2841. Hand-finished (Côtes de Genève).
Functions: hour, minute, small second, chronograph with 2 counters.
Case: 18 kt yellow gold, three-piece case, polished and brushed finish (Ø 40 mm, thickness 11,11 mm); curved sapphire crystal; yellow gold crown; snap-on back. Water-resistant to 2 atm. 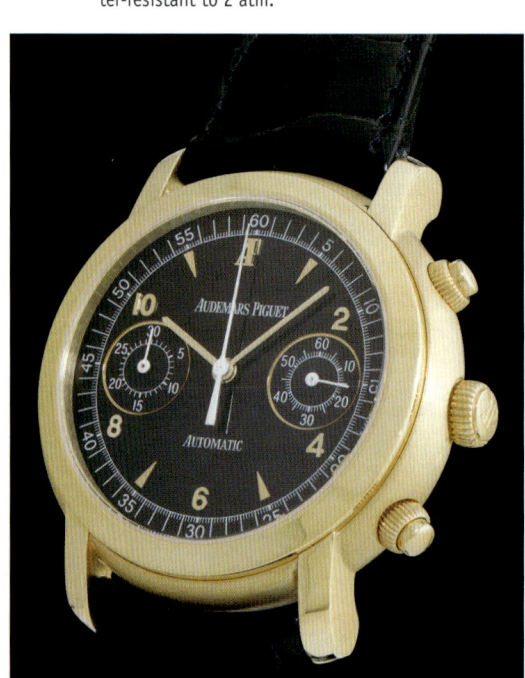
Dial: black; applied yellow gold pointed markers and Arabic numerals; yellow gold bâton hands.
Indications: small second at 3, minute counter at 9, center second counter (white painted hand), minute track with divisions for 1/5 of a second.
Strap: crocodile leather, padded and hand stitched; yellow gold fold-over clasp, in the shape of the firm's logo.
Price: 16'500 CHF.
Also available: stainless steel (on request); silvered dial.

AUDEMARS PIGUET

EDWARD PIGUET CHRONOGRAPH — REF. 25925OR.0.0001CR/01

Movement: mechanical, automatic winding, Audemars Piguet caliber 2385. 21 kt gold rotor. Hand-finished (Côtes de Genève).
Functions: hour, minute, small second, date, chronograph with 3 counters.
Case: 18 kt pink gold, two-piece rectangular-curved case (height 35 mm, width 28.m, thickness 12 mm); curved sapphire crystal; pink gold crown; pink gold oval pushers with case protection; case back attached by 4 screws. Moisture protection.
Dial: black, engine turned (guilloché); luminescent applied pink gold ellipsoidal markers; printed Arabic numerals and railway minute track; luminescent pink gold bâton hands.
Indications: minute counter at 3, date between 4 and 5, small second at 6, hour counter at 9, center second counter, minute track.
Strap: crocodile leather, padded and hand stitched; pink gold fold-over clasp in the shape of the firm's logo.
Price: 21'600 CHF.
Also available: white gold 21'600 CHF.

EDWARD PIGUET GENTS — REF. 15015OR.0.0001CR/01

Movement: mechanical, automatic winding, Audemars Piguet caliber 2140. Hand-finished (Côtes de Genève).
Functions: hour, minute, center second, date.
Case: 18 kt pink gold, two-piece rectangular-curved case (height 35,5 mm, width 27 mm, thickness 8,47 mm); curved sapphire crystal; pink gold crown; case back attached by 4 screws. Moisture protection.
Dial: white lacquered; printed Arabic numerals; printed center railway minute track; burnished pink gold bâton hands.
Indications: date at 3.
Strap: crocodile leather; pink gold fold-over clasp.
Price: 13'300 CHF.
Also available: stainless steel (on request).

JULES AUDEMARS — REF. 15056OR.0.0067CR/01

Movement: mechanical, manual winding, Audemars Piguet caliber 3090, autonomy 48 hours, 21 jewels, balance-spring in Anachron. Bridges beveled and decorated with the Côtes de Genève pattern, pillar-plate decorated with circular graining.
Functions: hour, minute, small second.
Case: 18 kt pink gold, three-piece case, polished and brushed finish (Ø 36 mm, thickness 7,9 mm); curved sapphire crystal; pink gold crown; case back attached by 6 screws. Water-resistant to 2 atm.
Dial: silvered, engine turned (guilloché); rosé printed bâton markers and Roman numerals; printed minute track; pink gold bâton hands.
Indications: small second at 6.
Strap: crocodile leather, padded and hand stitched; pink gold fold-over clasp, in the shape of the firm's logo.
Price: 8'300 CHF.
Also available: white gold (on request).

CANAPE TOURBILLON — REF. 25876OR.0002/01

Movement: mechanical, manual winding, Audemars Piguet caliber 2871. Hand-finished (Côtes de Genève).
Functions: hour, minute, small second.
Case: 18 kt pink gold, two-piece rectangular case (height 40.5 mm, width 23.7 mm, thickness 12.8 mm), polished finish; curved sapphire crystal of considerable thickness; pink gold crown; case back attached by 4 screws, displaying the movement through a sapphire crystal; mobile shaped lugs (the design of case and lugs reminds that of a sofa called "canapé", and got the idea from an Audemars Piguet model of the Fourties). Moisture protection.
Dial: silvered, aperture on the tourbillon; applied pink gold bâton markers and Arabic numerals; printed railway minute track; pink gold bâton hands.
Indications: small second at 6 integrated in the tourbillon carriage.
Strap: crocodile leather, hand stitched; pink gold fold-over clasp in the shape of the firm's logo.
Price: 116'000 CHF. Edition limited to 25 pieces.

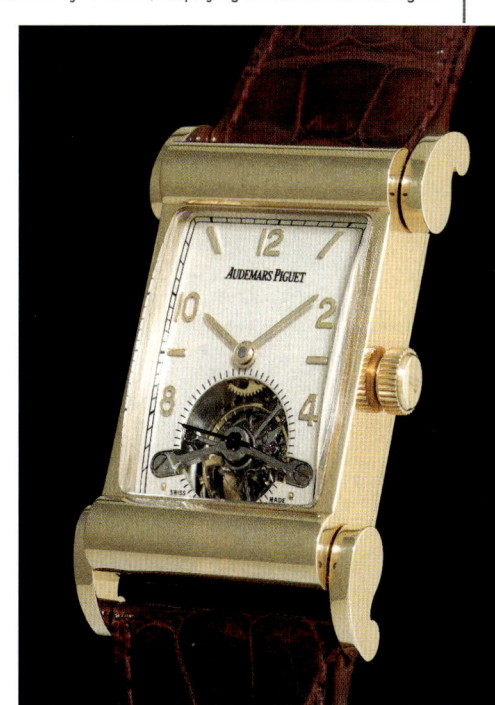

41

AUDEMARS PIGUET

MILLENARY PERPETUAL CALENDAR   REF. 25777BA.0.0002/01

Movement: mechanical, automatic winding, Audemars Piguet caliber 2120/2801 QP, extra-thin. Rotor with 21 kt gold segment. Hand-finished (Côtes de Genève).
Functions: hour, minute, perpetual calendar (date, day, month, year, week, moon phase).
Case: 18 kt yellow gold, three-piece oval case, polished and brushed finish (height 34 mm, width 39 mm); flat sapphire crystal; 3 correctors on case side; sapphire cabochon yellow gold crown; case back attached by 6 screws. 
Dial: white enameled; applied yellow gold bâton markers; printed minute track; blued gold Cathédrale hands.
Indications: date at 3, moon phase at 6, day at 9, month and four year cycle at 12, yellow gold pointed center week hand.
Strap: crocodile leather; yellow gold clasp.
Price: 49'800 CHF.
Also available: pink gold or white gold (on request).

MILLENARY CHRONOGRAPH   REF. 25822OR.0.0067CR/01

Movement: mechanical, automatic winding, Audemars Piguet caliber 2126/2840. Rotor with 21 kt gold segment. Hand-finished (Côtes de Genève).
Functions: hour, minute, small second, date, chronograph with 3 counters.
Case: 18 kt pink gold, three-piece oval case, polished and brushed finish (height 37 mm, width 41 mm, thickness 11 mm); flat sapphire crystal; sapphire cabochon pink gold crown; case back attached by 6 screws. 
Dial: silvered; printed luminescent Arabic numerals, printed minute track; luminescent burnished gold sword style hands.
Indications: date with magnifying glass at 3, hour counter at 6, minute counter at 9, small second at 12, center second counter, scroll tachymeter scale, telemeter scale on the beveled ring.
Strap: crocodile leather; pink gold clasp.
Price: 24.300.000 lire.
Also available: stainless steel with white dial and blue Arabic numerals (on request).

MILLENARY DUAL TIME   REF. 25778BA.0.0002/02

Movement: mechanical, automatic winding, Audemars Piguet caliber 2129/2845. Rotor with 21 kt gold segment. Hand-finished (Côtes de Genève).
Functions: hour, minute, date, second time zone, power reserve.
Case: 18 kt yellow gold, three-piece oval case, polished and brushed finish (height 35 mm, width 39, thickness 8,3 mm); flat sapphire crystal; sapphire cabochon yellow gold crown; case back attached by 6 screws. 
Dial: white enameled; applied yellow gold bâton markers, and printed minute track; yellow gold leaf style hands.
Indications: date at 2, second time-zone with double hand at 6, power reserve between 8 and 11.
Strap: crocodile leather; yellow gold clasp.
Price: 19'700 CHF.
Also available: pink gold with white enameled dial (on request).

MILLENARY AUTOMATIC   REF. 15016ST.0.0642/01

Movement: mechanical, automatic winding, Audemars Piguet caliber 2125. Rotor with 21 kt gold segment. Hand-finished (Côtes de Genève).
Functions: hour, minute, center second, date.
Case: stainless steel, three-piece oval case, polished and brushed finish (height 37 mm, width 41 mm, thickness 8,25 mm); flat sapphire crystal; stainless steel cabochon crown; case back attached by 6 screws. 
Dial: black; luminescent Arabic numerals; luminescent dots on the minute track; luminescent sword style hands.
Indications: date at 3.
Strap: calf, padded and hand stitched; stainless steel fold-over clasp.
Price: 5'900 CHF.
Also available: with silvered engine turned (guilloché) dial and printed Roman numerals.

AUDEMARS PIGUET

MILLENARY DAY-DATE MONTH   REF. 25816BA.0.0002/01

Movement: mechanical, automatic winding, Audemars Piguet caliber 2127/2827. Rotor with 21 kt gold segment. Hand-finished (Côtes de Genève).
Functions: hour, minute, small second, full calendar (date, day, month).
Case: 18 kt yellow gold, three-piece oval case, polished and brushed finish (height 37 mm, width 41 mm, thickness 10,85 mm); flat sapphire crystal; 2 correctors on case side; sapphire cabochon yellow gold crown; case back attached by 6 screws.
Dial: silvered, engine turned (guilloché); applied yellow gold bâton markers; blued gold Cathédrale hands.
Indications: small second at 6, day and month below 12, pointed center date hand.
Strap: crocodile leather; yellow gold clasp.
Price: 15'200 CHF.
Also available: pink gold (on request).

MILLENARY DAY-DATE   REF. 25779BA.0.0002/01

Movement: mechanical, automatic winding, Audemars Piguet caliber 2124/2810. Rotor with 21 kt gold segment. Hand-finished (Côtes de Genève).
Functions: hour, minute, day-date.
Case: 18 kt yellow gold, three-piece oval case, polished and brushed finish (height 35 mm, width 39, thickness 8 mm); flat sapphire crystal; sapphire cabochon yellow gold crown; case back attached by 6 screws.
Dial: white enameled; printed Roman numerals and railway minute track; burnished gold Cathédrale hands.
Indications: date at 3, day at 9.
Strap: crocodile leather; yellow gold clasp.
Price: 14'500 CHF.
Model only available with silvered dial (the white dial version in the photograph is out of stock).
Also available: pink gold (on request).

ROYAL OAK AUTOMATIC   REF. 14790ST.0.0789ST/01

Movement: mechanical, automatic winding, Audemars Piguet caliber 2125. Hand-finished (Côtes de Genève).
Functions: hour, minute, center second, date.
Case: stainless steel, three-piece brushed case (Ø 37 mm, thickness 8.5 mm); flat sapphire crystal; octagonal bezel with gasket and 8 recessed hexagon nuts in white gold fastening the 8 white gold through screws of the case back; hexagonal screw-down crown. Water-resistant to 5 atm.
Dial: dark blue, decorated with Clous de Paris pattern; luminescent white gold bâton markers; luminescent white gold bâton hands.
Indications: date at 3.
Bracelet: steel; fold-over safety clasp.
Price: 8'900 CHF.
Also available: with sapphire blue or white dial; yellow gold, slate-grey, ivory, white or gilt dial (on request); steel and yellow gold, slate-grey, ivory, white or gilt dial (on request); pink gold, slate-grey or ivory dial (on request).

ROYAL OAK FOUNDATION   REF. 15100ST.0.0789ST/01

Movement: mechanical, automatic winding, Audemars Piguet caliber 2225, 28,800 vibrations per hour (vph). Hand-finished (Côtes de Genève), celebrative pink gold rotor with embossed AP logo and oak leaves.
Functions: hour, minute, center second, date.
Case: stainless steel, three-piece brushed case (Ø 37 mm, thickness 8,3 mm); flat sapphire crystal; octagonal bezel with gasket and 8 recessed white gold hexagon nuts fastening the 8 white gold through screws of the case back; hexagonal screw-down crown; case back attached by 8 screws, displaying the movement through a sapphire crystal. Water-resistant to 5 atm.
Dial: blue, decorated with Clous de Paris pattern; in the central part great tapisserie with an embossed stylized oak as a symbol of the "Time for the Trees" Foundation; luminescent applied white gold markers; luminescent white gold bâton hands.
Indications: date at 3.
Bracelet: steel; fold-over safety clasp.
Price: 9'950 CHF. Edition limited to 450 pieces (the proceeds of sales contribute in sustaining the "Time for the Trees" Foundation).
Also available: yellow gold, silvered dial, 50 pieces (on request).

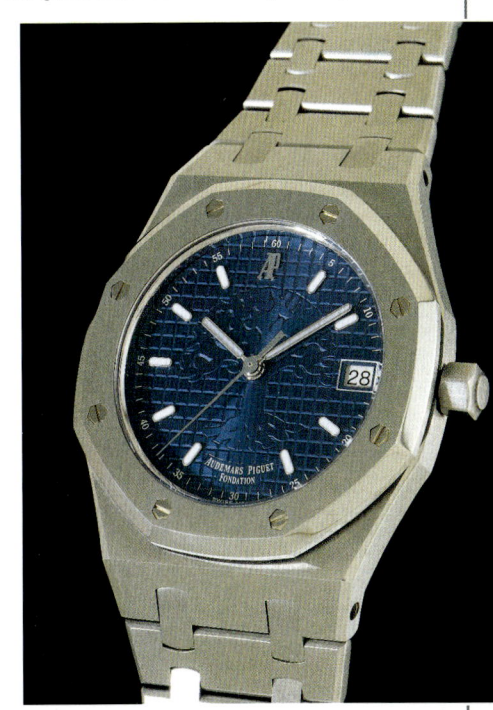

AUDEMARS PIGUET

ROYAL OAK PERPETUAL CALENDAR — REF. 25820ST.O.0944ST/01

Movement: mechanical, automatic winding, Audemars Piguet caliber 2120/2802. 22 kt white gold skeleton rotor. Hand-finished.
Functions: hour, minute, perpetual calendar (date, day, month, year, moon phase).
Case: stainless steel, three-piece brushed case (Ø 38.5 mm, thickness 9.5 mm); flat sapphire crystal; octagonal bezel with gasket and 8 recessed hexagon nuts in white gold fastening the 8 white gold through screws of the case back displaying the movement through a sapphire crystal; 4 correctors on case side; hexagonal screw-down crown. Water-resistant to 2 atm.
Dial: grey; applied white gold baton markers; printed minute track; white gold bâton hands.
Indications: date at 3, moon phase at 6, day at 9, month and four year cycle at 12.
Bracelet: stainless steel, satiny; fold-over safety clasp.
Price: 44'900 CHF.
Also available: yellow gold with gilt dial (on request). Squelette Ref. 25829: yellow gold or platinum (on request).

ROYAL OAK ANNUAL CALENDAR — REF. 25920BA.O.0789BA/01

Movement: mechanical, automatic winding, Audemars Piguet caliber 2224/2814, made up by 228 elements, autonomy 38 hours, 35 jewels (Ø 26 mm, 11 lines and 1/2, thickness 4.85 mm), 28,800 vibrations per hour (vph). Hand-finished.
Functions: hour, minute, annual calendar (date, month).
Case: 18 kt yellow gold, three-piece brushed case (Ø 37 mm, thickness 10 mm); flat sapphire crystal; octagonal bezel with gasket and 8 recessed hexagon nuts in white gold fastening the 8 white gold through screws of the case back; 2 correctors on case side; hexagonal screw-down crown. Water-resistant to 5 atm.
Dial: dark blue, decorated with Clous de Paris pattern; luminescent applied white painted bâton markers; luminescent white painted bâton hands.
Indications: month at 5 (months with 31 days in red), pointed center date hand.
Bracelet: 18 kt yellow gold, satiny; pink gold fold-over safety clasp.
Price: 30'500 CHF.
Also available: stainless steel with dark blue dial (on request).

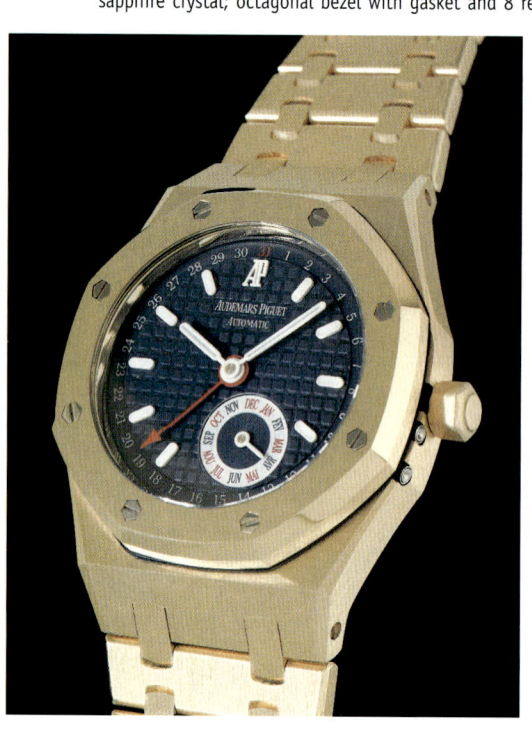

ROYAL OAK DUAL TIME — REF. 25730BA.O.0789BA/04

Movement: mechanical, automatic winding, Audemars Piguet caliber 2129/2845. Hand-finished (Côtes de Genève).
Functions: hour, minute, date, second time zone, power reserve.
Case: 18 kt yellow gold, three-piece brushed case (Ø 36 mm, thickness 9,5 mm); flat sapphire crystal; octagonal bezel with gasket and 8 recessed hexagon nuts in white gold fastening the 8 white gold through screws of the case back; hexagonal screw-down crown. Water-resistant to 5 atm.
Dial: ivory, decorated with Clous de Paris pattern; luminescent applied yellow gold baton markers; luminescent yellow gold bâton hands.
Indications: date at 2, second time-zone with double hand at 6, power reserve between 8 and 11.
Bracelet: yellow gold, satiny; fold-over safety clasp.
Price: 212'800 CHF.
Also available: white, black or slate-grey dial; steel with white, blue or black dial (on request); yellow gold & stainless steel, with ivory, white or black dial (on request).

ROYAL OAK DAY-DATE MOON PHASE — REF. 25594ST.O.0789ST/01

Movement: mechanical, automatic winding, Audemars Piguet caliber 2124/2825. Hand-finished (Côtes de Genève).
Functions: hour, minute, day-date, moon phase.
Case: stainless steel, three-piece brushed case (Ø 36 mm, thickness 8,5 mm); flat sapphire crystal; octagonal bezel with gasket and 8 recessed white gold hexagon nuts fastening the 8 white gold through screws of the case back; hexagonal screw-down crown. Water-resistant to 10 atm.
Dial: white, decorated with Clous de Paris pattern, zones with silvered crown; luminescent applied white gold markers; luminescent white gold bâton hands.
Indications: date at 3, moon phase at 6, day at 9.
Bracelet: stainless steel, satiny; fold-over safety clasp.
Price: 11'200 CHF.
Also available: stainless steel and yellow gold with slate-grey, gilt, ivory or black dial (on request); in yellow gold with ivory dial (on request).

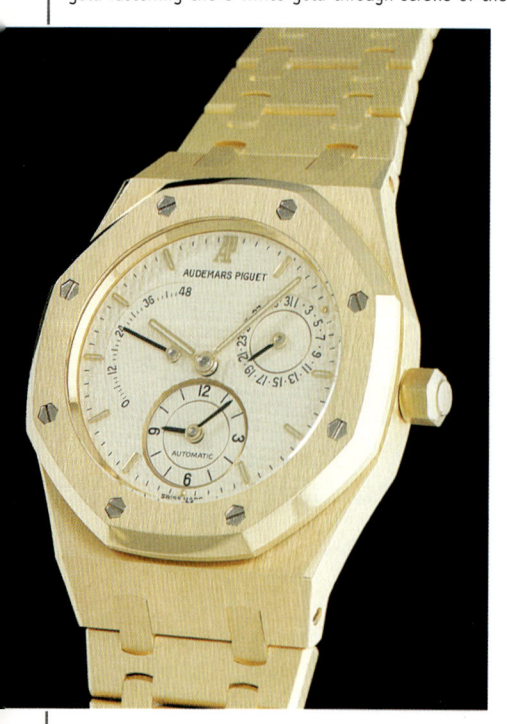

AUDEMARS PIGUET

ROYAL OAK CHRONOGRAPH — REF. 25860ST.O.1110ST/01

Movement: mechanical, automatic winding, Audemars Piguet caliber 2385. 21 kt gold rotor. Hand-finished (Côtes de Genève).
Functions: hour, minute, small second, date, chronograph with 3 counters.
Case: stainless steel, three-piece brushed case (Ø 41 mm, thickness 11 mm); flat sapphire crystal; octagonal bezel with gasket and 8 recessed hexagon nuts in white gold fastening the 8 white gold through screws of the case back; hexagonal screw-down crown with case protection; pushers with case protection. Water-resistant to 5 atm.
Dial: dark blue, decorated with Clous de Paris pattern; luminescent applied white painted bâton markers; luminescent white painted bâton hand.
Indications: date and minute counter at 3, small second at 6, hour counter at 9, center second counter, minute track.
Bracelet: stainless steel, satiny; fold-over safety clasp.
Price: 15'200 CHF.
Also available: yellow gold 39'900 CHF.

ROYAL OAK OFFSHORE CHRONOGRAPH — REF. 25770ST.O.0009/02

Movement: mechanical, automatic winding, A. Piguet caliber 2226/2840. Rotor with 21 kt gold segment. Hand-finished (Côtes de Genève). Protected against magnetic fields by a special ductile metal frame.
Functions: hour, minute, small second, date, chronograph with 3 counters.
Case: stainless steel, three-piece brushed case (Ø 42 mm, thickness 15 mm); flat sapphire crystal; octagonal bezel (joints in Therban) and 8 white gold recessed hexagon nuts fastening the 8 steel through screws (silver joints) of the case back (joints in Therban); hexagon screw down crown; pushers coated with a silicone layer. Water-resistant to 10 atm.
Dial: yellow, Clous de Paris and blue counter crowns; luminescent applied white gold oval markers; luminescent white gold bâton hands.
Indications: date with magnifying glass at 3, hour counter at 6, minute counter at 9, small second at 12, center second counter, minute track with divisions for 1/5 of a second, tachymeter scale on the beveled ring.
Strap: shark leather, padded and hand stitched; steel fold-over safety clasp.
Price: 36'200 CHF.
Also available: leather strap velcro or bracelet (on request); titanium bracelet (on request); yellow gold (on request); many dial colors and leather strap.

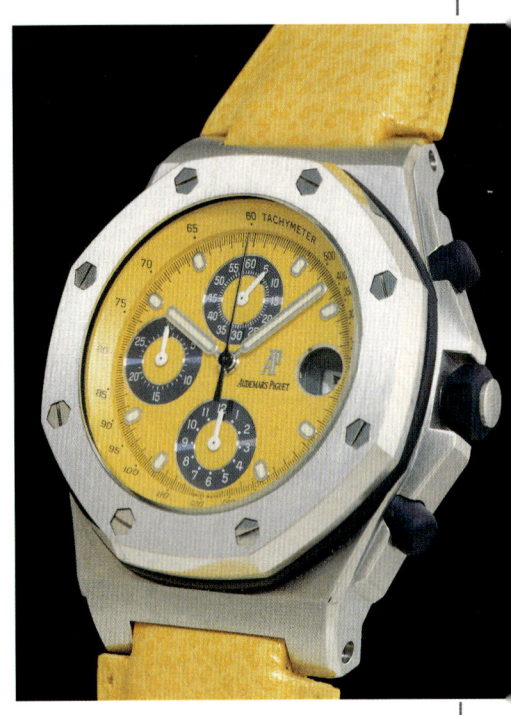

ROYAL OAK OFFSHORE DAY-DATE MONTH — REF. 25807ST.O.1010ST/01

Movement: mechanical, automatic winding, A. Piguet caliber 2127/2827. Rotor with 21 kt gold segment. Hand-finished (Côtes de Genève and circular graining). Protected against magnetic fields by a special ductile metal frame.
Functions: hour, minute, small second, full calendar (date, day, month).
Case: stainless steel, three-piece brushed case (Ø 37 mm, thickness 14,5 mm); flat sapphire crystal; octagonal bezel (joints in Therban) and 8 recessed hexagon nuts in white gold fastening the 8 steel through screws (silver joints) of the case back (joints in Therban); 2 correctors on case side; hexagonal screw-down crown coated with a silicone layer. Water-resistant to 10 atm.
Dial: black, Clous de Paris; applied white gold luminescent bâton markers; white gold luminescent bâton hands.
Indications: small second at 6, day and month below 12, white pointed center date hand with reading on the beveled ring.
Bracelet: steel; fold-over safety clasp.
Price: 12'800 CHF.
Also available: leather strap (on request); yellow gold, leather strap or bracelet (on request); many other color combinations of dial and leather strap.

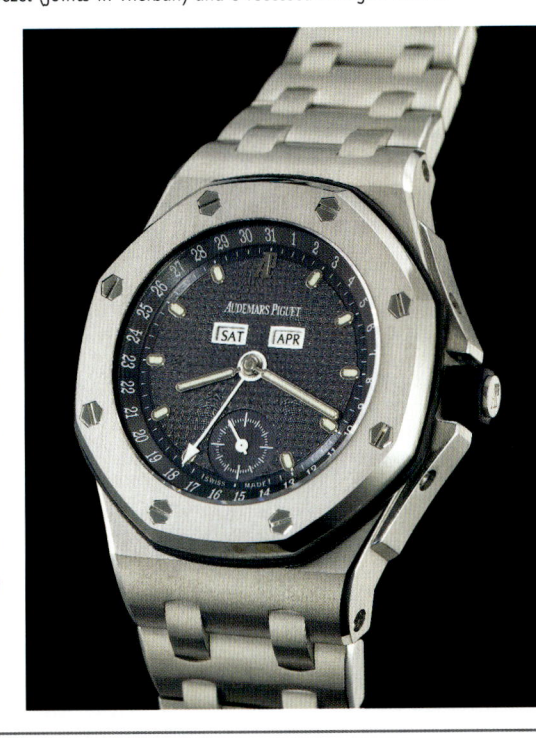

ROYAL OAK OFFSHORE AUTOMATIC LADY — REF. 77151ST.O.0009/01

Movement: mechanical, automatic winding, Audemars Piguet caliber 2140. Rotor with 21 kt gold segment. Hand-finished (Côtes de Genève). Protected against magnetic fields by a special ductile metal frame.
Functions: hour, minute, center second, date.
Case: stainless steel, three-piece brushed case (Ø 30 mm, thickness 10 mm); flat sapphire crystal; octagonal bezel with joints in Therban and 8 recessed hexagon nuts in white gold fastening the 8 steel through screws (silver joints), of the case back (joints in Therban); hexagonal screw-down crown coated with a silicone layer. Water-resistant to 10 atm.
Dial: blue, decorated with Clous de Paris pattern; luminescent applied white gold oval markers; railway minute track on the beveled ring; luminescent white gold bâton hands.
Indications: date at 3.
Strap: shark leather, padded and hand stitched; steel fold-over safety clasp.
Price: 7'850 CHF.
Also available: bracelet (on request); yellow gold, leather strap or bracelet (on request); many other color combinations of dial and leather strap.

Baume & Mercier

Baume & Mercier's headliner this past year was its gold Hampton Milleis, an addition to the company's best-selling Hampton collection of rectangular watches. The Milleis, whose name is meant to evoke thoughts of the millennium, is a luxury version of the Hampton, in 18k yellow or white gold. What's unusual about the watch is its case shape, curved both horizontally and vertically and fitted with a sapphire crystal that is also domed in two directions. The men's watch comes in quartz and automatic versions; the women's models all have ultra-thin quartz movements. All have silvered dials with a guilloché pattern designed specifically for the collection, plus Arabic numerals at 3 o'clock, 9 o'clock and 12 o'clock. The automatic version has a date window at 6 o'clock. The strap is made of alligator and has a folding clasp.

In the fall of 1998 Baume & Mercier broke new ground when it launched its CapeLand watch, a chunky, steel model that was heftier and more macho than most of its other men's models. Now it's come out with a chronograph version of the CapeLand in a limited edition of 99 pieces each in pink and white gold, each marked on the dial with a year from the past century. There is also a single piece made in platinum.

Another new offering from Baume & Mercier: a new Catwalk women's watch with a bracelet made of steel and rubber. Until the new version came out, the Catwalk came in all-steel or all-gold models. There is also a new steel-and-diamond Catwalk; the diamonds run along the sides of the watch face.

The Gala Collection, also launched just a few months ago, is a collection of women's watches in 14k or 18k gold. They're available with or without diamonds and have plain white, mother-of-pearl or silver dials.

The History

It was during the 16th Century that the French Calvinist Baume family moved to Switzerland where, in 1610, at Les Bois it organized its watchmaking company. Two centuries later, in 1830 (some say '34) the Société Baume Frères was founded, and in 1844, when four of the Baume brothers were working there, a branch was opened in London. Just a few years later their watches were exported to Australia and New Zealand, presented at world fairs and won various and many awards. In 1893 the English Observatory at Kew awarded exceptional marks for precision (91.9 over 100) to the keyless tourbillon chronometer. Then, in 1912, William Baume met Paul Cerecicenko, who was born in Paris, the son of a Russian army official and an embroideress, and who changed his name to Mercier. A self-made man, Mercier speaks seven languages fluently and manages Haas, the Geneva watch and jewellery shop. Their friendship grew and in 1918, Baume & Mercier came into being in Geneva.

1921 - Their production was hallmarked with the Geneva Seal
1937 - William Baume retires because of ill health and his place is taken by Constantin De Gorski, a Pole resident in Geneva.
1950's - Having gotten through the difficult war years, Baume & Mercier regains its place with its ladies watches; the Marquise, held in a buckleless rigid bracelet, becomes famous. De Gorski dies in 1958 and control of the Company passes to Marc Beuchat. Several foreign companies would like to take over the Company but the workers are behind Beuchat who, in 1965, signs an agreement with the Piaget family.
1964 - A new logo is adopted: the Greek letter Phi to signify the Company's search for perfection in details and in proportions.
1968 - The Baume & Mercier automatic watches are among the thinnest of all made at the time.
1971 - The Tronosonic models are presented with diapason, or tuning fork, mechanism.
1973 - Three different models, Galaxy, Mimosa and Stardust, are awarded the Golden Rose prize at Baden-Baden. This is also the year of the extremely fortunate collection, Riviera: these models with their distinguishing 12-sided cases, have, in twenty years, accounted for 25% of the Company's sales volume and 30-35% of its proceeds.
1988 - Baume & Mercier becomes part of the Vendôme Luxury Group.
1997 - Baume & Mercier suggest closing one eye to tradition. They choose the Rétro Hampton, automatic with cambered case, and the new Classima, a man's extra-thin chronograph with round case and integrated lugs - their steel cases are their characteristics. The new ladies watch, Catwalk, is also made in steel, both the square case and bracelet. Their feminine public is offered some "jewel" type models. Linea, instead, presents the essential aesthetic that was so much in favor in the '80's.
1998 - CapeLand is the expression of the rediscovery of more traditional "forms", filtered by new sensitivity and new technical and technological capacities. Simple, linear, nearly elementary forms and yet so new, the curved profile of the polished steel case recalling unconsciously the majesty as well as imperfection of the Earth, thus inviting us towards adventure. Adventure as well in the jewelled or plain gold versions of Catwalk. For its tenth anniversary, Linea is presented in a splendid, diamond set, pink gold version.

BAUME & MERCIER

CAPELAND CHRONOGRAPH AUTOMATIC   REF. MOA06907

Movement: mechanical, automatic winding, BM 13750 (Valjoux caliber 7750).
Functions: hour, minute, small second, date, chronograph with 3 counters.
Case: stainless steel, three-piece polished case (Ø 39 mm, thickness 15,4 mm); brushed bezel; curved sapphire crystal; screw-down crown, with logo; rectangular pushers; screwed-on case back. Water-resistant to 10 atm.
Dial: black; painted Arabic numerals and minute track; luminescent dots; luminescent stainless steel CapeLand hands.
Indications: date at 3, center second counter, hour counter at 6, small second at 9, minute counter at 12, minute track.
Strap: crocodile leather; fold-over safety steel clasp.
Price: 2'450 CHF.
Also available: with bracelet; silvered dial and black Arabic numerals. Prices on request.

CAPELAND AUTOMATIC   REF. MOA06856

Movement: mechanical, automatic winding, ETA caliber 2895-1.
Functions: hour, minute, small second, date.
Case: stainless steel, three-piece polished case (Ø 39 mm, thickness 12.4 mm); brushed bezel; curved sapphire crystal; screw-down crown, with logo; screwed-on case back. Water-resistant to 10 atm.
Dial: black; printed Arabic numerals and lozenge minute track marker; luminescent dots; luminescent stainless steel CapeLand hands.
Indications: date at 3, oval small second at 6.
Bracelet: polished stainless steel; recessed double fold-over clasp.
Price: 2'100 CHF.
Also available: leather strap with fold-over clasp; silvered dial. Smaller size (Ø 37 mm), with quartz movement and center seconds, steel black or silvered dial, leather strap with fold-over clasp or with bracelet. Prices on request.

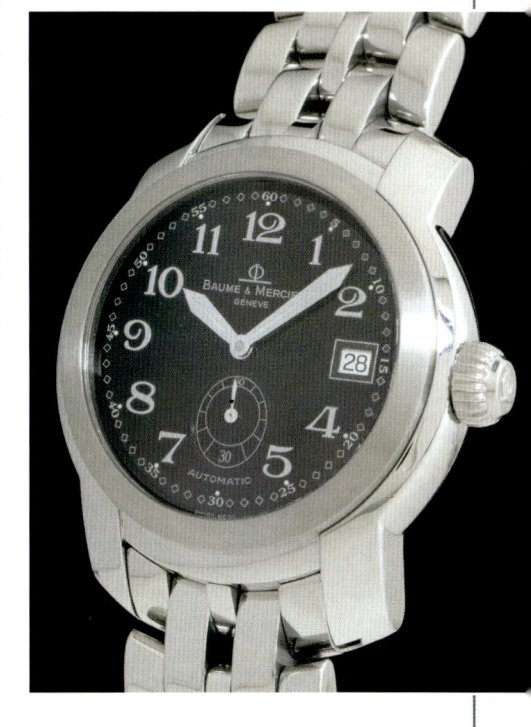

HAMPTON GRAND MODELE MILLEIS GOLD   REF. MOA06877

Movement: mechanical, automatic winding, ETA caliber 2000-1.
Functions: hour, minute, date.
Case: 18 kt yellow gold, two-piece polished rectangular case with longitudinal and transversal curving (height 34 mm, width 26 mm, thickness 8,2 mm); curved sapphire crystal; case back attached by 6 screws, with engraved individual number. Water-resistant to 3 atm.
Dial: silvered, engine turned (guilloché) with wave pattern; applied Arabic numerals and square markers; printed minute track; fan-shaped bâton hands.
Indications: date at 6.
Strap: crocodile leather; adjustable fold-over clasp, gold-plated.
Price: 3'750 CHF.
Also available: white gold; with quartz movement and small second at 6: in yellow gold, white or silvered dial and Arabic numerals; white gold, silvered dial and Arabic numerals. Lady's size with quartz movement and small second at 6, in yellow gold, silvered dial and Arabic numerals. Prices on request.

HAMPTON GRAND MODELE   REF. MOA06939

Movement: mechanical, automatic winding, ETA caliber 2000-1.
Functions: hour, minute, center second, date.
Case: stainless steel, two-piece polished rectangular-curved case (height at lugs 40 mm, width without crown 24,7 mm, thickness 8,3 mm); curved sapphire crystal; snap-on back. Water-resistant to 3 atm.
Dial: black; applied square markers and Arabic numerals; printed railway minute track; rhodium-plated fan-shaped bâton hands.
Indications: date at 6.
Strap: crocodile leather; stainless steel fold-over clasp.
Price: 1'800 CHF.
Also available: bracelet; white, blue or coppered dial with applied square markers and Arabic numerals or with blue, white or coppered dial, with printed bâton markers. In the big size, steel and black dial: automatic, Kevlar® leather strap or bracelet; quartz, Kevlar® leather strap or bracelet 1.950. Smaller size (height 26 mm, width 20 mm), quartz, steel with bracelet and black dial. Prices on request.

Bedat & Co

Innovation seamlessly melding with tradition — that is the hallmark of Bedat & Co., Switzerland's seasoned watchmakers who produce one of the youngest lines. Run by the mother and son team of Simone Bedat & Christian Bedat, the two are becoming a powerful force in the Swiss watchmaking industry with their line of contemporary, stylish timepieces. As testament, Bedat & Co.'s newest timepiece turns history upside down, just in time for the millennium, by giving an old timepiece a brand new look in the ChronoPocket, a chronograph wristwatch that is also a pocket watch, and a table clock, perfect for travelers. Christian Bedat calls the timepiece the first contemporary pocket watch. "For me, I have always liked pocket watches. I think the pocket watch is beautiful. But when other companies develop pocket watches they strive to recreate the look of old pocket watches rather than creating contemporary ones," says Bedat. When considering whether to launch either a chronograph or a pocket watch, it struck Bedat that he could offer one timepiece that combined both features. "It's important to propose something to the consumer that they appreciate and

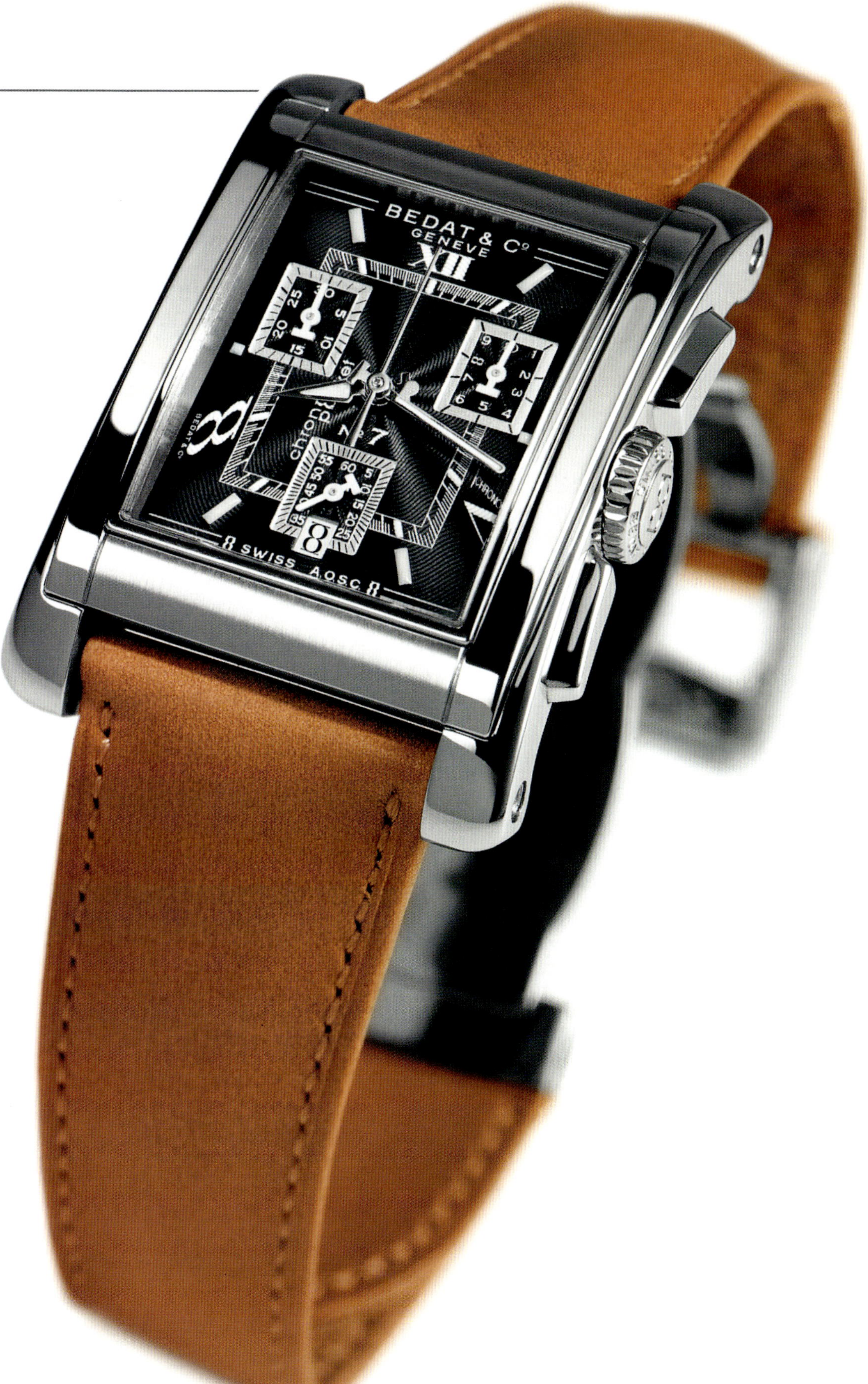
BEDAT & C°
GENEVE
SWISS

Bedat & Co

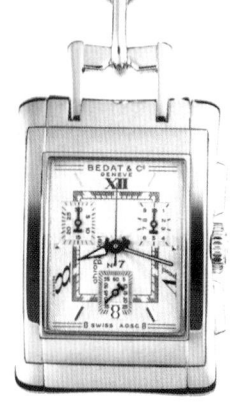

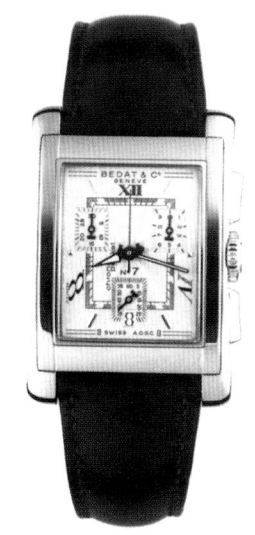

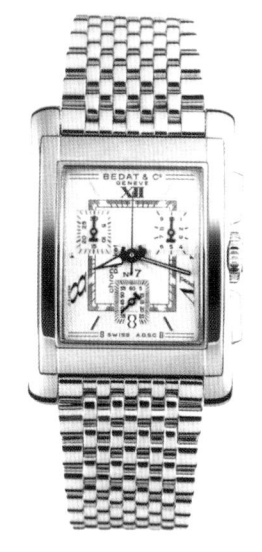

something they don't already have," says Christian Bedat. "We are creating an image by being innovative."

The ChronoPocket is housed in an elegant leather box lined with grey flannel, and contains up to three straps and the tool to convert the timepiece from wristwatch to pocket watch. Its sleek, rectangular face has three unusual rectangular windows to reveal the chronograph features, and it is available in steel, yellow and rose gold, white gold, or in platinum. "The name ChronoPocket refers 100 percent to the product. Few watch names define the product and that's one thing that gives the product the strength to become a classic." It is important to Bedat that his watches survive for generations. For this reason, the design of a Bedat & Co. timepiece is steeped in classic styling inspired by the work of artisans in the 1930s, yet updated with modern details.

The style of Bedat & Co. watches are suited to a particular niche of sophisticated watch wearers recognized by both Simone Bedat and Christian Bedat when the two decided to launch their own brand in 1997. The first collection drew remarkable acclaim from within the industry, where the Bedat's are well-known after committing several decades of experience to watchmaking. With the launch of their first collection of 52 pieces, it was evident that Bedat & Co. would not waver on standards. First, Bedat & Co. developed their own set of guidelines called the A.O.S.C, the "Certificate of Swiss Origin." "The A.O.S.C. guidelines were developed to instill confidence with the consumer," Bedat explains. The guidelines certify that each watch is made of only Swiss parts, and also guarantee the life of the watch for five years. The Bedat's also carefully defined the style consistency of the Bedat & Co. collection. Each dial is always comprised of the same Bedat & Co. details, from the exclusive Bedat watch hands, to the placement of the Bedat logo at the 8, to the appearance of the Bedat & Co name above the 12 and the A.O.S.C. insignia below the 6.

With the same precise detailing, Bedat & Co. also established firm rules on how each collection would be named and chose to refer to each collection by number,

Opening Page
Table clock positioned, 18K yellow and rose gold ChronoPocket.
Ref. 778.310.810

Previous Page
Very distinctive look for the steel ChronoPocket.
Ref. 778.010.320

Left
Christian Bedat.

Top (left to right)
The ChronoPocket transforms itself into a pocket watch, a desk watch, a chronograph with a leather or steel bracelet.

Below
The elegant leather and grey flannel box housing the ChronoPocket and its tools.

Bottom
"The name ChronoPocket refers 100 percent to the product."
Here featured in 18K yellow and rose gold.
Ref. 778.310.320.

symbols of time itself. When determining which numbers would be selected, the Bedat's understood they must appeal across continents, and chose the numbers with deep significance for many cultures. The ladies' collection is named No. 3, for the symbol of perfection; the Trinity, Buddhism's three jewels and the three

51

Bedat & C⁰

phases of existence, while the men's collection is called No.7, the symbol of eternal life; seven degrees of perfection and the seven heads of naja at AngkorWat, while the No.8 collection is represented by the symbol of infinity.

Although each watch boasts the trademark Bedat & Co. features, each collection has its own distinctive look. With its sensuously curved, rectangular face, the ChronoPocket is an obvious extension of the No.7 collection, which includes square, rectangular, and a slightly rounded rectangular shaped watch faces. While the No. 7 collection was developed for men, in 1999 Bedat adorned the symmetry of the square shape with diamonds, added a satin strap and created an irresistible evening timepiece. "We've come fur-

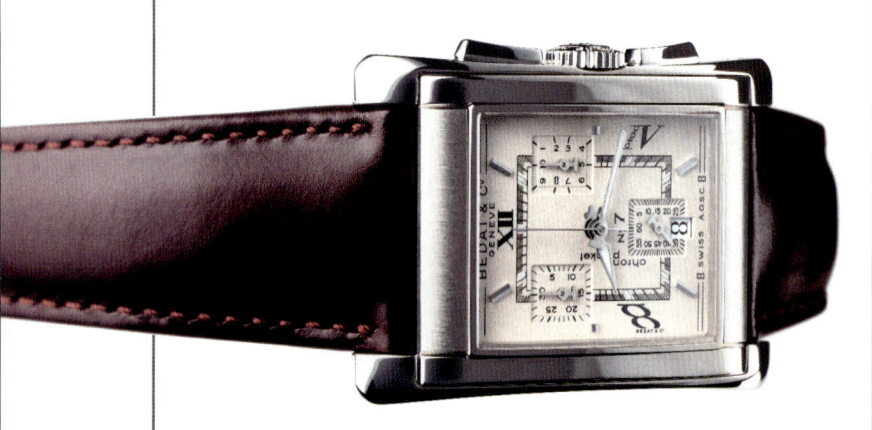

Above
This timepiece already has the beauty and distinction of a "classic" 18K white gold ChronoPocket.
Ref. 778.510.810.

Facing page
Top (left to right)
N°3, 101 diamonds set, steel.
Ref. 304.051.109.

N°7, Automatic, 185 diamonds set on steel.
Ref. 728.050.109.

N°7, Automatic, 205 diamonds on steel.
Ref. 788.050.109

Bottom
Sensuously curved rectangular automatic steel N°7.
Ref. 788.011.110.

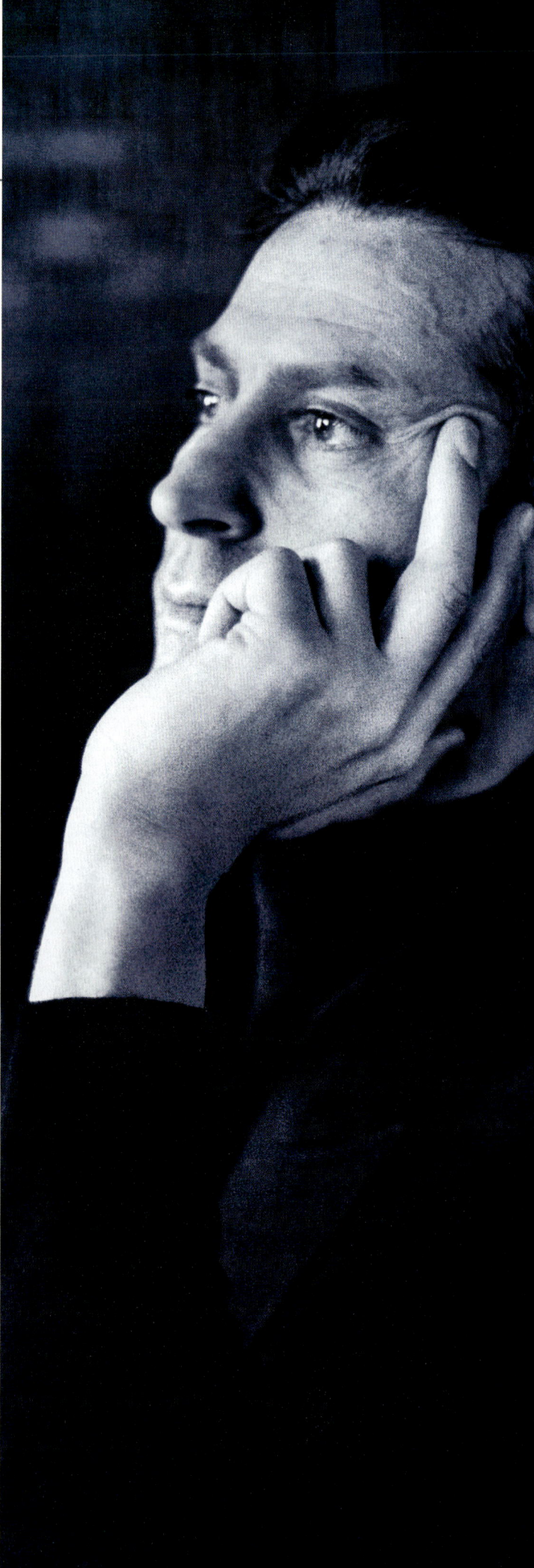

Bedat & Co

ther with setting our watches with diamonds, using more diamonds than ever before," says Bedat. Consumers can decide between the more refined diamond setting alongside the bezel, or a magnificent diamond watch whose bezel is completely set with diamonds.

The ladies No. 7 timepieces also come with colored stones and accent color strap, with one row of stones at the top and bottom of the bezel. Each reflects the sensational appeal now familiar from the Jeweler in Steel. "The use of color is comforting, reassuring," says Bedat. The jeweled No. 7 watches are the cosmopolitan counterpart to the extraordinary No. 3 collection which includes the bracelet watch with knitted steel links. Delicate and demure, the bracelet style looks like a family heirloom, or an item that would have been worn by your grandmother. Whether completely covered in diamond pave or delicately set with diamonds on the bezel, the timepiece evokes nostalgia for days gone by. A bracelet design may have as many as 592 diamonds accenting supple beauty.

From the sinuous barrel, manchette and hexagonal shapes of No. 3 to the smooth curved lines of each timepiece in No. 7 and the sporty round shape of No. 8, Bedat & Co. strives to offer elegance that transcends generations.

"Whatever we create should be a contemporary classic today and tomorrow," says Bedat.

Bedat & C⁰

The watch brand is attracting the attention of leading fashion magazines in the U.S., a development that has not gone unnoticed by Bedat, who oversees the development of the U.S market. "We are new and when people support us, I really appreciate it." His well-planned, yet subtle branding may be a part of the draw. Advertisements for Bedat & Co. products are captivating for what they don't say. Images of charismatic people in unidentifiable settings beg the viewer to ask, 'Where are they? Who are they? What are they thinking?.' Bedat explains that the ad targets the people who will buy his watch, those who will identify with the person in the ad and recognize that the ad demonstrates that a person has a choice which watch to wear, that they are not obligated to wear a Bedat & Co. or any other brand.

A watch lover himself, Bedat recognizes that there are many prestigious watches to own and is most pleased when the consumer chooses a Bedat & Co. watch because of an appreciation for the design, not because of a feeling of obligation. As a new watchmaker, Bedat says his goal is to develop Bedat & Co. into a "small institutional brand." Already, the watchmaker is stealing a great deal of limelight with its inspiring innovations, including the ChronoPocket, that are helping pave the way for the future of watchmaking.

Bedat & C° jeweller of steel

Below
Automatic N°7 steel set with princess cut blue topaze, pink tourmaline, yellow citrine or diamonds.
Ref. 728.810.109
Ref. 728.710.109
Ref. 728.610.109
Ref. 728.510.109

Bedat & Co

Below
From purely steel to tremendously diamond, N°3 bracelet watch.
Ref. 308.011.109
Ref. 308.022.109 (287 diamonds)
Ref. 308.035.109 (606 diamonds)

Blancpain

Measuring up to the vast and competitive jungle of top of the line watchmaking is certainly no easy task. Blancpain well knows this. And, season after season, success upon success, it is always at the top with its creations, in its constant search for perfection. Beautifully interpreting the style of our days - frenetic and vivacious - the Maison concentrated its attention in 1999 particularly on the sports collection 2100. Among the new proposals, the Tourbillon Split-second Chronograph with fly-back feature has extra-thin automatic movement with 8 day power reserve and military-style dial; the Minute repeater "Pièce Unique" with automatons (or Jaquemarts) that enliven the background; the Chronograph and the Calendar Demi-Savonnette, with the characteristic double back case. The first, solid and hinged, the second, traditional, screwed in place with viewing hole. A piece with classic lines justified by its classic origins: legend says that this type of watch was invented by Napoleon.

The Le Brassus' Company has also remembered the "citizens of the world" with the Time Zone, double time zone and day/night indication that shows at a glance, thanks to the particular geometry of the dial, the time in two distinct part of the world. After earth, water is the key element in Aqua Lung, the new automatic with water-resistant to 100 meters steel case.

Impossible not to remember Ladybird, the lucky successor of the 1956 model that used what was then the smallest manual movement in the world, and that can make the same boast today, automatic, of course…

The Special Series of Blancpain

The realization of preparatory models, or special series has always been one of the most distinctive characteristics of fine Swiss watchmaking.

Blancpain has respected this tradition which allows collectors and watch-lovers to acquire limited number versions that are sure to increase in value, and this year has create two interesting proposals.

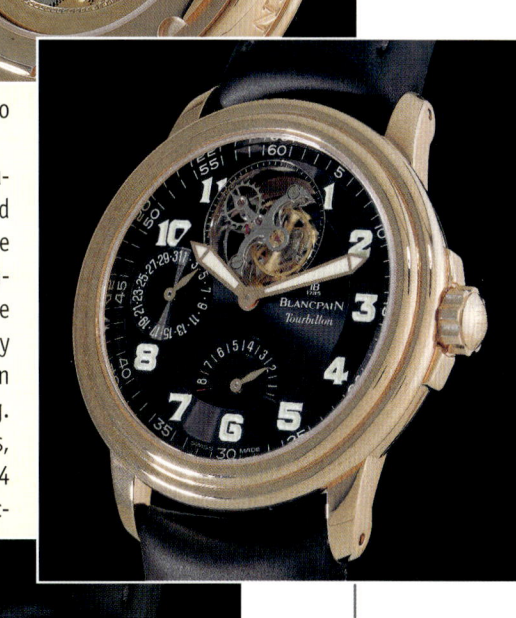

The first is Concept 99 that is substantially an evolution of the Trilogy (fifty Fathoms, Air Command and GMT). It is a special series that is characterized by the combination of steel and rubber on the crown, pushpieces, bezel and bracelet; a collection that recalls the sturdiness, durability and water resistance of the Fifty Fathoms, refining its functions and suggesting again its great wearableness, lightness and ease in reading. It was presented last year at Basel in limited numbers, Concept 99 includes: the GMT that through the "24 hours" function permanently shows the hour in a second time zone with a central independent hand, while a third time zone can be shown using the rotating bezel; the professional and military chronograph Air Command with fly-back feature in a futuristic presentation that is at the same time determined and tough, extremely light in design and as modern as space travel; the underwater Fifty Fathoms, the real ancestor of the whole series, is produced so rigorously that the person wearing it can face marine depths with the same equanimity as if strolling along the beach (single direction rotating bezel, screw-down crown, luminous markers and hands and water resistant to 300 m).

The second limited series is Desert Storm, a winning hand for sports lovers and whoever is active and dynamic. There are three sets, and eight of each are available: a Complete Calendar Moon Phases; a Chrono Fly-back Perpetual Calendar; a Tourbillon; a Chrono fly-back. The cases all have the design of the 2100 Collection, black dial with military type markers, the "techno" strap in crocodile covered with rubber. The sets will be available in the three gold colors (yellow, red, white) and will be sold in a solid wood case made of sycamore and macassar wood.

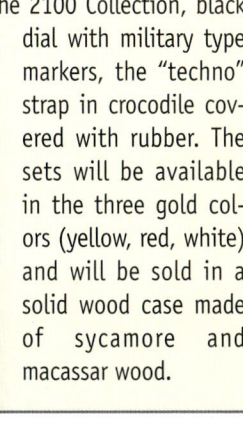

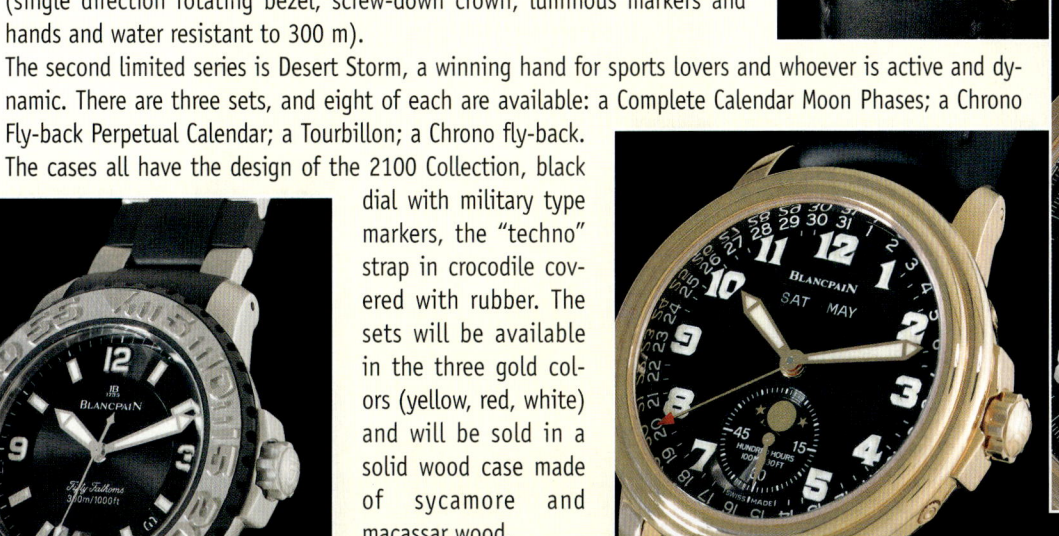

BLANCPAIN

1735 2100 — REF. 2735-1418-53BDA

Movement: mechanical, automatic winding, extra-thin, with tourbillon, produced exclusively for Blancpain caliber 1735, made up by 740 elements, autonomy 48 hours, skeleton platinum rotor, 44 jewels (Ø 31,5 mm, 13'''1/2, thickness 11 mm). Beryllium balance, 21,600 vibrations per hour (vph), flat balance-spring. Pillar-plates in 18 kt pink gold, decorated wheels, hand-polished steel parts.
Functions: hours, minutes; perpetual calendar (date, day, month, year, moon phase), minute repeater, split-second chronograph with 2 counters.
Case: 18 kt yellow gold, three-piece case (Ø 42 mm, thickness 17,5 mm); curved antireflective sapphire crystal; brand engraved on case side; screw-down yellow gold crown with split-second pusher; screw-down yellow gold pushers; 4 correctors on case side; screwed-on case back. Water-resistant to 3 atm.
Dial: white; applied yellow gold markers; luminescent cabochon on dial-train; luminescent skeletonized yellow gold sword style hands.
Indications: minute counter and date at 3, moon at 6, day at 9, month and four year cycle at 12, center split-second counters, minute track with divisions for 1/5 of a second.
Strap: crocodile leather, hand stitched; yellow gold fold-over clasp.
Price: 890'000 CHF.

2100 TOURBILLON AUTOMATIC — REF. 2125-1527-53

Movement: mechanical, automatic winding, extra-thin, produced exclusively for Blancpain caliber 25, with flying tourbillon; autonomy 8 days. Made up by 238 elements, 21 jewels, (Ø 25,6 mm, 11'''1/2, thickness 4,85 mm).
Functions: hour, minute, small second, date, power reserve.
Case: 18 kt white gold, three-piece case (Ø 38 mm, thickness 9,7 mm); antireflective curved sapphire crystal; brand engraved on case side; gold screw-down crown; shaped screwed-on back, displaying the movement through a sapphire crystal. Water-resistant to 10 atm.
Dial: white enameled, aperture on the tourbillon; applied white gold bâton markers (Roman numeral 6); luminescent cabochon on the printed minute track; luminescent skeletonized white gold sword style hands.
Indications: power reserve at 6, date at 9, small second at 12 integrated in the tourbillon carriage.
Strap: crocodile leather, hand stitched; white gold clasp.
Price: 74'800 CHF.
Also available: with fold-over clasp; with bracelet; with blue dial; in yellow gold and white or blue or pink gold dial and white dial (prices on request).

2100 MINUTE REPEATER — REF. 2135-1442-53

Movement: mechanical, automatic winding, produced exclusively for Blancpain caliber 35, autonomy 44 hours, 21 kt gold rotor. made up by 360 elements, 39 jewels, (Ø 23,5 mm, 10'''1/2, thickness 4,85 mm). **Functions:** hour, minute, small second, minute repeater. **Case:** 18 kt yellow gold, three-piece case (Ø 38 mm, thickness 11 mm); curved sapphire crystal; repeater slide provided with a safety lock fastened on the activation system, which makes it water-proof (once the lever is rotated, an inside spring is released and the sonnerie can work); pink gold screw-down crown; screwed-on case back, displaying the movement through a sapphire crystal. Water-resistant to 3 atm.
Dial: silvered, central part engine turned (guilloché) with shell pattern; applied yellow gold bâton markers and Roman numerals; luminescent cabochon on the printed minute track; luminescent yellow gold sword style hands.
Indications: small second at 6.
Strap: crocodile leather, hand stitched; yellow gold fold-over clasp.
Price: 136'500 CHF, also in pink gold and white gold, 10 pieces for each version.
Also available: classical: aut. Ref. 0035, yellow gold; red gold; platinum; manual Ref. 0033: yellow gold; red gold; platinum; with automata, lady Ref. 00342 yellow gold or platinum.

2100 CHRONO FLY-BACK PERPETUAL CALENDAR — REF. 2585F-3630-64BD

Movement: mechanical, automatic winding, Blancpain caliber 55F8, 18 kt gold rotor.
Functions: hour, minute, perpetual calendar (date, day, month, year, moon phase), chronograph with fly-back feature and 3 counters.
Case: 18 kt pink gold, three-piece case (Ø 38 mm, thickness 14 mm); antireflective curved sapphire crystal; 2 correctors and brand engraved on case side; screw-down crown and pushers; screwed-on case back. Water-resistant to 5 atm.
Dial: black-oxidized opaline; luminescent Arabic numerals; luminescent dots on the printed minute track; luminescent sword style hands.
Indications: minute counter and date at 3, moon phase at 6, hour counter and day at 9, month and four year cycle at 12, center second fly-back counter, minute track with divisions for 1/5 of a second.
Strap: rubber; pink gold fold-over clasp.
Price: 35'100 CHF. Edition limited to 50 pieces.
Also available: white gold with blue dial and calf leather strap, 50 pieces.

BLANCPAIN

2100 CHRONO RATTRAPANTE FLY-BACK TOURBILLON   REF. 2189F-3430-63

Movement: mechanical, automatic winding, extra-thin, produced exclusively for Blancpain caliber 2389A, with flying tourbillon. 18 kt yellow gold rotor.
Functions: hour, minute, center second, split-second chronograph with fly-back feature and 3 counters.
Case: platinum, three-piece case (Ø 38 mm, thickness 14.5 mm); antireflective curved sapphire crystal; brand engraved on case side; platinum screw-down crown and pushers; split-second pusher at 10; shaped screwed-on back, displaying the movement through a sapphire crystal. Water-resistant to 10 atm.
Dial: black-oxidized opaline, aperture on the tourbillon; luminescent Arabic numerals; luminescent dots on the printed minute track; luminescent skeletonized sword style hands.
Indications: off-center hour and minute at 12, minute counter at 3, small second at 6 integrated in the tourbillon carriage, hour counter at 9, center split-second fly-back counters, minute track with divisions for 1/5 of a second.
Strap: calf, hand stitched; platinum clasp.
Price: 160'000 CHF. Edition limited to 99 pieces.
Also available: white dial, crocodile leather strap, 99 pieces.

2100 FLY-BACK CHRONOGRAPH   REF. 2185F-1430-63BDA

Movement: mechanical, automatic winding, caliber F185, with fly-back feature (allowing the chronograph's second hand to start again immediately after a zero setting).
Functions: hour, minute, small second, date, chronograph with fly-back feature and 3 counters.
Case: 18 kt yellow gold, three-piece case (Ø 38 mm, thickness 12 mm); antireflective flat sapphire crystal; brand engraved on case side; yellow gold screw-down crown and pushers; screwed-on case back, displaying the movement through a sapphire crystal. Water-resistant to 10 atm.
Dial: black-oxidized opaline; luminescent Arabic numerals; luminescent skeletonized sword style hands.
Indications: minute counter at 3, small second and date at 6, hour counter at 9, center fly-back second counter, minute track with luminescent dots on the printed minute track and divisions for 1/5 of a second.
Strap: calf, hand stitched; yellow gold fold-over clasp.
Price: 17'800 CHF.
Also available: clasp; bracelet; steel and black dial, leather strap with clasp or fold-over clasp, bracelet; pink gold, leather strap, rubber fold-over clasp and black dial: 25 pieces; pink gold bracelet, 50 pieces; white gold bracelet and blue dial, 50 pieces.

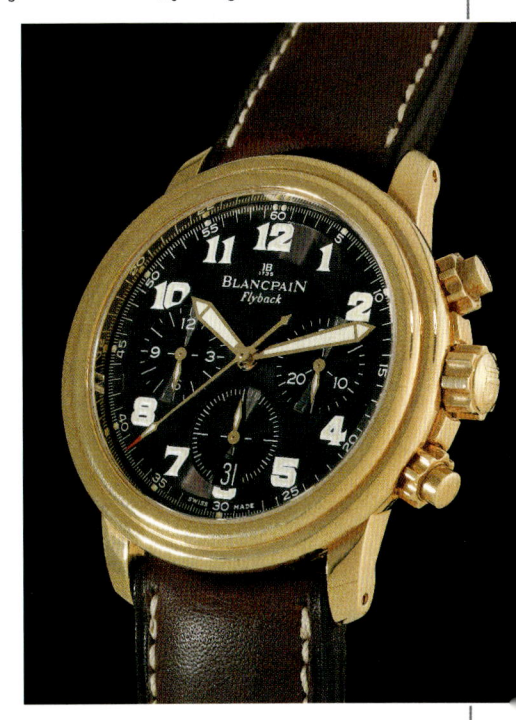

2100 TIME ZONE   REF. 2160-1130M-63

Movement: mechanical, automatic winding, extra-thin, produced exclusively for Blancpain caliber 5L60.
Functions: hour, minute, small second, date, second time zone, night & day indicator.
Case: stainless steel, three-piece case (Ø 38 mm, thickness 12 mm); antireflective curved sapphire crystal; brand engraved on case side; screw-down crown; shaped screwed-on back, displaying the movement through an antireflective sapphire crystal. Water-resistant to 10 atm.
Dial: black-oxidized opaline; zones with concentric-circles pattern; luminescent Arabic numerals; luminescent skeletonized sword style hands; printed minute track.
Indications: date at 3, small second at 6; night & day indicator at 9; hours and minute of the second timezone at 12, minute track.
Strap: calf, hand stitched; stainless steel clasp.
Price: 6'900 CHF.
Also available: white dial, crocodile leather strap; with bracelet and black dial. Edition limited to 333 pieces for each version, crocodile leather strap and opaline dial: pink gold; white gold.

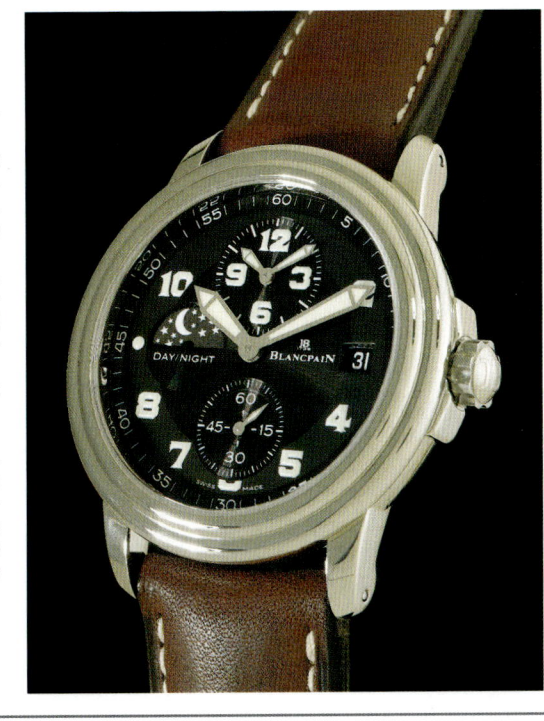

AQUA LUNG   REF. 2100-1130A-64BD

Movement: mechanical, automatic winding, caliber 1150, autonomy 100 hours. 18 kt yellow gold rotor.
Functions: hour, minute, center second, date.
Case: stainless steel, three-piece hand brushed case (Ø 38 mm, thickness 10 mm); antireflective curved sapphire crystal; brand engraved on case side; screw-down crown; screwed-on case back, displaying the movement through an antireflective sapphire crystal. Water-resistant to 10 atm.
Dial: black-oxidized opaline; luminescent applied white gold bâton markers and 4 military-fashioned Arabic numerals; printed white minute track; luminescent rhodium plated sword style hands.
Indications: date at 3, minute track with divisions for 1/5 of a second.
Strap: rubber, hand stitched; stainless steel fold-over clasp.
Price: 6'900 CHF. Edition limited to 1999 pieces.
Also available: with bracelet.

BLANCPAIN

2100 MOON PHASE CALENDAR — REF. 2763-1130-53

Movement: mechanical, automatic winding, caliber 1153, autonomy 100 hours. 18 kt gold rotor.
Functions: hour, minute, small second, full calendar (date, day, month, moon phase).
Case: stainless steel, three-piece case (Ø 38 mm, thickness 12 mm); antireflective curved sapphire crystal; 2 correctors and brand engraved on case side; screw-down crown; screwed-on case back displaying the movement through a sapphire crystal. Water-resistant to 10 atm. 
Dial: black-oxidized opaline; applied faceted bâton markers and 4 Roman numerals; printed minute track; luminescent skeletonized rhodium plated sword style hands.
Indications: moon phase and small second at 6, day and month at 12, red pointed center date hand.
Strap: crocodile leather, hand stitched; stainless steel clasp.
Price: 6'800 CHF.
Also available: white dial; fold-over clasp; bracelet; yellow gold, white or blue dial, leather strap, clasp or fold-over clasp, or bracelet; white gold, white or blue dial, leather strap, clasp or fold-over clasp, bracelet; pink gold, black dial, 300 pieces, leather strap, clasp or fold-over clasp; with "Military" dial, steel, leather strap, clasp or fold-over clasp, or bracelet.

CHRONOMETER — REF. 7002-1130-61

Movement: mechanical, manual winding, produced exclusively for Blancpain caliber 64/1, autonomy 40 hours.
Functions: hour, minute, small second.
Case: stainless steel, three-piece case (Ø 36 mm, thickness 6.8 mm); antireflective flat sapphire crystal; snap-on back displaying the movement through a sapphire crystal. Water-resistant to 3 atm. 
Dial: black-oxidized opaline; applied rhodium plated pointed markers and 4 Arabic numerals; luminescent dots on the printed minute track; luminescent rhodium plated leaf style hands.
Indications: small second at 6.
Strap: crocodile leather, hand stitched; stainless steel clasp.
Price: 5'800 CHF.

AIRCOMMAND — REF. 2285F-1540-64BDA

Movement: mechanical, automatic winding, caliber F185, with fly-back feature (allows the chronograph's second hand to start again immediately after a zero setting).
Functions: hour, minute, small second, date, chronograph with fly-back feature and 3 counters.
Case: 18 kt white gold, three-piece case (Ø 40 mm, thickness 13.5 mm); flat sapphire crystal; embossed minute track on the counter-clockwise turning bezel, useful for the calculation of diving times; brand engraved on case side; white gold screw-down crown and pushers; screwed-on case back. Sub 30 atm. 
Dial: bright blue; applied white gold bâton markers (Arabic numeral 12); luminescent dots on the printed minute track; luminescent skeletonized white gold sword style hands.
Indications: minute counter at 3, small second and date at 6, hour counter at 9, center fly-back second counter, minute track with divisions for 1/5 of a second.
Strap: crocodile leather, natural-rubber reinforced, water-repellent, hand stitched; white gold fold-over clasp.
Price: 20'900 CHF.
Also available: bracelet; steel, black dial, bracelet; yellow gold, black dial, leather strap, fold-over clasp, bracelet; pink gold, opaline dial, bracelet: 33 pieces.

GMT — REF. 2250-1430-63BDS

Movement: mechanical, automatic winding, caliber 5A50, autonomy of 100 hours. Tested and checked for 2,400 hours.
Functions: hour, minute, center second, date, second time zone, 24-hour indication.
Case: 18 kt yellow gold, three-piece case (Ø 40 mm, thickness 13,5 mm); flat sapphire crystal; bi-directional turning bezel, with embossed 24 hours scale, useful for time display of a second time-zone; brand engraved on case side; gold screw-down crown; screwed-on case back. Water-resistant to 30 atm. 
Dial: black-oxidized opaline; luminescent applied bâton markers and 4 Arabic numerals, in gold; luminescent dots on the printed minute track; luminescent skeletonized yellow gold sword style hands.
Indications: date between 4 and 5, luminescent red painted center second time-zone hand.
Strap: leather, natural-rubber reinforced, water-repellent and hand stitched; yellow gold fold-over clasp.
Price: 17'900 CHF.
Also available: bracelet; steel, black dial, bracelet; white gold, dial blue, leather strap and fold-over clasp or bracelet; pink gold, opaline dial, bracelet: 33 pieces.

BLANCPAIN

FIFTY FATHOMS   REF. 2200-1540-64BDA

Movement: mechanical, automatic winding, caliber 1151, autonomy of 100 hours. Tested and checked for 2,400 hours.
Functions: hour, minute, center second, date.
Case: 18 kt white gold, three-piece case (Ø 40 mm, thickness 13,5 mm); flat sapphire crystal; counter-clockwise turning bezel, with embossed minute track, useful for the calculation of diving times; brand engraved on case side; white gold screw-down crown; screwed-on case back. Water-resistant to 30 atm.
Dial: blue; luminescent rhodium plated applied bâton markers and 4 Arabic numerals; printed minute track; luminescent rhodium plated sword style hands.
Indications: date between 4 and 5.
Strap: crocodile leather, natural-rubber reinforced, water-repellent, hand stitched; white gold fold-over clasp.
Price: 8'500 CHF.
Also available: with bracelet; steel with bracelet and black dial; in yellow gold and black dial, leather strap and fold-over clasp or bracelet; pink gold with bracelet and opaline dial: 33 pieces.

AIR COMMAND PERPETUAL CALENDAR   REF. 2258F-3630-64BDS

Movement: mechanical, automatic winding, Blancpain caliber 55F8, with fly-back feature. 18 kt gold rotor.
Functions: hour, minute, perpetual calendar (date, day, month, year, moon phase), chronograph with fly-back feature and 3 counters.
Case: 18 kt pink gold, three-piece case (Ø 40 mm, thickness 15 mm); antireflective flat sapphire crystal; counter-clockwise turning bezel, with embossed minute track, useful for calculating diving times; 2 correctors and brand engraved on case side; pink gold screw-down crown and pushers; screwed-on case back. Water-resistant to 10 atm.
Dial: black-oxidized opaline; luminescent pink gold bâton markers; luminescent sword style hands.
Indications: minute counter and date at 3, moon phase at 6, hour counter and day at 9, month and four year cycle at 12, center fly-back second counter, minute track with divisions for 1/5 of a second.
Strap: crocodile leather, natural-rubber reinforced, water-repellent, hand stitched; pink gold fold-over clasp.
Price: 20'900 CHF. Edition limited to 99 pieces.

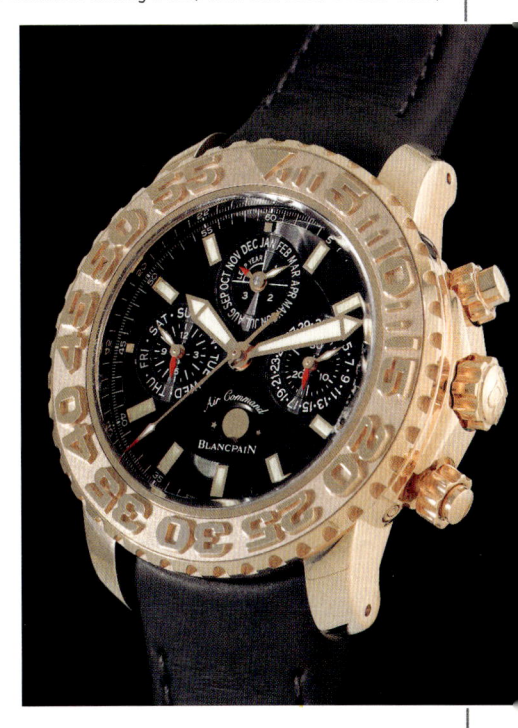

GMT PERPETUAL CALENDAR   REF. 2255A-3630-64BDS

Movement: mechanical, automatic winding, Blancpain caliber 55A5, autonomy of 100 hours.
Functions: hour, minute, perpetual calendar (date, day, month, year, moon phase), second time zone, 24-hour indication.
Case: 18 kt pink gold, three-piece case (Ø 40 mm, thickness 15 mm); antireflective flat sapphire crystal; bi-directional turning bezel, with embossed 24 hours scale, useful for displaying the time of a second time-zone; 2 correctors and brand engraved on case side; pink gold screw-down crown; screwed-on case back. Waterproof to 10 atm.
Dial: black-oxidized opaline; luminescent pink gold bâton markers; printed minute track; luminescent sword style hands.
Indications: date at 3, moon phase at 6, day at 9, month and four year cycle at 12, luminescent red painted center pointed second time-zone hand.
Strap: crocodile leather, natural-rubber reinforced, water-repellent, hand stitched; pink gold fold-over clasp.
Price: 34'400 CHF. Edition limited to 99 pieces.

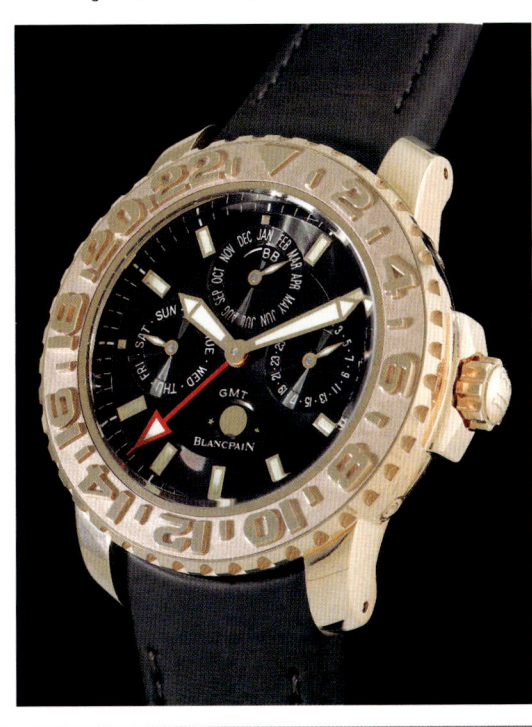

FIFTY FATHOMS PERPETUAL CALENDAR   REF. 22553-3630-64BDS

Movement: mechanical, automatic winding, Blancpain caliber 5553, autonomy of 100 hours.
Functions: hour, minute, perpetual calendar (date, day, month, year, moon phase).
Case: 18 kt pink gold, three-piece case (Ø 40 mm, thickness 15 mm); antireflective flat sapphire crystal; counter-clockwise turning bezel, with embossed minute track, useful for calculating diving times; 2 correctors and brand engraved on case side; pink gold screw-down crown; screwed-on case back. Waterproof to 10 atm.
Dial: black-oxidized opaline; luminescent pink gold bâton markers; printed minute track; luminescent sword style hands.
Indications: date at 3, moon phase at 6, day at 9, month and four year cycle at 12, center second counter, minute track.
Strap: crocodile leather, natural-rubber reinforced, water-repellent, hand stitched; pink gold fold-over clasp.
Price: 32'900 CHF.

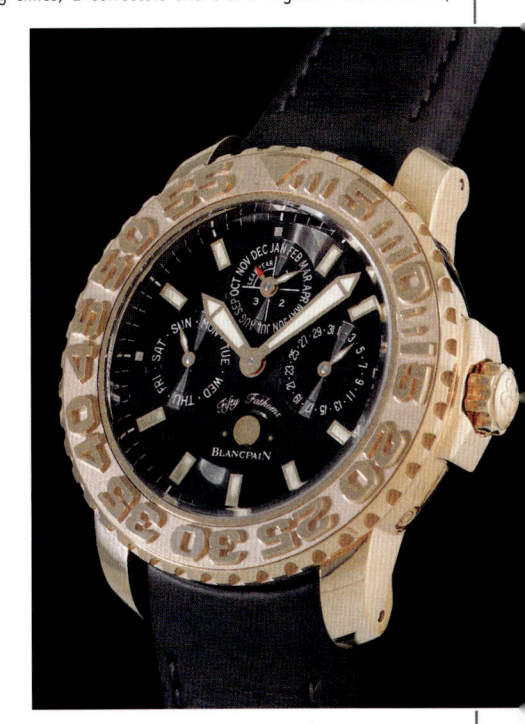

Boucheron

The great house of Boucheron boasts a prestigious place among the greatest jewelers of the world, not to mention its physical location at the heart of the haute-joaillerie world — Place Vendôme. This venerable jeweler has been creating immediately recognizable objects of art and sensational pleasures for well over a century. The title jeweler to imperial courts, shahs and maharajahs, Boucheron caters to international royalty, celebrities, corporate magnates and women of distinctly fine taste and spirit. Today, under the creative direction of fourth-generation Alain Boucheron, the company continues to follow the path of its founder: conveying emotion and passion in all of its creations — but with an enviable edge toward the future. In the past few years Alain Boucheron has brought the company to new heights, introducing incredible new jewelry and watches that reflect the company's artful eye, elegant past and well-poised future. It was Alain Boucheron's great grandfather, Frederic Boucheron, who opened his atelier in Paris in 1858 and immediately began creating high-jeweled celebrations of life, as well as opulent pendant, brooch

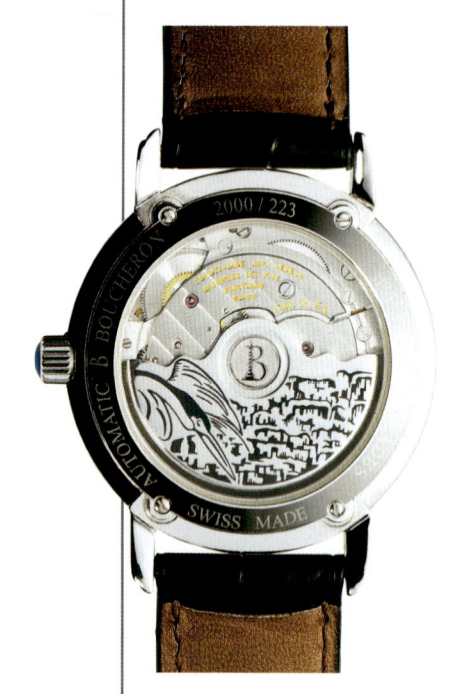

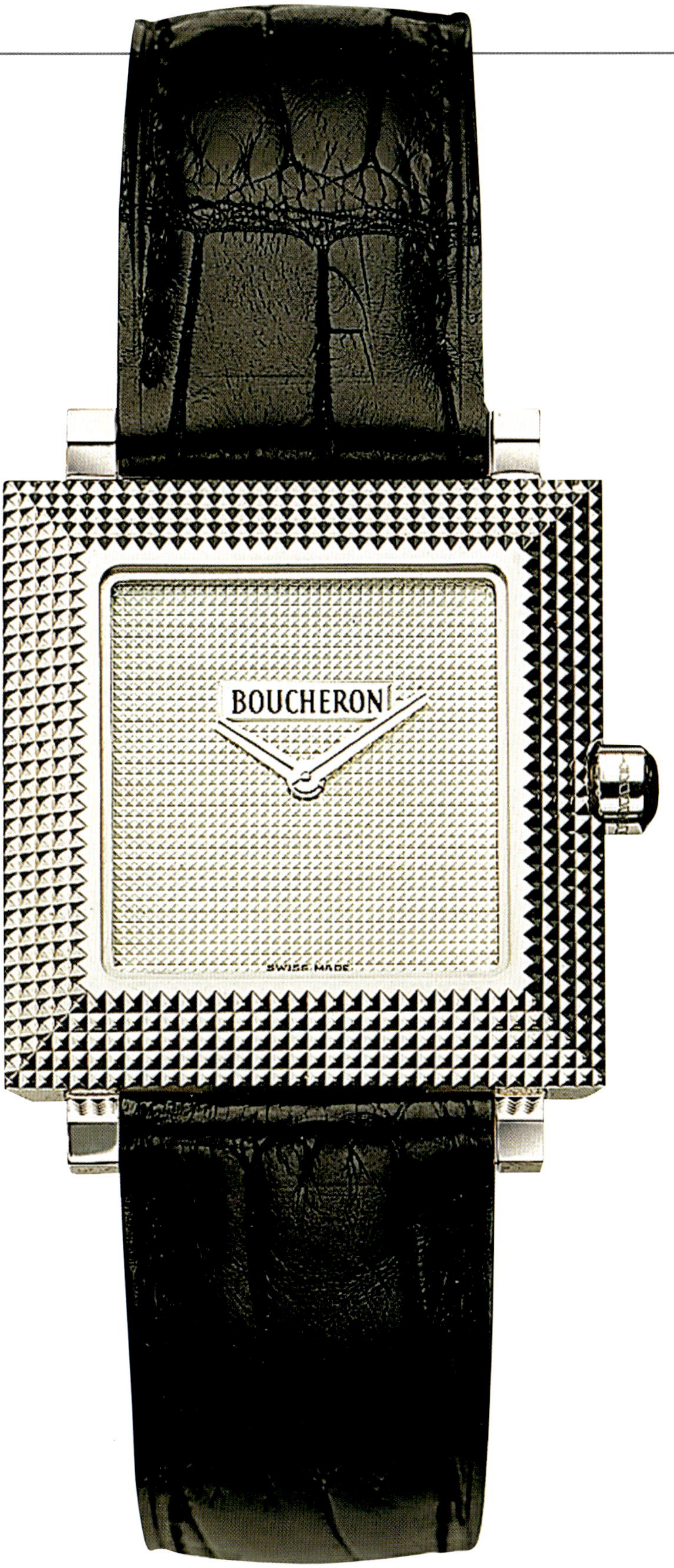
BOUCHERON
SWISS MADE

Boucheron

and pocket timepieces. His penchant for the finest of gemstones made his jewelry and timepieces coveted prizes of beauty. With his creations, the name of Boucheron was sealed — forever synonymous with elegance, innovation, and excitement.

Well ahead of his time, Boucheron opened his now famous boutique in Place Vendôme in 1893 — and adorned his windows with magnificent jewelry and watches. It may well have been his forward-thinking about timepieces that made the name Boucheron such a desirable and well-rounded company in its day. In an era when jewelers primarily offered jewelry and watchmakers offered watches — Boucheron offered both — masterfully — earning its reputation as the Jeweler of Time.

Throughout the next generations of Boucheron, the family continued to hold

Opening Page
Limited Edition platinum UNESCO watch with skeleton back featuring the Everglades World Heritage Site.

Previous Page
18K white gold automatic. "Diamant" watch.

Top left
18K white gold "Reflet" watch, set with 400 baguette diamonds.

Top right
18K white gold and diamond "Solis" watch with pavé diamond dial.

Center
18K white gold and diamond "Solis" watch with mother of pearl and diamond dial.

Left
18K yellow gold and diamond "Reflet" watch on a cultured pearl bracelet.

Boucheron

Above
Boucheron, Place Vendôme in Paris.

Center
18K white gold "Diamant" watches featured on crocodile straps.

Bottom
Limited Edition UNESCO automatic watch featured in 18K yellow gold and platinum.

timepieces as the most appealing and useful of jewels, and embarked on new ways to depict beauty in its watches. The design and innovations that epitomize the history of Boucheron watches defies time. From the first jewelry wristwatch to spherical watches, ring watches, and rock-crystal watches, Boucheron has always been a master at offering the unexpected.

In 1948 Boucheron created and patented an interchangeable invisible-clasp bracelet that set a new standard of excellence. The interchangeable straps and bracelets are slipped into an invisible clasp that is integrated into the watch case. The clasp closes once the watch strap is put into place. This unique system allows quick and easy interchanging of bracelets. It also features the BEST (Boucheron Easy System Technology) buckle system that allows the length of the bracelet to be perfectly adjusted to fit the wearer's wrist. Composing a world of harmony and emotion out of gemstones, pearls, platinum, gold and steel is a Boucheron passion that has remained intact for its more than 140 years. Even to this day, Boucheron continues in its ability to delight and surprise — a characteristic that Alain Boucheron has been careful to bring to Boucheron's objects d'art. While the timepieces created under Boucheron's attentive eye convey the same elegance and high style that his great-grandfather coined, they also offer a futuristic element of beauty and versatility.

"Today, Boucheron creates for the woman of the third millennium," says Alain Boucheron. "It imagines for her jewelry that will be the classics of tomorrow, and gives birth to a timeless value of emotion."

Indeed, from the high-jeweled masterpieces to the simply elegant sport watches, Boucheron timepieces offer flair, innovation

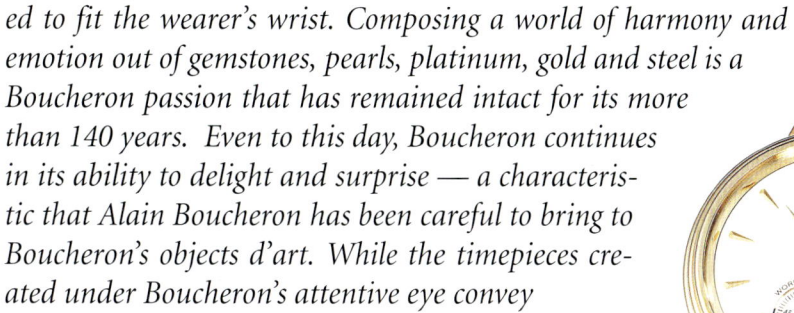

Boucheron

and a special sense of richness. Precious stones, pearls, and ornamental features grace Boucheron's timepieces — expressing personality, technique and sensitivity.

Artfully capturing the French spirit, Boucheron's timepieces embody a Swiss soul. All of the watches are designed and developed at Boucheron's workshops in Paris and are produced in the heart of the preeminent watchmaking country of Switzerland, where the time-honored tradition is world-renown.

Immediately recognizable for its striking lines and detailed craftsmanship, the Boucheron Montres Collection is at once complex, precise and elegant. It is focused, simply, around two design directions, one rectangular and the other circular. But that is where simplicity ends. Boucheron's rectangular design, Reflet, has been part of the company's collection since 1948. The round design, called Solis, was conceived of two years ago. Its contemporary style offers sporty, technical inspirations — and from it was born the Diver, Chronograph and Chronogolf — a unique timepiece that tracks golf scores.

Each timepiece collection features signature "godrons" - indented consecutive parallel lines that offer depth and dimension, emulating the female. Each, of course, incorporates the same patented interchangeable strap, invisible-clasp design from 1948 — offering today's watch wearer incredible versatility. The choices of bracelets range from the elegance of pearls, to the subtleness of satin,

Top left
18K yellow gold and diamond "Reflet" watch on a red lizard strap with fashion strap accessories.

Above
Stainless steel "Reflet" watch with pavé diamond dial.

Boucheron

Above
Stainless steel "Solis" watch with diamond bezel featured on a steel bracelet and interchangeable leather strap.

Top right
Stainless steel chronograph on interchangeable steel bracelet.

Bottom
Stainless steel "Solis" watch on blue leather strap with strap and bracelet accessories.

the allure of metal, and the casual comfort of denim. Twice a year, Boucheron introduces an array of metal bracelets and fabric straps that reflect the most up-to-date fashions and trends.

Finally, these elegant timepieces are adorned in varying degrees with diamonds and gemstones. Some are simply adorned with diamond markers, while others offer bezels and cases of sparkle. Still others are totally dripped in diamonds from bracelet to case to dial — offering the ultimate jewelry emotion — which is, of course, Boucheron's hallmark.

67

Breguet

Moving through the centuries with definite stylistic and technical coherence, Breguet arrives at the new millennium as a genuine point of reference for modern fine quality watchmaking. The tourbillon Chronograph is in the place of honor among the new products, practically a symbol for this Swiss company that had already presented it in a limited edition on its two-hundredth anniversary. It had cleverly combined two historic inventions of Abraham-Louis Breguet - the tourbillon and the double seconds chronometer, precursor of today's chronograph. This watch "classique", is a total expression of this Company's skill in building complication watches. Breguet, with its strong interest in continual improvement, aims at increasing the importance of the Héritage collection, adding a man's chronograph with a tonneau curved case.

The Marine, with its lady's model that has maintained its sporting style and robust structure (the case is reinforced, the crown is shielded) is a masterpiece of miniaturization thanks to its movement, the very smallest automatic chronograph made.

The Type XX (Aeronavale and Transatlantique) is the collection which demonstrates Breguet's interest in aviation. Both models have a "fly-back" chronograph hand. The new version of the Transatlantique (with date) is made in titanium or in steel.

Among the new proposals is the "Classique", an elegant wristwatch with an automatic movement, double barrel and date feature.

The History

1747 - Abraham-Louis Breguet is born at Neuchâ... on January 10th. He moves to France when he is 1... **1775** - Only 28, he sets up the Breguet company... Paris, at Quai de l'Horloge in the Ile de la Cité. 17... - Only 5 years later he shows the first automatic movements, the Perpetuals, with oscillati... weight and two barrels. **1783** - The year of the striking spring for repeater watches, allowi... the height of the case to be considerably lessened; this same year he designs the "Pomme"... apple-motif hands, still known as Breguet hands, and the typical Arabic numerals. **1786** - ... aesthetic improvement which will be a constant in the Breguet style: Arabesqued dials. In t... technical field, he perfects the English pallet lever escapement. **1789** - Two innovations: natural escapement which works without lubricants and the "cricket" key. From this point, t... rhythm of his inventions becomes almost unmanageable. **1790** - The first version of t... "parachute", an anti-shock mechanism which makes watches less fragile. **1791** - The fi... jumping seconds movements with independent seconds, and the "new calibre" which was d... rived from Lépine. **1792** - Exploring all the applications of microtechnology, in very fe... months he built the mechanism of the Chappe optical telegraph. The following year the fu... of the Revolution was such that he withdrew to his native Switzerland. **1793** - The two yea... of exile gave Breguet the opportunity to broaden international contacts. When the politic... situation was again calm, he returned to Paris. It is from this moment that his extraordina... ability as an inventor would stun the whole world. **1795** - He started by presenting an inve... tion he had been working on for fifteen years: the ruby cylinder escapement bearing. Th... same year he perfects the perpetual calendar and invents the balance spring which will ... given his name. **1796** - The first travelling watch, and he also perfects a new kind of optic... telegraph (this was done with the Spanish engineer Bethencourt). He sells the first "Souscri... tion". **1798** - He invents the constant force escapement, the Sympathetic Pendulum whi... corrects the time and regulates a clock placed in an appropriate niche and even a music... chronometer whose movement acts as a metronome. **1799** - He sells the first "touch-watch... one can tell what time it is by fingering the edge of the case. **1801** - The Tourbillon Regul... tor is patented and will be sold starting in 1805. **1810** - The first wristwatch model is ordere... by the Queen of Naples. Only two years earlier, Breguet had become the watchmaker of t... Tzar and of the Imperial Russian Navy and had started a branch shop in Moscow. **1812** - T... new wristwatch order for the Queen of Naples is completed. The first appearance of an o... center hours dial. **1815** - Breguet has in the meantime become a member of the "Bureau d... Longitudes", and perfects the double barrel navy chronograph; he is appointed Watchmaker ... the Royal French Navy. **1816** - He is welcomed in the Academy of Sciences and three yea... later receives the Legion of Honor from King Louis XVIII in unanimous recognition of his g... nius. **1819** - He was named Knight, and perfected the podometer, a military step counter th... would record the step of marching soldiers. This same year sees an astronomical counter ... the form of a telescope which for the first time allows fixing tenths of seconds, and, by a ... proximation, hundredths. **1820** - He invents what is considered the precursor of the mode... chronograph, that is the observation chronometer with double seconds hand. **1822** - Just o... year before his death he invents the ink chronograph, showing once again the great brillian... of his mind. **1823** - On the 17th of September, Abraham-Louis Breguet dies at 77. His was a... incredible life that has left indelible marks in the world of watchmaking. **1997** - The ye... that celebrates 250 years since the birth of Breguet with three commemorative watches: tw... tourbillons (manual winding), one with a perpetual calendar and minute repeater, the other ... a perpetual chronograph; one automatic two barrel index adjuster type, a homage to the f... mous possessors of Breguet watches whose names are inscribed on the back. And two mo... perpetuals: the first, covered by a patent, has the indications on a vertical axis through th... center of the dial, while on the second these indications have another unusual and admirab... placing. A beautiful tonneau curved automatic with sub-seconds is the last of this wonderf... collection of dress watches. Today as before, many Breguet have original movements; the... style, their neoclassic taste, is striking for its severity. Gold cases whose fine edges a... marked by careful fluting; gold dials, or enamelled or silvered and delicately finished wi... Guilloché pattern; Breguet hands in gold, hand burnished to a blue tone; elegant numera... designed by the Master. Breguet, through its part in the Groupe Horloger Breguet, can mo... easily from its grand tradition into advanced technology. Most of the high quality mechanic... watches currently produced are based on ideas, components and technology that origina... from one or another of the Companies in the group. Time has not stopped in the work sho... transferred to L'Abbaye and L'Orient, in the Vallée de Joux. And while Abraham-Louis alrea... invented practically everything, the valley watchmakers have succeeded in adding new refin... ment to the superb Palmarès. **1998** - Three new chronographs are presented this year. One ... the Type XX Transatlantique dedicated to Louis Breguet (one of Breguet's descendants and t... inventor of what was to become the modern helicopter), which differs from the "Type XX" ... having the date feature; the Split-Second Chronograph which has a crystal back and the lady... Marine Chronograph with automatic movement from 10''''1/2 of the Nouvelle Lemania. This ... the world's smallest in this category, in height, volume and for the extraordinary ratio b... tween size and performance. The new Héritage present the curved tonneau form and are vita... ized by an automatic calibre 8'''3/4.

BREGUET

TYPE XX AERONAVALE — REF. 3800ST.92.SW9

Movement: mechanical, automatic winding, Breguet caliber 582, with fly-back feature (allowing set the to chronograph zero and to let it start again by a simple pressure of the pusher at 4). 18 kt gold rotor, 27 jewels (13'''3/4). Numbered, personalized and hand-finished.
Functions: hour, minute, small second, chronograph with 3 counters.
Case: stainless steel, three-piece case (Ø 39 mm, thickness 14.5 mm); curved sapphire crystal; counter-clockwise turning bezel with engraved five-minute progression; fluted case side; screw-down crown; screwed-on case back. Water-resistant to 10 atm.
Dial: matte black; luminescent Arabic numerals; luminescent square markers on the minute track; luminescent white painted bâton hands.
Indications: minute counter at 3, hour counter at 6, small second at 9, center fly-back second counter, minute track.
Bracelet: steel; fold-over clasp.
Price: 8'200 CHF.
Also available: leather strap; pink gold and blue dial, leather strap or bracelet.

TYPE XX TRANSATLANTIQUE TITANIUM — REF. 4820TI.K2.T76

Movement: mechanical, automatic winding, Breguet caliber 582Q, with fly-back feature (allowing to set the chronograph to zero and to let it restart by a simple pressure on the pusher at 4). Steel rotor with tungsten peripheral mass, 27 jewels (13'''3/4). Numbered, personalized and hand-finished.
Functions: hour, minute, small second, date, chronograph with 3 counters.
Case: titanium, three-piece case (Ø 39 mm, thickness 14.5 mm); bombé sapphire crystal; counter-clockwise turning bezel with engraved five-minute progression; fluted case side; screw-down crown; screwed-on case back. Water-resistant to 10 atm.
Dial: carbon fiber on brass; luminescent Arabic numerals; applied square markers on the minute track; luminescent bâton hands.
Indications: minute counter at 3, date and hour counter at 6, small second at 9, center fly-back second counter, minute track.
Bracelet: titanium; fold-over clasp.
Price: 10'900 CHF.

MONTRE AGENDA — REF. 3860ST.92.SW9

Movement: mechanical, manual winding, Breguet caliber 579. One winding barrel. Numbered, personalized and hand-finished.
Functions: hour, minute, center second, date, alarm.
Case: stainless steel, three-piece case (Ø 39 mm, thickness 12.25 mm); curved sapphire crystal; counter-clockwise turning bezel with engraved five-minute progression; fluted case side with date corrector at 3; alarm crown at 2, screw-down winding crown at 4; screwed-on case back. Water-resistant to 10 atm.
Dial: matte black; turning center disc; luminescent Arabic numerals; applied square markers on the minute tracks; luminescent bâton hands.
Indications: date at 6, turning center disc, with luminescent triangular marker for the sonnerie.
Bracelet: steel; fold-over clasp.
Price: 9'700 CHF.
Also available: leather strap; yellow gold, leather strap or bracelet.

CLASSIC TOURBILLON CRHONOGRAPH — REF. 3577BA.15.9V6

Movement: hand winding, Breguet caliber 554 (base Lemania caliber 2387), tourbillon feature with polished steel carriage. Monometal screw balance, side pallet lever escapement, Breguet overcoil balance-spring, 25 jewels, switching of chronograph functions through a column wheel. Regulated in 6 positions. Hand-finished and hand-engraved.
Functions: hour, minute, small second, chronograph with 3 counters.
Case: 18 kt yellow gold, three-piece case (Ø 38 mm, thickness 11 mm); flat sapphire crystal; fluted case side; yellow gold crown; snap-on back displaying the movement through a sapphire crystal. Waterproof to 3 atm.
Dial: silvered solid gold, engine turned (guilloché) by hand, aperture on the tourbillon; printed Roman numerals; hand-blued and hand-made stainless steel Breguet hands.
Indications: minute counter at 3, hour counter at 6, small second at 9 integrated in the tourbillon carriage, center second counter, minute track with divisions for 1/5 of a second.
Strap: crocodile leather; yellow gold clasp.
Price: 120'900 CHF.
Also available: pink gold 122'500 CHF; white gold or platinum on request.

BREGUET

MARINE "HORA MUNDI"   REF. 3700BA.12.9V6

Movement: mechanical, automatic winding, Breguet caliber 563. Double winding barrel, 25 jewels, 22 kt gold rotor. Hand-finished.
Functions: hour, minute, center second, date, world time, 24-hour indication.
Case: 18 kt yellow gold, three-piece case (Ø 37 mm, thickness 9 mm); flat sapphire crystal; fluted case side; two yellow gold coaxial crowns with case protection, one external classical with three positions, one ring-shaped internal to select time-zone; case back attached by 6 screws. Water-resistant to 3 atm. 
Dial: silvered solid gold, engine turned (guilloché) by hand with meridians and parallels engraved in the central part; printed Roman numerals; hand-blued and hand-made stainless steel Breguet hands.
Indications: date at 6, double flange, the first outside with the names of reference towns for time-zones (mobile by means of the ring coaxial with the crown), the second inside with a 24-hours turning ring with night & day indication integrated with the main hour ("world hours" system invented by Louis Cottier in 1935).
Strap: crocodile leather; yellow gold fold-over clasp.
Price: 21'900 CHF.
Also available: bracelet on request; white gold, leather strap 23'500, bracelet on request.

MARINE CHRONOGRAPH LADY   REF. 8490BB.12.964

Movement: mechanical, automatic winding, Breguet caliber 550 (Lemania caliber 1050), with 38 jewels (10'''1/2 and 6 mm thickness), 21,600 vibrations per hour (vph), 18 kt gold rotor engine turned (guilloché). Hand-finished.
Functions: hour, minute, small second, date, chronograph with 3 counters.
Case: 18 kt white gold, three-piece case (Ø 29.5 mm, thickness 10.3 mm); flat sapphire crystal; fluted case side; white gold ogival-shaped crown with case protection and a ring signed at the base; case back attached by 6 screws. Water-resistant to 5 atm. 
Dial: silvered solid gold, engine turned (guilloché) by hand; printed Roman numerals; hand-blued and hand-made stainless steel Breguet hands.
Indications: minute counter at 3, date and small second at 6, hour counter at 9, center second counter, minute track with divisions for $1/5$ of a second.
Strap: crocodile leather; white gold fold-over clasp.
Price: 20'800 CHF.
Also available: with bracelet; yellow gold, leather strap or bracelet.

TOURBILLON   REF. 3357BA.12.986

Movement: mechanical, manual winding, with tourbillon (Lemania caliber 387). Hand-finished and hand-engraved.
Functions: hour, minute, small second.
Case: 18 kt pink gold, three-piece case (Ø 36 mm, thickness 9 mm); flat sapphire crystal; fluted case side; pink gold crown; snap-on back displaying the movement through a sapphire crystal. 
Dial: silvered solid gold, engine turned (guilloché) by hand and aperture on the tourbillon; hand-blued and hand-made stainless steel Breguet hands.
Indications: off-center hour and minute at 12 (satiny hour ring with printed Roman numerals, printed minute track and engraved secret signature); small second (hand with three tips, each indicating a sequence of 20 seconds) and tourbillon at 6.
Strap: crocodile leather; pink gold clasp.
Price: 85'700 CHF.
Also available: yellow gold 84'500 CHF; white gold 86'100 CHF; platinum 96'500 CHF. Squelette Ref. 3355: yellow gold 119'000 CHF; pink gold 120'200; white gold 120'600 CHF; platinum 131'000 CHF.

EQUATION OF TIME   REF. 3470BA.1G.986

Movement: mechanical, automatic winding, Breguet caliber 502DPE, 12 lines, 37 jewels, straight line lever escapement, 18 kt gold rotor. Hand-finished.
Functions: hour, minute, perpetual calendar (date, day, month, year, moon phase), power reserve, equation of time.
Case: 18 kt pink gold, three-piece case (Ø 36.5 mm, thickness 8 mm); flat sapphire crystal; 3 correctors on the Breguet finish case side; sapphire cabochon pink gold crown; snap-on back. 
Dial: silvered solid gold, engine turned (guilloché) by hand; printed Roman numerals and minute track; hand-blued and hand-made stainless steel Breguet hands.
Indications: equation of time between 1 and 2 (difference in minutes between true solar and civil time), date at 6, four year cycle between 8 and 9, power reserve between 10 and 11, day at 12, month at center.
Strap: crocodile leather; clasp and chain with special rod for calendar correction, pink gold.
Price: 148'000 CHF.
Also available: yellow gold; platinum 166'000 CHF.

BREGUET

HERITAGE CHRONOGRAPH   REF. 5460BA.12.996

Movement: mechanical, automatic winding, Breguet caliber 550 (Lemania 1050 base). 18 kt gold rotor engine turned (guilloché), 38 jewels (10'''1/2). Monometallic balance, straight line lever escapement. Numbered, personalized and hand-finished.
Functions: hour, minute, small second, date, chronograph with 3 counters.
Case: 18 kt yellow gold, three-piece tonneau-curved case (height 38.5 mm, width 32. mm, thickness 11.1 mm); curved sapphire crystal; fluted case side; yellow gold crown; oval pushers with case protection; case back attached by 8 screws. Water-resistant to 3 atm.
Dial: silvered solid gold, engine turned (guilloché) by hand, curved; printed Roman numerals and minute track; hand-blued and hand-made stainless steel Breguet hands.
Indications: minute counter at 3, date and small second at 6, hour counter at 9, center second counter, minute track with divisions for 1/5 of a second.
Strap: crocodile leather; yellow gold clasp.
Price: 26'900 CHF.
Also available: with bracelet; white gold, leather strap 28'400 CHF, bracelet on request; platinum, leather strap 37'900 CHF, bracelet on request.

HERITAGE   REF. 8670BB.12.BB0

Movement: mechanical, automatic winding, Breguet caliber 532 (8'''3/4), 25 jewels. Monometallic ring balance, straight line lever escapement. 22 kt gold rotor, engine turned (guilloché). Numbered, personalized and hand-finished.
Functions: hour, minute, small second.
Case: 18 kt white gold, three-piece tonneau case (height 30 mm, width 25 mm, thickness 8 mm); curved sapphire crystal; fluted case side; white gold crown; case back attached by 4 screws. Water-resistant to 3 atm.
Dial: silvered solid gold, engine turned (guilloché) by hand, curved; printed Roman numerals and minute track; hand-blued and hand-made stainless steel Breguet hands.
Indications: small second at 6.
Bracelet: white gold; gold clasp.
Price: 29'600 CHF.
Also available: leather strap; yellow gold, leather strap or bracelet. In men's size (height 34.5 mm, width 28.5 mm, thickness 8.2 mm), Ref. 3670: yellow gold, leather strap 15'900 CHF; white gold leather strap 17'400 CHF.

CLASSIQUE   REF. 5910BB.15.984

Movement: mechanical, automatic winding, Breguet caliber 591. Double winding barrel, 11'''1/2, straight line lever escapement, 25 jewels, 22 kt gold oscillating mass engine turned (guilloché). Hand-finished.
Functions: hour, minute, center second, date.
Case: 18 kt white gold, three-piece case (Ø 34.5 mm, thickness 7.5 mm); flat sapphire crystal; fluted case side; white gold crown; snap-on back. Water-resistant to 3 atm.
Dial: silvered solid gold, engine turned (guilloché) by hand; printed Roman numerals and minute track; hand-blued and hand-made stainless steel Breguet hands.
Indications: date at 3.
Strap: crocodile leather; white gold clasp.
Price: 13'400 CHF.
Also available: in yellow gold (price on request).

CALENDAR   REF. 3330BB.1F.986

Movement: mechanical, automatic winding. Hand-finished.
Functions: hour, minute, day-date, moon phase.
Case: 18 kt white gold, three-piece case (Ø 33 mm, thickness 6.6 mm); flat sapphire crystal; 3 correctors on the Breguet finish case side; sapphire cabochon white gold crown; snap-on back.
Dial: silvered solid gold, engine turned (guilloché) by hand.
Indications: off-center downward hour and minute with Roman numerals on the brushed ring with the secret signature and dial-train printed and hand-blued, hand-made stainless steel Breguet hands; date at 2, day at 10, moon phase at 12.
Strap: crocodile leather; white gold clasp.
Price: 34'100 CHF.
Also available: in yellow gold; pink gold; platinum (prices on request).

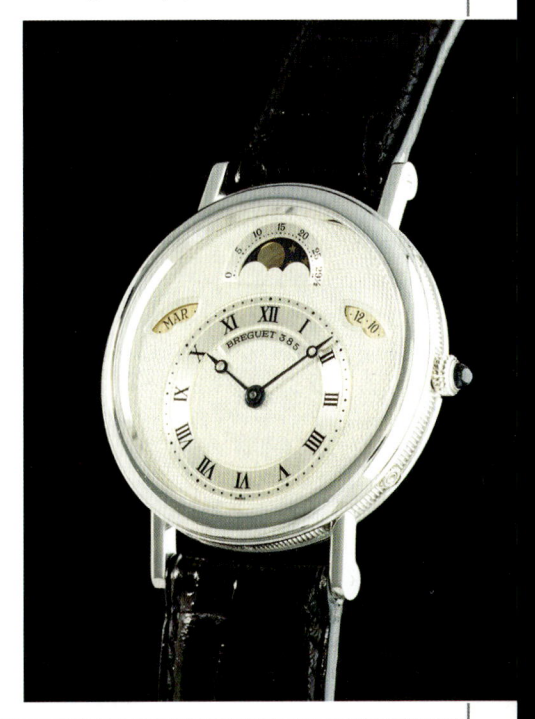

Breitling

Constant improvement of the performance of its wristwatches and constant perfection of the aesthetic aspects have always been the basis of Breitling's working creed. The result is that for the last several years most of the Breitling movements have the precision and working requirements necessary to obtain "chronometer" certificates. There was one last step: to bring the entire production to top quality watchmaking levels. This has been done, and Breitling has announced that from now on, all its watches, either mechanical or quartz, will be submitted to the COSC. Components selection, assembly, lubrication, the adjustment and control of its movements now meet the most demanding standards of the day. The decision to limit the production to chronometers alone at the same time strengthens the bonds which have always linked this name to aviation. And this is another sector where no detail is considered negligible and every check up is carried out rigorously. Regarding the new models, the presentation of the Crosswind Special must be stressed. This product has an automatic chronograph chronometer movement plus a large date function placed at two windows at 12 o'clock. Still in the field of mechanical chronographs, there is the Shadow Flyback, part of the Chronoliner collection. Its particularity is the "fly-back" feature which allows resetting and restarting the timekeeping with a single push-piece while the chronograph is running.

The most important of the Breitling collections, the Professional, was missing a women's version. This was resolved by the Colt Oceane, a product designed on ladies' proportions and that perfectly combines elegance and technology. It has a chronometer quartz movement.

The high technology sector presents the new B-2, mechanical automatic chronometer chronograph., with a slide rule function that works with the bi-directional rotating bezel.

The History

From the time Léon Breitling founded his Company in 1884 at St. Imier, he showed his overriding interest in chronographs and precision measuring instruments. This was a passion transmitted first to his son, Gaston, and then to his grandson, Willy. While the grandfather was, if not the first, then one of the first, to create in 1914 a chronograph to be worn on the wrist, the grandson accentuated the Company trend by specializing in the construction of watches to be used in aviation. This was during the 1930's.

1884 - Léon Breitling opens his first workshop; he produced pocket chronographs bearing his name and became interested in complications.
1892 - The workshop moves to La Chaux-de-Fonds. Here Léon dies in 1914.
1915 - Gaston Breitling follows the path his father indicated and builds a wrist model chronograph with a center mounted second counter and seconds totalizer at 30 minutes.
1923 - Patent registered for independent chronograph push-piece, or button.
1926 - Patent registered for the 1/10 seconds counter.
1933 - Breitling patents, at No. 172129, a two push-piece wrist model chronograph. The first button starts and stops the timing function sequentially in order to total the times; the second resets the hand. This is the birth of the modern chronograph, and was built according to an idea of Willy Breitling. As unusual as it might seem, several years later Breitling will patent a single button wrist chronograph.
1936 - More than 30 airline companies adopt the Breitling on-board chronograph.
1942 - Introduction of the Chronomat incorporating a slide rule function allowing mathematical calculation and fixing various sports competition data.
1952 - The Navitimer, a chronograph dedicated to aviation, becomes very useful for measuring speed and fuel consumption.
1958 - The Superocean is guaranteed water resistant even at great depths.
1962 - The Cosmonaute is a version of Navitimer with a space indication at 24 hours. The astronaut Scott Carpenter wore this model.
1966 - The first Breitling chronograph with a square case.
1968 - Electrosplit is an electronic sports time counter with a digital read out, two data pick-up systems and a memory.
1969 - The new automatic chronograph, Chronomat, is presented at Basel. This piece has the innovative Calibre 11, the first chronograph movement with "sandwich" construction. That is, a chronograph module developed by Breitling, Heuer-Leonidas and Hamilton-Buren is added to a Buren time base characterized by a "planetary" rotor, inserted within the movement in an off-center position. This movement, together with Zenith's El Primero (which, however, is an integrated calibre), marks the start of the era of the contemporary automatic chronograph.

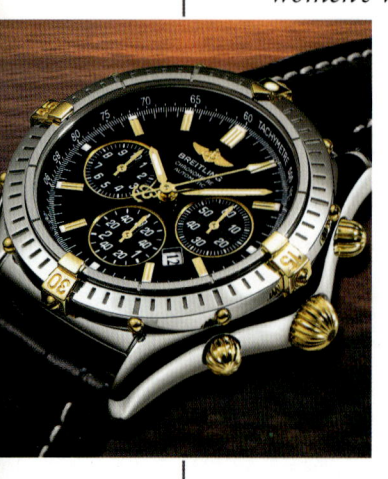

1971 - The chronograph Unitime shows the time simultaneously in two different zones.
1979 - An agreement between Ernest Schneider and Willy Breitling ensures the continuation of the company name, today led by Théodore Schneider.
1979/83 - The Navitimer chronographs adopt quartz movements; the GMT allows reading three time zones: two digital, one analog.
1984 - The Chronomat, undisturbed by 20 G acceleration, is chosen by the Italian acrobatic aviation team, the "Frecce Tricolori".
1986 - A Breitling watch resists at a depth of 1000 meters thanks to a valve that allows helium gas to escape.
1987 - An "anteprima" at Basel for "Emergency": its radio antenna can transmit an emergency signal.
1989 - The presentation of Chronomat Yachting, incorporating a regatta racing counter.
1990 - For the Globe Trotter, changing the time zone is a matter of pressing a button.
1992 - The Navitimer becomes more compact with automatic movement.
During the late '90's, the Grenchen based company fully completed the work on Emergency, which saved the lives of the 13 people aboard the raft Mata-Rangi. The Company continues to produce successful chronographs, among which Spatiographe automatic with digital visualized chronograph minutes and the underwater models such as the Colt Superocean, water resistant to 1000 meters.
1997 - Among the new products this year is the Montbrillant, the top of chronograph production with a perpetual calendar, and the Premier, a '30's model in a modern version. The Twinsixty has two simultaneous minute counters.
1998 - The new Montbrillant Eclipse, a chronograph with visualized moon phases, this is the latest product of the collection dedicated to the first Grenchen Company workshop. The Colt Superocean becomes Professional, is water resistant to 1500 meters and has a dulled metal military-type case. Two new chronographs are presented: both "rattrapante", that is with split seconds function, the Chronoracer with electronic movement, and the quartz movement Colt Chrono Ocean. The prize for watch-instrument of the year goes to the B-One, a multifunction watch created specifically for aviation pilots.
1999 - Breitling successfully participates in the first non-stop around the world balloon flight. The starting date was March 1st from Château d'Oeux in Switzerland, with an LTA craft named Orbiter 3 piloted by Bertrand Piccard and Brian Jones (in the photo). They arrived at Dakhla, Egypt on March 21st, after more than 19 days and 45,755 kilometers.

The slide rule

The slide rule is definitely one of the more fascinating and complex among the proposals made by modern wristwatch makers. Patented in 1941 by Graef & Cie. (obviously the patent refers to how the rule is fixed to and regulated by the watch, since the actual logarithmic scale was defined by Jost Burgi at the end of the 1500's), it became useful starting from the 1950's with Breitling's Navitimer.
The slide rule is immediately recognizable, what with the dozens of numbers and markers it has, but it often seems difficult to use, even to some of the sharpest watch lovers. Actually, the "ordinary slide rule" is a substantially simple instrument. It predates today's calculators and was used for years and years by engineers, surveyors and architects. It is an instrument used to multiply and to divide as well as to calculate velocity, average fuel consumption, the distance, either in ascent or descent, covered by an airplane; it can also handle converting miles, kilometers and nautical miles.
Looking at it closely, we see a white disk at the outer edge of the dial and part of the rotating bezel. It carries the numbers 10 to 10 that can be considered as multiples of 10 or sub-multiples, that is 1, 100, and so on. There is another, black, disk within the dial. The figures here are always in relation to miles (or kilometers) or miles per hour, feet (or meters), or feet per minute, gallons (or liters), or gallons per hour, and any other measurement which varies with time. The figures on the white disk show the minutes or the hours in all the problems regarding time. At 60 minutes on the black disk, we find an arrow marked MPH, which indicates the reference point for speed with respect to time, or the reference to "hours". This is used in all the problems which have hour quantities (both miles as well as kilometers, that is "Km"). The black disk also has a double time scale for sea-going pilots. It is possible to convert all the minutes over one hour (for example 70, 120, 450 on the external scale on the black disk) by reading the indications that match the lower black scale (=1:10, 2:00, 7:30, where 1:10 means one hour and ten minutes, etc.). In order to multiply, just start from the unit reference (the number 10 on the internal scale), choose the multiplier on the black disk and match it to the unit reference (10) on the external scale. Read the result on the black disk at the point of the multiplicand on the external scale on the white disk. The same operation in the opposite sense turns out to be division. Try it to believe it!

BREITLING

NAVITIMER MONTBRILLANT CHRONO PERPETUAL CALENDAR — REF. H2930

Movement: mechanical, automatic winding, Breitling caliber 29 (ETA base + Kelek chronograph/perpetual calendar module), 38 jewels.
Functions: hour, minute, small second, 24-hour indication, perpetual calendar (date, day, month, week, season, year, moon phase), chronograph with 3 counters.
Case: 18 kt pink gold, three-piece case (Ø 41.5, thickness 16.5 mm); curved sapphire crystal with antireflective treatment on both sides; bi-directional turning bezel, integrated with the flange; 5 correctors on case side; screwed-on case back with embossed medallion. Water-resistant to 3 atm.
Dial: silvered, antique fashion; applied pink gold plated lozenge markers; luminescent dots; printed minute track; luminescent pink gold plated lozenge hands.
Indications: moon phase and week at 3; day, hour counter and 24-hour display at 6; month, minute counter and 4 year cycle at 9; date, small second and season at 12, center second counter, minute track with divisions for $1/5$ of a second, normal slide rule with logarithmic and tachymetric scales.
Bracelet: Navitimer pink gold; fold-over clasp.
Price: on request.

NAVITIMER MONTBRILLANT RATTRAPANTE — REF. J3430

Movement: mechanical automatic, Breitling caliber 34 (base Frédéric Piguet caliber 1186), 39 jewels.
Functions: hour, minute, small second, date, split-second chronograph with 3 counters.
Case: 18 kt white gold, three-piece case, non-magnetic (Ø 38 mm, thickness 13.2 mm); curved sapphire crystal with antireflective treatment on both sides; bi-directional turning bezel, integrated with the flange; split-second pusher at 10; screwed-on case back. Water-resistant to 3 atm.
Dial: blue; counters silvered; luminescent Arabic numerals; printed minute track; luminescent gold plated sword style hands.
Indications: minute counter at 3, date between 4 and 5, hour counter at 6, small second at 9, center second and split-second counters, minute track with divisions for $1/5$ of a second; normal slide rule with logarithmic scale.
Strap: buffalo leather; white gold clasp.
Also available: platinum with blue dial and silvered counters.
Prices: on request.

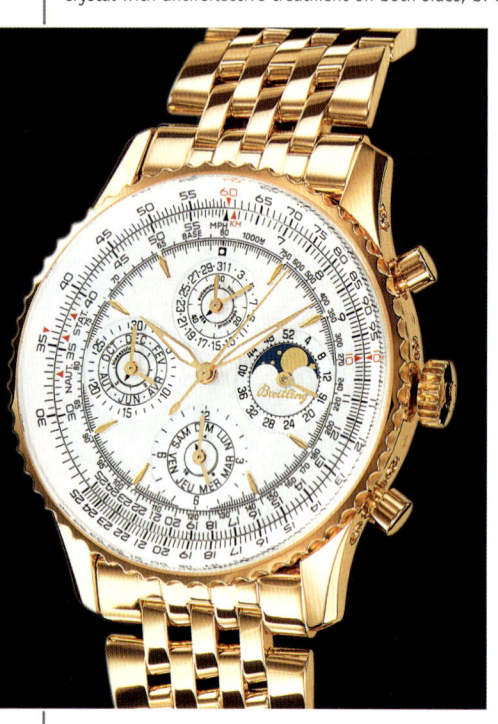

NAVITIMER MONTBRILLANT 1461 — REF. A19030

Movement: mechanical, automatic winding, Breitling caliber 19 (ETA caliber 2892-A2 + Kelek calendar module), 38 jewels.
Functions: hour, minute, small second, four year calendar (date, day, month, moon phase), chronograph with 3 counters.
Case: stainless steel, three-piece case (Ø 41.5, thickness 16.5 mm); curved crystal with antireflective treatment on both sides; bi-directional turning bezel, integrated with the flange; 4 correctors on case side; screwed-on case back with embossed medallion. Water-resistant to 3 atm.
Dial: silvered, antique-fashioned; applied yellow gold plated lozenge markers; luminescent dots; printed minute track; luminescent yellow gold plated lozenge hands.
Indications: moon phase at 3, hour counter and day at 6, month and minute counter at 9, small second and date at 12, center second counter, minute track with divisions for $1/5$ of a second, normal slide rule with logarithmic scale.
Strap: leather; stainless steel clasp.
Price: 5'500 CHF.
Also available: with Navitimer bracelet (on request); black dial.

NAVITIMER MONTBRILLANT ECLIPSE — REF. A4330C2

Movement: mechanical, automatic winding, Breitling caliber 43 (caliber Valjoux 7758 base), 25 jewels. Officially certified "chronometer" (C.O.S.C.).
Functions: hour, minute, small second, date, moon phase, chronograph with 2 counters.
Case: stainless steel, three-piece case (Ø 4.5 mm, thickness 15.5 mm); curved crystal with antireflective treatment on both sides; bi-directional turning bezel, integrated with the flange; screwed-on case back with embossed medallion. Water-resistant to 3 atm.
Dial: silvered, antique-fashioned; luminescent Arabic numerals; printed minute track; luminescent yellow gold plated lozenge hands.
Indications: date at 3, moon phase at 6, small second at 9, minute counter at 12 with telephone notches each 3', center second counter, minute track with divisions for $1/5$ of a second, normal slide rule with logarithmic scale.
Strap: leather; stainless steel clasp.
Price: 3'250 CHF.
Also available: (prices on request) with Navitimer bracelet; black dial, pink gold, leather strap and black dial.

BREITLING

NAVITIMER SPATIOGRAPHE MONTBRILLANT   REF. A36030

Movement: mechanical, automatic winding, Breitling caliber 36 (ETA caliber 2892-A2 + Dubois Dépraz module).
Functions: hour, minute, small second, chronograph with 3 counters.
Case: stainless steel, three-piece case, non-magnetic (Ø 41.5 mm, thickness 15 mm); curved crystal with antireflective treatment on both sides; bi-directional turning bezel, integrated with the flange; snap-on back. Water-resistant to 3 atm.
Dial: silvered, antique-fashioned; applied yellow gold plated lozenge markers; luminescent dots; printed minute track; luminescent yellow gold plated bâton hands.
Indications: small second at 3, hour counter (3 h) at 6, minute counter (10' digital display) at 9, center second counter, minute track with divisions for 1/5 of a second, normal slide rule with logarithmic scale.
Strap: crocodile leather; stainless steel clasp.
Price: 3'790 CHF.
Also available: (prices on request) with Navitimer bracelet; pink gold, leather strap: 50 pieces; platinum, leather strap: 25 pieces. All with silvered or black dial.

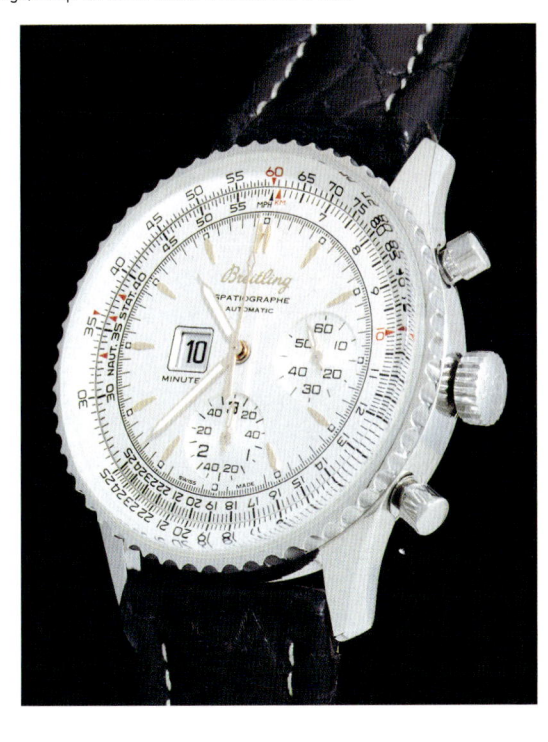

NAVITIMER MONTBRILLANT WITH DATE   REF. A4130C2

Movement: mechanical, automatic winding, Breitling caliber 41 (ETA caliber 2892-A2 + Dubois Dépraz module), 38 jewels. Officially certified "chronometer" (C.O.S.C.).
Functions: hour, minute, small second, date, chronograph with 3 counters.
Case: stainless steel, three-piece case, non-magnetic (Ø 38 mm, thickness 12.1 mm); curved mineral crystal with antireflective treatment on both sides; bi-directional turning bezel, integrated with the flange; snap-on back. Water-resistant to 3 atm.
Dial: black, silvered flange, antique-fashioned; applied rhodium plated lozenge markers (Arabic numeral 12); luminescent dots; printed minute track; luminescent rhodium plated lozenge hands.
Indications: small second at 3, date between 4 and 5, hour counter at 6, minute counter at 9, center second counter, minute track with divisions for 1/5 of a second, normal slide rule with logarithmic scale on the beveled ring, center hundredth scale.
Strap: leather; stainless steel clasp.
Price: 3'550 CHF.
Also available: (prices on request) bracelet Navitimer; silvered dial, black flange; pink gold, leather strap, black dial, silvered flange.

NAVITIMER COSMONAUTE II   REF. D1222C2

Movement: mechanical, manual winding, Breitling caliber 12 (Lemania caliber 1877 base). Officially certified "chronometer" (C.O.S.C.).
Functions: hour, minute, small second, chronograph with 3 counters.
Case: stainless steel and 18 kt yellow gold, three-piece case, non-magnetic (Ø 41.5 mm, thickness 13.3 mm); curved sapphire crystal with antireflective treatment on both sides; original patented rotating glass and ring system, the latter rotating in both directions and with deep engravings, which make the watch water-resistant to 3 atm.; screwed-on case back.
Dial: 24 hours, blue and silvered counters; luminescent bâton markers and Arabic numerals; printed minute track; gold plated luminescent sword style hands.
Indications: minute counter at 3, hour counter at 6, small second at 9, center second counter, minute track with divisions for 1/5 of a second; normal slide rule with logarithmic scale.
Strap: crocodile leather; stainless steel clasp.
Price: 4'440 CHF.
Also available: (prices on request) bracelet Navitimer steel, Navitimer steel/gold; yellow gold, leather strap; steel, leather strap, Navitimer bracelet. All with blue dial silvered zones or silvered champagne zones.

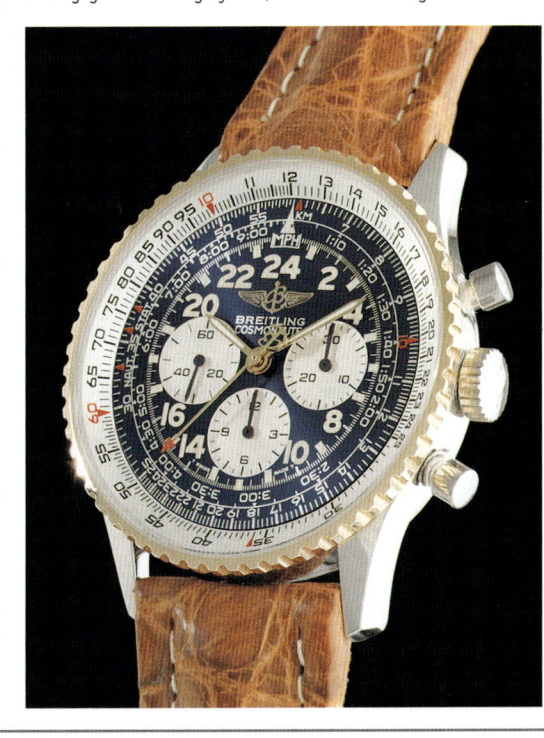

OLD NAVITIMER II   REF. D1322C2

Movement: mechanical, automatic winding, Breitling caliber 13 (Valjoux caliber 7750 base), 25 jewels. Officially certified "chronometer" (C.O.S.C.).
Functions: hour, minute, small second, date, chronograph with 3 counters.
Case: stainless steel and 18 kt yellow gold, three-piece case (Ø 41,5 thickness 14,4 mm), non-magnetic; curved sapphire crystal with antireflective treatment on both sides; bi-directional turning bezel, integrated with the flange; screwed-on case back with embossed logo and engraved temperature conversion scale from °C to °F. Water-resistant to 3 atm.
Dial: black with silvered counters; applied yellow gold plated bâton markers; luminescent dots; printed minute track; luminescent yellow gold plated sword style hands.
Indications: date at 3, hour counter at 6, small second at 9, minute counter at 12, center second counter, minute track with divisions for 1/5 of a second; normal slide rule with logarithmic and tachymetric scales.
Strap: crocodile leather; stainless steel clasp.
Price: 4'090 CHF.
Also available: (prices on request) with Navitimer steel bracelet, Navitimer steel/gold; steel, leather strap, Navitimer bracelet; yellow gold, leather strap. All with black or blue dial silvered zones or silvered gilded zones.

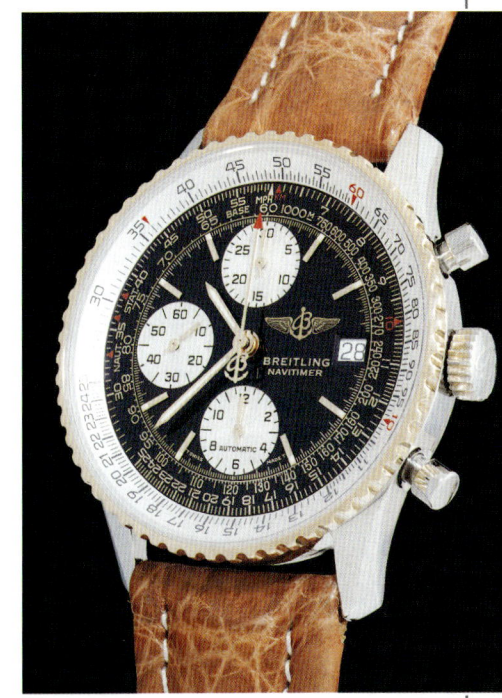

BREITLING

NAVITIMER GRAND PREMIER — REF. A13024

Movement: mechanical, automatic winding, Breitling caliber 13 (Valjoux caliber 7750 base), 25 jewels.
Functions: hour, minute, small second, date, chronograph with 3 counters.
Case: stainless steel, three-piece case, non-magnetic (Ø 39.7 mm, thickness 16.7 mm); curved crystal with antireflective treatment on both sides; screwed-on case back with embossed medallion. Water-resistant to 3 atm. 
Dial: black; luminescent Roman numerals; printed railway minute track; luminescent rhodium plated lozenge hands.
Indications: date at 3, hour counter at 6, small second at 9, minute counter at 12, center second counter, minute track.
Bracelet: Navitimer steel; fold-over safety clasp.
Price: 3'700 CHF.
Also available: (prices on request) leather strap; silvered dial.

NAVITIMER PREMIER WITH DATE — REF. H4235C2

Movement: mechanical, automatic winding, Breitling caliber 42 (ETA caliber 2892-A2 + Dubois Dépraz module), 38 jewels. Officially certified "chronometer" (C.O.S.C.).
Functions: hour, minute, small second, date, chronograph with 3 counters.
Case: 18 kt pink gold, three-piece case, non-magnetic (Ø 36.7 mm, thickness 13.5 mm); curved crystal with antireflective treatment on both sides; snap-on back. Water-resistant to 3 atm. 
Dial: black; luminescent Arabic numerals; printed minute track; luminescent pink gold plated lozenge hands.
Indications: small second at 3, date between 4 and 5, hour counter (on a three hours basis) at 6, minute counter (on a 10 minutes basis) at 9, center second counter, minute track with divisions for 1/5 of a second.
Strap: crocodile leather; pink gold clasp.
Price: 8'000 CHF.
Also available: (prices on request) stainless steel, non-chronometer, black or silvered dial, leather strap, with Navitimer bracelet.

WINGS AUTOMATIC — REF. B1050C2

Movement: mechanical, automatic winding, Breitling caliber 10 (ETA caliber 2892-A2 base). Officially certified "chronometer" (C.O.S.C.).
Functions: hour, minute, center second, date.
Case: in two colors, three-piece polished case (Ø 38 mm, thickness 12.9 mm), with aircraft wing profile; curved sapphire crystal with antireflective treatment on both sides, slightly recessed and of considerable thickness; counter-clockwise turning bezel with 12 hold screws, engraved minute track and 4 riders in 18 kt yellow gold at quarters; "Triplock" screw-down crown with case protection; screwed-on case back with embossed logo. Water-resistant to 10 atm. 
Dial: black, arabesqued at the center; applied yellow gold plated bâton markers and Arabic numerals; luminescent dots; printed minute track; luminescent gold plated bâton hands.
Indications: date at 3, 360° scale with cardinal points, useful as solar compass, and hundredth scale for aeronautical purposes on the beveled ring.
Strap: crocodile leather, stainless steel clasp.
Price: 2'390 CHF. **Also available:** (prices on request) Pilot steel bracelet, Rouleaux steel, Rouleaux steel/gold; steel, leather strap, Pilot bracelet, Rouleaux; yellow gold, leather strap. All with blue, black, silvered or slate-grey dial. Lady, quartz.

COLT OCEAN — REF. A1750C1

Movement: mechanical, automatic winding, Breitling caliber 17 (ETA caliber 2824/2 base), 25 jewels. Officially certified "chronometer" (C.O.S.C.).
Functions: hour, minute, center second, date.
Case: stainless steel, three-piece case (Ø 37.6 mm, thickness 12.6 mm); flat crystal; glassholder bezel with engravings at markers; counter-clockwise turning bezel (60 clicks) with 8 hold screws, 4 riders at quarters and brushed ring with engraved minute track; "Fliplock" screw-down crown with case protection; screwed-on case back. Water-resistant to 50 atm. 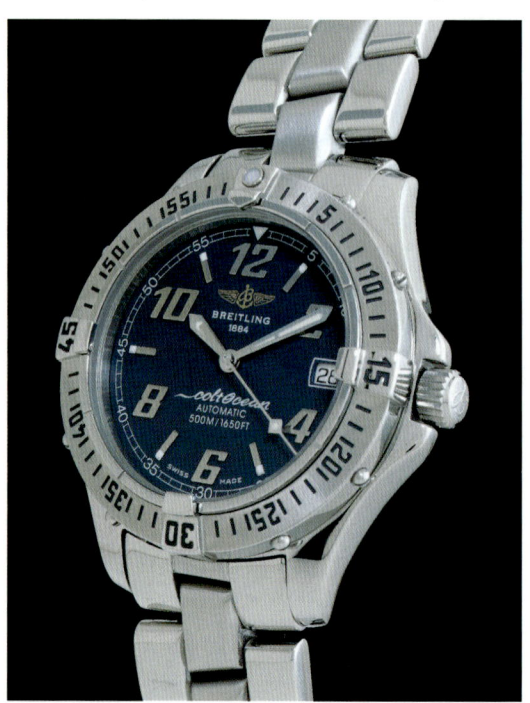
Dial: blue; applied rhodium plated Arabic "vitesse" numerals and bâton markers with luminescent dots; printed railway minute track; luminescent rhodium plated sword style hands.
Indications: date at 3.
Bracelet: Fighter steel; fold-over safety clasp.
Price: 1'530 CHF.
Also available: (prices on request) strap in shark-skin, Diver Pro, Plongeur; black or silvered dial; with quartz movement, steel, shark-skin strap, Diver Pro, Plongeur, Fighter bracelet.

BREITLING

B-2 — REF. A4262C

Movement: mechanical automatic winding, Breitling caliber 42 (ETA caliber 2892-A2 + Dubois Dépraz module), 38 jewels. Officially certified "chronometer" (C.O.S.C.).
Functions: hour, minute, small second, date, chronograph with 3 counters.
Case: stainless steel, three-piece case (Ø 43.5 mm, thickness 15 mm); flat sapphire crystal with antireflective treatment on both sides; bi-directional rotating bezel, with engraved 360° scale, provided with a supermultiplier pinion system allowing an extremely precise alignment of the slide rule figures; screwed-on case back with embossed medallion. Water-resistant to 10 atm.
Dial: black; luminescent bâton markers (Arabic numeral 12); printed minute track; luminescent rhodium plated sword style hands.
Indications: small second at 3, date between 4 and 5, hour counter (3 hours base) at 6, minute counter (10 minutes basis) a 9, center second counter, minute track with divisions for 1/5 of a second, normal slide rule with logarithmic scale on the beveled ring.
Strap: Diver Pro, water-repellent rubber; steel clasp.
Price: 2'870 CHF.
Also available: (prices on request) shark-skin strap, Fighter bracelet; yellow gold, coco leather strap; white gold, coco leather strap; with compass-watch, steel. All with silvered, black or blue dial.

CHRONO COLT AUTOMATIC — REF. A1335C1

Movement: mechanical, automatic winding, Breitling caliber 13 (Valjoux caliber 7750 base), 25 jewels. Officially certified "chronometer" (C.O.S.C.).
Functions: hour, minute, small second, date, chronograph with 3 counters.
Case: stainless steel, three-piece case (Ø 41.5 mm, thickness 15.5 mm), non-magnetic; curved crystal; glassholder bezel with engravings at markers; counter-clockwise turning bezel (60 clicks) with 8 hold screws, 4 riders at quarters and satiny ring with engraved minute track; screw-down crown with case protection; screwed-on case back. Water-resistant to 10 atm.
Dial: black with silvered counters; luminescent "vitesse" Arabic numerals; printed minute track; luminescent rhodium plated sword style hands.
Indications: date at 3, hour counter at 6, small second at 9, minute counter at 12, center second counter, minute track with divisions for 1/5 of a second, tachymeter scale on the beveled ring.
Bracelet: Professional steel; fold-over safety clasp.
Price: 2'680 CHF.
Also available: (prices on request) shark-skin strap, Plongeur, Diver Pro 3.305; with blue dial and silvered or white counters and black counters.

COLT SUPEROCEAN PROFESSIONAL — REF. A1745C9

Movement: mechanical, automatic winding, Breitling caliber 17 (ETA caliber 2824/2 base). Officially certified "chronometer" (C.O.S.C.).
Functions: hour, minute, center second, date.
Case: stainless steel, three-piece brushed case (Ø 41.5 mm, thickness 14.9 mm); curved mineral crystal with antireflective treatment on both sides (3.7 mm thickness); glassholder bezel with engravings at markers; counter-clockwise turning bezel (60 clicks) with 8 hold screws, 4 riders at quarters and satiny ring with engraved minute track; decompression valve at 10, allowing helium release during the reascent; "Fliplock" screw-down crown with case protection; screwed-on case back. Water-resistant to 150 atm.
Dial: yellow, grained; luminescent "aviation" Arabic numerals; luminescent markers on the beveled ring; printed minute track; luminescent rhodium plated sword style hands.
Indications: date at 3.
Strap: Diver Pro, water-repellent rubber; stainless steel clasp.
Price: 1'870 CHF.
Also available: (prices on request) shark-skin strap, with Professional bracelet; black dial.

COLT SUPEROCEAN — REF. K1040C1

Breitling, determined to make a technological challenge, in 1996 presented the first "1000 meters" in precious metal: Colt Superocean in 18 kt gold. For this watch an ingenious structure was used, reinforced by a patented titanium frame (slang name "cassolette"), compensating the inferior resistance of solid gold with respect to steel. Waterproof, professional, meeting the standard of the SEALs, the special scuba diver unit of the U.S. Navy, this is a C.O.S.C. chronometer equipped with an automatic winding movement Breitling caliber 17. The three-piece case (Ø 41.5, thickness 14.9 mm) is provided with a "Fliplock" screw-down crown with case protection and a decompression valve at 10 allowing helium release. The Superocean in gold version is available only with Professional gold bracelet and blue sun-pattern dial, protected by a curved mineral crystal with antireflective treatment on both sides, produced only on a 100 piece scale.
Price: 20'000 CHF.
Also available: (prices on request) steel, blue or black or orange dial, shark-skin strap, Plongeur, Professional bracelet.

BREITLING

CROSSWIND — REF. A1355C2

Movement: mechanical, automatic winding, Breitling caliber 13 (Valjoux caliber 7750 base), 25 jewels. Officially certified "chronometer" (C.O.S.C.).
Functions: hour, minute, small second, date, chronograph with 3 counters.
Case: stainless steel, three-piece case, non-magnetic (Ø 44 mm, thickness 15.5 mm), with aircraft wing profile; curved sapphire crystal with antireflective treatment on both sides; counter-clockwise turning bezel with 12 hold screws, engraved minute track and 4 riders at quarters; screw-down crown with case protection; screwed-on case back with embossed logo. Water-resistant to 10 atm.
Dial: black, arabesqued at center; luminescent applied rhodium plated Roman numerals; luminescent rhodium plated bâton hands; printed minute track.
Indications: date at 3, hour counter at 6, small second at 9, minute counter at 12, center second counter, minute track with divisions for 1/5 of a second, tachymeter and hundredths scale on the beveled ring.
Strap: shark-skin; stainless steel clasp. **Price:** 3'710 CHF. **Also available:** (prices on request) Pilot bracelet; two-color leather strap, Pilot steel bracelet, Pilot steel/gold; steel/gold, leather strap, Pilot bracelet; yellow gold leather strap, Pilot bracelet. All with white, black, brown, blue dial.

CROSSWIND SPECIAL — REF. A4455C2

Movement: mechanical, automatic winding, Breitling caliber 44 (ETA caliber 2892-A2 + Kelek module). 28,800 a/h, 38 jewels. Officially certified "chronometer" (C.O.S.C.).
Functions: hour, minute, small second, date, chronograph with 3 counters.
Case: stainless steel, three-piece case, non-magnetic (Ø 44 mm, thickness 16.5 mm), with aircraft wing profile; curved sapphire crystal with antireflective treatment on both sides; counter-clockwise turning bezel with 12 hold screws, engraved minute track and 4 riders at quarters; screw-down crown with case protection; rectangular pushers with apparent grooves; screwed-on case back. Water-resistant to 10 atm.
Dial: blue, silvered counters; applied rhodium plated bâton markers; luminescent dots; printed minute track.
Indications: big date at 12, small second at 3, hour counter at 6, minute counter at 9, center second counter, minute track with divisions for 1/5 of a second, tachymeter and hundredths scale on the beveled ring.
Strap: crocodile leather; stainless steel clasp.
Price: 5'120 CHF. **Also available:** (prices on request) without compass-watch: steel, leather strap, Pilot bracelet; yellow gold, leather strap; white gold leather strap. All with white, black, slate-grey or blue dial and silvered counters (gilded counters only for the yellow gold model).

CHRONOMAT VITESSE — REF. A1350C1

Movement: mechanical automatic winding, Breitling caliber 13 (Valjoux caliber 7750 base), 25 jewels. Officially certified "chronometer" (C.O.S.C.).
Functions: hour, minute, small second, date, chronograph with 3 counters.
Case: stainless steel, three-piece case, non-magnetic (Ø 40.5 mm, thickness 14.7 mm), with aircraft wing profile; curved sapphire crystal with antireflective treatment on both sides; counter-clockwise turning bezel with 12 hold screws, engraved minute track and 4 riders at quarters; screw-down crown with case protection; screwed-on case back with embossed logo. Water-resistant to 10 atm.
Dial: white; luminescent applied rhodium plated oversized Arabic numerals; printed minute track; luminescent rhodium plated bâton hands. **Indications:** date at 3, hour counter at 6, small second at 9, minute counter at 12, center second counter, minute track with divisions for 1/5 of a second, tachymeter and hundredths scale on the beveled ring.
Strap: leather; stainless steel clasp. **Price:** 3'100 CHF.
Also available: (prices on request) Pilot bracelet; two color leather strap, Pilot steel bracelet; steel/yellow gold, leather strap, Pilot bracelet; yellow gold leather strap, bracelet Pilot; with quartz watch and compass on the leather strap: steel; two colors. All with white, black or blue dial.

CHRONOMAT GRAND TOTALISATEUR — REF. B1350C1

Movement: mechanical automatic winding, Breitling caliber 13 (Valjoux caliber 7750 base), 25 jewels. Officially certified "chronometer" (C.O.S.C.).
Functions: hour, minute, small second, date, chronograph with 3 counters.
Case: two colors, three-piece case, non-magnetic (Ø 40.5 mm, thickness 14.7 mm), with aircraft wing profile; curved sapphire crystal with antireflective treatment on both sides; counter-clockwise turning bezel with 12 hold screws, engraved minute track and 4 riders at quarters 18 kt yellow gold; screw-down crown with case protection; screwed-on case back with embossed logo. Water-resistant to 10 atm.
Dial: green, gilded counters; applied yellow gold plated bâton markers; luminescent dots; printed minute track; luminescent gold plated bâton hands.
Indications: date at 3, hour counter at 6, small second at 9, minute counter at 12, center second counter, minute track with divisions for 1/5 of a second, tachymeter and hundredths scale on the beveled ring. **Strap:** crocodile leather; stainless steel clasp. **Price:** 3'490 CHF.
Also available: (prices on request) Pilot steel bracelet; steel, leather strap, Pilot bracelet; steel and yellow gold leather strap, Pilot bracelet; yellow gold, leather strap; many other dial colors.

BREITLING

CHRONOMAT LONGITUDE — REF. A2048C2

Movement: mechanical, automatic winding, Breitling caliber 20 (Valjoux caliber 7750 base), 25 jewels. Officially certified "chronometer" (C.O.S.C.). **Functions:** hour, minute, small second, date, three time zones on 12 hours, chronograph with 3 counters.
Case: stainless steel, non-magnetic, three-piece case (Ø 40.5 mm, thickness 13.80 mm); flat sapphire crystal with antireflective treatment on both sides; clockwise and counter-clockwise rotating bezel with minute track and 12 hours engraved, to set the time of a third time zone, 12 hold screws and 4 riders; screw-down crown with case protection; screwed-on case back with embossed logo. Water-resistant to 10 atm.
Dial: blue, arabesqued at center and silvered counters; luminescent applied rhodium plated bâton markers; luminescent rhodium plated bâton hands; printed minute track.
Indications: date at 3, hour counter at 6, small second at 9, minute counter at 12, center second counter and center second time zone (short hand with luminescent marker); 360° scale with cardinal points, useful as solar compass, on the beveled ring.
Bracelet: Pilot steel; fold-over safety clasp, steel.
Price: 4'420 CHF.
Also available: (prices on request) leather strap, Diver Pro; with black, blue, yellow or red dial and black counters.

CHRONORACER RATTRAPANTE — REF. A6948C2

Movement: quartz with mechanical chronograph module, Breitling caliber 69 (Frédéric Piguet caliber 1270 base), 23 jewels, chronography with column wheel. Côtes de Genève and circular graining finish. Officially certified "chronometer" (C.O.S.C.). **Functions:** hour, minute, small second, date, split-second chronograph with 3 counters. **Case:** stainless steel, three-piece case, non-magnetic (Ø 39.3, thickness 13.8 mm), with aircraft wing profile; curved sapphire crystal with antireflective treatment on both sides; counter-clockwise turning bezel with 12 hold screws, engraved minute track and 4 riders at quarters; screw-down crown with split-second pusher and case protection; oval pushers; screwed-on case back displaying the movement through a sapphire crystal. Water-resistant to 3 atm.
Dial: blue; luminescent "vitesse" Arabic numerals; printed minute track; luminescent rhodium plated bâton hands.
Indications: hour counter at 3, date between 4 and 5, small second at 6, minute counter at 9, center split-second counters, minute track with divisions for 1/5 of a second, tachymeter scale on the beveled ring.
Strap: calf; stainless steel clasp. **Price:** 4'630 CHF.
Also available: (prices on request) Diver Pro leather strap, Pilot bracelet; with black dial.

SHADOW FLYBACK — REF. B3512C2

Movement: mechanical, automatic winding, Breitling caliber 35 (ETA caliber 2892-A2 + Dubois Dépraz module), 38 jewels. Officially certified "chronometer" (C.O.S.C.).
Functions: hour, minute, small second, date, chronograph with 3 counters and "flyback" feature.
Case: two colors, three-piece case, non-magnetic (Ø 38 mm, thickness 13.5 mm), with aircraft wing profile; flat sapphire crystal with antireflective treatment on both sides; counter-clockwise turning bezel with 12 hold screws, engraved minute track and 4 riders at quarters in 18 kt yellow gold; slightly recessed crown; screwed-on case back with embossed logo. Water-resistant to 10 atm.
Dial: silvered; applied gold plated bâton markers; luminescent dots; printed minute track; luminescent gold plated bâton hands.
Indications: small second at 3, date between 4 and 5, hour counter (3h) at 6, minute counter (10') at 9, center fly-back second counter, minute track with divisions for 1/5 of a second.
Bracelet: Pilot polished steel with double central link "coiffé d'or"; steel fold-over safety clasp.
Price: 5'490 CHF.
Also available: (prices on request) Pilot steel bracelet, leather strap; black or blue dial.

CHRONO JETSTREAM — REF. B55048

Movement: quartz with mechanical chronograph module, Breitling caliber 55 (Frédéric Piguet caliber 1270 base). Officially certified "chronometer" (C.O.S.C.).
Functions: hour, minute, small second, date, chronograph with 3 counters.
Case: two colors, three-piece case (Ø 36.6 mm, thickness 11.3 mm); flat sapphire crystal with antireflective treatment on both sides; counter-clockwise turning bezel with 12 hold screws, engraved minute track and 4 riders at quarters in 18 kt yellow gold; slightly recessed screw-down crown; screwed-on case back with embossed logo. Water-resistant to 10 atm.
Dial: red and gilded counters; luminescent applied gold plated bâton markers (Arabic numeral 12); luminescent gold plated bâton hands.
Indications: hour counter at 3, date between 4 and 5, small second at 6, minute counter at 9, center second counter, minute track with divisions for 1/5 of a second, tachymeter scale on the beveled ring.
Bracelet: Pilot steel; fold-over safety clasp, steel.
Price: 4'130 CHF.
Also available: leather strap; white, black, blue, jade dial and gilded zones; yellow gold, leather strap and mother-of-pearl dial.

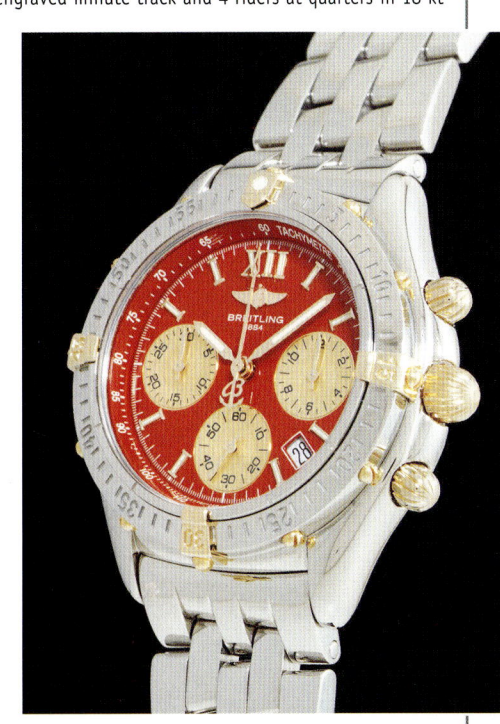

Bulgari

It should be no surprise that the biggest introduction from the famed Italian jewellery house of Bulgari is a new collection of jewellery watches just for women. The collection is named Ovale and it consists of 35 models, in 18k white or yellow gold, with elliptical cases and recessed white dials. The inner side of the bezel slopes down to meet the watch face in a graceful curve. Some models are adorned with diamonds set in a manner that accentuates the fluid shape of the case. Ovale watches come in two sizes, 27 mm and 32 mm (measured along the length of the case). All have quartz movements. They come with gold bracelets, made of elliptically shaped links that echo the case shape, or with leather straps in a choice of several colors. Celebrating what it calls "a year dedicated to diamonds", Bulgari is also offering new diamond-studded versions of several of its classic models. The Bulgari-Bulgari, Anfiteatro, Quadrato and Sport collections all now have models featuring diamonds on the indexes, the bezel and the dial. The Trika collection, know for its intricately linked bracelet, has a standard-sized and mini watch that has rows of diamonds on the perimeter of the case and in a ring on the watch face. Reflecting the increasingly strong trend toward steel and other white metals, Bulgari has also introduced a stainless steel version of the Tubogas watch, previously available only in gold. Bulgari lovers know the spiral-shaped Tubogas bracelet as one of Bulgari's signature designs. It's made from a single thread of metal hand-wrapped and hammered around a band. No soldering is used so the bracelet is smooth and flexible. Its name, by the way, is not nearly as elegant as its shape. It translates from Italian as "gas tube". Bulgari hasn't forgotten men, though. For them, it has a new chronograph version of its popular Aluminium watch, launched in 1998. Like the original Aluminium models, the chrono has an aluminum case. The bezel is made of rubber; the bracelet combines rubber and aluminum. The watch has an automatic movement. There's a date window between 4 o'clock and 5 o'clock, plus hour and minute totalizers at 6 o'clock and 9 o'clock respectively and a small seconds subdial at 3 o'clock.

The History

Bulgari has achieved great fame in the world of fine quality jewellery. The family's founder, Sotirio, heir to an ancient dynasty of Greek silver workers, opened his first shop in Rome on Via Sistina in **1884**. In **1905**, with his sons Costantino and Giorgio, he opened the shop on Via Condotti, and here the shop windows became an institution in the Old Center of the Italian capital, drawing tourists, the curious as well as fond clients from all over the world.

Bulgari's presence among fine watchmakers began during the **first half of the 20th Century**, when the Roman workshop was producing fabulous bracelets set with jewel-like watches. The movements were made by the Swiss company, Juvenia. Bulgari had in the meantime withdrawn from the rigid canons of the French school, and was creating his own style inspired by Graeco-Roman classicism, the Italian Renaissance and the 19th Century goldworking traditions.

During the '70's, Bulgari decides to make a decisive approach to fine quality watch production and, in what was to be the golden era of ultra thin wristwatches, he presented a model that was decidedly against the tide. Not only, but it also displays the name twice on the case with that pride and eloquence typical of the powerful. The mark, "Bvlgari-Bvlgari", invented in **1977**, is still unchanged and is the distinctive sign of one of the collections most sought after by those lovers of excellence and quality.

1980's - In order to follow the watch sector more closely, the Company founds Bulgari Time in Neuchâtel, Switzerland. Besides the boutiques in Rome, Paris, Geneva and Montecarlo, others were opened in New York, London, Milan, Monaco, St. Moritz, Hong Kong, Singapore, Osaka, Tokyo (there are now 44 shops in all).

1989 - An agreement is signed with GP Manufacture SA to produce the movements of the Bulgari watches that, starting in 1994, will be fitted with the new automatic GPM Calibre 3000 and 3100. The designers produce the collection Anfiteatro with an original, concave structured case, and "Alveare" (honeycomb) is presented for the jewelled watches.

1990 - Introduction of the quartz Chronograph.

1992 - The new, square "Quadrato" has the name engraved on the side of the case.

1993 - Bulgari watches are handled by the world's most exclusive jewellery shops.

1994 - Architectural and modern design produces the first Complications: a Tourbillon and a Minute Repeater. At the same time, the Sport collection is introduced that includes sports and underwater watches in a modern design and with automatic movements.

1995 - Trika is the first and most beautiful "soft" link bracelet, totally expressive of the skill of these masterly jewellers. On July 17th, Bulgari S.p.A. is quoted on the Italian Telematic Exchange and on the international SEAQ of London, proving itself to be an excellent deal.

1996 - The Sport collection grows to include a split second chronograph. Three more models are added to the Bvlgari-Bvlgari line: the Skeleton, the Perpetual Calendar whose dates are programmed up to 2099, and the GMT.

1997 - The new collection tends particularly towards steel, also used for the special series with automatic movements to celebrate the 20th anniversary of Bvlgari-Bvlgari. The more economic model, Just Time, is introduced that has, however, all the aesthetic and structural qualities that accompany this name. (see photo)

1998 - Bulgari sells its share participation in GP Manufacture SA. The new model Aluminium, is presented, an immediate worldwide success.

BULGARI

ALUMINIUM CHRONO — REF. AC38TAVD

Movement: mechanical, automatic winding, caliber MVA 080 (GP Manufacture cal. 3100 + chronograph module).
Functions: hour, minute, small second, date, chronograph with three counters.
Case: aluminum Anticorodal 900, three-piece brushed case (Ø 38 mm, thickness 11 mm); titanium bezel (inside) and rubber (outside); flat sapphire crystal; crown with black PVD coating, with case protection; oval pushers in titanium with black finish; snap-on titanium back. Water-resistant to 3 atm.
Dial: grey; printed bâton markers (Arabic numeral 12); printed minute track; bâton hands in rhodium plated brass, black painted.
Indications: small second at 3, date between 4 and 5, hour counter at 6, minute counter at 9, center second counter.
Strap: rubber and aluminum, clasp in aluminum.
Prices: on request.

ALUMINIUM — REF. AL38AVDAUTO

Movement: mechanical, automatic winding, caliber BV 220 (ETA 2892/A2 modified by GP Manufacture).
Functions: hour, minute, center second, date.
Case: aluminum Anticorodal 100, three-piece brushed case (Ø 38 mm, thickness 8.90 mm); bezel steel (inside) and rubber (outside); flat sapphire crystal; crown with black PVD coating, with case protection; snap-on case back steel with black PVD coating. Water-resistant to 3 atm.
Dial: grey; printed bâton markers (Arabic numerals 12 and 6); printed minute track; bâton hands in rhodium plated brass, black painted.
Indications: date at 3.
Strap: rubber and aluminum, aluminum clasp.
Also available: with quartz movement, in the medium size Ø 32, thickness 8.30 mm and small size Ø 29 mm, thickness 8.40 mm.
Prices: on request.

CHRONOGRAPHE RATTRAPANTE — REF. CH40PL

Movement: mechanical, automatic winding, cal. BV 900 (GP 9010 base deriving from Valjoux cal. 7750, modified so as to obtain the split-second function).
Functions: hour, minute, small second, split-second chronograph with 3 counters.
Case: platinum, three-piece brushed case (Ø 40 mm); antireflective flat sapphire crystal; fixed bezel with engraved brand; white gold crown and pushers (for flyback feature at 8); snap-on back displaying the movement through a sapphire crystal.
Dial: white; white gold bâton markers (Arabic numeral 12); white gold bâton hands.
Indications: minute counter at 3, hour counter at 6, small second at 9, center second and split-second counters, minute track.
Strap: leather; yellow gold fold-over clasp.
Also available: white gold; platinum.
Prices: on request.

SCUBA CHRONO — REF. SC38SV

Movement: mechanical, automatic winding, caliber GP 2282. Worked out, mounted, regulated and hand-decorated. Officially certified "chronometer" (C.O.S.C.).
Functions: hour, minute, small second, chronograph with 2 counters.
Case: stainless steel, brushed finish, three-piece case (Ø 38 mm, thickness 13.4 mm); flat sapphire crystal; counter-clockwise turning bezel with hold grooves and 5 engraved minute numerals; screw-down crown with case protection and screw-down pushers; screwed-on case back. Water-resistant to 20 atm.
Dial: black with white screen-prints; luminescent round markers and Arabic numerals; luminescent sport style hands.
Indications: small second at 3, minute counter at 9, center second counter, minute track.
Strap: rubber, with hinges reinforced with synthetic material; steel fold-over safety clasp.
Also available: with bracelet; yellow gold, leather strap or bracelet.
Prices: on request.

BULGARI

SCUBA — REF. SD38SSDAUTO

Movement: mechanical, automatic winding, caliber BV 220 (ETA 2892/A2 modified by GP Manufacture). Diameter 25.60 mm (11'''1/2), thickness 3.85 mm, 28,800 vibrations per hour (vph). Côtes de Genève finished and rhodium plated. Officially certified "chronometer" (C.O.S.C.).
Functions: hour, minute, center second, date.
Case: stainless steel, three-piece brushed case (Ø 38 mm, thickness 10 mm); flat sapphire crystal (thickness mm 2.40); counter-clockwise turning bezel (120 clicks) with hold grooves and engraved five-minute scale; screw-down crown with case protection; screwed-on case back. Water-resistant to 20 atm. 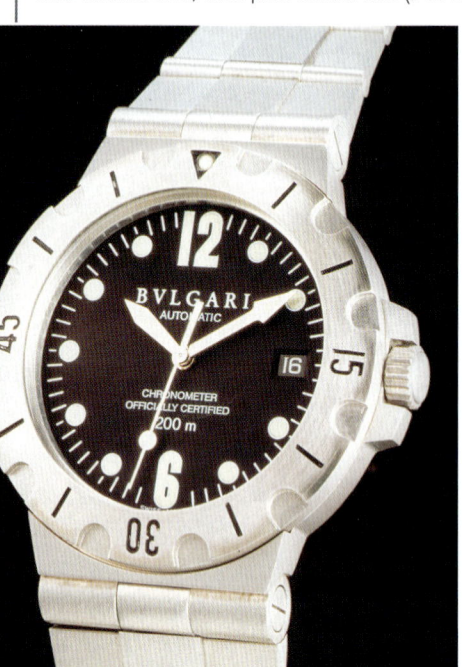
Dial: black; luminescent round markers and Arabic numerals; printed minute track; luminescent sport style hands.
Indications: date at 3.
Strap: rubber, with hinges reinforced with synthetic material; stainless steel fold-over clasp.
Also available: leather or rubber strap; in yellow gold, leather or rubber strap or bracelet.
Prices: on request.

SPORT — REF. LCV35WSSD

Movement: mechanical, automatic winding, caliber BV 220 (ETA 2892/A2 modified by GP Manufacture). Diameter 25.60 mm (11'''1/2), thickness 3.85 mm, 28,800 vibrations per hour (vph). Côtes de Genève finished and rhodium plated.
Functions: hour, minute, center second, date.
Case: stainless steel, three-piece brushed case (Ø 35.70 mm, thickness 8.65 mm); antireflective flat sapphire crystal; fixed bezel with engraved brand; snap-on back. Water-resistant to 3 atm. 
Dial: white; luminescent bâton markers and Arabic numerals; printed minute track; luminescent bâton hands.
Indications: date at 3.
Bracelet: steel; stainless steel fold-over clasp.
Also available: leather strap; steel and yellow gold, bracelet; yellow gold, leather strap; small size (Ø 29, thickness 7.40 mm) caliber GP 3002: steel (leather strap or bracelet); steel and yellow gold, leather strap; yellow gold, bracelet. The versions in steel or yellow gold are available with white or black dial, those in steel and yellow gold are available only with black dial.
Prices: on request.

ANFITEATRO MINUTE REPEATER — REF. AT40PLRM

Movement: mechanical, manual winding, caliber 9892. Diameter 27.60 mm (12'''1/4), thickness 5.70 mm, 32 jewels, Breguet overcoil balance-spring. Beveled and Côtes de Genève finished.
Functions: hour, minute, small second.
Case: platinum (gr 120 appr.), three-piece case (Ø 40 mm, thickness 11.05 mm); flat sapphire crystal; partially recessed white gold crown; repeater slide on case side; brushed case back attached by 8 white gold screws, displaying the movement through a sapphire crystal. 
Dial: 18 kt yellow gold, opaline silvered and big polished flange with engraved brand; applied white gold bâton markers (Roman numeral 12); white gold bâton hands.
Indications: small second at 9.
Strap: crocodile leather, hand stitched; platinum clasp (gr 7.20).
Also available: in yellow gold.
Prices: on request.

ANFITEATRO TOURBILLON — REF. AT40GLTB

Movement: mechanical, manual winding, Bulgari caliber 9902 (GP Manufacture cal. 9900 base). Diameter 28.6 mm (12'''1/2), thickness 5.7 mm, 20 jewels, 21,600 vibrations per hour (vph); Glucydur balance with 16 gold screws (12 for balancing and 4 for regulation purposes), Breguet overcoil balance-spring. Beveled and Côtes de Genève finished; bottom and tourbillon plate decorated with circular graining pattern, racket-wheel decorated with snailing pattern. 
Functions: hour, minute.
Case: 18 kt yellow gold (gr 90 appr.), three-piece case (Ø 40 mm, thickness 10.5 mm); flat sapphire crystal; partially recessed yellow gold crown; brushed case back attached by 8 yellow gold screws. Water-resistant to 3 atm.
Dial: 18 kt gold, opaline silvered, aperture on the tourbillon carriage (with steel bridge) and big polished flange with engraved brand; bâton markers, 12 Roman numerals, applied yellow gold; yellow gold bâton hands.
Strap: crocodile leather, hand stitched; yellow gold clasp (gr 5.5).
Also available: platinum.
Prices: on request.

BULGARI

ANFITEATRO — REF. AT35GLDAUTO

Movement: mechanical, automatic winding, caliber BV 220 (ETA 2892/A2 modified by GP Manufacture).
Functions: hour, minute, center second, date.
Case: 18 kt yellow gold, two-piece polished case (Ø 35 mm); antireflective flat sapphire crystal; partially recessed yellow gold crown. Water-resistant to 3 atm.
Dial: white and big polished gold flange with engraved brand; applied yellow gold plated bâton markers (Roman numeral 12); rolled gold bâton hands.
Indications: date at 3.
Strap: crocodile leather; yellow gold clasp.
Also available: platinum; in the small size (Ø 26 mm), yellow gold with quartz movement.
Prices: on request.

BVLGARI-BVLGARI — REF. BB33GLDAUTO

Movement: mechanical, automatic winding, caliber BV 220 G (ETA 2892/2 modified by GP Manufacture).
Functions: hour, minute, center second, date.
Case: 18 kt yellow gold, two-piece case, in the extra-large size (Ø 33 mm, thickness 7.35 mm); antireflective flat sapphire crystal; bezel with engraved brand; snap-on back. Water-resistant to 3 atm.
Dial: black; applied yellow gold bâton markers and Arabic numerals; bâton hands.
Indications: date at 3.
Strap: leather; yellow gold clasp.
Also available: stainless steel; with quartz movement, Ø 26 and 33 mm, steel or gold, leather strap or bracelet.
Prices: on request.

BVLGARI-BVLGARI GMT — REF. BB33GLDGMT

Movement: mechanical, automatic winding, ETA caliber 2893-2, 11'''1/2, 28,800 vibrations per hour (vph).
Functions: hour, minute, center second, date, second time zone, 24-hour indication.
Case: 18 kt yellow gold, two-piece case (Ø 33 mm, thickness 8.8 mm); antireflective flat sapphire crystal; bezel with engraved brand; snap-on back. Water-resistant to 3 atm.
Dial: black; applied yellow gold bâton markers and Arabic numerals; bâton hands.
Indications: date at 3, red painted center second-time-zone 24-hour hand.
Strap: leather; yellow gold clasp.
Also available: stainless steel.
Prices: on request.

BULGARI-BULGARI SQUELETTE — REF. BB33GLSK

Movement: mechanical, automatic winding, base 2892/A2, hand-skeletonized.
Functions: hour, minute.
Case: 18 kt yellow gold, two-piece case, in the extra-large size (Ø 33 mm); antireflective flat sapphire crystal; bezel with engraved brand; yellow gold crown; snap-on back displaying the movement through a sapphire crystal. Water-resistant to 3 atm.
Dial: bâton hands.
Strap: leather; yellow gold clasp.
Prices: on request.

83

Cartier

Over the past 20 years Cartier has brought out a parade of watches inspired by or based directly on noteworthy designs from its archives. Recently it presented another in the series: the Tank Basculante. The rectangular, steel watch has a specially constructed case that pivots on its horizontal axis and can be turned over so only the case back is visible. The watch is based on a Cartier design from 1932. At that time, before scratch-resistant sapphire glass was widely used for watch crystals, sportsmen who wore their wristwatches while golfing or playing polo or tennis often regretted it. Companies including Cartier came up with watch cases that could be reversed so the delicate crystal was out of harm's way. These watches had another benefit - like the Tank Basculante, they could be engraved on the back with a personal message or monogram.

The Tank Basculante comes in three sizes. The large model has a mechanical movement; the medium and small ones are quartz. All have the Roman numerals and railroad-tie-like markings around the dial for which the brand is well known. Although most of the models are steel (the Basculante is Cartier's first steel Tank watch on a strap - one made of blue alligator), the large size is also available in 18-karat gold. For more information on the original Basculante design and all Cartier Tank watches, see the newly published "Cartier: The Tank Watch", written by Franco Cologni, an executive at Cartier's parent company, the Vendôme Group, and published by Flammarion in Paris and New York.

Also new from Cartier this year - and underlining the tremendously strong trend toward steel cases and bracelets for all styles of watches - is a wide-bracelet ladies' quartz

The History

Louis-François Cartier founded what was to become his empire in the workshop he purchased in Paris in **1847**. Cartier quickly became world famous. His splendid jewellery was bought by members of royal families, by the aristocracy and by the growing upper middle class. He became justly known as "the king of jewellers and the jeweller of kings".

Cartier is proof of the rule that demands respect for tradition and careful regard for the future. Here we find the inimitable ability of catching the spirit of the times and objectifying it while keeping faith with a certain classicism which, without fail, makes of these creations new points of reference. This tenet applies not simply to jewellery, but to a great number of objects used from day to day. Such as watches, to which Cartier lends a touch that makes them precious, unique, inimitable. Almost archetypes. This magic can be seen, touched in every Cartier object, it makes of each piece a remarkable window overlooking the times and places it has inspired: sunset gleaming on the snowfield of the steppes and reflected on a window of the speeding Orient Express; the end of a smoky evening spent over the gaming table of a cruise ship, carrying languid Europeans towards the New World; the splendor of the Egyptian pyramids seen from the eyes of a gentleman seeking adventure. All this through the magic of Cartier.

1853 - The House records mention a watch probably purchased from a supplier and then decorated and made precious by Cartier.

1873 - An Egyptian-styled pocket watch, in gold, diamonds and rubies, signed Cartier.

1874 - Alfred Cartier, son of the founder, takes over the management of the House, an indication of one of Cartier's winning cards: a constant appreciation of new, youthful ideas.

1899 - The fourth change of address, this one at the hands of Louis Cartier, Alfred's son, brings the House to Rue de la Paix, 13, where it is today.

1904 - Louis Cartier designs the wristwatch for his rich Brazilian friend, Santos Dumont, which still bears his name. The Santos is sold starting in 1911.

1905 - Louis Cartier meets Edmond Jaeger. In 1907 they sign an agreement which will prove to be long lasting. Jaeger gives Cartier the exclusive commercial rights of his watch production, Cartier guarantees orders of at least 250,000 francs per year.

1913 - The first year of the Tortue and a small pendulum clock, "Mystérieuse".

1919 - The year of the Tank, perhaps inspired by the World War I tank tracks.

1930's - For the Pasha of Marrakech, who wished not to have to remove his watch while bathing, Cartier creates a watch, perhaps a Tank, using a locking system that makes the case water resistant.

1933 - Cartier patents the Vendôme with center-attached mobile lugs.

1040's through '60's - Many important watchmakers create models expressly for Cartier.

1972 - A group of investors, led by Joseph Kanouï buys Cartier Paris and, two years later, Cartier London.

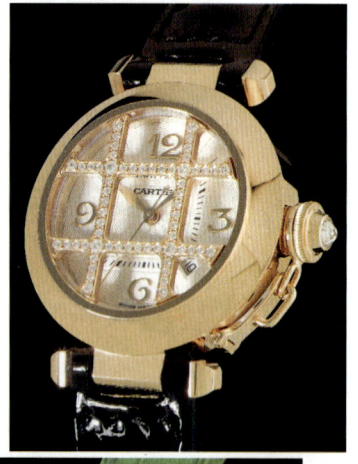

1976 - First appearance of the vérmeil watches for "Les Must de Cartier".
1978 - Santos is produced in gold and steel.
1979 - "Cartier Monde" is born, to unify all the interests of the House.
1983 - Presentation of the "Panthère".
1985 - Pasha is presented, taking its name for the '30's model.
1989 - Introduction of the Tank Américaine.
1996 - This is the year instead of the Tank Française.
1997 - Cartier celebrates its 150th anniversary with three limited editions of 150 pieces, each distinguished by a cabochon ruby. A 1930's Tank with jumping hours and rotating minute disk; a swinging levered Tank from 1923 (hand-engraved dial, apertures showing Skeleton movement - 15 pieces), and the Driver, with case curved to rest comfortably on top side of wrist while driving. Some other innovations are a Tank in platinum (15 pieces), a Tank Carrée Obus, a limited edition Pasha showing night and day hours with one double pointed hand, and an automatic Santos with two time zones and power reserve.
1998 - The Pasha Tourbillon with a single bridge formed by the Cartier entwined double C and arabesqued dial marks the year 1998 for the Parisian House. The refined Tortue collection has a single button manual chronograph and a Tourbillon with bridges and pillar plates cut from a single piece of rock crystal. The geometric clarity of the case of the Tank Française is highlighted by diamonds. The Three Diamond Trinity (the watch version of the famous "Three Golds" Ring) and the Manchette watches become objects of desire. Impossible not to remark the "Parrot": sumptuous example of a wristwatch with its 187 grammes of platinum, 1,013 diamonds and 2 emeralds. Or the "Pendulette Mystérieuse", in white gold and diamonds, geometric mother of pearl inlay and mechanical movement with an 8 day power reserve.

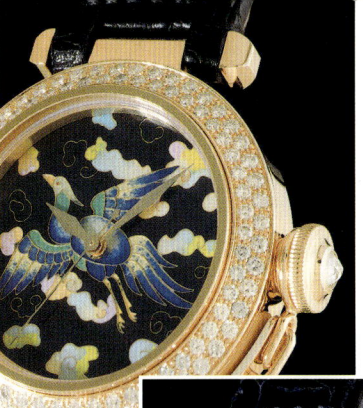

watch called the Panthère Ruban ("ribbon" in English). It has a panther link bracelet, mother-of-pearl dial - available in grey, white or pink - and triple deployant buckle.

Other new Cartier ladies' models include an 18-karat-white-gold and diamond version of the Trinity (half of all Cartier's gold watches are now white, not yellow gold - in keeping with an industry-wide trend toward white metal) and a new pink-gold version of the Pasha watch. Thirty-two millimeters in diameter, it has an automatic movement and removable grid set with pink diamonds that covers the watch face.

Cartier has also introduced the first models in a new collection called "Privée", aimed at watch collectors and others interested in high watchmaking. All the Privée watches will have mechanical movements (some will have complications), all will be made of 18-karat-gold and all will be based on Cartier models from the past. Among the 15 models recently introduced is the Tonneau, with a manual-wind, 21-jewel movement and 21,600-oscillations-per-hour balance. The large model is in pink or yellow gold or platinum, the smaller version in yellow gold. Cartier will bring out more Privée models next year.

Collection Privée Cartier

Each piece has a tale to tell and an identifying mark; each one is as well witness to exquisite craftsmanship and the finest watchmaking as shown in the "Collection Privée Cartier Paris", conceived precisely to enchant a restricted circle of people who cherish and collect, those lovers of precious, refined detail. Milestones in the history and the artistic properties of the Maison brought together here, each with its own particular spirit, that of the mechanical movement Manufacture, and well within the overall spirit of the best Swiss watchmaking tradition. Tonneau, Tank and Pasha of the Cartier Tourbillon with the famous bridge in the ornate form of two entwined "C's", the modern version of the Tortue, a one-button chronograph produced after five years of work: the dial of each watch is 18 karat, finely decorated gold, the single pieces are hand assembled; it is an object of great refinement and boasts only selected materials - steels, brasses, rubies. The choices can be seen in the details, like the ring of the gilded Glucydur balance, an alloy known for its resistance, elasticity and antimagnetic and stainless properties. The watches from the Collection Privée are distributed only in the best shops, and are presented in a red leather case lined with red velvet and mahogany.

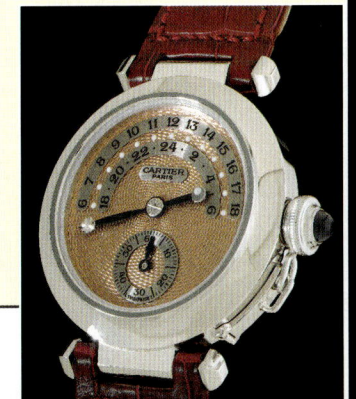

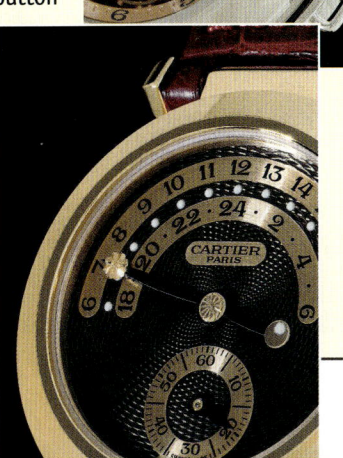

CARTIER

TANK FRANÇAISE CHRONOFLEX — REF. W50005R2

Movement: quartz with mechanical chronograph module, Cartier Chronoreflex caliber 212P, 25 jewels.
Functions: hour, minute, date, chronograph with 3 counters.
Case: 18 kt yellow gold, two-piece polished rectangular-curved case (height 24 mm, width 28 mm, thickness 6.5 mm); curved sapphire crystal; sapphire cabochon octagonal yellow gold crown; rectangular pushers with case protection; case back attached by 4 screws. Water-resistant to 3 atm.
Dial: silvered by granulation; printed Roman numerals and minute track; blued stainless steel sword style hands.
Indications: minute counter between 4 and 5, hour counter between 7 and 8, date at 12, center second counter, minute track with divisions for $1/5$ of a second.
Bracelet: yellow gold, polished and brushed finish links; double gold fold-over clasp, recessed.
Price: 25'700 CHF.
Also available: leather strap; yellow gold & stainless steel, with bracelet; steel with bracelet (prices on request).

TANK FRANÇAISE AUTOMATIC GRAND MODELE — REF. W50011S3

Movement: mechanical, automatic winding, Cartier caliber 120 (ETA caliber 2000 base).
Functions: hour, minute, center second, date.
Case: 18 kt white gold (30 gr), two-piece polished rectangular-curved case (height 24 mm, width 28 mm, thickness 7.6 mm); curved sapphire crystal; sapphire cabochon octagonal white-gold crown; case back attached by 4 screws. Water-resistant to 3 atm.
Dial: silvered, engine turned (guilloché) with sun pattern; printed Roman numerals and minute track; blued stainless steel sword style hands.
Indications: date at 6.
Bracelet: white gold, with polished links; double fold-over clasp in white gold, recessed.
Price: 25'200 CHF.
Also available: leather strap; in yellow gold, leather strap or bracelet; steel with bracelet. With quartz movement: medium size, steel with bracelet; small size, steel with bracelet; white gold, leather strap or bracelet (prices on request).

TANK AMERICAINE CHRONOFLEX — REF. W2601156

Movement: quartz with mechanical chronograph module, Cartier Chronoreflex caliber 212P, 25 jewels.
Functions: hour, minute, perpetual date, chronograph with 3 counters.
Case: 18 kt yellow gold, two-piece polished rectangular-curved case (height 37 mm, width 26.5 mm, thickness 8 mm); curved sapphire crystal; diamond set in octagonal yellow-gold crown; rectangular pushers with case protection; case back attached by 8 screws. Water-resistant to 3 atm.
Dial: grained, silvered, curved; printed Roman numerals and railway minute track; blued stainless steel sword style hands.
Indications: minute counter at 5, hour counter at 7, date at 12, center second counter, minute track with divisions for $1/5$ of a second.
Strap: crocodile leather; gold tongue clasp.
Price: 11'100 CHF.
Also available: with bracelet; white gold, with leather strap or bracelet; in yellow or white gold, with brilliants on case sides and leather strap (prices on request).

TANK AMERICAINE MOYEN MODELE — REF. WB702651

The Tank Américaine, a lengthened and curved version of the classical Tank, comes in a series of models meeting any possible request: from the chronograph Chronoreflex quartz with mechanical chronograph module to the automatic "only time, from the version for men to the lady version, with or without brilliants set on the case, with bracelet or leather strap. In this case we are in front of the medium size model, with white gold case and brilliants (25.30 gr gold, and 103 brilliants for a total of 1.28 kt). It is worthwhile noting that, as concerns the numeration on the dial, Cartier keeps th signature secret even on this model, hidden by the Roman numeral VII, whose reproduction is almost impossible on the false models diffused on the market. The two screws on case side perform the function of locking the movement reducer.
Price: 24'100 CHF.

86

CARTIER

CHRONO TORTUE   REF. W1525751

Movement: mechanical, manual winding, Cartier caliber 045, 11 lines, 22 jewels, 21,600 vibrations per hour (vph), switching of chronograph functions with column wheel. Decorated with Cartier's double "C" engraved on bridges; brushed chronograph levers.
Functions: hour, minute, small second, chronograph with 2 counters.
Case: 18 kt yellow gold, two-piece polished tonneau case (height 35 mm, width 34 mm, thickness 10 mm); curved crystal; chronograph pusher in the gold crown, octagonal, with faceted sapphire; case back attached by 8 screws, displaying the movement through a sapphire crystal. Water-resistant to 3 atm.
Dial: gold, silvered, engine turned (guilloché) with sun pattern; printed Roman numerals; printed railway minute track; blued stainless steel Breguet hands.
Indications: small second at 9, minute counter at 3, center second counter, minute track with divisions for 1/5 of a second.
Strap: crocodile leather, hand stitched; yellow gold fold-over clasp.
Price: 22'700 CHF.
Also available: white gold, silvered dial, engine turned (guilloché), applied white gold cabochon markers (prices on request).

TANK BASCULANTE GRAND MODELE   REF. W1011358

Movement: mechanical, manual winding, Cartier caliber 061.
Functions: hour, minute.
Case: stainless steel, four-piece rectangular case, polished and brushed finish (case: height 27.4 mm, width 18.4 mm, thickness 5.3 mm; with brancard: height 38.5 mm, width 25.3 mm, thickness 6.3 mm); flat sapphire crystal; circular grained flat crown; original longitudinal rocking bar system, with inside frame embellished with a blue cabochon. Water-resistant to 3 atm.
Dial: silvered, engine turned (guilloché) flinqué; printed Roman numerals and railway minute track; blued stainless steel sword style hands.
Strap: alligator leather, blue; tongue clasp.
Price: 5'400 CHF.
Also available: (prices on request) in yellow gold, leather strap (Collection Privée). With quartz movement, steel leather strap: medium or small size (prices on request).

BAIGNOIRE ALLONGEE DIAMANTS ROSES   REF. WL408031

Movement: mechanical, manual winding, Cartier caliber 078, 17 jewels.
Functions: hour, minute.
Case: 18 kt pink gold (41 gr), two-piece oval-curved case (height 52.5 mm, width 23.5 mm, thickness 8.5 mm), set with diamonds (233 pink diamonds, 1.49 kt); curved sapphire crystal; diamond set in pink gold crown; snap-on back.
Dial: grained, silvered, 18 kt gold (5.1 gr), curved; pink printed Roman numerals; pink gold sword style hands.
Strap: grey satin; adjustable fold-over clasp, 18 kt pink gold (11.8 gr).
Price: 129'000 CHF. Unique version.

CRASH WATCH DIAMANTS ROSES   REF. WL407931

Movement: mechanical, manual winding, Cartier caliber 160, 15 jewels.
Functions: hour, minute.
Case: 18 kt pink gold (21.2 gr), two-piece asymmetrically curved case (height 38.5 mm, width 23 mm, thickness 8.4 mm), set with diamonds (138 pink diamonds, 2.48 kt); curved sapphire crystal; diamond set in pink gold crown; snap-on back.
Dial: grained, silvered, 18 kt gold (3.6 gr), curved; printed Roman numerals; pink gold sword style hands.
Strap: in grey satin; adjustable fold-over clasp, 18 kt pink gold (11.6 gr).
Price: 91'500 CHF. Unique version.

CARTIER

PASHA QUANT. PERPETUEL TOURB. SQUELETTE   REF. HPI00040

Movement: mechanical, automatic winding, with tourbillon, Gérald Genta on an exclusive basis for Cartier caliber 039 (12''', 39 jewels). 22 kt gold rotor.
Functions: hour, minute, small second, perpetual calendar (date, day, month, year, moon phase).
Case: platinum, three-piece case (Ø 38.5 mm, thickness 11.5 mm); bezel with set diamonds with baguette cut; flat sapphire crystal; 4 correctors on case side; waterproof platinum crown, protected by a crown cover screwed on with a safety clip and a natural sapphire cabochon; case back attached by 8 screws, displaying the movement through a sapphire crystal. Water-resistant to 3 atm. 
Dial: skeletonized, crowns of zones in mother-of-pearl; applied white gold markers with luminescent cabochon; white railway minute track; luminescent blued stainless steel lozenge hands.
Indications: month and four-year cycle at 3, small second integrated in the tourbillon carriage and date at 6, day at 9, moon phases at 12.
Strap: crocodile leather; central attachment; adjustable fold-over clasp, white gold.
Price: on request.

PASHA CHRONO   REF. W3014051

Movement: mechanical, automatic winding, Cartier caliber 205 (11'''1/2), 37 jewels, 21,600 vibrations per hour (vph), monometallic balance with three arms, micrometer balance-spring regulation, Kif shock-resistant system. Decorated with Cartier's double "C" engraved. **Functions:** hour, minute, small second, date, chronograph with three counters. **Case:** 18 kt yellow gold, three-piece case (Ø 38 mm, thickness 11 mm); flat sapphire crystal; counter-clockwise turning bezel with slight knurling and engraved minute track; waterproof gold pushers and crown with screwed-on crown cover and safety clip, with cabochon sapphires; case back attached by 8 screws, displaying the movement through a sapphire crystal. Water-resistant to 3 atm. 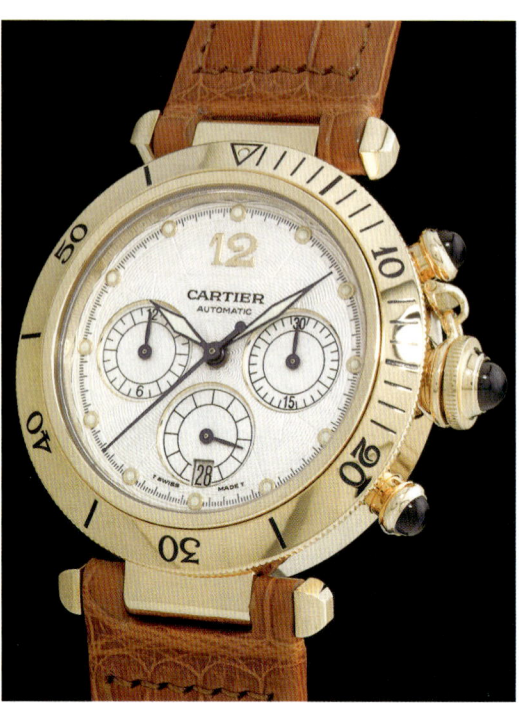
Dial: silvered, engine turned (guilloché); applied yellow gold Arabic numeral 12; applied yellow gold markers with luminescent cabochon on the printed minute track; luminescent blued stainless steel lozenge hands.
Indications: minute counter at 3, small second and date at 6, hour counter at 9, center second counter, minute track with divisions for 1/5 of a second.
Strap: crocodile leather; central attachment; yellow gold fold-over clasp.
Price: 21'500 CHF.
Also available: (prices on request) with bracelet; steel.

PASHA POWER RESERVE   REF. W3014456

Movement: mechanical, automatic winding, Cartier caliber 480 (11'''1/5), 27 jewels, 28,800 vibrations per hour (vph). Bridges and rotor engraved with Cartier's double "C".
Functions: hour, minute, center second, date, power reserve, second time zone, 24-hour. **Case:** 18 kt yellow gold, three-piece case (Ø 38 mm, thickness 10 mm); flat sapphire crystal; counter-clockwise turning bezel with slight knurling and engraved minute track; a corrector on case side; waterproof crown protected by a screwed-on crown cover with safety clip and cabochon sapphire; case back attached by 8 screws, displaying the movement through a sapphire crystal. Water-resistant to 10 atm. 
Dial: silvered by granulation and engine turned (guilloché - the decoration of the indicator at 12 reproduces a planetarium); applied yellow gold Arabic numerals; applied yellow gold markers with luminescent cabochon on the printed minute track; luminescent blued stainless steel lozenge hands. **Indications:** date between 4 and 5, power reserve at 6, second time zone 24-hour display at 12.
Strap: crocodile leather; central attachment; adjustable gold fold-over clasp.
Price: on request.
Also available: with bracelet; steel and yellow gold, leather strap or bracelet; steel, leather strap or bracelet (prices on request).

PASHA 35 MM   REF. W30145M9

Movement: mechanical, automatic winding, Cartier caliber 049 (ETA caliber 2892/A2 base).
Functions: hour, minute, center second, date.
Case: 18 kt white gold (143 gr), three-piece case, polished and brushed finish (Ø 35 mm, thickness 9.8 mm); flat sapphire crystal with magnifying lens on date; hollowed bezel; waterproof crown protected by a screwed-on crown cover with natural sapphire cabochon and safety clip; case back attached by 8 screws. Water-resistant to 10 atm. 
Dial: silvered by granulation; printed bâton markers; 4 applied Arabic numerals with luminescent dots; printed railway minute track; luminescent blued stainless steel lozenge hands.
Indications: date between 4 and 5.
Bracelet: white gold, brushed, with central attachment; recessed double fold-over clasp.
Price: 25'600 CHF.
Also available: crocodile leather strap Ref. W3014556 (prices on request).

CARTIER

PASHA EMAIL "DRAGON" — REF. WJ104751

Movement: mechanical, automatic winding, Cartier caliber 191, 27 jewels. Bridges and rotor engraved with Cartier's double "C".
Functions: hour, minute, center second.
Case: 18 kt yellow gold (54.59 gr), two-piece case (Ø 38 mm); flat sapphire crystal; bezel set with diamonds (105 stones, 1.81 kt); water-resistant yellow gold crown, protected by a crown cover screwed on with a safety clip bearing a set faceted diamond; case back attached by 8 screws, displaying the movement through a sapphire crystal. Water-resistant to 3 atm.
Dial: solid gold (5.9 gr), with polichrome hand-cloisonné enamels, representing a Chinese dragon; yellow gold lozenge hands. The Chinese dragon appeared for the first time on a pink gold black-enameled powder-compact designed by Cartier in 1925.
Strap: crocodile leather; central attachment; adjustable fold-over clasp in yellow gold (14.7 gr).
Price: 53'800 CHF.
Production limited to only 10 pieces for the whole world.

PASHA EMAIL "PANTHERE" — REF. WJ104551

It is not by chance that important creations by Cartier show animal figures. Some unforgettable masterpieces of the House, realized after the War under the guidance of Jeanne Toussaint, present the animal theme, preferred by Louis Cartier, in infinite different shapes: from the undying panther (the drawing in black enamel on a gold background on the dial of the Pasha photographed here uses just this theme), keeping on with tigers, dogs and cats, birds of any kind (see, for instance, the Oiseau Bleu with an extraordinary lyrebird on the opening page), turtles and snakes, but also dragons, medusas and chimaeras. A phantasmagoric zoo as a homage to the creativity of the founder of the House, but without neglecting the use of the most sophisticated technologies available and the respect of the unavoidable changes in taste, as is the case of the last Email collection proposed by Cartier at the occasion of the last Salon de Genève.
Price: 28'000 CHF.
Production limited to only 10 pieces for the whole world.

PASHA 32 MM — REF. WJ10551

Movement: mechanical, automatic winding, Cartier caliber 120 (ETA caliber 2000 base).
Functions: hour, minute, center second, date.
Case: 18 kt yellow gold (51.3 gr), three-piece case (Ø 32 mm, thickness 9 mm); flat sapphire crystal; bezel set with diamonds (39 stones, 1.62 kt); water-resistant yellow gold crown, protected by a crown cover screwed with a safety fastener with pavé diamond; case back attached by 8 screws. Water-resistant to 3 atm.
Dial: silvered by granulation; printed bâton markers; 4 applied yellow gold Arabic numerals; printed railway minute track; yellow gold lozenge hands.
Indications: date between 4 and 5.
Strap: crocodile leather; central attachment; gold tongue clasp.
Price: 24'500 CHF.
Also available: with bracelet; white gold, leather strap or bracelet; many other colors of crocodile leather strap (prices on request).

PASHA "GRILLE" 32 MM — REF. WJ104041

The Pasha, initially conceived as men's watch, was edited in many versions so as to meet also women's preferences for this model which has already become a symbol rather than a simple watch. By adopting again the grid for dial protection mounted for the soldiers of World War I, Cartier actualized it for a feminine public by adorning it with diamonds with brilliant cut (in the photograph a grid with 60 pink diamonds totalling 0.34 kt and bezel with 121 pink diamonds totalling 1.36 kt). The grids available are embellished with three different stone colors matching the gold color of the case: white, pink or "jonquille" with its unusual yellow tone. This is another possibility of transforming one's Pasha at pleasure. On the crown cover a faceted set diamond.
Price: 68'800 CHF.
Also available: in yellow gold, yellow diamonds; white gold, white diamonds. Bezel without diamonds: yellow gold with 3 interchangeable grids, leather strap, with 1 grid with yellow diamonds, bracelet; white gold 3 grids, leather strap, 1 grid with white diamonds, bracelet (prices on request).

89

Chaumet

Woman, Chaumet's eternal inspiration, keeps on being the self-evident essence of the creations of the Parisian Maison which is always capable of catching the desires of the feminine universe and materializing them in very prestigious realizations. Chaumet, which has been the reference name of international jewellery for more than two centuries, surprises each time with sumptuous and decidedly aristocratic jewels which capture and hypnotize the eye, as those presented at the occasion of the event "Diamonds Forever. The Millennium Celebration" by an exceptional witness, Ornella Muti. The first one among the models shown was the necklace Féminité, an extraordinary piece of outstanding quality in white gold, studded with brilliants, 43 cm long, for whose realization more than 400 working hours were needed at the atelier of Place Vendôme. The same essential style is adopted by Chaumet in watchmaking, a recent activity which brought them in little time to the Olympus of great names. The top model of this year's watch production is still Khésis, a bracelet watch with voluptuous and sinuous shapes, which at the Maison's début in this sector five years ago entailed a sort of revolution by its innovating shape (it was the first "manchette" watch) and the shocking combination of stainless steel and diamonds. The collection - including 50 versions - is today enlarged by the Top Lady model with double time zone indication, a novelty conceived for modern, active, dynamic and a little non-conformist women who want functionality from a timepiece, without renouncing the top quality of an absolutely feminine jewel. An unmistakable graphic line is still the distinctive sign of the Style de Chaumet models with ultra-thin shaped rectangular, square or round case design, in chronograph, quartz or automatic versions, conceived at the sign of the purity of design and a simplicity which becomes an indispensable value for the most exclusive elegance. The latest born is the 36 mm chronograph, animated by a quartz movement and proposed with a leather strap or a brand new Spirit Of bracelet with brushed central links and polished edges. Finally, the House introduces two unisex models into its universe, and gentlemen will like them: an underwater watch, Class One, a decidedly sportsmanlike piece with extremely reduced volumes (in automatic, quartz and jewel versions), and the "12", pay-

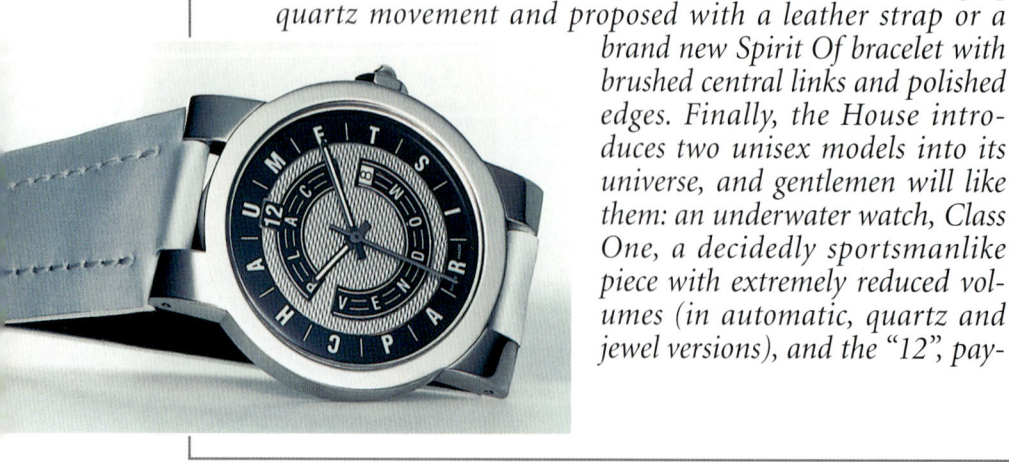

The History

Chaumet's history starts in **1780** when Marie-Etienne Nitot, a young and talented French jeweller establishes in rue Saint-Honoré in Paris. His talent is undeniable, but it is a fortuitous meeting with Napoleon, who was then first consul, that determines his success. Nitot succeeds in stopping the future emperor's restive horse pair. Napoleon, some years later, to repay the kindness, orders the young man to realize his coronation parure and appoints him official purveyor of the Court. The Emperor's glorious ascent increases Nitot's reputation, but the Maison's success is not tied to Nitot's name. When he retires, Jules Fossin takes on the business, but in **1861**, failing heirs, he is obliged to leave his propriety to Prosper Morel whose father had been the manager. At this point Joseph Chaumet comes on the scene, at first apprentice and then atelier executive and finally owner thanks to his marriage with Morel's daughter. From then on, under the brand name Chaumet, the Parisian Maison, established in **1907** at number 12, Place Vendôme, in a sumptuous palace which still houses the atelier, the illustrious goldsmith tradition commenced in rue Saint-Honoré is continued here, interlacing the history of persons and the great European history. During its two-century life, Chaumet never gave up relationships with aristocratic families all over the world, such as Queen Victoria, the Russian Tsars, Indian Maharajas and the cream of European aristocracy, for which reason the House is called "Kings' Jewellers".

1995 - Chaumet's début in the watchmaking sector with the Khésis model, bound to go down in history, the first watch with diamonds set in stainless steel and realized in two sizes exclusively for ladies.

1996 - Birth year of Style de Chaumet, a collection of over 30 versions with round or rectangular case in steel or steel and gold, automatic or quartz movement, showing a linear and extremely elegant design.

1997 - Extension of the Style de Chaumet collection with a square dial model and a chronograph.

1998 - The Style de Chaumet collection is enriched by a model produced in a limited series of 250 pieces for each version, a thin watch with mechanical hand-winding movement in platinum or yellow gold with a "guilloché" dial. First appearance of Class One, a new unisex underwater watch with a rubber strap whose design reminds a steel bracelet.

1999 - Top Lady enters the Khésis collection: a steel or white gold watch with double time zone indication. The new "12" model pays homage to the mythical number 12 at Place Vendôme.

Today - Without denying its past, the House Chaumet gives its destiny a new dimension thanks to the mighty backing of the international Investcorp group. Apart from jewellery, leatherware and valuables signed by Chaumet, today watchmaking plays a very important role in the Maison's production, so that this belongs already to the restricted number of great watchmakers. The boutiques of London (in cooperation with Harrod's), the USA (in cooperation with Saks Fifth Avenue), Japan (in cooperation with Mitsukoshi) and Hong Kong represent the milestones of an evolution just commenced which will lead Chaumet to run along the ways of the third millennium with the unconstraint of winners.

ing homage to the number 12 of Place Vendôme, a very trendy piece with a two-color dial overtly reminding night and day and a white boxcalf leather strap, produced in a limited series.
Ladies will certainly forgive this digression. The great can afford everything. It's a question of ... style.

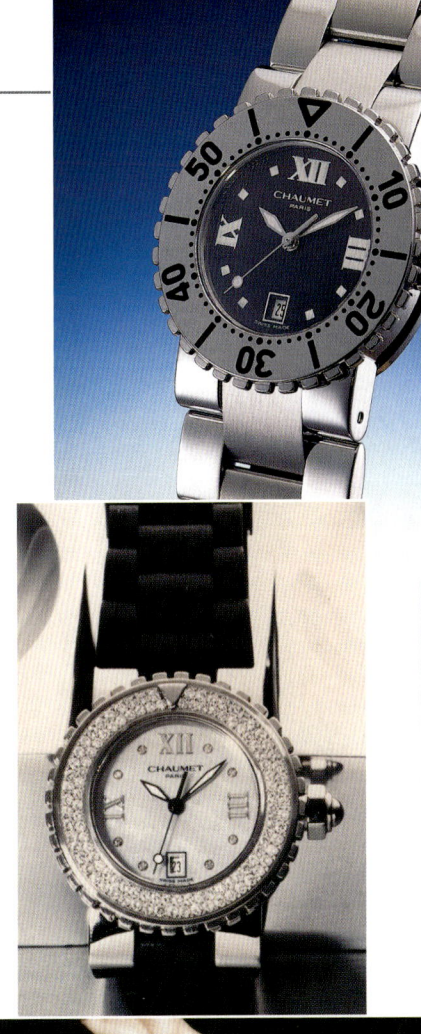

CHAUMET

STYLE DE CHAUMET CARRE   REF. W04290.036

Movement: mechanical, automatic winding, ETA caliber 2000.
Functions: hours, minutes, seconds, date.
Case: steel, two-piece, square shape (dim. 30x30 mm, thickness 8 mm); curved sapphire crystal; hexagonal crown with cabochon; case back fastened by 4 screws. Water-resistant to 3 atm.
Dial: silvered, engine-turned (guilloché) Clous de Paris in the central part; screen-printed Roman numerals and square markers; screen-printed minute track; sword style hands. 
Indications: date at 6.
Strap: crocodile leather; steel clasp with engraved "Chaumet Paris".
Also available: with Spirit Of bracelet; yellow gold, strap, Spirit Of bracelet. Medium, automatic: steel, strap, Spirit Of bracelet; yellow gold, strap, Spirit Of bracelet. With quartz movement, medium or small, steel or yellow gold with strap or Spirit Of bracelet, grey, silvered or white dial, Roman numerals or white or black, brilliant markers; in jewel version.
Prices: on request.

STYLE DE CHAUMET CARRE   REF. W04090.034

More than a name, "Style de Chaumet" is the emblem of high jewellery. The shaped design and wise volumes, the dynamic and highly personal look make it be a model of incontestable elegance, imitated many times but remaining beyond reach. Proposed in dozens of different versions, with round, rectangular or square cases, in gold or steel, leather strap or metal bracelet (gold, steel or steel/gold), with a "chemin de fer" white, grey, silvered or gilded dial, with the hours zone blued "ton sur ton", black with diamond markers, it perfectly combines simple shapes and volumes which distinguish it from the whole current production. The photograph shows the yellow gold version, with automatic movement and crocodile leather strap.
Price: on request.

STYLE DE CHAUMET RECTANGULAR   REF. W01635.030

Style de Chaumet in a few years became one among the most representative collections of the new trends in international watchmaking. It is based essentially on three case types: round, square and rectangular. The former two are produced with both automatic and quartz movement, while the latter is available only in the quartz version (this choice is virtually compulsory for the rectangular case if a watch must have an ideal size for a feminine wrist). Among the most recent novelties related to this model, a special rank is hold by the "Spirit Of" bracelet, realized in steel or gold. Though maintaining the concept of matte/polished it fits the wrist well and is elegant at the same time without betraying the original and unmistakable design of the collection.
The model shown in the photograph (size 35x23 mm, thickness 6 mm) has a silvered and guilloché dial with screen-printed Roman numerals and square markers.
Also available: strap; yellow gold, strap, bracelet Spirit Of; white gold, strap. Small size: steel; yellow gold, strap, bracelet Spirit Of; white gold, strap; in jewel version.
Prices: on request.

STYLE DE CHAUMET   REF. W02280.036

Movement: mechanical, automatic winding, ETA caliber 2892/A2.
Functions: hours, minutes, seconds, date.
Case: steel, two-piece (Ø 35 mm, thickness 8 mm); smooth sapphire crystal; hexagonal crown with cabochon; case back fastened by 6 screws. Water-resistant to 3 atm.
Dial: silvered, engine-turned (guilloché) Clous de Paris in the central part; screen-printed markers with Roman numerals; screen-printed minute track; sword style hands. 
Indications: date at 6.
Strap: crocodile leather; steel clasp with engraved "Chaumet Paris".
Also available: with Spirit Of bracelet; yellow gold with strap, bracelet. In the small size, automatic: steel; yellow gold with strap, with Spirit Of bracelet. With quartz movement, large or small size, steel or yellow gold with strap or bracelet or steel and yellow gold with bracelet.
Prices: on request.

CHAUMET

STYLE DE CHAUMET CHRONOGRAPH AUTOMATIC   REF. W03080.082

Movement: mechanical, automatic winding, extra-thin, Frédéric Piguet cal. 1185, rotor in yellow gold, engraved by hand.
Functions: hours, minutes, small seconds, date, chronograph with 3 counters.
Case: 18 kt yellow gold, two-piece (size 38.5x40 mm, thickness 11 mm), polished; curved sapphire crystal; hexagonal crown with cabochon and gold pushers; case back fastened by 6 screws with sapphire crystal bull's eye. Water-resistant to 3 atm.
Dial: silvered, engine-turned (guilloché) in the central part, with gold-colored hour and counter ring; applied gilded bâton markers and Arabic numerals; luminescent gilded bâton hands.
Indications: minute counter at 3, date between 4 and 5, small seconds at 6, hours at 9, center seconds, sexagesimal scale with division for $1/5$ sec. and luminescent markers.
Strap: crocodile leather; gold tongue clasp with engraved logo.
Also available: bracelet Style De; white gold, strap and black dial; steel, silvered dial and blue zones; quartz; in jewel version. Ø 36 mm, quartz, steel or yellow gold, silvered dial and gilded zones, black or white, strap or bracelet Spirit Of; in jewel version.
Prices: on request.

STYLE DE CHAUMET CHRONOGRAPH AUTOMATIC   REF. W03280.026

Within the Style de Chaumet collection, style and purity are combined with a contemporary strong and simple design, with well defined volumes. Such features are put into evidence in the chronograph model by which Chaumet affirms its presence within the segment of technical watches, but without preventing women to consider it one the most popular models (it is, in any case, available also in a version with quartz chronograph movement with a reduced diameter of 36 mm). The steel version shown in the photograph comes with a silvered dial with Arabic numerals and luminescent markers whose readability is enhanced by the blue color chosen for the hour ring and the perimeter of additional zones. Its movement is the automatic caliber 1185 by Frédéric Piguet. As an alternative to the leather straps available in many colors, there are the bracelets matching the case metal, with the particular design of their broad brushed links with polished edges.
Also available: with Style De bracelet.
Prices: on request.

CLASS ONE AUTOMATIC   REF. W06680.068

Movement: mechanical, automatic winding, Eta caliber 2000.
Functions: hours, minutes, seconds, date.
Case: steel, three-piece (Ø 35 mm, thickness 8 mm); domed sapphire crystal; counter-clockwise turning ring, with engraved graduated scale, useful to read diving times; screwed-on hexagonal crown with cabochon; screwed-on back. Water-resistant to 10 atm.
Dial: black, with wave pattern; applied and luminescent Roman numerals and square markers; luminescent lozenge hands.
Indications: date between 4 and 5, sexagesimal scale on the bezel.
Bracelet: brushed steel; steel fold-over clasp with engraved "Chaumet Paris".
Also available: grey silvered dial; with rubber strap; with black ring. Ø 33 mm, only quartz: steel, black ring or steel, dial white or black, rubber strap, bracelet; with pink or blue ring and black dial; steel, yellow gold ring, black dial, strap, bracelet; in jewel version.
Prices: on request.

CLASS ONE AUTOMATIC   REF. W06281.068

The Class One, Chaumet's first underwater watch, luckily combines excellent technical features and elegance, by which this Parisian jeweller distinguishes himself. Class One is a synthesis of antithetical factors - thanks to its size, it is a model perfect for both men and women. The models for both genders offer various combinations of dials, rings and straps or bracelets (hypoallergenic and water-repellent black rubber strap, as for the model shown in the photograph, or steel bracelet with adjustable fold-over clasp with double safety device). The movement is an automatic Eta 2000 caliber 200 (but quartz versions are available as well).
Price: on request.

Chopard

The world of Chopard is rich with history, technique, elegance and beauty. One of the most perfectly well-rounded watch and jewelry houses on the globe, Chopard's success story weaves myth, mystery, passion and allure. This legendary firm produces some of the world's most exquisite jewelry and timepieces—catering to men and women alike.

Since its inception 140 years ago, Chopard's craftsmen have managed a symbiosis of tradition, technology, design and elegance that is unparalleled. The talent and desire for perfection that Karl Scheufele, his wife Karin and their two children, Karl-Friedrich Scheufele and Caroline Gruosi-Scheufele have put into Chopard is what has propelled it to the forefront of the luxury jewelry and watch industry. The astute business acumen of Karl-Friedrich Scheufele, Chopard's vice president, and the exacting eye of Caroline Gruosi-Scheufele, vice president and creator of Chopard's most beautiful watches, come together in a brilliant mix of refreshing innovation.

As this family-owned business waltzes into the new millennium, it offers a wonderful array of exciting complicated timepieces, lush high-jeweled masterpieces, and invigorating sports marvels.

95

The genius that is Chopard today has its roots in 1860 when Louis-Ulysse Chopard founded his watchmaking company in a small village in the Jura Mountains of Switzerland. Even from the start, his timepieces were incredible works of art, elegantly designed with filigree, offering the finest enamel dials. Deeply dedicated to precision and quality, Chopard created wonderful pocket chronometers and exquisitely decorated watches for women. His family followed in his footsteps, keeping the company rooted in its heritage and building a worldwide reputation for its chronometers until 1963 when Karl Scheufele bought the firm from Chopard's grandson.

One of the finest jewelers of his time, Scheufele was a master goldsmith, innovative in gem setting and exquisite jewelry designs. His jewelry workshops were located near the great jewelry-making city of Pforzheim, Germany. It was his goal to bring his jewelry collection full circle, and to create elegantly jeweled wristwatches. The family firm had already been creating watchcases, table clocks and pocket watches with the name Eszeha on them. His purchase of "Le Petit Fils de L.U. Chopard"—now located in Geneva—gave him independence in the watch industry and the

Previous Page
The L.U.C Sport 2000 is equipped with the L.U.C 4.96 automatic movement, made by Chopard. It is a certified chronometer and features 65-hour power reserve and center seconds hand. It is water resistant to 100 meters and the rotor is finished with black nickel. It is created in a limited and numbered edition of 2000 in 18-karat gold and in a numbered edition of 2000 in steel.

Top left
Chopard is a family business — The Scheufeles, whose brilliance, poise, grace and passion shines through in the watches and jewelry they create. Karl, Caroline, Karin and Karl-Friedrich

Top center
This men's watch houses the L.U.C self-winding movement. It is available with either black, white or copper-colored dial in 18-karat yellow white or rose gold.

Above
In traditional beauty of form and function, Chopard's tonneau shaped watch features 45-hour power reserve, date and sub-seconds hand. It is crafted in 18 karat rose gold.

Left
Classical men's watch with automatic movement, double going barrel, power reserve of 100 hours.

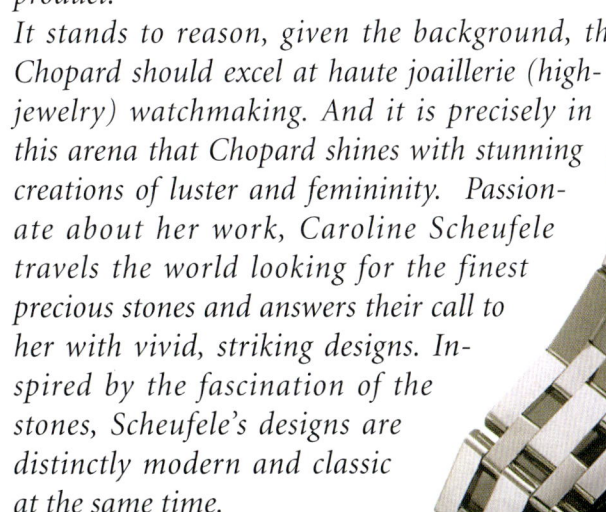

Chopard

Top
The La Strada Collection of timepieces features the "chic" of the Fifties.

Bottom
From the Imperiale collection, these 18-karat white gold watches are set with cabochon cut rubies or sapphires.

ability to produce whatever he chose. He spent several years streamlining his new possession, and relaunched Chopard as a top-of-the-line luxury hallmark.

Thanks to Scheufele's foresight and ingenious design, Chopard has grown to over 900 employees. Today the firm has a work force of more than 500 varied artisans, including goldsmiths, watchmakers, gem setters and mechanics. The Scheufele family took the fine firm one very important step further—making it a fully integrated, complete manufacturer.

Chopard today is one of the few luxury watch companies left that creates many of its own parts, builds up the basic movements it purchases, and assembles them all together in the Geneva workshops. It has even created its own superior watch movements.

Through regular family meetings, the Scheufeles determined that their watches, like their jewelry, should be hand made to the utmost standards of quality and craftsmanship. Today, Chopard embodies the epitome of technical prowess, hand-craftsmanship and tradition.

With this legendary reputation around the world, the newest generation of Scheufeles—Karl-Friedrich and Caroline—has spent the past years taking the company to new heights in terms of product.

It stands to reason, given the background, that Chopard should excel at haute joaillerie (high-jewelry) watchmaking. And it is precisely in this arena that Chopard shines with stunning creations of luster and femininity. Passionate about her work, Caroline Scheufele travels the world looking for the finest precious stones and answers their call to her with vivid, striking designs. Inspired by the fascination of the stones, Scheufele's designs are distinctly modern and classic at the same time.

Chopard

Each piece, once sketched and planned, is hand-made—sometimes taking hundreds of hours at the most detailed work. Goldsmiths must solder together anywhere from 3,000 to 4,000 points to provide the settings for these pieces of art. These pieces, too, often command the highest prices—reaching well into the multiple thousands and even hundreds of thousands depending upon their intricacy.

In the world of diamond watches Chopard also excels when it comes to uniqueness. Aside from its incredible haute joaillerie pieces, Chopard corners the market on inventive diamond-setting with its signature Happy Diamonds collection. It was 23 years ago that one of Chopard's top designers conceived of a watch in which diamond brilliants would reveal their full beauty and glitter roaming free on the watch dial. Inspired by a waterfall, the design was chosen by a panel of leading jewelers as the "most interesting watch of the year."

Great in concept, the execution of this design was a puzzle to accomplish—one that required incredible technical knowledge and open mindedness. Karl-Friedrich Scheufele rose to the challenge and set his Geneva craftsmen on to the task. At every step, new issues arose, including where to find a top and

Left
"Ice Cube" collection designed be de Grisogono for Chopard. Lady's watch in white gold. Bezel set with 16 emeralds and 60 square-cut diamonds. The buckle is set with diamonds.

Above
The Ice Cube is created in 18-karat white or yellow gold for shimmering appeal. Also available with diamonds and other precious stones.

Bottom left
Eva Herzigova wearing Chopard jewelry.

Chopard

bottom glass that the diamonds, when set between, would not scratch. The solution was to create a conical shaped sheath that ensconced the base of each diamond, so that with the lightest tap of the watchcase, the diamonds would rotate.

Borne of whim, the design won the 1976 Golden Rose of Baden-Baden competition. A year later, it was one of the most-demanded watches the firm created, and today, it is a legend.

Chopard creates the Happy Diamonds watches either with full gemstone-adorned cases and bracelets, or as simply elegant 18K gold watches with dancing diamonds within. What's more, the company has introduced new evolutions of the concept, from the Happy Diamonds perfume, with free-floating diamonds in the bottle to the Happy Diamonds watches collection with rubies, emeralds or sapphires merrily

Top
From the Spring 1999 "Casmir" collection, ladies' watches in white gold, bezel and dial set with black and white diamonds. Center Naomi Campbell wearing Chopard jewelry.

Center
Ophélie Winter wearing Chopard Happy Sport watch and Love ring.

Bottom
Chopard's Pushkin collection was inspired by the spires in St. Petersburg, and is elegantly translated in diamonds.

spinning on the dial, to the Happy Sport collection. In this series, intended to contrast with the Happy Diamonds, the diamonds roll elegantly around the dial, and the stones roll freely across the watchcase.

But for the Scheufele family, diamonds and gemstones simply are not enough. In tribute to its forefathers—of both its own and the Chopard family—precision and quality nagged at them. While the diamond pieces were perfectly set and exquisitely executed, their penchant for complexity drove them forward. Today, Chopard's great Geneva watchmakers also excel at the intricate art of classical, complicated watchmaking. Among its myriad timepieces of technical excellence are perpetual calendars, chronographs, dual time zones, skeletons and moonphase watches.

Symbolizing the company's return to its origins, fourth generation Karl-Friedrich Scheufele, on the threshold of the new millennium, initiated research into the creation of a Chopard movement, and set up factory in Fleurier—a top Swiss watchmaking region. Here it was that the Chopard automatic movement, named L.U.C. in tribute to Louis-Ulysse Chopard, was born. After three years of research and development, the L.U.C. brings the house of Chopard full circle making it a true "manufacture" in the strict Swiss sense of the term.

Of course, also behind this intriguing company is a boundless creative spirit that yields refreshing innovation in classical and sport watches. Chopard's

Top
The St. Moritz offers sporty elegance in its nautically inspired design.

Center
Mille Miglia Chronograph in steel, special Jacky ICKX edition. Case-back in sapphire crystal to admire the automatic movement, black dial, water-resistant up to 50 meters, date indicator, tachometer, hour counter, limited edition signed by Jacky Ickx.

Bottom
From the Imperiale collection, this lady's chronograph watch in steel with a blue dial are set with cabochon-cut sapphires (1.76ct), water-resistant.

100

Chopard

Top
La Strada Collection pair of ladies' watches in steel, steel bracelet with blue or white dial.

Center
Karl-Friedrich Scheufele and his wife participating in the Mille Miglia race in 1999 with a Porsche 550A Spider of 1955.

Bottom
The 1999 Mille Miglia chronograph features a rubber strap with the Dunlop racing tire design, engine-turned silver dial, automatic movement and tachometer bezel.

watch collections range the full gamut, from Art Deco inspired watches, to the sophisticated Tonneau, to the beveled, hand-engraved Skeleton. Sportier lines include the Gstaad and St. Moritz collections, and the Mille Miglia—produced in tribute to the legendary Mille Miglia vintage car rally that was held annually from 1927 to 1957. The Mille Miglia was revived in 1977 as a three-day showcase rally for vintage cars. Within years, Chopard became the sponsor of the race, and each year creates a watch in tribute to it and its drivers. Mille Miglia was another perfect match for Chopard—not only because cars and watches have always held true to the same ideals of high performance and elegance, but also because both Karl and Karl-Friedrich join in the race with their vintage automobiles.

So, by carefully keeping an eye on the traditions of the past, and by blending in the passion and drive of the present, Chopard is one of the most gracefully poised personalities in the luxury watch and jewelry business for the millennium.

CHOPARD

L.U.C "1.96" — REF. 16/1860/2

Movement: mechanical, automatic winding, Chopard caliber L.U.C 1.96. Hallmarked with the "Geneva Seal" (watchmaking's highest distinction of quality). Completely hand-made in the Swiss factory in Fleurier.
Functions: hour, minute, small second, date.
Case: 18 kt pink gold, three-piece case (Ø 36 mm, thickness 8 mm); slightly bombé sapphire crystal; pink gold crown; case back attached by 8 screws, displaying the movement through a sapphire crystal. Water-resistant to 3 atm. 
Dial: silvered gold, engine turned (guilloché) by hand at the center and brushed on the hour ring; zone with concentric-circles pattern; applied pink gold pointed markers; printed minute track; pink gold Dauphine hands.
Indications: small second and date at 6.
Strap: crocodile leather; pink gold clasp.
Price: 11'730 CHF. Numbered edition of 1860 pieces, a homage to Louis-Ulysse Chopard, who founded the firm in 1860.
Also available: black dial; white gold, silvered, black, gilded or coppered dial (same price); in yellow gold, black or silvered dial 11'630 CHF; platinum, silvered, black, gilded or coppered dial 14'930 CHF.

L.U.C "3.96" — REF. 16/1860

Movement: mechanical, automatic winding, Chopard caliber L.U.C 3.96. Completely hand-made in the Swiss factory in Fleurier.
Functions: hour, minute, small second, date.
Case: 18 kt white gold, three-piece case (Ø 36 mm, thickness 8 mm); slightly bombé sapphire crystal; white gold crown; case back attached by 8 screws, displaying the movement through a sapphire crystal. Water-resistant to 3 atm. 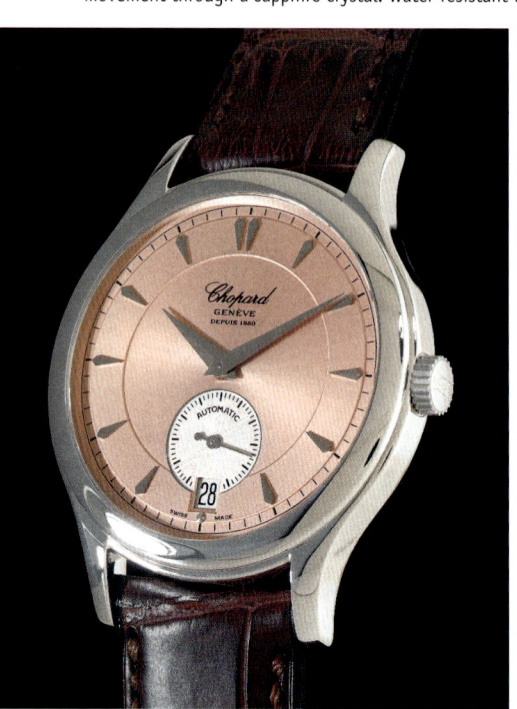
Dial: coppered and silvered; zone with concentric-circles pattern; applied white gold pointed markers and printed minute track; white gold Dauphine hands.
Indications: small second and date at 6.
Strap: crocodile leather; white gold clasp.
Price: 8'700 CHF. Limited edition of 1860 numbered pieces, a homage to Louis-Ulysse Chopard, who founded the firm in 1860.
Also available: pink gold (same price); yellow gold 8'600 CHF. Dials available white or coppered with silvered small second dial.

L.U.C "4.96" — REF. 16/1862

Movement: mechanical, automatic winding, Chopard caliber L.U.C 4.96 (caliber L.U.C 3.96 base), 34 jewels. Hallmarked with the "Geneva Seal" (watchmaking's highest distinction of quality). Completely hand-made in the Swiss factory in Fleurier.
Functions: hour, minute, center second, date.
Case: 18 kt yellow gold, three-piece case (Ø 36.3 mm, thickness 7.8 mm); slightly bombé sapphire crystal; yellow gold crown; case back attached by 8 screws, displaying the movement through a sapphire crystal. Water-resistant to 3 atm. 
Dial: gold, black; applied yellow gold pointed markers; printed minute track; yellow gold Dauphine hands.
Indications: date at 6.
Strap: crocodile leather; yellow gold clasp.
Price: 8'200 CHF. Numbered edition of 1860 pieces, a homage to Louis-Ulysse Chopard, who founded the firm in 1860.
Also available: pink or white gold 8'280 CHF. Dials available: silvered, white, black or coppered.

L.U.C SPORT 2000 — REF. 16/8200

Movement: mechanical, automatic winding, Chopard caliber L.U.C 4.96 (base caliber L.U.C 3.96), 34 jewels. Screw heads and rotor with "black nickel" finish. Hallmarked with the "Geneva Seal" (watchmaking's highest distinction of quality). Completely hand-made in the Swiss factory in Fleurier.
Functions: hour, minute, center second, date.
Case: stainless steel, three-piece case (Ø 40 mm, thickness 10 mm); slightly bombé sapphire crystal; screw-down crown; case back attached by 8 screws, displaying the movement through a sapphire crystal. Water-resistant to 10 atm. 
Dial: blue, engine turned (guilloché) with a basket pattern at the center and concentric-circles pattern on the hour ring; applied pointed markers; printed minute track with luminescent dots on the beveled ring; luminescent Dauphine hands.
Indications: date at 3.
Strap: rubber; stainless steel clasp.
Price: 6'340 CHF. Limited edition of 2000 numbered pieces in each version.
Also available: in yellow gold 11'690 CHF; pink or white gold 11'830 CHF. Dials available in grey, black or blue.

CHOPARD

CHRONOGRAPH "MILLE MIGLIA 1999"   REF. 16/8331-99

Movement: mechanical, automatic winding, caliber ETA 2892/A2 plus Dubois Dépraz module.
Functions: hour, minute, small second, date, chronograph with 3 counters.
Case: stainless steel, three-piece case (Ø 39 mm, thickness 11.5 mm); antireflective curved sapphire crystal; case back attached by 8 screws, displaying the movement through a sapphire crystal. Water-resistant to 5 atm.
Dial: silvered, with bouchonné finish (adopted in the Thirties for instrument panels of sporting cars); luminescent Superluminova Arabic numerals; luminescent stainless steel bâton hands.
Indications: small second at 3 (with the famous red arrow as a symbol for racing), date between 4 and 5, hour counter at 6, minute counter at 9, center second counter, minute track with divisions for 1/5 of a second, tachymeter scale on the beveled ring.
Strap: rubber reproducing the tread of Dunlop Racing tires of the Sixties); stainless steel clasp.
Price: 3'150 CHF.
Realized at the occasion of the 1999 "Mille Miglia" race, in limited edition of 1000 numbered pieces.
Also available: in yellow gold 8'990 CHF: 100 pieces; white gold 9'100 CHF: 100 pieces.

CHRONOGRAPH "MILLE MIGLIA" LADY   REF. 13/8355-23

The mythical Mille Miglia car race was run on a distance of 1000 miles from 1927 to 1957 on normal roads along the Brescia-Roma-Brescia route. Considered as dangerous, the race was abolished for many years, until in 1977 it was revived as a reliability trial for historical cars. Since 1988, Chopard is the main sponsor of this event, for which reason at the occasion of the last edition they celebrated the tenth anniversary of cooperation. Each year Chopard creates for the historical Mille Miglia an exclusive masterpiece to offer to each participant who has the surprise of seeing his start number engraved on the case back. A similar version is marketed, of course without personalized numbers. In the photograph the chronograph in lady's version (Ø 33, thickness 9 mm), with a quartz movement and Frédéric Piguet mechanical chronograph module, cassteel case and bezel in white gold with a circle of diamonds and sapphires.
Price: 10'380 CHF.
Also available: with brilliants and rubies 11'100 CHF; with brilliants and emeralds 13'850 CHF; with brilliants 11'550 CHF.

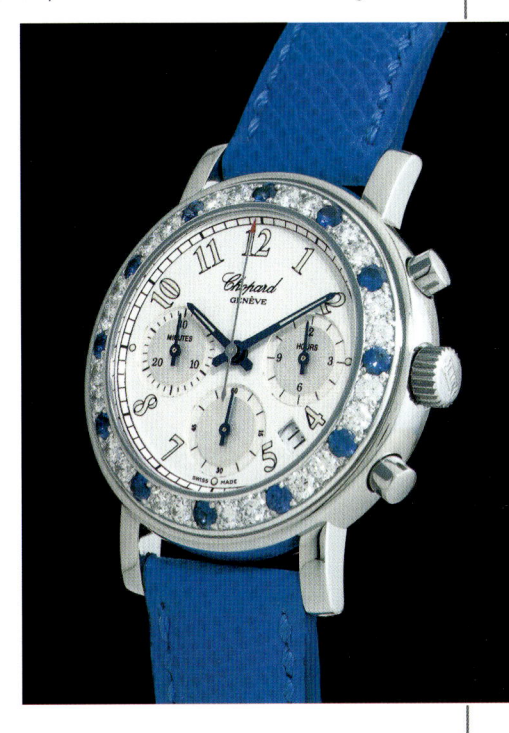

CHRONOGRAPH AUTOMATIC   REF. 34/1202

Movement: mechanical, automatic winding, Jaeger-Le Coultre caliber 889/1 plus chronograph module.
Functions: hour, minute, small second, date, chronograph with 3 counters.
Case: 18 kt yellow gold, three-piece case (Ø 37 mm, thickness 11 mm); antireflective flat sapphire crystal; bombé bezel with engraved minute track; screw-down yellow gold crown with case protection and yellow gold pushers; case back attached by 8 screws. Water-resistant to 10 atm.
Dial: white; applied bâton markers; luminescent bâton hands.
Indications: date with magnifying glass at 3, hour counter at 6, minute counter at 9, small second at 12, center second counter, minute track with luminescent dots and divisions for 1/5 of a second.
Strap: crocodile leather; hand-engraved yellow gold clasp.
Price: 11'750 CHF.
Also available: pink or white gold 11'850 CHF. Each version is available with white, black or pink dial.

CHRONOGRAPH MANUAL   REF. 34/8179

Movement: mechanical, manual winding, Lemania caliber 1874.
Functions: hour, minute, small second, chronograph with 3 counters.
Case: stainless steel, three-piece case, polished and brushed finish (Ø 37 mm, thickness 11.2 mm); antireflective flat sapphire crystal; bombé bezel with engraved tachymeter scale; crown with case protection; case back attached by 8 screws, displaying the movement through a sapphire crystal. Water-resistant to 3 atm.
Dial: white; silvered counters with concentric-circles pattern; luminescent applied bâton markers and railway minute track on the beveled ring; tritium-plated bâton hands.
Indications: minute counter at 3, hour counter at 6, small second at 9, center second counter, minute track with divisions for 1/5 of a second.
Strap: crocodile leather; stainless steel clasp.
Price: 4'990 CHF.
Also available: in yellow gold 11'450 CHF; white or pink gold 11'550 CHF. Each version is available with white or black dial.

103

CHOPARD

CHRONOGRAPH PERPETUAL CALENDAR WITH SEASON — REF. 36/1224

Movement: mech., automatic winding (autonomy 43 h), Jaeger-Le Coultre cal. 889/2152 base, Dubois-Dépraz perpetual calendar and chrono module. Balance with micrometer balance-spring regulation and Kif shock-resistant system. Beveled and Côtes de Genève finished; rotor on ball-bearing with 21 kt yellow gold peripheral mass, skeletonized, personalized and engine turned (circular graining). **Functions:** hour, minute, small second, 24-hour indication, perpetual calendar (data, day, month, weeks, seasons, year, moon phases), chronograph with 3 counters. **Case:** 18 kt yellow gold, three-piece case (Ø 40.80, thickness 12.60 mm); antireflective curved sapphire crystal; 4 correctors on case side; rectangular yellow gold crown and pushers; case back attached by 8 screws, displaying the movement through a sapphire crystal. Water-res. to 5 atm. **Dial:** in gold, white enameled, silvered zones; printed Roman numerals; leaf style hands. **Indic.:** moon phase and week at 3; day, hour counter and 24-hour display at 6; minute counter, month and four year cycle at 9; date, small second and season at 12; center second counter, minute track with divisions for 1/5 of a second. **Strap:** crocodile leather; hand-engraved yellow gold clasp. **Price:** 44'650 CHF. **Also av.:** (50 pieces each type), pink gold 44'790; PT 49'310; guilloché dial.

CHRONOGRAPH PERPETUAL CALENDAR — REF. 36/91208

Movement: mechanical, automatic winding, Jaeger-Le Coultre caliber 889/1 base with perpetual calendar and chronograph developed by Chopard. 18 kt gold rotor. **Functions:** hour, minute, small second, chronograph with 3 counters, perpetual calendar (date, day, month, year, moon phase). **Case:** platinum, three-piece case (Ø 40, thickness 12.30 mm); antireflective flat sapphire crystal; bezel with minute track engraved; 4 correctors on case side; platinum crown with case protection and platinum pushers; case back attached by 8 screws, displaying the movement through a sapphire crystal. Water-resistant to 3 atm. **Dial:** in gold, white; silvered zones with concentric-circles pattern; luminescent applied bâton markers; luminescent white gold bâton hands. **Indications:** moon phase at 3, day and hour counter at 6; minute counter, month and four year cycle at 9; date and small second at 12, center second counter, railway minute track with divisions for 1/5 of a second on the beveled ring. **Strap:** crocodile leather; hand-engraved platinum clasp. **Price:** 43'210 CHF. **Also available:** yellow gold 38'360 CHF; pink or white gold 38'500 CHF. Edition limited to 50 pieces for each version.

CHRONOGRAPH RATTRAPANTE — REF. 34/1243

Movement: mechanical, automatic winding, Frédéric Piguet 1186. Beveled, Côtes de Genève and circular graining finish. 18 kt gold rotor. **Functions:** hour, minute, small second, date, split-second chronograph with 3 counters. **Case:** 18 kt white gold, three-piece case (Ø 38 mm, thickness 11.7 mm); antireflective curved sapphire crystal; rectangular white gold crown and pushers (for fly-back feature at 10); case back attached by 8 screws, displaying the movement through a sapphire crystal. Water-resistant to 3 atm. **Dial:** gold, silvered; zones with concentric-circles pattern; printed Arabic numerals; white gold luminescent bâton hands. **Indications:** minute counter at 3, date between 4 and 5, small second at 6, hour counter at 9, center split-second counters, minute track with divisions for 1/5 of a second. **Strap:** crocodile leather; white gold clasp, hand-engraved. **Price:** 38'320 CHF. **Also available:** in yellow gold 38'180 CHF. Both versions available with white or silvered dial.

CHRONOGRAPH RATTRAPANTE

Among the men's watches contained in the Chopard catalog there is this outstanding chronograph with fly-back feature and case aesthetically halfway between the perpetual chronograph type with indication of season and the sporting Mille Miglia type. Through the aperture in the case back, protected by the usual sapphire glass it is possible to admire the splendid Frédéric Piguet movement, with its high-level decoration and finish: everything is ruled by the gold rotor emphasized by a circular graining decoration which characterizes also the bridges, except for the one of the automatic winding wheelwork showing the classical Côtes de Genève decoration. Furthermore, all the bridges are beveled and the chronograph levers are polished. Immediately above the rotor, just to the right, one sees the column wheel which controls the switching of the fly-back feature functions.

CHOPARD

TONNEAU PERPETUAL CALENDAR — REF. 36/92249

Movement: mechanical, automatic winding, Jaeger-Le Coultre caliber 888 base and perpetual calendar module developed by Chopard.
Functions: hour, minute, 24-hour indication, perpetual calendar (date, day, month, year, moon phase).
Case: platinum, three-piece tonneau case (height 36.50 mm, width 34.40 mm, thickness 8.85 mm); flat sapphire crystal; 4 correctors on case side; platinum crown; case back attached by 8 screws. Water-resistant to 3 atm.
Dial: silvered, engine turned (guilloché); printed Roman numerals and railway minute track; blued stainless steel Breguet hands.
Indications: month and four year cycle at 3, moon phase at 6, day and 24-hour display at 9, fan-shape date in the higher dial part with retrograde hand.
Strap: crocodile leather, hand stitched; platinum clasp.
Price: 42'670 CHF.
Also available: in yellow gold 37'430 CHF; pink or white gold 37'550 CHF.

TONNEAU POWER RESERVE — REF. 16/2248

Movement: mechanical, automatic winding, Frédéric Piguet caliber 9644.
Functions: hour, minute, small second, date, power reserve.
Case: 18 kt yellow gold, three-piece tonneau case (height 32.50 mm, width 30 mm, thickness 7.10 mm); antireflective flat sapphire crystal; sapphire cabochon yellow gold crown; case back attached by 8 screws. Water-resistant to 3 atm.
Dial: silvered, engine turned (guilloché); printed Roman numerals and railway minute track; blued stainless steel Breguet hands.
Indications: power reserve at 3, date at 6, small second at 9.
Strap: crocodile leather, hand stitched; hand-engraved yellow gold clasp.
Price: 8'900 CHF.
Also available: pink or white gold 8'970 CHF; platinum 15'290 CHF. Each version is available with white, silvered, anthracite, champagne or coppered dial.

TONNEAU AUTOMATIC — REF. 16/2247

Movement: mechanical, automatic winding, Frédéric Piguet caliber 9511.
Functions: hour, minute, center second, date.
Case: 18 kt yellow gold, three-piece tonneau case (height 37.8 mm, width 35.5 mm); flat sapphire crystal; sapphire cabochon yellow gold crown; case back attached by 8 screws. Water-resistant to 3 atm.
Dial: white; printed Roman numerals and railway minute track; sword style hands.
Indications: date at 6.
Strap: crocodile leather; hand-engraved yellow gold clasp.
Price: 7'230 CHF.
Also available: pink or white gold 7'310 CHF. Each version is available with white or silvered dial.

TONNEAU SMALL SECOND — REF. 16/2246

Movement: mechanical, manual winding, Jaeger-Le Coultre 818/4.
Functions: hour, minute, small second.
Case: 18 kt white gold, three-piece tonneau case (height 37.8 mm, width 35.5 mm, thickness 7.2 mm); flat sapphire crystal; sapphire cabochon white gold crown; case back attached by 8 screws. Water-resistant to 3 atm.
Dial: white; printed Roman numerals and railway minute track; sword style hands.
Indications: small second at 6.
Strap: crocodile leather; hand-engraved white gold clasp.
Price: 6'400 CHF.
Also available: pink gold (same price); yellow gold 6'320 CHF. Each version is available with white or silvered dial.

CHOPARD

PERPETUAL CALENDAR   REF. 36/1206

Movement: mechanical, automatic winding, Jaeger-Le Coultre caliber 888 base and perpetual calendar module developed by Chopard.
Functions: hour, minute, 24-hour indication, perpetual calendar (date, day, month, year, moon phase).
Case: 18 kt yellow gold, three-piece case (Ø 36 mm, thickness 9 mm); antireflective flat sapphire crystal; 4 correctors on case side; yellow gold crown with case protection; case back attached by 8 screws. Water-resistant to 3 atm.
Dial: gilded; applied yellow gold square markers on the railway minute track; luminescent bâton hands.
Indications: month and four year cycle at 3, moon phase at 6, day and 24-hour display at 9, fan-type date in the higher dial part with retrograde hand.
Strap: crocodile leather; hand-engraved yellow gold clasp.
Price: 27'150 CHF.
Also available: pink or white gold 27'250 CHF; platinum 36'730 CHF. Dials available: white, silvered or gilded.

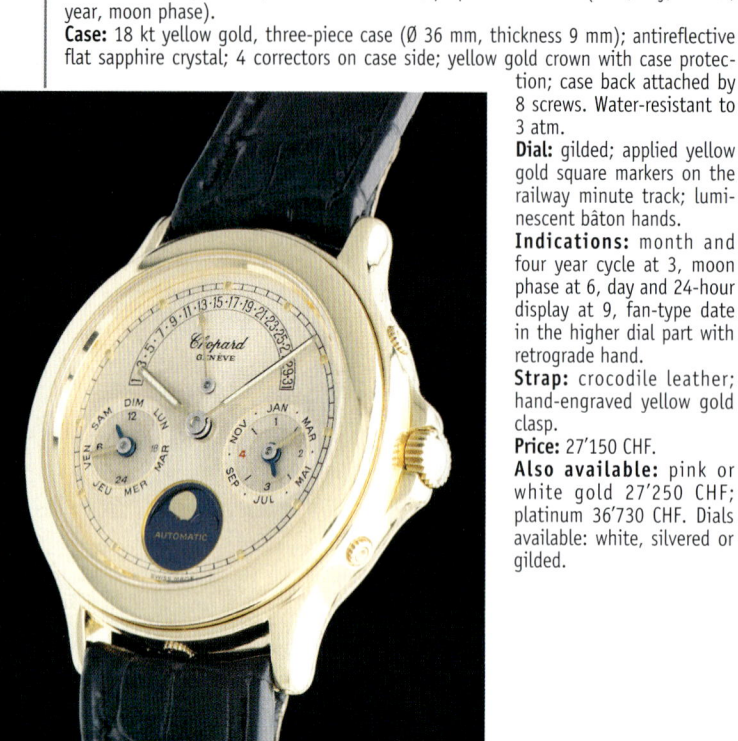

DUAL TIME   REF. 16/2240

Movement: two mechanical movements, manual winding, Jaeger-Le Coultre caliber 846.
Functions: hours and minutes of two different time zones.
Case: 18 kt yellow gold, two-piece rectangular-curved case; curved sapphire crystal; winding crowns at 2 and 4, in gold, with cabochon in black onyx.
Dial: white, curved; printed Roman numerals; leaf style hands.
Indications: off-center hour and minute: main time-zone time at 12, second time-zone time at 6, both with double hand.
Strap: crocodile leather; recessed attachment; yellow gold clasp.
Price: 3'690 CHF.
Also available: white gold 3'730 CHF; with quartz movements.

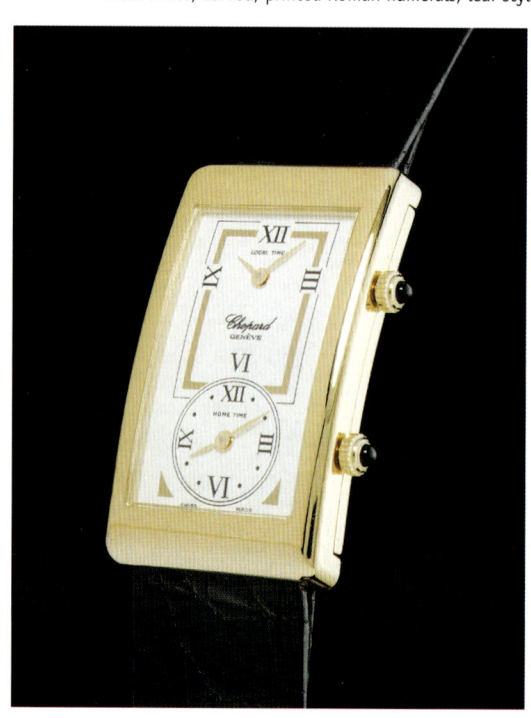

ST. MORITZ CHRONOGRAPH   REF. 26/8352

Movement: mechanical, automatic winding, Frédéric Piguet caliber 1185. 21 kt gold rotor.
Functions: hour, minute, center second, date, chronograph with 3 counters.
Case: stainless steel, three-piece case (Ø 37.5 mm, thickness 10.7 mm); antireflective flat sapphire crystal; bezel fastened by 8 steel screws; screw-down crown; rectangular pushers; case back attached by 8 screws, displaying the movement through a sapphire crystal. Water-resistant to 10 atm.
Dial: blue, soleil; applied stainless steel bâton markers, 12 in Roman numerals; luminescent dots; luminescent bâton hands.
Indications: minute counter at 3, date between 4 and 5, small second at 6, hour counter at 9, minute track with divisions for 1/5 of a second on the beveled ring.
Strap: Kevlar fiber; double fold-over clasp steel.
Price: 6'740 CHF.
Also available: with single clasp 6'280 CHF; with bracelet 7'590 CHF; black or white dial.

ST. MORITZ   REF. 26/8300

Movement: mechanical, automatic winding, Jaeger-Le Coultre caliber 889.
Functions: hour, minute, center second, date.
Case: stainless steel, three-piece case (Ø 37.5 mm, thickness 8.5 mm); antireflective flat sapphire crystal; bezel fastened by 8 steel screws; screw-down crown; case back attached by 8 screws. Water-resistant to 10 atm.
Dial: white; applied stainless steel black painted bâton markers and printed Roman numerals; luminescent dots on the railway minute track; luminescent bâton hands.
Indications: date between 4 and 5.
Bracelet: steel; double fold-over steel clasp.
Price: 3'930 CHF.
Also available: in yellow gold 20'990 CHF; white gold 21'370 CHF; yellow gold & steel, 7'730 CHF. Each version is available with white, grey, blue or coppered dial.

CHOPARD

ST. MORITZ LADY — REF. 25/8320

Movement: mechanical, automatic winding, Frédéric Piguet caliber 951.
Functions: hour, minute, center second, date.
Case: stainless steel, three-piece case (Ø 30.5 mm, thickness 7 mm); antireflective flat sapphire crystal; bezel fastened by 8 steel screws; screw-down crown; case back attached by 8 screws. Water-resistant to 10 atm.
Dial: coppered; applied bâton markers and Roman numerals, printed minute track; luminescent bâton hands.
Indications: date between 4 and 5.
Bracelet: steel; double fold-over steel clasp.
Price: 3'750 CHF.
Also available: stainless steel and yellow gold 6'420 CHF; in yellow gold 16'480 CHF; white gold 16'760 CHF. Each version is available with white, silvered, blue or coppered dial.

HAPPY SPORT CHRONOGRAPH — REF. 28/8267-23

Movement: quartz with mechanical chronograph module, Frédéric Piguet caliber 1270.
Functions: hour, minute, small second, date, chronograph with 3 counters.
Case: 18 kt white gold, three-piece case, polished (Ø 38.5 mm, thickness 10.5 mm); 7 top-Wesselton quality brilliants (totalling 0.39 kt) individually set fluctuating between two flat sapphire crystals; iolite cabochon crown, pushers and lugs; case back attached by 8 screws. Water-resistant to 3 atm.
Dial: lacquer white, counters silvered; printed Roman numerals and railway minute track; blued stainless steel sword style hands.
Indications: hour counter at 3, date between 4 and 5, small second at 6, minute counter at 9, center second counter.
Bracelet: white gold; double fold-over white gold clasp.
Price: on request.
Also available: Prices refer to the leather strap version: steel, cab. iolite 10'100, cab. sapphire. 10'990; cab. rubies 13'100; yellow gold, cab. sapphire. 18'810, cab. rubies 20'890; white gold, cab. sapphire. 18'950, cab. rubies 20'990; bezel brilliants: yellow gold, cab. sapphire. 37'590, cab. rubies 39'590; white gold, cab. sapphire. 37'820 CHF, cab. rubies 39'800; in many other jewel versions.

MINI — REF. 13/6636-20 - REF. 13/6632-23

Movement: mechanical, manual winding, caliber 2442.
Functions: hour, minute.
Case: 18 kt yellow gold (Square), 18 kt white gold (Round) and brilliants set on bezel and lugs, three-piece case (height 17 mm, width 17 mm and Ø 18 mm, thickness 7 mm); flat sapphire crystal; yellow gold crown and lugs studded with faceted diamonds (Square) or chabochon sapphires (Round); snap-on back. Water-resistant to 3 atm.
Dial: studded with brilliants (Square) and in mother-of-pearl (Round); yellow gold Dauphine hands.
Strap: satin (Square); lizard-skin (Round); yellow gold clasp (Round); gold and brilliants (Square).
Price: 14'440 CHF (Square), 9'650 CHF (Round).
Also available: with square case: pink or white gold 14'480 CHF; with ruby, emerald or sapphire cabochon (prices on request); with round case: pink or white gold 9'650 CHF, yellow gold 9'610 CHF; with ruby, emerald or faceted diamond cabochons on the crown and on lug sides (prices on request).

"LA STRADA" — REF. 41/6659/8

Movement: mechanical, manual winding, Omega caliber 730 (realized in 1968), rectangular shape, size 16.4x9 mm, thickness 3.2 mm, 17 jewels, 21,660 vibrations per hour (vph), power reserve of 48 hours.
Functions: hour, minute.
Case: 18 kt white gold, two-piece case (curved bombé rectangular case, made up by 4 full-volume elements and case back - size 30x18.5 mm, thickness 9 mm); with double brilliants paving on the two lateral bezel volumes; curved sapphire crystal; brand engraved on the left case side; emerald cabochon white gold crown; curved case back attached by 4 screws. Water-resistant to 3 atm.
Dial: white, curved; printed Arabic numerals and railway minute track; bâton hands black enameled.
Strap: crocodile leather, recessed and fastened by lateral screws; pink gold clasp.
Price: 15'830 CHF.
Also available: pink or yellow gold (same price); without brilliants: in yellow gold 5'430 CHF; pink or white gold 5'510 CHF; in other jewel versions; with quartz movement.

107

CHOPARD

IMPERIALE CHRONOGRAPH AUTOMATIC — REF. 37/8209.33

Movement: mechanical, automatic winding, Jaeger-Le Coultre caliber 889/1 and chronograph module.
Functions: hour, minute, small second, date, chronograph with 3 counters.
Case: stainless steel, four-piece case (Ø 37 mm, thickness 11 mm); flat sapphire crystal; brand and progressive number engraved on the left case side; iolite cabochon octagonal crown, pushers and lugs; case back attached by 8 screws. Water-resistant to 3 atm.
Dial: white with silvered counters; applied Roman numerals and faceted round markers on the railway minute track; stainless steel lozenge hands.
Indications: date with magnifying glass at 3, hour counter at 6, minute counter at 9, small second at 12, center second counter, minute track with divisions for 1/5 of a second.
Strap: crocodile leather; central attachment; stainless steel clasp.
Price: 5'710 CHF.
Also available: with bracelet 7'350 CHF; with cabochon steel (price on request); with blue, coppered or mother-of-pearl dial, or white with blue counters, silvered with white counters.

IMPERIALE CHRONOGRAPH — REF. 37/3157.23

Movement: quartz with mechanical chronograph module, Frédéric Piguet caliber 1270.
Functions: hour, minute, small second, date, chronograph with 3 counters.
Case: 18 kt pink gold, four-piece case (Ø 37 mm, thickness 9 mm); flat sapphire crystal; brand and progressive number engraved on the left case side; ruby cabochon pink gold octagonal crown, pushers and lugs; case back attached by 8 screws. Water-resistant to 3 atm.
Dial: white and counters silvered; applied round faceted markers on the railway minute track; pink gold sword style hands.
Indications: hour counter at 3, date between 4 and 5, small second at 6, minute counter at 9, center second counter.
Strap: crocodile leather; central attachment; pink gold clasp.
Price: 15'770 CHF.
Also available: white gold (same price); in yellow gold 15'650 CHF; with ruby cabochons: in yellow gold 19'670 CHF; pink or white gold 19'790 CHF; with brilliants on bezel and central attachment Ref. 37/3168-23: in yellow gold 30'520 CHF; white gold 30'640 CHF.

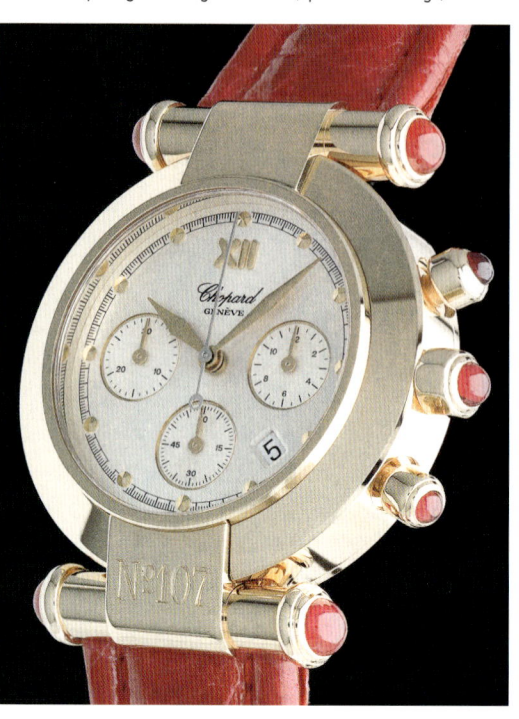

IMPERIALE CHRONOGRAPH MEDIUM — REF. 38/3469-20

The Imperial chronograph family includes a slightly smaller size than men's size (Ø 32 mm; thickness 9.5 mm) having the same movement, caliber 1270 by Frédéric Piguet, but without date indication. Conceived for the feminine public, this model was renewed recently in this version in white gold embellished by a grid studded with brilliants; four circles above the mother-of-pearl dial frame the auxiliary indicators and the firm's logo. Also the hour markers are adorned with brilliants as well as the chronograph keys, the crown and the lug ends. An important and precious watch, deriving its force and refinement from the use of only one color.
Price: 30'100 CHF.
Also available: yellow gold 29'960; with cab. sapphire: yellow gold 22'140; white gold 22'240. Ref. 38/3157, without brilliant ring and with sapphire cab.: yellow gold 14'700; red gold, white gold 14'800. Ref. 38/3168, bezel with brilliants and sapphire cab.: yellow gold 30'560; white gold 30'660. "Rapsody" Ref. 38/3180, dial studded with brilliants and sapphire at markers, bezel sapphire and brilliants, sapphire cab. sapphire and brilliants on central attachment: yellow gold 42'950; white gold 43'100.

IMPERIALE AUTOMATIC — REF. 37/8203

Movement: mechanical, automatic winding, ETA 2892/A2.
Functions: hour, minute, center second, date.
Case: stainless steel, four-piece case (Ø 37 mm, thickness 9.3 mm); flat sapphire crystal; brand and progressive number engraved on the left case side; iolite cabochon octagonal crown and lugs; case back attached by 8 screws. Water-resistant to 3 atm.
Dial: white; printed Roman numerals; applied faceted round markers on the railway minute track; blued stainless steel lozenge hands.
Indications: date at 3.
Strap: crocodile leather; central attachment; stainless steel clasp.
Price: 4'660 CHF.
Also available: with cabochon steel 3'870 CHF; in yellow gold: with iolite cabochon 10'760 CHF, with sapphire cabochon 14'800 CHF. Each version is available with white, blue, coppered or mother-of-pearl dial.

The History

It was in 1860, at Sonvilier in the Swiss Jura, that Louis-Ulysse Chopard founded his own watchmaking shop. He can't help but succeed: he comes from a family traditionally in this field from whom he has learned all the secrets of the trade, and he is anxious to put his many ideas into motion. He quickly built an excellent reputation particularly for his handcrafted production of pocket chronometers, so much so that he became one of the suppliers for that epitome of punctuality, the Swiss railroad.

1920's - Considering the success of his watches, Chopard takes the leap and transfers the shop to Geneva, which had already become the watchmaking capital of the world. Here, he began to produce increasingly precious watches, achieving extraordinary heights in this field. But quality and productivity don't always proceed together and during the course of the years the number of watches produced dropped (as did the number of workers).

1963 - Paul-André Chopard, the founder's grandson, decides to sell.

After a century of family management, the Chopard plant is purchased by Karl Scheufele, the third of that dynasty, who is running Eszeha, a German jewellery firm founded in 1904 at Pforzheim by his grandfather, and known throughout the world.

The new owner has an ambitious plan for those times: he would develop the company with the aid of new marketing methods while respecting the tradition of Chopard quality.

1975 - A new production plant is built in Meyrin-Genève and years of great prestige begin for Chopard. First to be set up is the Chopard distribution in France, and then, in New York, the Chopard Watch Company Corporation.

1976 - The designer, Romuald Kurowsky, draws sports models which are the first to use steel and diamonds together. The concept is epitomized by the famous "Happy Diamonds" with its gold set diamonds happily moving freely beneath the sapphire crystal.

1986 - The Gstaad collection is presented successfully, inspired by the elegance of the Swiss resort.

1990 - Introduction of a chronograph dedicated to the "Mille Miglia". The re-edition of this historic match has been sponsored each year by the House.

1991 - The younger generation, Caroline and Karl-Friedrich, Karl and Karolin Scheufele's sons, becomes more visible in the Company. Caroline designs the "Casmir" series, whose bracelets recall the designs of the far off land.

1993 - Karl-Friedrich decides to return to the heights of the former production. Research begins for a fine quality movement.

1995 - At Fleurier, in the Val de Travers in the Neuchâtel Jura, a plant is established which will produce and prepare the new calibre Chopard.

1997 - The movement conceived in 1993 will receive in '97 its official presentation in Basel. A traditional, round watch which carries the new Calibre L.U.C. automatic (the initials belong to the founder of the Company), will receive the Geneva quality mark for the precision creation of each component.

1998 - An intense image-building year. With the L.U.C. movement (the third 4.96 version with sweep seconds), Chopard becomes the first watchmaking industry to have been certified as excellent by the "ISO 9001" and by the "Swiss Association for Quality and Management Systems". During the Cannes cinema festival the Chopard boutique on the Croisette is inaugurated: the event-watch is Happy Star Watch in blue plastic and a diamond star with the Golden Palm engraved on the case back. The sponsors were Ornella Muti, Eva Herzigova and Carla Bruni. Among the sports events were the King Constantine Cup Polo Match, the New York City Marathon, the 1998 edition of the "Mille Miglia". For this event the commemorative watch is an automatic chronograph in steel (1000 pieces) or in yellow gold (100 pieces) with a very particular rubber watch band reproducing the famous Dunlop racing treads.

CALIBER L.U.C 1.96

Movement, automatic winding, with autonomy 65/70 hours and microrotor in 22 kt gold, bidirectional winding, off-center, included in the thickness of the movement and mounted on ball-bearings.
Functions: hours, minutes, small seconds; date.
Shape: round.
Diameter: mm 27.40.
Thickness: mm 3.30.
Jewels: 32.
Balance: in Glucydur, three spokes.
Frequency: 28,800 vibration per hour (vph).
Spiral: Breguet, Nivarox 1, with micrometer adjustment and swan-neck-shaped check spring.
Shock-absorber system: Incabloc.
Note: the pillar-plate is decorated with circular micrograining, all bridges decorated Côtes de Genève and beveled. The gold rotor is engraved and beveled. The movement is provided with two superimposed barrels series-connected so as to allow a greater power reserve and to mount additional complication modules. The quality of finish, the good functioning of different components and the compliance with specific standards permitted caliber L.U.C 1.96 to receive the "Poinçon de Genève".

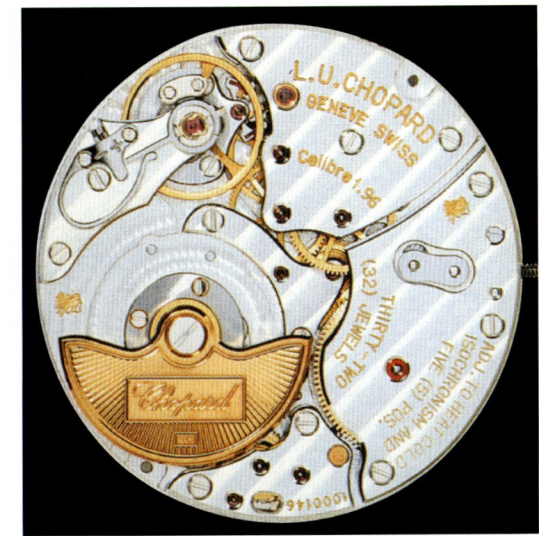

CALIBER L.U.C 3.96

The caliber 3.96 derives, for almost all of its components, from the very refined 1.96. It was upgraded by eliminating only some less important working processes, as for example the shot-peening finish replacing the circular graining finish of the pillar-plate, the bimetal microrotor (heavy metal coupled with a sight plate in 18 kt gold), the balance using a flat spiral instead of a Breguet type and the precise adjustment device (Triovis). The project aiming at providing the Chopard with a completely "home-made" movement, was commenced in Autumn 1993 at Fleurier, one of the cradles of Swiss watchmaking. The best local specialists were engaged, and only in 1995 the first prototype appeared, with a diameter of 26 mm (11''') and 21,600 vibrations per hour. The final decision, in line with the most recent tendencies, to adopt a frequency of 28,800 vibrations per hour (vph), suggested a revision of the initial project and to chose new sizes (Ø 27.40 - 12''') as well as to further improve the performance of the winding system through a general lowering of friction values. At the end of 1995 the L.U.C (a name chosen to pay a homage to the founder of the factory, 1860, Louis-Ulysse Chopard) was ready in its final arrangement and for series production at the workshop of Fleurier, equipped with the most sophisticated tools for planning and production under numerical control.
Derived calibers: L.U.C 4.96 (center second, 34 jewels, "Poinçon de Genève").

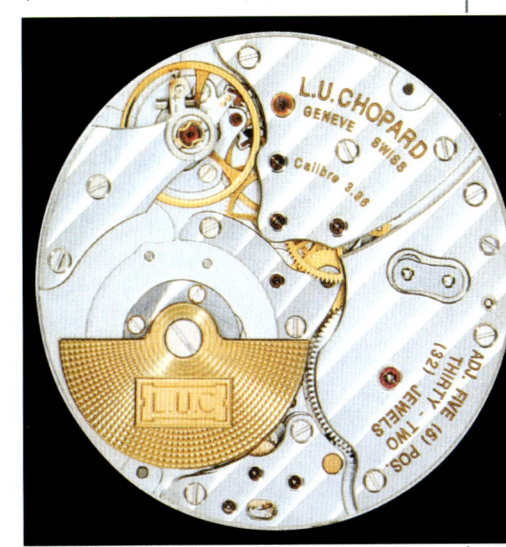

Concord

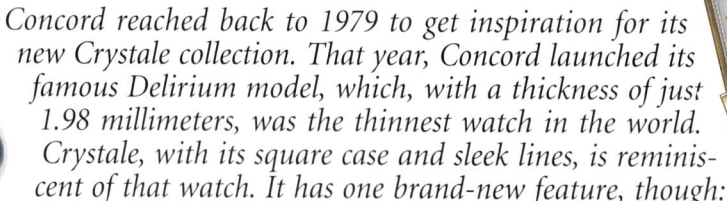

Concord reached back to 1979 to get inspiration for its new Crystale collection. That year, Concord launched its famous Delirium model, which, with a thickness of just 1.98 millimeters, was the thinnest watch in the world. Crystale, with its square case and sleek lines, is reminiscent of that watch. It has one brand-new feature, though: a crystal that wraps around the edges of the dial. It also has a two-tiered bezel on the north and south sides of the case. The second, outer tier bends to fit the shape of the wrist. The watch has a quartz movement and comes in men's and women's versions. It's made of yellow or white gold and is available with or without diamonds, on a black strap or gold bracelet.

The company has also expanded its La Scala collection with several new pieces. There are now round La Scala watches in three sizes--until now La Scala has only had square cases--with grey or mother-of-pearl dials. A new quartz chronograph La Scala model has a calendar window at 4 o'clock.

There's yet another new model in the collection, this one a haute joaillerie watch called La Scala Grande. It's set with nearly 24 carats of diamonds on its dial, bezel and bracelet.

Another new women's diamond watch from Concord: the Sportivo Chronograph. It has a quartz movement, mother-of-pearl dial and steel case. The strap comes in fuchsia, blue or black alligator. The diamonds run along the east and west sides of the rectangular bezel.

Lest anyone think the company makes only high-fashion quartz watches, note the two one-of-a-kind masterpieces of haute

The History

The Concord Watch Co., founded in Bienne in 1908, from the very beginnings shows a vocation towards exportation, in particular to the United States. It is perhaps indeed predestination, as during the following year the New York subsidiary is opened. Concord models conquer the American public in such a way that in 1968 they rank at the sixth place among the most imported watch brands. But Concord's entry into American history dates from 1945 when at the Peace Conference of Potsdam president Harry S. Truman chose two watches of the House of Bienne to make gifts to his "colleagues" Churchill and Stalin. In 1969, Gedalio Grinberg of the North American Watch Corporation acquires the brand that becomes his visiting card.

1979 - This is the year of Delirium, the legendary world's thinnest watch, realized by Eta technicians. It is presented for the first time in New York where this analogue quartz watch arouses a real "delirium" by its records: 1.98 mm thickness and movement integrated with the case. The challenge goes on the following year with Delirium II, whose thickness does not exceed 1.5 mm, and later with lady's Delirium III, whose overall dimension is reduced by 65%, and finally with Delirium IV having a thickness of only 0.98 mm.

1986 - Saratoga collection is the new pillar of Concord's production; it is made up of sporting, elegant or very precious models.

1991 - During the Nineties the leading brand in America triumphs at the Basel Show with its sparkling models, such as Sirius for men, with a platinum case and 295 brilliants totalling over 64 kt.

1992 - The occasion of the 5th centennial of the discovery of America gives life to Mariner V Centennial: five great complications sold to one customer for 3.2 million Swiss Franc. For the "normal" public the Mariner collection adopts quartz movements.

1995 - Saratoga Exor Double-face is a unique piece in platinum with brilliants, using a skeletonized manual movement, perpetual calendar with moon phases, minute repeater, tourbillon, thermometer for inside temperature measuring. Its price is unique too: two million Swiss Franc.

1997 - Four unique pieces, Saratoga Splendours Adamas, Esmeraude, Sapphirus and Rubeus combine the brightness of precious stones with complicated movements at the top level of watchmaking, all provided with minute repeaters, simple or combined with a perpetual calendar feature, power reserve indication and moon phases. More "approachable" are the automatic Saratoga SL (Sport Luxury) and the collections La Scala and Veneto. A Delirium, produced in only 90 pieces and reserved for the Italian market, is dedicated to Concord's 90th anniversary.

1998 - For the occasion of Concord's 90th birthday (1908-1998) the Impresario Répétition Minutes were much admired: six jewel-watches for gentlemen and ladies, in pink gold, platinum and platinum with brilliants, which will help another mysterious lover spending time. The men's version houses a movement developed by Concord's master watchmakers in cooperation with a small independent manufacture, while the movement adopted for Dame is the smallest repeater movement with chime ever produced. For the traditional market, the Impresario collection has the following models: a Chronograph with automatic El Primero movement, an automatic Small Seconds, a manual Power Reserve, an automatic GMT, all coming with a chronometer certificate, while the quartz models combine steel with brilliants. For ladies there are three magnificent versions of La Scala Diva, a luck collection dedicated to the Italian Opera House.

Crystale's magic

Twenty years after the launch of Delirium, the thinnest watch in the world, Concord once again presents a new revolutionary model that will mark a new epoch: Crystale. As a result of the best contemporary watch design, it adopts for the first time a sapphire crystal case treated in an absolutely innovatory way: in fact, it is not applied inside the bezel, as usually, but becomes itself a lateral case part, thus offering a new prospect of the dial (with a different and involving effect with respect to that offered by the polished glass models of the Fifties and Sixties).

The result obtained is of a great fascinating impact and beauty, with the dial which seems to come out of the case and hands and bridges brightened up by an unexpected luminosity.

On this page you can watch an absolutely special version, provided with a platinum case and an extra-thin mechanical hand-winding movement caliber 8.10 by Frédéric Piguet.

This is wholly skeletonized and hand-engraved with a flower pattern and remains totally at sight because of the complete absence of the dial, with time indicated by two Alpha type hands in blued steel.

The final result, emphasized by the bull's eye in sapphire crystal on the case back, exerts a great visual impact and repays with an elating glance a model which is successful and attractive by itself, thanks to a "delicate" and absolutely refined craftwork - the choice of the highest mechanical tradition is a best point more.

horlogerie the company has added to its Impresario collection. One is a chronograph with minute repeater and tourbillon, composed of 441 parts (it has 38 jewels.) The other is even more complicated: a chronograph with minute repeater, tourbillon and perpetual calendar. It has 525 parts. Both watches have transparent sapphire case backs.

CONCORD

MINUTE REPEATER CARILLON DAME

Movement: mechanical, hand winding with 45 hours autonomy.
Functions: hours and minutes; hour, quarter and minute repeater with chime.
Shape: round.
Diameter: mm 24.25.
Thickness: mm 5.00.
Jewels: 33.
Balance: with adjusting screws in gold, with two arms.
Frequency: 18,000 vibrations per hour.
Spiral: flat, first quality.
Shockabsorber system: Kif.
Note: the pillar-plate is decorated with circular graining pattern, the bridges with Côtes de Genève and beveled. The spiral adjustment system, the repeater hammers and the screw heads are specular-polished and beveled. A third hammer (not visible in the photograph because it is concealed under the other two), which strikes a third timbre, makes this very small-sized movement be the smallest wrist "Chime" that was ever produced. On the dial side (see photograph) between 5 and 8 there are the different components (with respect to the corresponding caliber used also by other Houses) realized on an exclusive basis for Concord to activate the chime function.

A MUSICAL CASKET

To celebrate its 90th anniversary, Concord (founded in Bienne in 1908) put together, in an extraordinary casket, three couples of unique pieces, all animated by refined movements with minute repeater and "dressed" with the Impresario case, presented last year in Basel. The six men's and lady's models have cases in pink gold, platinum and platinum with brilliants. The men's model (Ø 35 mm) is animated by a movement with hand winding, developed in cooperation with a specialized atelier. The following elements are worthwhile noting: the regulator adjustment system by micrometer screw and swan-neck shaped check spring, the endstone of the escapement wheel in a steel collet held in place by a screw and the gullet teeth of the ratchet wheel to improve the rolling and silencing. The lady version possibly mounts an even more sophisticated movement that the man version. In fact, the chime is housed in a very small sized space (here we see the dial face). As a result, the sound of the minute repeater is transformed into a little wrist concert. The lady version with a Ø 27 mm platinum case with diamonds on bezel and dial (bottom), houses a two-stage slide which, on that side of the case middle, interrupts the appearing knurling typical of the Impresario case.

IMPRESARIO MINUTE REPEATER   REF. 52-G4-0215-2204-31/977

Movement: mechanical, hand winding, developed by Concord in cooperation with a specialized atelier; regulator adjustment system by micrometer screw, endstone on the escapement wheel. Decorated with Côtes de Genève pattern and beveled.
Functions: hours, minutes, minute repeater.
Case: 18 kt pink gold, two-piece (Ø 35 mm, thickness 10.5 mm); smooth sapphire crystal; spider-shaped lugs; grooved case middle; pink gold crown; snap-on back with a sapphire crystal bull's eye. Water-resistant to 3 atm.
Dial: silvered with graining pattern, with the different levels profiled with a thin engine-turned (guilloché) thread, applied pink-gold-plated Roman numerals at the quarters; screen-printed dial-train; pink-gold-plated Alpha hands.
Strap: crocodile leather; pink gold clasp.
Price: on request. Unique piece.
Also available: in lady's size, unique piece Ref. 52-G5-02160-2205-31/977, (prices on request).

IMPRESARIO MINUTE REPEATER LADY   REF. 81-G5-0260-2205-31/999S

Movement: mechanical, hand winding, developed by Concord in cooperation with a specialized atelier; chime sonnerie with three hammers, endstone on the escapement wheel. Decorated with Côtes de Genève pattern and beveled.
Functions: hours, minutes, minute repeater, chime.
Case: platinum, two-piece (Ø 27.3 mm, thickness 10 mm); smooth sapphire crystal; spider-shaped lugs; bezel with baguette cut diamonds with invisible embedding (24 stones, 1.59 kt); grooved case middle; platinum crown with an embedded rosette cut diamond; snap-on back with a sapphire crystal bull's eye. Water-resistant to 3 atm.
Dial: white gold; diamonds with flush and invisible embedding in the central disc; trapezoidal cut diamond markers, with invisible embedding; screen-printed dial-train; blued steel leaf style hands.
Strap: crocodile leather; platinum clasp set with baguette diamonds.
Price: on request. Unique piece.

CONCORD

IMPRESARIO MAESTRO MASTERPIECE   REF. 80-J6-0212-0000-1/0019

Movement: mechanical, manual winding, Concord caliber J6, developed by the House in cooperation with a specialized factory; with tourbillon and steel carriage. Beveled three-block mirror finish and Côtes de Genève finished.
Functions: hour, minute, perpetual calendar (day, date, month), chronograph with 2 counters, minute repeater.
Case: platinum (platinum weight 86 gr.), two-piece (Ø 38 mm, thickness 14 mm); spider-shaped lugs; 2 correctors on the grooved case side; white gold repeater slide on case side; white gold crown and pushers; flat sapphire crystal; snap-on back displaying the movement through a sapphire crystal.
Dial: silvered, engine turned (guilloché), aperture on the tourbillon; applied bâton markers; printed minute track; Alpha hands.
Indications: minute counter and day at 3, month at 9, date at 12, second central counter, minute track with divisions for $1/5$ of a second.
Strap: crocodile leather; platinum clasp.
Price: 495'000 CHF. Single piece. 10 year guarantee.

IMPRESARIO MAESTRO MASTERPIECE   REF. 80-J6-0212-0000-1/0019

Once again Concord choose the stage of the Basel Show to present their last masterpieces of mechanic engineering. The two great complications are realized as single pieces and presented in the Impresario Maestro Masterpiece collection. The common features are the tourbillon (with hand-finished and hand-polishes steel carriage), the chronograph with 2 counters and the minute repeater. The platinum model has also the perpetual calendar feature, while the pink gold model has the power reserve. Their realization took one year and a half, due to both the intrinsic mechanic complexity (the first is made up by 525 parts and 38 jewels for a total of 9.25 mm height, and the second by 441 parts and 38 jewels for 7.65 mm), and the high general level of finish of all the components of the movement and case, even of the hidden ones. The Impresario Maestro Masterpieces are presented in a valuable case with an authenticity certificate and a 10 year guarantee.

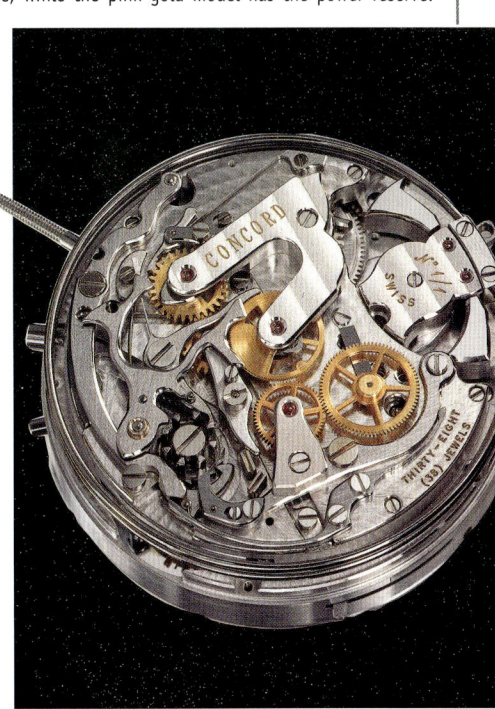

IMPRESARIO MAESTRO MASTERPIECE   REF. 52-J7-0212-0000-1/0020

Movement: mechanical, manual winding, Concord caliber J7, developed by the House in cooperation with a specialized factory; with tourbillon and steel carriage. Beveled three-block mirror finish and Côtes de Genève finished.
Functions: hour, minute, small second, chronograph with 2 counters, power reserve, minute repeater.
Case: 18 kt pink gold (gold weight 55 gr.), two-piece (Ø 38 mm, thickness 12 mm); spider-shaped lugs; grooved case side; pink gold crown and pushers; flat sapphire crystal; pink gold repeater slide on case side; snap-on back, displaying the movement through a sapphire crystal.
Dial: silvered engine turned (guilloché), aperture on the tourbillon; applied bâton markers; printed minute track; Alpha hands.
Indications: minute counter at 3, small second at 9, power reserve at 12, center second counter, minute track with divisions for $1/5$ of a second.
Strap: crocodile leather; pink gold clasp.
Price: 445'000 CHF. Single piece. 10 year guarantee.

IMPRESARIO MAESTRO MASTERPIECE

The "minor" model (though it is a relatively minor watch, because its price exceeds 250,000$) of the new complicated ones recently presented by Concord, belongs to the Maestro Masterpiece collection. Made of 18 kt pink gold, it combines a minute repeater and a two-counter chronograph with the indication of the power reserve. For its realization - and the same is true for the model provided with a perpetual calendar - technicians and watchmakers have been working for over one year and a half, due to its intrinsic mechanical complexity (its movement, a caliber J7 Concord, is made up by 441 parts) as well as to the general high level of its finish which involves all the components of movement and case, obviously including those which cannot be seen. The Impresario Maestro Masterpiece models are supplied in a prestigious case and are accompanied by a certificate of authenticity and 10-years guarantee.

113

CONCORD

IMPRESARIO CHRONOGRAPH   REF. 14-G9-0211-2202-1/231BA

Movement: mechanical, automatic winding, Zenith El Primero caliber 41.1. Côtes Circulaires finished rotor, circular graining finished bridges. Officially certified "chronometer" (C.O.S.C.).
Functions: hour, minute, small second, chronograph with 3 counters, full calendar (date, day, month).
Case: stainless steel, two-piece case (Ø 38 mm, thickness 12.2 mm); spider-shaped lugs; flat sapphire crystal; grooved case side; 1 corrector on case side; elliptic pushers; snap-on back displaying the movement through a sapphire crystal. Water-resistant to 3 atm. 
Dial: silvered, engine turned (guilloché); applied pointed markers (Arabic numeral 12); printed minute track; Alpha hands.
Indications: small second at 9, minute counter at 3, hour counter at 6, month at 2, date between 4 and 5, day at 10, center second counter, minute track with divisions for 1/5 of a second.
Strap: crocodile leather; stainless steel clasp.
Price: 5'400 CHF.
Also available: with bracelet 5'900 CHF; black dial; pink gold silvered dial, leather strap 9'900 CHF, with bracelet 19'900 CHF; brown or blue crocodile leather strap.

IMPRESARIO CHRONOGRAPH

In this model, as in many others of the Impresario collection, Concord adopted the Zenith movements, subsequently refined and decorated according to their high-level specifications. In this case we are in front of a Zenith El Primero caliber, in the version with complete calendar. It is worthwhile noting the personalization of decorations (Côtes Circulaires on the rotor and circular graining on bridges) and the eccentric screw system for the precise regulation of the regulator; the screw is flame-blued and its head is hand-polished. Zenith El Primero, up to now the only chronograph with a balance working frequency of 36,000 vibrations per hour (vph), underwent also the C.O.S.C. tests and obtained the chronometer certification.

IMPRESARIO CHRONOGRAPH   REF. 14-G9-0210-R45-4/231

The Impresario collection offers, for each model proposed, numerous versions: steel or pink gold construction, silvered or black dial, option between leather strap or bracelet of the same metal as the case material. In this case we see the Chronograph provided with steel case and bracelet and black dial. The central couple of links shows the same groove as the case side, which is one among the outstanding aesthetic features of the whole collection. The black dial has the same engine turned (guilloché) engravings as in the silvered version, with a horizontal ligné pattern at the center and with very thin hatchings to subdivide the different dial zones.
Price: 5'900 CHF.

IMPRESARIO POWER RESERVE   REF. 14-G8-0220-2204-4/261BA

Movement: mechanical, manual winding, Zenith Élite "HW". Officially certified "chronometer" (C.O.S.C.).
Functions: hour, minute, small second, date, power reserve.
Case: stainless steel, two-piece case (Ø 35 mm, thickness 8 mm); spider-shaped lugs; flat sapphire crystal; grooved case side; snap-on back displaying the movement through a sapphire crystal. Water-resistant to 3 atm. 
Dial: black, engine turned (guilloché); applied pointed markers (Arabic numerals 6 and 12); printed minute track; Dauphine hands.
Indications: date between 4 and 5, power reserve at 2, small second at 9.
Strap: crocodile leather; stainless steel clasp.
Price: 4'500 CHF.
Also available: silvered dial; pink gold, silvered dial 7'500 CHF; brown or blue crocodile leather strap.

CONCORD

IMPRESARIO GMT — REF. 14-G6-0220-2204-1/251

Movement: mechanical, automatic winding, Zenith Élite caliber 682. Côtes Circulaires finished rotor, circular graining finished bridges. Officially certified "chronometer" (C.O.S.C.).
Functions: hour, minute, small second, date, second time zone, 24-hour indication.
Case: stainless steel, two-piece case (Ø 35 mm, thickness 8 mm); spider-shaped lugs; flat sapphire crystal; grooved case side; 1 corrector on case side; crown for the adjustment of the second time zone; snap-on back displaying the movement through a sapphire crystal. Water-resistant to 3 atm.
Dial: silvered, engine turned (guilloché); applied pointed markers (Arabic numerals 6 and 12); printed minute track; Dauphine hands.
Indications: date at 3, red painted second-time-zone central hand, small second at 9.
Strap: crocodile leather; stainless steel clasp.
Price: 3'900 CHF.
Also available: black dial; pink gold, silvered dial, 3'900 CHF; brown, blue or bordeaux crocodile leather strap.

IMPRESARIO GMT — REF. 52-G6-0220-2204-1/252RE

Thanks to the Zenith movement, but also to the setting-up by Concord, the Impresario GMT is one among the few models in this watch class which styles itself with the Certificate of Chronometer issued by the C.O.S.C. In this version, Impresario GMT is characterized by a pink gold case, a silvered dial and a leather strap. The red-tipped center hand can be adjusted independently of the normal Dauphine hands, thus allowing to indicate the time of a different time zone. Its adjustment by means of a corrector on the case side is made by half-hour steps in a way as to allow to set also the times of the countries (mainly India, Iran, Afghanistan and Central Australia) whose time zone is offset by half an hour.
Price: 6'900 CHF.

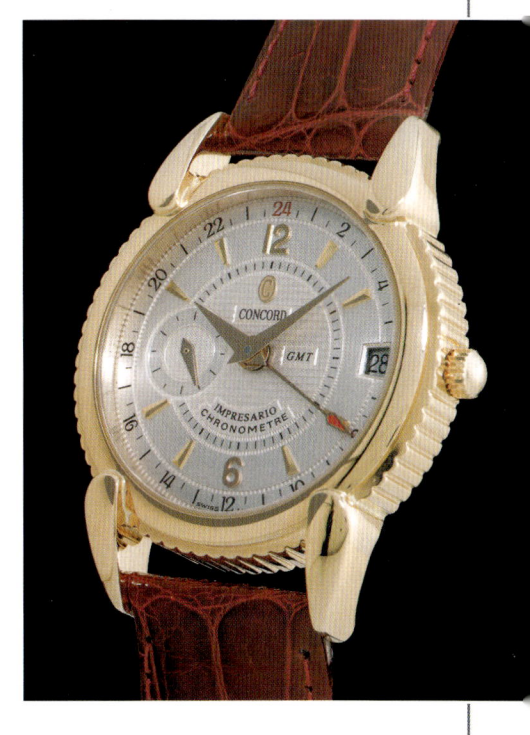

IMPRESARIO

Movement: mechanical, automatic winding, Frédéric Piguet caliber 1150. Pink gold Côtes de Genève finished rotor, beveled Côtes de Genève finished bridges. Officially certified "chronometer" (C.O.S.C.).
Functions: hour, minute, center second, date.
Case: 18 kt pink gold, two-piece case (Ø 35 mm, thickness 7.5 mm); lance-shaped lugs; flat sapphire crystal; grooved case side; snap-on back displaying the movement through a sapphire crystal. Water-resistant to 3 atm.
Dial: silvered, matte finish; applied pointed markers (Arabic numerals 6 and 12); dial-train with applied gilded cabochon; Alpha hands.
Indications: date at 3.
Strap: crocodile leather; pink gold clasp.
Limited edition presented in 1996.

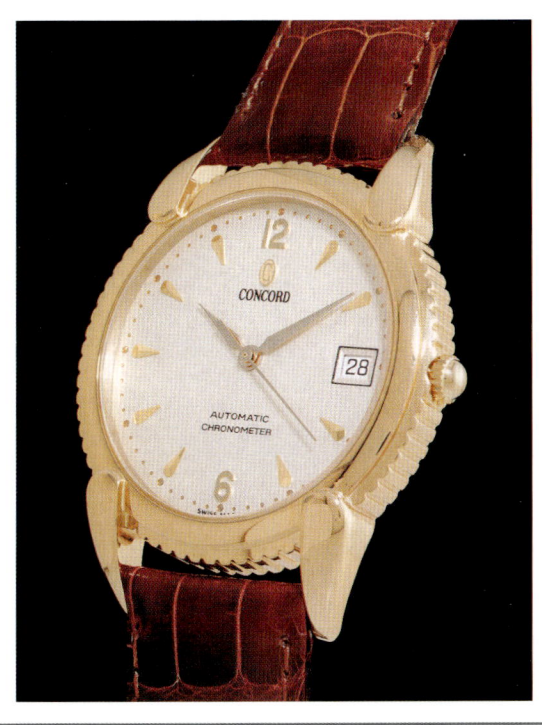

IMPRESARIO SMALL SECOND — REF. 52-G7-0220-2203-1/242RE

Movement: mechanical, automatic winding, Zenith Élite caliber 680. Côtes Circulaires finished rotor, circular graining finished bridges. Officially certified "chronometer" (C.O.S.C.).
Functions: hour, minute, small second, date.
Case: 18 kt pink gold, two-piece case (Ø 35 mm, thickness 7 mm); spider-shaped lugs; flat sapphire crystal; grooved case side; snap-on back displaying the movement through a sapphire crystal. Water-resistant to 3 atm.
Dial: silvered engine turned (guilloché); applied pointed markers (Arabic numerals 6 and 12); printed minute track; Alpha hands.
Indications: date between 4 and 5; small second at 9.
Strap: crocodile leather; pink gold clasp.
Price: 6'500 CHF.
Also available: black crocodile leather strap.

CONCORD

SARATOGA GENTS PERPETUAL CALENDAR — REF. 50-B3-0237-A12-3/430

Movement: mechanical, automatic winding, ETA caliber 2890/A9, 11'''1/2.
Functions: hour, minute, perpetual calendar (date, day, month, year, moon phase).
Case: 18 kt yellow gold, three-piece case, polished and brushed finish (Ø at the widest level 36 mm, thickness 9 mm); flat sapphire crystal; octagonal bezel with riders; 3 correctors on case side; screw-down crown; case back attached by 4 screws with embossed medallion. Water-resistant to 3 atm. 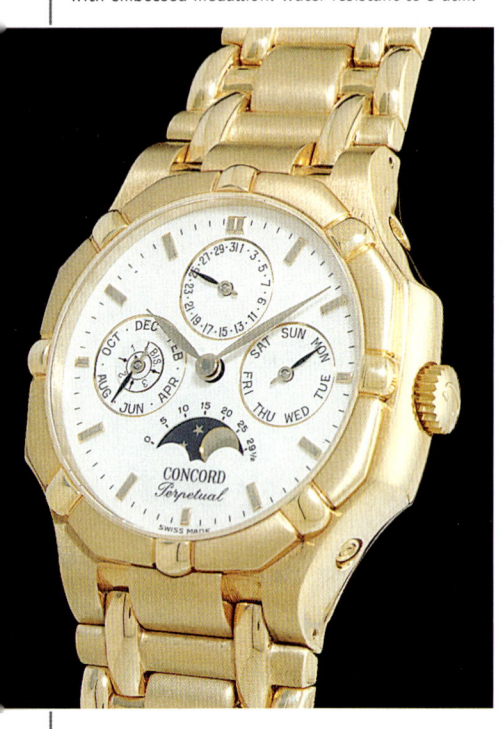
Dial: white; applied bâton markers; printed minute track; leaf style hands.
Indications: day at 3, moon phase at 6, month and four year cycle at 9, date at 12.
Bracelet: gold, with polished and brushed finished links; recessed double gold fold-over clasp.
Price: 30'350 CHF.

SARATOGA PERPETUAL CALENDAR "BOUTIQUE"

Concord, since the beginnings, made itself familiar with jeweller's craft. In fact, one must not forget that in 1915 they produced, for the account of clients such as Tiffany and Cartier, mostly very sophisticated watches, in platinum and studded with diamonds, emeralds, rubies and sapphires. It is the beauty of these stones that inspired the creation of four Perpetual Calendars of the Saratoga collection called "Boutique". The photograph shows the version with brilliants and emeralds set on the bezel, but there are also three models with rubies, sapphires or only diamonds, always set on the bezel riders and alternating with brilliants. These "colored" versions have also cabochons on the crown and leather straps of the same color tone as the stones chosen. All the dials of these jewel-watches are in mother-of-pearl (sky-blue for the version with sapphires) with silvered center zone decorated with refined engine turned (guilloché) pattern. 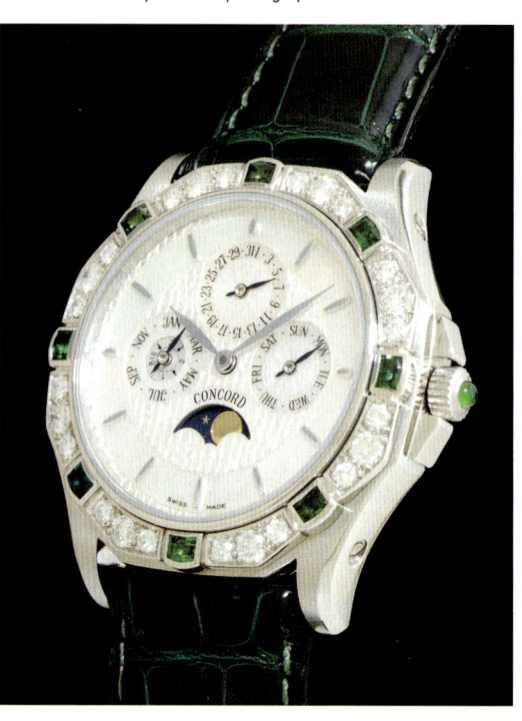
Also available: with rubies, sapphires or only diamonds.
Prices: on request.

SARATOGA GENTS POWER RESERVE — REF. 50-D3-0234-10/316

Movement: mechanical, automatic winding, Jaquet caliber 1/2897, 11'''.
Functions: hour, minute, center second, date, day, second time zone, 24-hour indication, power reserve.
Case: 18 kt yellow gold, three-piece case, polished and brushed finish; flat sapphire crystal; octagonal bezel with 8 riders; 2 correctors on case side; screw-down crown with case protection; case back attached by 4 screws. Water-resistant to 3 atm. 
Dial: blue; applied bâton markers; printed minute track; leaf style hands.
Indications: date at 3, power reserve at 6, day at 9, second time zone 24-hour display at 12.
Strap: crocodile leather; gold jewel-clasp.
Price: 11'200 CHF.
Also available: with gilt, white, black or silvered dial, Roman numerals; with bracelet, silvered dial with Roman numerals 19'950, white, blue or black dial, markers 19'700; steel and yellow gold, leather strap white, blue or black dial, markers, 3'450; bracelet, silvered dial, Roman numerals 5'600; blue, white or black dial, markers 5'500; stainless steel, leather strap, silvered dial, Roman numerals 3'600; blue, white or black dial, markers 3'200; bracelet, silvered dial, Roman numerals 4'050; blue, white or black dial, markers 3'950.

SARATOGA DIVER — REF. 14-A9-0238-V191-4/449BA

Movement: mechanical, automatic winding.
Functions: hour, minute, center second, date.
Case: stainless steel, three-piece case, polished and brushed finish (greatest Ø 39 mm, thickness 9.7 mm); flat sapphire crystal; counter-clockwise turning bezel, grooved, with blue metallized ring, tritium marker and graduated scale, useful for the calculation of diving times; screw-down crown with case protection; case back attached by 6 screws with embossed medallion. Water-resistant to 20 atm. 
Dial: bright blue; luminescent applied round and bâton markers; printed minute track; luminescent leaf style hands.
Indications: date at 3.
Bracelet: stainless steel, with polished and brush finished links; recessed double fold-over gold clasp.
Price: 2'550 CHF.
Also available: stainless steel and yellow gold 4'500 SFr.; white, black or champagne dial.

CONCORD

SARATOGA SPORT LUXURY MEDIUM   REF. 14-D9-0250-V40-5/871

Movement: mechanical, automatic winding, with gold rotor. **Functions:** hour, minute, center second, date.
Case: steel, three-piece brushed and polished case (Ø 33 mm, thickness 7.8 mm); flat sapphire crystal; octagonal bezel with 8 riders; crown with case protection; screw-on case back attached by 4 screws, displaying the movement through a sapphire crystal. Water-resistant to 5 atm.
Dial: anthracite, guilloché at center, brushed hour ring; applied bâton markers and Arabic numerals; printed minute track; leaf style hands.
Indications: date at 3.
Bracelet: steel, polished and brushed links; recessed double fold-over steel clasp.
Price: 2'350 CHF.
Also available: with strap 1'750; with silvered or anthracite dial; in steel/yellow gold, silvered dial, strap 1'800; bracelet 3'800; yellow gold, silvered dial, strap 5'700; bracelet 13'800. In the big size: steel, strap, silvered or anthracite dial 1'800; bracelet, silvered, green or anthracite dial 2'400; in steel/yellow gold, strap, silvered or blue dial 1'850; bracelet, silvered, blue or anthracite dial 3'950; yellow gold, strap, silvered or blue dial 6'200; bracelet, silvered or green dial 14'800.

SARATOGA GENTS CHRONOMETER   REF. 50-D4-0235-A43-1/808

Movement: mechanical, automatic winding, Jaquet caliber 2892-2 B0, 11'''1/2. Officially certified "chronometer" (C.O.S.C.).
Functions: hour, minute, center second, date.
Case: 18 kt yellow gold, three-piece polished and brushed case (Ø 36.6 mm, thickness 7.7 mm); flat sapphire crystal; octagonal bezel with 8 riders; crown with case protection; case back attached by 4 screws. Water-resistant to 3 atm.
Dial: silvered, guilloché at center and brushed hour ring; applied Roman numerals; rhodium plated leaf style hands.
Indications: date at 3.
Bracelet: 18 kt yellow gold, with polished and brushed links; gold fold-over clasp.
Price: 2'350 CHF.
Also available: with blue, white or black dial, markers 16'500; with strap, silvered dial, Roman numerals or blue, gilt, white or black markers 8'500; in steel/yellow gold, strap, silvered dial, Roman numerals or blue, white or black markers 2'400; bracelet, silvered dial, Roman numerals or blue, white or black markers 4'450; steel, strap, silvered dial, Roman numerals or blue, white or black markers 2'150; bracelet, silvered dial, Roman numerals 3'000; blue dial, white or black markers 2'900.

RECTANGULAR   REF. 14-36-0622-2113-4/131BA

Movement: quartz, next with mechanical movement and automatic winding.
Functions: hour, minute, center second, date.
Case: steel, two-piece rectangular-curved case, polished and brushed (at lugs and without crown 37.8 mm, width 26.3 mm, thickness 7.2 mm); curved sapphire crystal; crown with case protection; case back attached by 4 screws. Water-resistant to 3 atmospheres.
Dial: black, guilloché at center and brushed hour ring; applied pointed markers (Arabic numerals 6 and 12); luminescent dots on the printed railway minute track; luminescent sword style hands.
Indications: date at 3.
Strap: leather, stainless steel fold-over clasp.
Price: 990 CHF.
Also available: strap in brown, bordeaux, green or blue leather; with bracelet 1'390 CHF.; with dial bordeaux, silvered, green, blue or salmon. in the same versions, In lady's size (same prices).

DELIRIUM LIMITED EDITION   REF. 50-55-0619-2047-3/640CBA

Movement: mechanical, manual winding, extra-plat, Frédéric Piguet caliber 21. Decorated a Côtes de Genève, beveled bridges.
Functions: hour, minute.
Case: 18 kt yellow gold, two-piece case (dim. with lugs and without crown 34,5 mm, width 24,5 mm, thickness 4 mm); flat sapphire crystal; case back attached by 10 screws displaying the movement through a sapphire crystal. Water-resistant to 2 atmospheres.
Dial: white, with le date commemorative (1908-1998); applied cabochon markers and Roman numerals; bâton hands.
Strap: crocodile leather; yellow gold clasp.
Price: 7'900 CHF.
Realized to celebrate the 90th anniversary of the House, edition limited to 98 pieces for the Italian market.

Daniel JeanRichard

First revered more than one hundred years ago as the founder of watchmaking in Neuchâtel, Daniel JeanRichard's name is once again drawing great acclaim. Though a statue of JeanRichard has long loomed in the proud watchmaking town of Le Locle, and his name has graced the streets of many towns in the region, JeanRichard is re-emerging internationally through a new line of timepieces that carries with the collection his spirit of fine technical wizardry, as well as his name. Within a year of launching its phoenix line, JeanRichard is offering exceptional mechanical and complicated watches boasting sleek design. In particular, the TV Screen split-seconds chronograph, with its expansive face and slightly curved bezel shape appears to crow the hour in a style that is undoubtedly the star of the collection. Such extraordinary design coupled with fine craftsmanship is typical to the watch group responsible for bringing JeanRichard back to life, the Sowind Group, which also includes Girard-Perregaux and GP Manufacture. Under the direction of Sowinds CEO, Luigi Macaluso, Jean Richard is rising to its esteemed position as a master watchmaker.

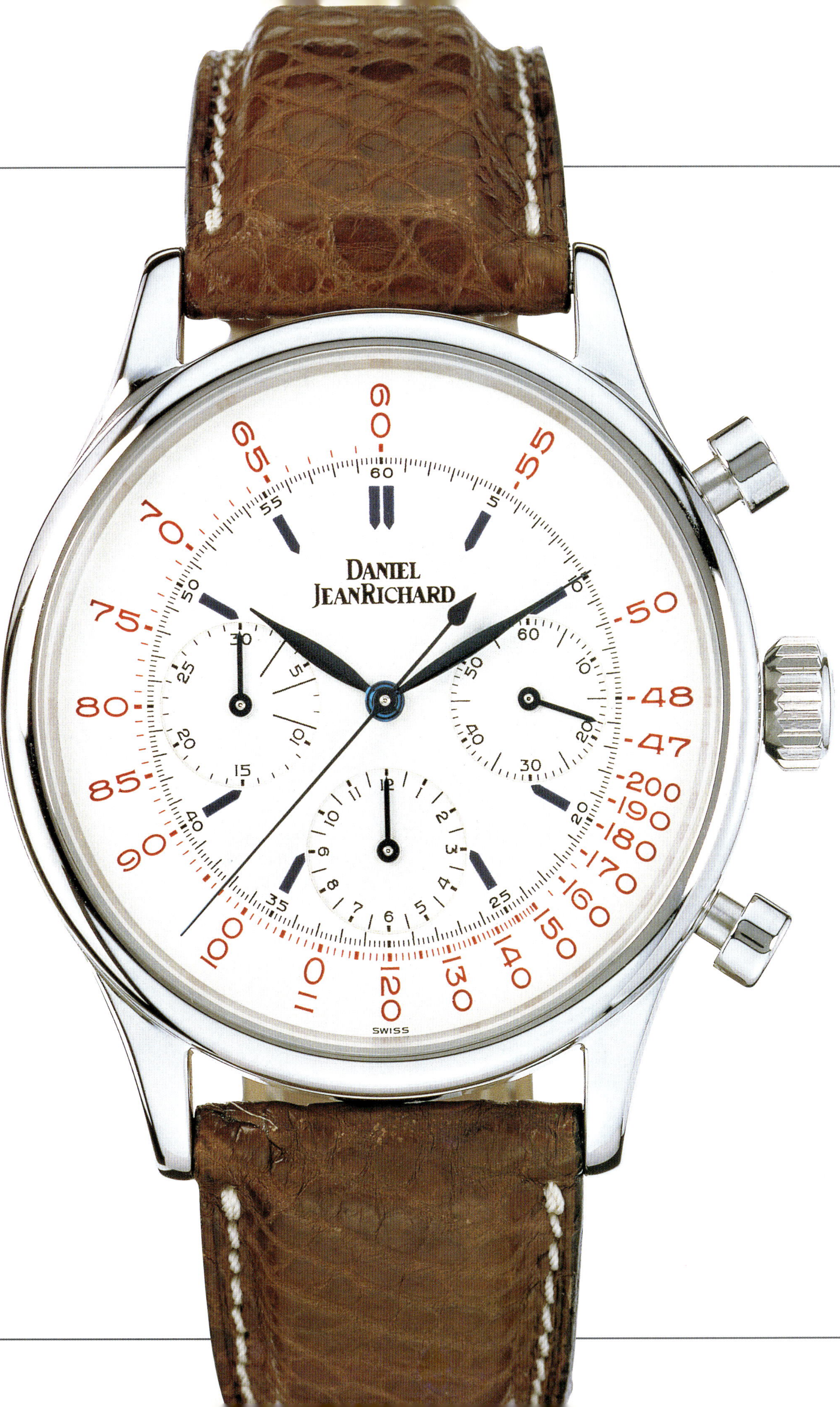
DANIEL
JEANRICHARD
SWISS

Daniel JeanRichard

Previous page
The Bressel Chronograph will catch the eye of all lovers of beautiful watches with its 51 ruby DJR 25 movement, with a frequency of 28,800v/h that is housed in a 316L steel case. It features a grained silver dial with vertical varnished blue hour markers and tone-on-tone counters. Produced in a limited numbered series of 500 pieces.

Below
The retro style Cambered Rectangle, one of Daniel JeanRichard's new 1999 models, features dials of a classic yet contemporary design, and it is finely engine-turned under a layer of translucent lacquer that gives i extra depth.

Facing page
Top
To meet market demand, Danie JeanRichard has manufactured a limited, numbered series of the classic TV Screen Chronograph in 25 yellow gold pieces and 25 pink gold pieces to mark the brand's first participation at the prestigious Salon International de la Haute Horlogerie in Geneva.

Center
The center piece of the DJR range, the TV Screen Split-seconds Chronograph has been produced in three limited series of 5 yellow gold, 5 pink gold and 50 steel pieces. This exceptional timepiece has a 44-hour power reserve and is water-resistant to 50 meters.

Possessing a celebrated history in watchmaking enables the seamless restoration to its solid foundations.

The son of a farmer, Daniel JeanRichard was highly skilled in working with machinery by the age of 18. As he began to seek out a means to express his love for mechanics, watchmaking caught his attention. At the time, only a few watchmakers existed in Geneva, and they were extremely guarded against the development of new competition. Yet by refusing to sell JeanRichard any of their wheels, the watchmakers merely fueled his passion. JeanRichard began crafting his own watch parts, ultimately inventing what is known as a divisor, which produced both pinions and wheels. The year spent laboring at the development of the divisor established firmly in Jean-Richard,s mind what would be required to run a thriving workshop. A remarkable insight, considering that when Daniel JeanRichard installed his first workshop in 1705 in the town of Le Locle, it was merely the dawn of modern watchmaking. Timepieces were crude mechanical items that were frustrating because of their inability to keep time, and during JeanRichards first

Daniel JeanRichard

decade of business, astounding leaps would be made in watchkeeping. For his part, JeanRichard's skills and passion for his craft were recognized by peers and citizens of the region, and more than a decade after his death, inspired the sculptor Iguel to create a statue in his likeness in 1888. It is a tangible testament to a man who is considered to have given birth to one of the key places for Swiss precision horology. This devotion to precision horology manifests itself in this new watch line, which first appeared in 1999. To celebrate its international launch, JeanRichard produced a special Gold TV Screen Chronograph in a limited series of 25 yellow gold and 25 pink gold pieces. At the same time, the company presented remarkable timekeeping pieces, such as the Bressel Chronograph and the Chronoscope. Evident at a glance that the wristwatches are highly specialized, the face of the Bressel Chronograph is unusual with blue hour markers

Daniel JeanRichard

reading the time and an outer perimeter of red numbered markings revealing its chronograph features.

The Chronoscope, the name is the correct term for chronograph, is similar in that the time is indicated at the center of the face, while the recording of the intervals of time are notched around the perimeter.

Considered a high-tech product, the Chronoscope features a rotating bi-directional bezel under the glass, activated by a second crown at 9 o,clock. Water-resistant to 100 meters, the watch is available with a choice of four different dials. As this collection of timepieces may indicate, JeanRichard is intimately involved in the racing industry, a reflection of its commitment to~and passion for~mechanics. Much like Girard-Perregaux, JeanRichard produces timepieces for major sports car manufacturers, such as Alfa Romeo and Lancia. The watchmaker also counts three races in which it is involved, and of course, in which it excels. First, JeanRichard,s co-driver Luis Moya received the best co-driver award in the World Rally Championship in 1999. For more than a year, Daniel JeanRichard has been a part of the Italian Two-wheel-drive Championship, with the cars of Stefano and Macaluso proudly bearing the JeanRichard name. And finally, the watchmaker is the official sponsor of the Swiss Historic Racing Team.

Watchmaking, perhaps more than any other craft, involves a profound respect for the past and an innate ability to grasp the skills that have

Left
A larger version of the flagship model, the Maxi TV Screen Chronograph houses a 51-ruby DJR movement. Water resistant to 50 meters and fitted with a sapphire crystal and rectangular pushpieces, this shaped 316L steel model perfectly reflects current watch fashions, while preserving all the characteristics that have made its predecessor so successful.

Below
The Maxi TV Screen Chronograph is a perfect illustration of the technological mastery achieved in Daniel JeanRichard's products.

Daniel JeanRichard

evolved for hundreds of years. With the revival of a leader in the industry from another century, Daniel JeanRichard is bound to return to its position of eminence, picking up where it left off, and once again paving the way for horological technology in the future.

Top
The Bressel line of 43mm watches has been a success since its launch in 1998, and it has been supplemented with this chronograph version.

Right
The Chronoscope, aptly named since this is the correct term for what is commonly called a chronograph, this high-tech timepiece has several distinct characteristics: a large dimension (43 mm), water-resistant to 100 meters, and a rotating bi-directional bezel under the glass activated by a second crown at 9 o'clock.

123

Daniel Roth

A close blend of traditional and modern exemplifies Daniel Roth's new collections. The new millennium meant presenting two new cases, the "Vantage". Maintaining the characteristic double semi-ellipse, which is the real symbol of the Company, the new forms have a gentler profile and a more compact line; the slight protrusion on the middle-case is gone, typical of the classic form, the "Master". This is more evident in the first type where the separation between the two parts is almost imperceptible, while in the second, even though the two pieces are joined, the separation is clearer.

Without turning their backs on the past, the watchmakers of Sentier tend toward the future with their new collections, keeping in mind the collectors who will find excellent watchmaking and refined styling in the Great Complications of the Master collection. Connoisseurs of exceptional watches will especially love the recent version of Papillon, a new model with jumping hours and a brand new system to visualize minutes.

Vantage aims at a younger market: definitely more dynamic, more current and more accessible - particularly for its prices. The double ellipse has been kept; dear as this form is to Roth, it has been reproportioned in tune with new tendencies: the case is slightly curved, the structure simplified and strengthened.

These model creations, naturally, nonetheless enjoy the masterly technique, the famous competence and the attention to detail that give Daniel Roth's collections exceptional prestige.

The History

Daniel Roth was lucky because of his passion, and its the word to use, for Abraham-Louis Breguet. The greatest master watchmaker of the past held no secrets for the young Roth. Swiss, but born in Nantua, France, Roth lived in Nice and there, at the age of 14, decided to become a watchmaker, like his grandfather. At the local technical school for this trade, one of the teachers convinced him that the most beautiful watches are made in the Vallée de Joux. An apprenticeship brings out his great talent, both at Jaeger-LeCoultre and at Audemars Piguet, while he continues to want to know more about the life and works of his idol, to bring his name back to the summit of the world of his vocation. Roth's approach to his work can be summed up in a kind of personal challenge: to make watches while strictly following the oldest craftsmen's traditions. He is upheld in this by the Chaumet brothers, fine Parisian jewellers who became owners of the Company during the 1970's, and allow Roth to follow his inclinations. Thus, Roth's able hands created the modern Breguets, which we have all learned to admire. But the dream ended when the Company was sold to Invest Corporation. Roth, however, was by that time able to face the market alone and he set up, at the end of the 1980's, his own workshop in the Vallée de Joux where, at Le Sentier, grand masterpieces of style and technique are produced. His first collection took two years of work; proud and wiley, he chose a single case form, a double semi-ellipse, and used it for every creation, from the Grand Complications to ladies' watches. He worked for a year and a half on the design of the metal bracelet, of which every element repeats the style of the case. His constant effort at improvement, to reach perfection are attitudes he shares with Breguet. Naturally, the first complication with which he celebrated the first anniversary of his workshop in 1990, was a Tourbillon. From then on each year Le Sentier sends off to every continent about 400 watches created by Daniel Roth and his craftsmen.

1990 - The Tourbillon, the first Complication to carry Daniel Roth's name. This was subsequently created in the Skeleton version as were many other models of future collections.
1991 - Chronograph, extra thin, manual winding with two counters.
1992 - For the Rétrograde, the entwining circle-arcs accentuate the beauty of the dial.
1993 - Roth creates his Perpetual Calendar.
1994 - The moment of the first sports models, three-sphere automatic and date function; its bracelet is made of elements which repeat the form of the case. The women's models draw great attention.
1995 - The Minute Repeaters are presented, some also with the perpetual calendar, as well as the Automatic Chronograph.
1996 - Alert to his public, Daniel Roth proposes the first colored dials and the first GMT.
1997 - He presents the Lunette Tournante chronograph on a electro-mechanic movement by Frédéric Piguet and a GMT rotating bezel.
1998 - The new Minute Repeater uses an extra-thin movement which allows a much finer case and the slide is moved upwards. The Quantième Perpétuel Instantané offers the special instant release function for its indications. The Jumping Papillon is completely new in the Roth catalogue, with two minute hands that appear one at a time.

DANIEL ROTH

MASTER MINUTE REPEATER PERPETUAL CALENDAR   REF. C189BB

Movement: mechanical, manual winding, caliber C189 (Lemania base + QP module), autonomy 47 hours, 32 jewels (height 29.5 mm, width 30.5x10.23). Balance with two arms in Glucydur, 18,000 vibrations per hour (vph), Breguet overcoil balance-spring. Hand-beveled, Côtes de Genève hand-finished, "soigné" finished; assembly, mounting and complete mechanism construction by Daniel Roth's watchmakers, totalling appr. 170 working hours.
Functions: hour, minute, perpetual calendar (date, day, month, year, moon phase); minute repeater.
Case: 18 kt pink gold, two-piece case, double ellipse (height 40 mm, width 37, thickness 13.6 mm); flat sapphire crystal; 3 correctors and repeater slide on case sides; pink gold crown; snap-on back. Dust and moisture protection.
Dial: silvered solid gold, ligné decorated by hand and silver appliques. Off-center hour and minute; printed Roman numerals and minute track; blued stainless steel hand-made pointed hands.
Indications: date and 4 year cycle at 6, center day and month, moon phases below 12.
Strap: crocodile leather; hand-made pink gold clasp.
Also available: yellow gold; white gold.
Prices: on request.

MASTER PERPETUAL CALENDAR   REF. C117BA

Movement: mechanical, automatic winding, caliber C117 (Lemania caliber 8810 base + QP module), with 2 barrels, autonomy 38 h, 26 jewels (height 27.50 mm, width 30.50, thickness 5.78 mm). Pink gold engine turned (guilloché) rotor. Balance with 3 arms, in Glucydur, 28,800 vph, flat balance-spring. Hand-beveled and hand-finished Côtes de Genève, "soigné" finish; assembled, mounted and constructed by D. Roth's watchmakers for a total of appr. 100 working hours.
Functions: hour, minute, perpetual calendar (date, day, month, year). **Case:** 18 kt yellow gold, two-piece case, double ellipse (height 38 mm, width 35, thickness 11 mm); flat sapphire crystal; 3 correctors on case side; yellow gold crown; snap-on case back, numbered, displaying the movement through a sapphire crystal. Dust and moisture protection. **Dial:** solid gold, black, ligné hand-decorated and with applied rings. **Indications:** off-center hour and minute (golden Roman numerals and minute track, yellow gold hand-made pointed hands); date and four year cycle at 6, center day and month. **Strap:** crocodile leather; hand-made yellow gold clasp. **Also available:** pink or red gold; white gold; platinum; silvered or white enameled, yellow, red, blue, green or black dial; day, month with hand. **Prices:** on request.

MASTER TOURBILLON DOUBLE FACE   REF. C187BB

Movement: mechanical, manual winding, with tourbillon caliber C187 (derived from DR307, Lemania caliber 387 base); autonomy 45 hours, 19 jewels. Officially certified "chronometer" (C.O.S.C.).
Functions: hour, minute, small second, date, power reserve.
Case: 18 kt pink gold, two-piece case, double ellipse (height 38 mm, width 35 mm, thickness 10.90 mm); flat sapphire crystal on both sides; pink gold crown; snap-on back displaying the movement through a sapphire crystal. Water-resistant to 3 atm.
Dial: silvered solid gold, ligné decorated by hand, with silver appliques, aperture on the tourbillon. **Indications:** off-center hour and minute; printed Roman numerals and minute track; blued stainless steel hand-made hands; small second at 6 (hand with 3 staggered arms, integral with the tourbillon, indicating 20 second sequences on concentric arcs); date and reserve on back dial.
Strap: crocodile leather; hand-made pink gold clasp.
Price: 138'000 CHF.
Also available: yellow gold, red gold (same price); white gold 151'800; platinum 161'000; non Double Face, closed bottom Ref. C186 yellow gold, red gold 92; white gold 101'200; platinum 115'000; sapphire bottom Ref. C186S.

MASTER PAPILLON 10TH ANNIVERSARY   REF. C317BB

Movement: mechanical, automatic winding, extra-thin caliber DR317 (GP caliber 3100 base, modified by Daniel Roth to obtain the jumping-dial hour indication and minutes on a 180° semicircle); autonomy of 45 hours. 18 kt gold rotor engine turned (guilloché). Hand-beveled, hand-finished Côtes de Genève.
Functions: jumping hour, minute, center second.
Case: 18 kt pink gold, two-piece case, in double ellipse shape (height 38 mm, width 35 mm, thickness 10.25 mm); flat sapphire crystal; pink gold crown; snap-on back displaying the movement through a sapphire crystal. Dust and moisture protection. **Dial:** silvered ruthenium, engine turned (guilloché) by hand, silver appliques; painted Arabic numerals and minute track.
Indications: jumping hour at 12, center minute (disk with 2-hours revolution with two retractable hands indicating alternatively 60 minutes on a 180° arc; when an hour runs out, the hand on the 60th minute goes off by 90° on its axis, completely concealing itself under the seconds disk, while the other appears on the 1st minute), sweep second.
Strap: crocodile leather; hand-made pink gold clasp.
Price: 27'600 CHF, 110 pieces. **Also available:** white gold 30'475 CHF, 110 pieces; platinum 40'250 CHF, 30 pieces.

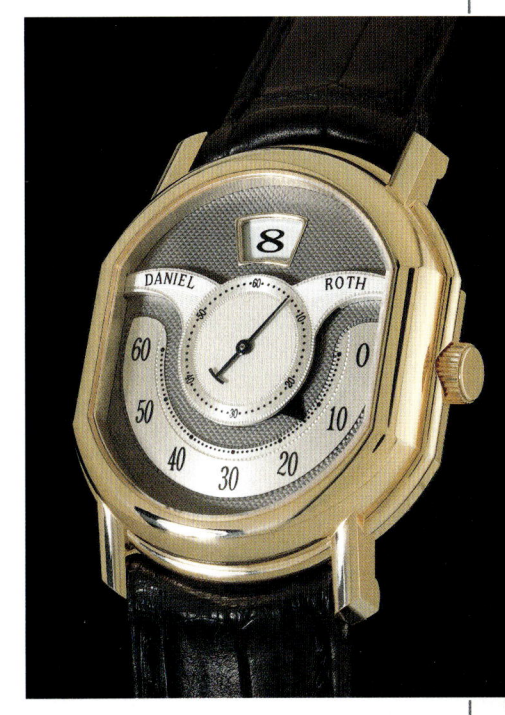

DANIEL ROTH

MASTER CHRONOGRAPH   REF. C448BB

Movement: mechanical, automatic winding, caliber DR101 (realized by GP on a D. Roth patent), autonomy of 40 hours, 38 jewels, balance with three arms in Glucydur, 28,800 vibrations per hour (vph), flat balance-spring (Ø 23.30, thickness 6.28). Chronograph with column wheel placed on dial side.
Functions: hour, minute, small second, date, chronograph with 2 counters.
Case: 18 kt pink gold, two-piece case, double ellipse (height 41 mm, width 38, thickness 10.8 mm); flat sapphire crystal; pink gold crown; water-resistant pushers with an exclusive shape conceived by Roth; snap-on back. Water-resistant to 3 atm. 
Dial: skeletonized and silvered brushed hour ring; printed Roman numerals and minute track; blued stainless steel hand-made pointed hands. **Indications:** minute counter at 3, date at 6, small second at 9, center second counter.
Strap: crocodile leather; hand-made pink gold clasp.
Price: 20'700 CHF.
Also available: white gold 22'770 CHF; platinum 34'500 CHF; with rosé dial.

MASTER CHRONOGRAPH LADY   REF. C447BA

Movement: mechanical, automatic winding, caliber DR101 (realized by Girard-Perregaux on a patent by D. Roth), autonomy of 40 hours, 38 jewels, balance with three arms in Glucydur, 28,800 vibrations per hour (vph), flat balance-spring (Ø 23.30, thickness 6.28 mm). Chronograph with column wheel placed on the dial side; solid gold rotor.
Functions: hour, minute, small second, chronograph with 2 counters. 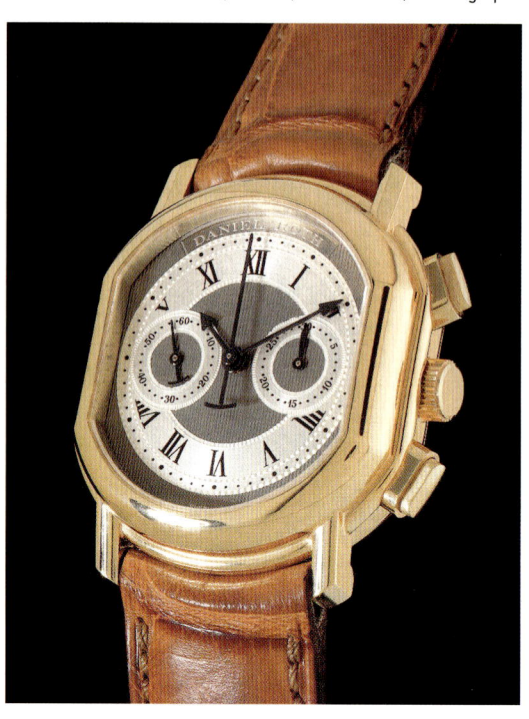
Case: 18 kt yellow gold, two-piece case, double ellipse (height 34.5 mm, width 31.5, thickness 11 mm); flat sapphire crystal; yellow gold crown; water-resistant pushers in an exclusive shape conceived by Roth; snap-on back displaying the movement through a sapphire crystal. Water-resistant to 3 atm.
Dial: silvered, ligné hand-decorated; printed Roman numerals and minute track; blued stainless steel hand-made pointed hands. **Indications:** minute counter at 3, small second at 9, center second counter.
Strap: crocodile leather; hand-made yellow gold clasp.
Price: 19'550 CHF.
Also available: white gold 21'505; platinum 33'350; steel 10'350.

MASTER RETROGRADE   REF. C127BC

Movement: mechanical, manual winding, caliber C127 (Lemania caliber NL27 base + module) autonomy of 40 hours, 14 jewels, balance with two arms in Glucydur, 18,000 vibrations per hour (vph), Breguet overcoil balance-spring (Ø 27.50 mm, thickness 6.70 mm). Hand-beveled, Côtes de Genève hand-finished, "soigné" finish; assembly, mounting and complete construction of the mechanism by Daniel Roth's watchmakers for a total of appr. 60 working hours. 
Functions: hour, minute, small second.
Case: 18 kt white gold, two-piece case, in double ellipse shape (height 38 mm, width 35, thickness 10.7 mm); flat sapphire crystal; white gold crown; snap-on back. Dust and moisture protection.
Dial: solid gold, black, ligné hand-decorated; printed Arabic numerals and minute track; pointed hands in stainless steel, hand-made, off-center, retrograde hours hand (at the stop limit it goes instantaneously back to the departure point). **Indications:** small second at 6.
Strap: crocodile leather; hand-made white gold clasp.
Price: 49'500 CHF.
Also available: yellow or pink gold 45'000; white gold and red 49'500; platinum 65'000; silvered dial.

SPORT AUTOMATIC   REF. S177ST

Movement: mechanical, automatic winding, caliber 0177, 33 jewels. Hand-beveled, hand-finished Côtes de Genève, "soigné" finish; assembly, mounting and adjustment of the mechanism made by Roth's watchmakers for a total of appr. 30 working hours.
Functions: hour, minute, center second, date.
Case: stainless steel, two-piece double ellipse case (height 38 mm, width 35 mm, thickness 7.5 mm); flat sapphire crystal; case back attached by 4 screws. Dust and moisture protection. 
Dial: black, ligné decorated by hand and brushed hour ring; printed Roman numerals and minute track; luminescent applied cabochon markers; luminescent stainless steel pointed hands. **Indications:** date at 6.
Bracelet: steel; fold-over clasp.
Price: 12'420 CHF.
Also available: in yellow or pink gold with bracelet 33'120 CHF; white gold with bracelet on request; with ivory, white, silvered, rosé, anthracite or yellow, red, blue and green enameled dial; as jewel-watch.

DANIEL ROTH

VANTAGE METROPOLITAN — REF. K857BC

Movement: mechanical, automatic winding, caliber DR710, autonomy of 42 h, 26 jewels, balance with three arms in Glucydur, 28,800 vibrations per hour (vph), flat balance-spring (Ø 31.40x34.80, thickness 6.35).
Functions: hours and minutes (of a second time zone as an alternative), night & day indicator.
Case: 18 kt white gold, two-piece double ellipse curved case (height 41 mm, width 38); curved sapphire crystal; screw-down crown; rectangular pusher at 9 for the selection of the second time zone; snap-on back. Water-resistant to 3 atm.
Dial: slate-grey, ligné decorated by hand and brushed hour ring; luminescent printed Arabic numerals and minute track; luminescent white-gold pointed hands.
Indications: two windows at the poles with the towns opposed on the planisphere, indicator of the window of the selected time zone at 12 and related night & day indicator at 6.
Strap: crocodile leather; white gold clasp.
Price: 18'700 CHF.
The piece shown is a prototype.
Also available: yellow or pink gold 17'000; steel 9'775; silvered or rosé dial.

VANTAGE PREMIER — REF. K807BC

Movement: mechanical, automatic winding, caliber DR700, autonomy of 42 hours, 27 jewels, balance with three arms in Glucydur, 28,800 vibrations per hour (vph), flat balance-spring (Ø 26 mm, thickness 5.15 mm).
Functions: retrograde hour and minute display, date.
Case: 18 kt white gold, two-piece double ellipse curved case (height 41 mm, width 35 mm, thickness 10.7 mm); curved sapphire crystal; screw-down crown; snap-on back. Water-resistant to 3 atm.
Dial: silvered, ligné decorated by hand and brushed zones; painted Arabic numerals and minute track; off-center luminescent blued stainless steel hand-made pointed hands, (retrograde hour hand).
Indications: date at 6.
Strap: crocodile leather; white gold clasp.
Price: 18'170 CHF.
The piece shown is a prototype.
Also available: in yellow or pink gold 16'502.50 CHF; steel 7'305.50 CHF; with rosé or anthracite dial.

CLASSIC GMT GENTS — REF. N238BB

Movement: mechanical, automatic winding, extra-thin caliber D237 (further developed on GP caliber 3100 base), autonomy 45 h, 32 jewels, Ø 25.60. Hand-beveled, hand-finished with Côtes de Genève pattern, "soigné" finish; assembled, mounted and adjusted by Roth's watchmakers for a total of appr. 20 working hours.
Functions: hour, minute, date, second time zone, 24-hour indication.
Case: 18 kt pink gold, two-piece case, double ellipse (height 38 mm, width 35, thickness 8.5 mm); flat sapphire crystal with magnifying lens on the second time zone; rectangular pusher at 2 for the second time zone; case back attached by 4 screws, displaying the movement through a sapphire crystal. Water-resistant to 3 atm.
Dial: silvered solid gold, ligné hand-decorated, with silver appliques; printed Roman numerals and minute track; luminescent blued stainless steel pointed hands. **Indications:** date at 6, second time zone 24-jumping hour display at 12 with instant leap.
Strap: crocodile leather; pink gold clasp.
Price: 18'400 CHF.
Also available: yellow gold (same price); white gold 20'240 CHF; steel 10'120 CHF; with blue, ivory, slate-grey, rosé or bordeaux, blue or black enameled dial.

CLASSIC EXTRA-PLATE AUTOMATIC GENTS — REF. N107BA

Movement: mechanical, automatic winding, extra-thin caliber N107 (Frédéric Piguet caliber 71 base), autonomy of 45 hours. Hand-beveled, Côtes de Genève hand-finished, "soigné" finish; assembly, mounting and mechanism adjustment by Daniel Roth's watchmakers for appr. 30 working hours.
Functions: hour, minute.
Case: 18 kt yellow gold, two-piece case, in double ellipse shape (height 38 mm, width 35 mm, thickness 6.4 mm); flat sapphire crystal; yellow gold crown; snap-on back. Dust and moisture protection.
Dial: silvered solid gold, ligné hand-decorated, silver appliques; printed Roman numerals and minute track; blued stainless steel hand-made pointed hands.
Strap: crocodile leather; hand-made yellow gold clasp.
Price: 28'520 CHF.
Also available: red gold, pink gold (same price); white gold 31'395; platinum 44'850; as jewel-watch (on request); with anthracite dial. Medium (height 34.5 mm, width 31.5, thickness 7.3 mm), manual winding Ref. O167: in yellow or pink gold, silvered dial 20'700; yellow gold, onyx dial 24'840.

Ebel

The protagonist of Ebel's latest production is the "Type E" model, an impeccable product originated from the mind of the Architects of Time and manufactured using the most recent technology. Senior and Lady's versions, provided with automatic movements, boast an essential and balanced structure. Their bracelet (or rubber strap) shows a row of "E", the House's well known logo, which provides for identity with discretion and elegance. The integration of case and bracelet represents the dominant motif of many Ebel collections. A "family" character is also lent by a play of alternating polished and matte surfaces which has been used successfully in the Maison's timepieces. The steel version with the rubber strap bears new printed numerals on the dial, that have slight grey shadows around, which makes them seem three-dimensional. On the whole, complex technology was used to produce this watch, and top-level process standards were adopted, which had been tuned up by the US space industry. In particular, Ebel was able to take advantage of such high technology for a civil application, especially as regards the MIM (Metal Injection Molding) process which allows to produce parts ready for finishing in an integrated cycle, starting from metal powder.

Among the other new products for the 1999/2000 season, we met also a new version of the chronograph Bouchonné, with "fausses côtes" decorations, a new dial for the 1911 Senior, the "Lady" version of Discovery and the new, automatic Sportwave Gent.

The brand new Satya, which recalls the divinity who gave light to gold, a symbol of absolute purity, is available with a quartz movement and in two sizes -

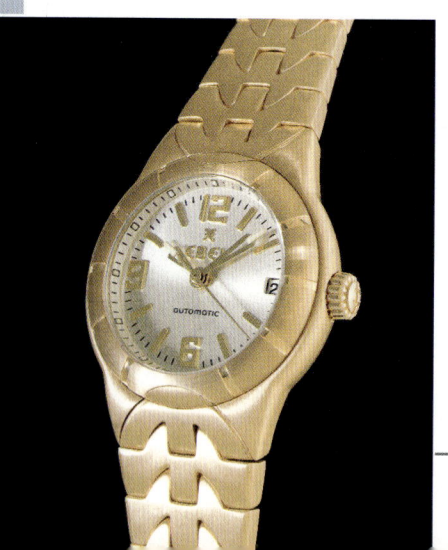

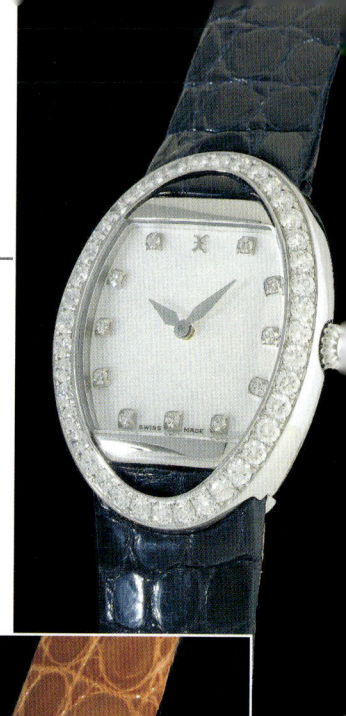

The History

In **1911**, at la Chaux-de-Fonds, Eugène Blum and his wife, Alice Lévy, founded Ebel. At the beginning the Company worked prevalently on outside commissions, even though taking part in some of the international fairs with its own watches. In **1914** Ebel won a prize at the Berne Exposition and in **1925** at the Art Déco Exhibit in Paris. Ebel's rise to great frame however began in the **1960's**, when Pierre Alain Blum, member of the third generation in the Company, was called back home from New York where he was having a successful career for an import-export company. Under his guidance the name became known throughout the world.

1928 - Ebello, a watch closed in a perfectly waterproof, patented case.

1935 - The Company began to use numerical control machines, first choosing Western Electric, then Vibrograf.

1945/47 - By the end of the Second World War, the Company decided to concentrate on the production of watch movements.

1973/79 - These are the years which produce Sport and Beluga. Pierre Alain Blum, the single owner of the Company, signs an agreement with Cartier for which Ebel will produce cases and movements. The Company purchases new plants for the production of cases, bracelets made up of hundreds of hand-assembled parts, watch movements, technical and jewelled watches.

1984 - The underwater diving model, Discovery, is shown.

1986 - For the 75th Anniversary, the presentation of "1911", a great success together with Voyager, an automatic World Time module.

1991 - Ahead of the tendency, Ebel proposes the White Gold collection and the new family, Lichine.

1995 - The first movement designed and produced by the Company: the Le Modulor Chronograph Chronometer. The name is chosen in honor of the architect, Le Corbusier, born in La Chaux-de-Fonds, and where his "Villa Turque" is bought by Ebel as a public relations center. This is also the year of Meridian, an innovative Time of the World.

1996 - Shanta is a splendid ladies watch with cover over the dial. Pierre Alain Blum gives the Company over to the Invest Corporation and takes up other activities. The few Swiss companies left in the hands of their original family descendants lose one of their most important representatives.

1997 - The Chrono Le Modulor is produced in steel and in a limited edition of 199 pieces in pink gold and 99 in platinum. Sport Classique celebrates 20 years of production.

1998 - Sportwave comes on the scene in steel or steel and titanium, a now-generation quartz watch; new versions for the classic men's 1911, Voyager and Discovery, with cases dimensioned to the sizes of the Chronograph.

1999 - Ebel ownership moves to the LVMH Group (Louis Vuitton Moët Hennessy), along with Chaumet, Zenith and TAG Heuer, giving life to an important group of haut-de-gamme (top scale) watchmakers.

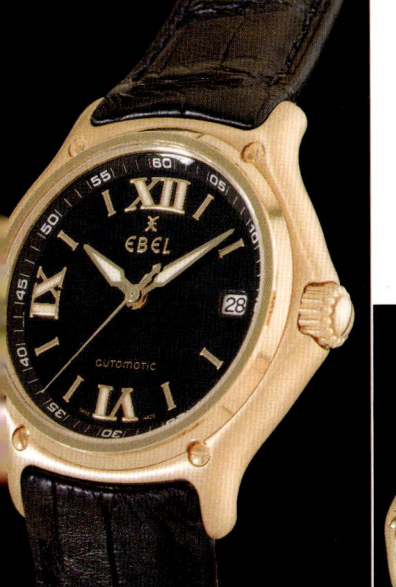

Mini and Lady. The tonneau-shaped dial, with Roman numerals fluently arranged on a luminous, mother-of-pearl or silvered, "soleil"-brushed background, occupies the center of a charming oval bezel. This is a timepiece for a lady who feels like a goddess within an ever more depersonalizing society. Finally, the new Beluga Manchette, more casual but always sparkling and refined, is again a quartz watch for "Her": steel case with brilliants, which form also the four markers on the dial, with a bracelet made up of shaped links with rounded angles and fold-over clasp.

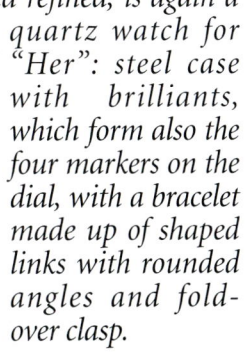

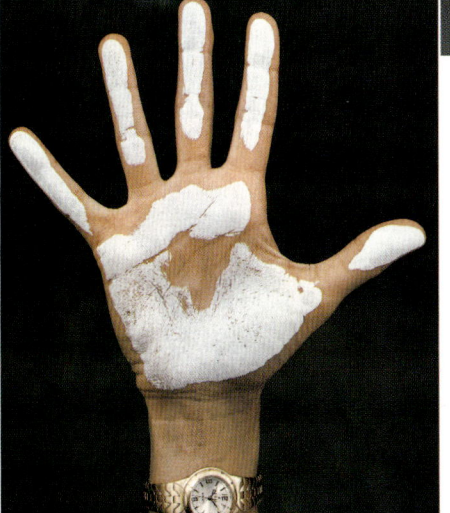

EBEL

CHRONOGRAPH PERPETUAL CALENDAR   REF. 3136901/35

Movement: mechanical, automatic winding, Ebel caliber 136 (Zenith El Primero caliber 40.0 base + perpetual calendar module realized by Ebel).
Functions: hour, minute, small second, perpetual calendar (date, day, month, year, moon phase), chronograph with 3 counters.
Case: 18 kt white gold, three-piece brushed case (Ø 40, thickness 12 mm); antireflective flat sapphire crystal; polished bezel fastened with 5 white gold screws; 4 correctors on case side; hexagonal white gold crown with case protection; snap-on back with gasket. Water-resistant to 3 atm. 
Dial: silvered; applied Roman numerals; white gold bâton hands.
Indications: minute counter and date at 3, moon phase and hour counter at 6, small second and day at 9, four-year cycle and month at 12, center second counter, minute track with divisions for $1/5$ of a second, tachymeter scale on the beveled ring.
Strap: crocodile leather; white gold fold-over clasp.
Also available: with bracelet; in yellow gold, leather strap or bracelet; pink gold or platinum, leather strap. All available versions only with silvered dial.
Prices: on request.

1911 CHRONOGRAPH   REF. 9137240/6635

Movement: mechanical, automatic winding, Ebel caliber 137. Hand-engraved rotor. Officially certified "chronometer" (C.O.S.C.). **Functions:** hour, minute, small second, date, chronograph with 3 counters. **Case:** stainless steel, three-piece brushed case (Ø 40 mm, thickness 12 mm); antireflective flat sapphire crystal; polished bezel fastened with 5 gold screws; crown with case protection; case back attached by 8 screws displaying the movement through a sapphire crystal. Water-resistant to 5 atm. 
Dial: silvered, "fausses côtes" decoration; applied faceted bâton markers (Arabic numeral 12); luminescent dots on the printed minute track; luminescent bâton hands.
Indications: date between 4 and 5, minute counter at 3, hour counter at 6, small second at 9, center second counter, minute track with divisions for $1/5$ of a second, tachymeter scale on the beveled ring.
Strap: rubber; stainless steel fold-over clasp.
Also available: bracelet; smooth blue, orange or black dial, Arabic numerals or white, black Roman numerals; steel and yellow gold, silvered, white, black or blue dial engine turned (guilloché), markers, leather strap or bracelet; yellow gold, smooth white, black or silvered dial, leather strap or bracelet.
Prices: on request.

NEW VOYAGER   REF. 9124341/5135

Movement: mechanical, automatic winding, ETA caliber 2892-A2, with Lemania 24 hour module, modified in Ebel 124 caliber. Decorated with Côtes Circulaires and circular graining pattern.
Functions: hour, minute, center second, date, world time.
Case: stainless steel, three-piece case (Ø 37.5 mm, thickness 10 mm), with 5 ornamental screws; antireflective flat sapphire crystal; brushed bi-directional turning bezel and knurled with engraved reference town names of the 24 time zones; screw-down crown with case protection; case back attached by 8 screws, with gasket. Water-resistant to 20 atm. 
Dial: black; luminescent bâton markers and Roman numerals; printed minute track; luminescent white painted bâton hands.
Indications: date at 3, world time (night & day indicator) on the counter-clockwise turning beveled ring, synchronized with the main time, in relation to the town names on the ring.
Strap: leather; stainless steel fold-over clasp.
Also available: white dial; with bracelet; with "Geo" dial, all silvered or black with silvered continents.
Prices: on request.

NEW DISCOVERY SENIOR   REF. 9080341/8635

Movement: mechanical, automatic winding, Ebel caliber 080 (Lemania caliber 8810 base), with two winding barrels. Côtes de Genève finished.
Functions: hour, minute, center second, date.
Case: stainless steel, three-piece brushed case (Ø 40 mm, thickness 11 mm), decorated by 5 screws, flat sapphire crystal, with magnifying lens on date; counter-clockwise turning bezel, knurled, with embossed minute track for the calculation of diving times; screw-down crown with case protection; case back attached by 8 screws, with gasket. Water-resistant to 20 atm. 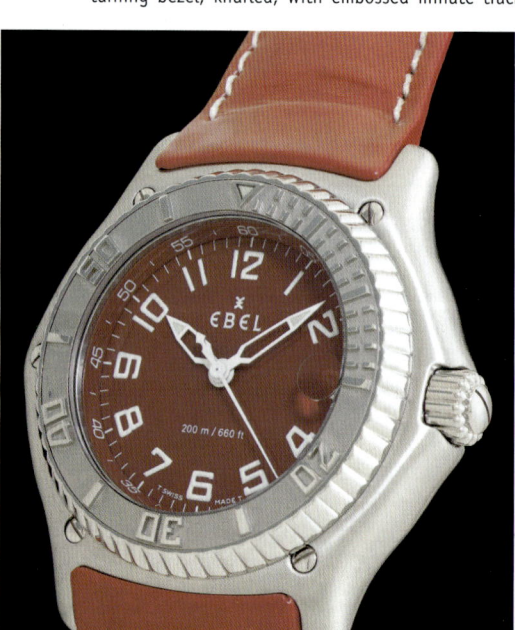
Dial: red; luminescent Arabic numerals; white printed minute track; luminescent skeletonized white painted Alpha hands; 5 minute markers on the beveled ring.
Indications: date at 3.
Strap: leather; stainless steel fold-over clasp.
Also available: white, blue or black dial; with bracelet.
Prices: on request.

EBEL

E-TYPE SENIOR   REF. 9330C41/3716

Movement: mechanical, automatic winding, Ebel caliber 330 (Girard-Perregaux caliber GP3300 base), 11 lines and $^1/_2$ (Ø 25.6 mm thickness 3.1 mm), brass and heavy metal oscillating mass with a stylized "E" as a symbol for the collection. Côtes de Genève finished. **Functions:** hour, minute, center second, date.
Case: stainless steel, three-piece brushed case (Ø 38 mm, thickness 10 mm) realized by means of the Metal Injection Molding technology (injection of thermally treated metal powder of aeronautical origin); antireflective curved sapphire crystal; fixed bezel with brushed surface and polished engraved hour markers; slightly recessed crown; case back attached by 8 screws with gasket, displaying the movement through a sapphire crystal. Water-resistant to 10 atm.
Dial: slate-grey; applied bâton markers and Arabic numerals; printed minute track with luminescent dots on the beveled ring; luminescent skeletonized hands.
Indications: date at 3.
Bracelet: brushed steel, with E-shaped links; stainless steel fold-over clasp
Also available: white or black dial; leather strap, black or white dial; yellow gold, slate-grey dial, black, silvered, leather strap or bracelet.
Prices: on request.

NEW 1911 SENIOR   REF. 9080241/5465P

Movement: mechanical, automatic winding, Ebel caliber 080 (Lemania caliber 8810 base), with two winding barrels. Côtes de Genève finished.
Functions: hour, minute, center second, date.
Case: stainless steel, three-piece brushed case (Ø 38 mm, thickness 9 mm); flat sapphire crystal; polished bezel with double gasket, fastened with 5 screws; screw-down crown with case protection; case back attached by 8 screws with gasket. Water-resistant to 10 atm.
Dial: black; luminescent applied bâton markers and Roman numerals; printed minute track on the beveled ring; luminescent Alpha hands.
Indications: date at 3.
Bracelet: stainless steel, made up by 190 polished and brushed links, assembled and finished by hand; stainless steel fold-over clasp.
Also available: white, silvered or blue dial; leather strap and black or white dial; yellow gold & stainless steel with bracelet and white, black, silvered dial; in yellow gold, silvered, black dial, leather strap or bracelet.

SPORTWAVE AUTOMATIC SENIOR   REF. 9120632/61P10

Movement: mechanical, automatic winding, Ebel caliber 120 (ETA 2892/A2 base), autonomy of 42 hours.
Functions: hour, minute, center second, date.
Case: stainless steel, three-piece brushed case (Ø 36 mm, thickness 8.8 mm); flat sapphire crystal; polished fixed bezel with cabochon markers, fastened by 4 screws at the cardinal points; crown with case protection; screwed-on case back. Water-resistant to 5 atm.
Dial: silvered, with two tones; luminescent printed Roman numerals; printed minute track; luminescent bâton hands.
Indications: date at 3.
Bracelet: stainless steel, made of polished undulating links; double fold-over steel clasp.
Also available: with blue or black dial.
Prices: on request.

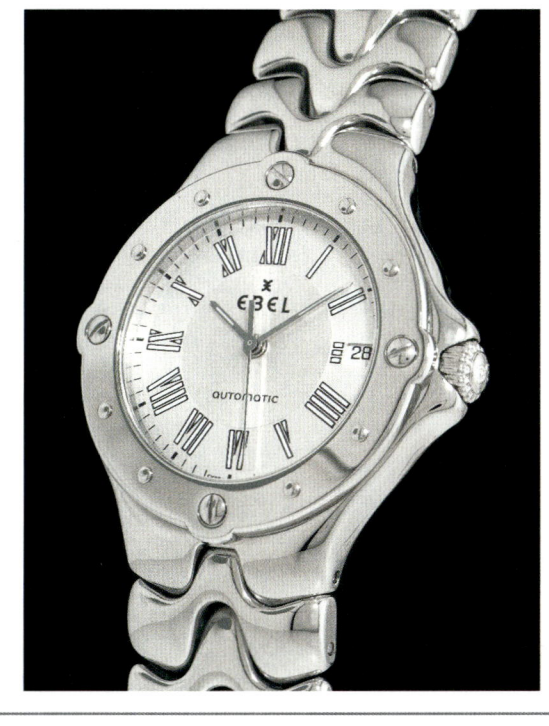

LICHINE TONNEAU AUTOMATIC   REF. 8172431/6435

Movement: mechanical, automatic winding, caliber ETA 2671, modified Ebel caliber 172. Decorated with Côtes de Genève pattern and circular graining.
Functions: hour, minute, center second, date.
Case: 18 kt yellow gold, two-piece tonneau case (height 39 mm, width 29 mm, thickness 9 mm); curved sapphire crystal; case back attached by 4 screws, with gasket. Water-resistant to 3 atm.
Dial: silvered, engine turned (guilloché) with sun pattern at the center; applied yellow gold triangular markers and Arabic numerals; tonneau-shaped printed minute track; yellow gold bâton hands.
Indications: date at 6.
Strap: crocodile leather; fold-over yellow gold clasp.
Also available: black dial; with bracelet; stainless steel, black or silvered dial, leather strap or bracelet.

131

Eberhard & Co.

Perhaps it is the attention paid to the technical detail, or the unmistakable personality of each creation that makes Eberhard a timeless classic. The Swiss Maison in any case reconfirms its position, after a one hundred year history, moving away from tradition, proud but never pompous. The new millennium is welcomed by the new version, "Gold Car Collection", of the mythical Tazio Nuvolari, the watch all motorists (and non) will be proud to wear and to admire with its transparent back, the fausses côtes, the miniature reproduction of the Alfa Romeo "C" engraved on the rotor, and the stylized image of the good-luck turtle. A sporting cast for the Aiglon, the new collection presented at Basel last year, and for the powerful Traversetolo Vitré, that now has a transparent back case.

The new Désirée is the priceless suggestion the Maison offers to ladies: with its slave bracelet, the icy jewel-watch gleams with its unusual steel "dress", practical and natural, perfect anytime, anywhere.

The History

The history of Eberhard & Co. begins at St. Imier, where Georges Emile Eberhard was born and where he worked as an apprentice. In 1887, he had moved to La Chaux-de-Fonds and founded his own Manufacture. In less than 20 years he was able to inaugurate a large establishment on Rue Robert after having personally carried his watches, produced with considerable technical skill, throughout Europe. In this shop, his sons and nephews carry on the tradition with fine quality watches. The first Eberhard wrist model chronograph dates from 1919; during the 20's/30's he creates the single button chronographs with a flip-up case cover (during the '30's, the Royal Italian Navy chooses these for its officers). The first two-button models are presented in 1935, and not until 1938 does the hour counter appear. Starting from 1939, the year a 15''' split time counter with column wheel, justly called Extrafort, is produced, and series production methods begin. Eberhard uses the Dubey & Schaldenbrand patent to create a split time chronograph, the Mobile Index, where the second hand keeps moving for about one minute. This system was sufficient to measure two times in rapid succession, and it allows lower production costs since the expensive column wheel mechanism is unnecessary. During the Second World Ward, Eberhard watches, because they are reliable and precise, become a valid instrument for the military. The first ladies collection dates from 1946, as does both the digital day-date function and the subsidiary date hand. New goals are set for the 1950's, such as the rapid date adjustment function (1955).

1962 - The granddaughter of the founder and her husband die in an automobile accident. Her father, Maurice, decides to put the Company management in other hands. Even though new and interesting models were being made (1967 is the presentation year of a quartz movement watch with a date function: the Beta 2.1, 6.2 mm high and was awarded recognition by the Neuchâtel Observatory), the Company undergoes a period of inactivity, common to the entire watch production sector, and that would end at the start of the 1980's.

1983 - Eberhard sponsors many sports events. In 1983 it perfects for "Azzurra", Italy's contender for the America's Cup, a watch with count-down function: it shows the last five minutes before the start of a regatta in five separate apertures.

1986 - The year of the collection dedicated to the "Frecce Tricolori", the Italian acrobatic flying team. This collection is to include the "diascope" versions which have a separate supplementary indication for 24 hours.

1987 - The centenary sees the presentation of Navymaster.

1991 - Great innovation in Basel is the Maréoscope, an automatic chrono which shows the tide changes, with a maximum 2 minute margin of error, and the moon phases.

1992 - The 100th year since the birth of Tazio Nuvolari, and Eberhard dedicates to the great racing pilot an automatic chronograph, sport model: the turtle that D'Annunzio gave the driver is on the dial. There is also a pocket version, and three years later, in 1995, the find split seconds wrist model is presented.

1993 - Besides the "Signée" and the "Marignan" crowns, distinguished by a patented screw closing, the "Sabord" is introduced, named for the submarine hatch. This is also the year of "Quadrangolo" with its squared-off case.

1995 - Eberhard dedicates attention to the new aesthetics of its production. The newly squared Chrono Screen takes up the Quadrangolo attitude; Hyperbole recalls a reverse hyperbole; Traversetolo is considerably large (43 mm diameter) and carries a 1950's calibre. The sports models using Scafomaster can be brought to 250 or to 500 meters in depth. The models dedicated to the Frecce Tricolori, with its logo on the dial, are not the only ones to pass stiff acceleration testing. The production of ladies watches brings out precious models in gold, with bracelets, using two different kinds of links to offer a real jewel and that is shown best on the new "My Way". The bracelets, as well as the crowns on the men's models already in the collection, show the care taken to perfect both old, successful themes as well as the newest, imaginative products.

1997 - The is the moment of the 8-day watch, with the power reserve shown on the dial: included in the "8-Day" and "Aqua 8". The chronograph Chieftain which simplifies the most essential characteristics of the collection, or Diascope. Eberhard creates ladies models which are jewelled watches, My Way, the elegant mix of white gold and diamonds.

EBERHARD & CO.

TAZIO NUVOLARI RATTRAPANTE — REF. 31055/CP

Movement: mechanical automatic winding (modified Valjoux caliber 7750 base), resists strong accelerations. **Functions:** hour, minute, small second, split-second chronograph with 3 counters. **Case:** stainless steel, 3-piece case (Ø 39.5, thickness 14.25 mm); antireflective curved sapphire crystal; bezel decorated with "fausses côtes" pattern, with engraved km-miles conversion table; screw-down crown; water-resistant rectangular pushers, fly-back pusher at 8 with Nuvolari's engraved initials; case back attached by 8 white gold screws, decorated with "fausses côtes" pattern, with Nuvolari's engraved signature, the stylized turtle as his good-luck piece and the dates of the centennial of his birth. Water-resistant to 3 atm.
Dial: matte black; stylized turtle in polychromic enamels; luminescent Arabic numerals; luminescent dots on the minute track; luminescent white painted bâton hands. **Indications:** minute counter at 3, hour counter at 6, small second at 9, center split-second counters, minute track with divisions for 1/5 of a second, tachymeter scale on the beveled ring.
Strap: crocodile leather; steel clasp.
Price: 9'090 CHF.
Also available: Charme steel bracelet, stylized gold turtle 9'890 CHF; yellow gold, leather strap 17'000 CHF, bracelet 23'440 CHF.

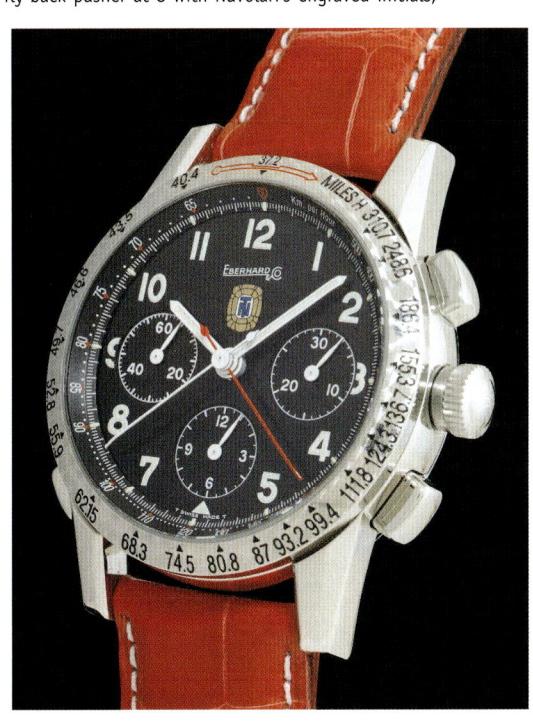

TAZIO NUVOLARI "GRANDE TAILLE" — REF. 31036/CP

Movement: mechanical, automatic winding (Valjoux caliber 7750 base), resisting strong accelerations.
Functions: hour, minute, chronograph with 3 counters.
Case: stainless steel, three-piece case (Ø 43 mm, thickness 13 mm); antireflective flat sapphire crystal; bezel decorated with "fausses côtes" pattern, with engraved km-miles conversion table; screw-down crown; rectangular screw-down pushers; case back attached by 8 screws decorated with "fausses côtes" pattern, with Tazio Nuvolari's engraved signature, the stylized turtle as his good-luck piece and the dates of the centennial of his birth. Water-resistant to 3 atm.
Dial: matte black; stylized turtle in polychromic enamels; luminescent Arabic numerals; luminescent dots on the printed minute track; luminescent white painted bâton hands. **Indications:** hour counter at 6, minute counter at 12, center second counter, minute track with divisions for 1/5 of a second, tachymeter scale on the beveled ring.
Strap: crocodile leather; stainless steel clasp.
Price: 3'650 CHF.
Also available: with Charme bracelet 4'450 CHF.

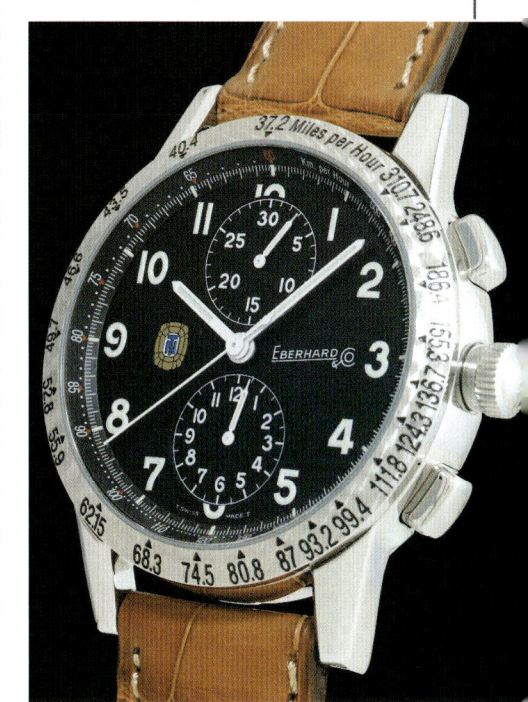

TAZIO NUVOLARI — REF. 31030/CA4

Movement: mechanical, automatic winding (Valjoux caliber 7750 base), resisting strong accelerations. **Functions:** hour, minute, chronograph with 3 counters.
Case: stainless steel, 3-piece case (Ø 39.5 mm, thickness 13.3 mm); antireflective flat sapphire crystal; bezel decorated with "fausses côtes" pattern, with engraved km-miles conversion table; screw-down crown; water-resistant rectangular pushers, with Nuvolari's signature, the stylized turtle as his good-luck piece and the dates of the centennial of his birth. Water-resistant to 3 atm.
Dial: black; stylized turtle in enamels; luminescent Arabic numerals; luminescent white painted bâton hands. **Indications:** hour counter at 6, minute counter at 12, center second counter, minute track with divisions for 1/5 of a second, tachymeter scale on the beveled ring.
Bracelet: Charme stainless steel, with polished flat links; fold-over clasp recessed, steel with 18 kt gold stylized turtle.
Price: 4'160 CHF.
Also available: leather strap 3'360 CHF; gold, Chronometer leather strap 11'000 CHF, bracelet 17'440 CHF; stainless steel, sapphire case back, engraved movement, leather strap or Charme bracelet on request; steel pocket watch 3'640 CHF; gold, Chronometer 12'260 CHF.

TAZIO NUVOLARI "GOLD CAR COLLECTION" — REF. 31037/CP

Special edition of the famous Tazio Nuvolari chronograph, characterized by its case back with a mineral glass bull's eye which allows to inspect the caliber chronograph by Valjoux in a particularly refined arrangement with 25 jewels, 16 blue steels screws and decoration with Côtes de Genève pattern. Its rotor is embellished by an applied 18 kt gold reproduction of the Alfa Romeo type "C" which had accompanied Nivola (this was the racing-car driver's nickname) to many great victories. The rotor shows also beautiful gilded engravings. 18 kt yellow gold screws fasten the case back decorated with a "fausses côtes" pattern. The case shows a slightly stronger thickness (14 mm) and on its front side it presents, as the only distinctive element with respect to series models, Tazio Nuvolari's signature on the dial at 9 below the stylized turtle in polychromic enamel. This had been drawn for Nuvolari by Gabriele D'Annunzio as a good-luck piece, accompanied by the dedication "To the fastest man, the slowest animal".
Price: 3'900 CHF.
Also available: Charme steel bracelet and 18 kt gold stylized turtle 4'700 CHF.

133

EBERHARD & CO.

CHRONOMASTER "FRECCE TRICOLORI" — REF. 32120/CP

Movement: mechanical, automatic winding (Lemania caliber 5100 base), anti-G tested (resisting strong accelerations). **Functions:** hour, minute, small second, date, 24-hour indication, chronograph with 3 counters. **Case:** stainless steel, three-piece case (Ø 40 mm, thickness 14.5 mm); antireflective flat sapphire crystal; counter-clockwise turning bezel (60 clicks) with gold details, luminescent oversized pointer; engraved minute track to be used for the calculation of diving times; small yellow-gold spheres on a "Marignan" type screw-down crown; pushers with case protection; case back attached by 8 screws. Water-resistant to 6 atm. **Dial:** white; logo "Pattuglia Acrobatica Nazionale"; luminescent bâton markers; printed minute track; luminescent bâton hands. **Indications:** date at 3, hour counter at 6, small second at 9, 24-hour display at 12, minute counter (airplane on the tip) and center second counter, minute track with divisions for 1/5 of a second, tachymeter scale on the beveled ring. **Strap:** crocodile leather; jointed attachment; stainless steel clasp. **Price:** 3'500 CHF. Dedicated to the National Acrobatic Group of the Italian Air Forces. **Also available:** with Charade steel bracelet 4'200 CHF; yellow gold, Chronometer, 3 atm., leather strap 12'500 CHF, Chardon bracelet 19'540 CHF. All with white or blue dial.

CHRONOMASTER "FRECCE TRICOLORI" DIASCOPE — REF. 32033/CA3

Movement: mechanical, automatic winding (Lemania cal. 5195 base), anti-G tested (resisting strong accelerations). **Functions:** hour, minute, small second, chronograph with 3 counters, second time zone, 24-hour indication. **Case:** stainless steel, 3-piece brushed case (Ø 40, thickness 16.7 mm); antireflective curved mineral crystal; counter-clockwise turning bezel with gold details, large luminescent pointer and engraved minute track, useful for the calculation of diving times; small yellow gold spheres on a "Marignan" type screw-down crown; case back attached by 8 screws. Water-resistant to 6 atm. **Dial:** blue, white counters; logo "Pattuglia Acrobatica Nazionale"; luminescent bâton markers; luminescent bâton hands. **Indications:** 2nd time zone 24-hour night & day display at 3, hour counter at 6, small second at 9, central minute (plane-shaped hand) and second counters, minute track with divisions for 1/5 of a second, tachymeter scale on the beveled ring. **Bracelet:** Charade brushed steel; recessed fold-over clasp. **Price:** 4'665 CHF. Dedicated to the Acrobatic Group of the Italian Air Forces. **Also available:** leather strap and jointed attachment 3'965 CHF; gold, water-resistant to 3 atm., leather strap 13'500 CHF, Chardon bracelet 20'540 CHF. All with white or blue dial, white counters.

SCAFOMASTER 500 DL — REF. 42016/CP

Movement: mechanical, automatic winding (ETA caliber 2892-2 base), anti-G tested (resisting strong accelerations). **Functions:** hour, minute, center second, date. **Case:** stainless steel with 18 kt yellow gold details, three-piece brushed case (Ø 39.5 mm, thickness 12.5 mm); antireflective flat sapphire crystal; counter-clockwise turning bezel with large luminescent pointer and engraved minute track, useful for the calculation of diving times; small yellow gold spheres on a "Marignan" type screw-down crown with case protection; case back attached by 8 screws. Water-resistant to 50 atm. **Dial:** blue, screened; luminescent applied bâton markers; luminescent bâton hands; printed minute track on the beveled ring. **Indications:** date at 3. **Strap:** water-repellent leather, salt-resistant; adjustable steel fold-over safety clasp. **Price:** 2'250 CHF. **Also available:** with Charade steel bracelet 2'950 CHF; steel, black dial Ref. 41005, leather strap 2'100 CHF, with Charade bracelet 2'800 CHF.

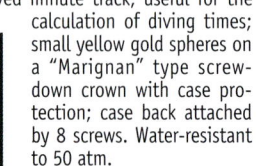

SCAFOMASTER 250 — REF. 41004/CA2

Movement: mechanical, automatic winding (ETA caliber 2892-2 base), anti-G tested (resisting strong accelerations). **Functions:** hour, minute, center second, date. **Case:** stainless steel with 18 kt white gold details, three-piece brushed case (Ø 37.3 mm, thickness 10.2 mm); antireflective flat sapphire crystal; counter-clockwise turning bezel with large luminescent pointer and engraved minute track, useful for the calculation of diving times; small yellow gold spheres on a "Marignan" type screw-down crown; case back attached by 8 screws. Water-resistant to 25 atm. **Dial:** black; luminescent bâton markers; printed minute track on the beveled ring; luminescent white painted bâton hands. **Indications:** date at 3. **Bracelet:** Charade steel; recessed fold-over clasp. **Price:** 2'250 CHF. **Also available:** leather strap 1'750 CHF.

EBERHARD & CO.

FLYMATIC — REF. 40010/OR

Movement: mechanical, automatic winding (ETA caliber 2892-2 base), anti-G tested (resisting strong accelerations). Officially certified "chronometer" (C.O.S.C.).
Functions: hour, minute, center second, date.
Case: 18 kt yellow gold, three-piece case (Ø 37.5 mm, thickness 9.5 mm); antireflective flat sapphire crystal; counter-clockwise turning bezel with large luminescent marker and engraved minute track; small spheres on a yellow gold "Marignan" type screw-down crown; case back attached by 6 screws. Water-resistant to 3 atm.
Dial: white; logo "Pattuglia Acrobatica Nazionale"; luminescent applied bâton markers (Arabic numeral 12); luminescent bâton hands. **Indications:** date at 3, minute track on the beveled ring.
Strap: crocodile leather; jointed coupling; gold-plated clasp.
Price: 7'425 CHF. Series dedicated to the Acrobatic Group of the Italian Air Forces.
Also available: stainless steel, gold details, non chronometer, 10 atm., leather strap 1'600 CHF, Charade steel bracelet 2'100 CHF; small size (Ø 335 mm, thickness 9 mm): steel and gold details, 6 atm., leather strap 1'600 CHF, Chardon steel bracelet 2'050 CHF; gold, chronometer, 3 atm., leather strap 6'050 CHF, Chardon bracelet 11'990 CHF. All with white or blue dial.

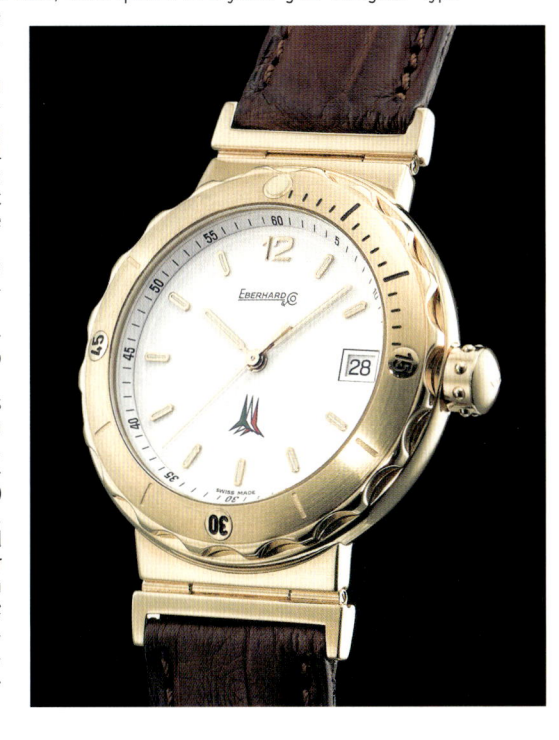

FLYMATIC DIASCOPE — REF. 42017/CP

Movement: mechanical, automatic winding (Lemania caliber 5195 base), anti-G (resisting strong accelerations).
Functions: hour, minute, center second, date, three time zones.
Case: stainless steel, three-piece case (Ø 37.5 mm, thickness 11.4 mm); antireflective flat sapphire crystal; ring, with gold details, rotating in both directions with blue-red engraved 24 hours; small yellow gold spheres on a "Marignan" type screw-down crown; case back attached by 8 screws. Water-resistant to 10 atm.
Dial: blue; logo "Pattuglia Acrobatica Nazionale"; luminescent applied bâton markers; printed minute track; luminescent bâton hands.
Indications: date at 3, independently adjustable center hand indicating the 24 hours of the second time zone on the fixed beveled ring and of the third one on the suitably turned ring.
Strap: crocodile leather; jointed coupling; stainless steel clasp.
Price: 2'100 CHF. Series dedicated to the Acrobatic Group of the Italian Air Forces.
Also available: with Charade steel bracelet 2'600 CHF; with blue dial and 24-hours ring painted in red and blue.

QUADRANGOLO CHRONO SCREEN — REF. 31034/CP

Movement: mechanical, manual winding (Lemania caliber 1872 base).
Functions: hour, minute, small second, chronograph with 2 counters.
Case: stainless steel, three-piece rectangular curved case (height 35.8 mm, width 34.5 mm, thickness 11 mm); antireflective flat sapphire crystal; smooth bezel; Signée-type crown, with embossed logo; pushers with case protection; case back attached by 8 screws, decorated with "fausses côtes" pattern. Water-resistant to 5 atm.
Dial: black; luminescent Arabic numerals; printed minute track; luminescent bâton hands.
Indications: minute counter at 3, small second at 9, center second counter, minute track with divisions for 1/5 of a second, tachymeter scale on the beveled ring.
Strap: crocodile leather; steel clasp.
Price: 4'600 CHF.
Also available: with Charade bracelet 5'340 CHF; steel and yellow gold, water-resistant to 5 atm., leather strap 5'110 CHF, steel bracelet and "coiffé or" 18 kt 7'080 CHF; gold, water-resistant to 3 atm., leather strap 11'000 CHF, bracelet 17'600 CHF. All with white or black dial and with smooth bezel or decorated with "fausses côtes" pattern.

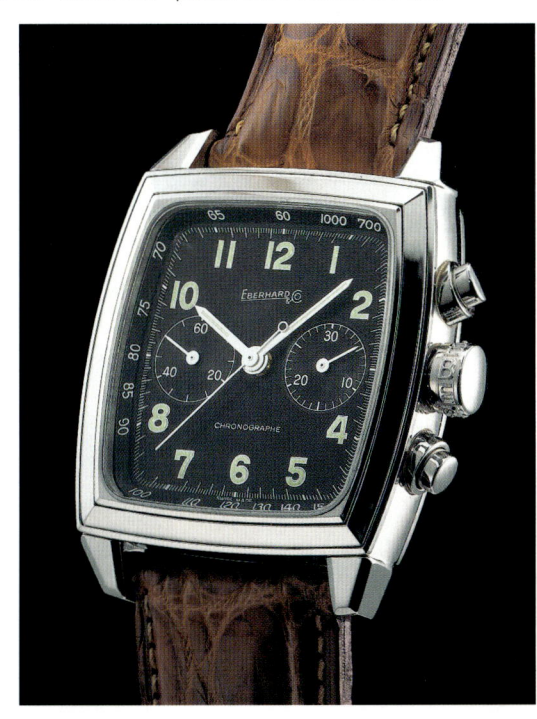

QUADRANGOLO — REF. 41010/CA

Movement: mechanical, automatic winding (Eta caliber 2892-2 base).
Functions: hour, minute, center second, date.
Case: stainless steel, three-piece rectangular curved case (height 33 mm, width 32 mm, thickness 9 mm); antireflective flat sapphire crystal; bezel decorated with "fausses côtes" pattern; Sabord-type crown, Eberhard patent, screwed inside a cylindric protection, with hinged liftable hold and engraved logo; case back attached by 8 screws. Water-resistant to 6 atm.
Dial: white; applied Arabic numerals; luminescent dots on the printed minute track; luminescent bâton hands.
Indications: date at 4, minute track on the beveled ring.
Bracelet: Charade steel; fold-over clasp.
Price: 3'645 CHF.
Also available: leather strap 2'950 CHF; yellow gold & stainless steel, leather strap 3'400 CHF, with bracelet 6'095 CHF; yellow gold, water-resistant to 3 atm., C.O.S.C. chronometer, leather strap 7'800 CHF, with bracelet 14'180 CHF. Each version is available with white or black dial and smooth bezel or decorated with "fausses côtes" pattern.

EBERHARD & CO.

CHEFTAIN CHRONOGRAPH — REF. 31040/CP

Movement: mechanical, automatic winding (Valjoux caliber 7750 base).
Functions: hour, minute, small second, date, chronograph with 3 counters.
Case: stainless steel, three-piece case (Ø 38.6 mm, thickness 13.2 mm); curved crystal; smooth bezel; screw-down octagonal crown; pushers with case protection; snap-on case back, polished with knurled edge. Water-resistant to 5 atm.
Dial: blue, silvered counter crowns; applied bâton markers; luminescent dots on the printed minute track; luminescent bâton hands.
Indications: date at 3, hour counter at 6, small second at 9, minute counter at 12, center second counter, tachymeter scale on the beveled ring.
Strap: leather; stainless steel clasp.
Price: 2'350 CHF.
Also available: with Chablis bracelet 2'900 CHF; with 12 markers engraved on the bezel; white dial, blue counter crowns, white with blue counters or blue with white counters and applied gold plated markers.

CHEFTAIN CHRONOGRAPH DIASCOPE — REF. 31058/CA

Movement: mechanical, automatic winding (Lemania caliber 5195 base).
Functions: hour, minute, small second, chronograph with 3 counters, second time zone, 24-hour indication.
Case: stainless steel, three-piece case (Ø 38.6 mm, thickness 13.8 mm); curved crystal; bezel with 12 engraved markers; screw-down octagonal crown; pushers with case protection; snap-on case back, polished with knurled edge. Water-resistant to 5 atm.
Dial: white, blue zones with concentric-circles pattern; applied bâton markers; luminescent dots on the printed minute track; luminescent bâton hands.
Indications: 24 hours second time zone at 3, hour counter at 6, small second at 9, center minute (red arrow-shaped hand) and second counters, tachymeter scale on the beveled ring.
Bracelet: Chablis steel; recessed fold-over clasp.
Price: 2'850 CHF.
Also available: leather strap 2'300 CHF; with blue dial and white counters; with smooth bezel.

CHEFTAIN — REF. 41014/CA

Movement: mechanical, automatic winding. **Functions:** hour, minute, center second, date. **Case:** stainless steel, three-piece case (Ø 37 mm, thickness 8.7 mm); curved crystal; screw-down octagonal crown; snap-on case back, polished with knurled edge. Water-resistant to 5 atm. **Dial:** black; luminescent bâton markers and Arabic numerals; printed minute track; luminescent white painted bâton hands. **Indications:** date between 4 and 5. **Bracelet:** Chablis steel; recessed fold-over clasp.
Price: 1'620 CHF.
Also available: with strap 1'200 CHF; steel/yellow gold, 5 atm., leather strap 1'650 CHF, Chablis bracelet 2'750 CHF; yellow gold, 3 atm., leather strap 3'650 CHF, Chablis bracelet 8'200 CHF. All with black dial, luminescent Arabic numerals, date between 4 and 5 or white or blue, applied markers and date at 3.

OLDFLYER VITRE — REF. 30056/OR45

Movement: precision chronograph, antique-fashioned, mechanical, manual winding (Valjoux caliber 7733 base). Decorated with circular graining and Vagues de Genève pattern.
Functions: hour, minute, small second, chronograph with 2 counters.
Case: 18 kt pink gold, three-piece case (Ø 36 mm, thickness 12 mm), numbered; antireflective curved sapphire crystal; pink gold rectangular pushers; pink gold crown; snap-on case back displaying the movement through a sapphire crystal (firm brand, model name and progressive number engraved on gold).
Dial: silvered; zones with concentric-circles pattern; applied rosé Arabic numerals; luminescent rosé bâton hands.
Indications: minute counter at 3, small second at 9, center second counter, minute track with divisions for 1/5 of a second and luminescent dots, tachymeter scale.
Bracelet: Charme pink gold; fold-over clasp.
Price: 12'515 CHF.
Limited edition of 449 numbered pieces to celebrate the 111th anniversary of the foundation of the House.
Also available: leather strap 6'900 CHF; applied triangular markers; in the same versions with closed bottom, non limited series, same prices.

136

EBERHARD & CO.

REPLICA GENTS — REF. 30022/OR.C

Movement: mechanical, manual winding (Valjoux caliber 7761 base). Officially certified "chronometer" (C.O.S.C.).
Functions: hour, minute, small second, full calendar (date, day, month), 24-hour indication, chronograph with 3 counters.
Case: 18 kt yellow gold, three-piece case (Ø 38 mm, thickness 14.2 mm); bombé hexalite glass; Onion crown and gold olive pushers; snap-on case back with engraving of the House of La Chaux-de-Fonds; double hinged case back and decorated with inside circular graining pattern containing a scroll for engravings.
Dial: white enameled; applied Roman numerals; printed minute track; bâton hands.
Indications: hour counter at 6, small second and 24-hour indication at 9, day, month and minute counter at 12, center date (half-moon-shaped hand) and second counter, minute track with divisions for 1/5 of a second.
Strap: crocodile leather; gold-plated clasp.
Price: 8'800 CHF.
Also available: silver 925; vérmeil (silver 925 yellow-gold-plated 20 micron), 3'620 CHF; with moon phases.

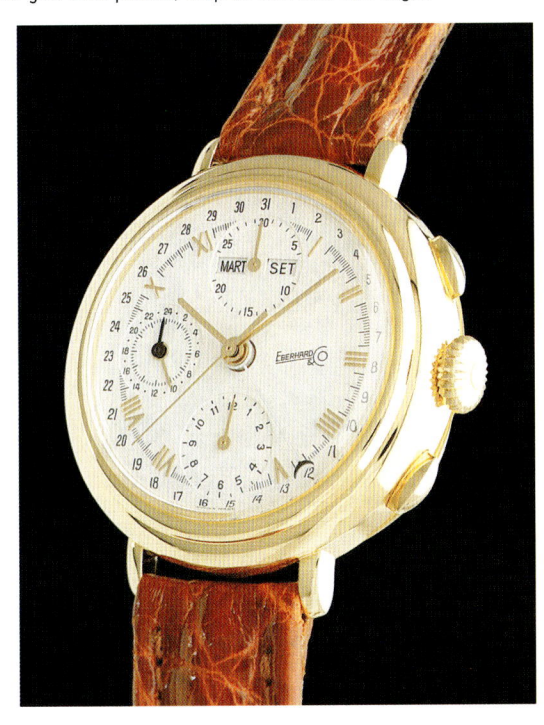

REPLICA LADY — REF. 30053/OR

Movement: mechanical, manual winding (Lemania caliber 1872 base).
Functions: hour, minute, small second, chronograph with 2 counters.
Case: 18 kt yellow gold, two-piece polished case (Ø 33 mm, thickness 10.3 mm); bombé hexalite glass; stepped bezel; case side with engraved brand; Louis XVth-style crown and olive pushers, yellow gold; snap-on back.
Dial: white enameled; applied Roman numerals; gilded bâton hands.
Indications: minute counter at 3, small second at 9, center second counter, minute track with divisions for 1/5 of a second, tachymeter scale.
Strap: crocodile leather; gold-plated clasp.
Price: 5'780 CHF.
Also available: silver 925, sold out; in vermeil (silver 925 yellow-gold-plated 20 micron), 3'010 CHF.

CHAMPION DIASCOPE — REF. 30051/OR40

Movement: mechanical, automatic winding (Lemania caliber 5195 base), antishock, anti-G (resisting strong accelerations). **Functions:** hour, minute, small second, second time zone, 24-hour indication, chronograph with 3 counters.
Case: 18 kt yellow gold, three-piece case (Ø 36 mm, thickness 14.25 mm) polished and brushed finish; bombé hexalite glass; bezel with engraved tachymeter scale and riders at quarters; yellow gold screw-down crown and yellow gold pushers; case back attached by 6 screws. Water-resistant to 3 atm.
Dial: silvered; zones with concentric-circle pattern; applied bâton markers; printed minute track; bâton hands.
Indications: second time zone 24-hour night & day indication at 3, hour counter at 6, small second at 9, center minute (plane-shaped hand) and second counters, minute track with divisions for 1/5 of a second.
Bracelet: Charme in yellow gold; polished and brushed finish; recessed fold-over clasp.
Price: 15'860 CHF.
Also available: Chance bracelet, same price; leather strap 9'810 CHF; blue or bordeaux dial, white counters. Champion model Ref. 30232, with Marignan crown, yellow gold, chronometer, blue, white or bordeaux dial and gilded counters, leather strap 8'800 CHF, Chance or Charme bracelet 14'850 CHF.

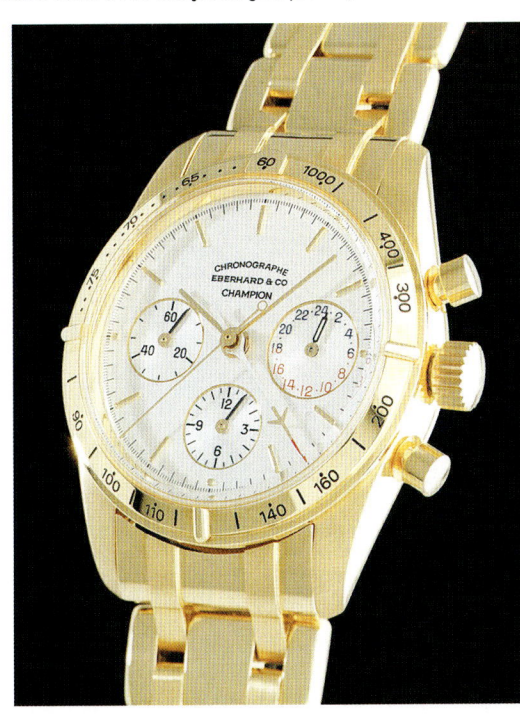

AQUADATE LADY — REF. 40026/OR18

Movement: mechanical, automatic winding. **Functions:** hour, minute, center second, date. **Case:** 18 kt yellow gold, two-piece brushed case (Ø 28 mm, thickness 8.8 mm); flat sapphire crystal with magnifying lens on date; polished bezel with engravings and raised markers; small spheres on the yellow gold "Marignan" type screw-down crown; case back attached by 6 screws. Water-resistant to 5 atm.
Dial: white; applied bâton markers; luminescent dots on the printed minute track; luminescent bâton hands.
Indications: date at 3.
Bracelet: Chance gold; fold-over clasp.
Price: 9'790 CHF.
Also available: with Charme bracelet 9'340, leather strap 4'500. With quartz movement: steel, Water-resistant to 10 atm., Chance or Charme bracelet 2'000, steel/gold, Water-resistant to 10 atm., Charme bracelet 4'250, Chance 3'800; yellow gold, water-resistant to 5 atm., leather strap 3'950, Charme bracelet 8'790, Chance 9'235; with brilliants on the dial and for the gold version also on the bezel. All the versions with quartz movement are available with white dial, applied bâton markers or black printed Roman numerals, or blue or slate-grey dial with applied bâton markers; the version with automatic movement only with white dial and applied bâton markers.

137

EBERHARD & CO.

TRAVERSETOLO — REF. 20019/VZOR

Movement: mechanical, manual winding (Unitas caliber 6498 base).
Functions: hour, minute, small second.
Case: 18 kt yellow gold, three-piece case (Ø 43 mm, thickness 10.7 mm); curved sapphire crystal; yellow gold crown; case back attached by 8 screws, stamped with embossed brand and model name. Water-resistant to 5 atm.
Dial: glossy white; printed Arabic numerals; luminescent dots on the printed minute track; luminescent black painted leaf style hands.
Indications: small second at 6.
Strap: leather; gold-plated clasp.
Price: 6'200 CHF.
Also available: stainless steel, with mineral glass: closed bottom, leather strap 1'400 CHF, Chaland bracelet 1'950 CHF; transparent case back, leather strap 1'660 CHF, bracelet 2'210 CHF. With hand winding movement and autonomy of 8 days, closed bottom and sapphire crystal, steel, leather strap 2.450, bracelet 3.050. Each version is available with matte black dial and luminescent Arabic numerals or white with screen-printed black Arabic numerals.

TRAVERSETOLO VITRE — REF. 21020/CA

Presented at the occasion of the International Watchmaking Show in Basel in 1996, Traversetolo includes the whole philosophy of the Swiss House: keeping faith to tradition and offering one's esteemers a mechanical watch whose movement keeps value in time. In this case it is a mechanical manual winding Unitas caliber, created in the Fifties for pocket watches and improved in the subsequent years. The version adopted for Traversetolo Vitré with mineral glass case back shows a valuable arrangement, with pillar-plate and bridges decorated with Perlé and 1 Côte pattern, intermediate winding wheel and trundle with the name Traversetolo engraved and blued on a snailing pattern finish, blued screws and gilded writings.
Price: 2'210 CHF.

8 JOURS — REF. 21017/VZCA

Movement: mechanical, manual winding, Eberhard caliber 896-8J, autonomy of 8 days and patented power reserve indicator.
Functions: hour, minute, small second, power reserve.
Case: stainless steel, three-piece polished case (Ø 39.7 mm, thickness 12 mm); curved sapphire crystal; bezel bombé; waterproof crown; case back attached by 6 screws. Water-resistant to 3 atm.
Dial: silvered; printed Roman numerals and minute track; black leaf style hands.
Indications: small second at 6, power reserve in days between 9 and 10.
Bracelet: Charade steel; fold-over clasp.
Price: 3'150 CHF.
Also available: leather strap 2'600 CHF; in yellow gold, leather strap (in the photograph). All with blue dial, Roman or Arabic numerals; silvered, Roman numerals or white, Arabic numerals. On the grounds of the concept that, if the mainspring is sufficiently strong or long, a watch can work for a longer time without needing winding, Eberhard & Co. in 1997 presented a highly technology intensive watch, featuring an autonomy of 8 days. This means that, unlike normal mechanical models.

8 JOURS — REF. 20017/VZOR

With hand or automatic winding, this watch may be wound only once a week and, even if one forgets to do so, it is still able to work. The watches with 8 days winding were widespread at the time of pocket watches, while wristwatches were - and still are - very rare: in fact, because of their small size they present many technical difficulties to overcome. To automatically extending their winding-keeping it is not sufficient to adopt a stronger spring because many other factors play a rôle, such as friction and the constant tension of the spring itself.
The great innovation introduced by the House consists of using two coupled superimposed springs housed in two coupled barrels (in the upper one the longer spring, in the lower one the second spring). During the winding operation, the upper spring winds up, pulling the second spring which is thus wound up in turn. In this way the duration of the mechanical energy accumulated is extended without causing pressure increases on pivots and gearing teeth.
Price: 5'000 CHF.

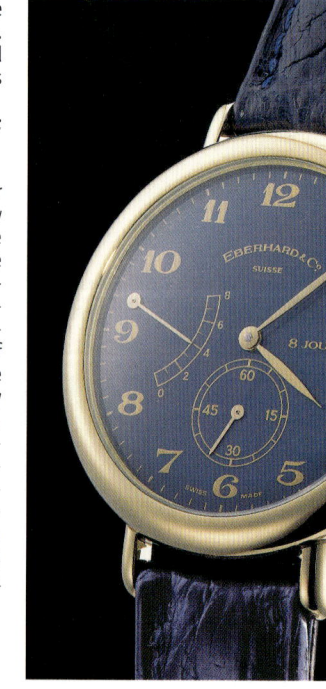

138

EBERHARD & CO.

AQUA 8 REF. 21018/CA3

Movement: mechanical, manual winding, Eberhard caliber 896-8J, autonomy of 8 days and patented power reserve indicator.
Functions: hour, minute, small second, power reserve.
Case: stainless steel, three-piece case (Ø 39 mm, thickness 10 mm) polished and brushed finish; flat sapphire crystal; bezel with engravings and raised markers; waterproof crown; case back attached by 6 screws. Water-resistant to 3 atm.
Dial: blue; applied silvered bâton markers; luminescent dots on the printed minute track; luminescent silvered bâton hands.
Indications: small second at 6, power reserve in days between 9 and 10.
Bracelet: Chaland stainless steel, with brushed inside link and polished outside links; recessed fold-over clasp.
Price: 3,000 CHF.
Also available: leather strap 2'450 CHF; white dial.

AQUADATE ECOPOWER REF. 41707/CA5

Movement: with electric drive controlled by a quartz crystal with an energy accumulation system by means of a traditional oscillating mass (ETA cal. 205.911 base); 11''' 1/2, 17 jewels; 100 days power reserve. **Functions:** hour, minute, center second, date. **Case:** stainless steel, 2-piece brushed case (Ø 35, thick. 9.3); flat sapphire crystal with magnifying lens on date; polished bezel with engravings and raised markers; small yellow gold spheres on the "Marignan" type screw-down crown; case back attached by 6 screws. Water-resistant to 10 atm. **Dial:** white; applied bâton markers; lumin. dots; lumin. bâton hands. **Indic.:** date at 3. **Brac.:** Charme stainless steel, polished and brushed flat links; fold-over clasp. **Price:** 2'360 CHF. **Also av.:** Chance brac. 2'360; blue dial; Ø 39 stainless steel, 10 atm., leather strap 1'700, Charme brac. 2'400. Automatic: Ø 35, steel, white dial, applied markers or painted Roman numerals, blue or slate-grey, applied markers, 10 atm., Chance or Charme brac. 2'360; steel/gold and white dial, applied markers or painted Roman numerals blue or slate-grey, applied markers, 10 atm., Chance brac. 4'500, Charme (steel w/gold-capped links) 4'300; gold, white or blue dial, applied markers, chronometer, 5 atm., leather strap 5'860, Chance or Charme brac. 11'690; Ø 39, steel, white or blue dial, applied markers, leather strap 1'700, Charme brac. 2'400.

AIGLON REF. 41016/CA

Movement: mechanical, automatic winding (ETA caliber 2892/2 base).
Functions: hour, minute, center second, date.
Case: stainless steel, three-piece case; polished and brushed finish (Ø 37.5 mm, thickness 9.2 mm); flat sapphire crystal; polished bezel; screw-down crown, with embossed logo; polished and engraved snap-on back. Water-resistant to 5 atm.
Dial: anthracite; applied bâton markers; luminescent dots on the printed minute track; luminescent nickel-plated bâton hands.
Indications: date at 3.
Bracelet: Chablis steel; recessed fold-over clasp.
Price: 1'420 CHF.
Also available: leather strap 1'000 CHF; silvered dial, glossy red, yellow or blue enameled with applied bâton markers, luminescent nickel-plated bâton hands and date at 3; silvered or anthracite sun-pattern decorated with luminescent Arabic numerals, luminescent nickel-plated bâton hands and date at 3; blue, sun-pattern decorated or white with 4 Roman numerals, luminescent nickel-plated leaf style hands and date at 6.

AIGLON REF. 41016/CP

The Aiglon collection, presented at the Basel 1999 Show, though maintaining its technical and aesthetic features unchanged, which always distinguish Eberhard's realizations, proposes a new "youthful" interpretation. Therefore, the display of simple functions has been carried to extremes, especially the hour reading feature, without adding any merely decorative element. Thus an absolutely essential dial, really personalized only inasmuch as the choice of markers and case back color are concerned, naturally contrasts an extremely sober and linear case with its polished finish and the only personalizing element consisting of the "E" on the external crown part. All this makes up an undoubtedly beautiful watch, showing an extremely positive quality/price ratio and at the same time agreeably neutral, once it is put on one's wrist. This detail is certainly welcome by the feminine public, which always prefers own individuality rather than the personality of objects.
Price: 1'000 CHF.

EBERHARD & CO.

AVIOMATIC 315 — REF. 40021/OR

Movement: mechanical, automatic winding (ETA caliber 2892/2 base). Officially certified "chronometer" (C.O.S.C.).
Functions: hour, minute, center second, date.
Case: 18 kt pink gold, three-piece case; polished and brushed finish (Ø 31.5 mm, thickness 8.7 mm); antireflective curved sapphire crystal; polished stepped bezel; screw-down crown; case back attached by 6 screws, with engraved chronometer certificate number. Water-resistant to 3 atm. 
Dial: white; applied Arabic numerals and luminescent applied triangular markers; luminescent dots on the printed minute track; luminescent Dauphine hands.
Indications: date at 3.
Strap: crocodile leather; pink-gold-plated clasp.
Price: 4'860 CHF.
Also available: with Charme bracelet 9'920 CHF; steel, leather strap lire 1'190 CHF. Each version is available with rosé, white or blue dial. Aviolady in 18K gold, chronometer C.O.S.C., leather strap 4'860 CHF. In the small size with quartz movement (Aviolady), pink gold and white or rosé dial, leather strap 3'050 CHF, with Charme bracelet 7'395 CHF.

AUTOMATIC GENTS — REF. 40028/OR

Movement: mechanical, automatic winding (ETA caliber 2892/2 base).
Functions: hour, minute, center second, date.
Case: 18 kt yellow gold, three-piece case (Ø 35 mm, thickness 7.5 mm); flat crystal; snap-on back.
Dial: silvered, engine turned (Guilloché) with "grain d'orge" pattern; printed Roman numerals and minute track; Breguet black enameled hands. 
Indications: date at 3.
Strap: hand-trimmed crocodile leather; gold-plated clasp.
Price: 2'750 CHF.
Also available: white dial, Arabic numerals applied at 3, 9, 12 and date at 6.

AUTOMATIC GENTS — REF. 40024/OR

Movement: mechanical, automatic winding (ETA caliber 2892/2 base).
Functions: hour, minute, center second, date.
Case: 18 kt yellow gold, three-piece case (Ø 34 mm, thickness 7 mm); flat sapphire crystal; small spheres on the yellow gold "Marignan" type screw-down crown; case back attached by 4 screws. Water-resistant to 3 atm.
Dial: silvered; applied bâton markers; printed minute track; bâton hands. 
Indications: date at 3.
Strap: hand-trimmed crocodile leather; gold-plated clasp.
Price: 3'950 CHF.
Also available: in men's size with hand winding movement, Ref. 20011, 3'500 CHF; in lady's size with quartz movement: Ref. 60047, 2'570 CHF; Ref. 60048, 2'750 CHF. Each version is available with blue or silvered dial.

NAVILE — REF. 40030/OR

Movement: mechanical, automatic winding (ETA caliber 2892/2 base).
Functions: hour, minute, center second, date.
Case: 18 kt yellow gold, two-piece square case (height 31.2 mm, width 30.4 mm, thickness 7.3 mm); flat sapphire crystal; small spheres on the yellow gold "Marignan" type screw-down crown; case back attached by 4 gold screws, with engravings. Water-resistant to 3 atm. 
Dial: opaline white, silvered minute square; applied markers, bâton markers and Roman numerals at 12, 6, 9; printed minute track; bâton hands.
Indications: date at 3.
Strap: hand-trimmed crocodile leather; gold-plated clasp.
Price: 3'850 CHF. Unique version.

EBERHARD & CO.

PALAZZO — REF. 20013/OR

Movement: mechanical, manual winding (Peseux caliber 7001 base), gilt finish, blue steel screws.
Functions: hour, minute, small second.
Case: 18 kt pink gold, two-piece case (Ø 35 mm, thickness 7 mm); flat sapphire crystal; snap-on case back, bombé, with engraving of the Eberhard House.
Dial: silvered; zone with concentric-circles pattern; applied pink bâton markers; printed minute track; pink bâton hands.
Indications: small second a hours 6.
Strap: crocodile leather; pink-gold-plated clasp.
Price: 3'210 CHF. Unique version.

VENISE — REF. 20010/OR

Movement: mechanical, manual winding (Peseux caliber 7001 base), gold finish, blue steel screws.
Functions: hour, minute, small second.
Case: 18 kt yellow gold, two-piece case, square curved shape (height 27 mm, width 27 mm, thickness 6.7 mm); curved crystal; small spheres on the yellow gold screw-down "Marignan" type crown; snap-on back.
Dial: white enamel; applied Arabic numerals; printed minute track; bâton hands.
Indications: small second at 6.
Strap: crocodile leather; central attachment with jointed handle-type lugs; gold-plated clasp.
Price: 3'300 CHF. Unique version.

HYPERBOLE — REF. 41011/1CA2

Movement: mechanical, automatic winding (ETA caliber 2000 base).
Functions: hour, minute, center second.
Case: stainless steel, two-piece tonneau-curved case (height 34 mm, width 27.1 mm, thickness 7.5 mm); antireflective curved sapphire crystal; small white gold spheres on the "Marignan" type crown; case back attached by 7 screws. Water-resistant to 3 atm.
Dial: white, curved; printed Roman numerals and minute track; bâton hands black enameled.
Bracelet: Charade steel; double fold-over safety clasp.
Price: 3'500 CHF.
Also available: leather strap 2'700 CHF; white dial with Roman numerals and applied markers; in yellow gold, white dial, applied gilded markers, leather strap 6'150 CHF, with bracelet 11'450 CHF.

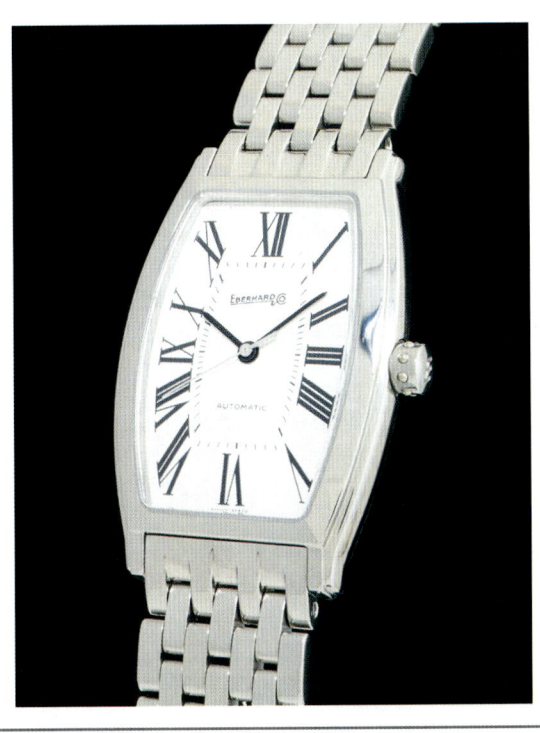

NEW YORK — REF. 20014/OR

Movement: mechanical, manual winding (Peseux caliber 7001 base), gold finish, blue steel screws.
Functions: hour, minute.
Case: 18 kt pink gold, two-piece rectangular case (only case size 32x25 mm, thickness 6.3 mm); curved crystal; case back attached by 4 screws.
Dial: white enamel, curved; applied rosé Arabic numerals; bâton hands rosé.
Strap: crocodile leather; pink-gold-plated clasp.
Price: 3'670 CHF. Unique version.

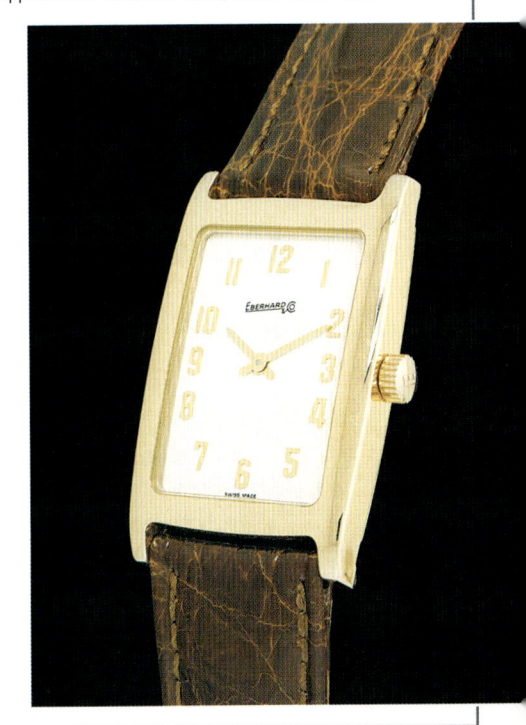

European Company Watch

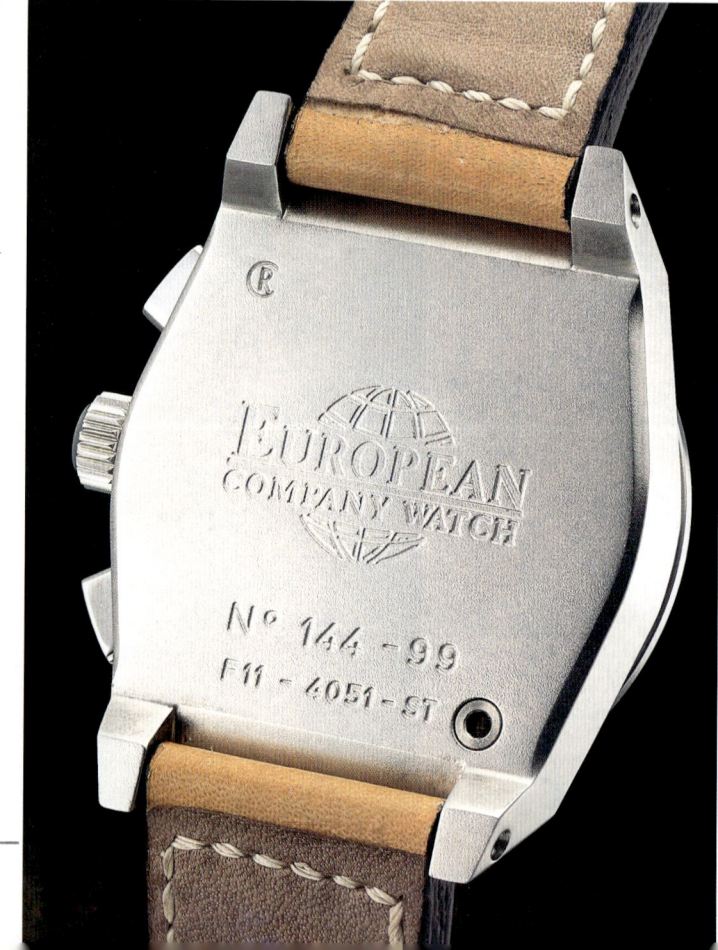

There are a great many "beautiful" watches produced today; very few, however, have strong enough a personality to impress effectively those who wear them. European Company Watch are among these. This is thanks to the steel case, with its flat back, the large lugs turned downwards, and the determined profile marked by the 8 edges that define its form. It is freely inspired by the armored vehicles designed by Panhard and that accompanied the French Foreign Legion on its campaigns, more mythical than heroic, choosing a "colonial" taste that is pleasantly suggested in the choice of dials and straps. Such exotic evocations could only belong to the cultural "baggage" of one of the most well known personalities of the Italian watch world: Roberto Carlotti. His are the thirty successful years as a distributor of luxurious fine watches and his as well is the dream of high quality watchmaking that is finally "made in Italy" and that is becoming reality with the ECW. The distinctive element of this new watch is, as we have said, its important case made of solid steel, (40x51 mm, 13 mm high), hand turned and polished. It is entirely built and assembled in Milan in a craftsmen's workshop. Here they follow the old time methods in which the steel is shaped in 15 different steps, which require alternating firings at 1000° C with coining in a 120 ton press. The final result, that calls for 5 working hours (a great many when compared to the times and automatic work procedures that are usual in modern fine watchmaking), is a monobloc perfectly polished piece with sharp edges that haven't a single sign of rounding, ready for subsequent turning and milling. Design and marketing for ECW are also done in Milan, while Switzerland provides only the mechanical movements. Two models have been presented: the chronograph Panhard F11 with a Dubois Dépraz caliber 2030 movement, and the hour and minute Panhard M8 caliber 2824A2. Some of their construction characteristics are interesting: the rectangular pushers are fixed with screwed collars; the screw-down crown is water-resistant to 200 m; the bezel has a new opening system using a titanium screw pivoted on the back side that raises it, making it easier to remove; the movement has rhodium plated finish with personalized rotor; the matte dial is technological with big luminous markers and the background is absolute black, blue, olive drab or sand-colored; the strap is of highest quality natural leather with hand-made steel buckle. Both the F11 and M8 are produced in two versions: the first has a highly polished steel case, the second with a sand-blast finish will be soon available only in a titanium case. This version with a military type style non-reflecting case is a necessary choice, considering that the watch was inspired by the armored vehicle designed by Panhard for the Foreign Legion. But his name mostly brings common people back to the dawn of the automobile racing. The first race to be held, the Paris-Rouen, in 1894, was won by a Panhard 4 HP. Among his pilots were, in different moments, Farman and Morane-Saulnier (who then became aircraft builders), Roland Garros (the first fighter pilot ace) and a fellow named Henry Renault, who will then go on to set up his "Atelier Automobilistique".

The chronograph Panhard F11, with the polished steel case, costs 3,073 Euro, the automatic M8, costs 2,040 Euro.

Franck Muller

The Master of Complications has recently launched a chronograph version of his well-known Master Banker watch, so-called because it displays the time in three time zones, allowing globe-trotting financiers to keep track of the time at three different stock markets. In order to fit the chronograph into the already super-complex, self-winding movement, Muller had to redesign the base plate to accommodate the chronograph gear wheels and the patented locking system. That system allows the chronograph to run without interfering with the rest of the mechanism. The watch has a small seconds hand at 9 o'clock. The additional time zones are shown on subdials at 6 and 12 o'clock. The 12 o'clock subdial also serves as a 30-minute counter for the chronograph. Muller has also expanded his Megapole collection with a new round style called Transamerica, a sporty-looking watch with big, luminous numerals. The watch is self-winding and equipped with a chronograph. Like other watches in the Megapole collection, the Transamerica shows the time in any of 14 international cities. The wearer sets the other-time-zone indicator by turning the dial, causing the city's name to appear in a window. The current hour in that city then appears in an aperture next to the window.

The Transamerica is available in a limited edition of 250 pieces in steel, 25 in white gold and 25 in platinum.

In celebration of the new millennium Muller is offering his 2000 Limited Edition Cintrée Curvex. Its shape harks back to the original Curvex of 1987, which was longer than the Curvex models of

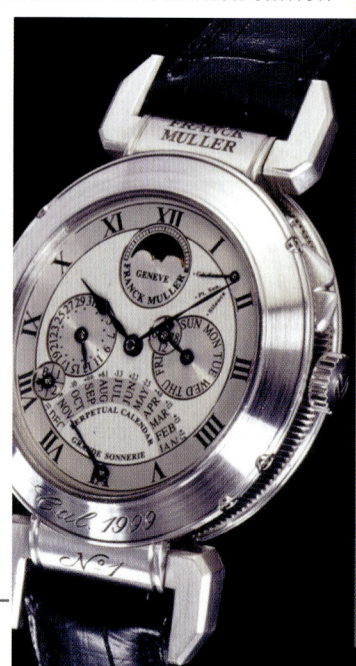

The History

Among the various specializations in the industry of watches on the whole, Franck Muller, even as a very young boy, certainly chose the most complicated. For years now he himself has created Complications that are creative masterpieces. His first work, "Wrist model Tourbillon, jumping hours and minutes and index-adjustment type dial" has generated, ever since 1986, a series of highly appreciated models. Muller put that watch together when he was barely 28 years old and it meant for him a leap in status. No longer a prodigy of the watch-building craft, but rather a protagonist of advanced research.

1958 - The year Franck Muller was born. After he finished school, his parents sent him to study watchmaking. He became impassioned, developed a love for the antique tools and instruments of watchmaking, taking apart and putting back together everything he can find, seeking out the secrets that made the Masters of the past so great. At the Ecole d'Horlogerie in Geneva he is among the best and designs a Rolex Quantième Perpétuel that astounds his teachers. He becomes truly famous as a restorer of antique clocks: he has been called upon from around the world and collaborates with the biggest auction houses.

1983/91 - Muller becomes an expert at the top of watchmaking creation: the Tourbillon. After three years of research and study, eighteen months of work at the bench, he wins world attention with a Jumping Hours Tourbillon. In 1987 the Tourbillon Minute Repeater comes to be; in 1989 a reversed Tourbillon with Repeater and Perpetual Calendar suggests that he present one or two super-complications each year. Thus in 1990 we have a Split-Seconds Tourbillon Chronograph, then a Minute, Hours of the World Repeater; in 1991 a single button, double face, Hours of the World Chronograph and a Tourbillon Split-Seconds Perpetual Calendar Chronograph.

1992 - A golden year for Muller: his unique piece: Grande and Petite Sonnerie, Minute Repeater, Perpetual Calendar with Retrograde Month, Moon Phases and 24 Hours, is the most complex ever made.

Muller decides to make his name into a real trademark. In Genthod, on the hill overlooking Lake Lemond, in the Geneva canton, and in a little workshop full of old fashioned time pieces, he is no longer "only" a designer, but a business man.

End of the '90's - Muller's curriculum is full of events, the world firsts, the unique pieces go along with patents such as the double-faced chronograph, the sonnerie hands for the minute repeaters, the indoor temperature indication. The collections are done on essential lines: the innovative form of the Cintrée Curvex or the more classic form of the Rondes move from discreet elegance to more aggressive sporting models with the assurance of one who knows exactly what he is about. Boutiques have been opened in Tokyo, Osaka and Geneva; Franck Muller Co. is a growing reality. New spaces are needed. The Master has taken over a splendid, early 1900's manor house and has moved the offices there. The old fashioned workbenches are now flanked by computers, his dream has come true. In very few years a new star has joined the constellation of the Great Names.

1997 - The two counter, round, manual Chronograph is spectacular, literally encrusted with precious stones. The three, jewelled Cintrée Curvex create a grand effect. The pocket Chronograph, "Royal Endurance", wins the enviable position of being the official chronometer of the 24 Hours of Le Mans. It is also available in a version with Minute Repeater and Perpetual Calendar. The Endurance has also inspired the Split-second wrist model and the manual Three Counter. The line of the new Cintrée Curvex Havana is highly unusual.

1998 - Franck Muller presents the latest collections at his house, in the beautiful castle of Genthod, thus leaving the SIHH. The innovations, as usual, are remarkable, particularly the Conquistador. Starting from the classic Cintrée Curvex, where the novelty is in the single-button chronograph and a Séconde Rétrograde, the new collection suggests more defined volumes and a degree of aggressiveness in the sporting design of the dials. Besides the bezel, the sapphire crystal is also more curved, giving a good indication of the new steps Franck Muller will be taking. The calibre '98 (there is a women's model for this same version) has a diamond cascade on the case and diamonds pavé on the dial of the "Mystérieuse", where a rotating disc, with a single large sapphire takes the place of the hands. The smallest tourbillon movement in the world is another of his exploits, breaking the record that had been set in 1945 by Robert Charrue. It is only 8,5''' in diameter, and is placed in an unusual jewel: a diamond encrusted egg.

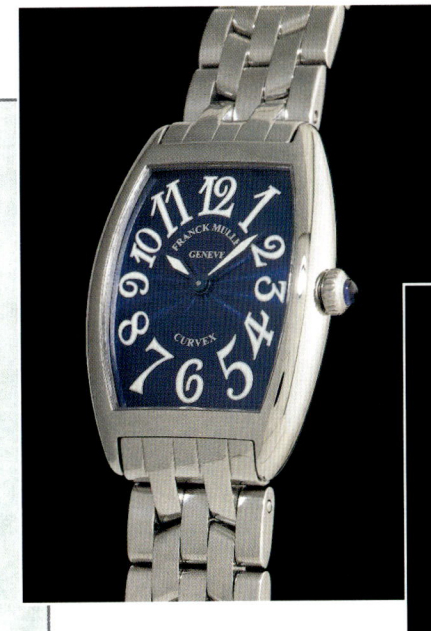

today. The watch has one entirely new feature: a large date window at 12 o'clock. Muller made 1,000 pieces of the watch in steel, 200 each in yellow, white, rose and red gold and 200 in platinum. For gamblers, Muller has launched his whimsical Las Vegas watch, which serves as a mini-roulette wheel. Using a slide on the winding button, the wearer starts and stops a center wheel, which spins quickly and then comes to rest pointing to a number on a ring on the dial. The watch has an automatic movement and comes in yellow, rose, red or white gold or platinum.

He has also produced an amazingly complicated one-of-a-kind piece: the Calibre 99 Double Mystery. For this watch, Muller has added a minute indicator to the Mystery watch he introduced in 1997. (The original Mystery showed only the hours.) The watch is reversible. On one side is the Double Mystery dial, composed of two disks rotating at different speeds. When you turn the watch over you see a perpetual calendar, moonphase indicator and 24-hour counter, and have access to a grande sonnerie, petite sonnerie and minute repeater.

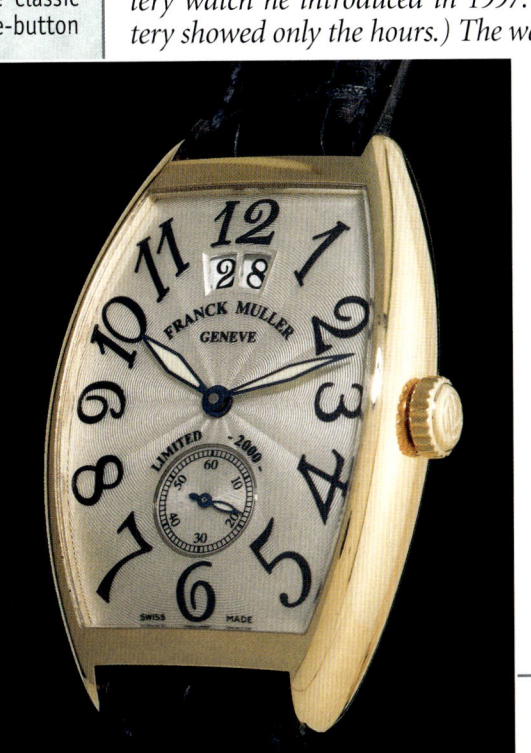

FRANCK MULLER

TRANSAMERICA CHRONO MASTER BANKER

Movement: mechanical, automatic winding, Franck Muller caliber 7000CC MB, autonomy of 42 hours, rotor with platinum segment, modified for the reading of two additional time zones. Beveled, Côtes de Genève and circular graining finished.
Functions: hour, minute, small second, three time zones, chronograph with 2 counters.
Case: stainless steel, three-piece case (Ø 40 mm, thickness 15.2 mm) polished and brushed finish; curved sapphire crystal; screw-down crown for the three time zones correction; screw pushers; screwed-on case back. Water-resistant to 5 atm. 
Dial: white; black peripheral ring and counters; luminescent Arabic numerals; luminescent blued stainless steel lozenge hands.
Indications: date at 3, 2nd and 3rd time zone, respectively at 12 and 6, with double hand, small second at 9, minute counter at 12 (with red hand), center second counter, minute track with divisions for 1/4 second.
Strap: crocodile leather, hand stitched; stainless steel clasp.
Price: 19'565 CHF.
Also available: white gold 27'090 CHF; platinum 37'840 CHF.

TRANSAMERICA MEGAPOLE

Movement: mechanical, automatic winding, Franck Muller caliber 7000, modified for the jumping-hour reading of 14 time zones, rotor with platinum segment. Beveled, Côtes de Genève and circular graining finished.
Functions: hour, minute, small second, second time zone with reference towns, chronograph with 3 counters.
Case: stainless steel, three-piece case (Ø 40 mm, thickness 15 mm) polished and brushed finish; curved sapphire crystal; screw-down crown for the two time zones correction; screw pushers; screwed-on case back. Water-resistant to 5 atm. 
Dial: black; white peripheral ring and counters; luminescent Arabic numerals; luminescent blued stainless steel lozenge hands.
Indications: second time zone (jumping-hour) and 14 reference towns at 3, hour counter at 6, small second at 9, minute counter at 12, center second counter, minute track with divisions for 1/4 of a second.
Strap: crocodile leather, hand stitched; stainless steel clasp.
Price: 15'910 CHF.
Also available: white gold 24'510 CHF; platinum 35'260 CHF.

TRANSAMERICA "GRAND GUICHET"

Movement: mechanical, automatic winding, Franck Muller (Eta base + Jaquet module), modified for the large date display at 12, autonomy of 47 hours, rotor with platinum segment. Beveled, Côtes de Genève and circular graining finished.
Functions: hour, minute, small second, date.
Case: stainless steel, three-piece case (Ø 40 mm, thickness 14.2 mm) polished and brushed finish; curved sapphire crystal; screw-down crown; screwed-on case back. Water-resistant to 5 atm. 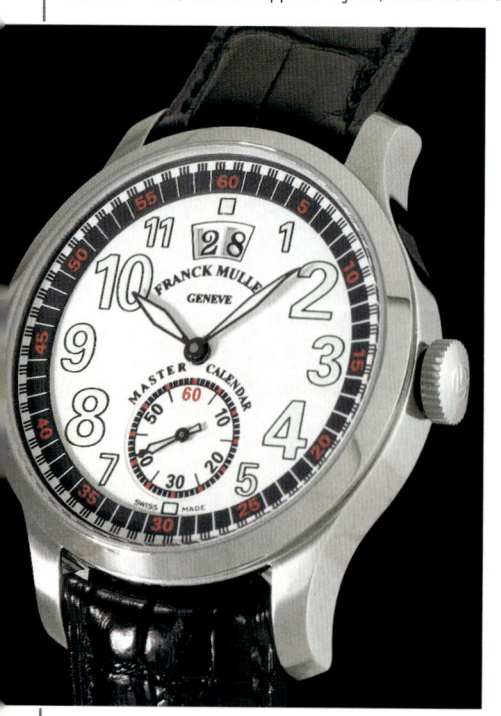
Dial: white; black peripheral ring; luminescent Arabic numerals; luminescent blued stainless steel lozenge hands.
Indications: small second at 6, big date at 12.
Strap: crocodile leather, hand stitched; stainless steel clasp.
Price: 10'535 CHF.
Also available: white gold 19,135 CHF; platinum 26'660 CHF.

RATTRAPANTE, PERPETUAL, TOURBILLON, EQUATION   REF. 1790 QPTRE

Movement: mechanical, manual winding, Franck Muller caliber 1790 (Venus 179 base strongly modified + Dubois Dépraz exclusive module), autonomy of 48 hours, tourbillon device, 26 jewels. Beveled, finished with Côtes de Genève and circular graining.
Functions: hour, minute, 24-hour indication, perpetual calendar (date, day, month, year, moon phase); split-second chronograph with 2 counters.
Case: 18 kt yellow gold, three-piece case (Ø 39 mm); curved sapphire crystal; 3 correctors on case side; split-function pusher on the yellow gold crown; snap-on back displaying the movement through a sapphire crystal. Water-resistant to 3 atm. **Dial:** silvered; applied blued stainless steel square faceted markers; blued stainless steel Pomme hands. **Indications:** minute counter and moon phase at 3, day and 24-hour display at 6, retrograde month hand at 9 (with relevant information on the time equation, i.e. the difference in minutes between civil and sidereal time), four year cycle at 11, date at 12, center second and split-second counters; minute track with divisions for 1/5 of a second. 
Strap: crocodile leather, hand stitched; screw connection; gold clasp.
Price: 264'450 CHF. Limited ed. **Also available:** red gold, white gold, pink gold (same price); PT (281'650 CHF); Double Face (on request).

FRANCK MULLER

CHRONOGRAPH, PERPETUAL CALENDAR, EQUATION   REF. 7000 QPE DF

Movement: mechanical, automatic winding, caliber Franck Muller 7000 (QP Dubois Dépraz exclusive module), autonomy of 42 hours, platinum rotor and 26 jewels. 28,800 vibrations per hour (vph), first-quality balance-spring. Beveled, finished with Côtes de Genève and circular graining. **Functions:** hour, minute, 24-hour indication, perpetual calendar (date, day, month, year, moon phase), chronograph with 2 counters.
Case: 18 kt pink gold, three-piece double-face case (Ø 39, thickness 14.5 mm); curved sapphire crystal; 4 correctors on case side; pink gold crown; snap-on case back in sapphire crystal. **Dial:** black; pink gold applied square markers; pink gold Pomme hands. **Indications:** day and 24-hour display at 3, month with retrograde hand at 6 (with relevant information on the time equation, i.e. the difference in minutes between civil and sidereal time), four-year cycle at 8, date at 9, minute counter and moon at 12, center second counter, minute track with divisions for 1/5 of a second. Telemeter, pulsometer and tachymeter scales on the case back. **Strap:** crocodile leather, hand stitched; screw connection; pink gold clasp. **Price:** 72'777 CHF.
Also available: yellow gold, white gold, pink gold (same price); PT 88'365; non Double Face (4 golds 64'930; PT 78'045); silvered dial; Ø 36 mm (on request); closed bottom.

PERPETUAL CAL., MIN. REPEATER, TOURBILLON, EQUATION   REF. RMQPTRE

Movement: mechanical, manual winding, caliber Muller (Lemania 389 base strongly modified + patented QP module), autonomy of 48 h, 38 jewels (Ø 28 mm, thickness 7.5); tourbillon device, 18,000 vibrations per hour (vph), Phillips overcoil balance-spring. Beveled, Côtes de Genève and circular graining finished.
Functions: hour, minute, 24-hour indication, minute repeater, perpetual calendar (data, day, month, year, moon phases).
Case: 18 kt yellow gold, three-piece case (Ø 36 thickness 13.5 mm); curved sapphire crystal; 4 correctors and repeater slide on case side; yellow gold crown; snap-on back displaying the movement through a sapphire crystal.
Dial: in mother-of-pearl and silvered; applied blued star-shaped markers (Roman numeral 12) and blued stainless steel Stuart hands. **Indications:** four year cycle at 2, date at 3, moon and sonnerie end indicator (patented) at 6, day and 24-hour display at 9, month with time equation information and retrograde hand at 12. **Strap:** crocodile leather, hand stitched; screw connection; gold clasp.
Price: 392'375 CHF. Edition limited to 20 pieces. **Also available:** white gold/red gold/pink gold (same price); platinum 408'500 CHF; silvered dial and screen-printed Roman numerals.

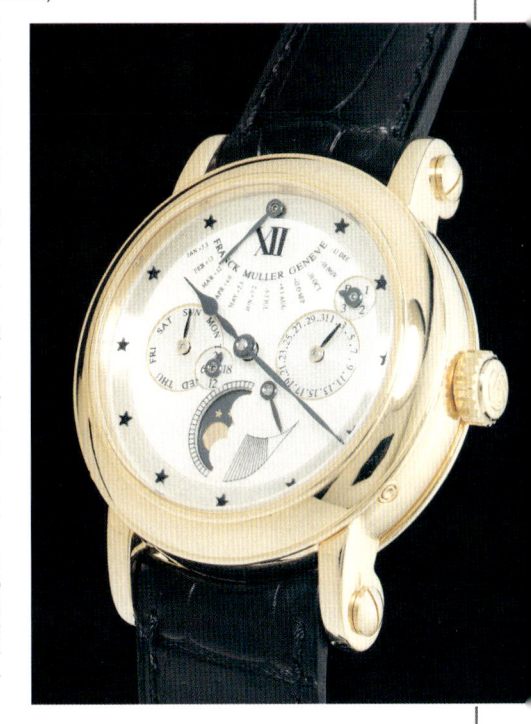

PERPETUAL CALENDAR   REF. 7000 QPA

Movement: mechanical, automatic winding, caliber Franck Muller 7000 (QP Dubois Dépraz exclusive module), autonomy of 42 hours, platinum rotor and 26 jewels. 28,800 vibrations per hour (vph), first-quality balance-spring, regulator system with micrometer adjustment, thermostable, Incabloc shock-resistant system. Beveled, Côtes de Genève and circular graining finished.
Functions: hour, minute, perpetual calendar (date, day, month, year, moon phase).
Case: 18 kt white gold, three-piece case (Ø 39, thickness 11 mm); curved sapphire crystal; 4 correctors on case side; white gold crown; snap-on case back in sapphire crystal.
Dial: white; blued stainless steel applied square markers; blued stainless steel Breguet hands.
Indications: day at 3, month with retrograde hand at 6, four-year cycle at 8, date at 9, moon phase at 12, minute track with divisions for 1/5 of a second. **Strap:** crocodile leather, hand stitched; screw connection; white gold clasp. **Price:** 40'850 CHF.
Also available: yellow, pink or red gold (same price); steel 31'175 CHF.

CHRONO MASTER BANKER   REF. 7000 CCMB

Movement: mechanical, automatic winding, Franck Muller caliber 7000CC MB, autonomy of 42 hours, rotor with platinum segment, modified for the reading of two additional time zones. Beveled, Côtes de Genève and circular graining finished.
Functions: hour, minute, small second, three time zones, chronograph with 2 counters.
Case: 18 kt red gold, three-piece case (Ø 39 mm, thickness 13.2 mm); curved sapphire crystal; red gold crown for the three time zones correction; snap-on back. Water-resistant to 3 atm.
Dial: porcellanized white; luminescent Arabic numerals; luminescent blued stainless steel lozenge hands.
Indications: date at 3, 2nd and 3rd time zone, respectively at 12 and 6, with double hand, small second at 9, minute counter at 12 (with red hand), center second counter, minute track with divisions for 1/5 of a second. **Strap:** crocodile leather, hand stitched; screw connection; red gold clasp. **Price:** 32'035.
Also available: yellow or white gold (same prices); platinum 43'860 CHF; steel 21'285 CHF.

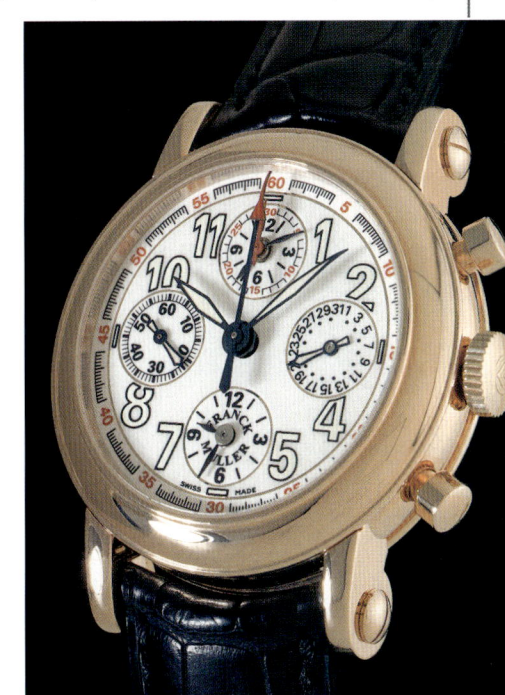

FRANCK MULLER

CHRONOGRAPH MASTER CALENDAR — REF. 7000 CC MC

Movement: mechanical, manual winding, caliber FM 1870 (Lemania base), autonomy of 50 h, 18 jewels (Ø 27, thickness 5.70); 21,600 vibrations per hour (vph), first-quality balance-spring, regulator system with micrometer adjustment, thermostable, Incabloc shock-resistant system, special patented escapement. Beveled, Côtes de Genève and circular graining finished. **Functions:** hour, minute, small second, 24-hour indication, full calendar (date, day, month), chronograph with 2 counters. 
Case: 18 kt pink gold, three-piece case (Ø 39, thickness 12.5 mm); curved sapphire crystal; 2 correctors on case side; pink gold crown; snap-on back displaying the movement through a sapphire crystal. Water-resistant to 3 atm.
Dial: silvered; applied blued star-shaped markers and blued stainless steel leaf style hands. **Indications:** minute counter at 3, 24-hour display at 6, small second at 9, day and month below 12, date with arrow-shaped center hand, center second counter, minute track with divisions for 1/5 of a second. **Strap:** crocodile leather, hand stitched; screw connection; red gold clasp. **Price:** 27'090 CHF.
Also available: yellow, red, white gold (same price); platinum 36'550; steel 20'640 CHF; with Roman numerals; Double Face on request; Ø 36 mm (same prices).

RONDE MASTER BANKER "HAVANA" — REF. 7000 MB HV

Movement: mechanical, automatic winding, caliber Franck Muller 2800, autonomy of 47 hours, platinum rotor and 21 jewels (Ø 26.20, thickness 3.60 mm), modified for the reading of two additional time zones; 28,800 vibrations per hour (vph), and balance-spring with micrometer adjustment, Incabloc shock-resistant system. Beveled, Côtes de Genève and circular graining finished.
Functions: hour, minute, center second, date, three time zones. 
Case: 18 kt pink gold, three-piece case (Ø 39, thickness 11 mm); curved sapphire crystal; crown for the three time zones and date correction, pink gold; case back attached by 4 screws. Water-resistant to 2.5 atm.
Dial: silvered; zones with concentric-circle pattern; luminescent Arabic numerals; printed railway minute track; blued stainless steel Stuart hands. **Indications:** date at 3, 2nd and 3rd time zone, respectively at 12 and 6, with double hand.
Strap: crocodile leather, hand stitched; screw connection; pink gold clasp.
Price: 22'360 CHF.
Also available: yellow gold/pink gold/white gold (same price); steel 12'900 CHF; Ø 39: steel 12'255 CHF, 4 golds 21'715 CHF; Ø 34 (steel 10,8; 4 golds 18,8; platinum 25,4); Ø 34 mm Ref. 2802 or Ø 36 mm Ref. 3802 white dial, black or "Havana" (on request).

CINTREE CURVEX CONQUISTADOR CHRONOGRAPH — REF. 8000 CC

Movement: mechanical, automatic winding, Franck Muller caliber 1185, autonomy of 40 hours, platinum rotor and 37 jewels (Ø 25.6 mm, thickness 5.5 mm); balance with 21,600 vibrations per hour (vph), and balance-spring with micrometer adjustment, thermostable, Kif shock-resistant system. Hand-finished.
Functions: hour, minute, date, chronograph with 3 counters.
Case: stainless steel, three-piece tonneau-curved case (height 40 mm, width 35 mm, thickness 13 mm); curved sapphire crystal; triangular pushers; screw-down crown; case back attached by 4 screws. Water-resistant to 3 atm. 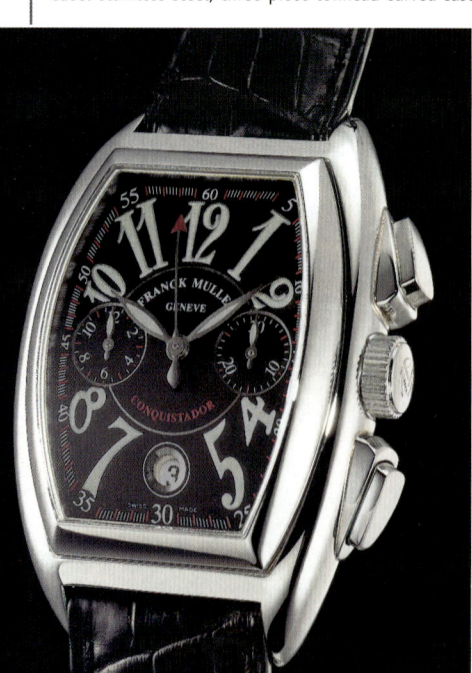
Dial: black, curved; luminescent Arabic numerals; printed minute track; luminescent leaf style hands.
Indications: minute counter at 3, date at 6, hour counter at 9, center second counter, minute track with divisions for 1/5 of a second.
Strap: crocodile leather, hand stitched; stainless steel clasp.
Price: 19'135 CHF.
Edition limited to 1000 pieces.
Also available: with bracelet 21'070 CHF; yellow, pink, red, white gold, leather strap, 250 pieces for each version 30'745 CHF; platinum, leather strap, 250 pieces 41'495 CHF; white dial.

CINTREE CURVEX CONQUISTADOR — REF. 8000 SC

Movement: mechanical, automatic winding, Franck Muller caliber 2800, autonomy of 44 hours, platinum rotor and 21 jewels (Ø 26.20 mm, thickness 3.6 mm); 28,800 vibrations per hour (vph), and balance-spring with off-center screw adjustment, thermostable, Incabloc shock-resistant system. Beveled, Côtes de Genève and circular graining finished.
Functions: hour, minute, center second, date. 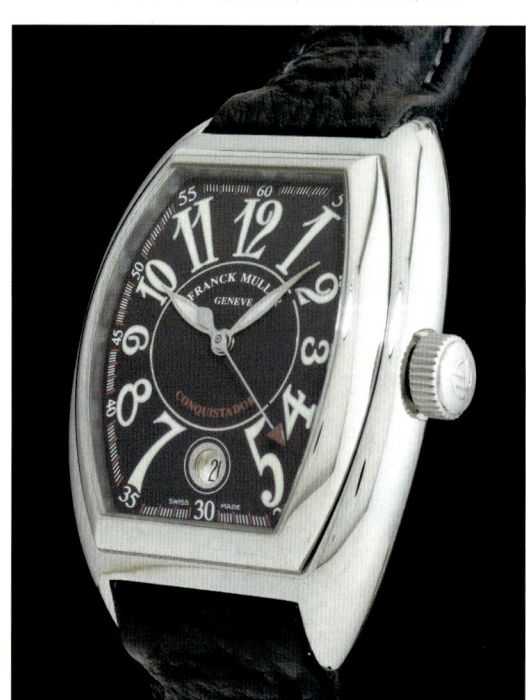
Case: stainless steel, three-piece tonneau-curved case (height 48 mm, width 35 mm, thickness 13 mm); curved sapphire crystal; case back attached by 4 screws. Water-resistant to 3 atm.
Dial: black, curved; luminescent Arabic numerals; printed minute track; luminescent leaf style hands.
Indications: date at 6.
Strap: shark-skin, hand stitched; stainless steel clasp.
Price: 8'815 CHF.
Edition limited to 1000 pieces.
Also available: with bracelet 10'750 CHF; yellow, pink, red, white gold, leather strap, 250 pieces for each version 17'845 CHF; platinum, leather strap, 250 pieces 24'080 CHF; white dial.

FRANCK MULLER

CINTREE CURVEX CHRONO PERPETUAL CALENDAR   REF. 6850 QPE

Movement: mechanical, automatic winding, caliber Franck Muller 7000 (QP Dubois Dépraz exclusive module), autonomy of 42 hours, platinum rotor and 26 jewels. 28,800 vibrations per hour (vph), first quality balance-spring. Beveled, Côtes de Genève and circular graining finished. **Functions:** hour, minute, 24-hour indication, perpetual calendar (date, day, month, year, moon phase), chronograph with one counter.
Case: 18 kt yellow gold, two-piece case, anatomically tonneau-curved (height 45 mm, width 34, thickness 13 mm); curved sapphire crystal; 4 correctors on case side; yellow gold crown and yellow gold oval pushers; case back attached by 4 screws. Water-resistant to 2.5 atm.
Dial: silvered (two tones), engine turned (guilloché) with sun pattern in the central part and on the external ring, curved; printed Arabic numerals; Stuart gold hands, blued.
Indications: day and 24-hour display at 3, month with retrograde hand at 6, four-year cycle at 8, date at 9, moon at 12, center second counter, minute track with divisions for 1/5 of a second.
Strap: crocodile leather, hand stitched; yellow gold clasp.
Price: 69'015 CHF.
Also available: red gold/white gold (same price); platinum 80'840 CHF.

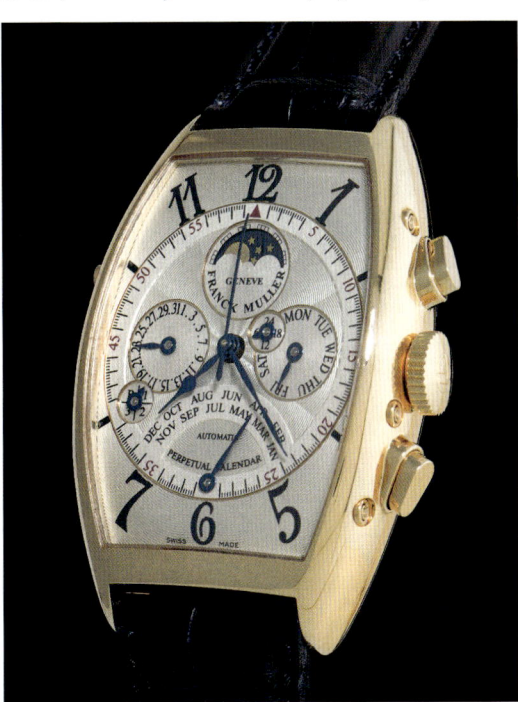

CINTREE CURVEX CHRONO MASTER CALENDAR   REF. 6850 CC MC

Movement: mechanical, manual winding, F. Muller caliber 1870 (Lemania base), autonomy of 50 hours, 18 jewels (Ø 27 mm, thickness 5.70 mm). 21,600 vibrations per hour (vph), first quality balance-spring with off-center screw adjustment, thermostable, Incabloc shock-resistant system. Beveled, Côtes de Genève and circular graining finished. **Functions:** hour, minute, small second, 24-hour indication, full calendar (date, day, month), chronograph with 2 counters. **Case:** Magnum 18 kt red gold, two-piece case, anatomically tonneau-curved (height 47 mm, width 34, thickness 11.50 mm); curved sapphire crystal; 3 correctors on case side; red gold crown and red gold oval pushers; case back attached by 4 screws. Water-resistant to 2.5 atm.
Dial: blue, engine turned (guilloché) with sun pattern, silvered ring and counters, curved; painted Arabic numerals; red gold Stuart hands. **Indications:** minute counter at 3, 24-hour display at 6, small second at 9, day and month at 12, date with arrow-shaped center hand, center second counter, minute track with divisions for 1/5 of a second.
Strap: crocodile leather, hand stitched; red gold clasp. **Price:** 39'560 CHF.
Also av.: yellow gold/red gold/white gold (same price); platinum 53'427 CHF; steel 28'595 CHF; Automatic, 4 golds 40'635 CHF; steel 29'670 CHF.

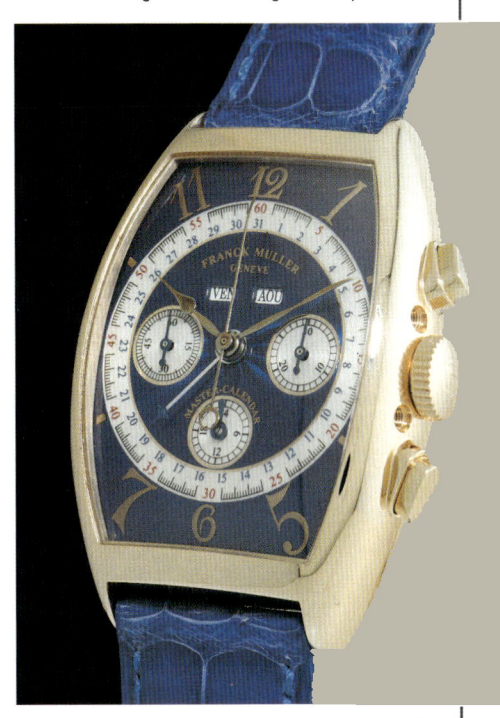

CINTREE CURVEX CHRONOGRAPH   REF. 5850 CC AT

Movement: mechanical, automatic winding, Franck Muller caliber 1185 (Frédéric Piguet base), autonomy of 40 hours and 37 jewels (Ø 25.6 mm, thickness 5.5 mm); balance with 21,600 vibrations per hour (vph), and balance-spring with micrometer adjustment, thermostable, Kif shock-resistant system. Hand-finished.
Functions: hour, minute, small second, date, chronograph with 3 counters.
Case: 18 kt white gold, two-piece case, anatomically tonneau-curved (height 45 mm, width 32 mm, thickness 12 mm); curved sapphire crystal; white gold crown and white gold oval pushers; case back attached by 4 screws. Water-resistant to 3 atm.
Dial: white, engine turned (guilloché) with sun pattern, curved; screen-printed Arabic numerals; blued stainless steel Stuart hands.
Indications: minute counter at 3, small second and date at 6, hour counter at 9, center second counter, minute track with divisions for 1/5 of a second.
Strap: crocodile leather, hand stitched; white gold clasp.
Price: 31'712 CHF. The watch in picture is a prototype.
Also available: yellow, pink, red gold (same price); steel 20'640 CHF; with "Havana" dial: steel 21'285 CHF, 4 golds 32'357 CHF, platinum 40'850 CHF.

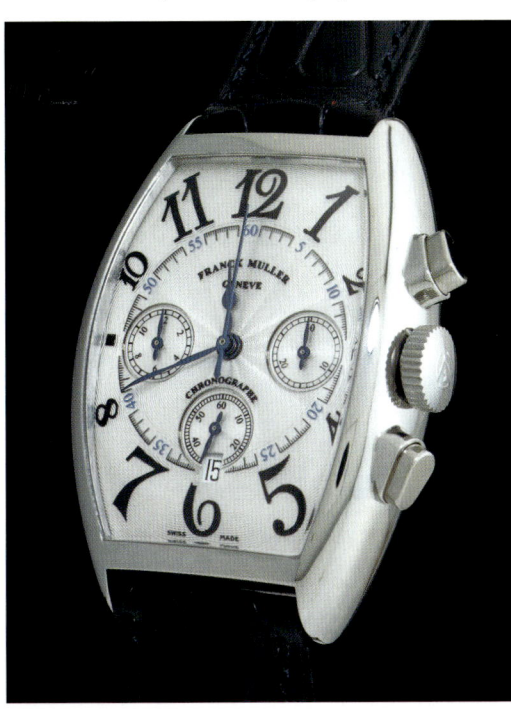

CINTREE CURVEX MONOPUSHER CHRONOGRAPH   REF. 7502 CC M

Movement: mechanical, manual winding, (Ø 24 mm, 10'''1/2, thickness 4.20 mm), 21 jewels, 21,600 vibrations per hour (vph), power reserve 40 hours. Beveled, Côtes de Genève and circular graining finished.
Functions: hour, minute, small second, chronograph with 2 counters.
Case: 18 kt yellow gold, two-piece case, anatomically tonneau-curved (height 38.5 mm, width 28, thickness 9 mm); curved sapphire crystal; yellow gold crown with pusher; case back attached by 4 screws. Water-resistant to 3 atm.
Dial: silvered, engine turned (guilloché) with sun pattern, curved; screen-printed Arabic numerals; blued stainless steel Stuart hands. **Indications:** minute counter at 3, small second at 9, center second counter, minute track with divisions for 1/5 of a second.
Strap: crocodile leather, hand stitched; yellow gold clasp.
Price: on request. The watch in picture is a prototype.
Also available: pink, red, white gold; platinum; steel; Grand Modèle Ref. 5850, mm 45x32: 4 golds or platinum.

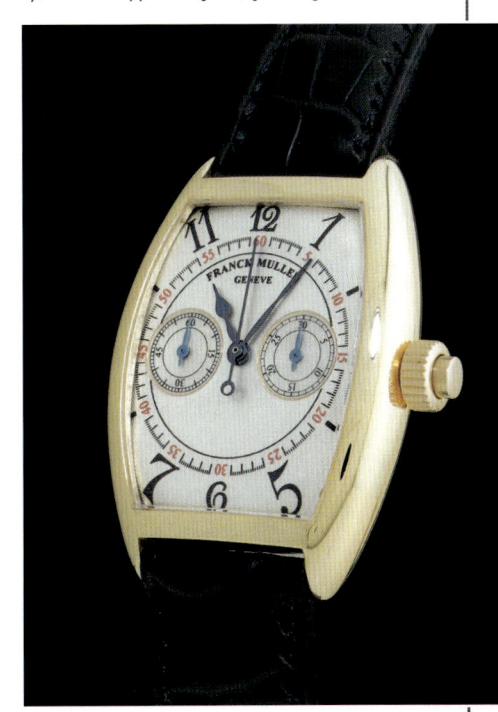

FRANCK MULLER

CINTREE CURVEX MIN. REPEATER TOURBILLON IMPERIALE REF. 5850 RM-T

Movement: mechanical, manual winding, tonneau-shaped caliber TRM95 completely modified by Franck Muller, autonomy of 48 hours and 32 jewels (height 28.80 mm, width 21.45 mm, thickness 6.10 mm); tourbillon device, 21,600 vibrations per hour (vph), Phillips overcoil balance-spring and fine regulation. Beveled and Côtes de Genève finished.
Functions: hour, minute, small second; minute repeater. 
Case: platinum, two-piece tonneau-curved case (height 45 mm, width 32 mm, thickness 11.40 mm); curved sapphire crystal; repeater slide on case side; platinum crown; case back attached by 4 screws, displaying the movement through a sapphire crystal.
Dial: silvered, engine turned (guilloché), curved, aperture on the tourbillon; screen-printed Arabic numerals; blued stainless steel Stuart hands.
Indications: small second at 6 integral with the tourbillon, sonnerie end indicator, patented, at 10 (to indicate when it is possible to reactivate the sonnerie).
Strap: crocodile leather, hand stitched; platinum clasp.
Price: 303'150 CHF, 25 pieces.
Also available: yellow, pink, red, white gold 288'100 CHF; steel 268'750 CHF.

CINTREE CURVEX TOURBILLON IMPERIALE "GRAVE" REF. 5850 T

Movement: mechanical, manual winding, tonneau caliber TFM95 completely modified by F. Muller, autonomy of 48 hours and 19 jewels (height 28.20 mm, width 21.45, thickness 6.10 mm); with tourbillon, Phillips overcoil balance-spring with fine regulation. Hand-finished and hand engraved.
Functions: hour, minute, small second.
Case: 18 kt white gold, two-piece case, anatomical tonneau (height 45 mm, width 32, thickness 12 mm); curved sapphire crystal; white gold crown; case back attached by 4 screws, displaying the movement through a sapphire crystal. 
Dial: blue, curved, aperture on the tourbillon; luminescent Arabic numerals; luminescent blued stainless steel lozenge hands.
Indications: small second at 6, integrated in the tourbillon carriage.
Strap: crocodile leather, hand stitched; white gold clasp. **Price:** on request. 10 pieces. **Also available:** yellow gold/red gold/pink gold/platinum (on request); Ref. 2852 (on request); Ref. 6850 (4 golds or platinum, on request); silvered dial; without engravings: Ref. 2852, yellow gold/red gold/pink gold/ white gold 101'587; platinum 116'637; Ref. 5850, yellow gold/red gold/pink gold/white gold 110'187; platinum 125'237; Ref. 6850 on request.

CINTREE CURVEX PERPETUAL CALENDAR MIN. REPEATER REF. 5850 RM QP

Movement: mechanical, manual winding, caliber RFM93 (RFM93 base + QP Dubois Dépraz 5100 exclusive module), autonomy of 42 hours and 34 jewels (Ø 24 mm, thickness 5 mm); bimetallic balance with compensation screws, 18,000 vibrations per hour, Phillips overcoil balance-spring, Incabloc shock-resistant system. Beveled, Côtes de Genève and circular graining finished.
Functions: hour, minute, perpetual calendar (date, day, month, year, moon phase); minute repeater. 
Case: 18 kt yellow gold, two-piece tonneau-curved case (height 45 mm, width 32 mm); curved sapphire crystal; 4 correctors and repeater slide on case side; yellow gold crown; case back attached by 4 screws.
Dial: silvered, matte finish, curved; printed Arabic numerals; blued stainless steel Stuart hands.
Indications: date at 3, moon phase at 6, day at 9, month and four year cycle at 12.
Strap: crocodile leather, hand stitched; yellow gold clasp.
Price: 275'200 CHF.
Also available: pink, red or white gold (same prices); platinum 290'787 CHF; sapphire case back (on request).

CINTREE CURVEX PERPETUAL CALENDAR REF. 5850 QP24

Movement: mechanical, automatic winding, Franck Muller caliber 2800 (FM base + QP Dubois Dépraz 5100 exclusive module), autonomy of 47 hours and 21 jewels (Ø 26.30 mm, thickness 3.60 mm); 28,800 vibrations per hour, flat balance-spring with off-center screw adjustment, Incabloc shock-resistant system. Beveled, Côtes de Genève and circular graining finished.
Functions: hour, minute, center second, 24-hour indication, perpetual calendar (date, day, month, year, moon phase). 
Case: 18 kt yellow gold, two-piece tonneau-curved case (size 45x32 mm, thickness 11.5 mm); curved sapphire crystal; 4 correctors on case side; yellow gold crown; case back attached by 4 screws.
Dial: silvered, matte finish, curved; printed Arabic numerals; blued stainless steel Stuart hands.
Indications: date at 3, moon phase at 6, day and 24-hour display at 9, month and four year cycle at 12.
Strap: crocodile leather, hand stitched; yellow gold clasp.
Price: 43'645 CHF.
Also available: pink, red, white gold (same price); platinum 54'287 CHF. Ref. 2852, 4 golds 42'570 CHF, platinum 52'782 CHF.

FRANCK MULLER

CINTREE CURVEX WORLD WIDE "EUROPE"   REF. 5850 WW

Movement: mechanical, automatic winding, caliber FM 2800, autonomy of 44 hours, platinum rotor and 21 jewels (Ø 26.20 mm, thickness 3.6 mm); 28,800 vibrations per hour (vph), balance-spring with off-center screw adjustment, thermostable, Incabloc shock-resistant system. Beveled, Côtes de Genève and circular graining finished.
Functions: hour, minute, second; second time zone, 24-hour indication.
Case: platinum, two-piece tonneau-curved case (height 45 mm, width 32 mm, thickness 11.20 mm); curved sapphire crystal; platinum crown; case back attached by 4 screws. Water-resistant to 2.5 atm.
Dial: engine turned (guilloché) with sun pattern and blue enamel, curved; center with Europe (or Oceania, Asia, Africa, America) in polychromic enamels; silvered 24-hour ring; gilded Arabic numerals; pink gold Stuart hands.
Indications: center second time zone 24-hour snaking hand.
Strap: crocodile leather, hand stitched; stainless steel clasp.
Price: 30'960 CHF.
Also available: yellow gold, red gold, pink gold, white gold 23'435 CHF; silvered dial; Ref. 2852, mm 43x31, yellow gold, red gold, pink gold, white gold 22'360 CHF; platinum 29'455 CHF.

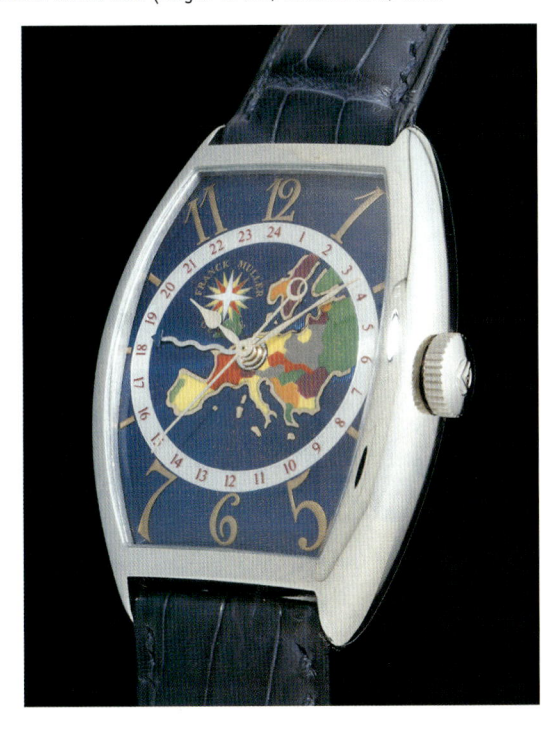

CINTREE CURVEX MASTER BANKER   REF. 6850 MB

Movement: mech., automatic winding, cal. Franck Muller 2800, autonomy 47 hours, platinum rotor (Ø 26.30, thickness 5.35 mm), modified for the reading of two additional time zones; 28,800 vph, and balance-spring with micrometer adjustment, Incabloc shock-resistant system. Beveled, Côtes de Genève and circular graining finished.
Functions: hour, minute, center second, date, three time zones.
Case: Magnum stainless steel, two-piece case, anatomically tonneau-curved (height 46, width 34, thickness 13.5 mm); curved sapphire crystal; crown for three time zones and date correction; case back attached by 4 screws. Water-resistant to 2.5 atm.
Dial: blue, engine turned (guilloché) with sun pattern, curved, zones silvered; luminescent Arabic numerals; luminescent blued stainless steel lozenge hands.
Indications: date at 3, 2nd and 3rd time zone at 12 and 6, with double hand.
Strap: crocodile leather, hand stitched; steel clasp.
Price: 12'255 CHF. **Also av.:** 4 golds 23'435; PT 32'035; Ref. 5850: steel 11'610; 4 golds 20'640; PT 29'240; Ref. 2852: steel 10'965; 4 golds 19'565; PT 28'164; white dial; "Havana" dial: Ref. 6850: steel 12'900; 4 golds 24'080; PT 32'680; Ref. 5850: steel 12'362; 4 golds 21'285; PT 30'530; Ref. 2852: steel 11'610; 4 golds 20'210; PT 29'455.

CINTREE CURVEX RETROGRADE SMALL SECOND   REF. 2852 RET

Movement: mechanical, manual winding, caliber Franck Muller 7500, autonomy of 44 hours and 17 jewels (Ø 23.30 mm, thickness 2.50 mm); 21,600 vibrations per hour (vph), and balance-spring with micrometer adjustment, Incabloc shock-resistant system. Patented retrograde small second system to avoid accumulating delay during the fly-back to zero. Beveled, Côtes de Genève and circular graining finished.
Functions: hour, minute, small second.
Case: 18 kt white gold, two-piece tonneau-curved case (height 48.3 mm, width 31 mm, thickness 10 mm); curved sapphire crystal; white gold crown; case back attached by 4 screws. Water-resistant to 3 atm.
Dial: silvered, engine turned (guilloché) with sun pattern, curved; printed Arabic numerals; printed railway minute track; blued stainless steel Stuart hands.
Indications: small second with retrograde snaking hand.
Strap: crocodile leather, hand stitched; white gold clasp.
Price: 16'555 CHF.
Also available: yellow, pink, red gold (same price); platinum 28'595 CHF; Ref. 5850, mm 45x32: 4 golds 17'630 CHF, platinum 29'670 CHF; Ref. 7501, mm 38,5x28,5: 4 golds 16'125 CHF, platinum 27'520 CHF.

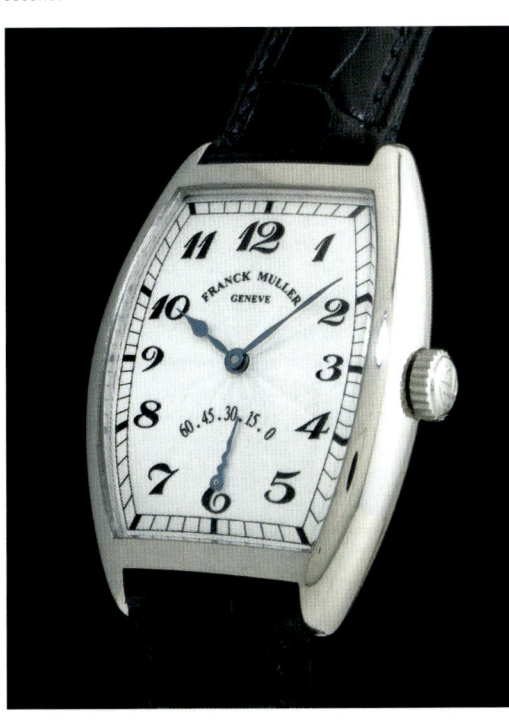

CINTREE CURVEX LIMITED   REF. 2851S6LTD

Movement: mechanical, automatic winding, caliber Franck Muller, autonomy of 47 hours, platinum rotor. Beveled, Côtes de Genève and circular graining finished.
Functions: hour, minute, center second, date.
Case: 18 kt white gold, two-piece tonneau-curved case (only case size 38.3x30 mm, thickness 11 mm); case back attached by 4 screws; curved sapphire crystal. Water-resistant to 3 atm.
Dial: blue, engine turned (guilloché) with sun pattern, curved; printed Arabic numerals; luminescent stainless steel leaf style hands.
Indications: small second at 6, big date at 12.
Strap: crocodile leather, hand stitched; white gold clasp.
Price: 20'210 CHF. Series limited to 2.000 pieces: 1.000 stainless steel, 200 for each of the four gold colors (yellow, pink, red, white), 200 in platinum.
Also available: yellow gold, pink gold, red gold (same price); platinum 27'735 CHF; steel 11'610 CHF; with rosé dial, luminescent Arabic numerals, or white dial, black Arabic numerals.

Gérald Genta

To go beyond the known limits of the complications seemed to be the challenge Gérald Genta accepted in 1994, when the Grande Sonnerie, a never-before triumph comprising more than 1000 parts, made its appearance, winking as it were at the great names of fine watchmaking. Today, thirty year after its founding, the Manufacture again goes the limit with "Grande Sonnerie 99", the latest great million-franc creation by the Geneva master. Here, he has turned the mechanical movement of the watch upside-down, the watch that had ensured its creator a place of honor in the Olympus of timepieces, and included the four striking hammers, the tourbillon, the carillon regulating mechanism and the Geneva Seal on one side of the dial where their exquisiteness can be admired, having moved the hours and minutes toward the right.

The Rétro Sport will meet definite success among those who consider measuring time to be an Art. This is the latest development of the brilliant collection which revolutionized the reading of hours and minutes with the ingenious mechanism of the jumping hours and retrograde minutes. In this version, with its strong structure and youthful design, Genta has kept faith with the technology of the entire series, combining two complications on the same dial. At every hour change, the hour disc jumps ahead, while the minute hand turns back to its starting point in an instant. The Rétro family has a new automatic tonneau with jumping hours and retrograde minutes and a retrograding small seconds. Among the complications, then, is a jumping retrograde minutes repeater with mother of pearl dial and printed parts with gold cabochon.

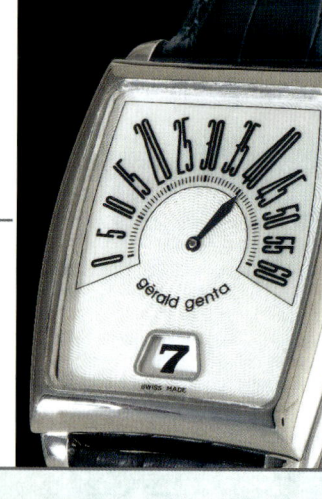

The History

Born in Geneva of a Piedmont family, Gérald Genta starts his career as a stylist at 23, after an old fashioned apprenticeship in a large Geneva jewellers. He was one of the best signatures for about twenty years in the world of traditional watchmaking, where he created such guide lines as Pasha, Royal Oak, Nautilus, Omega Titane, Bvlgari-Bvlgari. His youthful experiences in publicity and high fashion and his sensitivity for the public's desires which he acquired there, becomes extremely useful when he decides to start his own company. It is 1972: Van Cleef & Arpels and Fred, in Paris are his first clients. They order unique pieces for their own clients who don't care what they spend. Genta surrounds himself with a team of expert case builders, engravers, watchmakers, jewel setters; he goes beyond all expectations by creating models that are absolutely original. During the '80's he enjoys hearing himself defined as the Fabergé of watchmakers, but he is not satisfied with being only a grand stylist. He begins to cultivate technical ambitions that are realized by the production of complicated models like the Quantième Perpétuel with moon phases, the Grand Sonnerie pocket model, the wrist model Repeaters. The excellent quality of the movements will bring him the much desired Geneva Seal. Some years later the name is purchased by Hour Glass, the oriental group which is also the owner in Europe of Daniel Roth. Today Gérald Genta lives and works in Montecarlo. In a workshop in Geneva about 40 workers see to the production of cases and dials, and mounting and testing finished watches. In the Vallée de Joux another group of 22 construct the mechanisms, the cases and special crystals.

Early '60's - Genta designs watches for several prestigious Houses, like Omega (Constellation) and Universal Genève (Polerouter).
1968 - He signs the Audemars Piguet "Royal Oak".
1969 - The Gérald Genta Manufacture is founded.
Early '70's - He continues to design successful watches for the great Houses, like Nautilus for Patek Philippe.
1972 - He does several unique pieces for the Parisian jewellers Fred and Van Cleef & Arpels.
1980's - The Octo collection softens the octagonal shape of the case, harmonizing it to an elegant round bezel. The "Gefica" come into being for three friends who ask him for a watch worthy of their African safaris (the name comes from the initials of their names: GEoffroy, FIssore and CAnali). In the meantime he designs Titane for Omega and the Bvlgari-Bvlgari for the famous Italian jeweller.
1993 - The collection Success, which is Genta's inauguration of his patent for a sapphire crystal faceted on the underside.
1994 - To celebrate the 25th anniversary of the Manufacture, Gérald Genta creates the Wrist model of the Grande Sonnerie, one of the most complicated models in the world. The edition comprises 8 pieces, there are 8 complications and there are 8 ridges on the 8 sided case.
1996 - The Rétro Classic collection presents an ingenious mechanism for instant jumping hours and retrograde minutes, patented.
1997 - The Gérald Genta Manufacture becomes part of the Hour Glass group, a huge watch production organization spread over five continents.
1998 - Backtime is the watch with the count down of the days to the year 2000; 456 pieces like the days to go starting from October 1st 1998, when the watch was officially presented. The Geneva exhibition loved Night & Day, an automatic having an extremely simple appearance: a red hand to read the second time zone and the image of the sun or the moon to tell us if it is day or night in that "other time".

GERALD GENTA

RETRO SPORT   REF. G3694

Movement: mechanical, automatic winding, Gérald Genta caliber GG 4503 (Eta base + patented module for jumping hours and retrograde minutes), with 44 hours power reserve, 27 jewels. **Functions:** jumping hour 24-hour indication, retrograde minute display, center second.
Case: stainless steel, three-piece case (Ø 40.5 mm, thickness 12 mm); curved sapphire crystal; fluted case side; small spheres on screw-down crown with case protection; case back attached by 6 screws. Water-resistant to 10 atm.
Dial: carbon fiber; outer ring in rubber with embossed firm logo and luminescent minute Arabic numerals; white printed minute track.
Indications: retrograde center minute (patented) with luminescent blued stainless steel sword style hand, 24-jumping hour at 12, minute track with divisions for 1/5 of a second on the beveled ring.
Bracelet: steel; fold-over clasp.
Price: 6'900 CHF.
Also available: with fiber glass and white rubber dial; leather or rubber strap 5'950; with rubber bezel (same prices); with rubber and diamonds bezel, leather strap 13'900.
N.B. The photographs of the Sport model are reduced by 5% compared with the others.

RETRO TONNEAU   REF. G3671

Movement: mechanical, automatic winding, Gérald Genta caliber GG 4503 (Eta base + patented module for jumping hour and retrograde minutes).
Functions: jumping hour 24-hour indication, retrograde minute display.
Case: stainless steel, three-piece case (height 36 mm, width 31.5 mm, thickness 10.5 mm); curved sapphire crystal; case side with longitudinal groove; small spheres on crown; case back attached by 4 screws. Water-resistant to 3 atm.
Dial: black; painted Arabic numerals and minute track.
Indications: 24 jumping hour at 6, retrograde center minute (patented) with luminescent sword style hand.
Strap: crocodile leather; stainless steel clasp.
Price: 6'950 CHF.
Also available: in yellow or pink gold 13'850 CHF; white gold 15'235 CHF. Each version is available with white or black dial.

RETRO DOUBLE RETROGRADE 38 MM   REF. G3754

Movement: mechanical, automatic winding. **Functions:** jumping hour 24-hour indication, retrograde minute display, retrograde date display. **Case:** stainless steel, three-piece case (Ø 36, thick. 11 mm); curved sapphire crystal; fluted case side; small spheres on crown; case back attached by 6 screws. Water-resistant to 3 atm. **Dial:** in mother-of-pearl, engine turned (guilloché). **Indications:** fan-shaped date with retrograde hand at 6, jumping 24-hour display at 12, retrograde center minute (patented) with burnished steel sword style hand. **Strap:** crocodile leather; stainless steel clasp.
Price: 5'730 CHF.
Also available: brac. 6'680; steel+yellow gold/pink gold, leather strap 8'480; yellow gold/pink gold, leather strap 14'170; white gold, leather strap 15'600. Ø 36 mm Ref. 3734: steel, leather strap 5'730, brac. 6'840; steel+yellow gold/pink gold, leather strap 7'480, brac. 11'160; yellow gold/pink gold, leather strap 10'820, brac. 24'280; white gold, leather strap 11'770, brac. 26'530. Ø 33 mm Ref. 3714: steel, leather strap 5'730, brac. 6'840; steel+yellow gold/pink gold, leather strap 7'160, brac. 10'630; yellow gold/pink gold, leather strap 10'310, brac. 22'720; white gold, leather strap 11'210, brac. 24'860. All with silvered or porcellanized white dial (mother-of-pearl dial on request; blue or black enameled 350 SFr. extra-price).

RETRO FANTASY 33 MM   REF. G3612

In 1998 the Rétro Fantasy collection was enlarged by new versions, characterized by offset indications, jumping hour display at 4 and retrograde minute ring between 8 and 3. In the photograph shown with Walt Disney's figures playing golf, the hour display is at the same time the hole aimed at by the unlikely stroke which should come from the retrograde club-shaped hand. For these new versions there are the following case options: Moyen or Grand Modèle, in steel, steel and diamonds, steel and gold or gold. In the photograph a Moyen Modèle with Donald Duck on the dial, steel case and brilliants on the bezel. **Price:** 12'960 CHF. **Also available:** brac. 14'290 CHF; steel+yellow gold/pink gold, leather strap 14'660, brac. 18'710; in yellow or pink gold, leather strap 18'340, brac. 32'860; white gold, leather strap 19'400, brac. 35'360. Large Ref. 3632: steel, leather strap 13'730, brac. 15'030; steel+yellow gold/pink gold, leather strap 15'770, brac. 20'070; in yellow or pink gold, leather strap 19'670, brac. 35'410; white gold, leather strap 20'810, brac. 38'110. Lady's, quartz, Ref. 3622: steel, leather strap 10'340, brac. 11'640; steel+yellow gold/pink gold, leather strap 11'395, brac. 14'340; in yellow or pink gold, leather strap 14'340, brac. 26'190; white gold, leather strap 15'240, brac. 28'280. All with Walt Disney's figures on the dial.

GERALD GENTA

JOUR & NUIT — REF. G3706

Movement: mechanical, automatic winding. **Functions:** hour, minute, center second, date, second time zone, night & day indicator. **Case:** stainless steel, three-piece case (Ø 36 mm, thickness 10.5 mm); curved sapphire crystal; fluted case side; small spheres on crown; pusher at 9 for the adjustment of the second time zone hand; case back attached by 6 screws. Water-resistant to 3 atm. **Dial:** black; luminescent applied bâton markers; printed railway minute track; luminescent blued sword style hands. **Indications:** date at 6, night & day indicator window at 12, second time zone with center red hand. **Bracelet:** steel; fold-over clasp.
Price: 6'260 CHF.
Also available: leather strap 5'150; steel+yellow gold/pink gold, leather strap 6'890, bracelet 10'580; yellow gold/pink gold, leather strap 10'210, brac. 23'670; white gold, leather strap 11'160, brac. 25'920. Ø 38 mm Ref. 3707: steel, leather strap 5'150, brac. 6'100; steel+yellow gold/pink gold, leather strap 7'700; white gold, leather strap 14'650. Ø 33 mm Ref. 3705: steel, leather strap 5'150, brac. 6'260; steel+yellow gold/pink gold, leather strap 6'580, brac. 10'050; yellow gold/pink gold, leather strap 9'700, brac. 22'110; white gold, leather strap 10'660, brac. 24'330. All with blue, black, white porcellanized or mother-of-pearl dial; as jewel-watch (on request).

BACKTIMER — REF. 3806

Movement: mechanical, automatic winding.
Functions: hour, minute, center second, date, days back count.
Case: 18 kt white gold, three-piece case (Ø 38 mm, thickness 10 mm); curved sapphire crystal; fluted case side; small spheres on white gold crown; 3 pushers for digit adjustment on the dial; case back attached by 6 screws. Water-resistant to 3 atm.
Dial: silvered, "2000" engraved at the center; luminescent applied bâton and cabochon markers and Arabic numerals; printed railway minute track; luminescent blued sword style hands.
Indications: date at 6, tripartite aperture with magnifying lenses for the back count of the days left to go to 2000 or with numbering to select at pleasure.
Strap: crocodile leather; white gold clasp.
Price: 15'800 CHF.
Also available: medium size Ref. 3805, 14'740 CHF.

SECONDE RETRO — REF. G3610

Movement: mechanical, automatic winding.
Functions: hour, minute, retrograde second.
Case: stainless steel, three-piece polished case (Ø 36 mm, thickness 10 mm); carved case side; curved sapphire crystal; small spheres on crown; case back attached by 6 screws. Water-resistant to 3 atm.
Dial: beige; applied black painted bâton markers and Arabic numerals; luminescent black painted sword style hands.
Indications: second at 6 (patented) with retrograde black painted hand measuring 30 seconds sequences.
Strap: crocodile leather; stainless steel clasp.
Price: 5'450 CHF.
Also available: in yellow gold 12'000 CHF; in white gold 13'200 CHF.

TOURBILLON — REF. G4066

Movement: mechanical, automatic winding, with tourbillon. Hand-finished and hand-engraved.
Functions: hour, minute, small second, date, power reserve.
Case: 18 kt white gold, three-piece case (Ø 36 mm, thickness 10.50 mm); curved sapphire crystal; hollowed case side; small spheres on white gold crown; case back attached by 6 screws, displaying the movement through a sapphire crystal. Water-resistant to 3 atm.
Dial: black, carbon fiber, aperture on the tourbillon carriage; printed Roman numerals; luminescent sword style hands.
Indications: date with lozenge center hand, power reserve (in mother-of-pearl) at 12, small second integral with the tourbillon carriage at 6.
Strap: crocodile leather; white gold clasp.
Price: 74'100 CHF.
Also available: in yellow or pink gold 67'310 CHF. All with dial in carbon fiber or fiber glass or white or black "Fabergé". In the largest size (Ø 38 mm) Ref. 4166, white gold with carbon fiber dial 76'100 CHF; in yellow gold 69'310 CHF.

GERALD GENTA

PERPETUAL CALENDAR   REF. G3774

Movement: mechanical, automatic winding (Jaeger-Le Coultre base and perpetual calendar module).
Functions: hour, minute, center second, perpetual calendar (date, day, month, year, moon phase).
Case: 18 kt white gold, three-piece case (Ø 36 mm, thickness 10 mm); curved sapphire crystal; 4 correctors on the hollowed case side; small spheres on the white gold crown; case back attached by 6 screws, displaying the movement through a sapphire crystal. Water-resistant to 3 atm.
Dial: black "Fabergé", engine turned (guilloché), with rings of zones in mother-of-pearl; zones of moon phases in lapislasuli and white gold ring; luminescent applied cabochon markers; luminescent sword style hands.
Indications: month and four year cycle at 3, date at 6, day at 9, moon phase at 12.
Strap: crocodile leather; white gold clasp.
Price: 38'480 CHF.
Also available: in yellow or pink gold 34'980 CHF. Each version is available with green, red, blue, white or black "Fabergé" dial.

PERPETUAL CALENDAR MINUTE REPEATER   REF. G4163

Movement: mechanical, automatic winding. Hand-finished and hand-engraved.
Functions: hour, minute, perpetual calendar (date, day, month, year, moon phase), minute repeater.
Case: 18 kt white gold, three-piece case (Ø 38 mm, thickness 11 mm); curved sapphire crystal; 4 correctors on the hollowed case side; small spheres on the white gold crown; repeater white gold pusher at 9; case back attached by 6 screws, displaying the movement through a sapphire crystal. Water-resistant to 3 atm.
Dial: blue, engine turned (guilloché), with rings of zones in mother-of-pearl; moon phases zones in lapis-lasuli and white gold ring; luminescent applied cabochon markers; luminescent sword style hands.
Indications: month and four year cycle at 3, date at 6, day at 9, moon phase at 12.
Strap: crocodile leather; white gold clasp.
Price: 229'370 CHF.
Also available: in yellow or pink gold 208'700; in the smaller size (Ø 36, thickness 11) Ref. 4063, with blue, opaline or black "Fabergé" dial: in yellow or pink gold 206'700 CHF; in white gold 227'370 CHF.

GRANDE SONNERIE 99

Movement: mechanical, manual winding, Gérald Genta caliber GG31000; with tourbillon device. Westminster Carillon sonnerie with 4 hammers and 4 gongs tuned with the notes E-C-D-G. Hallmarked with the "Geneva Seal" (watchmaking's highest distinction of quality).
Functions: hours, minutes; petite and grande sonnerie; minute repeater; double power reserve indicator for the movement and for the carillon.
Case: 18 kt white gold, three-piece case (Ø 41 mm, thickness 13 mm); curved sapphire crystal; carved case side; crown and pushers (or repetition at 9, selection petite and grande sonnerie at 7, mute or sonnerie selection at 11) in white gold, adorned with small spheres; case back attached by 8 screws, displaying the movement through a sapphire crystal. Water-resistant to 3 atm.
Dial: silvered, engine turned (guilloché), Clous de Paris outside and with basket pattern inside, aperture on the tourbillon; applied Roman numeral markers.
Indications on the case back: carillon reserve at 7; watch reserve at 10; petite or grande sonnerie position at 2; mute or sonnerie position at 4.
Strap: crocodile leather, white gold clasp.
Price: 1'000'000 CHF.

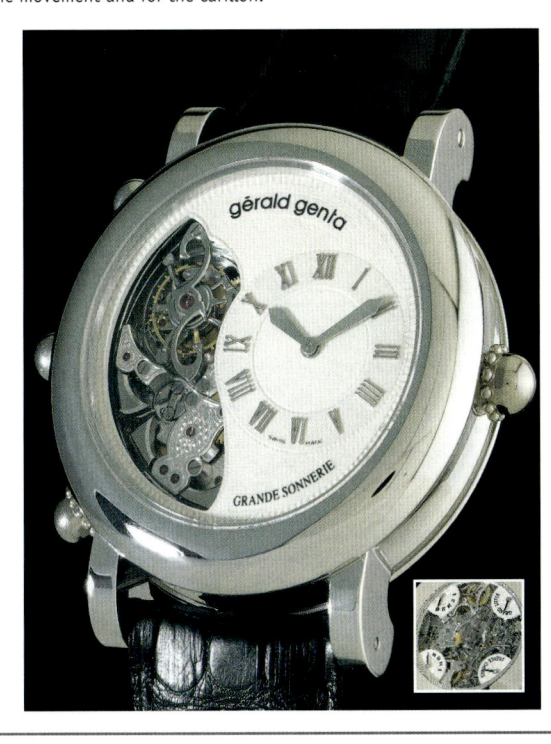

MINUTE REPEATER AUTOMATIC   REF. G4062

Movement: mechanical, automatic winding. Hand-finished and hand-engraved.
Functions: hour, minute, minute repeater.
Case: 18 kt yellow gold, three-piece case (Ø 36 mm, thickness 9.10 mm); curved sapphire crystal; hollowed case side; small spheres on yellow gold crown; repeater yellow gold pusher at 9; case back attached by 6 screws, displaying the movement through a sapphire crystal. Water-resistant to 3 atm.
Dial: opaline; applied bâton markers and Arabic numerals; printed railway minute track; luminescent sword style hands.
Strap: crocodile leather; yellow gold clasp.
Price: 159'000 CHF.
Also available: in pink gold (same price); in white gold 174'900 CHF. Each version is available with opaline, blue or black dial "Fabergé".

Girard-Perregaux

With utmost reverence to time itself, Girard-Perregaux crafts remarkable timepieces in classic tradition while bringing together innovations brought by progress. For more than 200 years, the watchmaker has produced timepieces in this manner because at Girard-Perregaux, goals and objectives remain constant: there will never be a compromise in watchmaking. As the rest of the world fixes its attention on the year 2000, Girard-Perregaux looks beyond the millennium and focuses on its continual evolution as a watchmaker. The timepiece Girard-Perregaux chose to honor the end of the millennium is as exceptional, and as traditional, as every watch produced at the manufactory in La Chaux-de-Fonds, Switzerland. The Vintage 1999 is a chronograph whose tank-shaped case is based on a model that first appeared in 1945. What is noteworthy is that the watch features a new movement that required three years for development. It is an integrated chronograph movement, featuring a column wheel used to transfer the power to the chronograph features. Yet the size of the movement is small, giving watchmakers greater flexibility with case shapes and sizes.

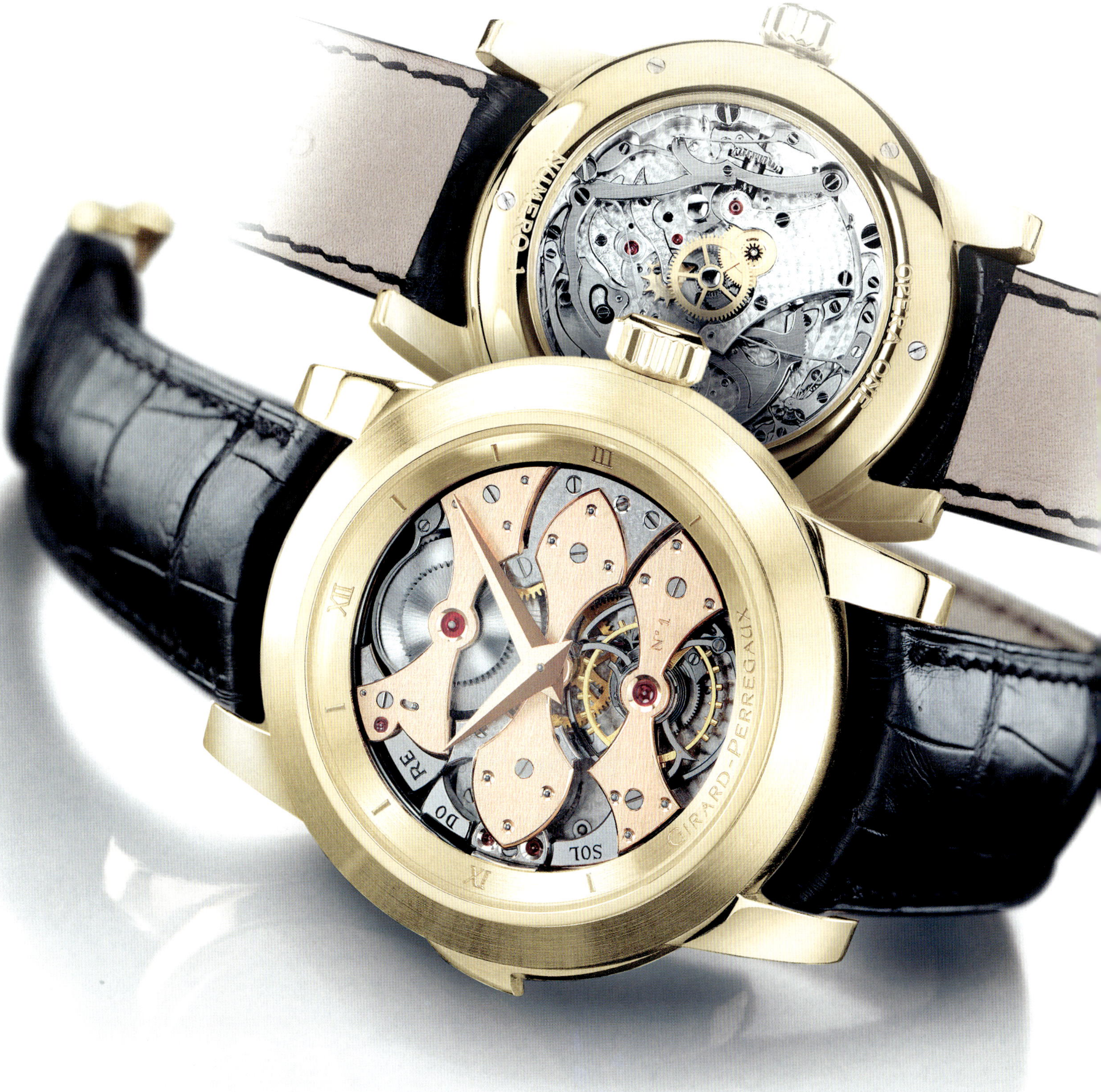
NUMERO 1
OPERA ONE
GIRARD-PERREGAUX
N°1
DO
RE
SOL

Girard-Perregaux

The Vintage 1999 is produced in a limited edition of 999 pieces in the workshops at Girard-Perregaux, an achievement that is both rare and admirable in Swiss watchmaking.

With most companies today it's very rare to possess the skills and infrastructure to create anything from within, whether it is the development of a concept or the manufacturing of the product. For Girard-Perregaux, all of the research, development and production is done in-house and it is accomplished by people employed within the infrastructure of the Girard-Perregaux company. It is this philosophy that served as the basis for watchmaking when J.F. Bautte founded the company in Geneva, Switzerland in 1791, and that continues to be embraced by owner Dr. Luigi "Gino" Macaluso. These principles enable the company to create its dynamic repertoire of watches today.

Indeed, perhaps the most difficult question ever asked of Girard-Perregaux is, "Which watch is most important?" The answer one is likely to receive takes some time. There are a number of important watches released every year. For example, at the same time that Girard-Perregaux presented the Vintage 1999, the watchmaker also offered an Opera One Tourbillon with Three Gold Bridges featuring a minute repeater with a Westminster chime, along with an Automatic Tourbillon with Three Gold Bridges, an S.F. Foudroyante split-seconds chronograph, the F1-047 and the F1-048.

Four gongs sound the first, second and third quarters and two gongs mark the hours and the minutes with a delicate warmth in the Opera One Tourbillon with Three Gold Bridges. The mechanical marvel is revealed through the face as a result of careful stylizing of the Three Gold Bridges.

The Three Gold Bridges architecture is held in special regard for its links to Girard-Perregaux's namesake, Constant Girard. After assuming the company in the mid-1800s from founder J.F. Bautte, Girard married Marie Perregaux and naturally, the name Gi-

Opening Page
VINTAGE 1999's dial, automatic column-wheel chronograph.

Previous Page
"OPERA ONE" minute repeater carillon and Tourbillon with three gold Bridges.

Top left
Mr. Luigi Macaluso, president of Girard-Perregaux, is a qualified architect. He also designs the Girard-Perregaux watches.

Top center
Tourbillon with three gold Bridges, automatic mechanical movement.

Above
"Opera One" minute repeater carillon and Tourbillon with three gold Bridges.

Below
The striking work of the "Opera One".

Facing page
Top
Villa Marguerite, built in 1918 is the Manufactory's new private museum.

Top Center
Vintage 1945 Gent. This model was named "Best watch of the year" in Japan. Vintage 1945 Lady.

Bottom
Vintage 1999, automatic column-wheel chronograph.

rard-Perregaux was born. It was Constant Girard who designed the now famous Tourbillon with Three Gold Bridges. The complex technology of the tourbillon is still today a difficult mechanism to craft, and a marvel because it corrects the inaccuracies effected by gravity. When Girard presented his Three Gold Bridges watch to the Paris Universal Exhibitions of 1867 and 1889, the judges deemed the timepiece too perfect to compete. Since, Girard-Perregaux's Three Gold Bridges timepieces have earned the same critical acclaim. In 1981, Girard-Perregaux confirmed its watchmaking virtuosity by releasing 20 replicas of the original Tourbillon with Three Gold Bridges. No small feat considering that each watch required six to eight months in production.

The Three Gold Bridges first moved to the wrist in 1991, as a commemorative timepiece for the company's 200th birthday, and generated enormous excitement for as a new style, as well as technical wonder.

Girard-Perregaux

It is testimony to Constant Girard's vision that the design dated to the turn of the century. The recent Tourbillon with Three Gold Bridges timepieces uphold the watchmaker's tradition while continuing to advance technology. In the Automatic Tourbillon with Three Gold Bridges, the rotor is fitted beneath the barrel, retaining the face of the watch as the focus of beauty: the Three Gold Bridges.

Once again, Girard-Perregaux delved into its rich history to develop the S.F. Foudroyante. The limited edition split-seconds chronograph was produced in only 750 pieces and is based on a concept that dates to 1860. On the watchface is an 1/8-second subdial that relates fractions of seconds and a separate power reserve.

Girard-Perregaux, operating today under a unique co-branding arrangement with Ferrari, is one of the only watchmakers who is inextricably involved in the racing industry. This is traced to the company's leader, Macaluso, a former Fiat race car driver and President of Club Italia, a 50-member group devoted to the preservation of Italian cars and motorbikes. As a result, the watch-

Left
Lady "F".

Center
"La Esmaralda" Tourbillon with three gold Bridges (late 19th century).

Below left
Lépine open-faced watch in gold is lodged inside a Florentine double Ducate (1820).

Below
Vintage 1945 Lady, a soft and subtle jewelry watch.

Facing page
Top
Vintage 1945 Lady.

Bottom
Lady "F", a jewelry watch with a strong character.

maker produces phenomenal chronographs, many specifically developed for the Italian car manufacturer, Ferrari. The "Tribute to Ferrari" series began in 1994 when Macaluso assumed leadership of Girard-Perregaux. He and the president of Ferrari were longtime friends, fortifying a natural union between watchmaking and car racing. The two also shared grand visions. "Because Ferrari is the dream car that is unique to the world, we decided to create something that was for the top collectors," Macaluso said.

Connoisseurs were delighted with the first pieces produced under the "Tribute to Ferrari" series. In 1995, Girard-Perregaux showcased a one-of-a-kind timepiece adorned with a Ferrari stallion insignia carved from a ruby. This exceptional collector's watch quickly sold for $150,000. Girard-Perregaux also created special timepieces to honor Ferrari's history.

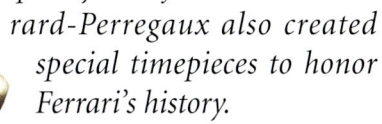

In 1997, Girard-Perregaux joined forces with the Italian automotive legend and created the F50 wristwatch in honor of the 50th anniversary of a vehicle that could only exist twice in one lifetime, the F50. Girard-Perregaux chose gold, platinum or titanium for the watchcase, which contains the F50 watch's complex mechanism. The F50 timepiece is an exceptional technical accomplishment. It boasts an automatic chronograph with a perpetual calendar capable of correcting the date, even in leap years, until the dawn of the 22nd century. Girard-Perregaux issued the Ferrari F50 watch in two very limited series. The first series of 349 watches was designed for the 349 owners of Ferrari F50 cars. Owners who acquired the F50 watch were cordially invited by Girard-Perregaux to have his name and serial number of his automobile engraved on the watch's case. A second series of 250 chronographs was then offered to distinguished collectors.

Drawing from its passion for racing, Girard-Perregaux recently launched the F1-047, which incorporates the innovative materials used in racing. The watch's alluminum case is created from an alloy that equals half the weight of titanium and was developed by Alcoa for the engine block of Ferrari F1 racing cars. Nearly weightless, the wearer only feels the weight of the mechanism inside the case. In the same spirit, Girard-Perregaux created the equally lightweight F1-048. The case is titanium, the dial is carbon, and the strap is rubber—resulting in a

Top left
Since 1971, a succession of talented watchmakers in the Manufactory's workshops has ensured the brand's continued success.

Top center
S.F. Foudroyante, automatic split-seconds chronograph, with coaxial pushpiece and jumping second function.

Center
Lady "F".

Below
In 1993, the Richeville chronograph model was named, "Best watch of the year" in Japan.

Bottom left
Vintage 1999, automatic column-wheel chronograph.

Girard-Perregaux

very light yet exceptional mechanical timepiece that can be worn racing, or while playing tennis and swimming. Girard-Perregaux assures the quality of its watches by producing only 18,000 each year. The watchmaker's peerless reputation draws acclaim from other leading watchmakers, and Girard-Perregaux creates some 20,000 watch movements for other watchmakers. With careful mastery, Girard-Perregaux is leaving this century much as it entered; as an esteemed watchmaker that holds the crafting of timepieces as an honored art form.

Above
Mr. Luigi Macaluso is a car lover.

Top center
F1 - 08, Girard-Perregaux pour Ferrari chronograph.

Center right
S.F. Foudroyante, automatic split-seconds chronograph, with coaxial pushpiece and jumping second function.

Bottom
Split-seconds chronograph and jumping seconds (1880).

163

GIRARD-PERREGAUX

TOURBILLON WITH GOLD BRIDGE REF. 99200

Movement: mechanical, manual winding, Girard-Perregaux caliber 9940, with tourbillon device mounted on a gold bridge, autonomy of 75 hours, 20 jewels (Ø 28.6 mm, 12'''1/2, thickness 12.8 mm dial included). Balance with 21,600 vibrations per hour (vph). Completely finished and decorated by hand by the firm's watchmakers.
Functions: hour, minute, small second, power reserve.
Case: platinum, three-piece polished case (Ø 39 mm, thickness 10 mm); antireflective curved sapphire crystal; white gold crown; case back attached by 6 screws, displaying the movement through a sapphire crystal. Water-resistant to 3 atm. 
Dial: solid gold, silvered, engine turned (guilloché) by hand, aperture on the tourbillon; applied white gold Roman numerals; blued stainless steel Stuart hands.
Indications: small second at 6, integrated in the tourbillon carriage, power reserve at 12.
Strap: crocodile leather; platinum clasp.
Price: 110'000 CHF.
Also available: in yellow or pink gold 89'000 CHF.

SKELETON TOURBILLON WITH THREE GOLD BRIDGES REF. 99050

Movement: mechanical, manual winding, Girard-Perregaux caliber 9905, with tourbillon device mounted on three 18 kt pink gold bridges, autonomy of 75 hours and 20 jewels. Balance with 21,600 vibrations per hour (vph). Bridges in solid pink gold, pillar-plate silvered and chased. Completely finished, decorated and skeletonized by hand by the firm's watchmakers.
Functions: hour, minute. 
Case: platinum, three-piece polished case (Ø 39 mm, thickness 10.6 mm); antireflective curved sapphire crystal; platinum crown; case back attached by 6 screws. Water-resistant to 3 atm.
Dial: 3 solid gold tourbillon bridges visible, as well as the engine turned (guilloché) pillar-plate, the skeletonized barrel and the tourbillon; Roman numerals and dial-train engraved on the beveled ring; blued stainless steel Stuart hands.
Strap: crocodile leather, hand stitched; screw connection; platinum clasp.
Price: 135'000 CHF.
Also available: in yellow or pink gold 125'000 CHF; white gold 130'000 CHF.

LITTLE TOURBILLON WITH THREE GOLD BRIDGES REF. 99020

Movement: mechanical, manual winding, Girard-Perregaux caliber 9700, with tourbillon device mounted on three 18 kt pink gold bridges, autonomy of 75 hours and 20 jewels. Balance with 21,600 vibrations per hour (vph). Bridges in solid pink gold, pillar-plate silvered and chased. Completely finished and decorated by hand by the firm's watchmakers.
Functions: hour, minute. 
Case: 18 kt pink gold, three-piece polished case (Ø 31 mm, thickness 9 mm); antireflective curved sapphire crystal; pink gold crown; case back attached by 7 screws. Water-resistant to 3 atm.
Dial: 3 solid gold tourbillon bridges visible, as well as the engine-turned (guilloché) pillar-plate, barrel and tourbillon; blued stainless steel leaf style hands.
Strap: crocodile leather, hand stitched; pink gold clasp.
Price: 79'000 CHF.
Also available: in yellow gold (same price); white gold 80'500 CHF; platinum 87'000 CHF.

SKELETON TOURBILLON WITH 3 GOLD BRIDGES MIN. REPEATER REF. 99550

Movement: mechanical, manual winding, Girard-Perregaux caliber 9892-070 with tourbillon device mounted on three 18 kt pink gold bridges. Chased, completely finished, decorated and skeletonized by hand by the firm's watchmakers.
Functions: hour, minute, minute repeater.
Case: 18 kt white gold, three-piece brushed case (Ø 39 mm, thickness 13.2 mm); antireflective curved sapphire crystal; bezel and lugs with square cut set brilliants; repeater slide on case side; diamond set in white gold crown; case back attached by 4 screws, displaying the movement through a sapphire crystal. Water-resistant to 3 atm. 
Dial: set brilliants on the beveled ring; blued stainless steel Stuart hands.
Strap: crocodile leather, hand stitched; white gold clasp.
Prices: on request.
Also available: yellow gold.

GIRARD-PERREGAUX

OPERA ONE — REF. 99750

Movement: mechanical, manual winding, Girard-Perregaux with tourbillon device mounted on three 18 kt pink gold bridges. Westminster carillon type sonnerie with 4 hammers and gongs tuned in the notes E-C-D-G (MI-DO-RE-SOL). Chased, entirely finished and decorated by hand by the firm's watchmakers.
Functions: hour, minute, minute repeater, carillon.
Case: 18 kt pink gold, three-piece case (Ø 40 mm, thickness 14 mm); antireflective curved sapphire crystal; repeater slide on case side; pink gold crown; case back attached by 6 screws, displaying the movement through a sapphire crystal. Water-resistant to 3 atm.
Dial: 3 solid gold bridges visible with the tourbillon at 6, as well as the barrel at 12, the G-C-D carillon hammers (E is hidden) and related gongs; Roman numerals on the beveled ring; pink gold Dauphine hands.
Strap: crocodile leather, hand stitched; pink gold clasp.
Prices: 450'000 CHF. Limited edition.
Also available: in yellow gold (same price).

OPERA ONE

The first watches with minute repeater by Girard-Perregaux appeared more than one hundred years ago, when the House of La Chaux-de-Fonds wanted to "tame" the sound of the bells, that scanned the rhythm of days, by transferring it into a sonnerie pocket watch. Today the Swiss factory, following its tradition, renews once again the most poetical indication of time - the minute repeater with carillon, combining it with the sophisticated tourbillon device. Opera One's precious mechanism reveals, through the transparent dial and case back, its wheels with parrot's beak teeth, the swan-neck-shaped regulator, the three pink gold bridges, the four hammers and gongs tuned in the notes E-C-D-G (MI-DO-RE-SOL) of the famous melody of the Big Ben (the first three quarters have a carillon sound, hours and minutes with two different tones). The whole is housed by a case specially conceived to amplify the sound, giving it a crystalline resonance.

TOURBILLON PRESIDENT WITH THREE GOLD BRIDGES — REF. 99800

Movement: mechanical, manual winding, Girard-Perregaux caliber 9800, with tourbillon device mounted on three 18 kt pink gold bridges, autonomy of 75 hours and 20 jewels. Balance with 21,600 vibrations per hour (vph). Movement mounted upside down, good hand-fitting at the pillar-plate. Bridges in solid pink gold, pillar-plate silvered and chased. Completely finished and decorated by hand by the firm's watchmakers.
Functions: hour, minute, small second.
Case: 18 kt yellow gold, three-piece case (Ø 38 mm, thickness 12.7 mm) polished and brushed finish; antireflective curved sapphire crystal; gold crown; case back attached by 6 screws, displaying the movement through a sapphire crystal. Water-resistant to 3 atm.
Dial: silvered; printed Roman numerals and railway minute track; blued stainless steel leaf style hands.
Indications: small second at 6, integrated in the tourbillon carriage.
Strap: crocodile leather, hand stitched; gold clasp.
Price: 87'500 CHF.
Also available: pink gold (same price); white gold 89'900. Each version is available with black dial and applied Arabic numerals or silvered dial and painted Roman numerals.

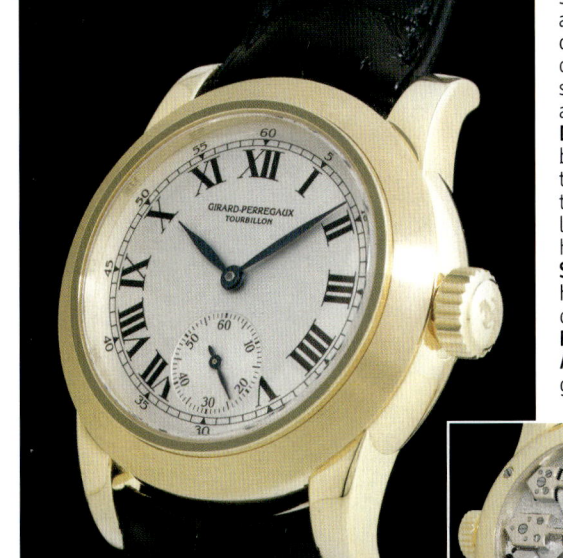

TOURBILLON AUTOMATIC WITH THREE GOLD BRIDGES — REF. 99250

Movement: mechanical, automatic winding, Girard-Perregaux caliber 9600, with tourbillon device mounted on three 18 kt pink gold bridges, autonomy of over 40 hours. Balance with 21,600 vibrations per hour (vph). Bridges in solid pink gold, pillar-plate silvered and chased. Completely finished and decorated by hand by the firm's watchmakers.
Functions: hour, minute.
Case: 18 kt pink gold, three-piece polished case (Ø 38 mm, thickness 10 mm); antireflective flat sapphire crystal; pink gold crown; case back attached by 6 screws. Water-resistant to 3 atm.
Dial: 3 solid gold tourbillon bridges visible, as well as the arabesqued pillar-plate, the barrel and the tourbillon; pink gold Dauphine hands.
Strap: crocodile leather, hand stitched; pink gold clasp.
Price: 100'000 CHF.
Also available: in yellow gold, same price; white gold 111'000; platinum 114'000.

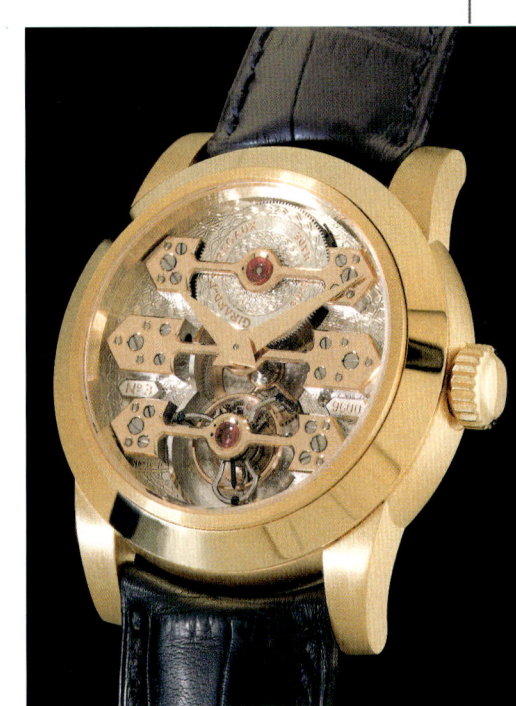

GIRARD-PERREGAUX

CHRONO TOURBILLON WITH THREE GOLD BRIDGES REF. 99150

Movement: mechanical, manual winding, Girard-Perregaux caliber 9981.
Functions: hour, minute, small second, chronograph with 3 counters.
Case: 18 kt yellow gold, three-piece case (Ø 39.7 mm, thickness 15.7 mm) polished and brushed finish; antireflective curved sapphire crystal; yellow gold crown and pushers; case back attached by 7 screws, displaying the movement through a sapphire crystal. Water-resistant to 3 atm. 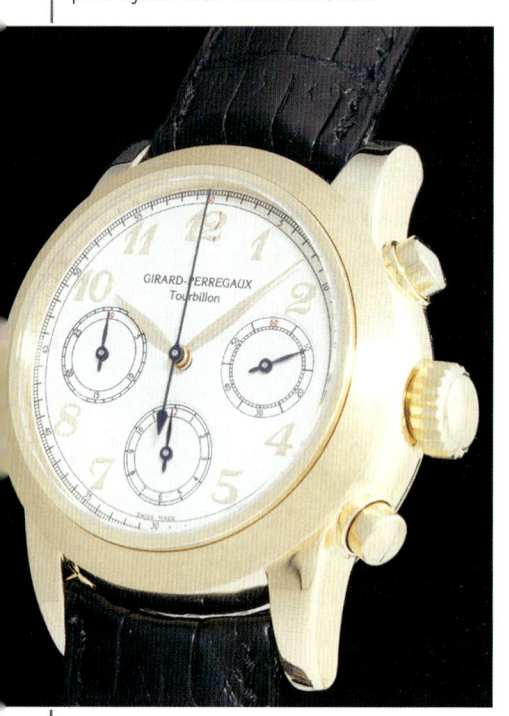
Dial: ivory; applied Arabic numerals; printed minute track; leaf style hands.
Indications: small second at 3, hour counter at 6, integrated in the tourbillon carriage, minute counter at 9, center second counter (blued stainless steel hands), minute track with divisions for 1/5 of a second.
Strap: crocodile leather, hand stitched; yellow gold clasp.
Price: 99'800 CHF.
Also available: pink gold (same price); white gold 102'000 CHF; platinum 110'000 CHF; titanium 95'000 CHF.

CHRONO RATTRAPANTE TOURBILLON MIN. REPEATER REF. 99700

Movement: mechanical, manual winding, Girard-Perregaux caliber 9898, with tourbillon device, autonomy of 32 hours, 44 jewels. Balance with 18,000 vibrations per hour (vph). Finished and decorated by hand by the firm's watchmakers.
Functions: hour, minute, small second, split-second chronograph with 2 counters, minute repeater.
Case: platinum, three-piece case (Ø 40, thickness 15 mm) polished and brushed finish; curved sapphire crystal; brushed bezel; white gold plated crown with pusher; white gold plated pushers; case back attached by 4 screws, displaying the movement through a sapphire crystal. Water-resistant to 3 atm. 
Dial: black; white painted Arabic numerals and minute track; Dauphine hands.
Indications: minute counter at 3, small second at 9, center second and split-second counters, minute track with divisions for 1/5 of a second.
Strap: crocodile leather, hand stitched; white gold clasp.
Price: 450'000 CHF. With black dial as a unique piece.
Also available: silvered dial: in yellow or pink gold 425'000 CHF; in white gold 427'500; in titanium 425'000 CHF.

CHRONOGRAPH RATTRAPANTE REF. 90170

Movement: mechanical, manual winding, Girard-Perregaux caliber 9780-070A, derived from an antique caliber Venus 185, autonomy of 45 hours and 26 jewels. Balance with 18,000 vibrations per hour (vph). Modified, mounted, adjusted and hand-finished by the firm's watchmakers. Officially certified "chronometer" (C.O.S.C.).
Functions: hour, minute, small second, split-second chronograph with 2 counters.
Case: 18 kt yellow gold, three-piece case (Ø 40 mm) polished and brushed finish; antireflective curved sapphire crystal; yellow gold crown with pusher; yellow gold pushers; case back attached by 7 screws, displaying the movement through a sapphire crystal. Water-resistant to 3 atm. 
Dial: ivory; applied Arabic numerals; printed minute track; Dauphine hands.
Indications: minute counter at 3, small second at 9, center split-second counters (blued stainless steel hands), minute track with divisions for 1/5 of a second.
Strap: crocodile leather, hand stitched; yellow gold clasp.
Price: 59'000 CHF.
Also available: pink gold (same price); white gold 61'950; platinum 77'500; titanium 49'000.

GP POUR FERRARI "F310B" REF. 90260

Movement: mechanical, automatic winding, Girard-Perregaux caliber 3170, 44 jewels, 28,800 vibrations per hour (vph).
Functions: hour, minute, small second, 24-hour indication, perpetual calendar (date, day, month, year, moon phase), chronograph with 3 counters.
Case: titanium, 3-piece case (Ø 40, thickness 13 mm) brushed; antireflective curved sapphire crystal; 2 correctors on case side; screw-down crown; case back attached by 8 screws, with silhouette of the "F310B" and the Grand Prix won. Water-resistant 3 atm. 
Dial: carbon fiber; luminescent Arabic numerals; luminescent sword style hands.
Indications: moon phase and 24-hour display at 3, day and hour counter at 6, months distributed over a four-cycle and minute counter at 9, date and small second at 12, center second counter, tachymeter scale.
Strap: crocodile leather, hand stitched; titanium fold-over clasp.
Price: on request.
Wooden case with red China lacquer with winding rotating device.
Also available: yellow gold/red gold; white gold; platinum. All available with black dial, luminescent Arabic numerals or ivory applied Arabic. "F50", realized in 1996 for the 205 years G.P. and 50 years Ferrari (same versions).

GIRARD-PERREGAUX

CHRONOGRAPH RATTRAPANTE S.F. FOUDROYANTE   REF. 90200

Movement: chronograph mechanical, manual winding. Modified and hand-finished by the firm's watchmakers.
Functions: hour, minute, small second, split-second chronograph with "lightning" feature with two counters.
Case: 18 kt pink gold, three-piece case polished and brushed finish (Ø 40, thickness 14.6 mm); antireflective "cushion-shaped" sapphire crystal; pink gold crown with pusher; pink gold pushers; case back attached by 7 screws. Water-resistant to 3 atm.
Dial: black; applied pink gold faceted triangular and Arabic numerals; printed minute track; leaf style hands.
Indications: minute counter at 3, eighths of a second counter with "lightning" hand at 9, center split-second counters, minute track with divisions for $1/5$ of a second, tachymeter scale.
Strap: crocodile leather, hand stitched; pink gold clasp.
Price: 32'000 CHF. Limited edition of 750 numbered pieces.
Also available: with bracelet 47'000; yellow gold (same prices); white gold, leather strap 33'000, bracelet 49'500. All with ivory dial and applied markers or black with luminescent or applied markers.

CHRONOGRAPH RATTRAPANTE S.F. FOUDROYANTE   REF. 90200

The originality of this model provided with a caliber with split-second chronograph, which is very complex in itself, consists of the small red "lightning" hand indicating the fractions of a second (eighths) on a separate dial at 9, thus ensuring a better chronometer display to be obtained by a mechanic movement. This "lightning" feature must be considered "classical" mechanic complication. In fact, the first watches with lightning seconds appeared in the XIXth century and were the ancestors of today's chronographs. The system adopted by Girard-Perregaux up to now virtually exploits the time division operated by the balance (in this case 28,800 vibrations per hour (vph) corresponding to 8 vibrations per second and to 1 vibration each $1/8$ of a second) to guarantee precise timing and a clear display of the time lapse measured. The photograph shows the version with titanium case and carbon fiber dial.
Price: 27'500 CHF.
Also available: bracelet 31'630.

GP POUR FERRARI "250 TR"   REF. 80900

Movement: mechanical, hand winding, Girard-Perregaux caliber 2280, autonomy 36 hours, bidirectional winding rotor and 48 jewels. Balance with 28,800 vibrations per hour (vph). Modified, mounted, adjusted and decorated by hand by the firm's watchmakers.
Functions: hour, minute, small second, 24-hour indication, chronograph with 3 counters.
Case: stainless steel, three-piece case (Ø 40 mm, thickness 14 mm) polished and brushed finish; curved sapphire crystal; case back attached by 8 screws, with the "Ferrari 250 TR" engraved. Water-resistant to 5 atm.
Dial: black; luminescent Arabic numerals; printed minute track; luminescent white painted bâton hands.
Indications: small second at 3, hour counter at 6, 24-hour indication at 9, center minute counter (with arrow-point shaped hand) and center second counter, tachymeter scale.
Strap: crocodile leather, hand stitched; stainless steel clasp.
Price: on request. Realized in a limited numbered edition of 2000 pieces, in memory of the prestigious Ferrari 250 TR.
Also available: with fold-over clasp; with bracelet.

GP POUR FERRARI "F1-048"   REF. 49550

Movement: mechanical, automatic winding, Girard-Perregaux caliber 2280, autonomy 36 hours, bidirectional winding rotor and 57 jewels. Balance with 28,800 vibrations per hour (vph). Modified, mounted, adjusted and decorated by hand by the firm's watchmakers.
Functions: hour, minute, small second, date, chronograph with 3 counters.
Case: titanium, 3 parts (Ø 40, thickness 13 mm) polished and brushed finish; antireflective curved sapphire crystal; back fastened by 7 steel screws with Ferrari logo and dedication "Manufacturé spécialement pour Ferrari". Water-resistant to 3 atm.
Dial: carbon fiber; screen-printed Arabic numerals and luminescent white painted bâton hands; printed minute track.
Indications: small second at 3, date between 4 and 5, hour counter at 6, minute counter at 9, center second counter, minute track and tachymeter scale.
Strap: titanium and Kevlar reinforced rubber, leather lining; titanium clasp.
Price: on request. Edition limited to 1000 pieces.

GIRARD-PERREGAUX

GP POUR FERRARI — REF. 80200

Movement: mechanical, automatic winding, Girard-Perregaux caliber 2280, autonomy 36 hours, bidirectional winding rotor, 57 jewels. Balance with 28,800 vibrations per hour (vph). Modified, mounted, adjusted and decorated by hand by the firm's watchmakers. **Functions:** hour, minute, small second, date, chronograph with 3 counters.
Case: stainless steel, three-piece brushed case (Ø 38 mm, thickness 13 mm); antireflective curved sapphire crystal; pushers with case protection; case back attached by 7 steel screws, with Ferrari logo and the dedication "Manufacturé spécialement pour Ferrari". Water-resistant to 3 atm. 
Dial: carbon fiber; polychromic Ferrari logo at 12; luminescent printed Arabic numerals; printed minute track; luminescent white painted bâton hands.
Indications: small second at 3, date between 4 and 5, hour counter at 6, minute counter at 9, center second counter.
Bracelet: brushed steel; double recessed fold-over clasp. Mahogany case.
Price: on request.
Also available: leather strap; colored dial: steel, leather strap, clasp, fold-over clasp, bracelet; yellow gold & stainless steel or pink leather strap, clasp8, fold-over clasp, bracelet; in yellow or pink gold, leather strap, fold-over clasp, bracelet; white gold, leather strap, clasp, fold-over clasp.

GP POUR FERRARI "F1-047" — REF. 49500

Movement: mechanical, automatic winding, Girard-Perregaux caliber 2200, autonomy of 36 hours, bidirectional winding rotor and 21 jewels. Balance with 28,800 vibrations per hour (vph). Modified, mounted, adjusted and decorated by hand by the firm's watchmakers.
Functions: hour, minute, center second, date.
Case: aluminum, three-piece case (Ø 38 mm, thickness 9.7 mm); antireflective curved sapphire crystal; case back attached by 7 screws. Water-resistant to 3 atm. 
Dial: carbon fiber; screen-printed Arabic numerals and luminescent white painted bâton hands; printed minute track.
Indications: date at 3.
Strap: titanium and Kevlar reinforced rubber, leather lining; aluminum clasp.
Price: on request.

GP POUR FERRARI PRESIDENT — REF. 80300

Movement: mechanical, automatic winding, Girard-Perregaux caliber 2200, autonomy of 36 hours, bidirectional winding rotor and 27 jewels. Balance with 28,800 vibrations per hour (vph). Modified, mounted, adjusted and decorated by hand by the firm's watchmakers.
Functions: hour, minute, small second.
Case: stainless steel, three-piece case (Ø 38, thickness 12.2 mm) polished and brushed finish; antireflective curved sapphire crystal; screw-down crown; case back attached by 6 screws, with the dedication "Manufacturé spécialement pour Ferrari". Water-resistant to 3 atm. 
Dial: silvered; applied Arabic numerals; printed minute track; Dauphine hands.
Indications: small second at 6.
Strap: crocodile leather, hand stitched; stainless steel clasp.
Price: on request.
Also available: in yellow gold. Both versions are available with black, silvered, bordeaux and yellow dial.

GP POUR FERRARI AUTOMATIC 36 MM — REF. 80250

Movement: mechanical, automatic winding, Girard-Perregaux caliber 2200, autonomy of 36 hours, bidirectional winding rotor and 21 jewels. Balance with 28,800 vibrations per hour (vph). Modified, mounted, adjusted and decorated by hand by the firm's watchmakers.
Functions: hour, minute, center second, date.
Case: stainless steel, three-piece case (Ø 36 mm, thickness 10,7 mm) polished and brushed finish; antireflective curved sapphire crystal; screw-down crown; case back attached by 6 screws. Water-resistant to 3 atm. 
Dial: black; white painted Arabic numerals and luminescent triangular markers on the printed railway minute track; Dauphine hands.
Indications: date at 3.
Strap: crocodile leather, hand stitched; stainless steel clasp.
Price: on request.
Also available: with bracelet; yellow gold & stainless steel or pink leather strap or bracelet; in yellow or pink gold, leather strap or bracelet; white gold, leather strap. All with silvered dial and applied bâton markers or black with applied bâton markers or white Arabic numerals.

GIRARD-PERREGAUX

LADY "F" — REF. 80390

Movement: mechanical, automatic winding, Girard-Perregaux caliber 2501, bidirectional winding rotor and 25 jewels. Balance with 28,800 vibrations per hour (vph). Modified, mounted, adjusted and decorated by hand by the firm's watchmakers.
Functions: hour, minute, center second, date.
Case: stainless steel, three-piece case (Ø 29 mm, thickness 9.5 mm) polished and brushed finish; antireflective curved sapphire crystal; screw-down crown; screwed-on case back. Water-resistant to 5 atm.
Dial: yellow; luminescent applied Arabic numerals and bâton markers; printed minute track; luminescent sword style hands.
Indications: date at 3.
Bracelet: stainless steel, polished and brushed finish; double recessed foldover clasp.
Price: on request.
Also available: stainless steel and yellow or pink gold with bracelet; yellow or pink gold, leather strap or bracelet; white gold, leather strap or bracelet. Each version is available with yellow, blue, black, white, rosé or red enameled dial with luminescent Arabic numerals and bâton markers or in mother-of-pearl with 11 brilliants at markers.

TRAVELLER II — REF. 49400

Movement: mechanical, automatic winding, Girard-Perregaux caliber 2291, with 31 jewels; balance with 28,800 vibrations per hour (vph). Modified, mounted, adjusted and decorated by hand by the firm's watchmakers.
Functions: hour, minute, center second, date, second time zone, 24-hour indication, alarm.
Case: stainless steel, three-piece case (Ø 38.2 mm, thickness 13.8 mm) polished and brushed finish; antireflective curved sapphire crystal; crown at 2 for hour, second time zone and date setting, at 4 for sonnerie setting; case back attached by 6 screws. Water-resistant to 3 atm.
Dial: silvered rosé; applied Arabic numerals; luminescent dots on the minute track, screen-printed; luminescent Dauphine hands.
Indications: date at 6 (referred to central time), second time zone–24-hour display below 12, sonnerie with red arrow-point center hand.
Strap: crocodile leather, hand stitched; stainless steel clasp.
Price: on request.
Also available: yellow or pink gold; white gold. All with ivory or rosé dial and applied Arabic numerals or black and luminescent or applied Arabic numerals.

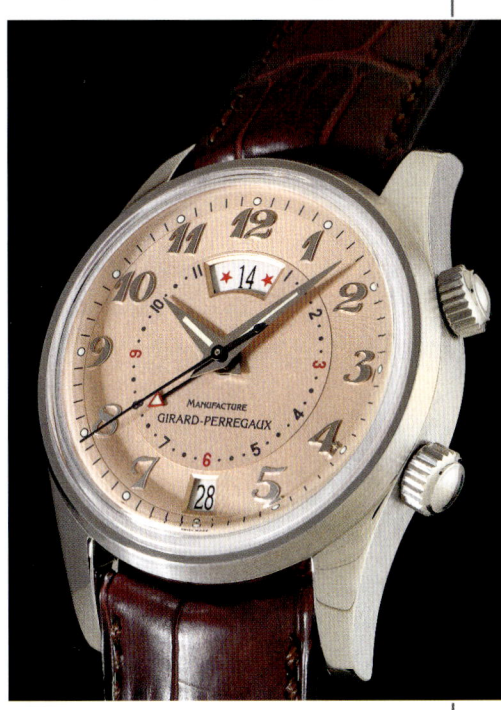

LAUREATO SPORT TOURBILLON WITH THREE GOLD BRIDGES — REF. 99070

Movement: mechanical, manual winding, Girard-Perregaux caliber 9900, with tourbillon device mounted on three 18 kt pink gold bridges and 20 jewels. Balance with 21,600 vibrations per hour (vph). Completely finished and decorated by hand by the firm's watchmakers.
Functions: hour, minute.
Case: 18 kt pink gold, three-piece case (Ø 40 mm, thickness 11.7 mm) polished and brushed finish; curved sapphire crystal; octagonal bezel with gasket; octagonal pink gold screw-down crown with case protection; case back attached by 6 screws. Water-resistant to 5 atm.
Dial: 3 bridges of the solid gold tourbillon visible, as well as the hand-chased pillar-plate, the barrel and the tourbillon; luminescent blued stainless steel lozenge hands.
Bracelet: pink gold, brushed finish, polished central links; double recessed foldover clasp in pink gold.
Price: 95'000 CHF.
Also available: in yellow gold (same price); white gold 97'000 CHF; steel 67'500 CHF.

LAUREATO CHRONOGRAPH — REF. 80170

Movement: mechanical, automatic winding, Girard-Perregaux caliber 3170, extra-thin. Hand-finished by the firm's watchmakers.
Functions: hour, minute, small second, date, chronograph with 3 counters.
Case: stainless steel, three-piece brushed case (with crown Ø 43.2 mm, thickness 13 mm); curved sapphire crystal; octagonal bezel with gasket; screw-down octagonal crown and pushers with case protection; case back attached by 6 screws. Water-resistant to 10 atm.
Dial: black; luminescent Arabic numerals; printed minute track; luminescent white painted bâton hands.
Indications: small second at 3, date between 4 and 5, hour counter at 6, minute counter at 9, center second counter, minute track with divisions for 1/5 of a second.
Bracelet: integrated brushed steel; steel foldover safety clasp.
Price: on request.

GIRARD-PERREGAUX

RICHEVILLE TONNEAU PERPETUAL CAL. MINUTE REPEATER   REF. 99600

Movement: mechanical, manual winding, Girard-Perregaux caliber 9896, autonomy of 36 hours and 30 jewels (Ø 28.2 mm, 12'''1/2, thickness 6.9 mm). Balance with 18,000 vibrations per hour (vph). Modified, mounted, adjusted and hand-finished by the firm's watchmakers.
Functions: hour, minute, center second, perpetual calendar (date, day, month, year, moon phase), minute repeater. 
Case: 18 kt yellow gold, three-piece polished tonneau case (height 37.5 mm, width 36 mm, thickness 11 mm); antireflective flat sapphire crystal; 3 correctors and repeater slide on case side; yellow gold crown; case back attached by 6 screws. Water-resistant to 3 atm.
Dial: solid gold, silvered; applied yellow gold Arabic numerals; printed railway minute track; yellow gold Breguet hands.
Indications: date at 3, moon phase at 6, day at 9, month and four year cycle at 12.
Strap: crocodile leather; yellow gold clasp.
Price: 195'000 CHF.
Also available: pink gold (same price); white gold 198'000 CHF.

RICHEVILLE TONNEAU PERPETUAL CALENDAR   REF. 27400

Movement: mechanical, automatic winding, Girard-Perregaux caliber 2290, autonomy of 45 hours and 21 jewels (Ø 25.9 mm, 11'''1/2, thickness 5.35 mm). Balance with 28,800 vibrations per hour (vph). Modified, mounted, finished, finished and decorated by hand by the firm's watchmakers.
Functions: hour, minute, center second, perpetual calendar (date, day, month, year, moon phase). 
Case: 18 kt yellow gold, three-piece polished tonneau case (height 36 mm, width 35 mm, thickness 10 mm); antireflective flat sapphire crystal; 4 correctors on case side; yellow gold crown; case back attached by 6 screws. Water-resistant to 3 atm.
Dial: silvered; applied yellow gold Arabic numerals; printed railway minute track; yellow gold Breguet hands.
Indications: date at 3, moon phase at 6, day at 9, month and four year cycle at 12.
Strap: crocodile leather; yellow gold clasp.
Price: 23'750 CHF.
Also available: pink gold (same price); white gold 24'900 CHF.

TOURBILLON TONNEAU WITH GOLD BRIDGE   REF. 99300

Movement: mechanical, manual winding, Girard-Perregaux caliber 9940, with tourbillon device mounted on a stainless steel bridge, autonomy of 75 hours and 20 jewels (Ø 28.6 mm, 12'''1/2, thickness 12.8 mm dial included). Balance with 21,600 vibrations per hour (vph). Finished and decorated by hand by the firm's watchmakers.
Functions: hour, minute, small second.
Case: 18 kt white gold, three-piece polished tonneau case (height 36 mm, width 35 mm, thickness 10 mm); antireflective flat sapphire crystal; white gold crown; case back attached by 6 screws. Water-resistant to 3 atm. 
Dial: silvered, engine turned (guilloché) by hand, aperture on the tourbillon; printed Roman numerals; blued stainless steel Stuart hands.
Indications: small second at 6, integrated in the tourbillon carriage.
Strap: crocodile leather; white gold clasp.
Price: on request.
Also available: in yellow or pink gold 67'500 CHF; platinum 69'000 CHF.

SKELETON TOURBILLON TONNEAU WITH 3 GOLD BRIDGES   REF. 99100

Movement: mechanical, manual winding, Girard-Perregaux caliber 990TO34, with tourbillon mounted on three 18 kt pink gold bridges, autonomy of 75 hours, 21,600 vibrations per hour, 20 jewels (Ø 36 mm, thickness 10 mm). Bridges in solid pink gold, pillar-plate silvered and chased. Completely finished, decorated and skeletonized by hand by the firm's watchmakers.
Functions: hour, minute, small second. 
Case: 18 kt pink gold, three-piece polished tonneau case (height 36 mm, width 35 mm, thickness 10 mm); antireflective flat sapphire crystal; pink gold crown; case back attached by 6 screws, displaying the movement through a sapphire crystal. Water-resistant to 3 atm.
Dial: silvered ring; printed Roman numerals; blued stainless steel Stuart hands; 3 bridges of the solid pink gold tourbillon visible, as well as the barrel with the mainspring and the silvered chased pillar-plate.
Indications: small second at 6, integrated in the tourbillon carriage.
Strap: crocodile leather, hand stitched; pink gold clasp.
Price: 89'000 CHF. Limited numbered edition.
Also available: yellow gold (same price); white gold 92'200 CHF; platinum 110'000 CHF.

GIRARD-PERREGAUX

RICHEVILLE TONNEAU CHRONOGRAPH — REF. 27500

Movement: mechanical, automatic winding, Girard-Perregaux caliber 2280.
Functions: hour, minute, small second, chronograph with 2 counters.
Case: stainless steel, three-piece polished tonneau case (height 37 mm, width 35 mm, thickness 11.5 mm); antireflective flat sapphire crystal; drop-shaped pushers, with case protection; case back attached by 7 screws. Water-resistant to 3 atm.
Dial: blue enameled, counters engine turned (guilloché); printed oversized Arabic numerals and railway minute track; luminescent lozenge hands. **Indications:** small second at 3, minute counter at 9, center second counter.
Strap: crocodile leather; stainless steel clasp.
Also available: steel and yellow gold or steel and pink gold; yellow gold; pink gold; white gold. Each version is available with white, black or blue enameled dial with Arabic numerals or Roman or silvered engine turned (guilloché) with Roman numerals.
Prices: on request.

GP 7000 — REF. 7000

Movement: mechanical, automatic winding, Girard-Perregaux caliber 8000, autonomy of 50 hours, bidirectional winding rotor and 39 jewels (Ø 30 mm, 13"'1/4, thickness 6.85 mm). Balance with 28,800 vibrations per hour (vph). Modified, mounted, adjusted and hand-finished by the firm's watchmakers.
Functions: hour, minute, small second, date, chronograph with 3 counters.
Case: stainless steel, three-piece case (Ø 38.3, thickness 11.6 mm) polished and brushed finish; antireflective flat sapphire crystal; bezel with engraved tachymeter scale; ogival pushers; case back attached by 6 screws. Water-resistant to 5 atm.
Dial: dark grey and black counters; applied Arabic numerals and a luminescent triangular marker; printed railway minute track with luminescent dots on the beveled ring; luminescent bâton hands.
Indications: date with magnifying glass at 3, hour counter at 6, minute counter at 9, small second at 12, center second counter.
Strap: crocodile leather, hand stitched; stainless steel clasp.
Also available: with bracelet; in yellow or pink gold & stainless steel, leather strap or bracelet; in yellow or pink gold, leather strap; various dials.
Prices: on request.

AUTOMATIC 3100 — REF. 90520

Movement: mechanical, automatic winding, Girard-Perregaux caliber 3000, extra-thin. Finished and decorated by hand by the firm's watchmakers.
Functions: hour, minute, center second, date.
Case: stainless steel, three-piece case (Ø 36 mm) polished and brushed finish; flat sapphire crystal; case back attached by 6 screws, displaying the movement through a sapphire crystal. Water-resistant to 3 atm.
Dial: white; applied Roman numerals; printed minute track; Dauphine hands.
Indications: date at 3.
Strap: crocodile leather, hand stitched; stainless steel clasp.
Also available: in yellow or pink gold; white gold. Each version is available with white or silvered dial and applied or printed Arabic or Roman numerals.
Prices: on request.

VINTAGE 1996 CHRONOGRAPH — REF. 49300

Movement: mechanical, automatic winding, Girard-Perregaux caliber 3170, autonomy of 36 hours, 18 kt gold rotor with bidirectional winding and 63 jewels, 13"'1/4. Balance with 28,800 vibrations per hour (vph). Modified, mounted, adjusted and hand-finished by the firm's watchmakers.
Functions: hour, minute, small second, date, chronograph with 3 counters.
Case: 18 kt white gold, three-piece case (Ø 36 mm, thickness 11.5 mm) polished and brushed finish; antireflective curved sapphire crystal; screw-down crown and pushers, in white gold; case back attached by 7 screws, displaying the movement through a sapphire crystal. Water-resistant to 3 atm.
Dial: black; applied Arabic numerals; printed minute track; leaf style hands.
Indications: small second at 3, date between 4 and 5, hour counter at 6, minute counter at 9, center second counter, tachymeter scale, minute track with divisions for $1/5$ of a second.
Strap: crocodile leather, hand stitched; white gold clasp.
Also available: yellow or pink gold. All with silvered, white or black dial, applied Arabic numerals or screen-printed Roman numerals, tachymeter or pulsometric scale.
Prices: on request.

GIRARD-PERREGAUX

VINTAGE 1997 CHRONOGRAPH RATTRAPANTE   REF. 90120

Movement: mechanical, automatic winding, Girard-Perregaux caliber 8298, with 31 jewels and Balance with 28,800 vibrations per hour (vph). Modified, mounted, adjusted and hand-finished by the firm's watchmakers.
Functions: hour, minute, small second, split-second chronograph with 2 counters.
Case: 18 kt yellow gold, two-piece brushed square curved case (height 38 mm, width 38 mm, thickness 14.8 mm); antireflective curved sapphire crystal; yellow gold crown with pusher; rectangular pushers; case back attached by 5 screws. Water-resistant to 3 atm. 
Dial: ivory; applied Arabic numerals; printed minute track; Dauphine hands.
Indications: minute counter at 3, small second at 9, center second and split-second counters, minute track with divisions for 1/5 of a second.
Strap: crocodile leather, hand stitched; gold clasp; precious wood case and authenticity certificate.
Also available: pink gold; steel. Each version is available with black dial and luminescent Arabic numerals or ivory dial and applied Arabic numerals.
Prices: on request.

VINTAGE 1960 CHRONOGRAPH   REF. 25980

Movement: mechanical, automatic winding, Girard-Perregaux caliber 2280. Balance with 28,800 vibrations per hour (vph). Modified, mounted, adjusted and hand-finished by the firm's watchmakers.
Functions: hour, minute, small second, 24-hour indication, chronograph with 2 counters.
Case: stainless steel, three-piece brushed case (height 30 mm, width 30 mm, thickness 14.8 mm); antireflective curved sapphire crystal; screw-down crown; rectangular pushers; case back attached by 7 screws. Water-resistant to 3 atm. 
Dial: silvered; applied Arabic numerals; printed minute track; leaf style hands.
Indications: small second at 3, 24-hour indication at 9, minute counter (with arrow-shaped point) and center second counter, minute track with divisions for 1/5 of a second.
Strap: crocodile leather, hand stitched; stainless steel clasp.
Price: on request.
Also available: in yellow, pink or white gold. Each version is available with silvered or black dial and applied Arabic numerals.

VINTAGE 1999 AUTOMATIC CHRONOGRAPH   REF. 25990

Movement: mechanical, automatic winding, Girard-Perregaux, caliber 3100 base with chronograph module (Ø23.3 mm, thickness 6.28 mm), 38 jewels, 28,800 vibrations per hour (vph), power reserve 36 hours. Finished and decorated by hand by the firm's watchmakers.
Functions: hour, minute, small second, chronograph with 2 counters.
Case: 18 kt pink gold, two-piece polished rectangular-curved case (height 31 mm, width 30 mm, thickness 13 mm); curved sapphire crystal; rectangular pushers; slightly recessed crown; snap-on back. Water-resistant to 3 atm. 
Dial: curved, anthracite, engine turned (guilloché) in the central part; applied Arabic numerals and faceted triangular markers; printed minute track; Dauphine hands.
Indications: minute counter at 3, small second at 9, center second counter.
Strap: crocodile leather, hand stitched; pink gold clasp.
Price: on request.
Also available: with bracelet; in yellow gold; white gold, leather strap or bracelet. All with smooth ivory or black or engine turned (guilloché), anthracite or pink dial.

VINTAGE 1945 GENTS   REF. 25940

Movement: mechanical, automatic winding, Girard-Perregaux caliber 3000, extra-thin. Finished and decorated by hand by the firm's watchmakers.
Functions: hour, minute, small second.
Case: 18 kt yellow gold, two-piece rectangular-curved case (with crown and lugs size 43x29.5 mm, thickness 10 mm) polished and brushed finish; curved sapphire crystal; slightly recessed crown; snap-on back. Water-resistant to 3 atm. 
Dial: curved, silvered brushed finish and zone engine turned (guilloché); printed Arabic numerals, digit 12 applied; printed railway minute track; Dauphine hands.
Indications: small second at 6.
Strap: crocodile leather, hand stitched; yellow gold clasp.
Price: on request.
Also available: red gold; steel, leather strap or bracelet; steel/yellow gold-pink gold, leather strap or bracelet. White, silvered, black dial. Lady Ref. 25900, manual, center second, silvered, pink, blue, anthracite dial: steel, leather strap or bracelet; yellow or pink gold & stainless steel, leather strap or bracelet; in yellow or pink gold, leather strap or bracelet; white gold, leather strap.

The History

Girard-Perregaux dates from 1791 and from that time has always expressed the combination of the two qualities that have most contributed to its success: technical skill and commercial instinct. Among the most exceptional watches under the Company's name is the Tourbillon Three Gold Bridges, awarded the Gold Medal at the World's Fair in Paris in 1867 and in 1889. The Company has become internationally known only fairly recently, and owes its rapid expansion to its own interpretation of "global manufacturing", that is, the real production capacity to move from making single components and all kinds of movements to the design and realization of exclusive, top quality pieces.

1966 - Girard-Perregaux designs and creates the first high frequency mechanical movement (36,000 A/h) on the base of a 1957 calibre. This is the Gyromatic H.F. calibre 16611. 1967 fully 73% of the chronometers certified by the Neuchâtel Observatory were Gyromatic H.F.

1968 - The Swiss industry is astounded by the potential of quartz: many of the old Houses step back from the new invention, but not Girard-Perregaux. It is the first to start industrial mass production of a Swiss made quartz model. Its oscillator frequency (32,768 Hertz) will subsequently be adopted as a world wide standard.

1987 - The GP 7000 is shown, a chronograph that is to become a great classic of contemporary sports watches and that will encourage the House to develop bonds with the sporting world of great competitions.

1991 - Influenced by the surge of revivals of the great complications of the past, Girard Perregaux presents a re-edition of the Tourbillon Three Bridges as a wristwatch at the Basel exhibition. This model is an indication of the ability and the ambitions of the Manufacture, which does not hesitate to test itself with an historical product while being attentive to the present and the future markets.

1993 - GP presents its Tribute to Ferrari, a split second automatic chronograph bearing the symbol known throughout the world: the rearing horse on a red ground, the Maranello flag. This was the start of an important association for the Swiss Company. The "pour Ferrari" group of watches will become a collection, in fact, enlarged year after year for a public devoted to its clean lines and elite and technological characteristics.

1994 - The capacity to make its own movements is an important and fundamental objective for all watchmaking companies. This year the movements GP 3000 and GP 3100 are introduced and will shortly equip all the House watches.

1995 - The collection "Laureato" is created, the first Girard-Perregaux "integrated" watch. The Company banks on this model that is characterized by an octagonal bezel and a decidedly sporting look. The chronograph version is chosen, in 1996 for the limited number edition of 999 pieces that the Manufacture has dedicated to each Olympic year since the turn of the last century.

1996 - Presentation of F50, an even stronger Ferrari link. Inspired by one of the most famous cars in the history of automobile racing, the chrono perpetual celebrates the 50th anniversary of the Maranello company and its own 205th anniversary. The new complication is a split second chrono with tourbillon and minute repeater. Two more models are added to the Vintage collection: the split second automatic chronograph, with a softened squared case, and the refined ladies model called Vintage Baguette. The new little automatic alarm calibre 2291 with a second time zone is mounted on Traveler II.

1998 - Girard Perregaux is recognizably among the most active companies in the field of quality watchmaking. Its new star is the Petit Tourbillon for which the GP craftsmen succeeded in miniaturizing the famous "Tourbillon Three Gold Bridges" movement in a 31 mm diameter case without distorting its technical characteristics. The ladies versions of Laureato and Vintage, dedicated to the alchemy of gold and diamonds, are greatly admired; the Lady "F", sports models dedicated to women and the Ferrari legend, are a natural development of the men's versions. Significant space is also given to the men's collections of the latest trends - like the Vintage 1945, "clothed" in fabulous cashmere and tasmanian wool from the Lanificio Loro Piana. The new "pour Ferrari" chronograph, the 250 TR, is dedicated to the Testa Rossa, whose silhouette is engraved on the back case. This, "three counters" model, with respect to the others, has a small section on the dial for the 24 hour counter in place of the traditional minute counter whose hand, in this instance, is next to the second counter.

Glashütte Original

After having won respect and admiration from collectors and from operators, thanks to a consistently high quality level, Glashütte Original enlarges its offer in that most difficult sector of the great complications with a model having absolutely innovative technology and construction: the PanoRetroGraph. It is a manual winding chronograph with fly-back feature, "panoramic date" indicator to which the count-down function has been added measured by the sweep second hand, with sector indication of the minutes on three ten-unit bands, that moves counter-clockwise. The acoustic system with striking hammer and circumference wire gong (already used in minute repeater watches) rings at the end of a time period set between 0 and 30 minutes. Its movement, made at the Glashütte Original manufacture, is the Calibre 60, 350 pieces, balance with compensation screws, regulator system with micrometer adjustment and regulator spring, gold jewel settings secured by screws, finely etched bridges. It will be officially presented in March at Basel 2000; production limited to 50 pieces, with platinum case and white gold dial; the price will be about 70-80 million Deutsche Marks.

Still at the top quality range, there is the new perpetual calendar Panorama Datum, automatic winding in the "Senator" line, available both in the Klassik collection (exclusively round cases) or in Karree (rectangular), while the "1845" line, distinguished by its manual winding movements also has the new power reserve - available in both Klassik and Karree.

Another innovation is the Karree Panoramadatum automatic with big date and moon phase. This last is always a fascinating indication that this German watchmaker has placed in an unusual aperture at 10 o'clock.

The History

Now that Time, frozen by the Iron Curtain, has again begun to fly, the elegance and reliability of the old Glashütte have returned intact thanks to the most sensitive spirits of those lands that have maintained their love for the beautiful in a dimension that, in the West, seems to have disappeared. The adventure begins again - but when did it really start?

1845 - Ferdinand Adolph Lange decides, one fine day, to give up his steady job as a watchmaker in Dresden to begin an adventure that promises to be fascinating. The object was to found a watch manufacture in the economically depressed region of Erzgebirge. When the Government of Saxony had suggested this, he was told that he would have to hire local workers who were absolutely without any notions of watchmaking. Lange had great faith in this own system of training, and accepted the risk. He did not simply succeed: he went far beyond his original aims. In a short time he convinced some of his collaborators to become independent, and thus was able to organize an autonomous network of watch parts production in Glashütte, that covered all sectors. Neither was Lange worried about the fact that in this way he was creating his own competition. He never forgot the initial urge behind his undertaking was his interest in the community, that is economic recovery by creating skilled workers as well as management. Other expert watchmakers began to arrive, attracted by the possibility of development in that area, such as Assman, Lange's future brother in law, who made a considerable contribution to the growth of the area.

1878 - This year the town of Glashütte experienced an event that would place it in the Gotha of watchmaking traditions. A school for the training of master watchmakers was founded, the Deutsche Uhrmacherschule. It would soon be recognized throughout the world as one of the best.

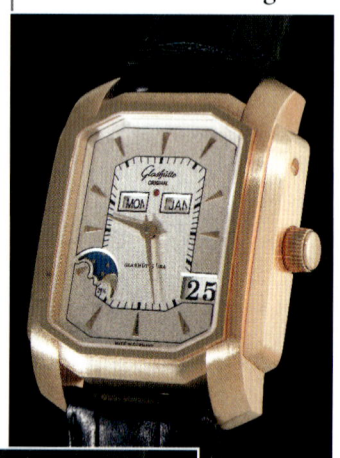

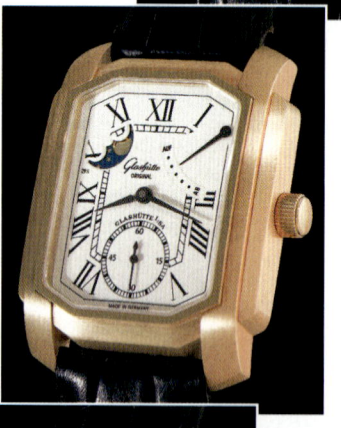

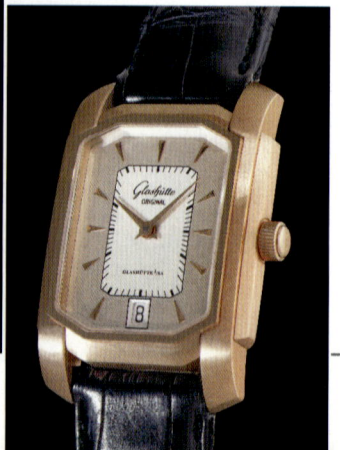

1920's - The end of World War I brought endless problems to Germany, not the least of which was economic. The world crisis became strangling in this area. The most serious problems in Glashütte depended upon the new, projectionist policies in Switzerland which risked isolating the town from its previous Swiss suppliers. Strangely, this new difficulty was instead a service rendered to the local industry, forced to create new factories and workshops to create on its own the components that had been imported. Glashütte became self-sufficient. And quality actually improved.

1940's - One war seems to lead to another only twenty years later. And Europe and the entire world were again at war. Adjusting to the situation, Glashütte produced prevalently watches for the navy and aviation..
On the 5th of August, 1945, just at the end of the war, a final bombardment devastated the watch industries there.

Post-War: The allied dismantling of German industry completed what the bombs had left unfinished. East Germany, including Erzgebirge, finds itself in the Soviet Union. In 1951 the main manufactures are united in a single company: Glashütter Uhrenbetrieb Gub.

1990 - The fall of the Berlin Wall and the unification of Germany allows the manufacture to consider a free market, without collective hobbles: the Company becomes Glashütter Uhrenbetrieb GmbH. It takes over the old buildings, the symbols of local watchmaking, and the time that begins to pass now has the taste of an old art.

1998 - It isn't hard to understand the philosophy of excellence at the base of this production, listening to the worlds of the president, Heinz W. Pfeifer, in Italy presenting the manufacture's historic collection. "The value of Glashütte Original watches, in 150 years, will be equal to or greater than that of today's museum pieces". For those who have gambled everything, taking up the challenge of remaking a company that had been blacked out under 50 years of Eastern Europe's nightmare, excellence and quality are necessarily the primary aspects to consider. The Company, in the last four years, has painstakingly rediscovered the transparent art of watchmaking, starting with the production of complicated movements. The latest production, the Karree, with austere rectangular lines, confirm the intuition of re-launching the manufacture. The first models presented in April, the Sub-seconds, the Perpetual Calendar and Lady, have manual winding movements (Calibre 42 for the fits two, Calibre 21 for the third). In September automatic winding models were presented, with the round Calibre 39 movement, and in particular the Karree Tourbillon, new classic, animated by a manual Calibre 43 and produced in a limited series of 25 pieces. The latest is the Flieger Panorama Datum which has an easy to read "panoramic" date function.

The New PanoRetroGraph

With its new PanoRetroGraph, once again Glashütte Original deal with "complicated" watches and this time chose not to base themselves on the most traditional types, such as tourbillons or perpetual calendars. On the contrary, they preferred the by far longer and hard way of absolute innovation which is here materialized in the count-down feature, very familiar to us through generations of multi-purpose chronographs with quartz movements (not to speak of the simpler kitchen timers) but absolutely new in the field of mechanical wrist chronographs. Figures confirm that it is a real "complication", especially those 360 elements which make up the movement as well as the complete list of features. In fact, it is a "fly-back" type chronograph with "panoramic" date display, to which the new count-down function has been added. This is read by the traditional sweep second hand, with sector minute indication on three counter-clockwise turning rings, of 10 units each, and a hammer and gong acoustic system with perimeter thread (already used in repeater watches) giving a sound at the end of the time set between 0 and 30 minutes (once the count-down is performed, the hand has come to 0 and the gong has been struck, the hand - if it is not stopped - keeps on moving counter-clockwise). The movement produced and realized by Glashütte Original, is the mechanical, hand-winding caliber 60 (ø 32 mm, thickness 7.2 mm) with balance and compensation screws, micrometer screw adjustment and swan-neck-shaped check spring, 28,800 vibrations per hour, screwed-on gold collets, finely decorated bridges.

Production will be limited to only 50 pieces, with platinum case and white gold dial, price approximative 70/80 thousand Deutsche Mark.

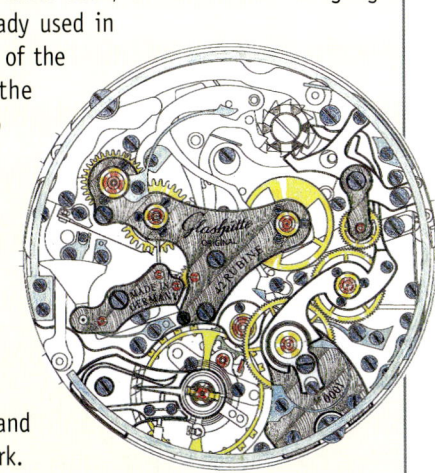

GLASHÜTTE ORIGINAL

1845 KLASSIK TOURBILLON ALFRED HELWIG — REF. 41.01.02.02.06

Movement: mechanical, manual winding, Glashütte Original caliber 41, with flying tourbillon.
Functions: hour, minute, small second.
Case: 18 kt pink gold, two-piece case (Ø 39 mm, thickness 9.5 mm) polished and brushed finish; flat sapphire crystal; knurled bezel; pink gold bulb-shaped crown; case back attached by 5 screws, displaying the movement through a sapphire crystal. Water-resistant to 5 atm. 
Dial: 18 kt white gold, silvered and rosé, color obtained in an electrolytic bath, aperture on the tourbillon.
Indications: off-center hour and minute at 6 with printed Arabic numerals and railway minute track, and blued stainless steel Breguet hands, small second at 12 integrated in the tourbillon carriage.
Strap: crocodile leather; pink gold clasp with applied logo.
Price: 113'980 CHF. Numbered edition limited to 25 pieces.

1845 KLASSIK PERPETUAL CALENDAR — REF. 49.01.04.01.04

Movement: mechanical, manual winding, Glashütte Original caliber 49/01.
Functions: hour, minute, center second, perpetual calendar (date, day of the week, month over a four-year cycle, moon phases).
Case: stainless steel, two-piece case (Ø 38.5 mm, thickness 11 mm) polished and brushed finish; flat sapphire crystal; knurled bezel; 3 correctors on case side; bulb-shaped crown; case back attached by 5 screws, displaying the movement through a sapphire crystal. Water-resistant to 5 atm. 
Dial: solid silver, white lacquered; zones with concentric-circles pattern; painted Arabic numerals and minute track; blued stainless steel Breguet hands.
Indications: date at 3, moon phase at 6, day at 9, months at 12 distributed over a four-cycle.
Strap: crocodile leather; stainless steel clasp with applied logo.
Price: 20'410 CHF.
Also available: silvered dial Ref. 49.01.03.01.04; pink gold silvered dial Ref. 49.01.03.02.04 or white Ref. 49.01.04.02.04, 25'820 CHF.

1845 KLASSIK WITH DATE INDICATOR — REF. 49.02.04.02.04

Movement: mechanical, manual winding, Glashütte Original caliber 49/02.
Functions: hour, minute, small second, date.
Case: 18 kt pink gold, two-piece case (Ø 38.5 mm, thickness 11.2 mm) polished and brushed finish; flat sapphire crystal; knurled bezel; pink gold bulb-shaped crown; case back attached by 5 screws, displaying the movement through a sapphire crystal. Water-resistant to 5 atm. 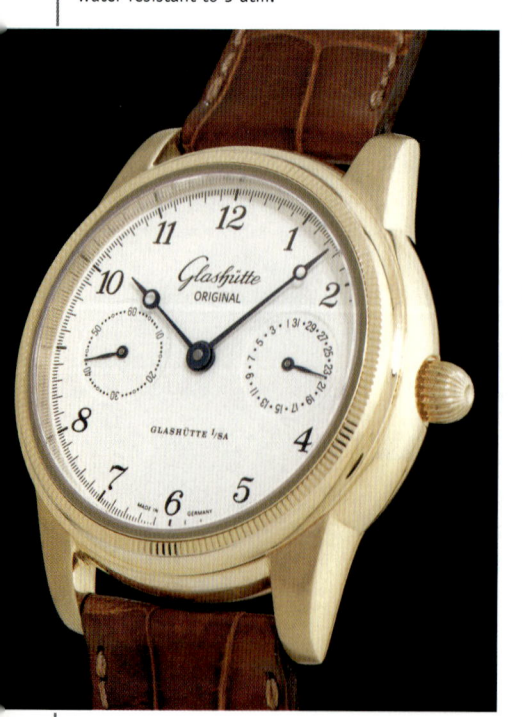
Dial: solid silver, white lacquered; painted Arabic numerals and minute track; blued stainless steel Breguet hands.
Indications: date at 3, small second at 9 (with stop device for hour setting).
Strap: crocodile leather; pink gold clasp with applied logo.
Price: 11'590 CHF.
Also available: with wholly silvered dial Ref. 49.02.03.02.04; stainless steel, silvered dial Ref. 49.02.03.01.04 or white lacquered dial Ref. 49.02.04.01.04, 8'690 CHF.

1845 KLASSIK POWER RESERVE — REF. 49.03.03.02.04

Movement: mechanical, manual winding, Glashütte Original caliber 49-03.
Functions: hour, minute, small second, date, power reserve.
Case: 18 kt pink gold, two-piece case (Ø 39 mm, thickness 12 mm) polished and brushed finish; flat sapphire crystal; knurled bezel; moon phase corrector at 10; pink gold bulb-shaped crown; case back attached by 8 screws, displaying the movement through a sapphire crystal. Water-resistant to 5 atm. 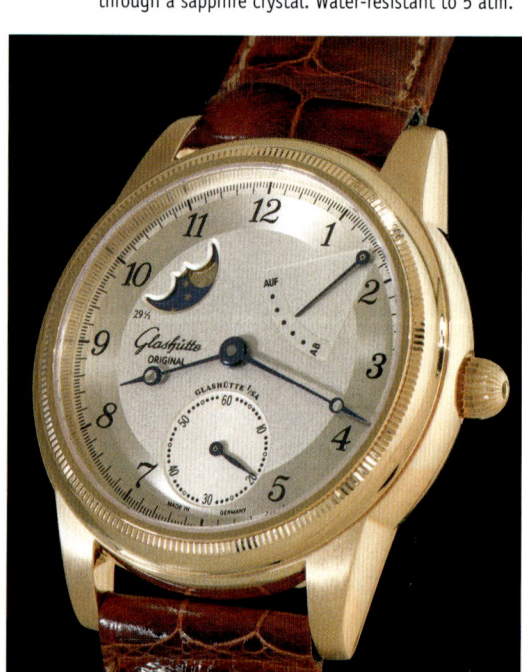
Dial: solid silver, silvered; zones with concentric-circles pattern; painted Arabic numerals and minute track; blued stainless steel Breguet hands.
Indications: power reserve between 1 and 2, small second at 6 (with stop device for hour setting), moon phases between 10 and 11.
Strap: crocodile leather; pink gold clasp with applied logo.
Price: 13'620 CHF.
Also available: with white lacquered dial Ref. 49.03.04.02.04; steel, silvered dial Ref. 49.03.03.01.04 or white dial Ref. 49.03.04.01.04, 11'110 CHF.

GLASHÜTTE ORIGINAL

1845 KLASSIK REGULATEUR — REF. 49.04.03.02.04

Movement: mechanical, manual winding, Glashütte Original caliber 49/04.
Functions: hour, minute, small second.
Case: 18 kt pink gold, two-piece case (Ø 38.5 mm, thickness 11.8 mm) polished and brushed finish; flat sapphire crystal; knurled bezel; pink gold bulb-shaped crown; case back attached by 5 screws, displaying the movement through a sapphire crystal. Water-resistant to 5 atm.
Dial: solid silver, silvered; zones with concentric-circles pattern; painted Arabic numerals and minute track; blued stainless steel Breguet hands.
Indications: off-center hour at 12, small second at 6.
Strap: crocodile leather; pink gold clasp with applied logo.
Price: 12'530 CHF.
Also available: with two-color silvered and pink dial Ref. 49.04.02.02.04 or white lacquered Ref. 49.04.04.02.04; stainless steel, wholly silvered dial Ref. 49.04.03.01.04 or two-color silvered and pink dial Ref. 49.04.02.01.04 or white lacquered dial Ref. 49.04.04.01.04, 9'580 CHF.

SENATOR KLASSIK PERPETUAL CAL. PANORAMADATUM — REF. 39.50.01.01.04

Movement: mechanical, automatic winding, Glashütte Original caliber 39/50.
Functions: hour, minute, center second, perpetual calendar (moon phases, month over a four-year cycle, day of the week, date).
Case: 18 kt pink gold, two-piece case (Ø 39 mm, thickness 12.5 mm) polished and brushed finish; flat sapphire crystal; 4 correctors on case side; knurled bezel; case back attached by 5 screws, displaying the movement through a sapphire crystal. Water-resistant to 5 atm.
Dial: silvered; applied golden bâton markers; golden brass Dauphine hands.
Indications: month window between 2 and 3, big date at 4 (two coaxial and coplanar disks), moon phase between 7 and 8, day window between 9 and 10, four-year cycle with digital display below 12.
Strap: crocodile leather; pink gold clasp with applied logo.
Price: 22'880 CHF.
Also available: stainless steel 15'830 CHF.

SENATOR PANORAMA DATUM — REF. 39.41.01.01.04

Movement: mechanical, automatic winding, Glashütte Original caliber 39/41.
Functions: hour, minute, center second, "panoramic" date, moon phase.
Case: 18 kt pink gold, two-piece case (Ø 38.5 mm, thickness 10.7 mm) polished and brushed finish; flat sapphire crystal; knurled bezel; case back attached by 5 screws, displaying the movement through a sapphire crystal. Water-resistant to 5 atm.
Dial: silvered; applied golden bâton markers (Arabic numeral 12) and cabochon minute track; golden brass Dauphine hands.
Indications: big date at 4 (two coaxial and coplanar disks), moon phase at 10.
Strap: crocodile leather; pink gold clasp with applied logo.
Price: 15'250 CHF.
Also available: steel Ref. 39.41.02.02.04, 8'770 CHF.

SENATOR KLASSIK AUTOMATIC — REF. 39.11.05.03.04

Movement: mechanical, automatic winding, Glashütte Original caliber 39/11.
Functions: hour, minute, center second, date.
Case: stainless steel, three-piece case (Ø 36.5 mm, thickness 9 mm) polished and brushed finish; flat sapphire crystal; knurled bezel; case back attached by 5 screws, displaying the movement through a sapphire crystal. Water-resistant to 5 atm.
Dial: white; printed Roman numerals and railway minute track; leaf style hands in blued brass.
Indications: date at 3.
Strap: crocodile leather; stainless steel clasp with applied logo.
Price: 3'490 CHF.
Also available: with black Roman numerals Ref. 39.11.050304; silvered dial, applied cabochon dial-train (Arabic numeral 12) Ref. 39.11.030304; pink gold, silvered dial, applied cabochon dial-train (Arabic numeral 12) Ref. 39.11.040204 or white, black Roman numerals Ref. 39.11.050204, 8'770 CHF.

GLASHÜTTE ORIGINAL

SENATOR KLASSIK CHRONOGRAPH   REF. 39.31.03.03.04

Movement: mechanical, automatic winding, Glashütte Original caliber 39/31.
Functions: hour, minute, small second, chronograph with 3 counters.
Case: stainless steel, three-piece case (Ø 39 mm, thickness 12 mm) polished and brushed finish; flat sapphire crystal; knurled bezel; ogival pushers; case back attached by 5 screws, displaying the movement through a sapphire crystal. Water-resistant to 5 atm. 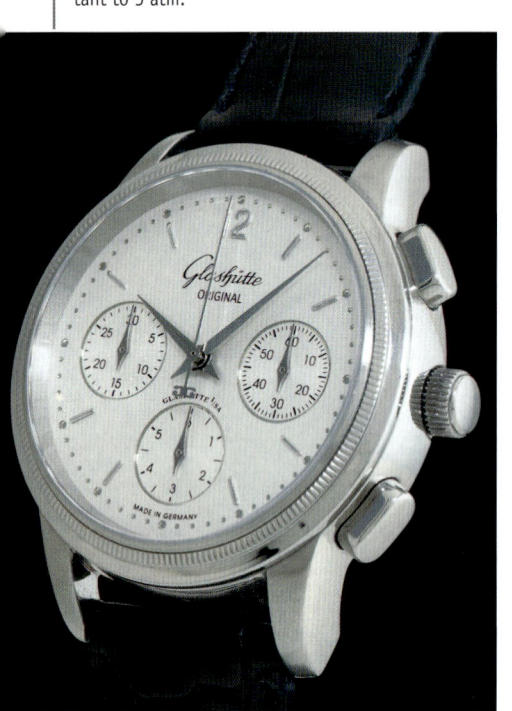
Dial: silvered; zones with concentric-circles pattern; applied bâton markers (Arabic numeral 12) and dial-train cabochon, in nickel-plated brass; nickeled brass Dauphine hands.
Indications: small second at 3, hour counter (6 h) at 6, minute counter at 9, center second counter.
Strap: crocodile leather; stainless steel clasp with applied logo.
Price: 4'580 CHF.
Also available: white dial, Roman numerals blue Ref. 39.31.02.03.04 or black Ref. 39.31.05.03.04; pink gold, silvered dial Ref. 39.31.04.02.04 or white Ref. 39.31.05.02.04, 10'050 CHF (gold models are available with applied bâton markers, Arabic numeral 12, or printed black Roman numerals).

SENATOR KLASSIK CHRONOGRAPH WITH DATE   REF. 39.32.05.02.04

Movement: mechanical, automatic winding, Glashütte Original caliber 39/32.
Functions: hour, minute, small second, date, chronograph with 3 counters.
Case: 18 kt pink gold, three-piece case (Ø 39 mm, thickness 12 mm) polished and brushed finish; flat sapphire crystal; knurled bezel; ogival pushers; pink gold crown; case back attached by 5 screws, displaying the movement through a sapphire crystal. Water-resistant to 5 atm. 
Dial: white lacquered; printed Roman numerals and railway minute track; leaf style hands in burnished brass.
Indications: small second at 3, hour counter (6 h) at 6, minute counter at 9, center second counter, date with magnifying glass at 12.
Strap: crocodile leather; pink gold clasp with applied logo.
Price: 10'180 CHF.
Also available: silvered dial Ref. 39.32.04.02.04; steel silvered dial Ref. 39.32.03.03.04 or white dial with blue Roman numerals Ref. 39.32.02.03.04 or black Roman numerals Ref. 39.32.05.03.04, 4'700 CHF.

SENATOR KLASSIK FLIEGER AUTOMATIC   REF. 39.11.07.06.04

Movement: mechanical, automatic winding, Glashütte Original caliber 39/11.
Functions: hour, minute, center second, date.
Case: 18 kt pink gold, three-piece case (Ø 36.5 mm, thickness 9 mm), completely brushed; flat sapphire crystal; case back attached by 5 screws, displaying the movement through a sapphire crystal. Water-resistant to 5 atm.
Dial: black enameled, matte; luminescent Arabic numerals and minute markers; luminescent white painted lozenge hands. 
Indications: date at 3.
Strap: calf, padded and hand stitched; pink gold clasp with applied logo.
Price: 10'320 CHF.
Also available: stainless steel Ref. 39.11.07.07.04, 4'800 CHF.

SENATOR KLASSIK FLIEGER PANORAMADATUM   REF. 39.42.07.01.04

Movement: mechanical, automatic winding, Glashütte Original caliber 39/42.
Functions: hour, minute, center second, date.
Case: 18 kt pink gold, three-piece case (Ø 37 mm, thickness 9 mm), completely brushed; flat sapphire crystal; pink gold crown; case back attached by 5 screws, displaying the movement through a sapphire crystal. Water-resistant to 5 atm.
Dial: black enameled, matte; luminescent Arabic numerals and minute markers; luminescent white painted lozenge hands. 
Indications: date at 4 (two coaxial and coplanar disks).
Strap: calf, padded and hand stitched; pink gold clasp with applied logo.
Price: 14'990 CHF.
Also available: stainless steel Ref. 39.42.07.02.04, 8'500 CHF.

GLASHÜTTE ORIGINAL

SENATOR KLASSIK FLIEGER CHRONO WITH DATE REF. 39.32.07.06.04

Movement: mechanical, automatic winding, Glashütte Original caliber 39/32.
Functions: hour, minute, small second, date, chronograph with 3 counters.
Case: 18 kt pink gold, three-piece case (Ø 39 mm, thickness 12 mm), completely brushed; flat sapphire crystal; bezel with engraved tachymeter scale; ogival pushers; pink gold crown; case back attached by 5 screws, displaying the movement through a sapphire crystal. Water-resistant to 5 atm.
Dial: black enameled, matte; luminescent Arabic numerals; printed minute track; luminescent white painted brass lozenge hands.
Indications: small second at 3, hour counter (6 h) at 6, minute counter at 9, date with magnifying glass at 12, center second counter, minute track with divisions for 1/5 of a second.
Strap: calf, padded and hand stitched; pink gold clasp with applied logo.
Price: 10'320 CHF.
Also available: stainless steel Ref. 39.32.07.07.04, 4'800 CHF.

1845 KARREE TOURBILLON REF. 43.01.01.01.06

Movement: mechanical, manual winding, Glashütte Original caliber 43/01, with flying tourbillon. Skeletonized and hand-decorated; back bridge with an engraving representing a watchmaker at work.
Functions: hour, minute, small second.
Case: 18 kt pink gold, four-piece case (height with lugs 44.5 mm, width 34.7 mm, thickness 11 mm) polished and brushed finish; curved sapphire crystal; pink gold crown; case back attached by 8 screws, displaying the movement through a sapphire crystal. Water-resistant to 3 atm.
Dial: 18 kt white gold, silvered, aperture on the tourbillon.
Indications: off-center hour and minute at 6 with printed Roman numerals, railway minute track and blued stainless steel Alpha hands, small second at 12 integrated in the tourbillon carriage.
Strap: crocodile leather; pink gold clasp with applied logo.
Price: 113'980 CHF.
Edition limited to 25 pieces for the whole world.

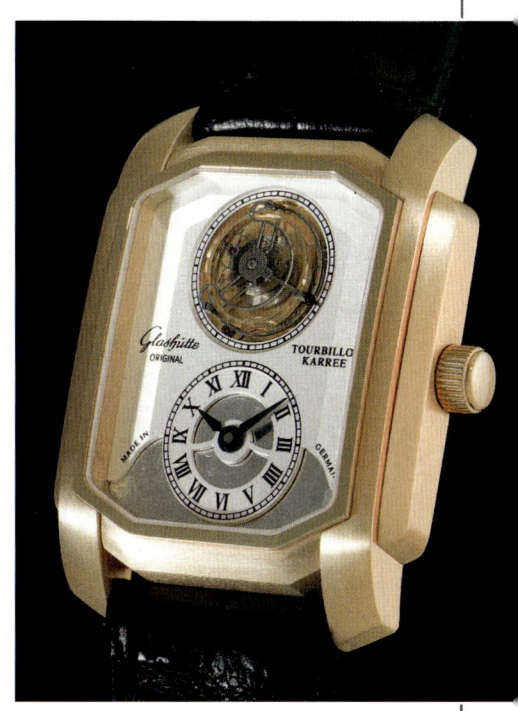

1845 KARREE PERPETUAL CALENDAR REF. 42.01.02.01.04

Movement: mechanical, manual winding, Glashütte Original caliber 42/01.
Functions: hour, minute, perpetual calendar (date, day of the week, month over a four-year cycle, moon phases).
Case: stainless steel, four-piece case (height with lugs 42.5 mm, width 30.5 mm, thickness 11.3 mm) polished and brushed finish; curved sapphire crystal; stainless steel crown; 3 correctors on case side; case back attached by 8 screws, displaying the movement through a sapphire crystal. Water-resistant to 3 atm.
Dial: solid silver, white lacquered; printed Roman numerals and railway minute track; blued stainless steel Alpha hands.
Indications: date at 3, moon phase at 6, day at 9, months at 12 distributed over a four-cycle.
Strap: crocodile leather; stainless steel clasp with applied logo.
Price: 22'970 CHF.
Also available: silvered dial, Arabic Ref. 42.01.01.01.04; pink gold, silvered dial, Arabic Ref. 42.01.01.02.04 or in silver, white lacquered Roman numerals Ref. 42.01.02.02.04, 28'380 CHF.

1845 KARREE POWER RESERVE REF. 42.03.01.01.04

Movement: mechanical, manual winding, Glashütte Original caliber 42/03.
Functions: hour, minute, small second, date, power reserve.
Case: stainless steel, four-piece case (height with lugs 44 mm, width 34.8 mm, thickness 11.3 mm) polished and brushed finish; flat sapphire crystal; stainless steel crown; moon phase corrector; case back attached by 8 screws, displaying the movement through a sapphire crystal. Water-resistant to 3 atm.
Dial: solid silver, silvered; printed Arabic numerals and railway minute track; blued stainless steel Alpha hands.
Indications: power reserve between 1 and 2, small second at 6 (with stop device for hour setting), moon phases between 10 and 11.
Strap: crocodile leather; stainless steel clasp with applied logo.
Price: 11'990 CHF.
Also available: white dial, Roman numerals Ref. 42.03.02.01.04; pink gold, silvered dial, Arabic Ref. 42.03.01.02.04 or white dial, Roman numerals Ref. 42.03.02.02.04, 14'890 CHF.

GLASHÜTTE ORIGINAL

SENATOR KARREE PANORAMADATUM — REF. 39.43.05.04.04

Movement: mechanical, automatic winding, Glashütte Original caliber 39/43.
Functions: hour, minute, date, moon phase.
Case: stainless steel, four-piece case (height with lugs 44.5 mm, width 35 mm, thickness 11.5 mm) polished and brushed finish; curved sapphire crystal; stainless steel crown; moon phase corrector; case back attached by 8 screws, displaying the movement through a sapphire crystal. Water-resistant to 3 atm. 
Dial: Art Déco, silvered with black external ring; applied pointed faceted markers; printed minute track; nickeled brass Dauphine hands.
Indications: big date at 4 (two coaxial and coplanar disks), moon phase at 10.
Strap: crocodile leather; stainless steel clasp with applied logo.
Price: 10'190 CHF. The Art Déco dial is available only for steel models.
Also available: silvered dial Ref. 39.43.040404; pink gold, silvered dial Ref. 39.43.07.05.04, 16'360 CHF.

SENATOR KARREE PERPETUAL CAL. PANORAMADATUM — REF. 39.51.02.02.04

Movement: mechanical, automatic winding, Glashütte Original caliber 39/51.
Functions: hour, minute, center second, perpetual calendar (date, day, month, year, moon phase).
Case: stainless steel, four-piece case (height with lugs 44 mm, width 35 mm, thickness 13 mm) polished and brushed finish; curved sapphire crystal; 4 correctors on case side; stainless steel crown; case back attached by 8 screws, displaying the movement through a sapphire crystal. Water-resistant to 3 atm. 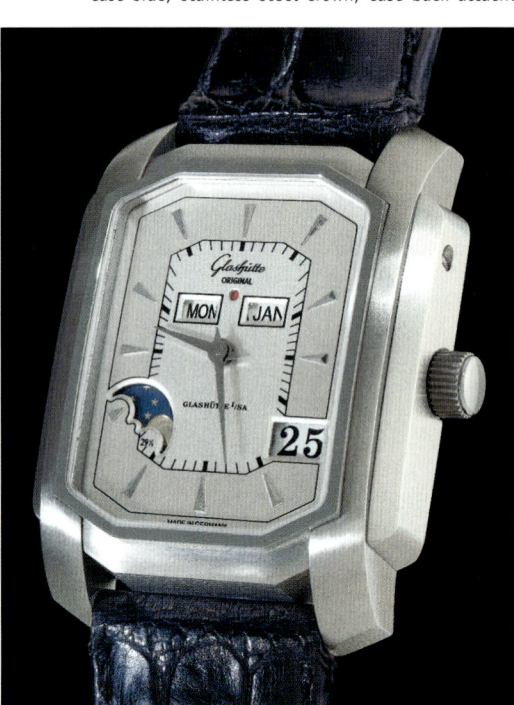
Dial: silvered; applied pointed faceted markers; printed minute track; nickeled brass Dauphine hands.
Indications: month between 2 and 3, big date at 4 (two coaxial and coplanar disks), moon phase between 7 and 8, day between 9 and 10, four-year cycle below 12.
Strap: crocodile leather; stainless steel clasp with applied logo.
Price: 15'700 CHF.
Also available: with Art Déco dial Ref. 39.51.03.02.04; pink gold Ref. 39.51.01.01.04, 24'150 CHF.

SENATOR KARREE CHRONOGRAPH — REF. 39.31.17.04.04

Movement: mechanical, automatic winding, Glashütte Original caliber 39/31.
Functions: hour, minute, small second, chronograph with 3 counters.
Case: stainless steel, four-piece case (height with lugs 45 mm, width 35 mm, thickness 13.5 mm) polished and brushed finish; slightly curved sapphire crystal; stainless steel crown; rectangular pushers (with axis parallel to the crown axis); case back attached by 8 screws, displaying the movement through a sapphire crystal. Water-resistant to 3 atm. 
Dial: Art Déco, silvered with black external ring; applied pointed faceted markers printed minute track; nickeled brass Dauphine hands.
Indications: small second at 3, hour counter (6 h) at 6, minute counter at 9, center second counter.
Strap: crocodile leather; stainless steel clasp with applied logo.
Price: 5'960 CHF.
Also available: silvered dial Ref. 39.31.06.04.04; pink gold, silvered dial Ref. 39.32.09.05.04, 12'300 CHF.

SENATOR KARREE CHRONOGRAPH WITH DATE — REF. 39.32.09.05.04

Movement: mechanical, automatic winding, Glashütte Original caliber 39/32.
Functions: hour, minute, small second, date, chronograph with 3 counters.
Case: 18 kt pink gold, four-piece case (height with lugs 45 mm, width 35 mm, thickness 13.5 mm) polished and brushed finish; slightly curved sapphire crystal; pink gold crown; rectangular pushers perpendicular to the case; case back attached by 8 screws, displaying the movement through a sapphire crystal. Water-resistant to 3 atm. 
Dial: silvered; zones with concentric-circles pattern; applied pink gold pointed faceted markers; printed minute track; golden brass Dauphine hands.
Indications: small second at 3, hour counter (6 h) at 6, minute counter at 9, center second counter, date with magnifying glass at 12.
Strap: crocodile leather; stainless steel clasp with applied logo.
Price: 12'430 CHF.
Also available: stainless steel, Art Déco dial Ref. 39.32.17.04.04 or silvered Ref. 39.32.06.04.04, 6'090 CHF.

GLASHÜTTE ORIGINAL

SENATOR KARREE AUTOMATIC — REF. 39.20.03.01.04

Movement: mechanical, automatic winding, Glashütte Original caliber 39/20.
Functions: hour, minute, date.
Case: stainless steel, four-piece case (height with lugs 42.4 mm, width 31 mm, thickness 9.5 mm) polished and brushed finish; curved sapphire crystal; stainless steel crown; case back attached by 8 screws, displaying the movement through a sapphire crystal. Water-resistant to 3 atm.
Dial: Art Déco, silvered with black external ring; applied pointed faceted markers; printed minute track; nickeled brass Dauphine hands.
Indications: date at 6.
Strap: crocodile leather; stainless steel clasp with applied logo.
Price: 4'410 CHF.
Also available: silvered dial Ref. 3920010104; pink gold, silvered dial Ref. 39.20.02.02.04, 9'040 CHF.

LADY SPORT AUTOMATIC — REF. 10.33.42.50.04

Movement: mechanical, automatic winding, Glashütte Original caliber 39-11 (from this year also the lady's model uses caliber 39-11 whose peculiarity is a skeletonized rotor personalized with the logo, 21 kt gold peripheral mass as all the automatic watches of this House).
Functions: hour, minute, center second, date.
Case: stainless steel, three-piece case, polished and brushed finish (Ø 31 mm, thickness 10.5 mm); flat sapphire crystal with magnifying lens on date; bezel 18 kt white gold, dodecagonal shape, with 24 set brilliants (0.60 kt); screw-down crown; screwed-on case back displaying the movement through a sapphire crystal. Water-resistant to 10 atm.
Dial: blue; applied faceted polished triangular markers; printed minute track in white; luminescent bâton hands.
Indications: date at 3.
Bracelet: steel; recessed double fold-over clasp, with engraved logo.
Price: 10'590 CHF.
Also available: white dial Ref. 10.33.41.50.04; in many other jewel versions; in non jewel version, blue or white dial Ref. 10.33.42.51.04, 4'460 CHF.

SPORT AUTOMATIC — REF. 10.33.18.12.04

Movement: mechanical, automatic winding, Glashütte Original caliber 39-11 (from this year it uses caliber 39-11 whose peculiarity is a skeletonized rotor personalized with the logo, 21 kt gold peripheral mass as all the automatic watches of this House).
Functions: hour, minute, center second, date.
Case: stainless steel and yellow gold, three-piece case (Ø 41, thickness 11 mm) polished and brushed finish; flat sapphire crystal with magnifying lens on date; counter-clockwise turning bezel (120 clicks), dodecagonal, with blue aluminum ring, luminescent marker and graduated scale, useful for the calculation of diving times; gold screw-down crown case back attached by 8 screws. Water-resistant to 20 atm.
Dial: white; luminescent applied geometric markers; printed minute track; luminescent Mercedes hands.
Indications: date at 3.
Strap: shark-skin; stainless steel clasp, with applied logo.
Price: 6'100 CHF.
Also available: bracelet 10'590 CHF; blue or black dial and bezel; steel, blue or black dial and bezel, leather strap 3'850 CHF, bracelet 5'280; yellow gold, blue or black dial and bezel, white dial and blue bezel, gilt dial and blue bezel, leather strap 12'350, bracelet 24'750.

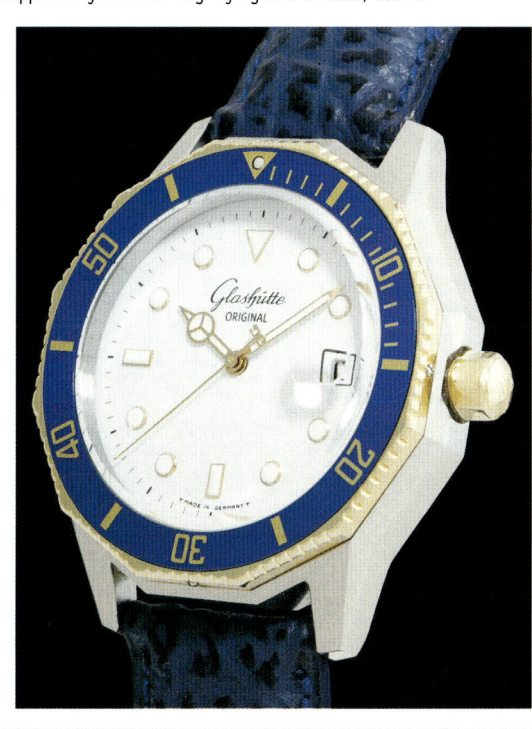

SPORT CHRONOGRAPH — REF. 10.66.16.14.04

Movement: mechanical, automatic winding, Glashütte Original caliber 39-31.
Functions: hour, minute, small second, chronograph with 3 counters.
Case: 18 kt yellow gold, three-piece case (Ø 41.5 mm, thickness 13.5 mm) polished and brushed finish; flat sapphire crystal; dodecagonal bezel with engraved tachymeter scale; yellow gold crown; faceted ogival pushers; case back attached by 8 screws, displaying the movement through a sapphire crystal. Water-resistant to 10 atm.
Dial: black; applied golden brass faceted triangular markers; luminescent golden brass bâton hands.
Indications: small second at 3, hour counter (6 h) at 6, minute counter at 9, center second counter, minute track with divisions for 1/5 of a second.
Strap: crocodile leather, padded and hand stitched; yellow gold clasp with applied logo.
Price: 13'150 CHF.
Also available: bracelet 25'550 CHF; yellow gold & stainless steel, leather strap 8'910; bracelet 11'400; steel, leather strap 4'690, bracelet 6'090; All the versions also with blue, green or white dial.

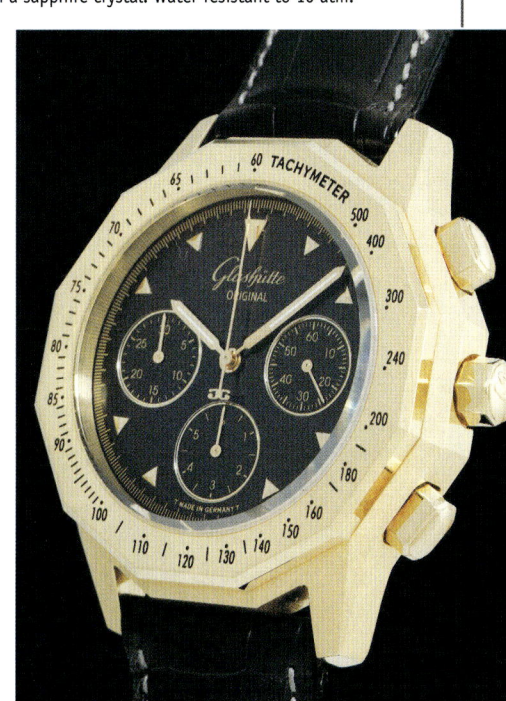

181

Hublot

From the discreet strength of the "Super Professional", to the elegance of the chronograph, from the refinement of the Automatique Dame to the originality of "Owl", Hublot meets the new year including new models in his collections that will meet with this public's approval, with that typical style of the House known for daring combinations and details that have become part of the myth. Like the watch strap, for instance, made of steel reinforced natural rubber, the unmistakable porthole form of the case, the original double deployant clasp, simple and safe.

"Super Professional 450" is dedicated to deep scuba divers, a genuine masterpiece, where an exclusive system blocks the rotating bezel to the typical refined case and offers the greatest reliability thanks to a special steel alloy.

The object set for "Automatique Dame" is also ambitious: very feminine, thoroughly sporting and elegant. Discreet scent of vanilla from the watch strap. This, plus its sturdiness and adaptability to the wrist, ensure that touch of vanity pleasing to the most modern woman.

Among the automatic models for men, is the new "Réserve de Marche", perfect proportions that have already made the series "Elegant" so famous; the new size, "Maxi" in the "Classic" collection, guarantees pure lines and absolute precision.

Classic and contemporary together describe the new Chrono Elegant. A pretty little owl finds it way among the colorful family of quartz movement watches inspired by animal life and the product of patient and expert work with champlevé enamels and touches of gold and diamonds.

Mouse, bear cub, frog, elephant - subjects in a series that is unique for its charm and for its rarity and value. Each watch is produced in a maximum of 30 copies. This year, there is something for everyone.

The History

"Almost everyone thought we were crazy". Carlo Crocco, president of MDM, remembers the day Hublot Watches were presented at the Basel Fair in 1980. He was 35, old enough to have gathered the necessary experience, young enough to throw himself into a stylistic and technical adventure as unusual as that of the porthole-watch. "There are those who love Hublot, and those who absolutely do not understand it". This peculiarity is rendered in the shocking combination of gold and rubber, and that has lasted through the years. These models still attract those looking for what is exclusive. But Hublot does not seek novelty for novelty's sake, because the convenience of the rubber strap is immediately seen, decidedly more durable that a leather strap. Even the double deployant clasp has become a classic, so much so that other houses use it. Also universally recognized is that particular charm of Italian design that gives Hublot its strong, classic and new personality for its wristwatch production.

1985 - The "Plongeur Professional" is presented at Montecarlo, water resistant to 300 meters, traditional single direction rotating bezel and new screw crown.

1986 - First change for the dial, a white version.

1987 - After having chosen quartz for its unarguable qualities of practicality, strength and precision, Carlo Crocco yields to the increasing demand for mechanical movements. He makes the first automatic Hublot. The new calibre, thicker than the quartz versions, forces him to redesign the case, which becomes softer; the bezel screws disappear. He chooses a calibre Frédéric Piguet for the movement.

1988 - Another great innovation: the Hublot chronograph. This is also a Piguet movement, electro-mechanical in this instance, technologically advanced and very practical and precise.

1990 - New models come one after the other, this is the moment for the GMT, useful for great travellers, and the second complication made by the House. It has a new water resistant system with a double gasket on the back held in place with 6 screws.

1991 - "Motor change" for the automatic: the Frédéric Piguet was too delicate for as sporting a watch as Hublot, and in went the classic ETA 2892, decidedly tougher and known to be reliable. This change brought with it the screw crown water resistant up to 5 atm, as well as a good number of new dials in various designs and colors.

1991 - The automatic chronograph, on an exceptional calibre 1185 Piguet, and the production is limited to 350 pieces: 250 in gold, the rest in platinum. This year the Hublot Service is inaugurated. A courtesy watch is "given" to the client in substitution for his own during maintenance.

1995 - The Hublot Classic presented with automatic movement.

1996 - The Colonial Bracelet is shown and production starts of a limited number of Cloisonné and Champlevé enamelled models.

1997 - Hublot again slightly changes its shape, it becomes bigger and more rounded: the presentation of Elegant, also as a chronograph.

1998 - Elegant improves: an automatic version with power reserve.

HUBLOT

CHRONOGRAPH ELEGANT   REF. 1810.410B.1

Movement: mechanical, automatic winding, ETA base + chronograph module Dubois Dépraz caliber 2021, personalized Hublot.
Functions: hour, minute, small second, date, chronograph 3 counters.
Case: stainless steel, three-piece case (Ø 40 mm, thickness 13 mm); flat sapphire crystal; bezel bombé and brushed; screw-down crown; olive pushers; case back attached by 6 screws. Water-resistant to 10 atm.
Dial: silvered; blued stainless steel bâton markers, applied Hublot logo at 12; luminescent dots on the printed minute track; luminescent blued stainless steel leaf style hands.
Indications: small second at 3, date between 4 and 5, hour counter at 6, minute counter at 9, center second counter, minute track with divisions for 1/5 of a second and tachymeter scale.
Strap: rubber, reinforced with integrated blades and inserted in patented attachment; double fold-over steel clasp.
Price: 4'800 CHF.
Also available: with black or blue dial, applied markers or luminescent Arabic numerals: steel (same price); yellow gold & stainless steel 6'250; in yellow gold 14'900; with bezel brilliants: steel 15'700; in yellow gold 25'400.

CHRONOGRAPH ELEGANT "NAVY"   REF. 1810.130.3

Chronograph Elegant "Navy", though it maintains Hublot's classical style prerogatives, is offered with a resolutely rounded and larger sized case (Ø 40 mm, thickness 13 mm). It comes in various available versions, with respect to both the case metal - stainless steel, steel and gold, 18 kt gold and even with diamonds - and the dial color. The "Navy" version is recognizable by its Arabic numerals in luminescent material, while a version standard comes with applied bâton markers and luminescent dots on the minute track. In the photograph we can see a model with 18 kt yellow gold case and black dial, with highly luminescent markers and hands in the "Navy" version. The movement adopted is a caliber Dubois Dépraz, made up by an ETA time base and a separate chronograph module. The famous Hublot rubber strap was broadened to fit the new case better and still has the steel reinforcement blades which guarantee its solidity and flexibility under any condition.
Price: 14'900 CHF.

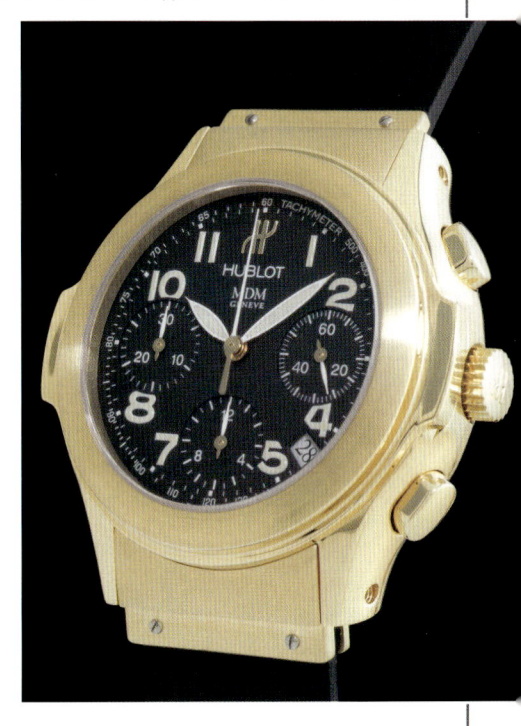

CHRONOGRAPH   REF. 1620.140.8

Movement: quartz with mechanical chronograph module, Frédéric Piguet caliber 1270.
Functions: hour, minute, small second, date, chronograph with 3 counters.
Case: 18 kt pink gold, three-piece case (Ø 37 mm, thickness 9 mm); flat sapphire crystal; brushed bezel with engraved tachymeter scale; 80 micron gold plated hexagonal crown; case back attached by 6 gold screws. Water-resistant to 5 atm.
Dial: black; luminescent cabochon markers; printed minute track; luminescent bâton hands.
Indications: hour counter at 3, date and small second at 6, minute counter at 9, center second counter, minute track with divisions for 1/5 of a second.
Strap: rubber, reinforced with integrated blades and inserted in a patented attachment; double fold-over gold clasp.
Price: 12'800 CHF.
Also available: in yellow gold with Colonial bracelet 18'950; yellow gold & stainless steel or pink strap 5'600, yellow gold & stainless steel, bracelet 8'170; steel, strap 4'400, bracelet 5'125. All with black, blue, white or green dial (for jewel version only black dial).

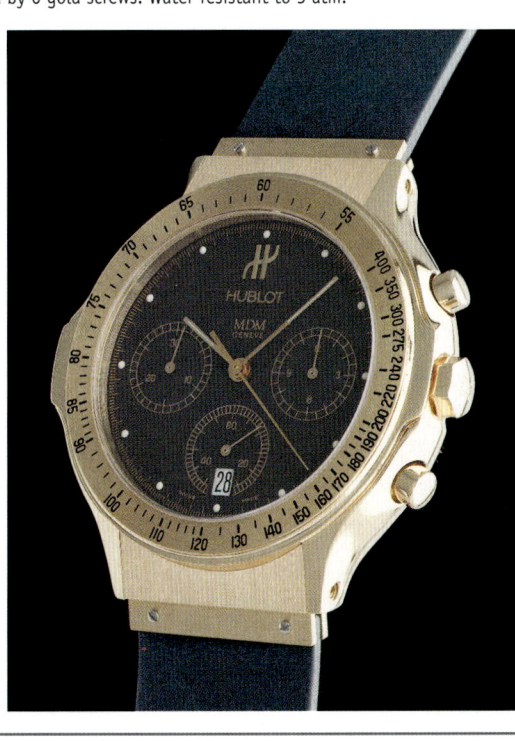

ELEGANT POWER RESERVE   REF. 1830.130.1

Movement: mechanical, automatic winding.
Functions: hour, minute, center second, date, power reserve.
Case: stainless steel, three-piece case (Ø 40 mm, thickness 12 mm); flat sapphire crystal; brushed bezel; screw-down crown; case back attached by 6 screws. Water-resistant to 10 atm.
Dial: black; luminescent Arabic numerals and applied Hublot logo at 12; printed minute track; luminescent stainless steel bâton hands.
Indications: date at 3, power reserve at 6.
Strap: rubber, reinforced with integrated blades and inserted in a patented attachment; double fold-over steel clasp.
Price: 4'200 CHF.
Also available: with applied bâton markers.

HUBLOT

ELEGANT AUTOMATIC — REF. 1710.410B.1

Movement: mechanical, automatic winding, ETA caliber 2892/A2, Hublot personalized.
Functions: hour, minute, center second, date.
Case: stainless steel, three-piece case (Ø 37 mm, thickness 8 mm); flat sapphire crystal; brushed bezel; screw-down crown; case back attached by 6 screws. Water-resistant to 5 atm. 
Dial: silvered with sun pattern; applied blued stainless steel bâton markers and Hublot logo at 12; printed minute track; luminescent blued stainless steel leaf style hands.
Indications: date at 3.
Strap: rubber, reinforced with integrated blades and inserted in a patented attachment; double fold-over steel clasp.
Price: 3'450 CHF.
Also available: with blue or black dial and applied bâton markers or luminescent Arabic numerals or white and applied bâton markers: steel (same price); yellow gold & stainless steel 4'400 CHF; in yellow gold 13'600 CHF; steel with bezel brilliants 11'600 CHF.

ELEGANT LADY — REF. 1430.110.1

Movement: mechanical, automatic winding, ETA caliber 2000, personalized Hublot.
Functions: hour, minute, center second, date.
Case: stainless steel, three-piece case (Ø 33 mm, thickness 8.5 mm); flat sapphire crystal; brushed bezel; screw-down crown; case back attached by 6 screws. Water-resistant to 5 atm.
Dial: black; applied bâton markers and Hublot logo at 12; luminescent dots on the printed minute track; luminescent leaf style hands. 
Indications: date at 3.
Strap: rubber, reinforced with integrated blades and inserted in a patented attachment; double fold-over steel clasp.
Price: 3'400 CHF.
Also available: with silvered dial, applied burnished markers; with luminescent Arabic numerals or white, applied markers or luminescent Arabic numerals; with blue dial, applied markers or luminescent Arabic numerals; steel and yellow gold, black or blue dial and applied markers or luminescent Arabic numerals or white and applied markers (same price); steel with bezel brilliants on request.

PROFESSIONAL 300 MT — REF. 1552.740.3

Movement: mechanical, automatic winding, ETA caliber 2892/2. Hand-finished.
Functions: hour, minute, center second, date.
Case: 18 kt yellow gold, three-piece case (Ø 36 mm, thickness 9 mm); flat sapphire crystal; counter-clockwise turning bezel with engraved minute track, useful for the calculation of diving times; yellow gold screw-down crown with case protection; case back attached by 6 titanium screws. Water-resistant to 30 atm. 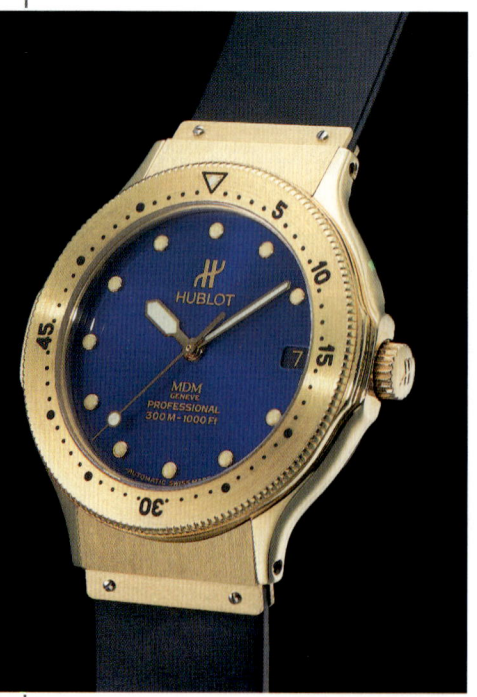
Dial: bright blue; luminescent applied cabochon markers; luminescent Index hands.
Indications: date at 3.
Strap: rubber, reinforced with integrated blades and inserted in a patented attachment; double fold-over gold clasp.
Price: 12'500 CHF.
Also available: Colonial bracelet 18'650 CHF; yellow gold & stainless steel, strap 4'900 CHF, bracelet 7'470 CHF; steel, strap 4'200 CHF, bracelet 4'925 CHF; with green or black dial (same prices).

SUPER PROFESSIONAL 450 MT — REF. 1850.140.1

Movement: mechanical, automatic winding, ETA caliber 2892/2. Hand-finished.
Functions: hour, minute, center second, date.
Case: special surgical purpose steel alloy, three-piece case (Ø 41 mm, thickness 12.5 mm); flat sapphire crystal; additional locking device of the counter-clockwise turning bezel which ensures the maintaining of the selected position (causing a counter-clockwise rotation force of the element placed between frame and ring acting upon the lateral juts, this shall snap in by appr. 5 mm in the "safety" position, thus preventing any accidental rotation); engraved minute track, useful for the calculation of diving times; screw-down crown with case protection; case back attached by 8 screws. Water-resistant to 45 atm. 
Dial: black; luminescent Super Luminova round markers; luminescent Super Luminova portion of the Index hands.
Indications: date at 3.
Strap: rubber, reinforced with integrated blades and inserted in a patented attachment; double fold-over clasp.
Price: 4'900 CHF.
Also available: with blue dial.

184

HUBLOT

CLASSIQUE LARGE — REF. 1880.100.1

Movement: mechanical, automatic winding, ETA caliber 2892/2.
Functions: hour, minute, center second, date.
Case: stainless steel, three-piece case (Ø 38.5 mm); flat sapphire crystal; brushed bezel with 12 screws at the hour markers; screw-down crown; case back attached by 6 screws. Water-resistant to 5 atm.
Dial: black; applied Hublot logo at 12; luminescent bâton hands.
Indications: date at 3.
Strap: rubber reinforced by integrated steel blades and inserted in the patented central attachment; double fold-over steel clasp.
Price: 3'550 CHF.
Also available: with quartz movement and white, black or blue dial 3'100 CHF; yellow gold & stainless steel: automatic movement on request, quartz movement 4'600 CHF; in yellow gold: automatic movement on request, quartz movement 10'900 CHF.

CLASSIQUE AUTOMATIC — REF. 1580.100.3

Movement: mechanical, automatic winding, ETA caliber 2892/2.
Functions: hour, minute, center second, date.
Case: 18 kt yellow gold, three-piece case (Ø 36 mm, thickness 8.6 mm); flat sapphire crystal; brushed bezel with 12 screws at the hour markers; gold screw-down crown; case back attached by 6 screws. Water-resistant to 5 atm.
Dial: black; applied Hublot logo at 12; luminescent bâton hands.
Indications: date at 3.
Strap: rubber, reinforced with integrated blades and inserted in a patented attachment; double fold-over gold clasp
Price: 10'700 CHF.
Also available: with Colonial bracelet 16'850 CHF; yellow gold & stainless steel, strap 4'800 CHF, bracelet 7'370; steel, strap 3'450 CHF, bracelet 4'175 CHF; with blue or white dial or engine turned (guilloché) with a honey-comb pattern, blue or green; white gold, leather strap and black dial on request; in the same versions with quartz movement (prices on request).

CLASSIQUE WITH COVER — REF. 1589.110.3

After a four year work and a million dollars invested in planning, in 1980 the Hublot was presented at the Basel Show. The first series was in two sizes and three variants (gold, steel/gold and steel; in the show-window there was also a model with a "cover" - the old would have said "with secret time" - bound to become the symbol of Hublot's philosophy. Absolutely in counter-tendency with respect to the speed imposed by modern times, it compels the user to carry out some small gestures to read the time (opening the cover and then possibly shutting it again). Therefore it maintains the charme of ancient taste, borrowed from the world of pocket watches which is rich of rituals. Its hinged cover, for whose opening it is sufficient to gently press the lower sides of the lugs, allows a large number of personalizations- engraving of emblems or monograms or setting of precious stones. The photograph shows the men's version in 18 kt yellow gold with engine turned (guilloché), blue enameled dial and markers made of brilliants.
Price: 18'270 CHF.
Also available: without brilliants 17'900 CHF.

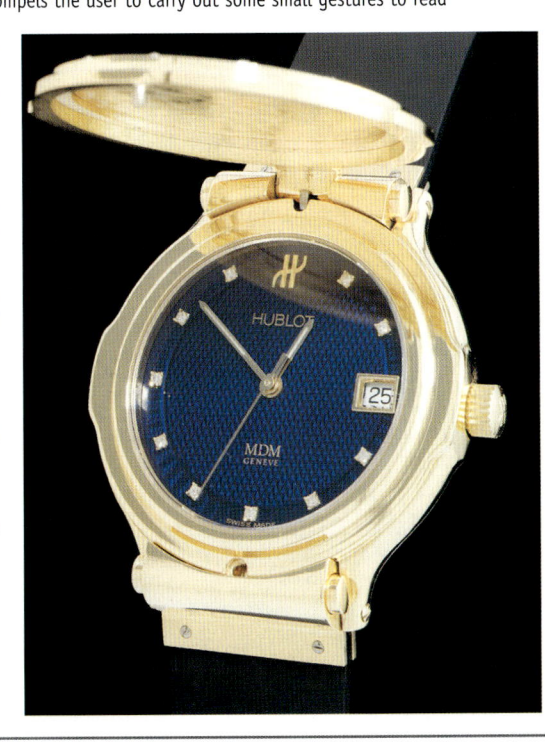

LES VAGUES

In 1993 the Hublot was embellished with an unusual and original element: Les Vagues (the waves). These are small gold or steel and gold bars with bendable ends to get fixed on the rubber strap. This is indeed a little masterpiece of jewellery but also of mechanics. Available in three basic shapes, they are personalized with the engraving of the owner's initials or by adding precious stones, until an infinite series of variants is realized. As ideal "gift mates", they may be bought at any moment even one by one, in order to make the Hublot of the beloved partner a unique piece. In this way, once a little collection of Vagues is made, perhaps with variously colored stones, the watch may be personalized according to the moment of the day, to the dress or (as far as women are concerned) to the mood. And all that in a perfect Hublot style.
Available "waves": with diamonds, sapphires, rubies and emeralds.
Prices: on request.

International Watch Co.

The era of electronics and cellular phones, greater demands for technology and practicality are well within the comprehension of International Watch Co. The President of the Schaffhausen's House claims "Men's watches that can attract and please women", and not without reason. Thanks to their high technical and aesthetic quality the IWC timepieces are tough, definitely masculine. They come from continuous research and technically advanced instrumentation guaranteeing precision, strength, endurance and excellent complications. We find all these characteristics in the GST, the group made up of two versions of the Chronograph, the Automatic Alarm, the underwater Aquatimer and, latest to join, the Deep One, a professional instrument for deep scuba divers. This has a rotating yellow ring on the dial to measure the length of the immersion and a mechanical depth gauge: two pointed hands showing the real depth and the greatest depth reached (it has a marginal protection limit of 45 meters). Both these systems permit easy measurement of the two essential parameters for scuba divers. The latest of the series for aviators, the Mark XV with a new automatic calibre 3745247 and an added internal case in soft iron for antimagnetic protection, retires the Mark XII.

Lastly there is a movement with tourbillon "volant" and large piller plate, the core of the new Da Vinci, made in a limited edition of 250 pieces to celebrate, along with the very limited and more sophisticated "Four Seasons", the end of the Millennium.

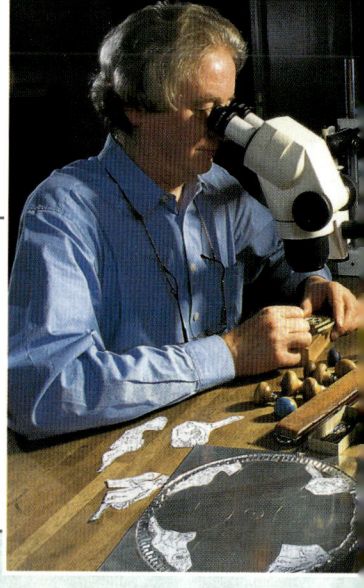

The History

For the people of Schaffhausen, it is simply "the Watch". On the other hand, simply the name "Schaffhausen" instantly brought to mind the IWC product. Since its beginning, far from the traditional Swiss centers of watchmaking, it had to become independent, training its own watchmakers and introducing instruments and production procedures that were unknown at the time. It became famous with pocket watches, strong, precise and excellent quality. Today IWC is part of the big German VDO Group and is directed by Günter Blümlein. Watch production employs about 300 people of whom 60 are watchmakers trained within the company. "The Watch" at this time has a broader production than all Swiss watchmaking, in the pocket watch field as well. Its motto, "Probus Scafusiae" (Schaffhausen's Quality) illustrates a company that has remained faithful to the excellent product levels reached in 1868.

1869 - The American watchmaker, Florentine Ariosto Jones and the watchmaker-businessman Johann Heinrich Moser found the International Watch Co. that begins its production of pocket watches with the famous and revolutionary high precision calibre Jones, among the first that can be wound from the crown.

1880 - The Company is acquired by the local industrialist Johannes Rauschenbach-Vogel (and will belong to the family for 4 generations) and begins to reap success for quality, reliability, strength, endurance and quiet refinement, all keys to future success.

1885 - The first watches with digital indication of hours and minutes.

1890 - The first Grand Complication in pocket version. It has more than 1300 mechanical parts. Some of the original "ébauches" still exist.

1900 - The first wristwatches that have the same, but smaller, movements as the pocket watches, highly precise watches made for the British Royal Navy and the Imperial German Navy and the first work-watches made for the Berlin public transport system. These were made antimagnetic to keep them correct on electric powered vehicles.

1904 - The Calibre 72, exceptionally beautiful, only 300 pieces were produced up to 1918.

1929 - Ernst Jakob Homberger, the Rauschenbach heir, becomes the single owner.

1940 - The beginning of the new era with the Portugieseruhr, classic and uncommon with its large size (a high precision pocket watch movement is used for the wristwatch case), and the first Fliegeruhr, antimagnetic watch for aviators, the largest wristwatch IWC ever made and mounted on a Calibre 83, a pocket model ancestor of a generation of calibers in wrist model version. Among these is the mythical "89" of the Mark XI.

1954 - During the post-war reconstruction, the automatic re-winding mechanism was perfected. It was then used for the

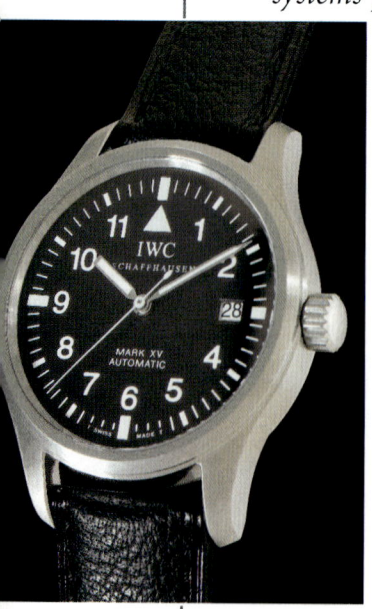

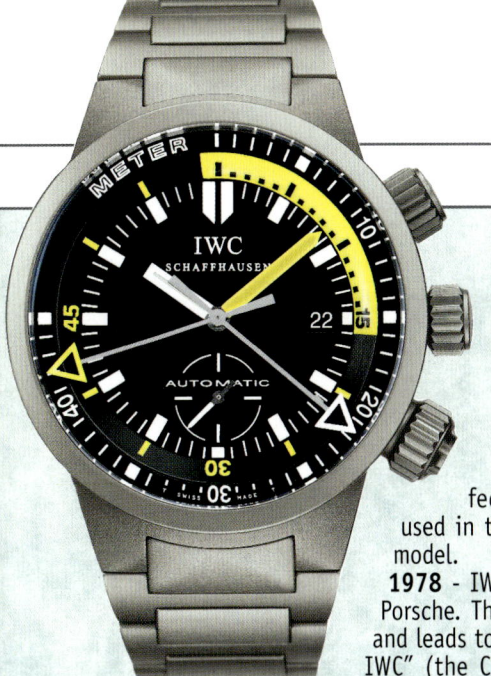

"Ingenieur" (particularly strong and functional, highly anti-magnetic, automatic rewinding and patented date indication), and for the "Yacht Club" (the best-selling IWC at that moment). Working with other famous Swiss companies, the mechanism "Beta 21" was perfected in those years. It will be used in the '70's for the first IWC quartz model.

1978 - IWC ties its name to Ferdinand A. Porsche. The link will last for twenty years and leads to the birth of "Porsche Design by IWC" (the Compass, the chrono Titan, the Ocean 2000). That same year Homberger's son sells to the German VDO Adolf Schindling AG.

1983 - Günter Blümlein takes over the management of the Company.

1985 - The module of a perpetual calendar is developed in collaboration with Jaeger-LeCoultre, the first where all the indications can be corrected from the crown. It recognizes the number of days in each month for the next 500 years and will not need a watchmaker until the year 2199, when the "centuries slide" will have to be substituted. IWC will deliver this carefully sealed in its own little box. Besides this, the moon phases are the most precise and will need to be corrected by one day only every 122 years and, lastly, the year is shown in four figures. This extraordinarily rational mechanism is used in the Da Vinci (made also in colored ceramic, derived from zirconium oxide with high tech procedures)...

1987 - ... in the Novecento, first rectangular automatic wristwatch, waterproof and perpetual calendar...

1990 - ... in the Grande Complication which, with its 9 hands and 659 mechanical parts in the limited space of a wristwatch, is the most complicated watch built up to then...

1993 - ... although overtaken on the occasion of IWC's 125th anniversary by the Destriero Scafusiae, where besides the manual winding mechanism it adds to the repeater and the perpetual calendar, a split-second function and the tourbillon with titanium cage.

1997 - The GST collection takes its name from the initials of the metals utilized (gold, steel, titanium). These are highbred chronographs: an automatic calibre 7922 with day and date, and a quartz-mechanical, calibre 631 still the most compact ever built. The Da Vinci SL suggests instead a trend evolution of the classic Da Vinci.

1998 - IWC again showed its superiority for highly technical sports watches; UTC is a typical aviator's watch, a class of instrument the IWC has known well since the '30's, and has perfected the reading of a second time zone. Setting the time for both zones, the automatic date change as well as setting the main time can all be done by using the crown alone. Two new models of the GST complete the sports models: Aquatimer, water resistant to 2000 meters, produced only in steel and titanium (gold cannot withstand such high pressure), the case is large (40 mm), and the watch has very highly technical qualities: special water-resistant seal for the back, multiple protection for the screw-down crown, the 3.2 mm thick crystal, the single direction rotating bezel that can be turned only by pressing the sides, the bracelet with a safety clasp that can be adapted to each wrist and that can be changed to a velcro strap so that it can be worn over the diving suit. The second model instead uses all three metals: a traditional alarm with double barrel (and two crowns).

The caliber 5000

IWC drew inspiration for its first movement of the new century from a production of 50 years ago when Albert Pellaton, at that time the technical manager of IWC, thought up the automatic winding mechanism that we find on the caliber 5000. It has the classic size of a "Lépine/pocket", 38.20 mm in diameter, 7.20 mm high; 46 jewels; balance with compensation screws and fine regulation using eccentric mass screws placed at the ends of both arms; 18,000 vph; Breguet balance spring with another fine regulation system. The winding system, exploiting the rotation of a heart cam like those, integral parts of the rotor, used to reset chronographs, causes the large lever to perform controlled oscillations (visible in the photo, where the rotor has been removed). Analogous to the caliber 8541, this one carries the two pawls to drag, alternately and clockwise, the adjacent gullet toothed wheel which, after a series of reductions, winds up the long, powerful mainspring. In this case there is autonomy of a good 8 and a half days, but a mechanical device collected to the visual system of the power reserve purposely stops the watch when there are another 36 hours of power felt. This is to prevent the watch from indicating the time less precisely, due to narrower oscillations of the balance. The first watch to carry this system is the unpresented "Portughese Automatic 2000", a good-sized timepiece that, as in the collection of the same name, is characterized by the two small dials, placed horizontally, for small seconds (at 9) and the power reserve (at 3). The movement is proudly shown through the case back and the gold medallion inserted in the rotor can be read: "Probus Scafusia".

INTERNATIONAL WATCH CO.

DOPPELCHRONOGRAPH — REF. 3713

Movement: mechanical, automatic winding, IWC caliber 79230 (Valjoux caliber 7750 base).
Functions: hour, minute, small second, day, date, split-second chronograph with 3 counters.
Case: platinum, three-piece brushed case (Ø 42 mm, thickness 16.5 mm); additional ductile iron inside case for the deviation of magnetic fields; curved very thick sapphire crystal, depressurization-resistant to 6 atm.; screw-down crown; pushers with case protection, split-second pusher at 10; screwed-on case back. Water-resistant to 5 atm.
Dial: blue; printed Arabic numerals and 4 luminescent markers; luminescent bâton hands.
Indications: day and date at 3, hour counter at 6, small second at 9, minute counter at 12, center second and split-second counters, minute track with divisions for 1/4 of a second.
Strap: crocodile leather; platinum clasp.
Price: 23'500 CHF.
Also available: stainless steel, black dial, white Arabic numerals, leather strap 8'500 CHF, bracelet 9'950 CHF.

FLIEGERCHRONOGRAPH AUTOMATIC — REF. 3706

Movement: mechanical, automatic winding, IWC caliber 7902 (Valjoux caliber 7750 base), autonomy of 44 hours, 25 jewels, shock-resistant and non-magnetic according to NICHS 91-10 standards.
Functions: hour, minute, small second, day, date, chronograph with 3 counters.
Case: stainless steel, three-piece brushed case (Ø 39 mm, thickness 15 mm); additional ductile iron inside case for magnetic field deviation; curved very thick sapphire crystal, depressurization-resistant to 6 atm.; screw-down crown; pushers with case protection; screwed-on case back with engraved logo. Water-resistant to 6 atm.
Dial: black; white printed Arabic numerals and 4 luminescent markers; luminescent bâton hands.
Indications: day and date at 3, hour counter at 6, small second at 9, minute counter at 12, center second counter, minute track with divisions for 1/4 of a second.
Strap: crocodile leather; stainless steel clasp.
Price: 3'950 CHF.
Also available: with bracelet 5'300 CHF.

FLIEGERCHRONOGRAPH — REF. 3741

Movement: quartz with mechanical chronograph module, IWC caliber 631 (Jaeger-Le Coultre base).
Functions: hour, minute, small second, date, chronograph with 3 counters.
Case: stainless steel, three-piece brushed case (Ø 36 mm, thickness 10.3 mm); additional ductile iron inside case for magnetic field deviation; curved very thick sapphire crystal, depressurization-resistant to 6 atmospheres; screw-down crown; pushers with case protection; screwed-on case back. Water-resistant to 5 atm.
Dial: black; white printed Arabic numerals and 4 luminescent markers; luminescent bâton hands.
Indications: hour counter at 3, date between 4 and 5, small second at 6, minute counter at 9, center second counter, minute track with divisions for 1/4 of a second.
Bracelet: brushed steel; double fold-over clasp.
Price: 3'950 CHF.
Also available: leather strap 3'100 CHF.

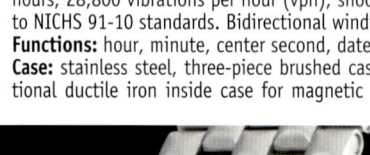

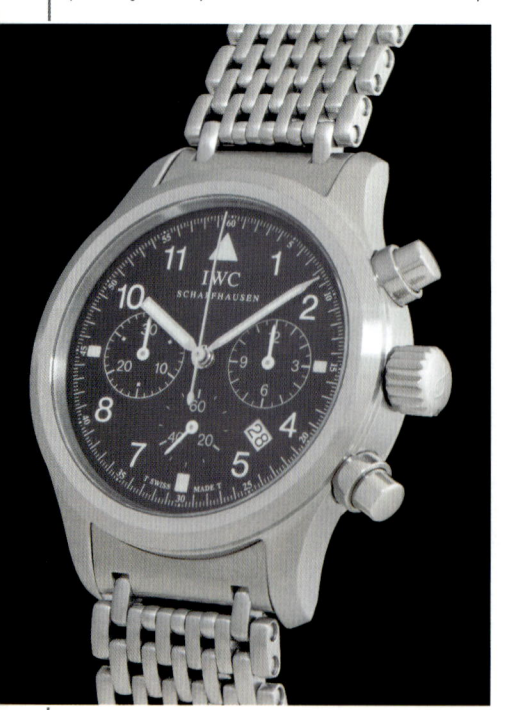

FLIEGERUHR UTC WORLD TIME — REF. 3251

Movement: mechanical, automatic winding, IWC caliber 37526, autonomy of 44 hours, 28,800 vibrations per hour (vph), shock-resistant and non-magnetic according to NICHS 91-10 standards. Bidirectional winding rotor.
Functions: hour, minute, center second, date, second time zone, 24-hour indication.
Case: stainless steel, three-piece brushed case (Ø 39 mm, thickness 12,4 mm); additional ductile iron inside case for magnetic field deviation; curved sapphire crystal; screw-down crown; screwed-on case back. Water-resistant to 6 atm.
Dial: black; Arabic numerals, luminescent bâton markers and minute track; luminescent lozenge hands (hour hand independently adjustable with crown pulled out at an intermediate notch).
Indications: date at 3, circle sector second time zone at 12.
Bracelet: brushed steel; fold-over clasp with safety pusher.
Price: 5'600 CHF.
Also available: leather strap 4'250 CHF; platinum, leather strap and blue dial 19'500 CHF.

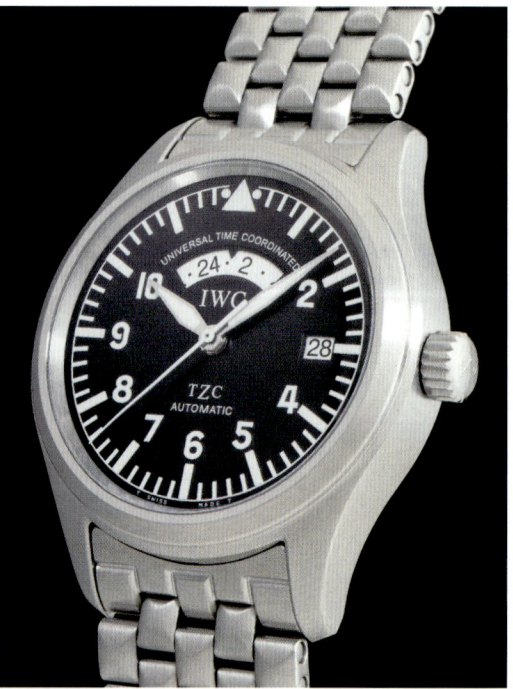

INTERNATIONAL WATCH CO.

FLIEGERUHR MARK XV — REF. 3253

Movement: mechanical, automatic winding, IWC caliber C.37524 (ETA base), shock-resistant and non-magnetic according to NICHS 91-10 standards.
Functions: hour, minute, center second, date.
Case: stainless steel, three-piece brushed case (Ø 38 mm, thickness 10.5 mm); additional ductile iron inside case for magnetic field deviation; curved very thick sapphire crystal, depressurization-resistant; screw-down crown; screwed-on case back. Water-resistant to 6 atm.
Dial: black; white printed Arabic numerals and 4 luminescent markers on the printed minute track; luminescent bâton hands.
Indications: date at 3.
Bracelet: brushed steel; double fold-over clasp.
Price: 4'250 CHF.
Also available: leather strap 3'400 CHF.

GST AUTOMATIC ALARM — REF. 9269

Movement: mechanical, automatic winding, IWC caliber 917 (Jaeger-Le Coultre base), autonomy of 44 hours, 22 jewels, 28,800 vibrations per hour (vph), made up by 220 elements.
Functions: hour, minute, center second, date, alarm.
Case: 18 kt yellow gold, three-piece case (Ø 39 mm, thickness 13.4 mm) polished and brushed finish; curved sapphire crystal; screw-down winding crown at 4, sonnerie crown at 2; screwed-on case back. Water-resistant to 3 atm.
Dial: silvered; applied bâton markers; luminescent dots; printed minute track; luminescent bâton hands.
Indications: date at 3, center hand with red point for the sonnerie.
Bracelet: in polished yellow gold, brushed finish; fold-over clasp with safety pusher.
Price: 23'500 CHF.

GST AUTOMATIC CHRONOGRAPH — REF. 3707

Movement: mechanical, automatic winding, IWC caliber 7922 (Valjoux caliber 7750 base), autonomy of 44 hours, 25 jewels, shock-resistant and non-magnetic according to NICHS 91-10 standards.
Functions: hour, minute, small second, day, date, chronograph with 3 counters.
Case: stainless steel, three-piece case (Ø 39.6 mm, thickness 14 mm) polished and brushed finish; sapphire crystal slightly bombé; screw-down crown; screwed-on case back. Water-resistant to 12 atm.
Dial: white, zones with concentric-circles pattern; applied golden bâton markers; luminescent dots; luminescent golden bâton hands.
Indications: day and date at 3, hour counter at 6, small second at 9, minute counter at 12, center second counter, minute track with divisions for 1/5 of a second.
Bracelet: stainless steel, polished and brushed finish; fold-over clasp with safety pusher.
Price: 4'950 CHF.
Also available: black dial; in titanium with bracelet and black dial 4'700 CHF; in yellow gold with bracelet and silvered dial Ref. 9277, 22'000 CHF.

GST CHRONOGRAPH — REF. 3727

Movement: quartz with mechanical chronograph module, IWC caliber 631 (Jaeger-Le Coultre base).
Functions: hour, minute, small second, date, chronograph with 3 counters.
Case: titanium, three-piece case, matte finish (Ø 36.6 mm, thickness 11 mm); sapphire crystal slightly bombé; screw-down crown; screwed-on case back. Water-resistant to 12 atm.
Dial: black, zones with concentric-circles pattern; applied bâton markers; luminescent dots; luminescent bâton hands.
Indications: hour counter at 3, date and small second at 6, minute counter at 9, center second counter, minute track with divisions for 1/5 of a second.
Bracelet: in titanium, matte finish; fold-over clasp with safety pusher.
Price: 3'950 CHF.
Also available: stainless steel with bracelet and white or black dial 4'200 CHF; in yellow gold with bracelet and silvered dial Ref. 9557, 19'500 CHF.

INTERNATIONAL WATCH CO.

GST AQUATIMER — REF. 3536

Movement: mechanical, automatic winding, IWC caliber 32524, autonomy of 42 hours, 21 jewels, 28,800 vibrations per hour (vph). Rotor with 22 kt peripheral mass.
Functions: hour, minute, center second, date.
Case: titanium, three-piece case, matte finish (Ø 42 mm, thickness 14,5 mm); curved sapphire crystal (thickness 3.2 mm); counter-clockwise turning bezel (only if simultaneously pressed at ends), detachable for maintenance purposes and with black ring and embossed minute track, useful for the calculation of diving times; screw-down crown; screwed-on case back, with embossed representation of a submarine. Water-resistant to 200 atm. 
Dial: black; luminescent bâton markers; printed minute track; luminescent bâton hands.
Indications: date at 3.
Bracelet: in titanium, matte finish; fold-over clasp with safety pusher. On request, with nylon and velcro strap to bear the watch over a diver's suit.
Price: 4'400 CHF.
Also available: stainless steel with bracelet and white or black dial 4'650 CHF.

DEEP ONE — REF. 3527

Movement: mechanical, automatic winding, IWC caliber 8914, autonomy of 38 hours.
Functions: hour, minute, small second, date, mechanical depth-gauge.
Case: titanium, three-piece case, matte finish (Ø 43 mm, thickness 14.5 mm); curved sapphire crystal (thickness 3.2 mm); screw-down crown at 3 for watch functions, crown at 2 for counter-clockwise adjustment of the diving time ring and as pusher to set the maximum depth reached to zero, crown at 4 for the water intake throttle of the depth-gauge and its zeroing; screwed-on case back. Water-resistant to 10 atm. 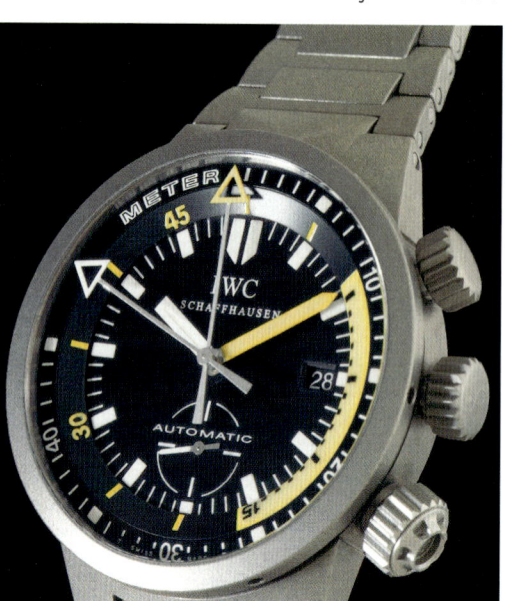
Dial: black; luminescent bâton markers; printed minute track; turning yellow/black flange with graduated scale to read diving time; luminescent bâton hands.
Indications: date at 3, small second at 6. Depth-gauge with display by two pointed hands: the white one for the depth in real time; the yellow one for the maximum depth reached measuring range of 45 meters.
Bracelet: in titanium, matte finish; fold-over clasp.; nylon case and strap with velcro and tester for the depth-gauge.
Price: 12'500 CHF.

DA VINCI SL CHRONOGRAPH — REF. 3728

Movement: quartz with mechanical chronograph module, IWC caliber 631 (Jaeger-LeCoultre base), with 25 jewels. made up by 233 elements.
Functions: hour, minute, small second, date, chronograph with 3 counters.
Case: stainless steel, three-piece brushed case (Ø 37 mm, thickness 10 mm); jointed lugs with central attachment; flat sapphire crystal; screw-down crown; polished rectangular pushers; case back attached by 5 screws. Water-resistant to 10 atm. 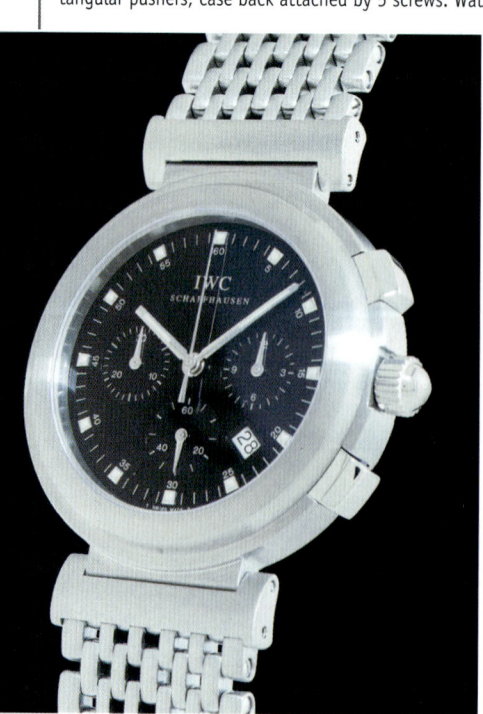
Dial: black, zones with concentric-circles pattern; luminescent applied rhodium plated square markers; luminescent bâton hands.
Indications: hour counter at 3, date between 4 and 5, small second at 6, minute counter at 9, center second counter, minute track.
Bracelet: stainless steel, brushed finish; fold-over clasp.
Price: 4'800 CHF.
Also available: leather strap 3'850 CHF; polished steel, white dial (same prices); in yellow gold, leather strap and white dial 9'250 CHF.

DA VINCI SL AUTOMATIC — REF. 3528

Movement: mechanical, automatic winding, IWC caliber 37524, with 21 jewels, 28,800 vibrations per hour (vph) and Nivarox balance-spring.
Functions: hour, minute, center second, date.
Case: 18 kt yellow gold, three-piece case (Ø 37 mm, thickness 10 mm); jointed lugs with central attachment; flat sapphire crystal; screw-down crown; case back attached by 5 screws. Water-resistant to 10 atm. 
Dial: white; luminescent applied golden square markers; printed minute track; luminescent bâton hands.
Indications: date at 3.
Strap: buffalo leather; yellow gold clasp.
Price: 8'000 CHF.
Also available: polished stainless steel, white dial or brushed steel, black dial, leather strap 2'900 CHF, bracelet 3'850 CHF.

INTERNATIONAL WATCH CO.

DA VINCI — REF. 3750

Movement: mechanical, automatic winding, IWC caliber 79261 (Valjoux base).
Functions: hour, minute, small second, perpetual calendar programmed until the year 2499 (date, day, month, year, moon phase), chronograph with 3 counters.
Case: stainless steel, three-piece case (Ø 39 mm, thickness 15 mm); jointed lugs with central attachment; curved plexiglass crystal (sapphire on request); screw-down crown for the correction of the whole calendar; snap-on back. Water-resistant to 3 atm.
Dial: black enameled; applied bâton markers; luminescent dots; luminescent bâton hands.
Indications: date at 3, month and hour counter at 6, four-digit year between 7 and 8, day and small second at 9, moon phase and minute counter at 12, center second counter, minute track with divisions for 1/5 of a second.
Strap: crocodile leather; stainless steel clasp.
Price: 14'500 CHF.
Also available: with bracelet 15'400 CHF; in yellow or white gold, white dial, leather strap 22'500 CHF. Adapted on request: spherically hollow ground sapphire glass, +1'750 CHF.

DA VINCI RATTRAPANTE — REF. 3751

Movement: mechanical, automatic winding, IWC caliber 79251 (Valjoux base).
Functions: hour, minute, small second, perpetual calendar programmed until the year 2499 (date, day, month, year, moon phase), split-second chronograph with 3 counters.
Case: 18 kt yellow gold, three-piece case (Ø 38.5 mm, thickness 16 mm); jointed lugs with central attachment; curved plexiglass crystal; screw-down crown for the correction of the whole calendar; split-second pusher at 10; snap-on back. Water-resistant to 3 atm.
Dial: silvered; applied bâton markers; luminescent dots; luminescent bâton hands.
Indications: date at 3, month and hour counter at 6, four-digit year between 7 and 8, day and small second at 9, moon phase and minute counter at 12, center second and split-second counters, minute track with divisions for 1/5 of a second.
Strap: crocodile leather; yellow gold clasp.
Price: 27'500 CHF. Realized for the tenth anniversary of the Da Vinci watch.
Also available: with bracelet 37'750 CHF; platinum with rhodium plated dial, leather strap 39'500 CHF, with bracelet 71'250 CHF. Adapted on request: spherically hollow ground sapphire glass, +1'750 CHF.

DA VINCI TOURBILLON — REF. 3752

Movement: mechanical, manual winding, IWC caliber 76061, with tourbillon, power reserve 44 hours.
Functions: hour, minute, small second, perpetual calendar programmed until the year 2499 (date, day, month, year, moon phase), chronograph with 3 counters.
Case: 18 kt yellow gold, two-piece case (Ø 39 mm, thickness 14 mm); jointed lugs with central attachment; curved sapphire crystal; screw-down crown for the correction of the whole calendar; snap-on case back displaying the movement through a sapphire crystal with hardness number 9. Water-resistant to 3 atm.
Dial: silvered; applied bâton markers; luminescent dots; luminescent bâton hands.
Indications: date at 3, month and hour counter at 6, four-digit year between 7 and 8, day and small second at 9, moon phase and minute counter at 12, center second counter, minute track with divisions for 1/5 of a second.
Strap: crocodile leather; yellow gold clasp.
Price: 72'500 CHF, 200 pieces.
Also available: platinum 95'000, 50 pieces; yellow gold, hand-engraved dial 82'500; yellow gold, gold dial with "4 seasons", 20 pieces (on request).

NOVECENTO PERPETUAL CALENDAR — REF. 3546

Movement: mechanical, automatic winding, IWC caliber 96061, with 47 jewels, 28,800 vibrations per hour (vph).
Functions: hour, minute, perpetual calendar (date, day, month, year, moon phase).
Case: 18 kt yellow gold, two-piece rectangular case (only case size 38x27 mm, thickness 8.3 mm); curved sapphire crystal; bulb-shaped screw-down crown for the correction of the whole calendar; case back attached by 6 screws. Water-resistant to 3 atm.
Dial: silvered; applied bâton markers on the printed railway minute track; leaf style hands.
Indications: moon phase at 3, date at 6, month at 9, two-digit year between 10 and 11, day at 12.
Strap: crocodile leather; yellow gold clasp.
Price: 19'750 CHF.
Also available: platinum, leather strap 32'750 CHF.

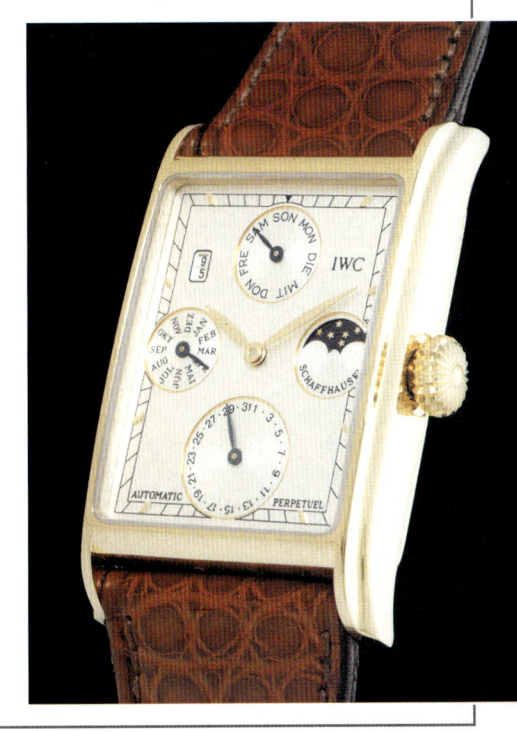

INTERNATIONAL WATCH CO.

PORTUGUESE AUTOMATIC CHRONOGRAPH — REF. 3714

Movement: mechanical, automatic winding, IWC caliber 79240 (Valjoux caliber 7750 base), autonomy of 44 hours, 31 jewels, 28,800 vibrations per hour (vph).
Functions: hour, minute, small second, chronograph with 2 counters.
Case: 18 kt white gold, three-piece case (Ø 41 mm, thickness 12.5 mm) polished and brushed finish; curved sapphire crystal; case back attached by 4 screws. Water-resistant to 3 atm. 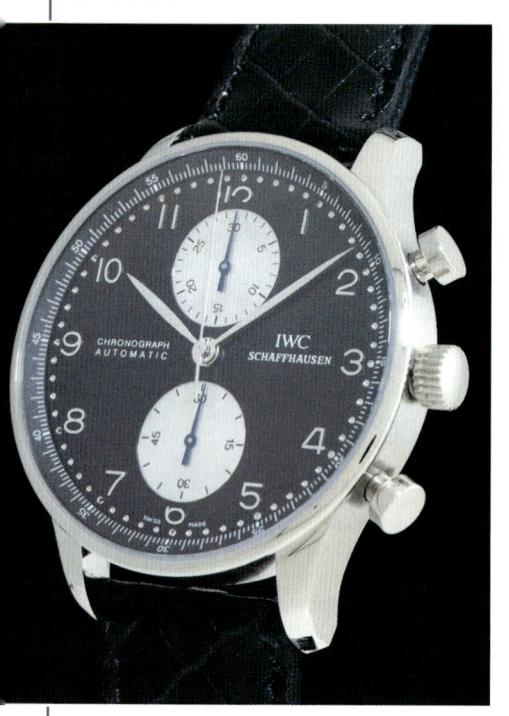
Dial: black with silvered counters; embossed rhodium plated Arabic numerals; recessed minute track; leaf style hands.
Indications: small second at 6, minute counter at 12, center second counter, minute track with divisions for 1/5 of a second on the beveled ring.
Strap: crocodile leather, hand stitched; white gold clasp.
Price: 13'500 CHF.
Also available: pink gold, silvered dial 13'500 CHF; steel, silvered dial 6'500 CHF.

PORTUGUESE CHRONOGRAPH RATTRAPANTE — REF. 3712

Movement: mechanical, manual winding, IWC caliber caliber 76240 (Valjoux caliber 776 base).
Functions: hour, minute, small second, split-second chronograph with 2 counters.
Case: 18 kt white gold, three-piece case (Ø 41 mm, thickness 125 mm); curved sapphire crystal; split-second pusher at 10; case back attached by 4 screws. Water-resistant to 3 atm. 
Dial: silvered; blued stainless steel embossed Arabic numerals and recessed minute track; leaf style hands.
Indications: small second at 6, minute counter at 12, center second and split-second counters, minute track with divisions for 1/5 of a second on the beveled ring.
Strap: crocodile leather, hand stitched; white gold clasp.
Price: on request.
Also available: pink gold 16'500 CHF; steel 9'500 CHF; platinum 32'500 CHF, 250 pieces.

PORTUGUESE MINUTE REPEATER — REF. 5240

Movement: mechanical, manual winding, IWC caliber 95290, derived from a Lépine pocket watch mechanic system.
Functions: hour, minute, small second, minute repeater.
Case: 18 kt yellow gold, three-piece brushed case (Ø 42 mm, thickness 11 mm); curved plexiglass crystal; polished convexed bezel; repeater slide on case side; snap-on back displaying the movement through a sapphire crystal. 
Dial: silvered, bombé; embossed golden Arabic numerals and recessed minute track; leaf style hands.
Indications: small second at 9.
Strap: crocodile leather; yellow gold clasp.
Price: 69'500 CHF.
Edition limited to 250 pieces.

PORTUGUESE AUTOMATIC — REF. 3532

Movement: mechanical, automatic winding, IWC caliber 887, with 36 jewels, 28,800 vibrations per hour (vph). Platinum rotor with bidirectional winding.
Functions: hour, minute, center second, date.
Case: platinum, three-piece brushed case (Ø 35 mm, thickness 8 mm); curved sapphire crystal; polished hollowed bezel; snap-on back displaying the movement through a sapphire crystal. Water-resistant to 3 atm. 
Dial: blue; embossed rhodium plated Arabic numerals and recessed minute track; leaf style hands.
Indications: date at 3.
Strap: crocodile leather, hand stitched; platinum clasp.
Price: 17'250 CHF.
Edition limited to 500 pieces.

INTERNATIONAL WATCH CO.

DESTRIERO SCAFUSIAE REF. 1868

Movement: mechanical, manual winding, IWC caliber 18680, with tourbillon and titanium carriage. Hand-finished and hand-engraved.
Functions: hour, minute, small second, perpetual calendar programmed until 2499 (date, day, month, year, moon phase), split-second chronograph with 3 counters, minute repeater.
Case: 22 kt pink gold (Ø 42.2 mm, thickness 18 mm); curved sapphire crystal; repeater slide on case side; crown for the correction of the whole calendar with cabochon split-second black pusher; rectangular pushers; case back attached by 6 screws, displaying the movement through a sapphire crystal. Waterproof and non-magnetic.
Dial: silvered; zones with concentric-circles pattern; printed Roman numerals; printed railway minute track; blued lozenge hands.
Indications: date at 3, hour counter and month at 6, four-digit year between 7 and 8, small second and day at 9, moon phase and minute counter at 12, center split-second counters, minute track with divisions for 1/5 of a second.
Strap: crocodile leather; pink gold clasp.
Price: 265'000 CHF. 125 pieces.

GRANDE COMPLICATION REF. 3770

Movement: mechanical, automatic winding, IWC caliber 79091. Hand-finished.
Functions: hour, minute, small second, perpetual calendar programmed until 2499 (date, day, month, year, moon phase), chronograph with 3 counters, minute repeater.
Case: 18 kt yellow gold (Ø 42.2 mm, thickness 16.3 mm); curved sapphire crystal; repeater slide on case side; screw-down crown for the correction of the whole calendar; rectangular pushers; case back attached by 6 screws. Waterproof and non-magnetic.
Dial: white enameled, zones with concentric-circles pattern; applied yellow gold bâton markers on the printed minute track; yellow gold bâton hands.
Indications: date at 3, hour counter and month at 6, four-digit year between 7 and 8, small second and day at 9, moon phase and minute counter at 12, center second counter.
Strap: crocodile leather; yellow gold clasp.
Price: 175'000 CHF. Edition limited to 50 pieces/year.
Also available: platinum, leather strap 197'500 CHF, 50 pieces.

PORTOFINO AUTOMATIC REF. 3513

Movement: mechanical, automatic winding, IWC caliber 37521. Autonomy 44 hours, diameter 25.6 mm (11'''1/2), thickness 3.75 mm, 21 jewels; Glucydur balance, 28,800 vibrations per hour (vph), Nivarox 1 balance-spring, Incabloc shock-resistant system.
Functions: hour, minute, center second, date.
Case: stainless steel, two-piece case (Ø 34 mm, thickness 8.5 mm); flat sapphire crystal; semi-recessed crown; case back attached by 4 screws. Water-resistant to 3 atm.
Dial: white; painted Arabic numerals and minute track; bâton hands black enameled.
Indications: date at 3.
Strap: "Peabody" leather; stainless steel clasp.
Price: 2'100 CHF.
Also available: with applied bâton markers or screen-printed Roman numerals; with rhodium plated dial, applied Arabic numerals or black, white Arabic numerals; with bracelet 3'100; yellow gold, leather strap and white or gilded dial, applied bâton markers or rhodium plated, applied Arabic numerals 5'950; with quartz movement.

INGENIEUR AUTOMATIC REF. 3521

Movement: mechanical, automatic winding, IWC caliber 887, modified. Autonomy 44 hours, platinum rotor and Nivarox 1 balance-spring. Officially certified "chronometer" (C.O.S.C.).
Functions: hour, minute, center second, date.
Case: stainless steel, three-piece brushed case (Ø 34 mm, thickness 9 mm); additional ductile iron inside case mounted on shock-absorbers resisting magnetic fields up to 80.000 A/m; flat sapphire crystal with magnifying lens on date; screwed-on bezel with polished side; screw-down crown; screwed-on case back. Water-resistant to 12 atm.
Dial: white; applied bâton markers; luminescent dots on the minute track; luminescent bâton hands.
Indications: date at 3.
Bracelet: stainless steel, brushed finish; fold-over clasp.
Price: 5'950 CHF.

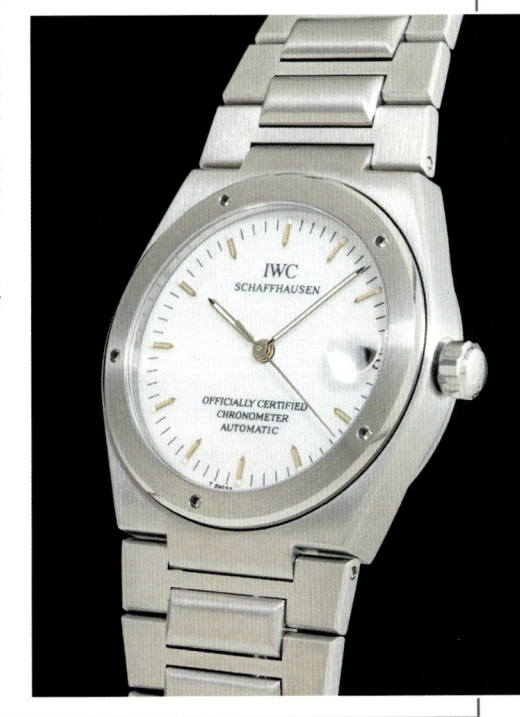

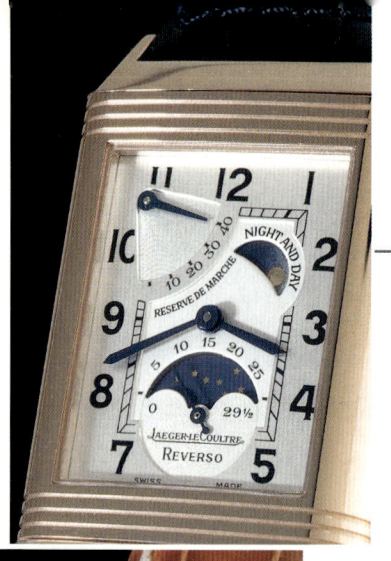

Jaeger-LeCoultre

During the relentless march of time there will be moments when we feel we must halt, stolen moments when we can dream of moving out of this hurrying, busy world… The Reverso Memory, the latest of the Jaeger-LeCoultre 1931 collection is the artifice of these personal, tranquil moments - hours captured from the universe ruled by Time. Invented by the watchmakers of the Manufacture of the Vallée de Joux, its strength lies in a function that has never been used to advantage: the chronograph with minute counter. In fact, the 146 elements of the calibre 862 (mechanical, manual winding, hand made and decorated) unite the utility of the function with the simplicity of use. Thus, the 60 minute counter which is on the second side of this original watch, is always in movement, and at simple pressure on the single button it returns to zero and automatically starts to measure the time desired.

The Reverso Sun Moon is a window to the sky. In its Grande Taille case, and moved by the new manual winding Calibre 823 composed of 212 elements, hand made and decorated, it is possible to see the power reserve (up to 45 hours), the moon phases, day and night-time hours.

The Reverso has another aspect in the Gran'Sport which, only six months after its appearance in 220 shops throughout the world, succeeded in creating an important niche for itself in the world of sports watches. Available in two versions, Automatique or Chronographe, it has attracted new attention to the Jaeger-LeCoultre product. From the case to the bracelet clasp, through the movement, it presents a great number of innovations (it is the result of 7 years of work) that make it really unique. Its commercial success, together with a positive trend registered by the House over the last ten years (while Swiss watchmaking on the whole increased its export by over 100%, this House increased the volume by 623%) so much so that a new plant has been set up at Porrentruy in the Swiss Jura. It will be active as of January 1, 2000 and within 5 years it should employ 50 specialized workers for a total cost of 2 million Swiss Francs.

Another of the historic models of Jaeger-LeCoultre has been touched up: Atmos, in its millennium mode shows, unique in the watchmaking world, hours and minutes, the month, the moon phases and the years from 2000 to 3000. Actually, at the 1st of January, 2000, Atmos will start a long, long voyage: an adventure a thousand years long. Its case seems styled to celebrate the history of this second millennium, suggesting two models: a classic version, Marqueterie with inlaid wood case made of numerous precious woods; a technological version, Atlantis, pure linear design made of transparencies and geometric solids, to dream about the next thousand years. Three irresistible objets d'art comprise the Reverso Trilogy of pocket watches, the fruit of the work of many different experts of the House. Carefully engraved and set with precious stones, "Feuilles", "Topaze" and "Améthyste" have an 18 carat white gold case, and are reversible with the same mechanism used for the wristwatch.

The History

Very few real manufactures make the majority of the components used in their watches. Jaeger-LeCoultre not only is one of these, but many, almost twice the movements it uses itself are used by a group of other, top of the line watchmakers. Since the Thirties, when the merger occurred between the Edmond Jaeger watch division, and LeCoultre, it has always been the most important company in the Vallée de Joux. It holds numberless patents, not exclusively linked to watchmaking. From its founding to today, Jaeger-LeCoultre has been able to keep up with the times without dropping to mass production, it has made its know-how technological, but not its production methods. Even today creations like Reverso and Atmos can observe the world from the heights of the most exclusive creative watchmaking.

1833 - Antoine LeCoultre opens a workshop at Le Sentier. Very inventive, he designs machines to facilitate the production of components. The first machine worked pinions are from this shop.
1834 - A brilliant invention, the "millionometer" can measure a thousandth of a millimeter, that is a micron, the equivalent of 0.001 mm.
1847 - The invention of a keyless winding system.
1880 - The Company specializes in complication watches: from chronographs to minute repeaters to alarm clocks.
1903 - The extra-thin movements created astonishment: a manual mechanism was only 1.38 mm., a chronograph 2.80 mm, a minute repeater 3.20 mm.
1928 - The presentation of "Atmos", the pendulum that "lives on air", the invention of the engineer Jean Léon Reutter, power is supplied by a metallic barometer.
1929 - The Calibre 101 is still the smallest mechanical movement in the world; it is made up of 74 elements and weighs only 0.9 grams.
1931 - The English army officers in India, great polo players, frequently broke their wristwatch crystals. The Reverso, whose case can be turned 180∞, was invented for them, brilliantly solving the problem.
1935 - For the first time the Company uses stainless steel and sapphire crystals.
1947 - The winding system of the early Atmos is definitively perfected. It exploits the property of gas whose volume changes according to the temperature. The ethyl chloride in a sealed expandable cylinder moves a small hood that transmits the movement to a powerful cylindrical spiral which, after passing through a system of pulleys, reaches the winding barrel.
1953 - Futurematic is a crownless automatic with power reserve indicator.
1956 - Memovox is the first automatic wristwatch alarm.
1958 - The Nautilus leaves for its explorations with Géophisic aboard, chronometer that is antimagnetic at 600 amp/meter.
1964 - A new automatic movement only 2.35 mm high.
1970's - The introduction of the "Mystery" watches, without the traditional hands, and the time is shown by an "invisible" rotating disc. 
1972 - Giorgio Corvo, Italian distributor for Jaeger-LeCoultre, discovers a deposit of Reverso and convinces the Company to re-present the model that had been abandoned years ago.
1982 - A quartz movement that is just barely 11.7 mm in diameter and 1.8 mm high.
1988 - Jaeger-LeCoultre and IWC jointly design the electromechanical movement Calibre 630, that will allow construction of much smaller chronographs.
1989 - The Grand Réveil, the first and still only automatic wrist-alarm with a perpetual calendar. 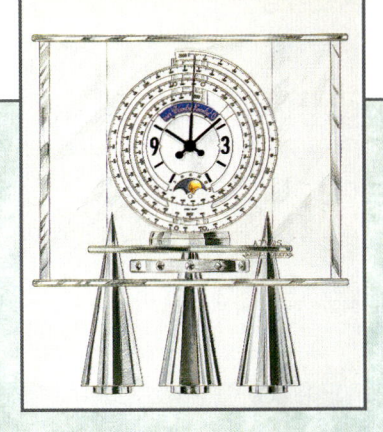
1990 - The Géographic is a revolutionary instantaneous "World Time"
1991 - The 60th anniversary of Reverso is celebrated by an exhibition presenting the history of Jaeger-LeCoultre mounted on an enormous Reverso case. The commemorative watch in pink gold is made in 500 numbered pieces with power reserve.
1992 - The year of the "Master Control", the first of a family of round shaped watches whose movements have been subjected to a thousand hours of testing. The Reverso Grande Taille is particularly adapted to modern taste.
1993 - Reverso Tourbillon and Art Déco in limited edition, and Master Date.
1994 - The Reverso Duo Face has a single movement, shows two time zones on two opposite dials. The Minute Repeater dial has the control for the "sonnerie". The Master Réveil is the first wristwatch to use a diapason for the alarm.
1995 - The Master family is complete: Chronograph, Réserve de Marche, Lady and Ultra-Plat. The Le Sentier Company, concentrating on women's models, produces the splendid Jewellery Reverso and the automatic movement for the Master Lady: the Calibre 960, the product of three and a half years of research has 226 components and 31 rubies, the diameter is 20 mm and thickness is 3.95. The Mini Reverso is a masterpiece of watchmaking technology and fine jewellery making. A reversible case, 1.3 by 3 centimeters holds the smallest mechanical movement in the world, the Calibre 101 from 1929, a volume of 0.2 cubic centimeters.
1996 - The Reverso chronograph Rétrograde is breathtaking. Time can be worn around the neck with the Reverso Pendentif. The Perpetual, the Memovox and the Classic appear among the Master collection.
1997 - Duetto is the Reverso for women, with hands showing the same time on two opposite dials: simple, day-time on one, "precious", and right for the evening, night-time on the other. Reverso Florale is steel and diamonds. Reverso Date, for men, has off-center aperture for the day, the date is shown with a hand, and uses the new manual calibre 836. The Master collection introduces two limited series of 250 pieces in platinum: the Master Geographic and the Master Perpetual, with a night-blue dial. The Master Réserve de Marche is in steel and the commemorative Reverso Juvecentus has the Turin Football Club's logo in enamel on the back for its 100th anniversary.
1998 - The event of the year is the Reverso Gran'Sport, a sporting modernization of the original Reverso, both Automatique and Chronographe with manual winding. The product of seven years of work - it called for a new building doubling the laboratory space - the Reverso Gran'Sport is entirely different but faithful to the spirit of the original, the water resistant, form-fitting case, the clasp, the movement are the same. The Reverso Géographic shows, on the first dial hours, minutes, seconds, sunset and dawn, and on the second dial has hours, minutes, the logo of city airports in each of the 24 time zones showing the time and indicating day or night for each. The Reverso Blue, very refined has a quartz movement and date at 6 o'clock and the special black dial Master series. The women's models are simple or precious versions of the successful collections, "Jewellery" and "Duetto".

195

JAEGER-LE COULTRE

MASTER PERPETUAL "BLACK" — REF. 140.840.807.SB

Movement: mechanical, automatic winding, Jaeger-Le Coultre caliber 889/440/2. Rotor with 22 kt pink gold peripheral mass. Côtes de Genève and circular graining finished. Tested for 1000 hours.
Functions: hour, minute, perpetual calendar (date, day, month, year, moon phase).
Case: stainless steel, three-piece case (Ø 37, thickness 10 mm); bezel fastened from behind with 4 screws; curved sapphire crystal; date corrector at 8; crown for the correction of the whole calendar; case back attached by 4 screws, displaying the movement through a sapphire crystal. Water-resistant to 5 atm. 
Dial: black, slightly bombé; applied rhodium plated pointed markers; luminescent dots on the printed minute track; luminescent rhodium plated Dauphine hands, skeletonized on the "prohibited hours".
Indications: day at 3, moon phase at 6, date at 9, month and two-digit year at 12, central sector for the indication, in red, of the period in which calendar corrections are not allowed.
Strap: crocodile leather, padded and hand stitched; fold-over steel clasp.
Also available: pink gold; with silvered dial and closed bottom, pink gold.
Prices: on request.

MASTER GEOGRAPHIC "BLACK" — REF. 142.840.927.SB

Movement: mechanical, automatic winding, Jaeger-Le Coultre caliber 929/3. Rotor with 22 kt pink gold peripheral mass. Vagues de Genève and circular graining finished. Tested for 1000 hours. **Functions:** hour, minute, center second, date, world time, second time zone, power reserve. **Case:** stainless steel, three-piece case (Ø 38 mm, thickness 11 mm); curved sapphire crystal; winding crown at 3 for the synchronization of secondary zones with the main time zone; crown at 10 for world time; date corrector at 2; case back attached by 4 screws, displaying the movement through a sapphire crystal. Water-resistant to 5 atm. 
Dial: black, slightly bombé; applied rhodium plated pointed markers and printed minute track, on the beveled ring; luminescent rhodium plated Dauphine hands.
Indications: date at 2, second time zone (hour and minute hands, night & day indicator) and window with bidirectional disk for reference town names of the 24 time zones at 6, power reserve at 10.
Strap: crocodile leather; fold-over steel clasp.
Also available: pink gold, leather strap; with silvered dial, closed bottom, steel, leather strap; red gold, sapphire bottom and cover hinged on case, leather strap. A steel bracelet is available as well.
Prices: on request.

MASTER CHRONOGRAPH "BLACK" — REF. 145.840.317.SB

Movement: quartz with mechanical chronograph module, Jaeger-Le Coultre caliber 631. Côtes de Genève finished. Tested for 1000 hours.
Functions: hour, minute, small second, date, chronograph with 3 counters.
Case: stainless steel, three-piece case (Ø 34 mm, thickness 8.2 mm); bezel fastened from behind with 4 screws; curved sapphire crystal; case back attached by 4 screws, displaying the movement through a sapphire crystal. Water-resistant to 5 atm. 
Dial: black, slightly bombé; applied rhodium plated pointed markers (Arabic numeral 12); luminescent dots on the printed minute track; luminescent rhodium plated Dauphine hands.
Indications: hour counter at 3, date between 4 and 5, small second at 6, minute counter at 9, center second counter, minute track with divisions for 1/5 of a second, tachymeter scale.
Strap: crocodile leather; fold-over steel clasp.
Also available: pink gold, leather strap and fold-over clasp. A steel bracelet is available as well.
Prices: on request.

MASTER GRANDE TAILLE — REF. 140.140.892B

Movement: mechanical, automatic winding, Jaeger-Le Coultre caliber 889/1. Vagues de Genève and circular graining finished. Tested for 1000 hours.
Functions: hour, minute, center second, date.
Case: 18 kt yellow gold, three-piece case, with additional ductile iron non-magnetic case back (Ø 37 mm, thickness 9.8 mm); bezel fastened from behind with 4 screws; curved sapphire crystal; yellow gold crown; case back attached by 4 screws, numbered, with yellow gold "1000 hours" seal. Water-resistant to 8 atm. 
Dial: silvered, slightly bombé; applied yellow gold Arabic numerals and pointed markers; luminescent cabochon markers on the printed minute track; luminescent yellow gold Dauphine hands.
Indications: date at 3.
Strap: crocodile leather; yellow gold fold-over clasp.
Also available: pink gold, leather strap and fold-over clasp; stainless steel, leather strap and fold-over clasp. Classic (Ø 34 mm): stainless steel, leather strap and fold-over clasp; yellow gold, leather strap and fold-over clasp; pink gold, leather strap and fold-over clasp. Only steel bracelet.
Prices: on request.

JAEGER-LE COULTRE

MASTER MEMOVOX — REF. 144.240.942B

Movement: mechanical, manual winding, Jaeger-Le Coultre caliber 914. Vagues de Genève and circular graining finished. Tested for 1000 hours.
Functions: hour, minute, center second, alarm.
Case: 18 kt pink gold, three-piece case (Ø 36 mm, thickness 12 mm); curved sapphire crystal; winding crown at 4, for the sonnerie at 2 (rings for 20 seconds), pink gold; case back attached by 4 screws, numbered, with pink gold "1000 hours" seal. Water-resistant to 5 atm.
Dial: silvered, slightly bombé; turning center disc; applied pink gold Arabic numerals and pointed markers; luminescent dots on the minute track, screen-printed; luminescent pink gold Dauphine hands.
Indications: turning center disc with luminescent sonnerie pointer.
Strap: crocodile leather; pink gold fold-over clasp.
Also available: stainless steel, ostrich-skin strap, fold-over clasp; with "Black" dial, sapphire case back, crocodile leather strap, fold-over clasp: steel or pink gold.
Prices: on request.

MASTER REVEIL — REF. 141.240.972B

Movement: mechanical, automatic winding, Jaeger-Le Coultre caliber 918. Vagues de Genève and circular graining finished. Tested for 1000 hours.
Functions: hour, minute, center second, date, alarm.
Case: 18 kt pink gold, three-piece case (Ø 38.7 mm, thickness 13 mm); bezel fastened from behind with 4 screws; curved sapphire crystal; winding crown at 4, for the sonnerie at 2 (rings for 20 seconds), pink gold; case back attached by 4 screws, numbered, with pink gold "1000 hours" seal. Water-resistant to 5 atm.
Dial: silvered, slightly bombé; turning center disc; applied pink gold Arabic numerals and pointed markers; luminescent dots on the printed minute track; luminescent pink gold Dauphine hands.
Indications: date at 3, turning center disc with luminescent sonnerie pointer.
Strap: crocodile leather; pink gold fold-over clasp.
Also available: in yellow gold, leather strap and fold-over clasp; steel, leather strap and fold-over clasp. A steel bracelet is available as well.
Prices: on request.

MASTER MOON PLATINE — REF. 140.640.986FB

Movement: mechanical, automatic winding, Jaeger-Le Coultre caliber 891/448. Rotor with platinum peripheral mass. Vagues de Genève and circular graining finished. Tested for 1000 hours.
Functions: hour, minute, small second, full calendar (date, day, month, moon phase).
Case: platinum, three-piece case (Ø 37 mm, thickness 11.5 mm); curved sapphire crystal; 2 correctors on case side; white gold crown; case back attached by 4 screws, displaying the movement through a sapphire crystal protected by a hinged snap-in cover. Water-resistant to 5 atm.
Dial: deep blue, slightly bombé; applied white gold pointed markers and Arabic numerals; 4 luminescent dots; white gold Dauphine hands.
Indications: small second and moon phases at 6, day and month in apertures at 12, date with half-moon center hand.
Strap: crocodile leather; platinum fold-over clasp.
Also available: Non limited series, "Black" dial, sapphire case back without hinged cover: steel leather strap and fold-over clasp; pink gold leather strap and fold-over clasp. A steel bracelet is available as well. **Prices:** on request. Edition limited to 20 numbered pieces.

MASTER DATE — REF. 140.840.872B

Movement: mechanical, automatic winding, Jaeger-Le Coultre caliber 889/447. Vagues de Genève and circular graining finished. Tested for 1000 hours.
Functions: hour, minute, small second, full calendar (date, day, month).
Case: stainless steel, three-piece case (Ø 37 mm, thickness 11 mm); curved sapphire crystal; 2 correctors on case side; case back attached by 4 screws, numbered, with yellow gold "1000 hours" seal. Water-resistant to 8 atm.
Dial: silvered, slightly bombé; applied rhodium plated pointed markers and Arabic numerals; 4 luminescent dots; luminescent rhodium plated Dauphine hands.
Indications: small second at 6, center day and month in apertures, date with half-moon center hand.
Strap: crocodile leather; fold-over steel clasp.
Also available: pink gold, leather strap and fold-over clasp. Only steel bracelet.
Prices: on request.

JAEGER-LE COULTRE

MASTER RESERVE DE MARCHE PLATINE   REF. 140.640.936.B

Movement: mechanical, automatic winding, Jaeger-Le Coultre caliber 928. Rotor with platinum peripheral mass. Vagues de Genève and circular graining finished. Tested for 1000 hours.
Functions: hour, minute, small second, date, power reserve.
Case: platinum, three-piece case (Ø 37 mm, thickness 11.5 mm); curved sapphire crystal; date corrector on case side; white gold crown; case back attached by 4 screws, displaying the movement through a sapphire crystal protected by a hinged snap-in cover. Water-resistant to 5 atm.
Dial: deep blue, slightly bombé; applied white gold Arabic numerals and pointed markers; luminescent dots on the printed minute track; white gold Dauphine hands.
Indications: date at 2, small second at 6, power reserve at 10.
Strap: crocodile leather; platinum fold-over clasp.
Also available: Non limited series, "Black" dial, sapphire case back without hinged cover or silvered dial, closed bottom: steel, leather strap and fold-over clasp; pink gold, leather strap and fold-over clasp. A steel bracelet is available as well.
Prices: on request. Edition limited to 250 numbered pieces.

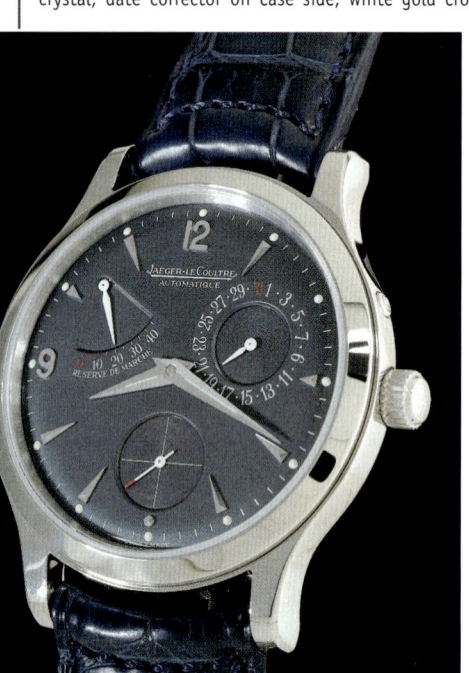

MASTER ULTRA-THIN "BLACK"   REF. 145.840.797.SB

Movement: mechanical, manual winding, Jaeger-Le Coultre caliber 849 extra-thin. Vagues de Genève and circular graining finished. Tested for 1000 hours.
Functions: hour, minute.
Case: stainless steel, three-piece case (Ø 34 mm, thickness 5.6 mm); bezel fastened from behind with 4 screws; curved sapphire crystal; pink gold crown; case back attached by 4 screws, displaying the movement through a sapphire crystal. Water-resistant to 5 atm.
Dial: black, slightly bombé; applied rhodium plated Arabic numerals and pointed markers; rhodium plated Dauphine hands.
Strap: crocodile leather; fold-over steel clasp.
Also available: with clasp; pink gold, leather strap and fold-over clasp; with silvered dial, closed bottom: steel, leather strap and fold-over clasp; pink gold, leather strap and fold-over clasp.
Prices: on request.

REVERSO GRAN'SPORT CHRONOGRAPHE RETROGRADE   REF. 295.110.592

Movement: mechanical, manual winding, Jaeger-Le Coultre caliber 859 (derived from caliber 829), 38 jewels, 28,800 vibrations per hour (vph). Made up by 317 elements. Beveled and Côtes de Genève hand-finished. **Functions:** hour, minute, center second, date, chronograph with 2 counters, chronograph working indicator. **Case:** 18 kt yellow gold, tonneau, reversible (with brancard size 43 mm, width 28, thickness 11.5 mm; only case size 32 mm, width 28, thickness 10 mm), engraved with transverse grooves, matte finish; curved sapphire crystal on both sides; yellow gold crown and rectangular pushers, beveled; case back attached by 4 screws, brancard with brushed finish and engine turned (circular graining). Waterproof.
Dial: silvered, engine turned (guilloché) with panels in the central part; luminescent applied pointed markers and Arabic numerals; printed minute track; luminescent blued stainless steel lozenge hands; chronograph on/off indicator at 5, date at 6; second face silvered, engine turned (guilloché) subdials with circular anthracite borders; minute counter with retrograde hand at 6, off-center second counter.
Bracelet: polished and brushed gold; double fold-over clasp and safety pushers. **Also available:** stainless steel with bracelet, anthracite or silvered dial. **Prices:** on request.

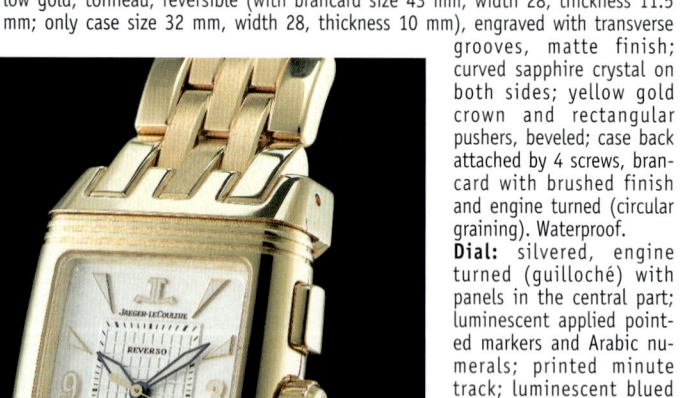

REVERSO GRAN'SPORT AUTOMATIQUE   REF. 290.880.602

Movement: mechanical, automatic winding, Jaeger-Le Coultre caliber 960R, 31 jewels, 28,800 vibrations per hour (vph). Made up by 226 elements. Beveled and hand-finished (Côtes de Genève).
Functions: hour, minute, center second, date.
Case: stainless steel, tonneau type, reversible, engraved with transverse grooves, matte finish (with brancard size 43 mm, width 26.5 mm, thickness 10 mm; only case size 30.5 mm, width 26.5 mm, thickness 4 mm); curved sapphire crystal; screw-down crown; case back attached by 4 screws, brancard with brushed finish and decorated with circular graining pattern. Waterproof.
Dial: silvered, engine turned (guilloché) with panels in the central part; luminescent applied pointed markers and Arabic numerals; printed minute track; luminescent blued stainless steel lozenge hands.
Indications: date at 6.
Bracelet: stainless steel, polished and brushed; double fold-over clasp with safety pushers.
Also available: with anthracite dial; in yellow gold with bracelet and silvered dial.
Prices: on request.

JAEGER-LE COULTRE

REVERSO CHRONOGRAPHE RETROGRADE   REF. 270.240.692B

Movement: mechanical, manual winding, rectangular shape, extra-thin, Jaeger-Le Coultre caliber 829 patented.
Functions: hour, minute, date, chronograph with 2 counters, chronograph working indicator.
Case: 18 kt pink gold, rectangular, reversible (with brancard size 42 mm, width 26, thickness 9 mm; case size 30.5 mm, width 26, thickness 8.5 mm); curved sapphire crystal on both sides; pink gold rectangular crown and pushers. Waterproof.
Dial: solid silver, engine turned (guilloché) and hand-finished; painted Arabic numerals and minute track; blued stainless steel sword style hands; chronograph on/off indicator 5 and date at 6 on the first face; minute counter at 6 (with retrograde hand) and off-center minute counter, perfectly integrated with the bridges and other movement components, on the second face.
Strap: crocodile leather; pink gold fold-over clasp. Edition limited to 500 pieces numbered 1996.
Also available: with bracelet.
Prices: on request.

REVERSO GEOGRAPHIQUE   REF. 270.240.582B

Movement: mechanical, manual winding, Jaeger-Le Coultre caliber 858, patented.
Functions: hour, minute, small second, night & day indicator; second time zone, night & day indicator with reference towns.
Case: 18 kt pink gold, rectangular, reversible (with brancard size 42 mm, width 26, thickness 9.8 mm; case size 30.5 mm, width 26, thickness 8.5 mm); curved sapphire crystal, on both sides; pink gold second time zone corrector and reference town rectangular corrector pusher on case side; pink gold crown. Water-resistant.
Dial: solid silver, engine turned (guilloché) center; painted Arabic numerals and minute track, blued stainless steel sword style hands, small second at 6, night & day indicator at 12; black second dial, engine turned (guilloché), white Arabic Chinese-style numerals, luminescent lozenge hands, reference towns at 5 and 7, GMT ± between 7 and 8, am/pm indicator between 4 and 5.
Strap: crocodile leather; pink gold fold-over clasp.
Also available: with bracelet.
Prices: on request.

REVERSO DUOFACE   REF. 270.240.544B

Movement: mechanical, manual winding, Jaeger-Le Coultre caliber 854, patented.
Functions: home time hour, minute, small second; second time zone hour, minute, 24-hour.
Case: 18 kt pink gold, rectangular, reversible (with brancard size 42 mm, width 26, thickness 9.8 mm; case size 30.5 mm, width 26, thickness 8.5 mm); curved sapphire crystal, on both sides; second time zone corrector on case side; pink gold crown. Waterproof.
Dial: solid silver, Art Déco design, silvered and engine turned (guilloché) in the central part, with printed Arabic numerals and minute track, blued stainless steel sword style hands and small second at 6; the rear dial, black, engine turned (guilloché), with applied white gold pointed markers and luminescent Arabic numerals, luminescent white gold lozenge hands and 24-hour display at 6.
Strap: crocodile leather; fold-over clasp in pink gold.
Also available: with both dial silvered; bracelet; in yellow gold; steel, leather strap and fold-over clasp or bracelet; white gold and black-rosé dials, leather strap and fold-over clasp or bracelet.
Prices: on request.

REVERSO ART DECO   REF. 270.340.625B

Movement: mechanical, manual winding, tonneau-curved, 14 kt pink gold, Jaeger-Le Coultre caliber 822/AD. Skeletonized, hand-finished and engine turned, made up by 193 worked-out and hand-decorated elements.
Functions: hour, minute, small second.
Case: 18 kt white gold, rectangular shape, reversible (with brancard size 42 mm, width 26 mm, thickness 9.8 mm; only case size 30.5 mm, width 26 mm, thickness 8.5 mm); curved sapphire crystal; white gold crown; numbered case back attached by 4 screws, displaying the movement through a sapphire crystal. Waterproof.
Dial: solid silver, rosé, engine turned (guilloché) and hand-finished; pointed markers and cabochon applied white gold; white gold Dauphine hands.
Indications: small second at 6.
Strap: crocodile leather; white gold fold-over clasp.
Also available: with bracelet; pink gold with dial in solid silver, engine turned (guilloché), leather strap and fold-over clasp or bracelet.
Prices: on request.

JAEGER-LE COULTRE

REVERSO MEMORY   REF. 255.840.822B

Movement: mechanical, manual winding, Jaeger-Le Coultre caliber 862.
Functions: hour, minute, small second, fly-back "memento" counter.
Case: stainless steel, rectangular shape, reversible (with brancard 38.5 mm, width 23 mm, thickness 10 mm; case only 27 mm, width 23); curved sapphire crystal; stainless steel crown; rectangular counter pusher at 4; case back attached by 8 screws, with gasket. Waterproof. 
Dial: silvered, engine turned (guilloché) in the central part; painted Arabic numerals and minute track; luminescent blued stainless steel sword style hands. On the back, black, engine turned (guilloché) in the central part, luminescent central sword style hand.
Indications: small second at 6, on the back 60 minutes "memento" counter with simultaneous zeroing and restart (fly-back) by the pusher at 4.
Strap: ostrich skin; fold-over steel clasp.
Also available: with bracelet; in steel/yellow gold, leather strap and fold-over clasp or bracelet; in yellow gold, leather strap and fold-over clasp or bracelet.
Prices: on request.

REVERSO MEMORY   REF. 255.140.822B

Undoubtedly conceived for the estimator of mechanical "complications", the new Reverso Memory includes the essence of chronograph technology, by resuming their functions in only one fly-back 60 minutes counter. The origins of this construction typology, better known under the name chrono-stop, go back to the Fifties and Sixties. The most famous models were realized by Longines, Pierce, Minerva, Lemania, ma above all by Rolex with its rare Zerographe of 1940. Their way of working was rather simple: by only one pressure on the pusher it was possible to stop, zero and restart the hand of the only second counter. It was mainly used to measure production times with working processes or aeronautical counters to calculate routes. The new Memory by Jaeger-Le Coultre is again provided with the chrono-stop feature, with the only substantial difference of the minute counter, and not second counter; placed separately on a rear dial.
In the photograph the back of the yellow gold version with same dials and crocodile leather strap.
Price: on request.

REVERSO SUN MOON   REF. 270.340.637SB

Movement: mechanical, manual winding, Jaeger-Le Coultre caliber 823.
Functions: hour, minute, small second, night & day indicator, moon phase, power reserve.
Case: 18 kt white gold, rectangular shape, reversible (with brancard size 42 mm, width 26 mm, thickness 9.8 mm; only case size 30.5 mm, width 26 mm, thickness 8.5 mm); curved sapphire crystal; white gold crown; case back attached by 8 screws displaying the movement through a sapphire crystal. Waterproof. 
Dial: black; white painted Arabic numerals inspired by the style of Chinese ideograms; white painted railway minute track; luminescent white gold leaf style hands.
Indications: night & day indicator window at 2, small second and moon phase window at 6, power reserve between 10 and 11.
Strap: crocodile leather; fold-over clasp in white gold.
Also available: with bracelet; pink gold and silvered dial, leather strap and fold-over clasp or bracelet.
Prices: on request.

REVERSO DATE   REF. 270.840.362.B

Movement: mechanical, manual winding, Jaeger-Le Coultre caliber 836.
Functions: hour, minute, small second, day-date.
Case: stainless steel, rectangular shape, reversible (with brancard size 42 mm, width 26 mm, thickness 9.8 mm; only case size 30.5 mm, width 26 mm, thickness 8.5 mm); curved sapphire crystal; date corrector on case side; stainless steel crown; case back attached by 8 screws. Waterproof. 
Dial: silvered opaline, zone engine turned (guilloché); printed Arabic numerals and round railway minute track; blued stainless steel sword style hands.
Indications: small second at 6, day at 11, pointed center date hand.
Strap: ostrich skin; fold-over steel clasp.
Also available: with bracelet; pink gold, leather strap and fold-over clasp or bracelet.
Prices: on request.

JAEGER-LE COULTRE

REVERSO GRAND TAILLE OR DECO   REF. 270.240.627.EB

Movement: mechanical, manual winding, Jaeger-Le Coultre caliber 822.
Functions: hour, minute, small second.
Case: 18 kt pink gold, rectangular shape, reversible (with brancard size 42 mm, width 26 mm, thickness 9.8 mm; only case size 30.5 mm, width 26 mm, thickness 8.5 mm); curved sapphire crystal; pink gold crown; case back attached by 8 screws. Waterproof.
Dial: black enameled; Arabic numerals inspired by the style of Chinese ideograms and railway minute track, white painted; luminescent pink gold sword style hands.
Indications: small second at 6.
Strap: crocodile leather; pink gold fold-over clasp.
Also available: with bracelet; white gold, leather strap and fold-over clasp or bracelet. With silvered dial and classical Arabic numerals, steel, leather strap and fold-over clasp or bracelet; yellow gold & stainless steel, leather strap and fold-over clasp or bracelet; in yellow gold, leather strap and fold-over clasp or bracelet.
Prices: on request.

REVERSO CLASSIC OR DECO   REF. 250.340.867.EB

Created in 1931 on request of British officers in India, who were "Polo" fans, and planned by the engineer René-Alfred Chauvot, the Reverso, an expression of pure Art Déco style, can be considered as the masterpiece of one among the pioneers of industrial design. Undying as myths are, this is an avant-garde model of the last decade. In this version with "Chinese" numerals and hand winding movement caliber 846, it is available only with a white gold or pink case, in the three classical sizes of the Reverso line: Grande Taille, Classic (in the photograph, with the following sizes: with brancard 38.5 mm, width 23 mm, thickness 7.3 mm; case only 27 mm, width 23 mm, thickness 6.3) and Lady.
Also available: pink gold leather strap and fold-over clasp or bracelet.
Prices: on request.

REVERSO CLASSIC   REF. 250.140.862B

Movement: mechanical, manual winding, Jaeger-Le Coultre caliber 846.
Functions: hour, minute, small second.
Case: 18 kt yellow gold, rectangular shape, reversible (with brancard 38.5v23 mm, thickness 7.3 mm; case only 27 mm, width 23 mm, thickness 6.3); curved sapphire crystal; yellow gold crown; case back attached by 8 screws, with gasket. Waterproof.
Dial: silvered; printed Arabic numerals and railway minute track, blued stainless steel sword style hands.
Strap: ostrich skin; fold-over clasp in yellow gold.
Also available: with bracelet; in yellow gold and bezel diamonds, leather strap and fold-over clasp or bracelet; pink gold, silvered or black dial, leather strap and fold-over clasp or bracelet; white gold, black or pink dial, leather strap and fold-over clasp; steel and yellow gold, silvered dial, leather strap and fold-over clasp or bracelet; stainless steel, silvered dial, leather strap and fold-over clasp or bracelet; with quartz movement.
Prices: on request.

REVERSO DUETTO   REF. 266.342.440B

Movement: mechanical, manual winding, Jaeger-Le Coultre caliber 844.
Functions: double hour indication, minute.
Case: 18 kt white gold, rectangular shape, reversible, double face, with 32 set brilliants on the second face (with brancard size 33v21 mm, thickness 8.5 mm; only case size 22.5 mm, width 21 mm, thickness 7.5 mm); curved sapphire crystal on both sides; white gold crown set with diamond. Waterproof.
Dial: solid silver, engine turned (guilloché) at the center; printed Chinese style numerals; applied white gold drop style markers; blued stainless steel sword style hands; solid silver, engine turned (guilloché) rear face, off-center white mother-of-pearl subdial with white gold Dauphine hands.
Strap: crocodile leather; fold-over clasp in white gold.
Also available: with bracelet; yellow gold, leather strap and fold-over clasp or bracelet; red gold, leather strap and fold-over clasp or bracelet; steel+yellow gold, leather strap and fold-over clasp or bracelet; steel, leather strap and fold-over clasp or bracelet; in many other jewel versions.
Prices: on request.

Officine Panerai

There are watches that have written history. They have gone far beyond fashion and commercial success. Panerai is among these. Brilliant example of Italian technology, they are still on the crest 60 years after their creation, confirmation of total reliability in their technical responses. Designed and built, as they are, to work under the most demanding conditions, they are solid, beautiful, they cleverly combine refinement with daring creativity, they create perfect proportion between form and content, between quality and price. Contemporary production takes nothing away from the originals, thanks to the artistic direction of Giampiero Bodino, the designer Vendôme called to bring the name back to the world's attention. His hand succeeded in stylishly matching the heroic suggestions in Luminor with the peaceful life of today, keeping the sense of determination and technical authority that had made Panerai the watches the world envies us for, and rightly so…

The History

1935 - On the requests made by the 1st Submarine Group of the Italian Navy, the Commission whose job this was began research to give special military corps a watch that was absolutely water resistant and also readable in the absence of light. Initial research regarding products being traded gave unacceptable results.

The company, "Guido Panerai & Figlio", was contacted, as the historical supplier of the Royal Navy since 1864 (Panerai was a Florentine). It suggested a watch absolutely unheard of at the time: the Radiomir. Tested at length at sea, night and day, it passed its trials easily and in March, 1936, was chosen as the official timepiece for the special services group within the submarine section of the Navy. This group, named the X Squadron MAS, received the first Panerai Radiomir produced in series starting from 1938.

Panerai often had a decisive part in the extraordinary exploits of the small group of men who were able to intimidate the powerful British Mediterranean Fleet. In all military operations, time and synchronization are fundamental variables. The extreme reliability of the watch made it invaluable. The Radiomir had an exceptionally heavy steel case. Almost square, the slightly convex plexiglas watch crystal was fixed beneath the bezel. The robust case back was screwed on and held in place a circular rubber seal. Like every other part of the watch, the lugs were primarily functional and generally made of a simple soldered steel wire. The screw crown was supplied by Rolex Switzerland.

Later on, Panerai will make its own system. The crown was water resistant with a cam lever which, fastened to a bridge screwed onto the case side, pressed against the crown keeping the seal under pressure. Simple. Genial. Even today it resists at well over 30 atm. Like all good sub watches, the graphics on the Panerai made the dial easily readable in all light conditions. Its size, therefore, was justified, as were the size of the white florescent markers and the black contrasting background. It had a manual winding mechanical movement, made by Rolex on a Cortébert ébauche. It was a separate bridged 15 line Lépine, plated in highly polished steel, 17 rubies, Breguet balance-spring in Elinvar, at 18,000 vph.

Going back to the dial and its readability, since experiments involving a battery powered light were failures, this concept was discarded in favor of a simpler solution and more effective markers based on radioactive radium. The dial was frequently made like a sandwich, where the upper part was black metal with apertures for the markers, and the lower part spread with radium which shone through the holes. The yellow-greenish light was so strong as to be seen not just by the divers but also by the men on the surface.

Simple solutions follow one another and they simply covered the watch faces with a handkerchief. Less radioactive, a tritio based material subsequently replaced the radium. The watch was named Luminor. Interestingly, the Panerai dials had no name on them, purportedly not to reveal the nationality of the men wearing them on secret missions during the war. Luminor remained in production until well after the war and was made in many variations and versions. The most famous was a "gigantic" 8-day with an Angelus calibre 240, requested by the Egyptian air-strikers in 1956; only fifty were made.

Panerai again became active in the early 1990's, thanks to pressure from collectors who wanted a historically valid re-edition of the Luminor.

From **1997** on, since the watchmaking department of the Florentine company was acquired by the powerful Vendôme Group, the House is seeing a second youth, and will be distributed alongside historical names like Cartier and Vacheron Constantin.

Officine Panerai's photographs reduced by 15% with respect to the other pieces.

OFFICINE PANERAI

LUMINOR MARINA — REF. PAM00001

Movement: mechanical, manual winding, Panerai caliber OP II (Unitas caliber 6497-2 base). Hand-finished; hand-engraved (Panerai finish) bridges. Officially certified "chronometer" (C.O.S.C.).
Functions: hour, minute, small second.
Case: steel with black PVD (Phisical Vapor Deposit) matte coating, three-piece "cushion-shaped" case (Ø 44 mm, thickness 16.8 mm); curved sapphire crystal (3.5 mm thick); stainless steel crown, waterproofed by a patented system made up by a bridge fastened on the case side by two screws and a pressing lever pivoted on the bridge which, by pushing the crown on to the o-ring, ensures its tightness; screwed-on case back. Water-resistant to 30 atm.
Dial: black; luminescent Arabic numerals and bâton markers; luminescent bâton hands.
Indications: small second at 9.
Strap: leather, linked with the lugs by two screwed-on pins; black anodized steel clasp (available also with a black rubber strap).
Also available: polished steel, black or white dial. With crown on the left, polished steel or steel with black PVD matte coating, black dial.
Prices: on request.

LUMINOR MARINA AUTOMATIC — REF. PAM00050

Movement: mechanical, automatic winding, Panerai caliber OP III (Valjoux caliber 7750-P1 base). Hand-finished; hand-engraved (Panerai finish) bridges. Officially certified "chronometer" (C.O.S.C.).
Functions: hour, minute, small second, date.
Case: stainless steel, three-piece polished case, "cushion-shaped" (Ø 40 mm); curved sapphire crystal (3.5 mm thick) with magnifying glass on date; stainless steel crown, waterproofed by a patented system made up by a bridge fastened on the case side by two screws and a pressing lever pivoted on the bridge which, by pushing the crown on to the o-ring, ensures its tightness; screwed-on case back. Water-resistant to 30 atm.
Dial: black; luminescent Arabic numerals and bâton markers; luminescent bâton hands.
Indications: date at 3, small second at 9.
Bracelet: stainless steel, with a link whose design reminds the crown-protecting bridge, made of two superimposed and screwed parts; stainless steel personalized clasp.
Also available: white dial; leather strap.
Prices: on request.

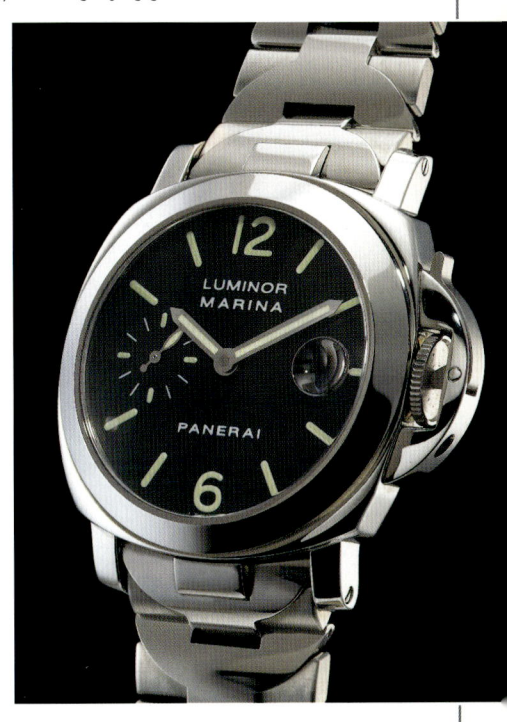

LUMINOR — REF. PAM00002

Movement: mechanical, manual winding, Panerai caliber OP I (Unitas caliber 6497-2 base). Hand-finished; hand-engraved (Panerai finish) bridges.
Functions: hour, minute.
Case: stainless steel, three-piece polished case, "cushion-shaped" (Ø 44 mm, thickness 16.8 mm); curved sapphire crystal (3.5 mm thick); stainless steel crown, waterproofed by a patented system made up by a bridge fastened on the case side by two screws and a pressing lever pivoted on the bridge which, by pushing the crown on to the o-ring, ensures its tightness; screwed-on case back. Water-resistant to 30 atm.
Dial: black; luminescent Arabic numerals and bâton markers; luminescent bâton hands.
Strap: leather, linked to the lugs by two pins closed by screws; stainless steel personalized clasp (available also with a black rubber strap).
Also available: white dial; steel with black PVD (Phisical Vapor Deposit) coating.
Prices: on request.

LUMINOR GMT — REF. PAM00023

Movement: mechanical, automatic winding (ETA caliber 2893/2 base). Hand-finished; hand-engraved bridges (Panerai finish). Officially certified "chronometer" (C.O.S.C.).
Functions: hour, minute, center second, date, second time zone, 24-hour indication.
Case: stainless steel, three-piece polished case, "cushion-shaped" (Ø 44 mm); curved sapphire crystal (3.5 mm thick) with magnifying glass on date; brushed bezel, fixed, with 24 hours engraved; stainless steel crown, waterproofed by a patented system made up by a bridge fastened on the case side by two screws and a pressing lever pivoted on the bridge which, by pushing the crown on to the o-ring, ensures its tightness; screwed-on case back. Water-resistant to 30 atm.
Dial: black; luminescent Arabic numerals and bâton markers; luminescent skeletonized bâton hands.
Indications: date at 3, second time zone–24-hour with arrow-point center hand.
Strap: leather; stailness steel personalized clasp (available also with a black rubber strap).
Also available: black dial with a vertical wave pattern.
Prices: on request.

OFFICINE PANERAI

LUMINOR POWER RESERVE — REF. PAM00027

Movement: mechanical, automatic winding, Panerai caliber 9040 (ETA caliber 2892 base modified by Soprod). Hand-finished; hand-engraved bridges (Panerai finish). Officially certified "chronometer" (C.O.S.C.).
Functions: hour, minute, center second, date, power reserve.
Case: stainless steel, three-piece polished case, "cushion-shaped" (Ø 44 mm); curved sapphire crystal (3.5 mm thick) with magnifying glass on date; stainless steel crown, waterproofed by a patented system made up by a bridge fastened on the case side by two screws and a pressing lever pivoted on the bridge which, by pushing the crown on to the o-ring, ensures its tightness; screwed-on case back. Water-resistant to 30 atm.
Dial: black; luminescent Arabic numerals and bâton markers; printed minute track; luminescent bâton hands.
Indications: date at 3, power reserve at 6.
Strap: leather; stainless steel personalized clasp (available also with a black rubber strap).
Also available: black dial with "Clous de Paris" pattern.
Prices: on request.

LUMINOR SUBMERSIBLE — REF. PAM00024

Movement: mechanical, automatic winding, Panerai caliber "OP III" (Valjoux caliber 7750-P1 base). Hand-finished. Hand-engraved (Panerai finish) bridges. Officially certified "chronometer" (C.O.S.C.).
Functions: hour, minute, center second, date.
Case: stainless steel, three-piece polished case, "cushion-shaped" (Ø 44 mm, thickness 16.8 mm); curved sapphire crystal (3.5 mm thick) with magnifying glass on date; counter-clockwise turning bezel with graduated scale made of small recessed cylinders; stainless steel crown, waterproofed by a patented system made up by a bridge fastened on the case side by two screws and a pressing lever pivoted on the bridge which, by pushing the crown on to the o-ring, ensures its tightness; screwed-on case back. Water-resistant to 30 atm.
Dial: black; luminescent Arabic numerals and round markers; luminescent skeletonized bâton hands.
Indications: date at 3, small second at 9.
Strap: crocodile leather; stainless steel personalized clasp (available also with a black rubber strap).
Prices: on request.
Also available: titanium, black dial with engraved diamonds.
Prices: on request.

RADIOMIR CHRONOGRAPH RATTRAPANTE — REF. PAM00047

Movement: mechanical, manual winding, Venus caliber 179 of the Fourties. Beveled and Côtes de Genève finished. Officially certified "chronometer" (C.O.S.C.).
Functions: hour, minute, small second, split-second chronograph with 2 counters.
Case: stainless steel, three-piece polished "cushion-shaped" (Ø 40 mm); curved sapphire crystal (3.5 mm thick); flush lugs; crown with split-second pusher; screwed-on case back displaying the movement through a sapphire crystal. Water-resistant to 3 atm.
Dial: black; luminescent Arabic numerals and bâton markers; luminescent bâton hands.
Indications: minute counter at 3, small second at 9, center second and split-second counters; minute track with divisions for 1/5 of a second and luminescent dots; tachymeter scale.
Strap: crocodile leather; stainless steel personalized clasp.
Price: on request. Edition limited to 20 pieces.

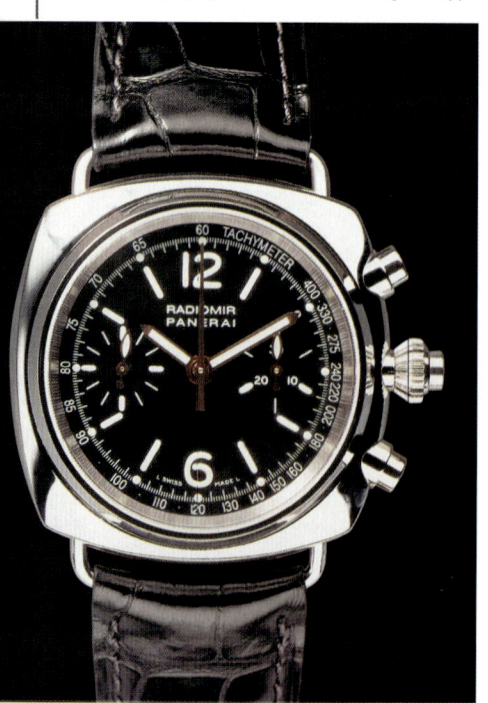

RADIOMIR CHRONOGRAPH RATTRAPANTE

The Radiomir, a model of great historical importance, was ordered to Panerai of Firenze in 1936, and its production commenced two years later. It became part of the equipment of the famous "Xth MAS Brigade", and the popular imagination associated it with the Brigade's heroic acts. Its name stems from the radium used to make its markers and hands luminescent (later on, radium was replaced by tritium, in the Luminor and, today, in the Superluminova models currently produced). The new formal edition of Radiomir (the original wasn't a chronograph watch) presented in 1999 also in the split-second chronograph version with alarm, proposed the historical cushion-shaped case in polished steel, with the classical removable flush lugs.
The movement is a rare "chronographe rattrapante", caliber 179 by Venus, realized in the Fourties and now out of production.

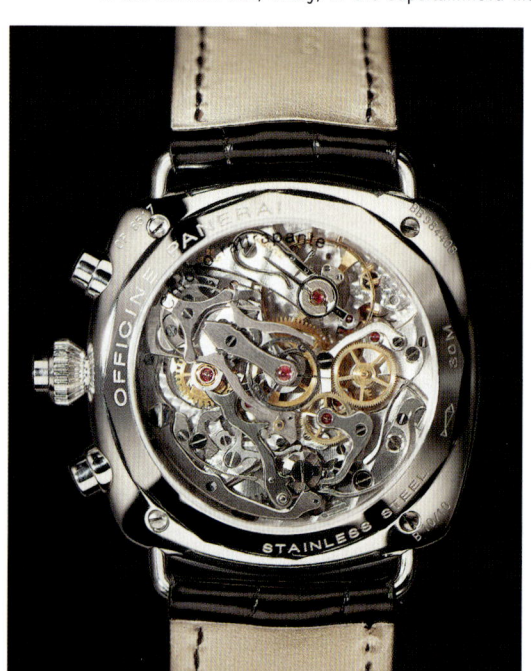

OFFICINE PANERAI

RADIOMIR ALARM/GMT   REF. PAM00046

Movement: mechanical, automatic winding, Panerai caliber 59 (GP caliber 2291 base), autonomy of 47 hours, 31 jewels. Hand-engraved rotor (Panerai finish). Beveled and Côtes de Genève finished.
Functions: hour, minute, center second, date, second time zone, 24-hour indication, alarm.
Case: 18 kt white gold, three-piece polished "cushion-shaped" case (Ø 40 mm); curved sapphire crystal (3.5 mm thick) with magnifying glass on date; flush lugs; white gold crown at 2 for hour, second time zone and date setting, at 4 for sonnerie setting; screwed-on case back displaying the movement through a sapphire crystal. Water-resistant to 3 atm.
Dial: black; luminescent Arabic numerals and bâton markers; printed minute track with luminescent dots; luminescent bâton hands.
Indications: date at 3 (referred to central time), second time zone–24-hour display at 6; sonnerie with arrow-point center hand, 24-hour indication.
Strap: crocodile leather; white gold personalized clasp.
Price: on request. Edition limited to 60 pieces.

LUMINOR CHRONO TITANIUM/STEEL   REF. PAM00052

Movement: mechanical, automatic winding, Panerai caliber "OP IV" (base Zenith caliber 40.0 El Primero). Hand-finished; hand-engraved bridges (Panerai finish). Officially certified "chronometer" (C.O.S.C.).
Functions: hour, minute, small second, chronograph with 3 counters.
Case: titanium, three-piece polished case, "cushion-shaped" (Ø 40 mm); steel bezel; curved sapphire crystal (3.5 mm thick); pushers integrated in the design of the crown-protection bridge; crown in stainless steel, with a patented system made up by a steel bridge fastened on the case side by two screws and a titanium pressing lever pivoted on the bridge which, by pushing the crown on to the o-ring, ensures its tightness; screwed-on case back displaying the movement through a sapphire crystal. Water-resistant to 20 atm.
Dial: black; luminescent Arabic numerals and bâton markers; printed minute track; luminescent bâton hands. **Indications:** minute counter at 3, hour counter at 6, small second at 9, center second counter with a precision of $1/10$ of a second.
Bracelet: stainless steel and titanium, with a link made of two superimposed and screwed parts; stainless steel personalized clasp.
Price: on request. Edition limited to 500 pieces.

LUMINOR CHRONO 2000   REF. PAM00045

Movement: mechanical, automatic winding, Panerai caliber "OP V" (Frédéric Piguet caliber 1185 base). Hand-finished; hand-engraved bridges (Panerai finish). Officially certified "chronometer" (C.O.S.C.). **Functions:** hour, minute, small second, chronograph with 3 counters.
Case: 18 kt white gold, three-piece polished case, "cushion-shaped" (Ø 40 mm); bezel with engraved tachymeter scale; curved sapphire crystal (3.5 mm thick); white gold pushers integrated in the design of the crown-protecting bridge; white gold crown with a patented system made up by a white gold bridge fastened on the case side by two screws and a gold pressing lever pivoted on the bridge which, by pushing the crown on to the o-ring, ensures its tightness; screwed-on case back displaying the movement through a sapphire crystal. Water-resistant to 20 atm.
Dial: black; embossed "Panerai 2000" writing; luminescent bâton markers (Arabic numeral 12); printed minute track; luminescent bâton hands. **Indications:** minute counter at 3, date between 4 and 5, small second at 6, hour counter at 9, center second counter.
Strap: crocodile leather; white gold personalized clasp.
Price: on request. Edition limited to 100 pieces.

LUMINOR CHRONO 2000

Inspired to the famous Luminor realized by Panerai for the raider units of the Italian Navy, Chrono 2000 proposes some substantial differences with respect to its illustrious predecessor. The first and also the most evident difference is that it is a chronograph, equipped with an automatic winding movement with gold rotor and C.O.S.C. chronometer certificate. The second and also very important difference is that its precious white gold case (waterproof to 200 m) was reduced to a diameter of 40 mm, thus fitting also people who prefer smaller sized watches. And all this without betraying traditional values and maintaining excellent quality standards, as the adoption of Swiss movements (chosen among the best of contemporary high quality level produce) witnesses, finished and personalized by hand and mostly provided with the chronometer certificate.

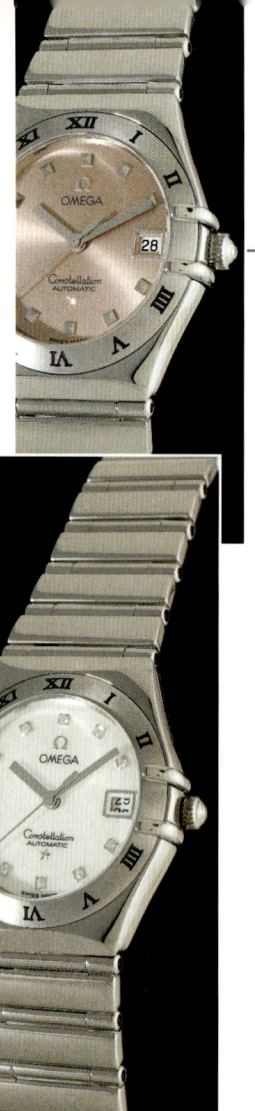

Omega

There's no doubt which watch Omega regards as its most important introduction of the year and probably of the decade. It's the Co-Axial De Ville. What makes it noteworthy is its escapement, which both its inventor, the famous watchmaker George Daniels, and Omega say represents the first real improvement on the traditional lever escapement since the British watchmaker Thomas Mudge conceived it in the 18th century. What's so great about this new escapement? Well, say its champions, it needs to be serviced less frequently and is more accurate than the traditional lever escapement. That's because it generates much less friction. In a standard escapement, friction is created when the pallet jewels slide along the escape-wheel teeth, providing the impulses that make the balance oscillate. In Daniels's co-axial escapement, the impulse-giving pallets don't slide against the teeth, but merely flick them. The watch has a self-winding, COSC-certified movement (calibre 2500) with 44-hour power reserve. The watch was produced in a limited edition and is hard to come by. If you can't get your hands on one now, though, don't despair. Omega says that within a few years it will be incorporating the co-axial movement into many of its watches. In the meantime the company has several other new models to choose from, including new additions to its Speedmaster Professional collection: the first rattrapante, certified chronometer, automatic movement, two chronographs with, respectively, date, day-date, and moonphase displays. A new Speedmaster, manufactured in a limited edition of 9,999 pieces and bearing on its case back a commemorative engraving, was launched to mark the 30th anniversary of man's first landing on the moon.

Omega has also brought out new additions to its "My Choice" collection of women's Constellation watches, for which Cindy Crawford serves as spokesperson. These include new automatic versions and small and mini models with a variety of dials including mother-of-pearl, copper and gray.

The History

1848 - The Company was founded by 23-year old Louis Brandt, it was a simple assembly plant where pocket watches were put together. In just a few decades, his sons, César and Louis-Paul, turned it into a manufacture where what were then considered avant-garde techniques were used. **1880** - The new plant is set up at Bienne, where the House has moved after the founder's death. The first caliber with cylinder escapement are made mechanically which means considerable commercialization for the new names: Jura, Patria, Helvetica, Celtic, Gurzelen. **1885** - The appearance of the new Calibre Labrador. **1894** - The famous pocket model Calibre 19 is made which, following the suggestion of a banker friend, is named Omega, the last letter of the Greek alphabet to stress the concept of "the definitive watch" - there was never to be anything better at that price. **1900** - For the first time the company adopts the name Omega. **1932** - After successfully participating in various sports events, Omega was named Official Timekeeper for the Los Angeles Olympics and will keep this place for more than 20 Games. The Marine is presented, the first underwater watch with a double case. **1930's** - Omega is the official supplier of the Italian and the British military aviation. **1948** - The first Seamaster. **1952** - The Constellation collection is introduced, all chronometers, and three years later the ladies Sapphette, that takes its name from the crystal cut like a diamond. During this decade, Omega perfects special instrumentation for incontrovertible results at sports events. **1957** - The mythical Speedmaster. In 1965 it will be chosen as the NASA official chronograph and in 1969 it will land on the moon attached to the wrist of Neil Armstrong. It will save the Apollo XIII mission crew, and for this receive the Snoopy Award. **1960** - Presentation of the De Ville collection. **1970** - The first Swiss quartz calibre, Beta 21, is at the base of the Electroquartz f8, 192 Hz. Two years later the competition sectors of Omega and Longines will be unified under the name, Swiss Timing. Omega receives its 2-millionth chronometer certificate. **1974** - The Marine Chronometer is the only wristwatch to obtain the "Marine Chronometer" certificate. Two years later the Chrono Quartz, analogue and digital, is at the Montreal Olympics. **1980** - Quartz production is intensified with the extraflat Dinosaur, Magic, Sensor with memories and the Megaquartz 4,190 which was elaborated for the French Navy. **1980's** - This decade sees many prizes for technology - for example in '88 the analogue chronograph Seamaster precise up to $1/100$ of a second - and for aesthetics: Omega receives six Diamonds International Award and seven Golden Rose at Baden Baden. **1990's** - The House honors its founder, Louis Brandt, and special editions celebrate the anniversaries of the Speedmaster. In 1993 it presents the Seamaster Professional Diver, water resistant to 30 atm, with a helium escape valve on the case. 1996 - The new Constellation collection is shown at Basel. **1997** - The Seamaster Ω-Matic is introduced, on the new calibre Omega 1400, that uses quartz technology associated with a recharging system in which a rotor stimulates a microgenerator. The Dynamic collection, with one chrono and an automatic, takes its inspiration from 1900's aviators. General renewal and restyling for the Constellation line; news for the De Ville Prestige as well; the Speedmaster's Racing Cart with its blue dial; on the new Sapphette, inspired by a 1944 Art Déco model, the facets of its crystal play with the light from the gold and diamonds defining the case and the handsome barleycorn finished bracelet. **1998** - Omega celebrates 150 years; the mythical Speedmaster Moonwatch celebrates 40 years, and there is a reproduction of the first 1957 Speedmaster. Forty is also the number of the special cases (lined with authentic photosensitive material spacesuits are made of) with the 22 watches commemorating many space missions. On every dial is the emblem of a particular mission, from Gemini V, to Skylab SL-4. There is electronic technology for Professional "X-33" with its titanium case, a model supplied to the NASA since 1992; it was designed in collaboration with astronauts and professional pilots. The Constellation My Way - worn by Cindy Crawford - comes in white gold, diamonds and mother of pearl, and the first chronograph with Frédéric Piguet electromechanical movement is introduced. A GMT is now included in the Seamaster line and has great visual impact.

OMEGA

Omegas's photographs reduced by 8% with respect to the other pieces.

SPEEDMASTER PROFESSIONAL MOON PHASE   REF. 3689.30.31

Movement: mechanical, manual winding, Omega caliber 1866 (Lemania 1883 base), power reserve of 40 hours. Hand-finished and hand polished.
Functions: hour, minute, small second, date, moon phase, chronograph with 3 counters.
Case: 18 kt white gold, 3 pieces (Ø 38.8 thickness 14.7 mm) polished, brushed finish; curved sapphire crystal with antireflective treatment on both sides; bezel with black aluminum ring and tachymeter scale; crown and partially recessed pushers, in white gold; screwed-on case back. Water-resistant to 3 atm.
Dial: silvered; applied rhodium plated bâton markers and luminescent dots on the printed minute track; luminescent blued stainless steel bâton hands.
Indications: minute counter at 3, hour counter at 6, small second at 9, date and moon phases at 12, center second counter, minute track with divisions for 1/5 of a second.
Strap: crocodile leather; fold-over clasp in white gold.
Price: 14'500 CHF, coming in a black leather case.

SPEEDMASTER "REPRODUCTION"   REF. 3594.50.00

Movement: mechanical, manual winding, Omega caliber 1861 (Lemania 1874 base). Hand-finished and hand polished.
Functions: hour, minute, small second, chronograph with 3 counters.
Case: stainless steel, three-piece case (Ø 42 mm, thickness 14.5 mm) polished and brushed finish; bombé hexalite glass; bezel with tachymeter scale; crown and partially recessed pushers; screwed-on case back with embossed medallion. Water-resistant to 3 atm.
Dial: black matte; original Omega logo applied at 12; luminescent bâton markers; luminescent "Speedmaster" hands.
Indications: minute counter at 3, hour counter at 6, small second at 9, center second counter, minute track with divisions for 1/5 of a second.
Bracelet: brushed steel, polished central links; fold-over safety clasp and spare leather strap.
Price: 3'200 CHF, coming in a black leather case.
Also available: leather strap.

SPEEDMASTER PROFESSIONAL MOONWATCH   REF. 3570.50.00

Movement: mechanical, manual winding, Omega caliber 1861 (Lemania 1874 base). Hand-finished and hand polished.
Functions: hour, minute, small second, chronograph with 3 counters.
Case: stainless steel, 3 pieces (Ø 42, thickness 14.5 mm) polished, brushed finish; bombé hexalite glass; bezel with black ring and tachymeter scale; crown and partially recessed pushers; screwed-on case back with embossed medallion (dragon with a horse head) and writing declaring its adoption by the NASA. Water-resistant to 3 atm.
Dial: black; luminescent bâton markers; luminescent white painted bâton hands.
Indications: minute counter at 3, hour counter at 6, small second at 9, center second counter, minute track with divisions for 1/5 of a second.
Bracelet: brushed steel, polished central links; fold-over safety clasp.
Price: 3'100 CHF, 999 pieces, coming in a black leather case.
Also available: leather strap; with sapphire case back caliber 1863, steel with bracelet. Numerous tests carried out by the NASA proved its reliability and aptitude for space flights, as it is non-magnetic, waterproof, shock-resistant, perfectly resistant to low temperatures and strong accelerations.

SPEEDMASTER MISSION "APOLLO 11"

Movement: mechanical, manual winding, Omega caliber 1861 (Lemania 1874 base). Hand-finished and hand polished.
Functions: hour, minute, small second, chronograph with 3 counters.
Case: stainless steel, three-piece case (Ø 42 mm, thickness 14.5 mm) polished, brushed finish; bombé hexalite glass; bezel with black ring and tachymeter scale; crown and partially recessed pushers; screwed-on case back, with embossed medallion. Water-resistant to 3 atm.
Dial: black; logo "Apollo 11" at 9; luminescent bâton markers; luminescent white painted bâton hands.
Indications: minute counter at 3, hour counter at 6, small second at 9, center second counter, minute track with divisions for 1/5 of a second.
Bracelet: brushed steel, polished central links; fold-over safety clasp.
Price: On request. Small suit-case produced in a limited edition of 40 pieces, with 22 commemorative pieces in steel, one of which is the copy of the original of 1957.

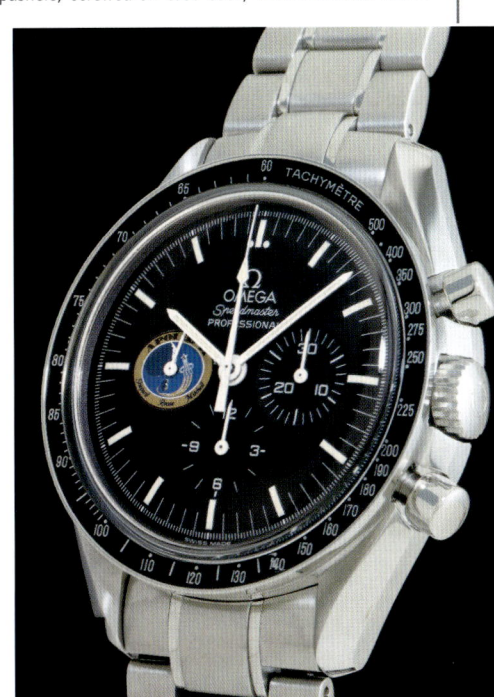

207

OMEGA

SPEEDMASTER DAY-DATE AM-PM — REF. 3623.50.31

Movement: mechanical, automatic winding, Omega caliber 1151 (Valjoux caliber 7751 base).
Functions: hour, minute, small second, full calendar (date, day, month), 24-hour indication, chronograph with 3 counters.
Case: 18 kt red gold, three-piece case (Ø 39 mm, thickness 14 mm) polished, brushed finish; antireflective curved sapphire crystal; bezel with tachymeter scale; day and month corrector on case side; crown and partially recessed pushers, in red gold; snap-on case back with embossed medallion. Water-resistant to 3 atm. 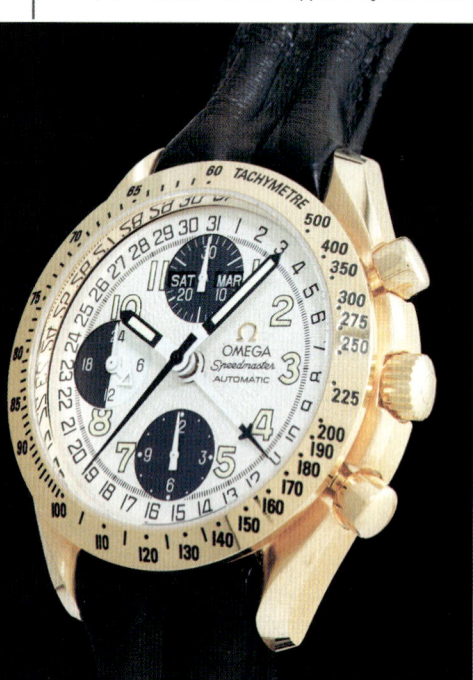
Dial: silvered, engine turned (guilloché) at the center; luminescent Arabic numerals; luminescent black and white painted bâton hands.
Indications: hour counter at 6, small second and 24 hours on the background of the night & day indicator at 9, minute counter, day and month at 12, second counter and date (with airplane at the point) at the center, minute track with divisions for 1/5 of a second.
Strap: crocodile leather; clasp red gold plated steel.
Price: 6'300 CHF.
Also available: stainless steel, black dial and 24 hours black-blue or all silvered, all blue dial with sun pattern or "Moon Look" black, leather strap or bracelet.

SPEEDMASTER DATE — REF. 3513.50.00

Movement: mechanical, automatic winding, Omega caliber 1152 (Valjoux 7750 base).
Functions: hour, minute, small second, date, chronograph with 3 counters.
Case: stainless steel, three-piece case (Ø 39 mm, thickness 14 mm) polished and brushed finish; antireflective curved sapphire crystal; bezel with tachymeter scale; crown and partially recessed pushers; snap-on case back with embossed medallion. Water-resistant to 3 atm. 
Dial: silvered; hour ring and zones with concentric circles pattern; applied bâton markers and luminescent dots; luminescent bâton hands.
Indications: date at 3, hour counter at 6, small second at 9, minute counter at 12, center second counter, minute track with divisions for 1/5 of a second.
Bracelet: polished steel with brushed finish; extensible clasp, with steel safety pusher with Omega symbol, patented.
Price: 2'200 CHF.
Also available: leather strap; in yellow gold leather strap or bracelet. All with black or silvered dial.

CONSTELLATION GENTS — REF. 1502.40.00

Movement: mechanical, automatic winding, Omega caliber 1120, 11'''1/2 (Ø 25.60, thickness 3.60 mm), autonomy of 44 hours and 23 jewels; Glucydur balance, 28,800 vibrations per hour (vph). Rhodium plated, Côtes de Genève and circular graining finished. Officially certified "chronometer" (C.O.S.C.).
Functions: hour, minute, center second, date.
Case: stainless steel, three-piece brushed case (Ø 36 mm, thickness 10 mm); antireflective curved sapphire crystal; bezel with Roman numerals engraved with 4 riders above, polished; snap-on case back with embossed medallion. Water-resistant to 5 atm. 
Dial: silvered, engine turned (guilloché) with a diamond point pattern; applied bâton markers and logo; luminescent dots on the printed minute track; luminescent Dauphine hands.
Indications: date at 3.
Bracelet: stainless steel, polished and brushed finish; fold-over clasp.
Price: 2'100 CHF.
Also available: stainless steel and yellow gold, silvered **Dial:** half-bar link, full bar; yellow gold, silvered or gilded dial.

CONSTELLATION LADY — REF. 1292.70.00

Movement: mechanical, automatic winding, ETA 2000, personalized Omega caliber 725, 8'''3/4 (Ø 19.40, thickness 3.60 mm), autonomy of 42 hours and 20 jewels; Glucydur balance, 28,800 vibrations per hour (vph). Côtes de Genève and circular graining finished.
Functions: hour, minute, center second, date.
Case: stainless steel and 18 kt yellow gold, three-piece brushed case (Ø 27 mm, thickness 9 mm); antireflective curved sapphire crystal; bezel with Roman numerals engraved with 4 riders above, polished; snap-on case back with embossed medallion. Water-resistant to 5 atm. 
Dial: silvered, engine turned (guilloché) with a diamond point pattern; applied bâton markers and logo; printed minute track; luminescent Dauphine hands.
Indications: date at 3.
Bracelet: steel and yellow gold, full link, polished and brushed finish; stainless steel and gold fold-over clasp.
Price: 3'150 CHF.
Also available: with gilt dial; with half-bar link; stainless steel, silvered dial; yellow gold, silvered dial.

OMEGA

SEAMASTER PROFESSIONAL CHRONO DIVER   REF. 2298.80.00

Movement: mechanical, automatic winding, Omega caliber 1154 (Valjoux caliber 7750 base). Officially certified "chronometer" (C.O.S.C.).
Functions: hour, minute, small second, date, chronograph with 3 counters.
Case: titanium, three-piece brushed case (Ø 41, thickness 16.3 mm); antireflective curved sapphire crystal; counter-clockwise turning shaped ring, with blue ring and graduated scale; screw-down crown with case protection; pushers with case protection, functional for scuba diving; pressure compensation valve with screwed protection crown 10; screwed-on case back with embossed medallion, non-slip. Water-resistant to 30 atm.
Dial: blue, decorated with wave pattern; luminescent round markers; luminescent skeletonized stainless steel hands.
Indications: date at 3, hour counter at 6, small second at 9, minute counter at 12, center second counter, minute track with divisions for 1/5 of a second.
Bracelet: "Sport" in titanium, polished-brushed; fold-over clasp with 2 safety pushers, extensible, Omega symbol in gold, patented.
Price: 4'100 CHF.
Also available: in titanium and yellow gold, blue dial; in titanium, tantalum, pink gold, blue dial; steel, with blue steel or aluminum ring, blue dial.

SEAMASTER 300 MT GMT   REF. 2834.50.91

Movement: mechanical, automatic winding, Omega caliber 1128 (ETA caliber 2893-2 base). Officially certified "chronometer" (C.O.S.C.).
Functions: hour, minute, center second, date, second time zone, 24-hour indication.
Case: stainless steel, three-piece case (Ø 41 mm, thickness 13 mm) polished and brushed finish; antireflective curved sapphire crystal; bidirectional turning shaped ring, with polished ring and 24h-scale divided by colors into night and day indication zones for pointing at a third time zone; screw-down crown with case protection; screwed-on case back with embossed medallion, non-slip. Water-resistant to 30 atm.
Dial: black, decorated with wave pattern; oversized luminescent markers; luminescent sword style hands.
Indications: date at 3, second time zone with arrow-point red center hand.
Strap: rubber with fold-over safety clasp.
Price: 2'400 CHF.
Also available: with bracelet.

SEAMASTER PROFESSIONAL DIVER 300 MT   REF. 2231.80.00

Movement: mechanical, automatic winding, Omega caliber 1109 (ETA caliber 2892-A2 base), protected by a cover. Officially certified "chronometer" (C.O.S.C.).
Functions: hour, minute, center second, date.
Case: titanium, three-piece brushed case (Ø 41 mm, thickness 11.5 mm); antireflective curved sapphire crystal; counter-clockwise turning shaped ring, with aluminum ring and engraved minute track, useful for the calculation of diving times; screw-down crown with case protection; pressure compensation valve with screwed protection crown 10; screwed-on case back with embossed medallion, non-slip. Water-resistant to 30 atm.
Dial: blue, decorated with wave pattern; oversized luminescent markers; luminescent sword style hands.
Indications: date at 3.
Bracelet: "Sport" in polished titanium, brushed finish; extensible fold-over clasp with safety pusher and gold logo.
Price: 3'200 CHF.
Also available: steel, ring in stainless steel, white or blue dial or blue aluminum ring, blue dial. Lady (Ø 29, thickness 9), quartz, stainless steel with steel ring, white or blue dial or blue aluminum ring, blue dial.

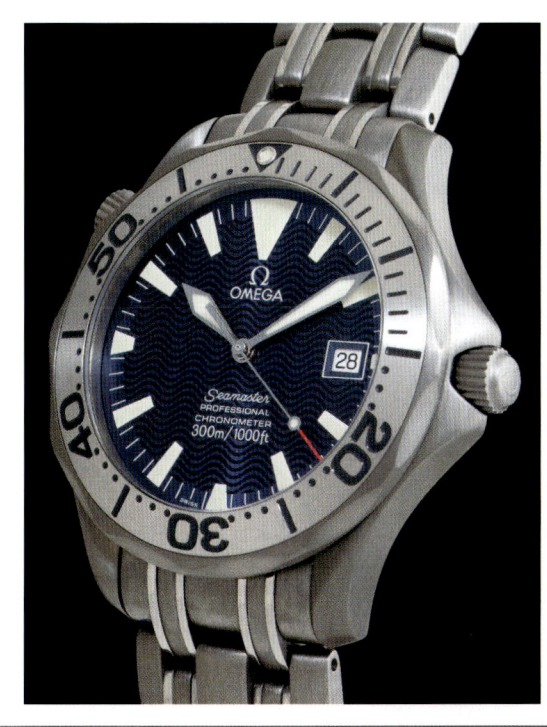

DE VILLE CO-AXIAL   REF. 5911.31.22

Movement: mechanical, manual winding, Omega caliber 2500 (ETA 2892 base), developed by George Daniels, with coaxial escapement and balance/balance-spring without regulator (system reducing the friction exerted by the pallet lever wheel on the pallet lever, thus solving any lubrication problem and improving precision). Officially certified "chronometer" (C.O.S.C.).
Functions: hour, minute, center second, date.
Case: 18 kt yellow gold, three-piece case (Ø 38 mm, thickness 9 mm.); curved sapphire crystal; screw-down yellow gold crown with case protection; screwed-on case back, numbered, with embossed medallion; inside bottom in ductile iron for the deviation of magnetic fields. Water-resistant to 3 atm.
Dial: silvered, with dodecahedron-shaped sloped and faceted peripheral part; luminescent Superlight applied yellow gold lozenge markers and Roman numerals; luminescent leaf style hands.
Indications: date at 3.
Strap: crocodile leather, hand stitched; yellow gold fold-over clasp.
Price: 7'900 CHF, 1000 pieces. **Also available:** pink gold, dark blue dial (same price, 1000 pieces). With skeletonized movement, 109 pieces (on request).

Parmigiani Fleurier

This four-year-old watch and clock brand, founded in the Swiss town of Fleurier by master watchmaker Michel Parmigiani, has introduced in 1999 four new watches.

The Ionica 1999 is an addition to the company's Ionica collection, which gets its name from the fact that the cases' curved lugs recall the forms of Ionic capitals. This men's model has an eight-day movement designed in a tonneau shape to fit neatly into the watch's tonneau case. The watch is manual-wind and has a power reserve indicator at 12 o'clock and a date window at 3 o'clock. The seconds subdial is at 6 o'clock. It comes in 18 kt gold or platinum. Its Javeline-shaped hands are a hallmark of the Parmigiani manufacture.

The Torus Quantième Perpétuel is an addition to the Torus collection, launched in 1998. It's a self-winding men's watch with perpetual calendar, moonphase, retrograde date indicator - which automatically returns to 1 at the end of each month - windows that show the day and month, and a round aperture at 12 o'clock that shows the number of years since the last leap year. The case comes in 18 kt gold or platinum and has a see-through back. The dial is made of 18 kt gold.

The piece de resistance, from a technical standpoint, is the Chrono Rattrapante. It's a manual-wind split-seconds column-wheel chronograph with the split-seconds hand controlled independently through the crown. Just 10 pieces were produced, all in 18k white gold. The continuous-seconds subdial is at 9 o'clock and the minute counter at 3 o'clock. It also has a see-through case back.

On a much simpler note: the aptly named Basica watch. Named for its basic styling, the watch has a round case, Arabic numerals and date window at 3 o'clock. Designed as a unisex style, it comes in two sizes, 37.3 millimeters or 32.5 millimeters in diameter. The case is 18 kt gold and is available with either a see-through or solid, engravable back. There are two color choices for the dial: ivory and bluish white.

The History

At fifty, Michel Parmigiani, designer of watches, still has the look in his eyes of the child at Couvet who would stand, mesmerized, staring upward at the statue dedicated to Ferdinand Berthoud, watchmaker to the Royal French Navy in the 18th Century. That same child loved to visit père Bernet, the town watchmaker who built "Neuchâteloises" pendulum clocks, and from that strange alchemy between monumental magnificence and the meekness of the everyday, he has drawn the most precious teaching to form the character of the man he is today. Humility and genius, serenity and determination to get to the top.

In any case, the fundamental encounter for Michel Parmigiani, watchmaker, was with Marcel JeanRichard, whom he considers his "spiritual father". He was a descendent of Daniel who was the real founder of the watch industry of Neuchâtel. JeanRichard was a precious master for him, and he taught him that "excellence is the flame that helps you remain humble with respect to what you have done and still must do". What still must be done. Exactly. And since his age no longer permitted him to follow with due attention those pieces still to be completed, he left the work to young Michel who, from then on is thought of as having a magic touch, because of his very uncommon skill and dedication. From **1975** he becomes an independent watchmaker and founds his own company, "Parmigiani Mesure et Art du Temps" (PMAT), concentrating on building complicated movements and on the restoration of rare, extremely beautiful antique clocks (even today his manufacture, which employs 60 people, also has four watchmakers who are dedicated wholly to this art). While working on ever more incredible restorations, he has a fourth "encounter" which changes his life. He comes across the Sandoz Family Foundation for which he restores several unique pieces. The directors of this Swiss colossus are so enthusiastic about the person that they decide to become his partner. It is **1994** and the name Parmigiani Fleurier takes flight. Three years later it will present a complete collection of 60 models with movements made by the Maison at the Geneva Salon of Fine Watchmaking. And just to make it clear where he stands, he opens a shop in Dubai, a bridgehead in the Arab world, the very rich market for the most precious watches on the market. The very small yearly production (about 300 pieces) that is rigorously top of the line, means that the wishes of the clients, even regarding functions, can be met on a personal basis.

Parmigiani himself cuts his own pinions, sculpts his own wheels, gives the right shape to the hands, to the jewel bearings... he even takes the photographs himself of his work in the patrician house where he has a show room. His entire workshop is in harmony, each piece is a note on the score, because Michel Parmigiani is not simply and excellent watchmaker, he is an artist of watchmaking. And the relationship of this artist with as powerful a partner as Sandoz (that acquired 51% of Parmigiani's shares in 1995) is ideal since it leaves him free space for creativity. And with this Parmigiani is climbing to the very top of his world.

1995 - For the launch of Parmigiani Fleurier one of the most important table clocks of the modern era is presented, the Fleur d'Orient. The construction of its original mechanism, a Grande Complication, more than 10,000 working hours were needed and the remarkable exterior of the object, set with jewels, called for the same commitment from the goldsmiths.

1998 - The presentation of the tonneau shaped watch with an exclusive 8-day movement and the automatic chronograph whose base is an El Primero movement. The collection Classic includes a man's model, very traditional with visible automatic movement, and several elegant and refined models for women.

Minute Repeater "Unique Object"

The Master Swiss watchmaker of Italian origin, Michel Parmigiani, unearthed an extraordinary antique calibre 994 by Audemars Piguet, 10 and 172 lines that was an ébauche, and built a unique piece around it. The movement was refined, decorated and engraved entirely by hand: polished bevelling on the bridge perimeters and the surfaces engraved with triangular motifs; the striking hammers, heads of screws, the balance spring stud and index were all hand polished. Another noteworthy characteristic is that the teeth of the wheels are carved in such a way as to improve smoothness and silence during action. The balance is bimetallic, with large compensation screws in gold, a Breguet spring and Phillips overcoil.

The placement of the striking hammers is unusual, pivoted on two separate structures instead of beneath the same bridge. The gold jewel setting is on the jewel which has to bear the greater load of the driving power from the barrel spring. It will probably need more frequent substitution in time.

The three-part case is entirely made by hand in platinum. Its principal decoration is the hand engraved reeding on the bezel, a characteristic of all his models. The dial is silver plated solid gold, guilloché in a basket weave design. The hour band is always gold, as is the logo placed at 12 o'clock. Another distinctive Parmigiani element is the gold "Javeline" hands.

211

PARMIGIANI FLEURIER

TORUS PERPETUAL CALENDAR   REF. C 04000

Movement: mechanical, automatic winding, caliber 13501 (base derived from Lemania caliber 8815 + module), 11'''1/2, 25 jewels, 28,800 vibrations per hour (vph); balance-spring regulator system with micrometer adjustment; 22 kt pink gold rotor, engraved and personalized by hand. Mounted by hand, beveled, decorated by hand with Côtes de Genève pattern.
Functions: hour, minute, center second, perpetual calendar (date, day, month, year, moon phase). 
Case: platinum, three-piece case (Ø 40 mm, thickness 11 mm); bezel with double hand-engraved knurling; curved sapphire crystal; natural sapphire cabochon platinum crown; snap-on case back, knurled, displaying the movement through a sapphire crystal. Water-resistant to 3 atm.
Dial: solid gold, anthracite, engine turned (guilloché) with basket pattern; minute and calendar ring in gold, applied with printed minute track; logo in white gold, applied; white gold Javeline hands.
Indications: month at 3, moon phase at 6, day at 9, four year cycle at 12, retrograde date with arrow-shaped center hand.
Strap: crocodile leather; platinum tongue clasp.
Also available: yellow gold. Both versions are available with eggshell dial.
Prices: on request.

CHRONOGRAPH RATTRAPANTE   REF. C 03860

Movement: mechanical, manual winding, caliber 27001, derived from Venus caliber 179 (14'''), 26 jewels, 18,000 vibrations per hour (vph); Breguet Phillips overcoil balance-spring, balance-spring regulator system with micrometer adjustment and regulator spring. Beveled and Côtes de Genève finished.
Functions: hour, minute, small second, split-second chronograph with 2 counters.
Case: 18 kt white gold, three-piece case (Ø 40 mm, thickness 14 mm); bezel with double hand-engraved knurling; curved sapphire crystal; white gold crown with pusher and case protection; white gold oval pushers; snap-on case back, knurled, displaying the movement through a sapphire crystal. Water-resistant to 3 atm. 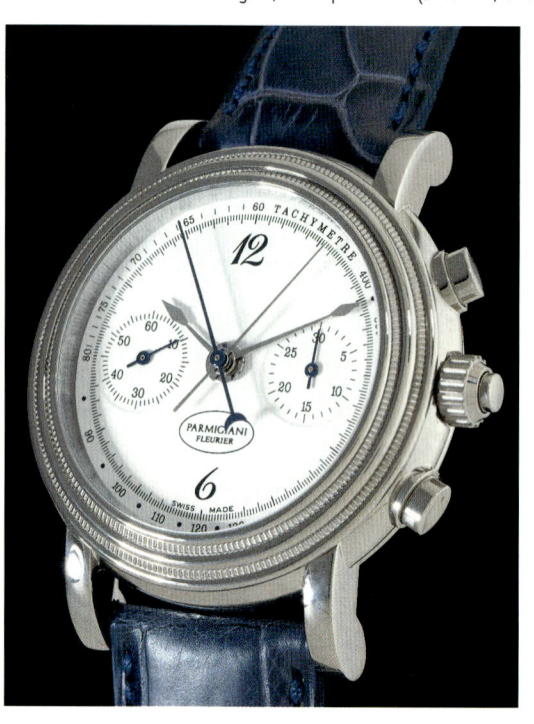
Dial: solid gold, white enameled; painted Arabic numerals and minute track; white gold Javeline hands.
Indications: minute counter at 3, small second at 9, center second and split-second counters, minute track with divisions for 1/5 of a second, tachymeter scale.
Strap: crocodile leather; white gold tongue clasp.
Price: on request.
Series limited to 10 pieces.

AUTOMATIC CHRONOGRAPH   REF. C 00900

Movement: mechanical, automatic winding, caliber 19001, derived from Zenith El Primero 400 (13'''), 31 jewels, 36.000 vibrations per hour (vph); regulator with off-center screw adjustment; 22 kt pink gold rotor engraved and personalized by hand. Mounted by hand, beveled, decorated by hand with Côtes de Genève pattern.
Functions: hour, minute, small second, date, chronograph with 3 counters.
Case: platinum, three-piece case (Ø 40 mm, thickness 12.5 mm); bezel with double hand-engraved knurling; curved sapphire crystal; natural sapphire cabochon white gold crown; oval pushers; snap-on case back, knurled, displaying the movement through a sapphire crystal. Water-resistant to 3 atm. 
Dial: solid gold, anthracite, engine turned (guilloché) with basket pattern; printed Roman numerals and minute track, logo in white gold, applied; white gold Javeline hands.
Indications: date between 1 and 2, minute counter at 3, hour counter at 6, small second at 9, center second counter, minute track with divisions for 1/5 of a second.
Strap: crocodile leather; platinum tongue clasp.
Also available: yellow, pink or white gold. All available with slate-grey, anthracite or eggshell dial.
Prices: on request.

AUTOMATIC CHRONOGRAPH   REF. C 00921

All the Parmigiani Fleurier watches - in men's or lady's versions, time only or complicated - have certain common technical and aesthetic features: bezel with simple or double knurling, the brand name inserted in an oval tag, elliptic lugs, Javelin type hands, a natural sapphire cabochon on the crown, pushers always of the same material as the case and the whole showing a quality without compromises, also certified by an international 10 years guarantee. Parmigiani chose their movements very accurately - regardless if they are rare antique calibers or modern and sophisticated mechanisms - as is the case of the El Primero high frequency device used for the automatic chronograph. The photograph shows the version with yellow gold case (ref. C 00921) and silvered dial, with screen-printed Roman numerals.
Price: on request.

PARMIGIANI FLEURIER

MINUTE REPEATER — REF. C 03501

Movement: mechanical, manual winding, caliber Christophe Claret 250 (12'''). Modified bridge design, 33 jewels; Glucydur balance with compensation screws, 18,000 vibrations per hour (vph), Breguet Phillips overcoil balance-spring, regulator system with micrometer adjustment and regulator spring, counter-pivot stone on the escape wheel. Beveled and Côtes de Genève finished.
Functions: hour, minute, small second; minute repeater.
Case: platinum, three-piece case (Ø 39, thickness 11.5 mm); bezel with hand-engraved double knurling; curved sapphire crystal; repeater slide on case side; natural sapphire cabochon white gold crown; snap-on case back, knurled, displaying the movement through a sapphire crystal. Water-resistant to 3 atm.
Dial: solid gold, slate-grey, engine turned (guilloché) with basket pattern; 2 white enameled Arabic numerals; applied white gold logo; white enameled minute track; white gold Javeline hands.
Indications: small second at 9.
Strap: crocodile leather; platinum tongue clasp.
Also available: anthracite dial; yellow gold, eggshell or anthracite dial.
Prices: on request.
Series limited to few pieces each year.

MEMORY TIME — REF. C 00843

Movement: mechanical, automatic winding, caliber 13201, derived from Lemania 8815 (11'''1/2) modified by eliminating the center seconds, 28 jewels, 28,800 vibrations per hour (vph); balance-spring regulator system with micrometer adjustment; 22 kt pink gold rotor, engraved and personalized by hand. Mounted by hand, beveled, decorated by hand with Côtes de Genève pattern.
Functions: hour, minute, second time zone, 24 hour.
Case: 18 kt pink gold, three-piece case (Ø 36 mm, thickness 8.5 mm); bezel with double hand-engraved knurling; curved sapphire crystal; natural sapphire cabochon pink gold crown; snap-on case back, knurled and displaying the movement through a sapphire crystal. Water-resistant to 3 atm.
Dial: solid gold, eggshell, engine turned (guilloché) with basket pattern; hour ring in pink gold, applied, with screen-printed Roman numerals; applied gold logo; printed minute track; pink gold Javeline hands.
Indications: second time zone 24-hour at 12.
Strap: crocodile leather; pink gold tongue clasp.
Also available: pink or white gold; platinum. All available with slate-grey or eggshell dial.
Prices: on request.

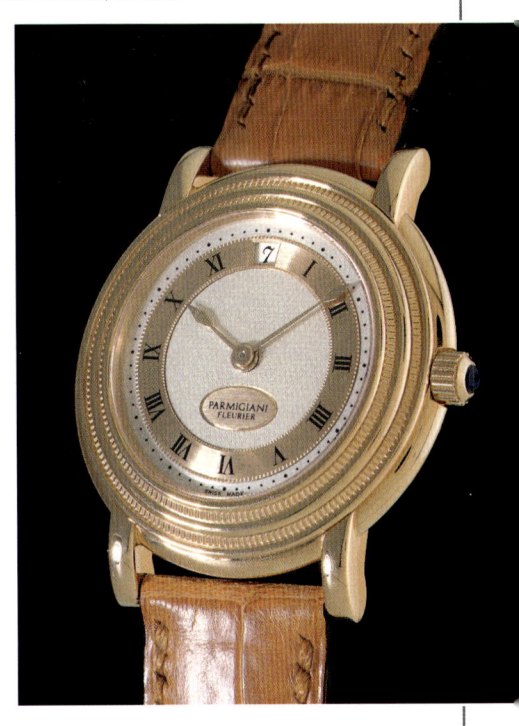

IONICA "8 DAYS" — REF. C 02021

Movement: mechanical, manual winding, manufacture caliber 110 (13'''x10'''), tonneau-curved, with power reserve of 8 days, 28 jewels; balance-spring regulator system with micrometer adjustment and regulator spring. Mounted by hand, beveled, hand-decorated with Côtes de Genève pattern.
Functions: hour, minute, small second, date, power reserve.
Case: 18 kt yellow gold, three-piece tonneau case (height 42.5 mm, width 34.5 mm, thickness 11 mm); bezel with double hand-engraved knurling; curved sapphire crystal; natural sapphire cabochon yellow gold crown; case back attached by 8 gold screws, knurled and displaying the movement through a sapphire crystal. Water-resistant to 3 atm.
Dial: solid gold, eggshell, engine turned (guilloché) with basket pattern; printed Arabic numerals, and applied gold logo; yellow gold Javeline hands.
Indications: date at 3; small second at 6; power reserve at 12 (applied gold sector).
Strap: crocodile leather; yellow gold clasp.
Also available: pink or white gold; platinum. All available with eggshell, anthracite or slate-grey dial.
Prices: on request.

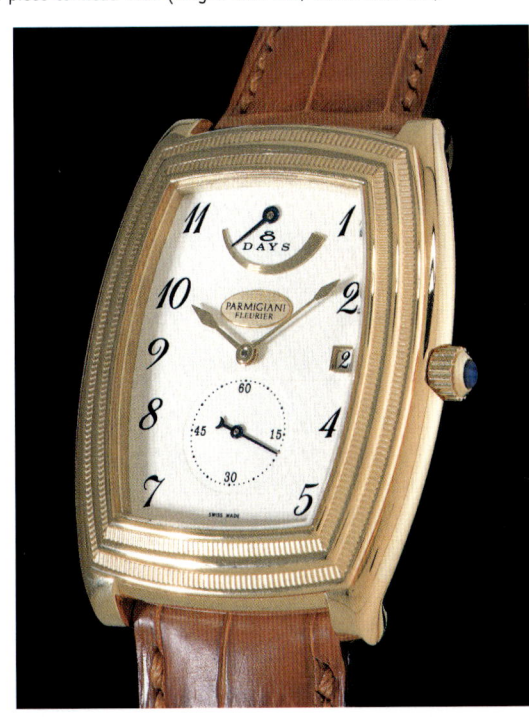

IONICA "8 DAYS" — REF. C 02000

Contrasting the iron law of the market and following the certainly more expensive and complex way of the best watchmaking tradition for his Ionica tonneau, Michael Parmigiani choose to create "his" tonneau-curved movement (while today commercial logics impose also for shaped models the use of round standard movements). As a result, we have now manufacture caliber 110 of Parmigiani's Mesure et Art du Temps (this is the name of the division specialized in micromechanics inside Parmigiani Fleurier).

The construction by separate bridges, which must take into account the tension exerted by the main spring dimensioned for a power reserve of 8 days, is really beautiful. In line with the best tradition are also the balance-spring regulator system with micrometer adjustment and regulator spring (swan-neck shaped). The photograph shows the version with platinum case, anthracite dial, hands and logo in white gold.
Price: on request.

213

PARMIGIANI FLEURIER

TORUS   REF. C 00742

Movement: mechanical, automatic winding, caliber 13301, derived from Lemania caliber 8815 (11'''1/2), 25 jewels, 28,800 vibrations per hour (vph); balance-spring regulator system with micrometer adjustment; 22 kt pink gold rotor, engraved and personalized by hand. Mounted by hand, beveled, hand-decorated with Côtes de Genève pattern.
Functions: hour, minute, center second, date.

Case: 18 kt pink gold, three-piece case (Ø 40 mm, thickness 8.8 mm); bezel with double hand-engraved knurling; curved sapphire crystal; natural sapphire cabochon pink gold crown; snap-on case back, knurled, displaying the movement through a sapphire crystal. Water-resistant to 3 atm.
Dial: solid gold, eggshell, engine turned (guilloché) with basket pattern; hour ring pink gold, applied, with printed Roman numerals; applied gold pink logo; printed minute track; pink gold Javeline hands (second hand in blued stainless steel).
Indications: date at 3.
Strap: crocodile leather; pink gold tongue clasp.
Also available: yellow or white gold; platinum. All available with slate-grey, anthracite or eggshell dial.
Prices: on request.

CLASSIC WITH DATE   REF. C 00443

Movement: mechanical, automatic winding, caliber 13301 (Lemania caliber 8815 base) 11'''1/2, 25 jewels, 28,800 vibrations per hour (vph); balance-spring regulator system with micrometer adjustment; 22 kt pink gold rotor, engraved and personalized by hand. Mounted by hand, beveled, hand-decorated with Côtes de Genève pattern.
Functions: hour, minute, center second, date.

Case: 18 kt pink gold, three-piece case (Ø 36 mm, thickness 8.3 mm); knurled bezel, hand-engraved; curved sapphire crystal; natural sapphire cabochon pink gold crown; snap-on case back, knurled, displaying the movement through a sapphire crystal. Water-resistant to 3 atm.
Dial: solid gold, eggshell, engine turned (guilloché) with basket pattern; two pearl-shaped markers and applied white gold logo; pink gold Javeline hands (seconds hands in blued stainless steel).
Indications: date at 3.
Strap: crocodile leather; pink gold clasp.
Also available: yellow or white gold. All available with slate-grey or eggshell dial.
Prices: on request.

CLASSIC   REF. C 00401

Movement: mechanical, automatic winding, caliber 13001 (Lemania caliber 8815 base) 11'''1/2, modified by eliminating center seconds and date, 25 jewels, 28,800 vibrations per hour (vph); balance-spring regulator system with micrometer adjustment; 22 kt pink gold rotor, engraved and personalized by hand. Mounted by hand, beveled, hand-decorated with Côtes de Genève pattern.
Functions: hour, minute.

Case: platinum, three-piece case (Ø 36, thickness 8.3 mm); knurled bezel, hand-engraved; curved sapphire crystal; natural sapphire cabochon white gold crown; snap-on case back, knurled, displaying the movement through a sapphire crystal. Water-resistant to 3 atm.
Dial: in black onyx with applied logo in white gold; flower pattern engraved on the beveled platinum ring; white gold Javeline hands.
Strap: crocodile leather; platinum clasp.
Also available: Greek fret engraved and black enameled on the beveled ring; lapislasuli dial; pink gold.
Prices: on request.

BASICA   REF. C 04460

Movement: mechanical, automatic winding, caliber 34001 (Frédéric Piguet 1150 base), 28,800 vibrations per hour (vph), balance-spring regulator system with micrometer adjustment. Mounted by hand, beveled, hand-decorated with Côtes de Genève pattern. Officially certified "chronometer" (C.O.S.C.).
Functions: hour, minute, center second, date.
Case: 18 kt white gold, three-piece case (Ø 37 mm, thickness 8 mm); polished bezel; curved sapphire crystal; natural sapphire cabochon white gold crown; snap-on case back, displaying the movement through a flat sapphire crystal. Water-resistant to 3 atm. 
Dial: solid gold, white "porcelainized"; printed Arabic numerals; blued stainless steel Javeline hands.
Indications: date at 3.
Strap: crocodile leather; white gold clasp.
Also available: yellow or pink gold, ivory dial.
Prices: on request.

PARMIGIANI FLEURIER

BASICA   REF. C 04320

Movement: mechanical, automatic winding, caliber 34001 (Frédéric Piguet 1150 base), 28,800 vibrations per hour (vph), balance-spring regulator system with micrometer adjustment. Mounted by hand, beveled, hand-decorated with Côtes de Genève pattern. Officially certified "chronometer" (C.O.S.C.).
Functions: hour, minute, center second, date.
Case: 18 kt yellow gold, three-piece case (Ø 32.5 mm, thickness 8 mm); polished bezel; curved sapphire crystal; natural sapphire cabochon yellow gold crown; snap-on case back, displaying the movement through a flat sapphire crystal. Water-resistant to 3 atm.
Dial: solid gold, ivory dial; printed Arabic numerals; blued stainless steel Javeline hands.
Indications: date at 3.
Strap: crocodile leather; white gold clasp.
Also available: pink gold, ivory dial; white gold, white "porcelainized" dial.
Prices: on request.

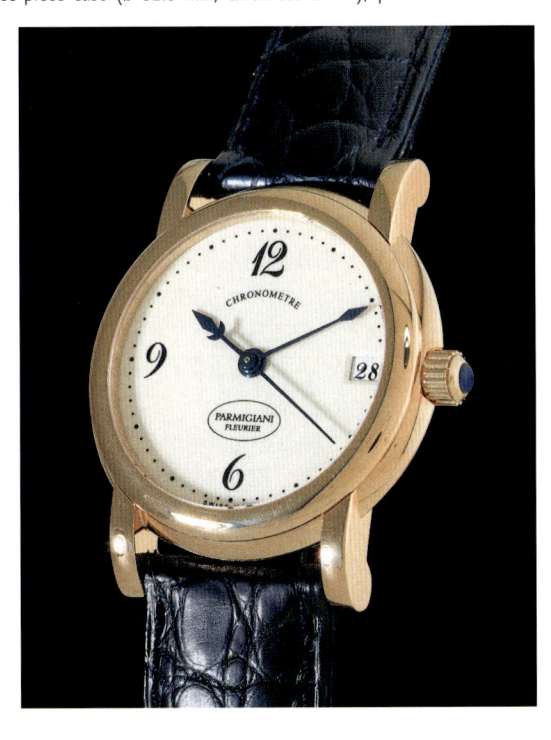

ELEGANCE   REF. C 00509

Movement: mechanical, manual winding, caliber 14001, derived from Frédéric Piguet caliber 8.10 (8'''), 20 jewels, 21,600 vibrations per hour (vph). Mounted by hand, beveled, hand-decorated with Côtes de Genève pattern.
Functions: hour, minute.
Case: platinum, three-piece case (Ø 28 mm, thickness 7.2 mm); knurled bezel, hand-engraved; curved sapphire crystal; natural sapphire cabochon platinum crown; snap-on back. Water-resistant to 3 atm.
Dial: in mother-of-pearl; diamond cut brilliants (totalling 0.73 kt) set on the beveled platinum ring; white gold Javeline hands.
Bracelet: platinum, with links reproducing a cobblestone paving.
Also available: yellow or pink gold; in many other jewel versions.
Prices: on request.

ELEGANCE "GENTS SKELETON"   REF. C 4SQ20

Movement: mechanical, automatic winding, caliber 13301 (Lemania caliber 8815 base) 11'''1/2, 25 jewels, 28,800 vibrations per hour (vph); balance-spring regulator system with micrometer adjustment; 22 kt pink gold rotor. Skeletonized, chased, mounted and finished by hand.
Functions: hour, minute, center second.
Case: 18 kt yellow gold, three-piece case (Ø 36 mm, thickness 8.3 mm); knurled bezel, hand-engraved; curved sapphire crystal; natural sapphire cabochon yellow gold crown; snap-on back displaying the movement through a sapphire crystal. Water-resistant to 3 atm.
Dial: made up by the pillar-plate of the movement, skeletonized and hand-chased; flange hand-chased, decorated with a flower pattern, in yellow gold; blued stainless steel Javeline hands.
Strap: crocodile leather; yellow gold tongue clasp.
Also available: pink gold or platinum; hand-chased beveled ring, decorated with geometric pattern.
Prices: on request.

"LADIES' SKELETON"   REF. C 5SQ40

Movement: mechanical, manual winding, caliber 14105, derived from Frédéric Piguet cal 8.10 (8'''), 20 jewels, 21,600 vibrations per hour (vph). Skeletonized, chased, mounted and finished by hand.
Functions: hour, minute.
Case: 18 kt pink gold, three-piece case (Ø 28 mm, thickness 7.2 mm); knurled bezel, hand-engraved; curved sapphire crystal; natural sapphire cabochon pink gold crown; snap-on back displaying the movement through a sapphire crystal. Water-resistant to 3 atm.
Dial: made up by the pillar-plate of the movement, skeletonized and hand-chased, flange hand-chased, decorated with a tile pattern, pink gold; Javel hands in blued stainless steel.
Strap: crocodile leather; pink gold tongue clasp.
Also available: hand-chased beveled ring, decorated with geometric or flower pattern: yellow or pink gold; platinum.
Prices: on request.

Patek Philippe

Patek Philippe, known chiefly for its classic men's watches, has now turned its attention to women with the introduction of its Art Deco-inspired Twenty-4 watch. The watch is a departure for the company - it's aimed at a younger, more fashion-oriented consumer than are its other ladies' watches. The Twenty-4 (Ref. 4910-10A) is also Patek's first steel and diamond model. Its curved, rectangular case is based on the cases used for the company's Gondolo collection. The watch comes in three choices of dial color: black, grey and white. Its quartz movement (calibre E15) is the smallest and thinnest of the three quartz movements the company uses in its watches. The name "Twenty-4" comes from the fact that the watch can be worn for any occasion - i.e. 24 hours a day.

Patek executives say the watch, which garnered much attention when it was introduced at the Basel Fair in April 1999, is the start of a campaign to build awareness of the brand among women. "We will commit time and energy to become a major player in this market in the same way that our status is truly established in the field of men's classical, technical watches", said Philippe Stern, president of Patek Philippe.

Patek's other big news is in a more traditional mode. It's a new automatic men's watch (Ref. 5054) with moon phase, analog date and power

The History

The most prestigious Swiss manufacture is named after its two founders. The first, Antoine Norbert de Patek, Polish aristocrat refugee in Switzerland, and the second, Adrien Philippe, a young French watchmaker, became partners in 1845. The Company really dates from six years earlier, when Patek joined forces with François Czapeck, a Bohemian watchmaker. The Company's name began to grow thanks to the innovation introduced by Adrien Philippe: a keyless winding system. In 1929, the Company was purchased by the Stern brothers and it is still owned today by Philippe Stern, a grandson. The Company is specialized in the production of very high quality and extremely complicated watches and, probably, Patek Philippe is today the most prestigious manufacture in the world. This is also thanks to the essential combination of a great watchmaking tradition and technological innovation. Its quality is easily demonstrated by the prices awarded to these watches when old models come up at the most important international auctions: always the absolute highest. Among famous figures of the past who were clients of the Company, we have Queen Victoria in 1851 (the year Patek makes the smallest watch in the world), Lev Tolstoy, Marie Curie, Piotr Ilic Tchiakovski, Richard Wagner, Rudyard Kipling, Albert Einstein.

1854 - Adrien Philippe patents the crown winding system.
1863 - Patent for the sliding mainspring, prevents break down due to overwinding.
1867 - The Patek Philippe complications are presented at the Paris World's Fair.
1868 - Patek builds the first Swiss wristwatch, purchased by the Countess Kocewicz.
1881 - This is the date of the patent for a special eccentric regulation of the index. This system was used for the Gondolo pocket models that then gave its name to a series of wristwatches.
1889 - Patent for a perpetual calendar mechanism (it adjusts automatically to the varying length of the months and to leap years).
1902 - Patent for a split-second chronograph.
1910 - The Duca di Regla watch was constructed, with Westminster sonnerie on 5 tones: unique and still unrivalled.
1915 - The first Patek complicated wristwatch (this, too, is a women's model), with hour, quarter hour and 5 minute repeater.
1925 - Introduction of wristwatch with perpetual calendar.
1927 - The first wrist model chronograph is sold for 2145 Swiss Francs.
1932 - The Calatrava is created; it will turn out to be one of the great classics of all times.
1941 - The wrist model chronographs with perpetual calendar start regular production.
1949 - On May 15th, with patent no. 261431, Patek introduces the Gyromax balance, a refined example of micromechanics that allows a more accurate definition of the number of oscillations and makes the watch more practical to use (the watch's speed can be regulated without involving the index, which is always a source of disturbance).
1956 - The first electronic watch for industrial uses is built.

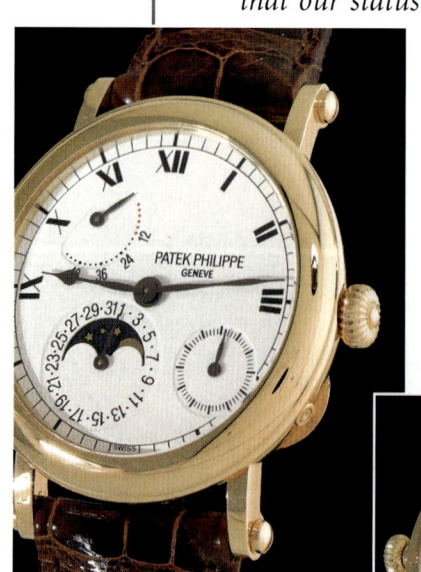

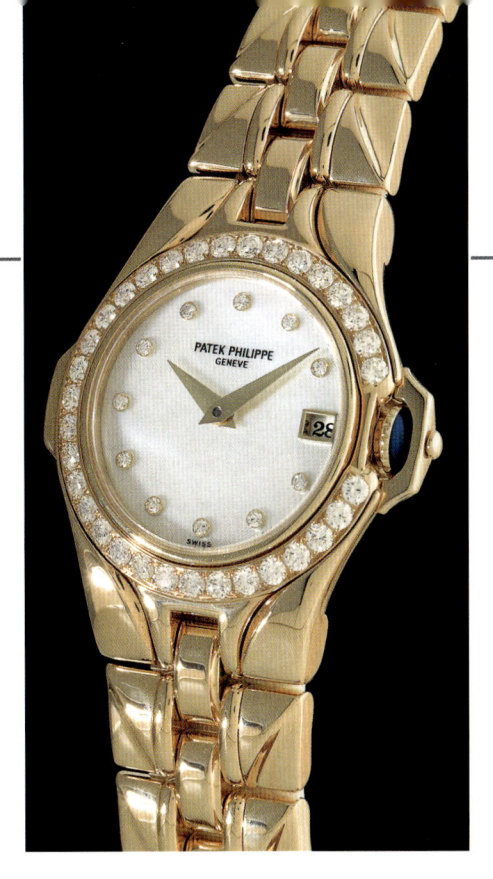

reserve indicator and seconds subdial. The ultra-slim movement (calibre 240) gives the watch a svelte contour - it's just 3.98 millimeters thick. The movement has a decentralized minirotor sunk into the baseplate and is hallmarked with the Geneva seal.

Both the date and moonphase can be set independently by push-pieces on the side of the case. A safety device prevents damage to the movement should you attempt to adjust the indicators while the automatic date change is engaged (around midnight). The 5054 comes in gold or platinum and has a hinged dust cover over a sapphire crystal back. The case is water resistant to 25 meters. The dial is white porcelain; the indicators slightly recessed to give a sense of depth. The top half of the dial bears Roman numeral hour markers and a railway track scale runs around the entire face.

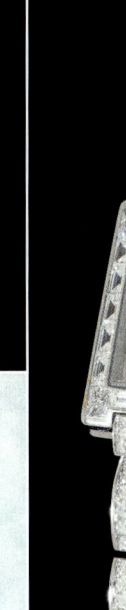

1959 - Introduction of a double time zone watch (with two hands)
1962 - Patek Philippe sets a record for precision for mechanical watches (that has not been bettered) at the Geneva observatory.
1964 - Patent for the outer rotor for automatic winding.
1968 - The model Ellipse was presented with its distinctive oval shape.
1976 - Nautilus is the first underwater sports watch ever made by the Maison.
1977 - The crown wheel rotor is introduced, placed off center and inserted through the movement.
1985 - Patek is the first to create (in its own workshop) a complication mechanism to indicate the exact date of Easter.
1986 - Another patent, this for a century perpetual calendar with retrograde indicator. It needs no regulation for 400 years.
1989 - The Calibre 89, the most complicated watch in the world. It has 33 different functions. Five years of research and more than 1728 components for a masterpiece boasting the most refined complications in watchmaking: grande sonnerie, minute repeater, century perpetual calendar, moon phases, retrograde date, date of Easter, split-second chronograph and supplementary mechanism allowing visualization of sidereal indications on the back dial.
1996 - The annual calendar keeps count of months with 30 and 31 days, carries digital indication of the date instead of a hand as on the traditional perpetual ones. The movement is not based on the usual mechanism of springs, cams and levers, but on a mechanism that is almost entirely rotative, on wheels and pinions.
1997 - The Pagoda, inspired by a rectangular model of the 1940's, is part of the limited series commemorative collection of 1997. There is also an automatic chronometer with minute repeater and round case in platinum with hinged cover and back case in sapphire crystal. Travel Time is a manual winding model and has the original characteristic of being able to conceal the supplementary hand beneath the main one when there is no need to indicate a second time zone. Aquanaut, steel automatic, has an unusually decorated dial in tone with the "Tropical" strap.
1998 - Patek Philippe returns to the "pure" chronograph, without added complications with the ref. 5070 made in only 250 pieces. The Quantième Perpétuel Ref. 5059 is also presented, this is an automatic with retrograde date, sweep seconds (calibre 315/136) and "officer" type case with a hinged back. Nautilus adds the Jumbo version with power reserve at 12 o'clock that emphasizes its air of power and solidity. Neptune adopts the ultra-thin calibre 240, and becomes the first all-steel complication of the Patek production. Specifically dedicated to a younger public it has a decidedly more accessible price with respect to the models in precious metals.

PATEK PHILIPPE

PERPETUAL CALENDAR MINUTE REPEATER — REF. 5013

Movement: mechanical, automatic winding, caliber Patek Philippe R 27 PS QR. Beveled and Côtes de Genève finished. Hallmarked with the "Geneva Seal" (watchmaking's highest distinction of quality).
Functions: hour, minute, small second, perpetual calendar until the year 2700 (date, day, month, year, moon phase), minute repeater.
Case: platinum, three-piece tonneau-shaped case (height 34 mm, width 34 mm) polished and brushed finish; curved sapphire crystal; 4 correctors and repeater slide on case side; platinum crown; snap-on back displaying the movement through a sapphire crystal. 
Dial: gold, silvered; printed Arabic numerals and railway minute track; white gold leaf style hands.
Indications: month at 3, moon phase and small second at 6, day at 9, four year cycle at 12, retrograde date with half-moon center hand.
Strap: crocodile leather; platinum clasp.
Also available: in yellow gold; pink gold; white gold; dial with applied Arabic numerals.
Prices: on request.

PERPETUAL CALENDAR MINUTE REPEATER TOURBILLON — REF. 5016

Movement: mechanical, manual winding, with tourbillon caliber Patek Philippe RTO 27 PS QR. Hallmarked with the "Geneva Seal" (watchmaking's highest distinction of quality).
Functions: hour, minute, small second, perpetual calendar until the year 2700 (date, day, month, year, moon phase), minute repeater.
Case: 18 kt yellow gold, three-piece case (Ø 36 mm, thickness 14 mm); curved sapphire crystal; 4 correctors and repeater slide on case side; yellow gold crown; furnished with two snap-on case backs, a closed one and one with a sapphire crystal. 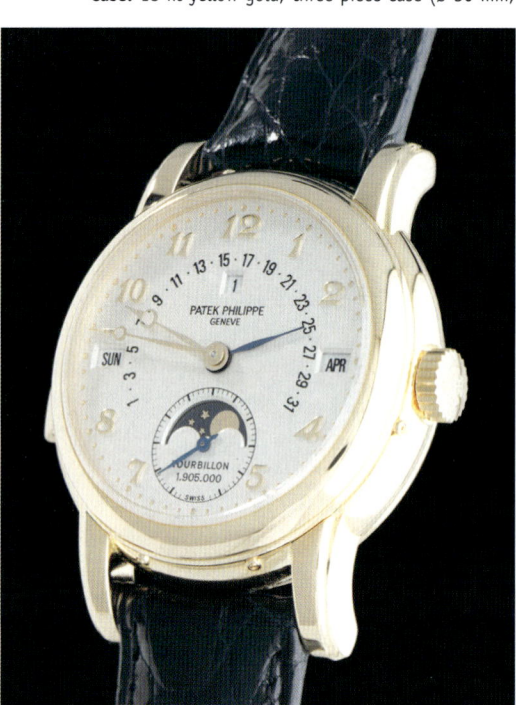
Dial: gold, silvered; applied yellow gold Arabic numerals and cabochon minute track; yellow gold Pomme and blued gold leaf style hands.
Indications: month at 3, moon phase and small second at 6, day at 9, four year cycle at 12, date with retrograde center hand.
Strap: crocodile leather; yellow gold clasp.
Also available: pink or white gold, 2 case backs; platinum with closed bottom.
Prices: on request.

MINUTE REPEATER TOURBILLON — REF. 3939 H

Movement: mechanical, manual winding, with tourbillon caliber Patek Philippe RTO 27 PS. Hallmarked with the "Geneva Seal" (watchmaking's highest distinction of quality).
Functions: hour, minute, small second, minute repeater.
Case: 18 kt yellow gold, three-piece case (Ø 33 mm); curved sapphire crystal; repeater slide on case side; yellow gold crown; furnished with two snap-on case backs, a closed one and one with a sapphire crystal. 
Dial: gold, white; applied yellow gold Arabic numerals; printed minute track; yellow gold Pomme hands.
Indications: small second at 6.
Strap: crocodile leather; yellow gold clasp.
Also available: pink or white gold, 2 case backs; platinum with closed bottom.
Prices: on request.

MINUTE REPEATER — REF. 3979 H

Movement: mechanical, automatic winding, caliber Patek Philippe R 27 PS. Hallmarked with the "Geneva Seal" (watchmaking's highest distinction of quality).
Functions: hour, minute, small second, minute repeater.
Case: 18 kt yellow gold, three-piece case (Ø 34 mm); curved sapphire crystal; repeater slide on case side; yellow gold crown; furnished with two snap-on case backs, a closed one and one with a sapphire crystal. 
Dial: gold, white; printed Roman numerals and railway minute track; leaf style hands black oxidized gold.
Indications: small second at 6.
Strap: crocodile leather; yellow gold clasp.
Also available: white gold, 2 case backs; platinum with closed bottom.
Prices: on request.

PATEK PHILIPPE

PERPETUAL CALENDAR MINUTE REPEATER — REF. 3974

Movement: mechanical, automatic winding, caliber Patek Philippe R 27 Q. Beveled and Côtes de Genève finished. Hallmarked with the "Geneva Seal" (watchmaking's highest distinction of quality).
Functions: hour, minute, 24-hour indication, perpetual calendar (date, day, month, year, moon phase), minute repeater.
Case: 18 kt yellow gold, three-piece case (Ø 36 mm); curved sapphire crystal; 4 correctors and repeater slide on case side; yellow gold crown; furnished with two snap-on case backs, a closed one and one with a sapphire crystal.
Dial: gold, silvered; applied yellow gold bâton markers and cabochon minute track; yellow gold Dauphine hands.
Indications: month and four year cycle at 3, moon phase and date at 6, day and 24-hour display at 9.
Strap: crocodile leather; yellow gold clasp.
Also available: pink or white gold, 2 case backs; platinum with closed bottom.
Prices: on request.

PERPETUAL CALENDAR — REF. 5050

Movement: mechanical, automatic winding, caliber Patek Philippe 315/136. Beveled and Côtes de Genève finished. Hallmarked with the "Geneva Seal" (watchmaking's highest distinction of quality).
Functions: hour, minute, center second, perpetual calendar (date, day, month, year, moon phase).
Case: platinum, three-piece case (Ø 35 mm, thickness 10.5 mm); curved sapphire crystal; hollowed bezel; 4 correctors on case side; platinum crown; screwed-on case back. Water-resistant to 2.5 atm.
Dial: gold, silvered; applied white gold Roman numerals and cabochon minute track; white gold leaf style hands.
Indications: month at 3, moon phase at 6, day at 9, four year cycle at 12, date with retrograde center hand, black oxidized gold.
Strap: crocodile leather; platinum clasp.
Price appr.: 66'100 CHF.
Also available: in yellow gold 55'000 CHF; pink or white gold 55'500 CHF. The gold versions are furnished with two screwed case backs, a closed one and one with a sapphire crystal.

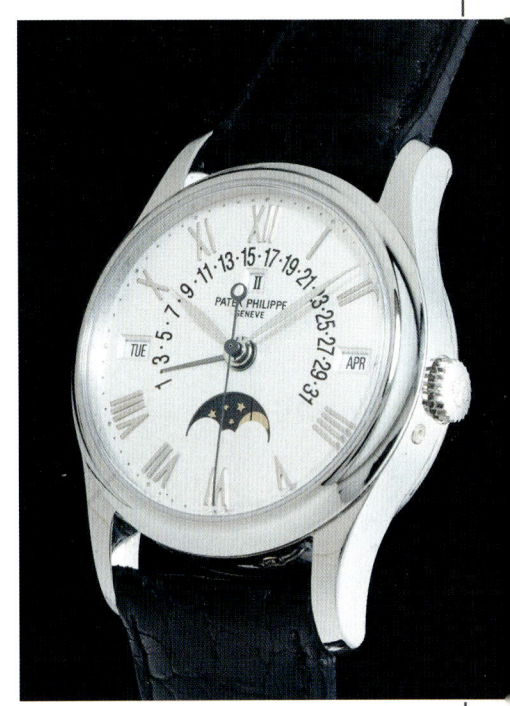

PERPETUAL CALENDAR — REF. 5059

Movement: mechanical, automatic winding, caliber Patek Philippe 315/136. Beveled and Côtes de Genève finished. Hallmarked with the "Geneva Seal" (watchmaking's highest distinction of quality).
Functions: hour, minute, center second, perpetual calendar (date, day, month, year, moon phase).
Case: 18 kt white gold, four-piece case (Ø 36 mm, thickness 12.8 mm); curved sapphire crystal; hollowed bezel; 4 correctors on case side; white gold crown with case protection; snap-on case back displaying the movement through a sapphire crystal, protected by a hinged cover. Water-resistant to 2.5 atm.
Dial: gold, white; applied black oxidized gold Roman numerals and cabochon minute track; black oxidized gold leaf style hands.
Indications: month at 3, moon phase at 6, day at 9, four year cycle at 12, date with retrograde center hand, black oxidized gold.
Strap: crocodile leather; screw connection; white gold fold-over clasp, with logo.
Price appr.: 57'000 CHF.
Also available: pink gold (same price); in yellow gold 56'500 CHF; platinum 67'100 CHF.

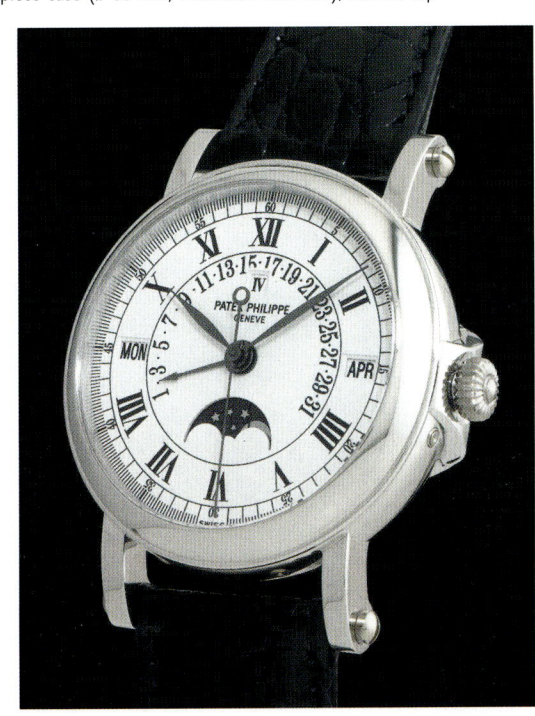

PERPETUAL CALENDAR TONNEAU — REF. 5040

Movement: mechanical, automatic winding, caliber Patek Philippe 240 Q. 22 kt gold rotor. Beveled and Côtes de Genève finished. Hallmarked with the "Geneva Seal" (watchmaking's highest distinction of quality).
Functions: hour, minute, 24-hour indication, perpetual calendar (date, day, month, year, moon phase).
Case: 18 kt pink gold, two-piece tonneau-shaped case (height lugs included 41 mm, width 35 mm, thickness 8.5 mm); curved sapphire crystal; 4 correctors on case side; pink gold crown; furnished with two snap-on case backs, a closed one and one with a sapphire crystal. Water-resistant to 2.5 atm.
Dial: gold, silvered; applied pink gold Arabic numerals; printed round railway minute track; pink gold leaf style hands.
Indications: month and four year cycle at 3, date and moon phase at 6, day and 24-hour indication at 9.
Strap: crocodile leather; pink gold clasp.
Price appr.: 50'400 CHF.
Also available: white gold, silvered or black dial (same price); yellow gold, silvered dial 49'900 CHF; platinum, closed bottom and silvered or black dial 61'000 CHF.

219

PATEK PHILIPPE

PERPETUAL CALENDAR — REF. 3940

Movement: mechanical, automatic winding, caliber Patek Philippe 240 Q. 22 kt gold rotor. Beveled and Côtes de Genève finished. Hallmarked with the "Geneva Seal" (watchmaking's highest distinction of quality).
Functions: hour, minute, 24-hour indication, perpetual calendar (date, day, month, year, moon phase).
Case: 18 kt pink gold, three-piece case (Ø 36 mm, thickness 8.5 mm); curved sapphire crystal; 4 correctors on case side; pink gold crown; furnished with two snap-on case backs, a closed one and one with a sapphire crystal. 
Dial: in gold, silvered; applied pink gold bâton markers and cabochon minute track; pink gold Dauphine hands.
Indications: month and four year cycle at 3, moon phase and date at 6, day and 24-hour indication at 9.
Strap: crocodile leather; pink gold clasp.
Price appr.: 48'700 CHF.
Also available: white gold (same price); in yellow gold 48'200 CHF; platinum with closed bottom 59'300 CHF.

PERPETUAL CALENDAR — REF. 5039

Movement: mechanical, automatic winding, extra-thin caliber Patek Philippe 240 Q. 22 kt gold rotor. Beveled and Côtes de Genève finished. Hallmarked with the "Geneva Seal" (watchmaking's highest distinction of quality).
Functions: hour, minute, 24-hour indication, perpetual calendar (date, day, month, year, moon phase).
Case: 18 kt yellow gold, three-piece brushed case (Ø 35 mm, thickness 8.5 mm); curved sapphire crystal; bezel decorated with Clous de Paris pattern; 4 correctors on case side; yellow gold crown; furnished with two snap-on case backs, a closed one and one with a sapphire crystal. 
Dial: silvered; applied yellow gold bâton markers and cabochon minute track; yellow gold Dauphine hands.
Indications: month and four year cycle at 3, moon phase and date at 6, day and 24-hour indication at 9.
Strap: crocodile leather; yellow gold clasp.
Price appr.: 48'200 CHF.
Also available: pink or white gold 48'700 CHF.

ANNUAL CALENDAR — REF. 5035

Movement: mechanical, automatic winding, caliber Patek Philippe 315 SQA 24 H, autonomy of 48 hours, 21 kt gold rotor and 35 jewels (Ø 30 mm, thickness 5.22 mm). Gyromax balance, 21,600 vibrations per hour (vph), flat balance-spring. Made up by 316 elements. Hallmarked with the "Geneva Seal" (watchmaking's highest distinction of quality). **Functions:** hour, minute, center second, 24-hour indication, annual calendar (date, day, month - keeps automatically the count of the days for a whole year).
Case: 18 kt yellow gold, three-piece case (Ø 36,5 mm, thickness 11 mm); curved sapphire crystal; hollowed bezel; 3 correctors on case side; yellow gold crown; screwed-on case back displaying the movement through a sapphire crystal. Water-resistant to 2.5 atm. 
Dial: silvered; luminescent applied yellow gold Roman numerals; printed railway minute track; luminescent yellow gold leaf style hands.
Indications: month with hand at 3, 24 hours and digital date at 6, day of the week with hand at 9.
Strap: crocodile leather; yellow gold clasp.
Price appr.: 20'700 CHF.
Also available: black dial; pink gold, silvered dial or black or white gold, dial copper or black 21'200 CHF; platinum, black dial 30'300 CHF.

ANNUAL CALENDAR PLATINUM — REF. 5056P

Patek Philippe's Annual Calendar - as an intermediate step between the classical watch with calendar (typically automatic, with date and/or day of the week in a window and seconds at the center) and the complex perpetual calendar (typically with date with hand and without seconds), recognizes the months of 30 and 31 days for a whole year, starting from the 1st of March until the end of February of the following year (when the date must be advanced manually). The latest version, ref. 5056P presented at the last Basel Show, is a revised edition, mainly as regards coloring, based on the new platinum case. This is perfectly matched by the safari-grey crocodile leather strap and the slate-grey dial, with hands and markers in white gold. A new distinctive sign of Patek Philippe's platinum watches, the Top Wesselton Pure diamond set between the lugs at 6, characterizes this exceptional piece, realized in 1999 in a series of 250 pieces.
Price appr.: 33'000 CHF.

PATEK PHILIPPE

CHRONOGRAPH — REF. 5070

Movement: mechanical, manual winding, caliber Patek Philippe 27-70/157. Beveled and Côtes de Genève finished. Hallmarked with the "Geneva Seal" (watchmaking's highest distinction of quality).
Functions: hour, minute, small second, chronograph with 2 counters.
Case: 18 kt yellow gold, two-piece case (Ø 42 mm, thickness 11.7 mm); curved sapphire crystal; stepped bezel; yellow gold crown; rectangular pushers; screwed-on case back displaying the movement through a sapphire crystal. Water-resistant to 2.5 atm.
Dial: black; applied yellow gold Arabic numerals; yellow gold leaf style hands.
Indications: minute counter at 3, small second at 9, center second counter, minute track with divisions for 1/5 of a second, tachymeter scale.
Strap: crocodile leather; fold-over clasp with logo, in yellow gold.
Price appr.: 35'000 CHF. Yearly production limited to 250 pieces.

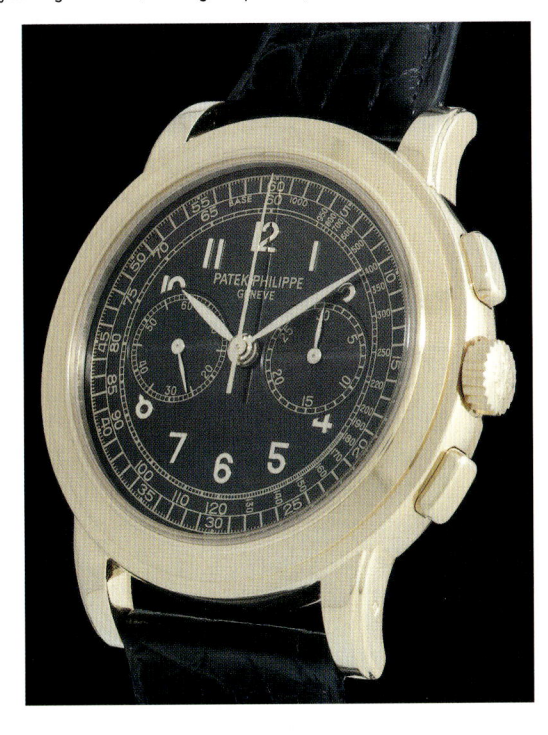

CHRONOGRAPH RATTRAPANTE PERPETUAL CALENDAR — REF. 5004

Movement: mechanical, manual winding, caliber Patek Philippe CHR 27-70 Q. Beveled and Côtes de Genève finished. Hallmarked with the "Geneva Seal" (watchmaking's highest distinction of quality).
Functions: hour, minute, small second, 24-hour indication, split-second chronograph with 2 counters, perpetual calendar (date, day, month, year, moon phase).
Case: 18 kt yellow gold, three-piece case (Ø 37 mm); curved sapphire crystal; 4 correctors on case side; yellow gold crown with pusher; furnished with two snap-on case backs, a closed one and one with a sapphire crystal. Water-resistant to 2.5 atm.
Dial: opaline silvered; applied yellow gold Arabic numerals; yellow gold leaf style hands.
Indications: minute counter and four year cycle at 3, moon phase and date at 6, small second and 24-hour indication at 9, day and month at 12, center second and split-second counters, minute track with divisions for 1/5 of a second.
Strap: crocodile leather; yellow gold clasp.
Price appr.: 158'000 CHF.
Also available: pink or white gold 159'000 CHF; platinum 168'500 CHF.

CHRONOGRAPH PERPETUAL CALENDAR — REF. 3970 E

Movement: mechanical, manual winding, caliber Patek Philippe CH 27-70 Q. Beveled and Côtes de Genève finished. Hallmarked with the "Geneva Seal" (watchmaking's highest distinction of quality).
Functions: hour, minute, small second, 24-hour indication, chronograph with 2 counters, perpetual calendar (date, day, month, year, moon phase).
Case: 18 kt white gold, three-piece case (Ø 36 mm, thickness 12 mm); curved sapphire crystal; hollowed bezel; 4 correctors on case side; white gold crown; furnished with two screwed-on case backs, a closed one and one with a sapphire crystal. Water-resistant to 2.5 atm.
Dial: in gold, silvered; applied white gold bâton and square markers; white gold bâton hands.
Indications: minute counter and four year cycle at 3, moon phase and date at 6, small second and 24-hour indication at 9, day and month at 12, center second counter, minute track with divisions for 1/5 of a second.
Strap: crocodile leather; white gold clasp.
Price appr.: 86'700 CHF.
Also available: pink gold (same price); in yellow gold 86'200 CHF; platinum, black dial and brilliants at markers 98'500 CHF.

CHRONOGRAPH PERPETUAL CALENDAR — REF. 5020

Movement: mechanical, manual winding, caliber Patek Philippe CH 27-70 Q. Beveled and Côtes de Genève finished. Hallmarked with the "Geneva Seal" (watchmaking's highest distinction of quality).
Functions: hour, minute, small second, 24-hour indication, chronograph with 2 counters, perpetual calendar (date, day, month, year, moon phase).
Case: platinum, two-piece tonneau-shaped case (height 37 mm, width 37 mm, thickness 12 mm); sapphire crystal tonneau, curved; 4 correctors on case side; platinum crown; snap-on back. Water-resistant to 2.5 atm.
Dial: in gold, black; applied white gold square markers set with diamonds; white gold bâton hands.
Indications: minute counter and four year cycle at 3, moon phase and date at 6, small second and 24-hour indication at 9, day and month at 12, center second counter, minute track with divisions for 1/5 of a second.
Strap: crocodile leather; platinum clasp.
Price appr.: 99'000 CHF.
Also available: yellow gold 87'900 CHF; pink or white gold 88'400 CHF. Versions in gold, available with silvered dial and applied Arabic numerals without brilliants, are furnished with a closed and a transparent bottom.

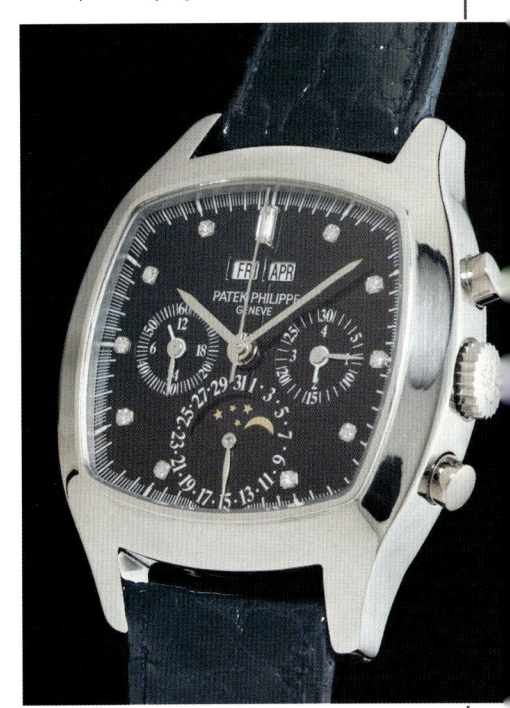

PATEK PHILIPPE

POWER RESERVE — REF. 5055

Movement: mechanical, automatic winding, caliber Patek Philippe 240/164. 22 kt gold rotor. Hallmarked with the "Geneva Seal" (watchmaking's highest distinction of quality).
Functions: hour, minute, small second, date, power reserve, moon phase.
Case: 18 kt pink gold, two-piece case (Ø 36 mm, thickness 9 mm); curved sapphire crystal; 2 correctors on case side (at 4 and at 8); pink gold crown; screwed-on case back displaying the movement through a sapphire crystal. Water-resistant to 2.5 atm. 
Dial: rosé; applied pink gold Arabic numerals; luminescent dots on the printed railway minute track; luminescent pink gold bâton hands.
Indications: small second between 4 and 5, date and moon phase at 7, power reserve between 10 and 11.
Strap: crocodile leather; pink gold fold-over clasp with round buckle, skeletonized in the Houses logo (Maltese cross).
Price appr.: 22'900 CHF.
Also available: white gold, black dial (same price); yellow gold, white dial 22'400 CHF.

POWER RESERVE — REF. 5054

Movement: mechanical, automatic winding, Patek Philippe caliber 240PS IRM-C-LU. Hallmarked with the "Geneva Seal" (watchmaking's highest distinction of quality).
Functions: hour, minute, small second, date, moon phase, power reserve.
Case: platinum, two-piece case (Ø 35.7 mm, thickness 9.75 mm) in Directoire style; curved sapphire crystal; winding crown in "turban" style, platinum; case back displaying the movement through a sapphire crystal, protected by a hinged cover. 
Dial: in gold, white porcelainized; printed Roman numerals and railway minute track; black oxidized Stuart gold hands.
Indications: small second between 4 and 5, date and moon phase at 7, power reserve between 10 and 11.
Strap: crocodile leather; screw connection; platinum clasp.
Price appr.: 34'000 CHF.
Also available: in yellow gold 24'000 CHF; pink or white gold 24'800 CHF.

POWER RESERVE — REF. 5085/1A

Movement: mechanical, automatic winding, caliber Patek Philippe 240/164. 22 kt gold rotor. Hallmarked with the "Geneva Seal" (watchmaking's highest distinction of quality).
Functions: hour, minute, small second, date, power reserve, moon phase.
Case: stainless steel, three-piece case (Ø 37 mm, thickness 10 mm) polished and brushed finish; curved sapphire crystal; 2 correctors on case side (at 4 and at 8); screw-down crown with case protection; screwed-on case back displaying the movement through a sapphire crystal. Water-resistant to 2.5 atm. 
Dial: black; white painted Arabic numerals and railway minute track with luminescent dots; luminescent white painted bâton hands.
Indications: small second between 4 and 5, date and moon phase at 7, power reserve between 10 and 11.
Bracelet: steel; double fold-over clasp.
Price appr.: 16'000 CHF.
Also available: in yellow gold, white dial 33'000 CHF.

PATEK PHILIPPE NEPTUNE — REF. 5080/1A

Movement: mechanical, automatic winding, caliber Patek Philippe 315 SC. 21 kt gold rotor. Hallmarked with the "Geneva Seal" (watchmaking's highest distinction of quality).
Functions: hour, minute, center second, date.
Case: stainless steel, three-piece case (Ø 36 mm, thickness 8 mm); curved sapphire crystal; bezel decorated with sun pattern, with raised hour markers; screw-down crown with case protection; screwed-on case back. Water-resistant to 6 atm. 
Dial: rosé; luminescent applied Roman numerals; printed railway minute track; luminescent leaf style hands.
Indications: date at 3.
Bracelet: steel; double fold-over clasp.
Price appr.: 10'300 CHF.
Also available: steel/yellow gold, black dial Ref. 5080/1JA; yellow gold, black dial, leather strap Ref. 5081, bracelet Ref. 5081/1; with bezel and brilliant markers Ref. 5081/10. Lady's size, quartz: bezel and brilliant markers Ref. 4881/10; yellow gold; white gold; brilliant markers: yellow gold Ref. 4881/1; steel and yellow gold Ref. 4880/1JA; 12 brilliants in bezel and 8 at markers Ref. 4881/30; without brilliants, steel Ref. 4880/1A. Prices on request.

PATEK PHILIPPE

NAUTILUS "JUMBO" — REF. 3710/1A

Movement: mechanical, automatic winding, caliber Patek Philippe 330 SC IZR. 21 kt gold rotor. Hallmarked with the "Geneva Seal" (watchmaking's highest distinction of quality).
Functions: hour, minute, center second, date, power reserve.
Case: stainless steel, two-piece tonneau case (height 38 mm, width 38 mm, thickness 8.3 mm), polished and brushed finish; curved sapphire crystal; crown with case protection, with two gaskets; screwed-on case back displaying the movement through a sapphire crystal. Water-resistant to 12 atm.
Dial: black; luminescent applied white gold Roman numerals; white printed minute track; luminescent bâton hands.
Indications: date at 3, power reserve at 12 (comet and hand rotating to indicate different situations of the winding charge).
Bracelet: brushed steel with polished central links; double fold-over safety clasp.
Price appr.: 11'500 CHF.

NAUTILUS — REF. 5060

Movement: mechanical, automatic winding, caliber Patek Philippe 330 SC. 21 kt gold rotor. Hallmarked with the "Geneva Seal" (watchmaking's highest distinction of quality).
Functions: hour, minute, center second, date.
Case: 18 kt yellow gold, two-piece tonneau case (height 34 mm, width 34 mm, thickness 8 mm) polished and brushed finish; flat sapphire crystal; screw down yellow gold crown with case protection, with two gaskets; screwed-on case back. Water-resistant to 12 atm.
Dial: black; luminescent applied yellow gold Roman numerals; golden minute track; luminescent yellow gold leaf style hands.
Indications: date at 3.
Strap: crocodile leather; fold-over yellow gold clasp.
Price appr.: 15'800 CHF. Limited production.
Also available: with bracelet Ref. 5060/002.

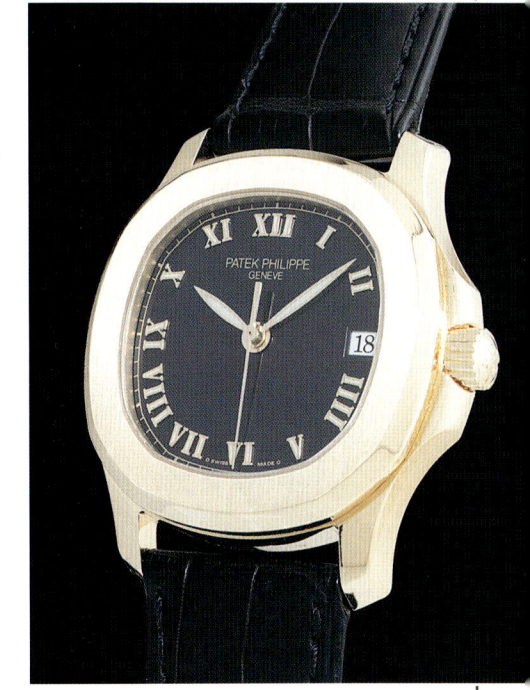

AQUANAUT — REF. 5065/A

Movement: mechanical, automatic winding, caliber Patek Philippe 315 SC. 21 kt gold rotor. Hallmarked with the "Geneva Seal" (watchmaking's highest distinction of quality).
Functions: hour, minute, center second, date.
Case: stainless steel, three-piece tonneau case (height 37 mm, width 37 mm, thickness 8.2 mm), polished and brushed finish; flat sapphire crystal; screw-down crown with case protection, with two gaskets; screwed-on brushed case back, displaying the movement through a sapphire crystal. Water-resistant to 12 atm.
Dial: semi-brilliant black, with embossed center decoration; applied white gold Arabic numerals; peripheral ring with white dial-train and large luminescent markers; luminescent white gold oversized bâton hands.
Indications: date at 3.
Strap: "Tropical" in composite materials, water-repellent and salt-resistant, made of more than 20 elements; double fold-over steel clasp with square shaped element with engraved logo, brushed finish.
Price appr.: 8'500 CHF.
Also available: with bracelet Ref. 5065/1A; yellow gold, leather strap Ref. 5065, bracelet Ref. 5065/1.

AQUANAUT — REF. 5066

Starting from 1998, the Aquanaut collection was enriched with new models. The version with the "Tropical" leather strap (realized in composite materials according to Patek's definition) is available in 3 sizes with stainless steel case: large (Ref. 5065/A), medium (Ref. 5066/A) and small (Ref. 4960/A, water-resistant to 6 atm.). The movements are automatic for the large and medium, quartz for the medium (in this case Ref. 5064/A) and small sizes. Some versions were presented with a new and exclusive bracelet in stainless steel, whose links show the same chequered design which characterizes the dial, but only for large (Ref. 5065/1A) and medium (Ref. 5066/1A) case sizes. The models with bracelet use only automatic movements. There is also a new version with case in yellow gold and "Tropical" leather strap (Ref. 5066), as shown in the photograph, available only with medium sized case. This model is told to be available in future also with a bracelet in gold. All the Aquanaut models of the latest generation with automatic winding movement are provided with case backs displaying the movement through a sapphire crystal.
Price appr.: 15'800 CHF.

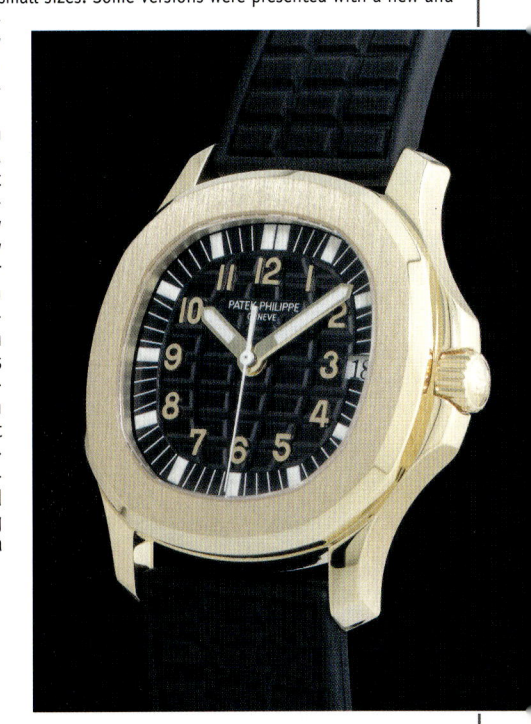

223

PATEK PHILIPPE

PATEK PHILIPPE SCULPTURE — REF. 5091/1A

Movement: mechanical, automatic winding, caliber Patek Philippe 315 SC. 21 kt gold rotor. Hallmarked with the "Geneva Seal" (watchmaking's highest distinction of quality). **Functions:** hour, minute, center second, date.
Case: stainless steel, two-piece case (Ø 37 mm, thickness 10.5 mm) polished and brushed finish; curved sapphire crystal; winding crown in imperial-blue cloisonné enamel, with a white gold protection above; screwed-on case back. Waterproof to 2.5 atm. 
Dial: black; luminescent Arabic numerals; white printed minute track with luminescent dots; luminescent bâton hands.
Indications: date at 3.
Bracelet: steel, integrated, with polished links; fold-over safety clasp.
Price appr.: 9'900 CHF. Production limited to 300 pieces each version, totalling 2700 watches.
Also available: with smooth white dial; steel and yellow gold, silvered engine turned (guilloché) dial; yellow gold, silvered engine turned (guilloché) dial; yellow gold, bezel brilliants, silvered engine turned (guilloché) dial; yellow gold, leather strap, smooth black or silvered engine turned (guilloché) dial. Ref. 5090/J, 21.306; Lady's size, quartz (prices on request).

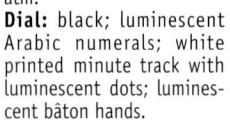

CALATRAVA — REF. 5032

Movement: mechanical, automatic winding, caliber Patek Philippe 240, extra-thin. Hallmarked with the "Geneva Seal" (watchmaking's highest distinction of quality). **Functions:** hour, minute.
Case: 18 kt yellow gold, three-piece case (Ø 36 mm), "bassiné" (the parts making up the case are accurately polished, so that this seems to be made in one piece); curved sapphire crystal; hollowed bezel; yellow gold crown; screwed-on case back. Water-resistant to 2.5 atm. 
Dial: silvered; applied yellow gold bâton markers and cabochon minute track; yellow gold Dauphine hands.
Strap: crocodile leather; yellow gold clasp.
Price appr.: 12'400 CHF.
Also available: white dial, Roman numerals.

CALATRAVA — REF. 5026

Movement: mechanical, automatic winding, caliber Patek Philippe 240 PS, extra-thin. 22 kt gold rotor. Hallmarked with the "Geneva Seal" (watchmaking's highest distinction of quality).
Functions: hour, minute, small second.
Case: 18 kt yellow gold, three-piece case (Ø 33 mm, thickness 7.4 mm); curved sapphire crystal; yellow gold crown; screwed-on case back displaying the movement through a sapphire crystal. Water-resistant to 2.5 atm. 
Dial: silvered; applied yellow gold Arabic numerals and cabochon minute track; yellow gold Pomme hands.
Indications: small second between 4 and 5.
Strap: crocodile leather; yellow gold clasp.
Price appr.: 14'000 CHF.
Also available: pink gold, black or silvered dial 14'300 CHF; white gold, black dial 14'300 CHF; platinum, anthracite grained dial 24'000 CHF.

CALATRAVA OFFICIER — REF. 5022/1

Movement: mechanical, manual winding, caliber Patek Philippe 215 PS. Hallmarked with the "Geneva Seal" (watchmaking's highest distinction of quality).
Functions: hour, minute, small second.
Case: 18 kt white gold, three-piece case (Ø 33.3 mm, thickness 6.85 mm) in "Officer" style; curved sapphire crystal; white gold crown; snap-on back. Water-resistant to 2.5 atm. 
Dial: porcelain white; printed Arabic numerals and railway minute track; gold Pomme hands.
Indications: small second at 6.
Bracelet: white gold; double fold-over clasp.
Price appr.: 23'500 CHF.
Also available: leather strap; with anthracite dial, engine turned (guilloché), and silvered external ring; pink gold and dial rosé or white (same prices); in yellow gold and dial gilded, silvered or white, leather strap or bracelet; platinum, leather strap and anthracite or white dial. Prices on request.

224

PATEK PHILIPPE

CALATRAVA — REF. 3796

Movement: mechanical, manual winding, caliber Patek Philippe 215/45. Hallmarked with the "Geneva Seal" (watchmaking's highest distinction of quality).
Functions: hour, minute, small second.
Case: 18 kt pink gold, three-piece case (Ø 30 mm, thickness 7 mm); curved sapphire crystal; pink gold crown; snap-on back. Water-resistant to 2.5 atm.
Dial: rosé; applied pink gold bâton markers and cabochon minute track; pink gold Dauphine hands.
Indications: small second at 6.
Strap: crocodile leather; pink gold clasp.
Price appr.: 10'800 CHF.
Also available: silvered dial; in yellow gold and silvered dial 10'500 CHF; platinum, silvered dial and brilliants at markers 23'500 CHF.

CALATRAVA — REF. 5023

Movement: mechanical, manual winding, caliber Patek Philippe 215/45. Hallmarked with the "Geneva Seal" (watchmaking's highest distinction of quality).
Functions: hour, minute, small second.
Case: 18 kt yellow gold, three-piece case (Ø 33 mm); curved sapphire crystal; hollowed bezel; yellow gold crown; screwed-on case back. Water-resistant to 2.5 atm.
Dial: silvered; applied yellow gold bâton markers and cabochon minute track; yellow gold Dauphine hands.
Indications: small second at 6.
Strap: crocodile leather; yellow gold clasp.
Price appr.: 10'600 CHF.

CALATRAVA — REF. 3998

Movement: mechanical, automatic winding, caliber Patek Philippe 315/130. Hallmarked with the "Geneva Seal" (watchmaking's highest distinction of quality).
Functions: hour, minute, center second, date.
Case: 18 kt white gold, three-piece case (Ø 33 mm, thickness 8 mm); flat sapphire crystal; white gold crown; screwed-on case back. Water-resistant to 2.5 atm.
Dial: silvered; applied white gold bâton markers and cabochon minute track; white gold Dauphine hands.
Indications: date at 3.
Strap: crocodile leather; white gold clasp.
Price appr.: 14'300 CHF.
Also available: black dial; pink gold, silvered dial (same price); in yellow gold, silvered dial 14'000 CHF; platinum, silvered or black dial and markers in brilliants 24'800 CHF; with bracelet Ref. 3998/1: yellow gold; white gold.

CALATRAVA — REF. 3820

Movement: mechanical, manual winding, caliber Patek Philippe 177/02, extra-thin. Hallmarked with the "Geneva Seal" (watchmaking's highest distinction of quality).
Functions: hour, minute.
Case: 18 kt pink gold, two-piece case (Ø 31 mm); drop-shaped lugs; flat sapphire crystal; pink gold crown; screwed-on case back. Water-resistant to 2.5 atm.
Dial: silvered; applied pink gold Arabic numerals and cabochon minute track; pink gold Pomme hands.
Strap: crocodile leather; pink gold clasp.
Price appr.: 13'400 CHF.

PATEK PHILIPPE

CALATRAVA — REF. 3802/200

Movement: mechanical, automatic winding, caliber Patek Philippe 315 SC. Hallmarked with the "Geneva Seal" (watchmaking's highest distinction of quality).
Functions: hour, minute, center second, date.
Case: 18 kt pink gold, three-piece case (Ø 33 mm, thickness 7.8 mm) polished and brushed finish; flat sapphire crystal; bezel decorated with Clous de Paris pattern; pink gold crown; snap-on back. Water-resistant to 2.5 atm. 
Dial: white; printed Roman numerals and minute track; black oxidized gold bâton hands.
Indications: date at 3.
Strap: crocodile leather; pink gold clasp.
Price appr.: 14'300 CHF.
Also available: white gold (same price); in yellow gold 14'000 CHF; with bracelet Ref. 3802/208: yellow gold; pink gold; white gold.

CALATRAVA — REF. 3919

Movement: mechanical, manual winding, caliber Patek Philippe 215 PS. Hallmarked with the "Geneva Seal" (watchmaking's highest distinction of quality).
Functions: hour, minute, small second.
Case: 18 kt yellow gold, three-piece case (Ø 33 mm, thickness 7 mm); curved sapphire crystal; bezel decorated with Clous de Paris pattern; yellow gold crown; snap-on back. Water-resistant to 2.5 atm. 
Dial: white; printed Roman numerals; leaf style hands in black oxidized gold.
Indications: small second at 6.
Strap: crocodile leather; yellow gold clasp.
Price appr.: 10'600 CHF.
Also available: pink or white gold 10'900 CHF; with bracelet Ref. 3919/8: yellow gold or white gold.

GONDOLO — REF. 5014

Movement: mechanical, manual winding, caliber Patek Philippe 215 PS. Hallmarked with the "Geneva Seal" (watchmaking's highest distinction of quality).
Functions: hour, minute, small second.
Case: 18 kt pink gold, two-piece rectangular convex case (height lugs included 27 mm, width 33 mm); curved sapphire crystal; pink gold crown; case back attached by 4 screws. Water-resistant to 2.5 atm. 
Dial: Art Déco style, black; applied pink gold Arabic numerals; white printed railway minute track; pink gold bâton hands.
Indications: small second at 6.
Strap: crocodile leather; pink gold clasp.
Price appr.: 11'200 CHF.
Also available: white gold, black dial, white Arabic numerals (same price); yellow gold, white porcelainized dial, screen-printed Roman or Arabic numerals 10'900 CHF.

GONDOLO — REF. 5024

Movement: mechanical, manual winding, caliber Patek Philippe 215 PS. Hallmarked with the "Geneva Seal" (watchmaking's highest distinction of quality).
Functions: hour, minute, small second.
Case: 18 kt yellow gold, two-piece rectangular-curved case, with side juts (height lugs included 30 mm, width 38 mm, thickness 7.7 mm); curved sapphire crystal; yellow gold recessed crown; case back attached by 4 screws. Water-resistant to 2.5 atm. 
Dial: porcelainized white; printed Arabic numerals and railway minute track; leaf style hands in black oxidized gold.
Indications: small second at 6.
Strap: crocodile leather; yellow gold clasp.
Price: 11'500 CHF.
Also available: white gold 11'800 CHF; with bracelet Ref. 5024/1: yellow gold or white gold.

PATEK PHILIPPE

TRAVEL TIME — REF. 5034/1

Movement: mechanical, manual winding, caliber Patek Philippe 215 PS FUS, autonomy of 44 hours and 18 jewels (Ø 21.90 mm, thickness 3.35 mm). Gyromax balance, 28,800 vibrations per hour (vph), flat balance-spring. Made up by 178 elements. Hallmarked with the "Geneva Seal" (watchmaking's highest distinction of quality).
Functions: hour, minute, small second, second time zone, 24-hour indication.
Case: 18 kt white gold, two-piece case (Ø 34 mm, thickness 8 mm); curved sapphire crystal; knurled bezel; 2 pushers on case side (at 8 to move the GMT hand forward, at 10 to move it backward); Louis XV white gold crown; snap-on back. Water-resistant to 2.5 atm.
Dial: black; applied white gold bâton markers; printed railway minute track; white lacquered gold leaf style hands (burnished gold GMT hand).
Indications: small second at 6, 24-hour indication at 12.
Bracelet: white gold; double fold-over clasp.
Price appr.: 27'400 CHF.
Also available: yellow gold 26'400 CHF; white gold leather strap, white dial Ref. 5034; yellow gold, white dial, strap Ref. 5034, bracelet Ref. 5034/1; pink gold, leather strap, white dial Ref. 5034; Lady's Ref. 4864 (prices on request).

ELLIPSE — REF. 5028

Movement: mechanical, automatic winding, extra-thin caliber Patek Philippe 240 PS. 22 kt gold rotor. Hallmarked with the "Geneva Seal" (watchmaking's highest distinction of quality).
Functions: hour, minute, small second.
Case: 18 kt white gold, two-piece elliptic case (height 35.4 mm, width 31 mm, thickness 6 mm); flat sapphire crystal; white gold crown; snap-on back. Water-resistant to 2.5 atm.
Dial: black; printed Arabic numerals and railway minute track; white enameled bâton hands.
Indications: small second at 4.
Strap: crocodile leather; white gold fold-over clasp, with round buckle skeletonized in the Houses logo (Maltese cross).
Price appr.: 14'300 CHF.

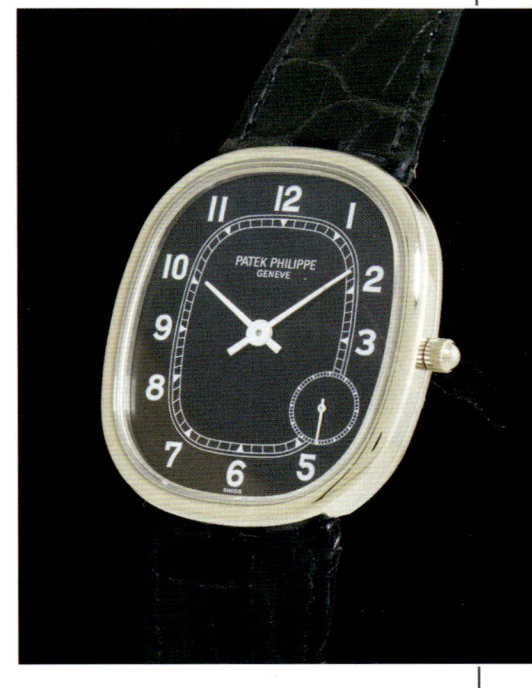

SMALL SECOND MOON PHASE — REF. 4857

Movement: mechanical, manual winding, caliber Patek Philippe 16-250PS/LU. Hallmarked with the "Geneva Seal" (watchmaking's highest distinction of quality).
Functions: hour, minute, small second, moon phase.
Case: 18 kt white gold, three-piece case (Ø 29 mm, thickness 7.8 mm); curved sapphire crystal; one corrector on case side; sapphire cabochon white gold crown; snap-on back. Water-resistant to 2.5 atm.
Dial: grey with sun pattern; applied white gold Roman numerals set with diamonds; printed minute track; white gold leaf style hands.
Indications: moon phase at 4, small second at 8.
Strap: crocodile leather; white gold clasp.
Price appr.: 9'600 CHF.
Also available: in yellow gold, white dial, blue zones 9'300 CHF.

SMALL SECOND MOON PHASE — REF. 4856

Movement: mechanical, manual winding, caliber Patek Philippe 16-250PS/LU. Hallmarked with the "Geneva Seal" (watchmaking's highest distinction of quality).
Functions: hour, minute, small second, moon phase.
Case: 18 kt yellow gold, three-piece case (Ø 26 mm, thickness 7.5 mm); curved sapphire crystal; hollowed bezel; one corrector on case side; sapphire cabochon yellow gold crown; snap-on back. Water-resistant to 2.5 atm.
Dial: white; applied yellow gold Roman numerals and cabochon minute track; yellow gold bâton hands.
Indications: moon phase at 4, small second at 8.
Strap: crocodile leather; yellow gold clasp.
Price appr.: 9'100 CHF.

Paul Picot

As the world focuses on the turning of the millennium, time becomes more important than ever before. And when it comes to time, time measured with true precision, who can we trust more than those craftsmen who have made watchmaking a science as well as an art for centuries? One outstanding leader in the industry is surprisingly new to the field. n Celebrating its 25th anniversary in 2001, Paul Picot is a comparatively young company, but one that has already achieved an undeniable stature in its field. Although a newcomer in historical terms, Paul Picot effectively combines two traditions: Swiss precision watchmaking and Italian artistic creativity. With a reputation forged by its well-informed, discerning and decidedly individualistic clientele, the company's special combination of technical prowess, innovation and attentive design will continue to be the best choice for leading citizens in the 21st century.

TACHY
MON SON SAM
DIE MIT DON FRE
CHRONOMETER
Nº37
Paul Picot
GENEVE
SWISS
MADE

Paul Picot

The story of this company began in the seventies, when Japanese and American factory-produced quartz watches hit the Swiss watchmaking industry badly, forcing many historical brands either to go out of business or to accept compromises in their methods. Contemporaries regarded the marketplace as too fragile for a new firm. But Mario Boiocchi focused instead on preserving Switzerland's rich watchmaking tradition of Switzerland, which was really in danger. Boiocchi's ambition was to re-create a true craftsman's company. In 1976, the quality watchmaking company Paul Picot was born. In the following years, the company's philosophy's summarized in its motto: Nobility of Detail—was reflected in its strict compliance with traditional Swiss standards of quality, combined with Boiocchi's experience as a jeweler and goldsmith in the classic Italian style.

However, the strenuous defense of tradition has not precluded technological innovation. And it is this powerful combination of tradition and innovation that has taken Paul Picot, within its brief life span, into the top ranks of the industry. In what is truly a craftsman's company, watches are designed, refined piece by piece and then assembled entirely by hand at the company's own workshops in Le Noirmont. This almost obsessive attention to the making of precision timepieces has contributed to a restoration of the proud traditions of watchmaking. And Paul Picot has done much to preserve the best of tradition.

As part of this effort, many first-quality, extremely complicated movements or the relevant rights have been ac-

Opening Page
The manufacture Paul Picot in Le Noirmont.

Previous Page
Technicum in yellow gold, calibre PP 8888, is a self-winding, split-seconds chronograph and certified Chronometer by the C.O.S.C. with solid silver dial, engine-turned and double sapphire crystal.

Top left
Mr. Boiocchi, Chairman and founder of Paul Picot.

Bottom
Atelier 1200 in yellow gold set with diamonds features 44-hour power-reserve indicator, self-winding movement calibre PP 1200 and is a certified Chronometer by the C.O.S.C. Right: Atelier classic in yellow gold.

Bottom left
Back view of Atelier 1200.

Paul Picot

quired by the company. The exquisite 1937 tonneau movement featured in the "Firshire 1937" is an excellent example of this policy.

Firshire—a collection for the "nostalgic"—is dedicated to the region of the Jura Mountains, which provided inspiration for the name and where the tradition of precision watchmaking was born, and three firs are engraved on the back of each piece. A classic from the standpoint of both watchmaking technology and aesthetics, any improvement in the tonneau movement—a true masterpiece—may truly be considered a very remarkable exploit. And yet this is exactly where Paul Picot has excelled. This movement, and others, have been enhanced and technically redesigned, in some cases with the addition of a number of very sophisticated functions.

In the "Firshire 1937" model, jewels were added and a shockproof system adopted. The product reflects the spirit of watchmaking of a by-gone age, but refined and enhanced with the incorporation of today's high technology.

Center
Firshire 1937. JA set consisting of two platinum watches, hand wound with a basic movement made in 1937. Each watch features a double sapphire crystal, crown set with a diamond, dial in solid silver, engine-turned. Ladies, model with a diamond on 3 and 9 o,clock. Limited series of 25 pieces each.

Bottom
Firshire Movement 1937 in platinum, calibre PP 88. Differential power reserve (28 components), pearl-milled openings and hand-beveled bridges.

Paul Picot

Then there is the "Firshire Perpetual Calendar," a classic like the other models of the Firshire collection, but featuring a self-winding movement and a perpetual calendar programmed until the year 2100! The movement requires no correction for months or leap years, and it is not affected by the notorious Y2K bug. Each of these watches has a rotating presentation case, and forms part of a limited series of thirty pieces.

The company's flagship model, the "Technicum," is part of the Atelier line. A first time ever, as it incorporates a power-reserve indicator, it is a unique split-second chronograph. An official C.O.S.C. chronometer certificate is issued with each piece. Launched in 1991, it has received numerous awards in the years since then and continues to maintain its distinctive role in the market.

The "Rattrapante 310," another watch in the Atelier line, is fitted with a special calibre movement based on the Venus 179, a movement developed between the two world wars. Paul Picot had the good fortune to buy the last 250 movements, and by refurbishing each original piece and adding 83 new parts, created a masterpiece called the Paul Picot 310 movement. With a full calendar, including the phases of the moon, the truly unique "Rattrapante 310" was pro-

Top
Firshire Perpetual Calendar in white gold. Self-winding movement, modul PP. Limited series of 30 pieces.

Left
Technicum in platinum is a self-winding, split-seconds chronograph and certified Chronometer by the C.O.S.C.

Paul Picot

Top
Rattrapante 310 in yellow gold. Hand-winding split-seconds chronograph, calibre PP 310 features dial in solid silver and double sapphire crystal.

Bottom
Atelier 1200 pavé is a C.O.S.C. certified Chronometer with self-winding movement, rhodium-plated and features 44-hour power-reserve indicator.

duced in a limited series of 200 pieces, due to the scarcity of the remaining original parts.

These and other pieces crafted by Paul Picot are highly prized by collectors, though by no means limited to that market. The company's steady rise to the top ranks of fine Swiss watchmaking is a result of diligent compliance with its corporate philosophy, rather than a particularly aggressive sales pitch. Paul Picot is dedicated to serve those who prize individuality and uniqueness as qualities inseparable from the Nobility of Details. In the early days of the company, the pieces were sold in Europe only, and they gained an especially strong following in Italy and Germany. Expansion to Middle-Eastern, Far-Eastern and Japan markets came next.

Chairman Boiocchi insists that growth should never interfere with quality and the defense of true craftsmanship. Paul Picot's guiding mission is to preserve the traditions of aesthetic and technological mastery, the hallmarks of fine watchmaking, by making the highest quality timepieces available on the market. The uniqueness of each Paul Picot timepiece demands strict standards of workmanship, attention to detail, and innovative performance. A young company with classic ideals and thoroughly modern pieces, Paul Picot has a fine future guaranteed in the world of Swiss precision watchmaking.

PAUL PICOT

FIRSHIRE TONNEAU CHRONOGRAPH — REF. 5058-33

Movement: mechanical, manual winding, (Lemania 1872, 12''' base), autonomy of 50 hours and 15 jewels. Balance with 21.000 vibrations per hour (vph), flat balance-spring with off-center screw adjustment, Incabloc shock-resistant system. Decorated with Vagues de Genève pattern.
Functions: hour, minute, small second, chronograph with 2 counters.
Case: stainless steel and 18 kt pink gold, three-piece tonneau case (with lugs size 42x32 mm, thickness 9 mm); flat sapphire crystal; drop-shaped pushers and screw-down crown, pink gold; case back attached by 4 screws. Water-resistant to 3 atm. 
Dial: black; zones decorated with concentric-circle pattern; luminescent Arabic numerals; luminescent lozenge hands.
Indications: minute counter at 3, small second at 9, center second counter, minute track.
Strap: crocodile leather; stainless steel clasp.
Price: 6'350 CHF.
Also available: in yellow or pink gold 9'900; white gold 10'750; steel strap 4'450, bracelet on request. Each version is available with silvered dial and applied Arabic numerals or Roman numerals, or in black with applied Roman numerals or luminescent Arabic numerals.

FIRSHIRE TONNEAU POWER RESERVE — REF. 4034/B

Movement: mechanical, automatic winding, caliber PP 1230. Vagues de Genève finish. Officially certified "chronometer" (C.O.S.C.).
Functions: hour, minute, small second, date, power reserve.
Case: stainless steel, three-piece tonneau case (with lugs size 42x32 mm, thickness 8 mm); curved sapphire crystal; one corrector on case side; case back attached by 4 screws. Water-resistant to 3 atm. 
Dial: silvered, engine turned (guilloché); applied Roman numerals; printed minute track; Pomme hands in blued stainless steel.
Indications: power reserve at 3, small second at 6, date at 9.
Bracelet: steel; fold-over safety clasp.
Price: 5'150 CHF.
Also available: leather strap 4'450 CHF; yellow or pink gold & stainless steel, leather strap 5'750; in yellow or pink gold, leather strap 9'900; white gold, leather strap 12'400. Each version is available with silvered dial and applied Arabic or Roman numerals, or black with applied Roman numerals.

FIRSHIRE TONNEAU CLASSIC — REF. 4044/B

Movement: mechanical, automatic winding, autonomy of 47 hours, 21 jewels; Glucydur balance, Nivarox balance-spring, Incabloc shock-resistant system. Vagues de Genève finish.
Functions: hour, minute, center second, date.
Case: stainless steel, three-piece tonneau case (size 34 mm, width 33 mm, thickness 7 mm); flat sapphire crystal; screw-down crown; case back attached by 4 screws. Water-resistant to 5 atm. 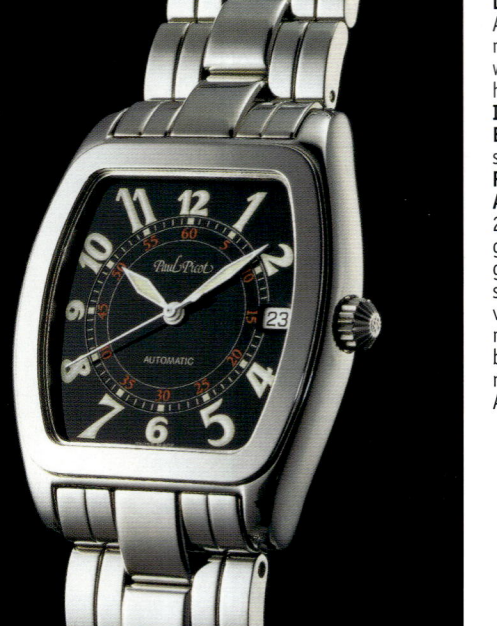
Dial: black; luminescent Arabic numerals; printed minute track; luminescent white painted lozenge hands.
Indications: date at 3.
Bracelet: steel; fold-over safety clasp.
Price: 3'200 CHF.
Also available: with strap 2'500 CHF; in yellow or pink gold, strap 7'900; white gold, strap 9'600. Each version is available with silvered dial and applied Roman or Arabic numerals or black with applied Roman numerals or luminescent Arabic numerals.

FIRSHIRE 2000 AUTOMATIC MEDIUM — REF. 4085

Movement: mechanical, automatic winding, Eta caliber 2000. Decorated with Vagues de Genève pattern.
Functions: hours, minutes, seconds, date.
Case: steel, three-piece, tonneau-curved (with lugs size 32x29 mm, thickness 10 mm); domed sapphire crystal; case back fastened by 4 screws. Water-resistant to 5 atm. 
Dial: black; luminescent screen-printed Roman numerals; luminescent sword style hands.
Indications: date at 3.
Strap: crocodile leather; steel clasp.
Price: 3'350 CHF.
Also available: bracelet 3'950 CHF; with brilliants, leather strap 8'200, bracelet 8'800; with Arabic numerals; with white dial and Arabic or Roman numerals.

PAUL PICOT

FIRSHIRE HAND WINDING PLATINUM GENTS — REF. 6003

Movement: mechanical, manual winding, caliber Paul Picot 88, autonomy of 42 hours, 17 jewels; Glucydur balance, 18,000 vibrations per hour (vph), Nivarox 1 balance-spring, Incabloc shock-resistant system. Beveled, Vagues de Genève and circular graining finished.
Functions: hour, minute, small second, power reserve.
Case: platinum, three-piece tonneau case (size 36 mm, width 33 mm, thickness 10.5 mm); curved sapphire crystal; screw-down crown; case back attached by 4 screws, displaying the movement through a sapphire crystal. Water-resistant to 5 atm.
Dial: solid silver, silvered with engine turned (guilloché) decoration; applied bâton markers (Arabic numeral 12); printed minute track; sword style hands.
Indications: power reserve at 1, small second at 6.
Strap: crocodile leather; platinum clasp.
Price: 23'700 CHF. Limited edition. Sold only in a case combined with lady's version (total price 45'600 CHF).

FIRSHIRE HAND WINDING PLATINUM LADY REF. 6004K

The Firshire 1937 model, which was presented in a limited series (pink gold, white gold and steel) in 1998 in a collection case, this year it was the turn of the complete series. As it had been promised to the first 50 customers, the new models will have a dial different from the 1998 version and will be numbered from 51 on. A limited production was also commenced for the platinum version, sold only in a case containing a men's and a lady's version (with the same movements, and two brilliants set on the dial). Its main feature is the caliber PP88, tonneau-curved movement, built in 1937 and completely restyled by Paul Picot. This involved the adoption of an Incabloc antishock system, a Glucydur balance, a Nivarox balance-spring, a Paul Picot proprietary power reserve indication module and beveled profiles finished with a Vagues de Genève and circular graining decoration for of the bridges.
Price: 22'200 CHF. Limited edition. Sold only in a case together with a men's version (total price 45'600 CHF).

FIRSHIRE 1937 HAND WINDING — REF. 4070

Movement: mechanical, manual winding, caliber Paul Picot 88 (basic movement ETA cal. 735, 1937 production), autonomy of 42 hours, 17 jewels; Glucydur balance, 18,000 vibrations per hour (vph), Nivarox 1 balance-spring, Incabloc shock-resistant system. Beveled, Vagues de Genève and circular graining finish.
Functions: hour, minute, small second, power reserve.
Case: stainless steel, three-piece tonneau case (size 36 mm, width 33 mm, thickness 10.5 mm); curved sapphire crystal; screw-down crown; case back attached by 4 screws, displaying the movement through a sapphire crystal. Water-resistant to 5 atm.
Dial: solid silver, silvered with engine turned (guilloché) decoration of the hour ring; applied burnished pointed markers and Arabic numerals 3, 9, 12; printed minute track; burnished sword style hands.
Indications: power reserve at 1, small second at 6.
Strap: crocodile leather; stainless steel clasp.
Price: 6'950 CHF. Limited edition.
Also available: pink gold 13'500; lady's version donna pink gold and yellow gold 12'000 CHF.

FIRSHIRE TONNEAU PERPETUAL CALENDAR — REF. 154-33

Movement: mechanical, automatic winding, caliber DD 5100, autonomy of 47 hours; Glucydur balance, Nivarox balance-spring, Nivaflex main spring. Decorated with Vagues de Genève pattern. Completely mounted, finished and checked by Paul Picot.
Functions: hour, minute, perpetual calendar (date, day, month, year, moon phase).
Case: 18 kt white gold, three-piece tonneau case (with lugs size 42x34 mm, thickness 10 mm); curved sapphire crystal; screw-down crown in gold with embossed logo, for the correction of the whole calendar; case back attached by 4 screws. Water-resistant to 5 atm.
Dial: solid silver, engine turned (guilloché); applied Arabic numerals, in gold; printed railway minute track; white gold Pomme hands.
Indications: date at 3, moon phase at 6, day at 9, month and four year cycle at 12.
Strap: crocodile leather; white gold clasp.
Price: Price: 30'450 CHF. Edition limited to 30 numbered pieces.
Also available: in yellow or pink gold 29'750 CHF.

235

PAUL PICOT

FIRSHIRE RONDE POWER RESERVE — REF. 4045/B

Movement: mechanical, automatic winding, caliber PP 1230. Vagues de Genève finished.
Functions: hour, minute, small second, date, power reserve.
Case: stainless steel, three-piece case (Ø 34 mm, thickness 9.5 mm); curved sapphire crystal; one corrector on case side; screw-down crown; case back knurled, fastened by 4 screws. Water-resistant to 3 atm. 
Dial: black, engine turned (guilloché) with sun pattern in the central part; zones and external ring decorated with concentric-circle pattern; applied pointed markers (Arabic numeral 12); printed minute track; Pomme hands.
Indications: power reserve at 3, small second at 6, date at 9.
Bracelet: steel; fold-over safety clasp.
Price: 4'350 CHF.
Also available: leather strap 3'600; silvered, blue or pink dial.

FIRSHIRE RONDE — REF. 4071/B

Movement: mechanical, automatic winding, caliber PP 1220. Vagues de Genève finish.
Functions: hour, minute, small second, date.
Case: stainless steel, three-piece case (Ø 35 mm, thickness 9.5 mm); curved sapphire crystal; one corrector on case side; screw-down crown; case back knurled, fastened by 4 screws. Water-resistant to 5 atm. 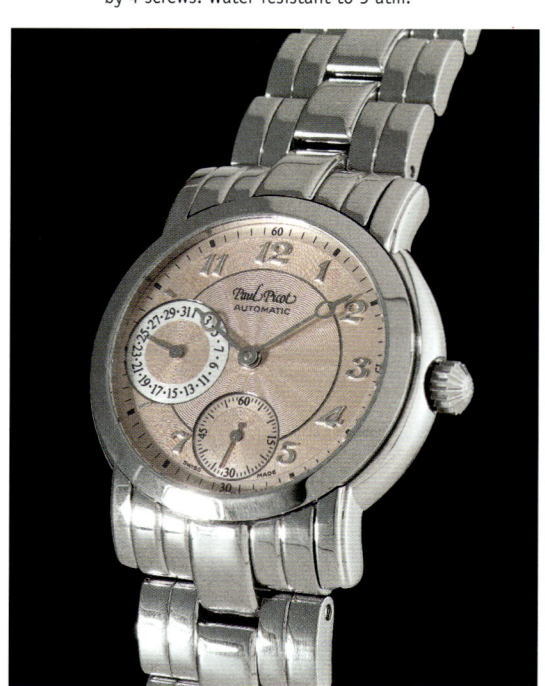
Dial: silvered rosé, engine turned (guilloché) with sun pattern in the central part; zones and external ring decorated with concentric-circle pattern; applied Arabic numerals; printed minute track; Pomme hands.
Indications: small second at 6, date at 9.
Bracelet: steel; fold-over safety clasp.
Price: 4'100 CHF.
Also available: leather strap 3'350 CHF; silvered, blue or pink dial.

FIRSHIRE RONDE 2-BARRELS AUTOMATIC — REF. 4082/B

Movement: mechanical, automatic winding, with Double winding barrel, autonomy of 100 hours. Vagues de Genève finish.
Functions: hour, minute, center second, date.
Case: stainless steel, three-piece case (Ø 37 mm, thickness 8 mm); curved sapphire crystal; snap-on case back knurled. Water-resistant to 5 atm.
Dial: silvered, engine turned (guilloché); applied Roman numerals and burnished; printed minute track; Dauphine hands, burnished.
Indications: date at 3.
Bracelet: steel; fold-over safety clasp.
Price: 3'600 CHF.

FIRSHIRE RONDE REGULATEUR — REF. 4081

Movement: mechanical, automatic winding, caliber PP 1120. Vagues de Genève finish.
Functions: off-center hour, center minute, small second, date.
Case: stainless steel, three-piece case (Ø 37.5 mm, thickness 9.5 mm); curved sapphire crystal; snap-on back. Water-resistant to 5 atm.
Dial: black, with zones silvered and engine turned (guilloché) with basket pattern; printed Arabic hour numerals; luminescent Arabic minute numerals; luminescent markers on the white printed minute track; Pomme hour hand, white painted Pomme minute hand.
Indications: small second at 6, date at 9, off-center hour at 12.
Strap: crocodile leather; stainless steel clasp.
Price: 3'300 CHF.
Also available: silvered dial and black zones (same price).

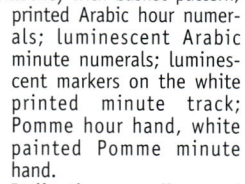

PAUL PICOT

FIRSHIRE RONDE ANNUAL CHRONODATE   REF. 4090

Movement: mechanical, automatic winding (ETA caliber 2892 base + Dubois-Dépraz chrono/calendar plate). Vagues de Genève finish.
Functions: hour, minute, small second, annual calendar (date and month - keeps automatically the count of months with 30 and 31 days, and needs correction only in February), chronograph with 3 counters.
Case: stainless steel, three-piece case; curved sapphire crystal; rectangular pushers; snap-on back. Water-resistant to 5 atm.
Dial: black; zones decorated with concentric-circle pattern; applied Roman numerals; printed minute track; Dauphine hands.
Indications: small second at 3, month between 4 and 5, hour counter at 6, minute counter at 9, center second counter, big date at 12; minute track with divisions for 1/5 of a second, tachymeter scale on the beveled ring.
Strap: crocodile leather; stainless steel clasp.
Price: 5'250 CHF.
Also available: silvered dial (same price)

FIRSHIRE RONDE CHRONODATE   REF. 4089

Movement: mechanical, automatic winding (ETA caliber 2892 base + Dubois-Dépraz chrono/calendar plate). Vagues de Genève finish.
Functions: hour, minute, small second, date, chronograph with 3 counters.
Case: stainless steel, three-piece case; curved sapphire crystal; rectangular pushers; snap-on back. Water-resistant to 5 atm.
Dial: black; zones decorated with concentric-circle pattern; applied Roman numerals; printed minute track; Dauphine hands.
Indications: small second at 3, hour counter at 6, minute counter at 9, center second counter, big date at 12; minute track with divisions for 1/5 of a second, tachymeter scale on the beveled ring.
Strap: crocodile leather; stainless steel clasp.
Price: 3'700 CHF.
Also available: silvered dial (same price).

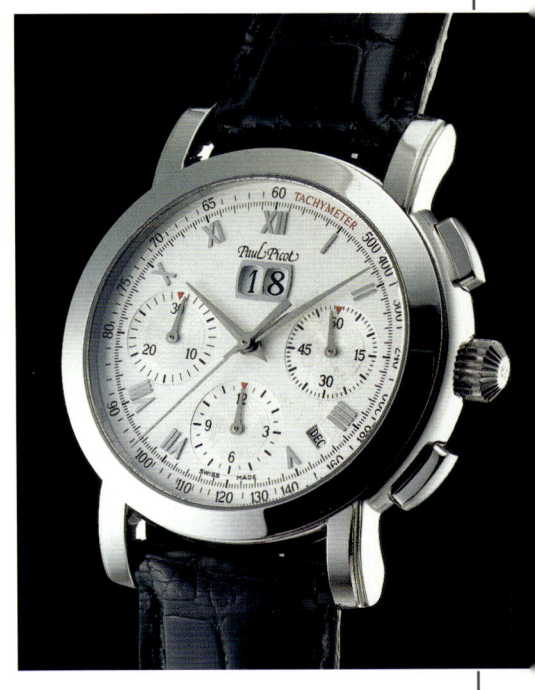

FIRSHIRE RONDE AUTODATE   REF. 4091

Movement: mechanical, automatic winding, Paul Picot caliber PP1120. Vagues de Genève finish.
Functions: hour, minute, small second, date.
Case: stainless steel, three-piece case; curved sapphire crystal; snap-on back. Water-resistant to 5 atm.
Dial: silvered; applied bâton markers; printed minute track; bâton hands.
Indications: small second at 6, big date at 12.
Strap: crocodile leather; stainless steel clasp.
Price: 3'250 CHF.

ATELIER MINUTE REPEATER

Movement: mechanical, manual winding, caliber PP 818 (Lemania 399 base).
Functions: hour, minute, small second, minute repeater.
Case: 18 kt yellow gold, three-piece case (Ø 37 mm); bezel and case side knurled; flat sapphire crystal; repeater slide on case side; yellow gold crown; knurled case back attached by 4 screws, displaying the movement through a sapphire crystal. Water-resistant to 3 atm.
Dial: solid silver, engine turned (guilloché); applied yellow gold Roman numerals; printed minute track; yellow gold Pomme hands.
Indications: small second at 9.
Strap: crocodile leather; yellow gold clasp.
Price: 150'000 CHF, appr. Limited edition.

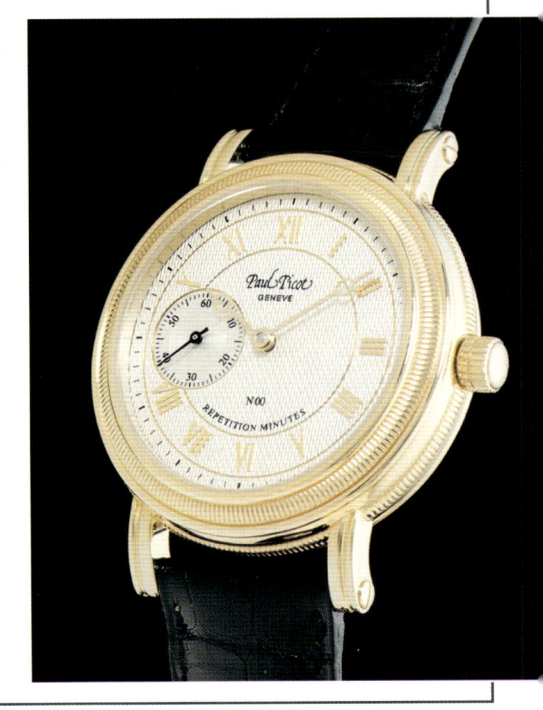

237

PAUL PICOT

ATELIER MARRAKECH REGULATEUR "1100"   REF. 4029

Movement: mechanical, automatic winding, caliber PP 1100, gold rotor. Vagues de Genève finish. Officially certified "chronometer" (C.O.S.C.).
Functions: off-center hour, central minute, small seconds, date, power reserve.
Case: stainless steel, three-piece case (Ø 40 mm, thickness 10 mm), knurled; flat sapphire crystal; one corrector on case side; screw-down crown protected by two shoulders fastened on the case by two screws; case back knurled, fastened by six screws, displaying the movement through a sapphire crystal. Water-resistant to 3 atm.
Dial: black, luminescent Arabic hour numerals; luminescent white painted sword style hands; luminescent Arabic minute numerals; white printed minute track.
Indications: off-center hour at 12, center minute, power reserve at 3, small second at 6, date at 9.
Strap: leather, quilted by hand; stainless steel clasp.
Price: 5'750 CHF.
Also available: with bracelet 22'400 CHF; pink gold (same prices); yellow gold & stainless steel, strap 7'250, bracelet 8'850; steel, strap 5'750 CHF, bracelet 6'700 CHF. All available with silvered or black dial.

ATELIER MARRAKECH POWER RESERVE "1200"   REF. 4028

Movement: mechanical, automatic winding, caliber PP 1200, gold rotor. decorated with circular graining pattern. Officially certified "chronometer" (C.O.S.C.).
Functions: hour, minute, center second, date, power reserve.
Case: stainless steel, three-piece case (Ø 37 mm, thickness 10.3 mm), knurled; flat sapphire crystal; one corrector on case side; screw-down crown protected by two shoulders fastened on the case by two screws; case back knurled, fastened by six screws, displaying the movement through a sapphire crystal. Water-resistant to 5 atm.
Dial: black, luminescent Arabic numerals; luminescent white painted sword style hands; luminescent markers on the white printed minute track.
Indications: power reserve at 3, date at 9.
Strap: leather, hand quilted; stainless steel clasp.
Price: 5'400 CHF.
Also available: with bracelet 6'400; steel and yellow gold strap 6'850, bracelet 8'450; yellow or pink gold, strap 12'400, bracelet 22'150; lefthander version (crown on the left, same prices). Medium (Ø 35 mm, thickness 9,3): steel, strap 4'950, bracelet 5'900; steel and yellow gold, strap 5'900, bracelet 7'500; yellow or pink gold, strap 10'750, bracelet 20'450. All with silvered dial, the pink gold also with black dial and pink sectors.

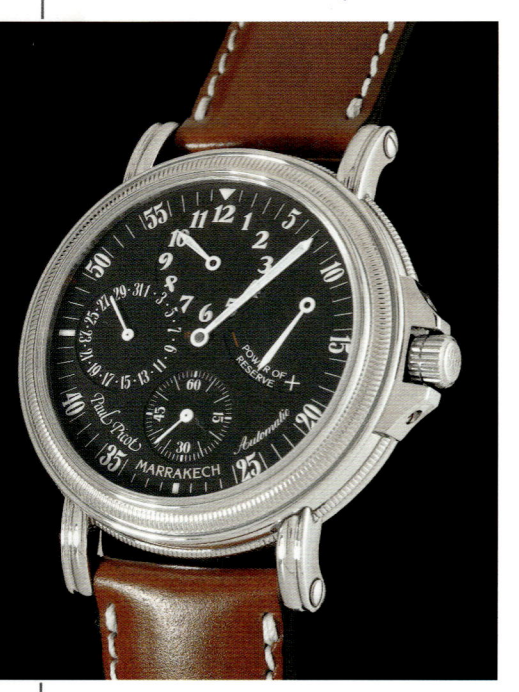

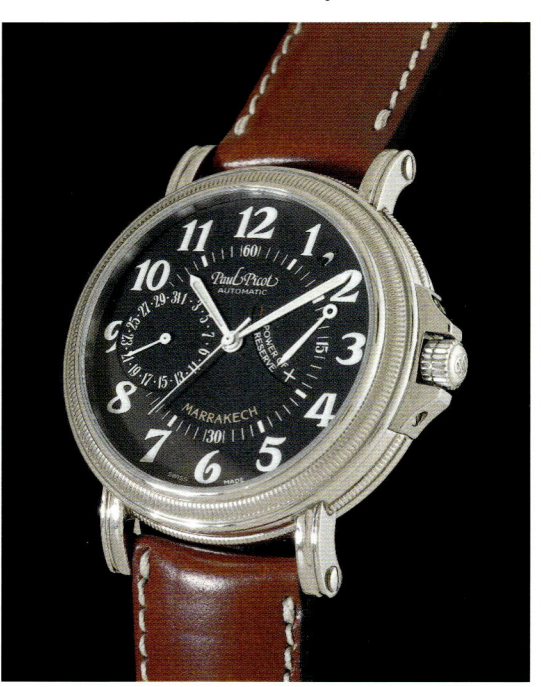

ATELIER AUTOMATIC   REF. 4026/B

Movement: mechanical, automatic winding, autonomy of 47 hours, 21 jewels; Glucydur balance, non-magnetic, Nivarox balance-spring, Incabloc shock-resistant system. Vagues de Genève finish. **Functions:** hour, minute, center second, date.
Case: stainless steel, three-piece case, knurled (Ø 37 mm, thickness 9 mm); flat sapphire crystal; screw-down crown protected by two shoulders fastened on the case by two screws; case back knurled, fastened by six screws. Water-resistant to 5 atm.
Dial: black; luminescent Arabic numerals; white printed minute track; luminescent skeletonized sword style hands.
Indications: date at 3.
Bracelet: stainless steel, fold-over safety clasp.
Price: 3'100 CHF.
Also available: with strap 2'150 CHF; with silvered or black dial, applied Roman numerals; steel and yellow gold, silvered, gilded or black dial, applied Roman numerals or black, luminescent Arabic numerals, strap 3'750 CHF, bracelet 5'350; yellow gold, silvered, gilded or black dial, applied Roman numerals or black, luminescent Arabic numerals, strap 7'400 CHF, bracelet 17'150 CHF; pink gold, silvered, pink or black dial, applied Roman numerals or black, luminescent Arabic numerals, strap 7'400 CHF, bracelet 17'150 CHF.

ATELIER AUTOMATIC   REF. 82

Paul Picot is at its best with the Atelier collection. Also the basic models, as the Automatic in yellow gold (Ø 33 mm, thickness 9), are finished at the highest quality level. The movement is a caliber ETA 2892-A2, completely revised and corrected by Paul Picot's technicians. Each individual element is unmounted and the raw piece is hand-finished. Glucydur balance, balance-spring in Nivarox 1 and Nivaflex winding spring are adopted, i.e. virtually the best with respect to stable performances and resistance to temperature changes. But this is not all - the bridges of the whole movement are decorated with circular graining pattern and finished by hand, screws are flame-blued, the rotor in 21 kt gold is skeletonized, engine turned (guilloché) and Paul Picot personalized.
Price: 6'750 CHF.
Also available: bracelet 15'650 CHF; gilded or black dial, applied Roman numerals or black luminescent Arabic pink gold, silvered, pink or black dial, applied Roman numerals or black, luminescent Arabic, strap 6'750 CHF, bracelet 15'650 CHF; steel and yellow gold, silvered, gilded or black dial, applied Roman numerals or black, luminescent Arabic, strap 3'500 CHF, br. 4'900 CHF; steel, silvered or black dial, applied Roman numerals or black, luminescent Arabic, strap 2'150 CHF, br. 3'100 CHF.

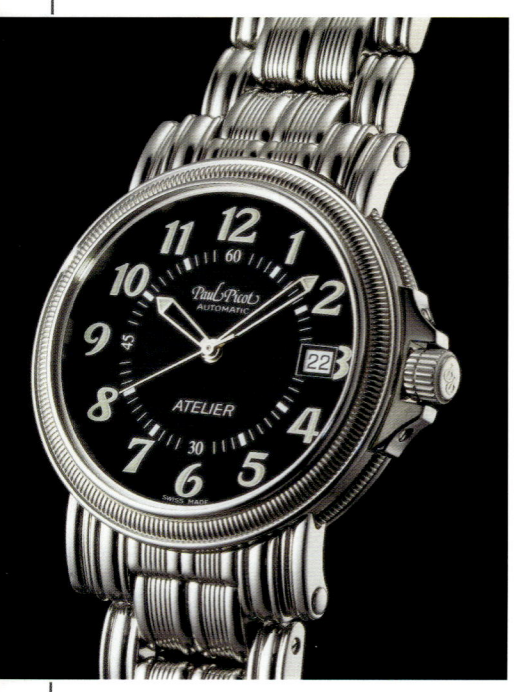

PAUL PICOT

ATELIER TECHNICUM REF. 103.33

Movement: mechanical, automatic winding, caliber PP 8888. Hand-finished. Officially certified "chronometer" (C.O.S.C.).
Functions: hour, minute, small second, day-date, power reserve, split-second chronograph with 2 counters.
Case: 18 kt white gold, three-piece case (Ø 40.5 mm, thickness 15 mm); curved sapphire crystal; white gold screw-down crown with case protection; split-second pusher between 7 and 8; one corrector on case side; case back attached by 6 screws, displaying the movement through a sapphire crystal. Water-resistant to 5 atm.
Dial: solid silver; applied pointed markers in white gold; Pomme hands in blued stainless steel.
Indications: date at 3, power reserve at 6, small second at 9, minute counter and day at 12, center second and split-second counters, minute track with divisions for 1/5 of a second, tachymeter scale on the beveled ring.
Strap: crocodile leather; white gold clasp.
Price: 27'400 CHF.
Also available: in yellow gold, strap 24'100, bracelet 32'400; pink gold, strap 24'100; yellow gold & stainless steel, strap 17'100; steel, strap 13'950, bracelet 14'700.

ATELIER CHRONOGRAPH RATTRAPANTE REF. 100

Movement: mechanical, manual winding, caliber PP 310 (Venus 179 base, of the Forties, modified to obtain the complete calendar), autonomy of 38 hours, Glucydur balance, Breguet overcoil balance-spring, regulator system with micrometer adjustment and regulator spring, Incabloc shock-resistant system. Finished and decorated by hand with Vagues de Genève pattern. **Functions:** hour, minute, small second, full calendar (date, day, month, moon phase), split-second chronograph with 2 counters.
Case: 18 kt yellow gold, three-piece case, knurled; curved sapphire crystal; yellow gold crown with pusher; yellow gold oval pushers; case back attached by 8 screws, displaying the movement through a sapphire crystal. Water-resistant to 5 atm.
Dial: solid silver, engine turned (guilloché); screen-printed Roman numerals; Pomme hands in blued stainless steel.
Indications: minute counter at 3, month and moon at 6, small second at 9, day-date at 12, center second and split-second counters, minute track with divisions for 1/5 of a second, tachymeter scale.
Strap: crocodile leather; yellow gold clasp.
Price: 82'100 CHF.
Edition of 200 pieces.
Also available: platinum, 110'000 CHF, 3 pieces.

ATELIER FLINQUE REF. 84/S

Movement: mechanical, automatic winding, autonomy of 47 hours, 21 jewels; Glucydur balance, non-magnetic, Nivarox balance-spring, Incabloc shock-resistant system. Vagues de Genève finish.
Functions: hour, minute, center second, date.
Case: 18 kt yellow gold, three-piece case (Ø 37, thickness 9 mm); flat sapphire crystal; flinqué and green enameled bezel; knurled case side; screw-down crown in gold with embossed logo, protected by two shoulders fastened on the case by two gold screws; case back attached by 6 screws, knurled, engine turned (guilloché) by the champlevé technique and enameled. Water-resistant to 5 atm.
Dial: silvered, engine turned (guilloché); applied yellow gold Roman numerals; printed minute track; yellow gold Pomme hands.
Indications: date at 3.
Strap: crocodile leather; screw connection; gold clasp.
Price: 12'400 CHF.
Edition of 30 numbered pieces for each bezel color.
Also available: pink gold (same price); with blue, white or red enameled bezel. With case diameter 33 mm, in yellow gold, 12'400 CHF.

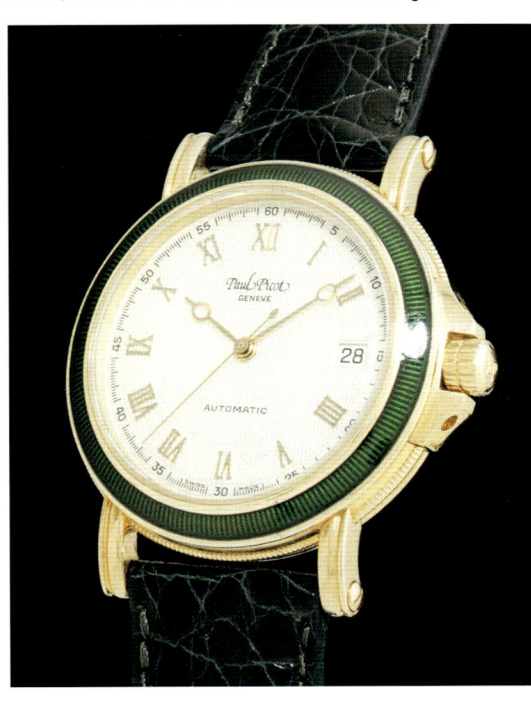

MINICHRON REF. 4032/B

Movement: mechanical, automatic winding (Lemania 283A base), 39 jewels. Balance in Glucydur, 28.000 vibrations per hour (vph). Hand-finished and decorated with Côtes de Genève pattern.
Functions: hour, minute, small second, date, chronograph with 3 counters.
Case: stainless steel, three-piece case (Ø 36 mm, thickness 12 mm); flat sapphire crystal; knurled bezel with engraved tachymeter scale; screw-down crown; screwed-on case back, with engraving. Water-resistant to 5 atm.
Dial: black; zones silvered, decorated with concentric-circle pattern; applied pointed markers; luminescent dots on the minute track; luminescent Alpha hands.
Indications: date with magnifying glass at 3, hour counter at 6, small second at 9, minute counter at 12, center second counter; minute track with divisions for 1/5 of a second, pulsometer scale on the beveled ring.
Bracelet: steel; fold-over safety clasp.
Price: 2'900 CHF.
Also available: leather strap 2'450 CHF; yellow gold & stainless steel, leather strap 2'900 CHF, bracelet 3'750 CHF; white, silvered, blue, champagne, bordeaux, green, grey dial, counters with the same or contrasting color.

239

PAUL PICOT

MONZA CHRONOGRAPH   REF. 4003/AB

Movement: mechanical, automatic winding, PP 284/1 (Lemania 283A base), autonomy of 42 hours, 39 jewels, 28,000 vibrations per hour (vph). Beveled bridges and Côtes de Genève finished pillar-plates.
Functions: hour, minute, small second, date, chronograph with 3 counters.
Case: stainless steel, three-piece case (Ø 42 mm, thickness 13); flat sapphire crystal; knurled bezel with engraved tachymeter scale; tag with the model name fixed on the case side by two titanium screws; crown with case protection and patented screw-down pushers; screwed-on case back displaying the movement through a sapphire crystal. Water-resistant to 10 atm.
Dial: yellow; logo Monza motor-racing track; printed Arabic numerals; luminescent dots on the minute track; luminescent black painted bâton hands.
Indications: date with magnifying glass at 3, hour counter at 6, minute counter at 9, small second at 12, center second counter, telemeter scale on the beveled ring.
Bracelet: steel; fold-over safety clasp.
Price: 4'150 or 4'450 CHF. Realized for the 75th anniversary of the Monza motor-racing track, 225 numbered pieces for each dial.
Also available: black, blue, red or white dial; leather strap 3'600 CHF.

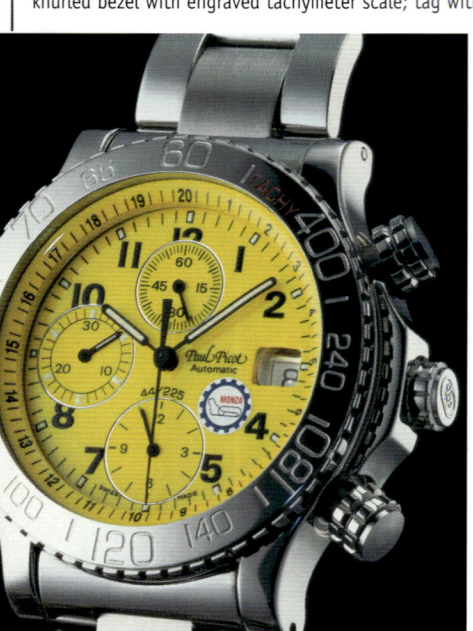

CHRONOGRAPH   REF. 5265

Movement: mechanical, automatic winding, cal. PP 284/1 (Lemania 283A base), 21 kt gold rotor, realized on an exclusive basis, 39 jewels. Balance in Glucydur, 28.000 vph. Hand-finished and decorated with Côtes de Genève pattern. **Functions:** hour, minute, small second, date, chronograph with 3 counters. **Case:** 18 kt yellow gold, three-piece case (Ø 42, thickness 13); flat sapphire crystal; knurled counter-clockwise turning bezel, sapphire ring and minute track; tag with model name fixed on the case side with 2 gold screws; crown with case protection and patented screw-down gold pushers; sapphire glass screwed-on case back. Waterproof 10 atm. **Dial:** black; luminescent applied square markers; luminescent bâton hands. **Indications:** date with magnifying glass at 3, hour counter at 6, minute counter at 9, small second at 12, center second counter, telemeter. on the beveled ring. **Strap:** crocodile leather, screw connection; gold clasp.
Price: 14'100 CHF.
Also available: br. 21'600; steel, strap 3'800, br. 4'650; steel/gold, strap 5'950, br. 7'450; fixed tachymeter bezel (steel, strap 3'700, br. 4'550; steel/yellow gold-red gold, strap 5'750, br. 6'700; yellow gold/red gold, strap 14'100, br. 21'600); white dial or silv. guill., Roman numerals; "5009", dial blue, black, white, strap 4'950, br. 5'950; "Mito", red dial, strap 5'950, br. 7'450.

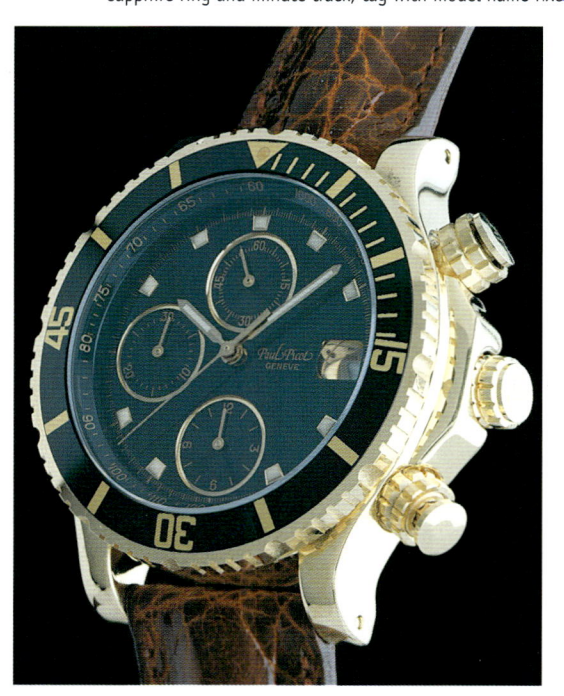

CARRE GALBE   REF. 65/B

Movement: mechanical, manual winding, caliber PP 775. Balance in Glucydur. Completely rhodium plated and decorated with Vagues de Genève pattern. Platelet on upper bridge with engraved brand name.
Functions: hour, minute.
Case: 18 kt yellow gold, two-piece square-curved case (height 26 mm, width 25 mm, thickness 6.5 mm); curved sapphire crystal; crown-protecting side element fixed by 2 gold screws; gold screw-down crown, case back attached by 4 screws. Water-resistant to 3 atm.
Dial: silvered, curved; applied Roman numerals and bâton markers; printed minute track; bâton hands.
Bracelet: in yellow gold; fold-over safety clasp.
Price: on request. Limited edition.
Also available: with strap 5'700; red gold, strap 5'700 CHF; steel, strap 2'250 CHF, bracelet 3'000 CHF; steel/gold strap 3'300 CHF; lady's size: steel, strap 2'250 CHF, bracelet 3'000 CHF; steel/gold, strap 2'750, bracelet on request; yellow or pink gold, strap 11'600 CHF. Each version is available with black, silvered or white dial and as jewel watch.

CARRE GALBE LADY   REF. 4019/B

The shaped watch, which came back into fashion at the end of the Nineties, is perhaps the most suitable to identify the ideal "classical" watch. However its realization involves great technical problems, mainly with respect to its water-tightness, which is more difficult to obtain with an angled case than with a curved one, but also style-related problems, in order to maintain visual balance among the different components (dial, case and bracelet). This task was brilliantly accomplished by Paul Picot with this Carré Galbé. It is a model accurately worked out as to its proportions, with a slightly curved case, lugs longer than average, and a discrete and elegant dial. The result is a watch easy to use at any occasion. The photograph shows the lady's version (height 26 mm, width 25 mm, thickness 10 mm).
Price: on request.

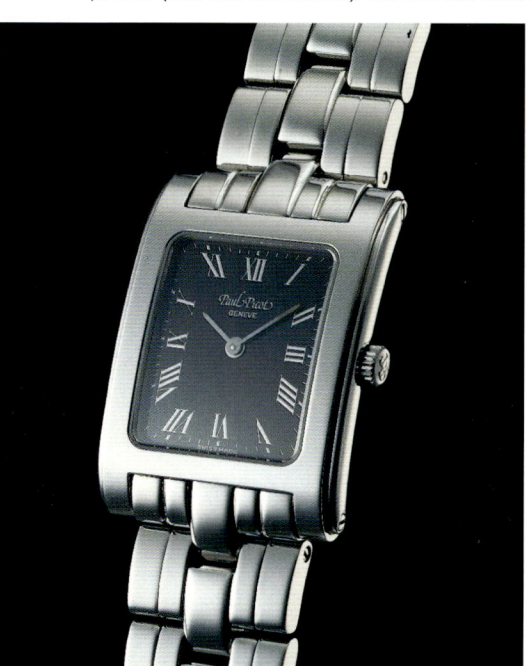

PAUL PICOT

AMERICAN BRIDGE — REF. 4075

Movement: mechanical, automatic winding, Eta caliber 2000. Vagues de Genève finish.
Functions: hour, minute, center second, date.
Case: stainless steel, two-piece square case curved both horizontally and vertically (size 42 mm, width 26 mm); curved sapphire crystal matching the bezel profile; case back attached by 4 screws, with an engraving. Water-resistant to 5 atm.
Dial: silvered (two tones), curved; printed Roman numerals and railway minute track; luminescent sword style hands.
Indications: date at 6.
Strap: colonial leather; stainless steel fold-over clasp.
Price: 2'200 CHF.
Also available: with bracelet 2'550 CHF; with copper, black or blue dial; applied Arabic or Roman numerals. Also with quartz movement.

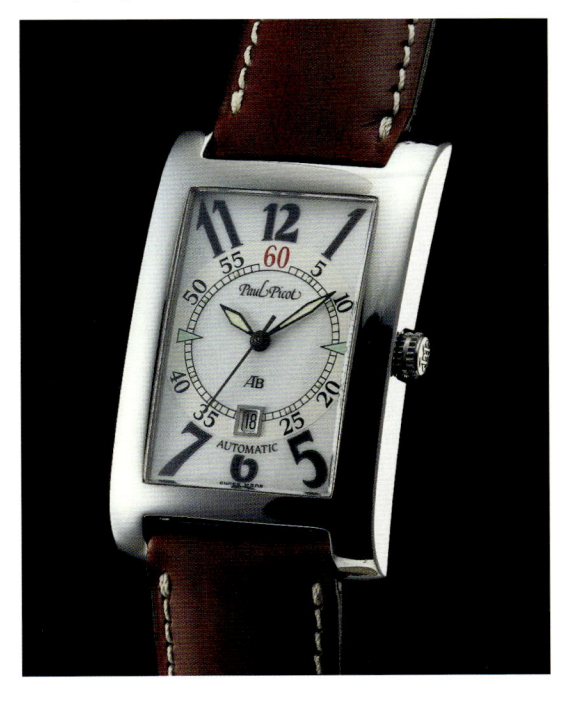

"4889" CHRONOGRAPH — REF. 5190

Movement: mechanical, manual winding (Lemania 1874 base), autonomy of 50 hours and 17 jewels (Ø 27 mm, 12''', thickness 6.8 mm). Balance with 21,600 vibrations per hour (vph), flat balance-spring with micrometer adjustment, Incabloc shock-resistant system. hand-decorated with Côtes de Genève pattern.
Functions: hour, minute, small second, chronograph with 3 counters.
Case: 18 kt yellow gold, three-piece case (Ø 35 mm, thickness 13 mm); curved sapphire crystal; pushers with case protection and crown, in gold; case back attached by 8 screws, displaying the movement through a sapphire crystal. Waterproof to 5 atm.
Dial: white enameled; bâton hands; applied bâton markers.
Indications: minute counter at 3, hour counter at 6, small second at 9, center second counter, minute track, tachymeter scale on the beveled ring.
Strap: crocodile leather; yellow gold clasp.
Price: 8'650 CHF.
Also available: pink gold (same price); yellow or pink gold & stainless steel 4'750 CHF; steel 4'250 CHF. Each version is available with black dial, bâton markers or white dial, bâton markers or Roman numerals.

"4888" CHRONOGRAPH — REF. 4888/B

Movement: mechanical, manual winding, autonomy of 50 hours and 17 jewels (Ø 27 mm, 12''', thickness 6.8 mm). Balance with 21,600 vibrations per hour (vph), flat balance-spring with micrometer adjustment, Incabloc shock-resistant system.
Functions: hour, minute, small second, chronograph with 3 counters.
Case: stainless steel gold-plated, two-piece case (Ø 35 mm, thickness 13 mm); bombé glass; steel crown and pushers; case back attached by 8 screws. Water-resistant to 3 atm.
Dial: ivory and gilded counters; Roman numerals; bâton hands black enameled.
Indications: minute counter at 3, hour counter at 6, small second at 9, center second counter, minute track with divisions for 1/5 of a second.
Strap: crocodile leather; central attachment with handle-type lugs; stainless steel clasp.
Price: 2'700 CHF.
Also available: stainless steel 2'450 CHF.

"4888 MOON PHASE" CHRONOGRAPH — REF. 4973

"4888" is the reference which has been characterizing Paul Picot's chronographs since October 1984. Simple rounded shapes and proportions agreeable at touch and sight, winding curves, a bombé glass matching the case shape and the two typical "handles" as lugs for the leather strap allowed it to overcome the fashion of super-sporting angled chronographs and to become a reference point within the world of chronographs. Thanks to its style, this model has been associated also with golf, which gave it an extremely suggestive image, inducing many imitation attempts during the last years. The chronograph 4888 is proposed in stainless steel or gold-plated with a wide choice of colors for the crocodile leather straps and dials with counters having the same or - conversely - contrasting colors. The photograph shows the version in stainless steel, blue dial and date and moon phase indication at 12.
Price: 2'850 CHF.
Also available: gold-plated stainless steel 3'100 CHF; with Roman numerals; white dial, bâton markers or Roman numerals.

241

Piaget

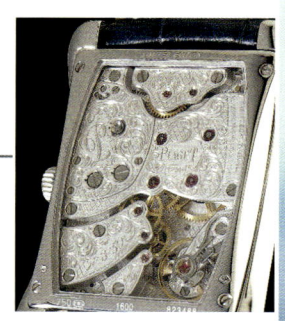

This venerable Swiss company marks its 125th anniversary with two limited-edition models. One is the rectangular "à l'Ancienne", in 18k white or pink gold. It has a 20-jewel mechanical movement (calibre 441P) with small seconds subdial, power reserve indicator at 6 o'clock, calendar at 3 o'clock and 40-hour power reserve. A total of 125 pieces have been produced, 10 of them in pink gold, the rest in yellow. The other commemorative watch is the eight-day Emperador. It has an eight-day power reserve, an extremely rare feature, with power reserve indicator at 12 o'clock. It also has a jumping hours indicator, right below the power reserve indicator. There's a small seconds subdial at 6 o'clock. The caseback is made of transparent sapphire crystal. The dial is guilloched and has gold hour markers. Fifty pieces were produced in 18k yellow, white and pink gold. Piaget also has several new designs for women. The company's Dancer collection now includes square-cased models with Manchette bracelets made of tiny interlocked yellow- or white-gold bars. One version has a pave diamond bezel; another is entirely covered with pave diamonds. Also new are gem-set Protocole models, one with a pave bezel, the other with a pave bezel and dial. The company's Haute Joaillerie collection has been expanded with a women's model with a mechanical movement. The elaborate, extravagant watch is set with 179 diamonds, plus 6 rubies and a 37-carat pink spinel that serves as a cover for the watch dial. When the wearer wants to read

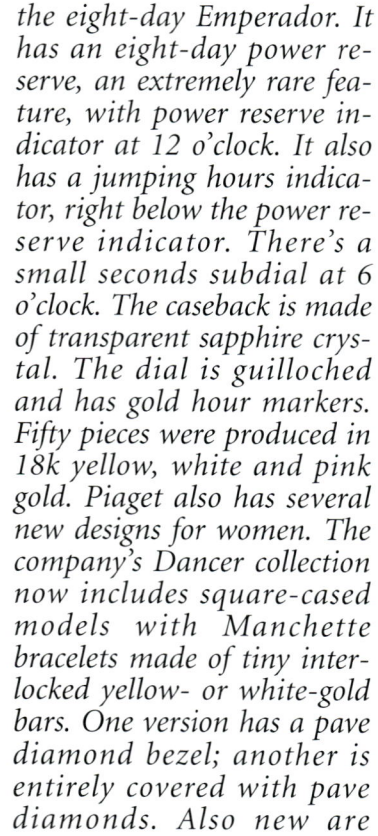

The History

In the remote Val de Travers, during the last century, the first economic activity to flourish besides the original agricultural vocation of the area, was lace making. Only after a while did matchmaking begin to interest a broader and broader part of the working population, and the deep memory of those light pieces of precious lace must have permanently colored the imagination of those master watchmakers... This can certainly be seen in the jewelled watches created by Piaget.

Founded in 1874 in La Côte-aux-Fées by nineteen-year-old Georges Piaget - but there are precious pocket watches dating earlier than this bearing the name Piaget and of the place it was built - the shop for a long time produced components, movements and even complete watches for other Houses, such as Rolex, Omega, Zenith, Vacheron Constantin, Cartier and more. With so much experience, second and third generation descendants threw themselves confidently into the watchmaking arena, building a plant in Geneva as well.

1944 - Géraldin and Valentin Piaget, Georges grandchildren, take over the Company. Géraldin managed the commercial and styling sectors, and Valentin the production of movements. The next year a new modern plant was inaugurated with 200 workers.

1950's - Géraldin Piaget travels throughout the world and makes watches for wealthy clients. There is a story about an Eastern ruler who wanted to give a watch to each of his wives, but it is impossible for a foreigner to meet them even in order to discover their tastes. Using a stratagem, the Piaget representative enters the apartments in their absence and, studying the furnishings, succeeds in understanding the types they are. Back in Geneva, those rapid glances at toilettes and dormeuses are translated into fabulous watches that obviously meet with enormous success. Valentin builds the famous Calibre 9P in 1956, an extra thin manual, 2 mm high. This piece, with few modifications, is still in use. At the end of the decade, 1960, Piaget patents the automatic Calibre 12P with gold rotor, 2.3 mm high and confirms his decision to construct watches only in gold, platinum and precious stones. Géraldin's son, Yves, comes into the Company.

1956-57 - The collaboration with the Master Louis Cottier and the painter Carlo Poluzzi, a great enamelist, leads to the creation of a unique piece: a pocket watch studded with diamonds. On the back of the case is a hunting scene; on the front, hours and minutes are shown on two half-circles; pressing a button, a serpent moves to indicate the hour, a bird in flight instead points out the minutes.

1964 - Piaget acquires Baume & Mercier.

1970's - Piaget by this time creates trend, and the female public is in love with the pendent watches, worn on long chairs around the neck, and with those set in splendid bracelets with diamonds and precious stones. There are also many original models for men, either pocket or wristwatch models. One memorable pocket model was formed from a small, 24 karat gold ingot that opened like a case to disclose a little watch with an 18 kt. gold case and black dial. Among the most curious wristwatches was one with gold bracelet and case. Onyx and mother of pearl were used on the gold to imitate a piano keyboard, and it fact it had been created for a jazz pianist.

1974 - More that 1,200 watches and jewelled watches are shown in the Company catalogue.

1976 - Piaget, that had been part of the development of the first Swiss quartz movement, Beta 21, presents Calibre 7P that, in 3.1 mm, encloses

...the time, she lifts the hinged cover to reveal the mother-of-pearl, diamond and ruby encrusted dial. Another new haute joaillerie watch, also with a mechanical movement, has a 6.3-carat pear-shaped emerald resting next to the pave-diamond pear-shaped dial. It incorporates 123 diamonds. The buckle alone has 1.5 carats of them.

an electronic module with 900 transistors, perpetual memory for the exact time and changes time zones instantaneously.
1979 - The Polo collection is introduced: extra thin case, 7P quartz.
1981 - The production of fabulous jewelled watches continues. Phoebus, created for a Japanese client, uses 154 grams of platinum and 296 diamonds for a total of 87.87 karats; in the midst of this is a splendid 3.85 karat blue diamond. At the time it cost 3.5 million Swiss francs. Piaget in any case recalls the extra thin models and builds the manual Calibre 20 that wins Guinness recognition for its size: 20.4 mm in diameter, 1.2 mm high. The automatic 25P is constructed around this and its height is 2 mm.
1986 - The Calibre 30P, used especially in the Polo collection, is a very intelligent quartz. The date function is, practically, a perpetual calendar. Should the movement for some reason be disactivated, once it is put back in motion, simply by pressing a button on the back of the case the hands will show the exact hour. The Dancers are invented.
1988 - Cartier, part of the Vendôme Group, acquires Piaget and Baume & Mercier. Piaget produces about 20,000 watches each year.
1990 - The jewellery line, Tanagra, is presented. Almost immediately, precious watches join the line, equipped with mechanical or quartz movements.
1992 - All the Vendôme Group names are present at the 2nd international salon of fine watchmaking at Geneva, and Piaget presents a manual winding in gold. Five Hundred of these watches are made: 200 in yellow gold, 150 in white gold, 50 in pink gold, 100 in platinum. The name is that of Piaget's founder, his signature is engraved on the back.
1994 - To celebrate its 120 years, Piaget builds a diamond studded pocket model split seconds chronograph with minute repeater. There are also four special series of wristwatches with yellow, pink and white gold cases and in platinum; they have mechanical movements and power reserve.
1995 - Piaget stresses its production of mechanical movement watches. The Gouverneur line is increased and at the S.I.H.H. at Geneva in 1996 it has a 35 mm automatic chronometer and a model with the moon phases. Another of this successful series is a wristwatch Grande Sonnerie in pink gold, whose Calibre 13''' is 6.8 mm high. The Citéa aims at a public that loves refined details like decorated gold dials. There is also a new extra-thin and precious dials for the Rectangle à l'Ancienne. The jewelled watches include a minute repeater with diamonds and sapphires, equipped with an antique manual movement restored and carefully engraved, visible behind a crystal case back. 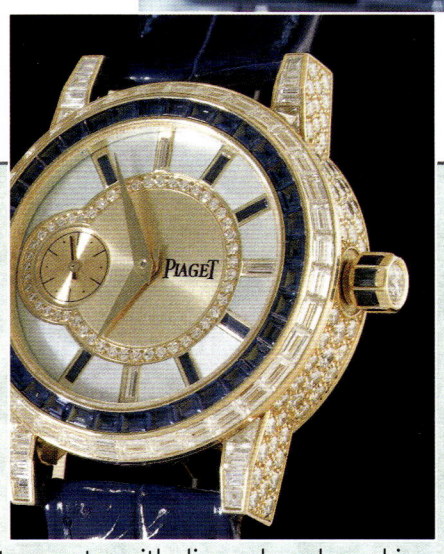
1997 - The production of the Calibre 500P's begins - for women's models or special forms - as well as the 430P. The first Piaget professional underwater model is absolutely new: the Polo Key Largo, two-color gold case surrounded by a vigorous, two directional rotating bezel and Cordura strap, or the new, flexible bracelet formed by little grooved cylinders.
1998 - The year of the Polo Key Largo chronograph, water resistant to 20 atm. The Protocole, an elegant, rectangular watch, slightly curved to make it more pleasing to wear; the new bracelet alternates polished and grooved matte links. A chrono and a quartz are also included in this series,. The versatile Citéa proposes a GMT in white or yellow gold, elegant and simple. The Miss Protocole are pretty and especially unmistakable models for women, with asymmetrical lugs, studded with diamonds or in sophisticated brushed gold, with vertical grooving on one side. The new jewellery line - rings and bracelets have the same names as the most successful models of the watches, combining modern with irresistibly delicate lines.

PIAGET

TRADITION EXTRA-PLAT CHRONOMETER   REF. GOA 22141

Movement: mechanical, automatic winding, extra-thin, Piaget caliber 199P. Officially certified "chronometer" (C.O.S.C.).
Functions: hour, minute, center second, date.
Case: 18 kt white gold, two-piece case (Ø 34 mm, thickness 6 mm); flat sapphire crystal; sapphire cabochon white gold crown with case protection; case back attached by 6 screws. Water-resistant to 3 atm. 
Dial: solid gold, black enameled; bâton markers, 3 printed Breguet numerals; printed minute track; white gold leaf style hands.
Indications: date at 6.
Strap: crocodile leather, hand stitched; white gold tongue clasp.
Also available: in yellow gold; white dial, 4 Breguet digits; silvered or white dial and Roman numerals.
Prices: on request.

ALTIPLANO   REF. GOA 24050

Movement: mechanical, manual winding, extra-thin, Piaget caliber 430P manufacture (derived from the famous caliber Piaget 9P, realized in 1956).
Functions: hour, minute.
Case: 18 kt yellow gold, three-piece case; polished and brushed finish (Ø 34 mm, thickness 5 mm), polished bezel; flat sapphire crystal; yellow gold crown; case back attached by 6 screws, displaying the movement through a sapphire crystal. Water-resistant to 3 atm. 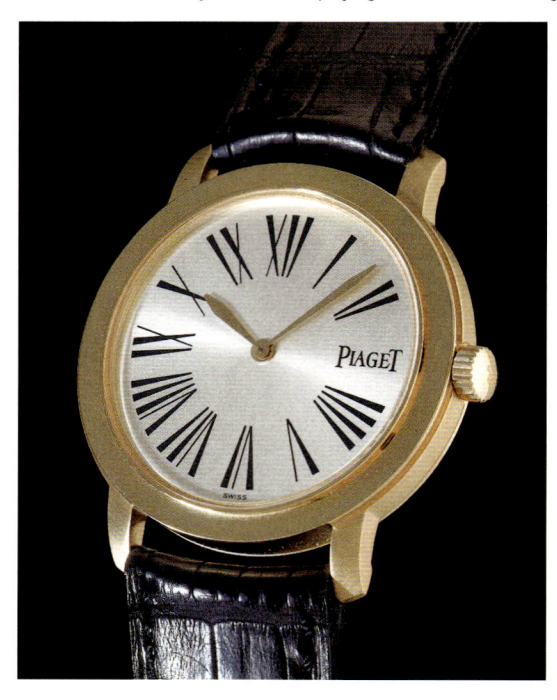
Dial: solid gold, silvered; printed Roman numerals; leaf style hands, in gold.
Strap: crocodile leather, hand stitched; gold tongue clasp.
Also available: white gold with blue metallized dial and screen-printed silvered Roman numerals; with quartz movement caliber 690P.
Prices: on request.

ALTIPLANO CARRE   REF. GOA 24048

Movement: mechanical, manual winding, extra-thin, Piaget caliber 430P manufacture (derived from the famous caliber Piaget 9P, realized in 1956).
Functions: hour, minute.
Case: 18 kt white gold, three-piece square case; polished and brushed finish (height 30 mm, width 30 mm, thickness 5.1 mm); flat sapphire crystal; white gold crown; case back attached by 8 screws, displaying the movement through a sapphire crystal. Water-resistant to 3 atm. 
Dial: solid gold, metallized blue; screen-printed silvered Roman numerals; leaf style hands, in white gold.
Strap: crocodile leather, hand stitched; white gold tongue clasp.
Also available: in yellow gold silvered dial and screen-printed black Roman numerals; with quartz movement caliber 690P.
Prices: on request.

CARRE   REF. GOA 23093

Movement: mechanical, manual winding, extra-thin, Piaget caliber 430P manufacture (derived from the famous caliber Piaget 9P, realized in 1956).
Functions: hour, minute.
Case: 18 kt white gold, two-piece square case (height 29 mm, width 29 mm, thickness 4.3 mm); flat sapphire crystal; sapphire cabochon white gold crown with case protection; case back attached by 8 screws. Water-resistant to 3 atm. 
Dial: solid gold, black enameled; printed Arabic numerals; white gold leaf style hands.
Strap: crocodile leather, hand stitched; gold tongue clasp.
Also available: white dial, screen-printed black Roman numerals; in yellow gold white dial, Arabic numerals or screen-printed black Roman numerals.
Prices: on request.

PIAGET

LEGENDE "EMPERADOR" 8 DAYS JUMPING HOUR   REF. GOA 24064

Movement: mechanical, manual winding, Piaget manufacture caliber 125P (caliber 110 Parmigiani Fleurier base), tonneau-curved (13'''x10''') with double barrel and autonomy of 8 days; balance-spring regulator system with micrometer adjustment and regulator spring. Mounted, engraved and hand-chased.
Functions: jumping hour, minute, small second, power reserve.
Case: 18 kt pink gold, three-piece rectangular case (height 41 mm, width 32 mm, thickness 10 mm); curved sapphire crystal; pink gold crown; case back attached by 4 screws, displaying the movement through a sapphire crystal.
Dial: solid gold, curved, silvered with inside zone engine turned (guilloché); applied pink gold bâton markers.
Indications: small second at 6, jumping hours below 12 with the power reserve indication window above, center minute with gold Dauphine hand.
Strap: crocodile leather, hand stitched; gold tongue clasp.
Also available: yellow gold, 10 pieces.
Prices: on request.
Realized for the 125th anniversary of the House, in a limited edition of 20 pieces. Realized for the 125th anniversary of the House, in a limited edition of 20 pieces.

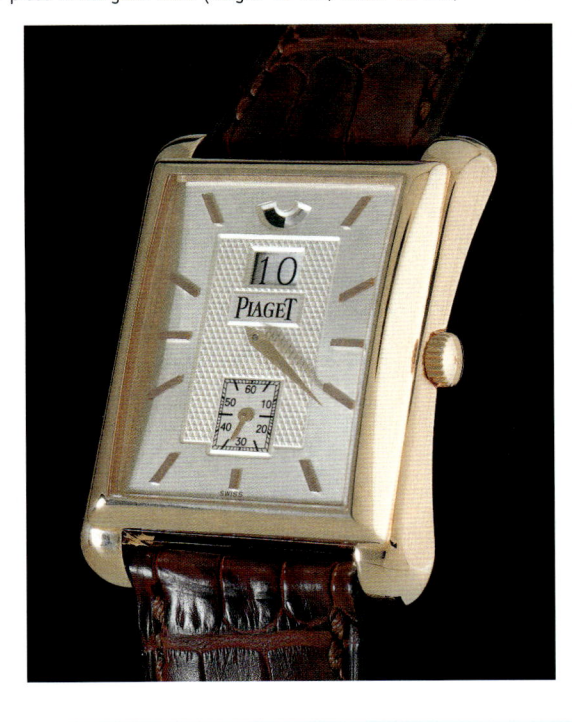

LEGENDE "RECTANGLE A L'ANCIENNE"   REF. GOA 23096

Movement: mechanical, automatic winding, Piaget caliber 500P.
Functions: hour, minute, center second, date.
Case: 18 kt pink gold, two-piece rectangular case (height 35 mm, width 24 mm, thickness 8 mm); curved sapphire crystal; pink gold crown; case back attached by 4 screws. Water-resistant to 3 atm.
Dial: solid gold, silvered, curved; pointed markers and applied pink gold Roman numerals; printed minute track; pink gold Dauphine hands.
Indications: date at 6.
Strap: crocodile leather, hand stitched; recessed coupling; pink gold tongue clasp.
Also available: white gold, pink dial, applied pointed markers and Roman numerals.
Prices: on request.

LEGENDE "RECTANGLE A L'ANCIENNE"   REF. GOA 24061

Movement: mechanical, manual winding, Piaget caliber 431P.
Functions: hour, minute, center second, date, power reserve
Case: 18 kt white gold, two-piece rectangular case (height 35 mm, width 24 mm, thickness 7.8 mm); curved sapphire crystal; white gold crown; case back attached by 4 screws. Water-resistant to 3 atm.
Dial: solid gold, rosé, curved; bâton markers and screen-printed Roman numerals with background in polished natural metal; white gold Dauphine hands.
Indications: date at 3, power reserve at 6, small second at 10.
Strap: crocodile leather, hand stitched; recessed coupling; white gold tongue clasp.
Also available: pink gold with white dial, realized in only 10 pieces exclusively for the Boutiques Piaget.
Prices: on request. Edition limited to 125 pieces to celebrate the 125th anniversary of the House.

PROTOCOLE CAMBRE   REF. GOA 23061

Movement: mechanical, automatic winding, Piaget caliber 520P.
Functions: hour, minute, date.
Case: 18 kt white gold, three-piece rectangular case with beveled angles (height 30 mm, width 26 mm, thickness 7 mm); curved sapphire crystal; bezel decorated with ligné pattern; white gold crown; case back attached by 4 screws. Water-resistant to 3 atm.
Dial: solid gold, white enameled; printed Roman numerals; white gold Dauphine hands.
Indications: date at 6.
Bracelet: white gold with central links decorated with ligné pattern; double fold-over clasp in white gold.
Also available: in yellow gold; with gilt dial and engine turned (guilloché).
Prices: on request.

PIAGET

GOUVERNEUR CHRONOGRAPH RATTRAPANTE   REF. GOA 19118

Movement: mechanical, automatic winding, Piaget caliber 1186P.
Functions: hour, minute, small second, date, split-second chronograph with 3 counters.
Case: 18 kt yellow gold, three-piece case (Ø 34 mm, thickness 11.5 mm); curved sapphire crystal; split-function pusher at 10; yellow gold crown; case back attached by 4 screws. Water-resistant to 3 atm. 
Dial: solid gold, silvered opaline, engine turned (guilloché); logo and applied yellow gold bâton markers; screen-printed Roman numerals; yellow gold Dauphine hands.
Indications: minute counter at 3, small second and date at 6, hour counter at 9, center second and split-second counters, minute track.
Strap: crocodile leather, hand stitched; gold tongue clasp.
Also available: pink gold; applied gold markers.
Prices: on request.

GOUVERNEUR CHRONOGRAPH   REF. GOA 20106

Movement: mechanical, automatic winding, caliber 1185P.
Functions: hour, minute, small second, date, chronograph with 3 counters.
Case: platinum, two-piece case (Ø 34 mm, thickness 10 mm); curved sapphire crystal; case back attached by 4 screws. Water-resistant to 3 atm.
Dial: solid gold, white enameled; printed Arabic numerals; white gold Dauphine hands. 
Indications: minute counter at 3, small second and date at 6, hour counter at 9, center second counter, minute track with divisions for $1/5$ of a second.
Strap: crocodile leather, hand stitched; platinum tongue clasp.
Also available: white gold, brown or pink dial, white Arabic numerals; yellow gold, white dial, black Roman numerals; pink gold, white dial, black Roman numerals.
Prices: on request.

GOUVERNEUR CHRONOMETER   REF. GOA 22094

Movement: mechanical, automatic winding, Piaget caliber 195P, autonomy of 50 hours; pink gold rotor. Officially certified "chronometer" (C.O.S.C.).
Functions: hour, minute, center second, date.
Case: 18 kt white gold, two-piece case (Ø 34 mm, thickness 7 mm); flat sapphire crystal; white gold crown; case back attached by 6 screws. Water-resistant to 3 atm.
Dial: solid gold, silvered, engine turned (guilloché) with sun pattern at the center; printed Roman numerals and railway minute track; white gold Dauphine hands. 
Indications: date at 6.
Strap: crocodile leather, hand stitched; white gold tongue clasp.
Also available: pink gold, engine turned (guilloché) ruthenium dial; yellow gold, white dial or nickel; pink gold, black dial hand-engraved, case back attached by 6 screws, displaying the movement through a sapphire crystal, limited edition of 199 numbered pieces.
Prices: on request.

NOUVELLE CLASSIQUE   REF. GOA 22535

Movement: mechanical, manual winding, extra-thin, Piaget caliber 430P manufacture (derived from the famous caliber Piaget 9P, realized in 1956).
Functions: hour, minute.
Case: 18 kt yellow gold, two-piece case (Ø 31.5 mm, thickness 5.3 mm); flat sapphire crystal; yellow gold crown; snap-on back. Water-resistant to 3 atm.
Dial: solid gold, white enameled; printed Roman numerals; burnished gold leaf style hands. 
Strap: crocodile leather, hand stitched; gold tongue clasp.
Price: on request.

PIAGET

CITEA GMT   REF. GOA 23071

Movement: mechanical, automatic winding, Piaget caliber 428P (28,800 vibrations per hour (vph)).
Functions: hour, minute, center second, date, 24-hour indication, second time zone.
Case: 18 kt yellow gold, three-piece case (Ø 38 mm, thickness 10.5 mm), polished and brushed finish; curved sapphire crystal; yellow gold crown; pusher at 2, in gold, for independent time adjustment; case back attached by 6 screws, displaying the movement through a sapphire crystal. Water-resistant to 3 atm.
Dial: solid gold, silvered; printed Roman numerals; luminescent dots on the printed minute track; silvered gold flange, with 24 hours; luminescent yellow gold Dauphine hands.
Indications: date at 6, luminescent skeletonized second time zone center hand.
Strap: crocodile leather, hand stitched; gold tongue clasp.
Also available: silvered dial, bâton markers and Arabic numerals; white gold.
Prices: on request.

CITEA   REF. GOA 23079

Movement: mechanical, automatic winding, Piaget caliber 197P (10'''1/2), autonomy of 42 hours.
Functions: hour, minute, center second, date.
Case: 18 kt white gold, three-piece case (Ø 35 mm, thickness 8 mm), polished and brushed finish; curved sapphire crystal; white gold crown; case back attached by 6 screws. Water-resistant to 3 atm.
Dial: solid gold, silvered, engine turned (guilloché) with sun pattern; printed Roman numerals; silvered gold flange, engine turned (guilloché); white gold Dauphine hands.
Indications: date at 6.
Strap: crocodile leather, hand stitched; white gold tongue clasp.
Also available: in yellow gold.
Prices: on request.

PIAGET POLO "KEY LARGO" CHRONOGHRAPH   REF. GOA 23033

Movement: mechanical, automatic winding, Piaget caliber 1185P.
Functions: hour, minute, small second, date, chronograph with 3 counters.
Case: 18 kt white gold, three-piece case (Ø 38 mm, thickness 13 mm); grooved lugs; curved sapphire crystal with magnifying lens on date; embossed white gold counter-clockwise turning bezel, luminescent triangular marker at 12 and engraved black painted minute track, useful for the calculation of diving times; white gold screw-down crown with case protection; white gold screw-down pushers; case back attached by 6 small bolts. Water-resistant to 20 atm.
Dial: solid gold, grey enameled and silvered, with with sun pattern decoration; applied white gold pointed markers with luminescent dots; railway minute track; luminescent white gold Dauphine hands.
Indications: minute counter at 3, small second and date at 6, hour counter at 9, minute track with divisions for $1/5$ of a second.
Strap: in "cordura" fabric; white gold fold-over clasp.
Also available: with bracelet; yellow gold, silvered dial, leather strap or bracelet.
Prices: on request.

PIAGET POLO "KEY LARGO"   REF. GOA 22036

Movement: mechanical, automatic winding, Piaget caliber 191P. Officially certified "chronometer" (C.O.S.C.).
Functions: hour, minute, center second, date.
Case: 18 kt yellow gold, three-piece case (Ø 38,5 mm, thickness 11 mm); lugs grooved; curved sapphire crystal with magnifying lens on date; embossed yellow and white gold counter-clockwise turning bezel with luminescent triangular marker at 12 and embossed minute track useful for the calculation of diving times; yellow gold screw-down crown with case protection; case back attached by 6 small bolts. Water-resistant to 20 atm.
Dial: solid gold, black enameled; applied yellow gold pointed markers with luminescent dots; golden railway minute track; luminescent yellow gold Dauphine hands.
Indications: date at 6.
Strap: in "cordura"; yellow gold fold-over clasp.
Also available: with blue dial; white gold, white dial and bezel pink gold and white, leather strap simple or with inlays in white gold, with bracelet.
Prices: on request.

247

Raymond Weil

Raymond Weil reached fame by uniting to a watchmaker's precision and know-how, an extraordinary intuition for anticipating fashion tendencies. Success has not altered the authentic character of the Company for which the founder, Raymond Weil, is the source of professional inspiration and Oliver Bernheim, President and C.E.O., is the point of reference for future development.

The value-references chosen for the latest models are rigor and emotion, expressed almost like a melody in the new Parsifal watches, as eternal seduction among the Don Giovanni line and the variations of Tema, where steel knows how to become precious. These last, characteristically rectangular and in their simplicity and elegance directed towards a feminine public, where luxury equals modernity and is clearly inspired by Art Déco, are made precious with mother of pearl and diamond dials. In the same way, the best known model, Parsifal, continues its evolution and today, in both the men's and women's versions, presents the perfection of its sculpted case.

The History

Each Raymond Weil watch is inspired by a piece of music - a melody, a movement of a sonata, a variation, or a tempo. Parsifal, Saxo, Don Giovanni, Tema, W1, Allegro, Tango, Chorus, Tradition. They are like notes on a musical score written by the Geneva Company.

1976 - Raymond Weil and Simone Bédat create the Raymond Weil in Geneva, when the Swiss market is in a deep recession.
1979 - The Company decides to concentrate on quartz movements and launches the Golden Eagle series: steel, sports watches in octagonal cases.
1983 - Raymond Weil participates with the Milos Forman film, Amadeus, and launches a collection by the same name. From now on his main collections have names inspired by classical music and opera.
1984 - Start of the publicity campaign for Amadeus.
1985 - The Fidelio collection is introduced; the models are refined and slender, mounted on an 18 kt gold-plated link bracelet.
1986 - Another new collection, Othello, the synthesis of advanced technology (quartz ultra-thin movement, only 1.2 mm high) and refined design. These watches, no longer being produced, made an important contribution to the success of the Company.
1988 - Introduction of the Traviata collection. These are watches which bring to mind the stained glass cathedral windows that, in their time, convulsed traditional aesthetics.
1989 - Having sold 500,000 watches throughout the world, Raymond Weil reinforces his position in the Olympus of Swiss watchmaking. A new advertising campaign is presented: Iceland.
1990 - Christian Bédat takes over the management of the design and production departments of the Company.
1991 - The Parsifal collection is presented; it is the first with steel and 18 kt gold versions.
1992 - Introduction of the Amadeus 200 collection, the first with sports models water resistant to 200 meters. At the same time the jewellery collection linked to Parsifal is presented; the pieces are executed in gold and diamonds.
1993 - Parsifal has three new models: GMT, square case and automatic.
1994 - Raymond Weil modifies his image; the new advertising campaign draws on "Precision Moments" and the world of the dance. The new collection, Traditions Mécaniques, is introduced, with manual or automatic movements.
1995 - Two new collections, Tango and Toccata: steel case, young sporting design.
1996 - Five years after its presentation, Parsifal proves to be one of the best selling of Swiss watches: 70.000 of these watches are produced each year. This calls for 10 tons of molybdenum steel and a transformation process that unites the best of modern technology to the traditions of watchmaking; it has been awarded the ISO 9002 certificate.
1998 - Once gain, two new collections: Allegro and Tema: modern watches interpreting classic themes.

RAYMOND WEIL

SAXO AUTOMATIC   REF. 2292030

Movement: mechanical, automatic winding, ETA caliber 2824/2, 25 jewels.
Functions: hours, minutes, seconds, date.
Case: steel, three-piece (Ø 37 mm, thickness 9.2 mm); smooth sapphire crystal; brushed bezel; screwed-on crown; case back fastened by 4 screws, with raised medallion in the central part. Water-resistant to 10 atm.
Dial: white enameled; black screen-printed Roman numerals and minute track; bâton hands, skeletonized and luminescent.
Indications: date at 3.
Bracelet: steel, polished and brushed; steel fold-over safety clasp.
Price: on request.

SAXO CHRONOGRAPH   REF. 2772036

Movement: mechanical, automatic winding, Valjoux caliber 7750.
Functions: hours, minutes, small seconds, date, three-counter chronograph.
Case: steel, three-piece (Ø 37 mm, thickness 13 mm); smooth sapphire crystal; brushed bezel; screwed-on crown; round pushers; case back fastened by 4 screws. Water-resistant to 10 atm.
Dial: white enameled; raised blue Roman numerals; bâton hands, skeletonized and luminescent, blue lacquered.
Indications: date at 3, hours at 6, small seconds at 9, minute counter at 12, center second, minute track with division for $1/5$ second.
Bracelet: steel, polished and brushed; steel fold-over safety clasp.
Price: on request.
Also available: gold-plated steel. Both versions are available with white or blue dial.

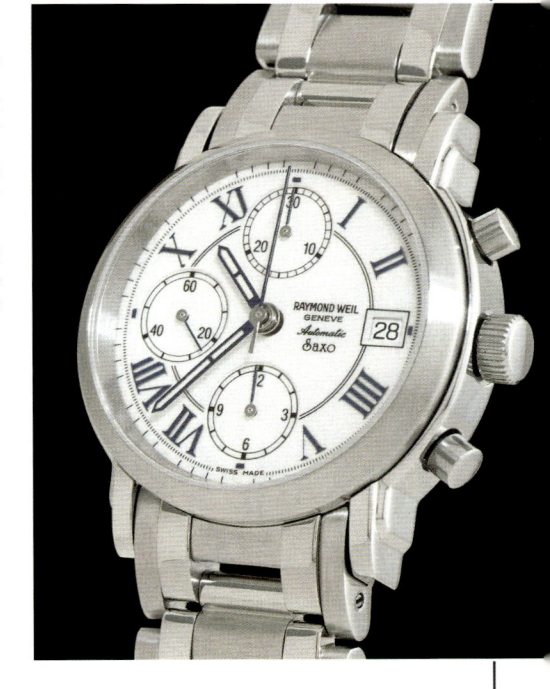

PARSIFAL ASPIRATION CHRONOGRAPH   REF. 2723163

Movement: mechanical, automatic winding, Raymond Weil caliber 7200 (ETA 2892-2 base + Dubois Dépraz chronograph module.
Functions: hours, minutes, small seconds, date, three-counter chronograph.
Case: steel, three-piece (Ø 39 mm, thickness 11 mm); antireflective smooth sapphire crystal; bezel polished with raised riders; protected crown and blue lacquered pushers; screwed-on back. Water-resistant to 10 atm.
Dial: "soleil" blue, counters decorated with circular beads; applied bâton markers; bâton hands.
Indications: small seconds at 3, hours at 6, minute counter at 9, date at 12, center second, minute track with division for $1/5$ second.
Bracelet: steel, polished and brushed; steel fold-over safety clasp.
Price: on request.
Also available: with white dial and Roman numerals; with strap and white dial with Roman numerals; steel and yellow gold (see photograph).

PARSIFAL ASPIRATION CHRONOGRAPH   REF. 2723025

By its Parsifal collection, presented for the first time in Basel in 1991, Raymond Weil officially entered the absolutely selective market of luxury watches. Elegant and precious together, reliable and of a refined simplicity, this line is diversified in various shapes and dial types - thin quartz movements for shaped and lady models and, instead, sophisticated mechanisms for the complicated watches and chronographs. Among the latter, the Parsifal Aspiration model, recently presented, holds a very special position. Its sportsmanlike and attractive look is characterized by a bezel with raised riders and its crown protection wings with screws and bars, which make the model immediately recognizable. Cases are available in steel, steel and gold (as the model shown in the photograph) with bracelet or the new original sporting leather strap, curved at the lugs to perfectly fit the case.
Price: on request.
Also available: with pink dial, Roman numerals; with bracelet and pink or white dial, Roman numerals.

249

Roger Dubuis

The latest invention from the Geneva watchmaker Roger Dubuis is the self-winding Three-Retrograde wristwatch. Featuring three central retrograding hands, for hour, minute and date, it's the most elaborate retrograde model so far from the man who has made this type of watch something of a specialty. The first series of the Three-Retrograde watch was made in platinum. As with most of Dubuis's watches, only 28 pieces were produced. Dubuis does not consider it a limited edition, however. In his rarefied world, a limited edition consists of five pieces or fewer. Like all his other watches, the Three-Retrograde bears the Geneva Seal, awarded to movements assembled in Geneva that measure up to certain strict standards for the quality of their finishing. The watch has also been awarded a certificate from the National Observatory of Besançon attesting to its accuracy.

Among Dubuis's other new offerings is his first watch for women, the Lady Sympathie, with a manual-wind movement. It's a smaller version of the men's Sympathie, whose unusual case shape - a square with concave sides - is a hallmark of the Dubuis brand. The women's version comes with an ivory-colored or black dial, both decorated with a red heart at 8 o'clock. (According to some Oriental traditions, the number eight symbolizes love.) It is available in rose or white gold. Dubuis does not use yellow gold for any of his watches because, he explains, when he was young and learning watchmaking, only pink or white gold were considered unusual enough for use in the finest watches.

The Lady Sympathie also comes in diamond-set versions with a variety of dials. All models are delivered with both a sapphire and a metal back. Another new model is the MuchMore. It's a rectangular watch available in five sizes, up to a very large 34 millimeters in width (hence the watch's name). It has a manual-wind or automatic movement and is also available with a single-pusher, column-wheel chronograph and a window perpetual calendar. The case back is fitted with a circular sapphire window so you can admire the movement's finish.

The History

Roger Dubuis was born in 1939 in Vevey, a little Swiss city on the shores of Lake Leman. The watchmaker's shop was where his passion for the mechanics within this craft grew. He began studying in 1953 at the Geneva School of Watchmaking and received his first diploma after only 4 years. He was immediately able to put his talent to work for some of the best known names in the field.

1980 - Once he became independent, he opened his own workshop in Geneva, where he repairs and restores complication watches the belong to private collectors from all over the world. At the same time he continues to contribute to the design and creation of complication models, where he himself has thought of the new movements, sold by some of the most important Geneva Companies. During these years he becomes a friend of Carlos Dias.

1995 - With Dias' participation the "independent" Manufacture Roger Dubuis S.A. opens in Geneva. Only two watchmakers work there and there is only one essential premise: each watch must be perfect from every point of view. 1996 - The first basic collections are officially presented, placed among the top of Swiss production: Sympathie and Hommage. The first has an original squared design with harmonious curves on each side, and the second is round, classic and decidedly severe. Both have many, more or less complicated, versions. At the same time the patent for the Double-Rétrograde day and date indication on perpetual calendar models, was awarded. There are also the so-called "master" complications, minute repeaters and the chronograph. All the creations of this Geneva watchmaker stand out for the great care with which each detail has been studied and executed. All the models have the Geneva mark of quality, the "Poinçon de Genève" and many have been recognized for precision by the Observatory. There are now 30 employees, the Company has an average annual growth rate of +125% for 1995-1998.

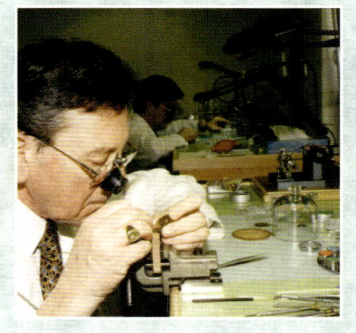

1999 - The third collection is introduced, Much-More; it has an anatomically designed case, exquisitely reproducing the 1920's. There are five sizes (22, 25, 28, 31, and 34 mm in width) and have versions with manual winding, automatic winding and single button chronograph. A new mechanical-automatic patent is presented, the Tri-Rétrograde, with jumping hours, minutes and instantaneous date, all central and retrograde.

ROGER DUBUIS

HOMMAGE CHRONO MONOPUSHER PERP. CAL BI-RETR.   REF. H40.6532.0

Movement: mechanical, manual winding, caliber RD6532. Beveled, Côtes de Genève and circular graining finished. Hallmarked with the "Geneva Seal" (watchmaking's highest distinction of quality); "chronometer class" certified by an official Observatory.
Functions: hour, minute, small second, perpetual calendar (date, day, month, year, moon phase), chronograph with 2 counters.
Case: 18 kt grey gold, three-piece case (Ø 40 mm, thickness 12.5 mm); concave bezel; curved antireflective sapphire crystal; 3 screw-down correctors on case side; grey gold crown with pusher; furnished with two case backs, one closed and the other in sapphire crystal. Water-resistant to 5 atm.
Dial: black enameled; painted Arabic numerals; grey gold Alpha hands.
Indications: date and day of the week with retrograde hands at 3 and at 9, minute counter at 3, moon phase at 6, small second at 9, month and four year cycle at 12, center second counter, minute track with divisions for $1/5$ of a second.
Strap: crocodile leather, hand stitched; grey gold clasp.
Price: 78'800 CHF.
Also available: pink gold 75'570 CHF; platinum (on request). All available with cream or black dial.

HOMMAGE MINUTE REPEATER PERP. CAL. BI-RETR.   REF. H37.2607.0

Movement: mechanical, manual winding, caliber RD2607, 12'''$1/4$, 32 jewels. Beveled, Côtes de Genève and circular graining finished. Hallmarked with the "Geneva Seal" (watchmaking's highest distinction of quality); "Chronometer class" certified by an official Observatory.
Functions: hour, minute, perpetual calendar until 2100 (date, day, month over a four-year cycle, moon phases), minute repeater.
Case: 18 kt grey gold, three-piece case (Ø 37 mm); concave bezel; curved antireflective sapphire crystal; 3 screw-down correctors and repeater slide on case side; grey gold crown; furnished with two screwed-on case backs, one closed and the other in sapphire crystal.
Dial: black enameled; applied grey gold cabochon markers; painted railway minute track; grey gold Alpha hands.
Indications: date and day of the week with retrograde hands at 3 and 9, moon phase at 6, months distributed over a four year cycle at 12.
Strap: crocodile leather, hand stitched; grey gold clasp.
Also available: pink gold; platinum (on request). All available with cream, white or black dial.
Prices: on request.

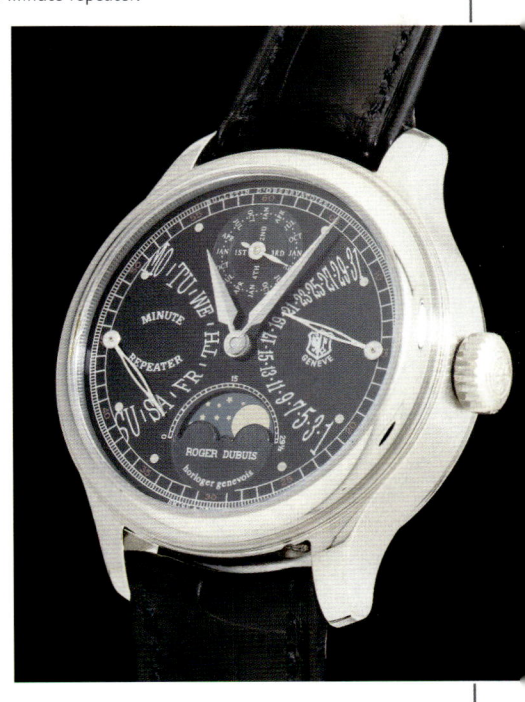

HOMMAGE CHRONO, PERP. CAL. BI-RETROGRADE   REF. H40.5632.5

Movement: mechanical, manual winding, caliber RD5632, 12''', 21 jewels. Beveled, Côtes de Genève and circular graining finished. Hallmarked with the "Geneva Seal" (watchmaking's highest distinction of quality); "chronometer class" certified by an official Observatory. **Functions:** hour, minute, small second, perpetual calendar (date, day, month, year, moon phase), chronograph with 2 counters.
Case: 18 kt pink gold, three-piece case (Ø 40 mm, thickness 12.5 mm); concave bezel; curved antireflective sapphire crystal; 3 screw-down correctors on case side; pink gold crown; non-slip pushers; furnished with two screwed-on case backs, one closed and the other in sapphire crystal. Water-resistant to 5 atm.
Dial: black enameled; painted Arabic numerals; pink gold Alpha hands.
Indications: date and day with retrograde hands at 3 and 9, minute counter at 3, moon phases at 6, small second at 9, month and four year cycle at 12, center second counter, minute track with divisions for $1/5$ of a second.
Strap: crocodile leather, hand stitched; pink gold clasp.
Price: 67'990 CHF.
Also available: grey gold 70'680 CHF; platinum (on request). All with cream or black dial.

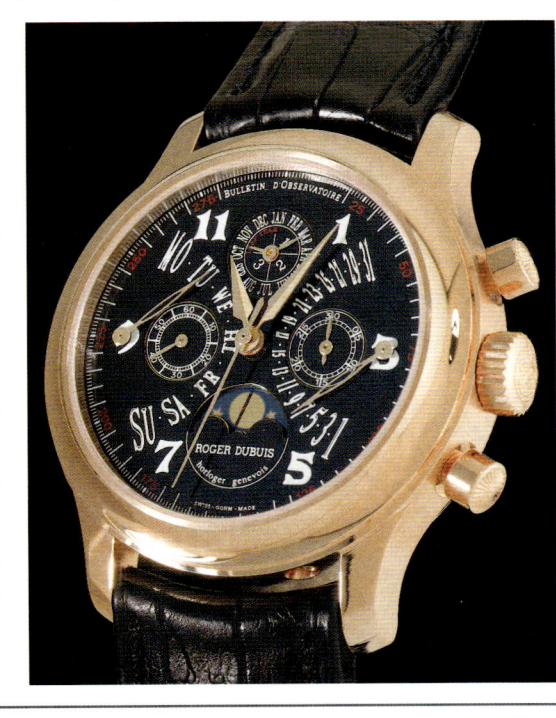

HOMMAGE PERPETUAL CALENDAR "A GUICHET"   REF. H40.5739.5

Movement: mechanical, automatic winding, caliber RD5739, 11'''$1/2$, 25 jewels. Beveled, Côtes de Genève and circular graining finished. Hallmarked with the "Geneva Seal" (watchmaking's highest distinction of quality); "chronometer class" certified by an official Observatory.
Functions: hour, minute, center second, perpetual calendar (date, day, month, year, moon phase).
Case: 18 kt pink gold, three-piece case (Ø 40 mm, thickness 10.67 mm); concave bezel; curved antireflective sapphire crystal; 3 screw-down correctors on case side; pink gold crown; furnished with two screwed-on case backs, a closed one and one with a sapphire crystal. Water-resistant to 5 atm.
Dial: black enameled; faceted pointed markers and Arabic numerals, applied pink gold; printed minute track; pink gold Alpha hands.
Indications: 4-year cycle digital display at 3, date at 4, moon phase at 8, day and month below 12.
Strap: crocodile leather, hand stitched; pink gold clasp.
Price: 43'860 CHF.
Also available: in grey gold 47'090 CHF; in platinum (on request). All available with cream, white or black dial.

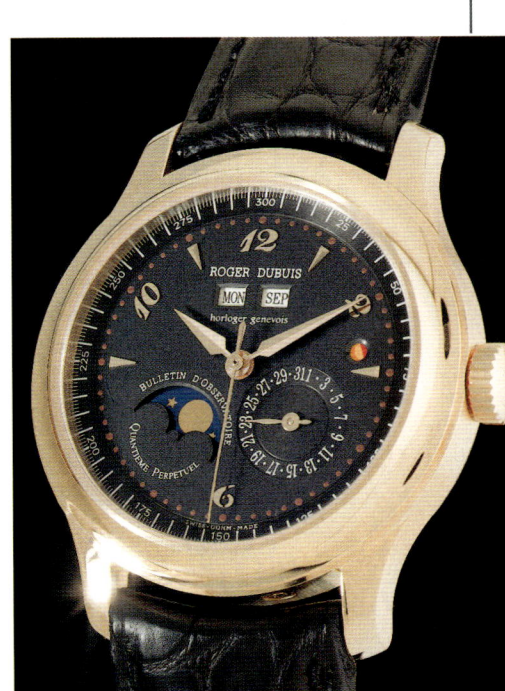

ROGER DUBUIS

HOMMAGE PERPETUAL CALENDAR BI-RETROGRADE — REF. H37.5772.5

Movement: mechanical, automatic winding, caliber RD5772. Beveled, Côtes de Genève and circular graining finished. Hallmarked with the "Geneva Seal" (watchmaking's highest distinction of quality); "chronometer class" certified by an official Observatory.
Functions: hour, minute, center second, perpetual calendar (date, day, month, year, moon phase). 
Case: 18 kt pink gold, three-piece case (Ø 37 mm, thickness 10.8 mm); concave bezel; curved antireflective sapphire crystal; 3 screw-down correctors on case side; grey gold crown; furnished with 2 screwed-on case backs, one closed and the other with a sapphire crystal. Water-resistant to 5 atm.
Dial: black enameled; applied pink gold faceted pointed markers; printed minute track; pink gold Alpha hands.
Indications: date and day of the week with retrograde hands at 3 and 9, moon phase at 6, month and four year cycle at 12.
Strap: crocodile leather, hand stitched; pink gold clasp.
Price: 43'590 CHF.
Also available: grey gold 46'820 CHF; platinum (on request). All available with cream or black dial.

HOMMAGE PERPETUAL CALENDAR BI-RETROGRADE — REF. H37.5771.0

Movement: mechanical, automatic winding, caliber RD5771. Beveled, Côtes de Genève and circular graining finished. Hallmarked with the "Geneva Seal" (watchmaking's highest distinction of quality); "chronometer class" certified by an official Observatory.
Functions: hour, minute, center second, perpetual calendar (date, day, month, year, moon phase). 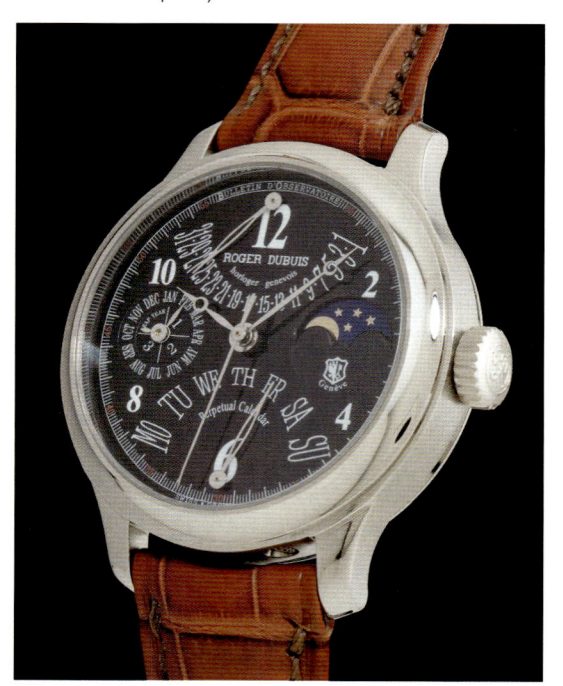
Case: 18 kt grey gold, three-piece case (Ø 37 mm); concave bezel; curved antireflective sapphire crystal; 3 screw-down correctors on case side; grey gold crown; furnished with two screwed-on case backs, a closed one and one with a sapphire crystal. Water-resistant to 5 atm.
Dial: black enameled; printed Arabic numerals and railway minute track; grey gold Pomme hands.
Indications: day-date with retrograde hands at 6 and 12, moon phase at 3, month and four year cycle at 9.
Strap: crocodile leather, hand stitched; grey gold clasp.
Price: on request.
Also available: pink gold; platinum (on request). All available with cream or black dial.

HOMMAGE CHRONO MONOPUSHER — REF. H40.65.0

Movement: mechanical, manual winding, caliber RD65, 12''', 21 jewels, balance-spring regulator system with micrometer adjustment and regulator spring, mobile balance-spring stud holder. Beveled, Côtes de Genève and circular graining finished. Hallmarked with the "Geneva Seal" (watchmaking's highest distinction of quality); "chronometer class" certified by an official Observatory. **Functions:** hour, minute, small second, chronograph with 2 counters. **Case:** 18 kt grey gold, three-piece case (Ø 40, thickness 11 mm); curved sapphire crystal; concave bezel; grey gold crown with pusher; furnished with two screwed-on case backs, one closed and the other provided with a sapphire crystal. Water-resistant to 5 atm. 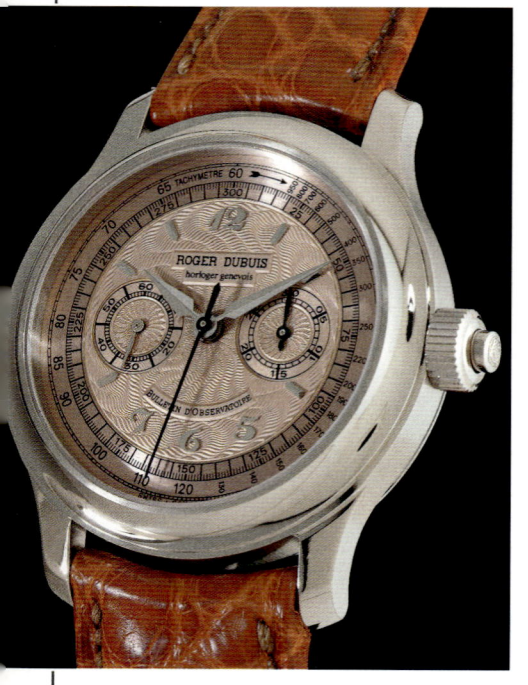
Dial: rosé, engine turned (guilloché); applied grey gold bâton markers and Arabic numerals; grey gold Alpha hands.
Indications: minute counter at 3, small second at 9, center second counter, railway minute track with divisions for 1/5 of a second and related adder (until 300), tachymeter scale.
Strap: crocodile leather, hand stitched; grey gold clasp. **Price:** 40'215 CHF.
Also available: pink gold 36'990; platinum (on request); with black engine turned (guilloché); with rosé, cream or black smooth dial: pink gold 34'620; grey gold 37'850; platinum (on request).

HOMMAGE CHRONOGRAPH — REF. H40.56.0

Movement: mechanical, manual winding, caliber RD56. Beveled, Côtes de Genève and circular graining finished. Hallmarked with the "Geneva Seal" (watchmaking's highest distinction of quality); "chronometer class" certified by an official Observatory. **Functions:** hour, minute, chronograph with 2 counters.
Case: 18 kt grey gold, three-piece case (Ø 40 mm, thickness 10.63 mm); curved sapphire crystal; concave bezel; grey gold crown; non-slip pushers; furnished with two screwed-on case backs, one closed and the other provided with a sapphire crystal. Water-resistant to 5 atm. 
Dial: white lacquered; applied grey gold bâton markers and Arabic numerals; pink gold leaf style hands.
Indications: minute counter at 3, small second at 9, center second counter, railway minute track with divisions for 1/5 of a second and related adder (until 300), tachymeter scale.
Strap: crocodile leather, hand stitched; grey gold clasp.
Price: 34'620 CHF.
Also available: pink gold 31'390; platinum (on request); rosé or black smooth dial: pink gold 33'750; grey gold 36'980; platinum (on request). Ø 37 mm: black, cream or silvered smooth dial: pink gold 28'170; grey gold 29'240; platinum 37'950.

ROGER DUBUIS

HOMMAGE TRI-RETROGRADE　　REF. H37.5799

Movement: mechanical, automatic winding, caliber RD5799 (caliber 57 base + module), 11'''1/2, over 300 components. Patented system with retrograde center hands for hours, minutes and date. Beveled, Côtes de Genève and circular graining finished. Hallmarked with the "Geneva Seal" (watchmaking's highest distinction of quality); "chronometer class" certified by an official Observatory.
Functions: hour, minute, date.
Case: platinum, three-piece case (Ø 37 mm, thickness 10.6 mm); curved antireflective sapphire crystal; concave bezel; platinum crown; furnished with two screwed-on case backs, one closed and the other provided with a sapphire crystal. Water-resistant to 5 atm.
Dial: white, stoving enameled; painted Roman numerals and railway minute track; Poire Stuart hands for hours and date, bâton minute hands.
Indications: hour, minute and date with retrograde center hand.
Strap: crocodile leather, hand stitched; platinum clasp.
Price: 90'000 CHF.

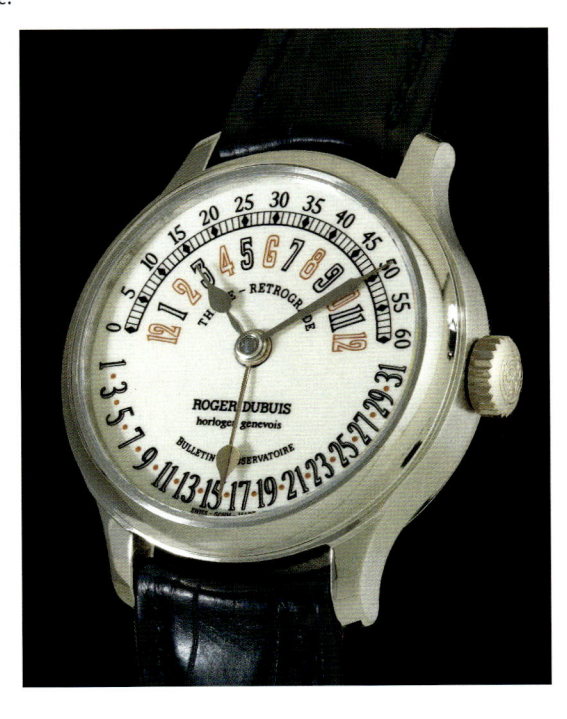

HOMMAGE CALENDAR À GUICHET　　REF. H40.5749.5

Movement: mechanical, automatic winding, caliber RD5749, 11'''1/2. Beveled, Côtes de Genève and circular graining finished. Hallmarked with the "Geneva Seal" (watchmaking's highest distinction of quality); "chronometer class" certified by an official Observatory.
Functions: hour, minute, center second, full calendar (date, day, month).
Case: 18 kt pink gold, three-piece case (Ø 40 mm, thickness 11 mm); curved antireflective sapphire crystal; concave bezel; corrector on case side; pink gold crown with embossed logo; furnished with two screwed-on case backs, one closed and the other with a sapphire crystal. Water-resistant to 5 atm.
Dial: white lacquered; pointed markers and Arabic numerals, applied pink gold; cabochon dial-train; pink gold Alpha hands.
Indications: date at 6, day and month below 12, minute track with divisions for 1/5 of a second and related adder (until 300).
Strap: crocodile leather, hand stitched; pink gold clasp.
Price: 34'610 CHF.
Also available: grey gold 37'840 CHF; platinum (on request). Ø 37, thick. 10,67, Ref. H37.5749, cream dial: pink gold 31'390 CHF; grey gold 34'080 CHF; platinum (on request).

HOMMAGE CONDOTTIERI　　REF. H40.27.0

Movement: mechanical, manual winding, caliber RD27, 15'''. Beveled, Côtes de Genève and circular graining finished. Hallmarked with the "Geneva Seal" (watchmaking's highest distinction of quality); "chronometer class" certified by an official Observatory.
Functions: hour, minute, small second.
Case: 18 kt grey gold, three-piece case (Ø 40 mm, thickness 9.04 mm); curved antireflective sapphire crystal; concave bezel; grey gold crown; furnished with two screwed-on case backs, one closed and the other provided with a sapphire crystal. Water-resistant to 5 atm.
Dial: white, stoving enameled; Roman numerals and railway minute track, painted; blued stainless steel leaf style hands.
Indications: small second at 6.
Strap: crocodile leather, hand stitched; grey gold clasp.
Also available: pink gold; platinum.
Prices: on request.

HOMMAGE CLASSIC　　REF. H37.57.5

Movement: mechanical, automatic winding, caliber RD57, 11'''1/2, 25 jewels. Beveled, Côtes de Genève and circular graining finished. Hallmarked with the "Geneva Seal" (watchmaking's highest distinction of quality); "chronometer class" certified by an official Observatory. **Functions:** hour, minute, center second. **Case:** 18 kt pink gold, three-piece case (Ø 37 mm, thickness 8.28 mm); curved antireflective sapphire crystal; concave bezel; pink gold crown; furnished with two screwed-on case backs, one closed and the other provided with sapphire crystal. Water-resistant to 5 atm. **Dial:** black, engine turned (guilloché) by hand; Arabic numerals applied pink gold; painted railway minute track; pink gold Pomme hands. **Strap:** crocodile leather, hand stitched; pink gold clasp. **Price:** on request.
Also available: grey gold; platinum (on request); same versions, white or blue enameled dial and painted markers (same prices); white enameled dial and applied pink gold Arabic numerals: pink gold; grey gold; platinum (on request); smooth black dial, cream-silvered or cream-rosé: pink gold; grey gold; platinum (on request). Medium size, Ø 34 mm, white enameled dial, applied Arabic numerals: pink gold; grey gold; platinum (on request); black dial, cream-silvered or cream-rosé: pink gold; grey gold; platinum (on request).

ROGER DUBUIS

SYMPATHIE CHRONO PERP. CAL. BI-RETROGRADE   REF. S37.5637.5

Movement: mechanical, manual winding, caliber RD5637. Beveled, Côtes de Genève and circular graining finished. Hallmarked with the "Geneva Seal" (watchmaking's highest distinction of quality); "chronometer class" certified by an official Observatory.
Functions: hour, minute, small second, perpetual calendar (date, day, month, year, moon phase), chronograph with 2 counters.
Case: 18 kt pink gold, curved square (height 37 mm, width 37, thickness 12 mm); flat antireflective sapphire crystal; 3 screw-down correctors on case side; pink gold crown; oval pushers; case back attached by 8 screws, displaying the movement through a round sapphire crystal. Water-resistant to 3 atm. 
Dial: cream; applied pink gold markers decorated with "Clous de Paris" pattern; pink gold Alpha hands.
Indications: date and day of the week with retrograde hands at 3 and 9, minute counter at 3, moon phases at 6, small second at 9, months distributed over a four year cycle at 12, center second counter, railway minute track with divisions for 1/5 of a second.
Strap: crocodile leather, hand stitched; pink gold clasp.
Also available: grey gold; platinum. All with cream or black dial.
Prices: on request.

SYMPATHIE CHRONOGRAPH   REF. S37.56.0

Movement: mechanical, manual winding, caliber RD56. Beveled, Côtes de Genève and circular graining finished. Hallmarked with the "Geneva Seal" (watchmaking's highest distinction of quality); "chronometer class" certified by an official Observatory.
Functions: hour, minute, chronograph with 2 counters.
Case: 18 kt grey gold, curved square (height 37 mm, width 37 mm, thickness 9.4 mm); flat antireflective sapphire crystal; grey gold crown; oval pushers; case back attached by 8 screws, displaying the movement through a round sapphire crystal. Water-resistant to 3 atm. 
Dial: black enameled; applied grey gold Arabic numerals; painted cabochon markers; grey gold leaf style hands.
Indications: minute counter at 3, small second at 9, center second counter, railway minute track with divisions for 1/5 of a second and related adder (until 300), tachymeter scale.
Strap: crocodile leather, hand stitched; grey gold clasp.
Price: 33'770 CHF.
Also available: pink gold 30'000 CHF; platinum (on request). All available with cream or black dial.

SYMPATHIE PERPETUAL CALENDAR BI-RETROGRADE   REF. S37.5707.5

Movement: mechanical, automatic winding, caliber RD5707. Beveled, Côtes de Genève and circular graining finished. Hallmarked with the "Geneva Seal" (watchmaking's highest distinction of quality); "chronometer class" certified by an official Observatory.
Functions: hour, minute, center second, perpetual calendar (date, day, month, year, moon phase). 
Case: 18 kt pink gold, curved square (height 37 mm, width 37 mm, thickness 9.6 mm); flat antireflective sapphire crystal; 3 screw-down correctors on case side; pink gold crown; case back attached by 8 screws, displaying the movement through a round sapphire crystal. Water-resistant to 3 atm.
Dial: black; applied Clous de Paris markers; printed railway minute track; pink gold Alpha hands.
Indications: date and day of the week with retrograde hands at 3 and 9, moon phase at 6, months distributed over a four year cycle at 12.
Strap: crocodile leather, hand stitched; pink gold clasp.
Price: on request.
Also available: in grey gold; platinum (on request). All with cream or black dial.

SYMPATHIE PERPETUAL CALENDAR À GUICHET   REF. S37.5739D.5

Movement: mechanical, automatic winding, caliber RD5739, 11'''1/2, 25 jewels. Beveled, Côtes de Genève and circular graining finished. Hallmarked with the "Geneva Seal" (watchmaking's highest distinction of quality); "chronometer class" certified by an official Observatory. **Functions:** hour, minute, center second, perpetual calendar (date, day, month, year, moon phase).
Case: 18 kt pink gold, curved square (height 37 mm, width 37, thickness 9.7 mm); flat antireflective sapphire crystal; 3 screw-down correctors on case side; pink gold crown; case back attached by 8 screws, displaying the movement through a round sapphire crystal. Water-resistant to 3 atm. 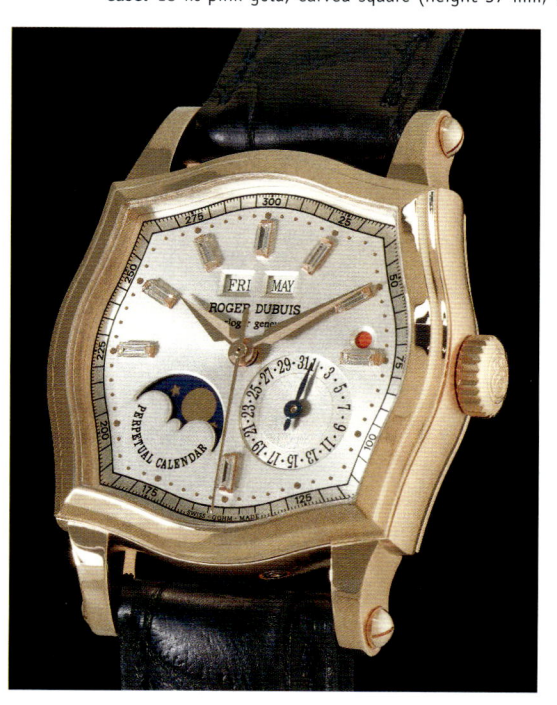
Dial: silvered; applied pink gold rectangular markers set with 8 baguette diamonds; cabochon minute track; pink gold Alpha hands.
Indications: 4-year cycle digital display at 3, date at 4, moon phase at 8, day and month below 12.
Strap: crocodile leather, hand stitched; pink gold clasp.
Price: on request.
Also available: cream dial; grey gold; platinum (on request). Without brilliants at markers, cream dial and painted or applied Arabic numerals or whit silvered dial and applied Arabic numerals: pink gold; grey gold; platinum (on request).

ROGER DUBUIS

SYMPATHIE CAL. BI-RETROGRADE NEW MILLENARY   REF. S34.5740.0

Movement: mechanical, automatic winding, caliber RD5740. Beveled, Côtes de Genève and circular graining finished. Hallmarked with the "Geneva Seal" (watchmaking's highest distinction of quality); "chronometer class" certified by an official Observatory.
Functions: hour, minute, center second, date, day, moon phase).
Case: 18 kt grey gold, curved square (height 34 mm, width 34 mm, thickness 9.6 mm); flat antireflective sapphire crystal; 3 screw-down correctors on case side; grey gold crown; case back attached by 8 screws, displaying the movement through a round sapphire crystal. Water-resistant to 3 atm.
Dial: white lacquered; applied grey gold cabochon markers; printed railway minute track; grey gold Alpha hands.
Indications: date and day of the week with retrograde hands at 3 and 9, moon phase at 6.
Strap: crocodile leather, hand stitched; grey gold clasp.
Price: 30'110 CHF.
Also available: pink gold 26'880 CHF; platinum (on request). All with cream or black dial.

MUCH MORE PERPETUAL CALENDAR À GUICHET   REF. M34.5739.0.

Movement: mechanical, automatic winding, caliber RD5739, 11'''1/2, 25 jewels. Beveled, Côtes de Genève and circular graining finished. Hallmarked with the "Geneva Seal" (watchmaking's highest distinction of quality); "chronometer class" certified by an official Observatory.
Functions: hour, minute, center second, perpetual calendar (date, day, month, year, moon phase).
Case: 18 kt grey gold, three-piece rectangular-curved case (size 46.7x34 mm, thickness 11.3 mm); curved sapphire crystal; 3 screw-down correctors on case side; grey gold crown with embossed logo; case back attached by 8 screws, displaying the movement through a little sapphire crystal. Water-resistant to 3 atm.
Dial: silvered; applied grey gold Arabic numerals; cabochon minute track; grey gold Poire hands.
Indications: 4-year cycle digital display at 3, date at 4, moon phase at 8, day and month below 12.
Strap: crocodile leather, hand stitched and fastened by 4 screws; grey gold clasp.
Price: 57'090 CHF.
Also available: cream dial and applied or painted Arabic numerals; pink gold 53'220 CHF; platinum (on request).

MUCH MORE CHRONO MONOPUSHER CO-AXIAL   REF. M31.28.5

Movement: mechanical, manual winding, caliber RD28, 10''', 21 jewels, balance-spring regulator system with micrometer adjustment and regulator spring, mobile balance-spring stud holder. Beveled, Côtes de Genève and circular graining finished. Hallmarked with the "Geneva Seal" (watchmaking's highest distinction of quality); "chronometer class" certified by an official Observatory.
Functions: hour, minute, small second, chronograph with 2 counters.
Case: 18 kt pink gold, three-piece rectangular-curved case (size 42.8x31 mm, thickness 10.7 mm); curved sapphire crystal; pink gold crown with pusher; case back attached by 8 screws, displaying the movement through a little sapphire crystal. Water-resistant to 3 atm.
Dial: ivory lacquered; printed Arabic numerals; printed minute track; pink gold Alpha hands.
Indications: minute counter at 3, small second at 9, center second counter, minute track with divisions for 1/5 of a second and related adder (until 300).
Strap: crocodile leather, hand stitched and fastened by 4 screws; pink gold clasp.
Price: 31'390 CHF.
Also available: silvered dial and painted Arabic numerals; grey gold 33'870 CHF; platinum (on request).

MUCH MORE AUTOMATIC GENTS   REF. M34.57.5

Movement: mechanical, automatic winding, caliber RD57, 11'''1/2, 25 jewels. Beveled, Côtes de Genève and circular graining finished. Hallmarked with the "Geneva Seal" (watchmaking's highest distinction of quality); "chronometer class" certified by an official Observatory.
Functions: hour, minute.
Case: 18 kt pink gold, three-piece rectangular-curved case (size 46.7x34 mm, thickness 9.1 mm); curved sapphire crystal; pink gold crown; case back attached by 8 screws, displaying the movement through a little sapphire crystal. Water-resistant to 3 atm.
Dial: ivory lacquered; printed Arabic numerals; printed minute track; pink gold Poire hands.
Strap: crocodile leather, hand stitched and fastened by 4 screws; pink gold clasp.
Price: 19'990 CHF.
Also available: applied Arabic numerals; silvered dial and painted Arabic numerals; grey gold, 22'360 CHF; platinum (on request).

255

Rolex

Rolex, one of the most successful watch brands that's ever existed, seldom feels the need to introduce dramatically new and different models. Why should they? This year, however, the company came up with something completely unprecedented - a watch that combines platinum and steel.

The unlikely duo are combined in Rolex's new Yacht-Master Rolesium model, which has an engraved and graduated platinum bezel, a platinum dial, and a steel case and bracelet. The watch is yet another example of the current craze for white metals - steel, white gold, titanium, platinum, aluminum, rhodium plate and silver - a craze that has set watch manufacturers scurrying to find new and interesting white-metal combinations and treatments (the tremendous number of steel-and-diamond watches introduced this year is part of the same trend). The platinum and steel combination harks back to earlier unorthodox metal pairings by Rolex. In 1933, the company combined steel and gold in the same watch and christened the duo "Rollesor".

Like the other Yacht-Masters, the Rolesium has a self-winding certified chronometer movement and a rotating bezel which allows the wearer to measure elapsed time.

It comes in three sizes: ladies', medium and men's.

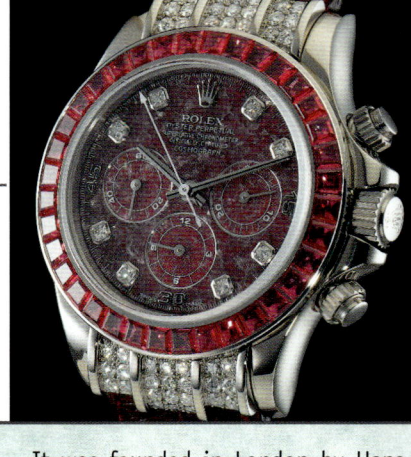

The History

It was founded in London by Hans Wilsdorf in 1905 and has become a world class colossus in the field of watchmaking. And, nonetheless, it produces great quality that has shown great endurance and that it often tends to increase in value. It is considered with admiration by all its competitors and is, at the present time, the most universally known name in the sector. Wilsdorf's intuition, extraordinary at the turn of the century, that wristwatches would undergo enormous development, depended upon two innovations: the water-resistance of the cases and automatic winding. And the name itself, so familiar today, is also due to Wilsdorf, who chose "Rolex" because he wanted a term easy to pronounce in every language. Another aspect that is also Wilsdorf's merit is to have gambled on precision and to have introduced, decades before the others, a watch produced in series with the chronograph certificate, and in fact, as of today, there are a good ten million Rolex watches produced and tested according to the regulations of the observatories first of all and also of the COSC. The sports models made in a special, factory-secret alloy, are of exceptional quality. This, plus the fact that the watches are air-tight, means that even very old watches work perfectly and are still look very good. The Oyster Perpetual could be considered the archetype of the modern wristwatch and its numerous variations and are among the best selling models at auctions; of these the most popular is the Daytona and its descendants. The auction levels reached by the classic chronographs are also very high. As for the models with different shapes, Rolex became famous in the 1930's for its "Prince", rectangular (with a Duo type dial where the sub-seconds are very evident) which is still considered a masterpiece of elegant design.

1908 - The name Rolex is registered, an anagrammatic exercise with the words, "horloge excellent".

1912 - The Company moves to Bienne.

1914 - First Class A chronograph certificate from the Kew Observatory, in Great Britain, for an 11 line movement tested with the same criteria used for the Royal Navy chronometers. At this point Wilsdorf decides that every Rolex calibre must be made as though it were to pass the same tests.

1925 - The five point crown, that is to become the symbol of the Company, makes its first appearance.

1926 - The Oyster case is patented.

1927 - Mercedes Gleitze swims across the English Channel. She's wearing a Rolex Oyster - the myth begins here.

1928 - The balances, "Prima", "Extra-Prima" and "Ultra-Prima" are constructed. The unmatched doctor's watch, Prince, is made with its characteristic double dial (the upper one for hours and minutes, the lower for seconds). The "Brancard" version is undoubtedly one of the form models most sought and appreciated by collectors throughout the world.

1931 - The production in series of certified chronometers begins, and the first automatic rotor winding movement is presented, "Perpetual".

1938 - The presentation of "Ovetto", with the typical connection between the lugs and the considerably curved back due to the voluminous rotor of the automatic movement (and this explains the nick-name "bubble-back"), nowadays absolutely one of the most sought pieces.

1945 - The triple date Chronographs, ref. 4767 and better known as "Datacompax" is placed on sale. It was produced up to 1955 as reference 6036 and known to collectors as "Killy Watch" (from the name of the 1960's ski champion). Datejust is presented; the first chronometer with automatic date change.

1950 - Presentation of the complete calendar with moon phases, ref. 6062 and better known as "Starlets" because of the star shaped markers.

1952 - Production of the Turn-o-graph begins, which, the following year, will become the Submariner ref. 6204 (known by collectors like James Bond and recognizable by the lack of protective horns at either side of the crown).

1954 - The GMT Master model with double time zone and the first ladies Oyster Perpetual chronometer are presented.

1956 - The automatic date change is perfected and the day shown in letters is added. The Day-Date is born.

1961 - The manual chronograph, Cosmograph Daytona (ref. 6239-6241), starts production and will continue until 1976.

1970 - The Cosmograph Daytona is presented with an "exotic" two-tone dial, today known as the "Paul Newman".

1971 - The Sea Dweller is the first watch to have a special helium escape valve. Its water resistance is demonstrated to 610 meters and will be increased to today's 1220 meters.

Today - It has become, in recent years, a world myth - so much so that its models, along with those of Cartier, are the ones most imitated and falsified - and it has such a strong position at the top of the desires of the international public, that it certainly doesn't share the anxiety about innovations that keeps its direct competitors in a state of worry. The Geneva House is one of the few that can allow itself long periods of reflection before actually launching a new product. And these are in fact rare and memorable events, carefully prepared and tested. The latest member of the family is Yacht-Master, an elegant diver's model with its case made in gold, in steel and gold or in steel-platinum in the Rolesium version, and in three different sizes. There is instead constant activity regarding keeping the classics up to date. The Company antenna are always ready to catch changes of mood, of taste, clients' requests. The present range substantially follows two lines: Cellini, or the classic, elegant models made in gold, and Oyster. Among these last, which in turn are divided between men's and ladies' models, the most important pieces are first of all the Chronograph Daytona in the steel case version, followed by the technical models, like Explorer, Submariner and the GMT. The vitality shown in the sector dedicated to ladies watches - a top of the range segment in continuous growth - multiplies the Rolex dedication to the really elitist field of fine, stupefying jewellery to accompany the watches: band rings, colliers and earrings. Things for a fortunate few, you will say. But, admiring and dreaming is free, and in any case, much of the passion "common mortals" feel about watches is, in fact, the stuff dreams are made of.

Other new Rolex models include two new versions of the Oyster Perpetual Day-Date (also known as the President). One has a dial made of authentic meteorite set with eight brilliant and two baguette diamonds and a bezel set with 42 baguette diamonds. The other new Day-Date has a dial covered entirely with pave diamonds. Its bezel is set with 40 brilliant diamonds. Both have a Tridor bracelet (so called because it's made of tri-colored 18-karat gold - pink, white and yellow).

The Rolex Cellini line has been expanded with a new pink-gold model with a manual-wind movement and leather strap. It comes in a ladies', medium, and men's size.

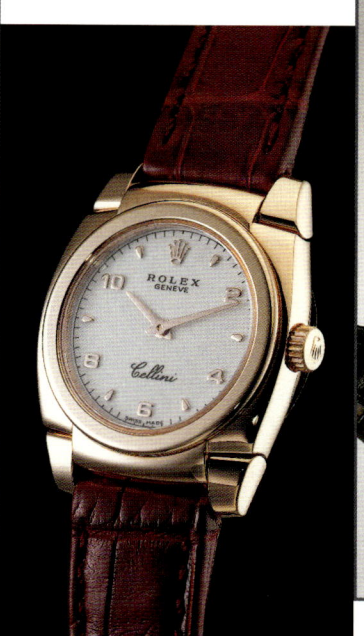

ROLEX

OYSTER PERPETUAL COSMOGRAPH DAYTONA — REF. 16559SACO

Within the "Daytona" family, each version, as Rolex is in the habit of doing, can become a watch for itself, almost a unique piece. Apart from the manifold proposals related to case metal or dial color and leather straps, the chromatic inventions allowed by the use of precious stones (chosen by Rolex among the most beautiful and purest offered by nature) permit to differentiate watches in such a way as to make exclusive jewels of them, as the Daytona shown in the photograph demonstrates: a precious chronograph in white gold with bezel adorned by 36 square cut cognac-color sapphires (appr. 4.92 kt), and on the connecting element between the lugs 24 brilliants (appr. 0.66 kt) and 6 baguette cut cognac-color sapphires (appr. 1.43 kt); on the guided dial in mother-of-pearl there are 8 brilliants at the markers. 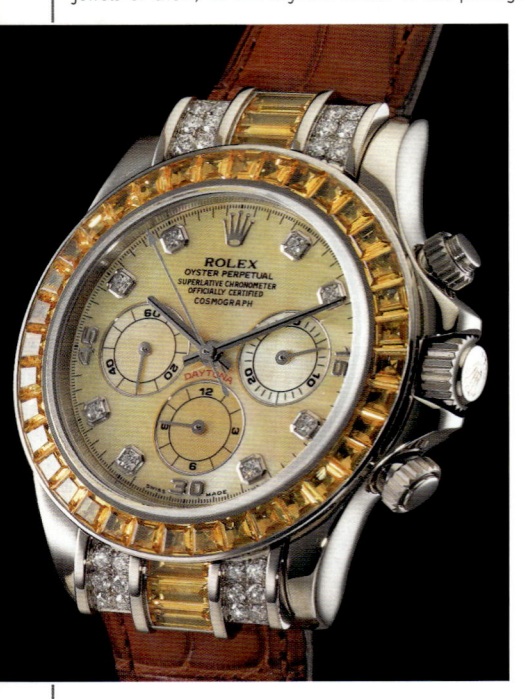
Part of the movement is the famous Perpetual rotor, patented by Rolex, which in 1931 revolutionized the concept of watch winding by transforming arm movements in a power reserve, while maintaining the spring in an optimal tension state and ensuring a constant working precision.
Price: on request.

OYSTER PERPETUAL COSMOGRAPH DAYTONA — REF. 16528

Movement: mechanical, automatic winding, caliber Rolex 4030, 31 jewels; "microstar" balance in Glucydur with micrometer adjustment, 28,800 vibrations per hour (vph), Breguet overcoil balance-spring, Parechoc shock-resistant system. Officially certified "chronometer" (C.O.S.C.).
Functions: hour, minute, small second, chronograph with 3 counters.
Case: 18 kt yellow gold, three-piece case (Ø 40 mm, thickness 12.5), polished and brushed finish; sapphire crystal; fixed bezel with engraved tachymeter scale; screw-down gold crown with threefold safety device and case protection; screwed-on round pushers; screwed-on case back. Water-resistant to 10 atm. 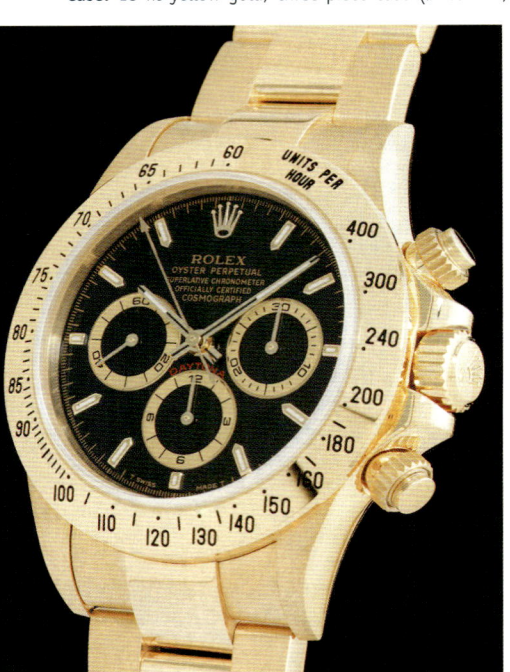
Dial: black enameled; champagne-color counters crowns; printed minute track; luminescent applied yellow gold bâton markers; luminescent yellow gold bâton hands.
Indications: minute counter at 3, hour counter at 6, small second at 9, center second counter, minute track with divisions for $1/5$ of a second.
Bracelet: Oyster in brushed gold, polished central links; fold-over clasp.
Also available: white or champagne-color dial; with brilliants at markers.
Prices: on request.

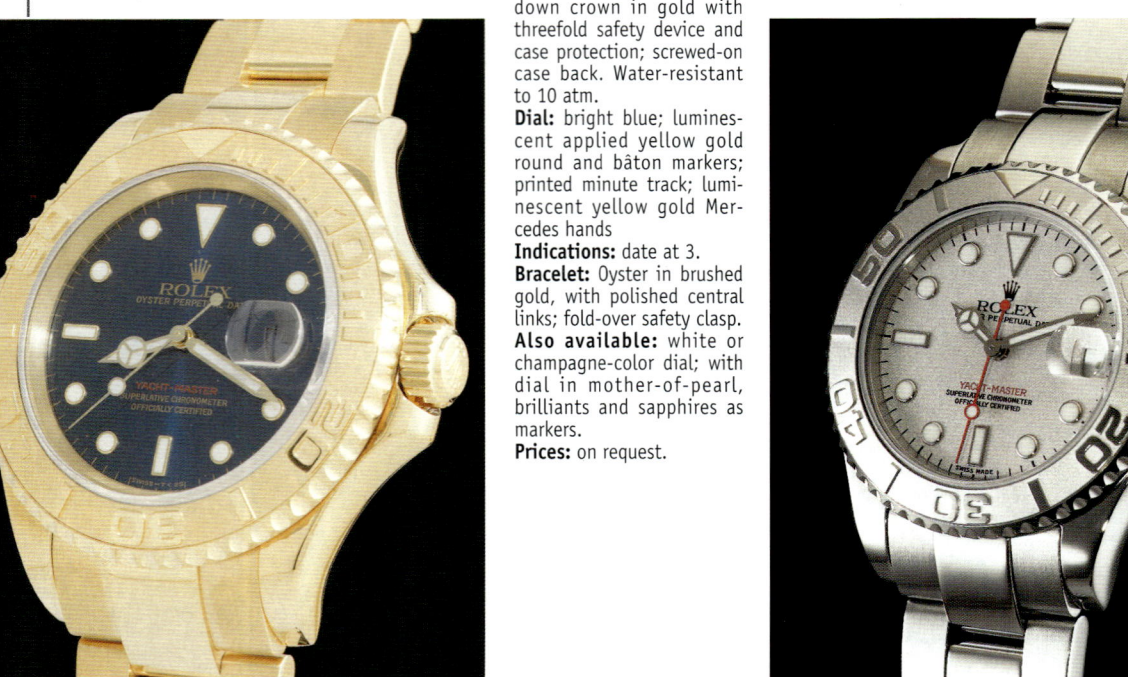

OYSTER PERPETUAL DATE YACHT-MASTER — REF. 16628

Movement: mechanical, automatic winding, Rolex caliber 3135. Officially certified "chronometer" (C.O.S.C.).
Functions: hour, minute, center second, date.
Case: 18 kt yellow gold, three-piece case (Ø 40 mm, thickness 12 mm); sapphire crystal with Cyclope magnifying glass on date; bi-directional turning bezel, matte finish, embossed polished minute track, useful for the calculation of diving times; screw-down crown in gold with threefold safety device and case protection; screwed-on case back. Water-resistant to 10 atm. 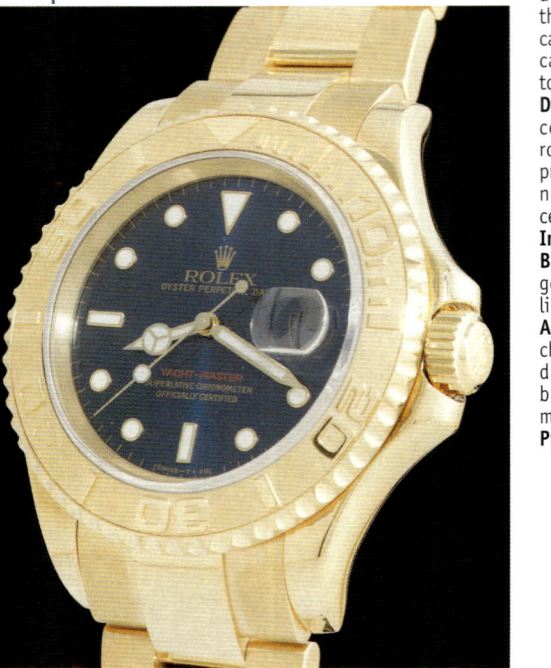
Dial: bright blue; luminescent applied yellow gold round and bâton markers; printed minute track; luminescent yellow gold Mercedes hands.
Indications: date at 3.
Bracelet: Oyster in brushed gold, with polished central links; fold-over safety clasp.
Also available: white or champagne-color dial; with dial in mother-of-pearl, brilliants and sapphires as markers.
Prices: on request.

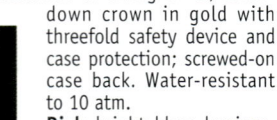

OYSTER PERPETUAL DATE YACHT-MASTER ROLESIUM — REF. 168622

The waterproof Yacht Master, the most recent among the creations of the Genevan House is realized with three case sizes: large - diameter 40 millimeters, medium - diameter 34 millimeters, small - diameter 29 millimeters. Through solutions based on the light-and-shade effects of the metals (gold or stainless steel and gold) used for cases and bracelets, the Yacht Master medium size models come with traditional dials showing steel, blue, white or champagne-color backgrounds or the white reflexes of mother-of-pearl, also combined with markers made of precious stones.
In the photograph the version presented at the Basel 1999 show, called Rolesium, with case and bracelet in stainless steel, stepped bezel and platinum dial.
Also available: Ø 40 mm Ref. 16622; Ø 29 mm Ref. 169622.
Prices: on request.

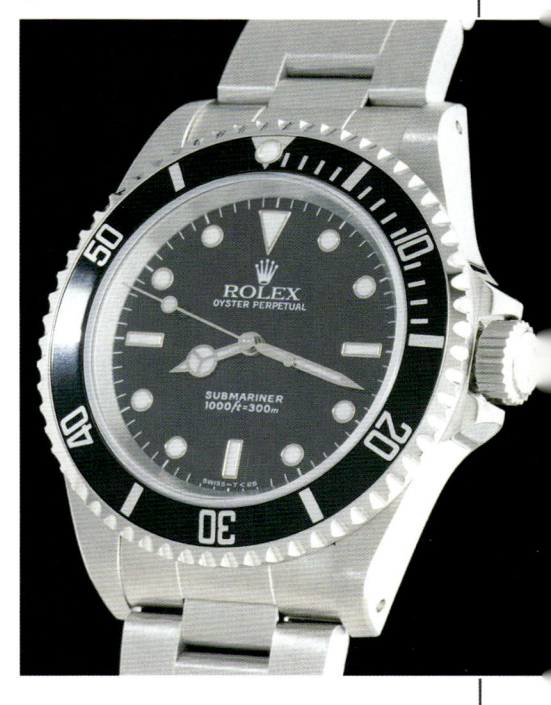

ROLEX

OYSTER PERPETUAL DATE SEA-DWELLER 4000   REF. 16600

Movement: mechanical, automatic winding, caliber Rolex 3135. Officially certified "chronometer" (C.O.S.C.).
Functions: hour, minute, center second, date.
Case: stainless steel, two-piece case (Ø 40 mm, thickness 15 mm), polished and brushed finish; sapphire crystal of considerable thickness, resisting high pressures, pressure compensation valve for the release of helium and other very light gases (penetrating after long lasting exposures to high pressures); counter-clockwise turning bezel with black ring and graduated scale, useful for the calculation of diving times; screw-down crown with threefold safety device and case protection; screwed-on case back. Water-resistant to 122 atm.
Dial: black enameled; luminescent applied white gold round and bâton markers; printed minute track; luminescent white gold Mercedes hands.
Indications: date at 3.
Bracelet: Oyster in brushed steel; Fliplock fold-over safety clasp; furnished with an additional link, an extension sheet of the clasp and a screw-driver to extend it and put it on over the suit.
Price: on request.

OYSTER PERPETUAL SUBMARINER   REF. 14060

Movement: mechanical, automatic winding, caliber Rolex 3000.
Functions: hour, minute, center second.
Case: stainless steel, three-piece case (Ø 40 mm, thickness 13 mm), polished and brushed finish; sapphire crystal; counter-clockwise turning bezel with black ring and graduated scale, useful for the calculation of diving times; screw-down crown with threefold safety device and case protection; screwed-on case back. Water-resistant to 30 atm.
Dial: black enameled; luminescent applied white-gold round and bâton markers; printed minute track; luminescent white gold Mercedes hands.
Bracelet: Oyster in brushed steel; fold-over safety clasp.
Price: on request.

OYSTER PERPETUAL DATE SUBMARINER   REF. 16618

The Submariner, the most popular and sought-after waterproof watch by the enthusiasts all over the world, is proposed here in the 18 kt yellow gold version with blue ring and a luminous champagne-color dial with brilliants and sapphires set on hour markers. The winding crown with a protection consisting of two juts on the case, is characterized by an inside thread receiving the outside thread of the small little tube integrated in the case side: two axial gaskets and a radial gasket ensure its perfect tightness. The Oyster bracelet is a special version expressly conceived for the diving models. The Fliplock clip, on which the bracelet design is printed, is provided with a release safety device and includes extension and folding plates. The latter allow, when they are unfold, to put on the watch over a light diver suit.
As all the models of the Genevan House, the Submariner too is available in a rich series of color combinations of ring and dial and, the most elegant ones, in many "precious" variants.
Also available: without stones on the dial; Ref. 16610 steel, black bezel and dial; steel and yellow gold: blue or black bezel and dial, blue bezel, acier dial, brilliants and sapphires markers.
Prices: on request.

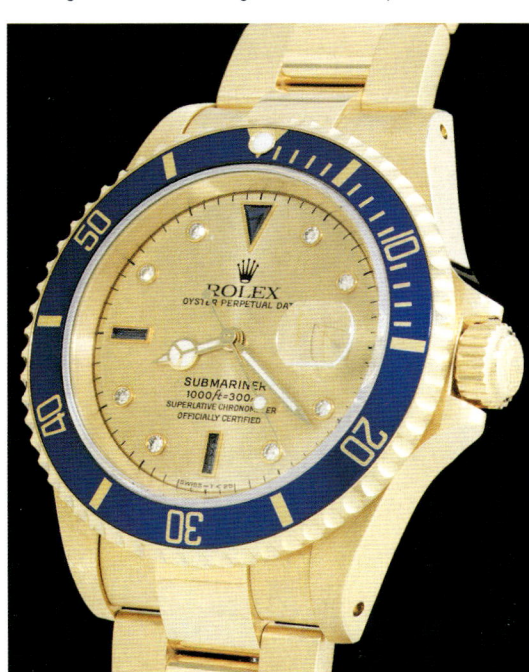

OYSTER PERPETUAL DAY-DATE   REF. 18239

Realized starting from 1956, Oyster Perpetual Day-Date, is not only one among the best known and most imitated models in the history of modern watchmaking, but it holds also the record of being the first wrist-chronometer which can indicate the day of the week, written in full letters and in 26 languages inside special dial zones. The photograph shows the version entirely in white gold with a knurled bezel. This bezel type was introduced by Rolex not only for aesthetic reasons but also in order to distinguish the steel models with white gold bezels from those which are entirely in steel. On the silvered metallized dial, where markers bear brilliants and luminescent dots on the printed minute track, a large window at 12 houses the indication of the day of the week. The Superpresident bracelet, which is brush finished with polished central links, has an invisible fold-over clasp.
Also available: in yellow gold with Superpresident bracelet, bezel brilliants, silvered dial, brilliant markers Ref. 18348.
Prices: on request.

259

ROLEX

OYSTER PERPETUAL DATE GMT MASTER — REF. 16700

Movement: mechanical, automatic winding, caliber Rolex 3175. Officially certified "chronometer" (C.O.S.C.).
Functions: hour, minute, center second, date, second time zone, 24-hour indication.
Case: stainless steel, three-piece case (Ø 40 mm, thickness 12 mm), polished and brushed finish; sapphire crystal with Cyclope magnifying glass on date; bi-directional turning bezel, with black 24-hours ring, useful for displaying the time of a second time zone; screw-down crown with double safety device and case protection; screwed-on case back. Water-resistant to 10 atm. 
Dial: black enameled; luminescent applied white-gold round and bâton markers; printed minute track; luminescent white gold Mercedes hands.
Indications: date at 3, 24 hours domestic time (position the time on the ring, corresponding to that of the main hands, on the arrow-shaped center hand) or second time-zone time (position the time on the ring, corresponding to the second time zone, on the arrow-shaped center hand).
Bracelet: Oysterlock in brushed steel; fold-over clasp.
Also available: with red-blue ring; with Jubilé bracelet.
Prices: on request.

OYSTER PERPETUAL DATE GMT MASTER II — REF. 16718

The GMT by Rolex is undoubtedly the most famous one among the multi-time-zone watches. The typical Oyster and Jubilé bracelets make its so essential design unmistakable, a perfect synthesis of class and sportsmanship. The initials GMT (Greenwich Mean Time) were used for the first time by Rolex, in the Sixties, for a watch with two time-zone indications. GMT Master II, the peak model of the present collection provides the time indication of three time zones thanks to the independent adjustment of the main hour hand with respect to the "GMT" (arrow-shaped) hand, which thus indicates the local time. To read the time of a third time zone, it is necessary to turn the ring so as to make the GMT-hand coincide with the time of the town chosen. To come back to the time zone previously set, one must bring the triangular marker on the bezel in the position corresponding to the 12 on the dial.
The photograph shows the version in yellow gold with champagne-color dial and brilliants and rubies as markers. 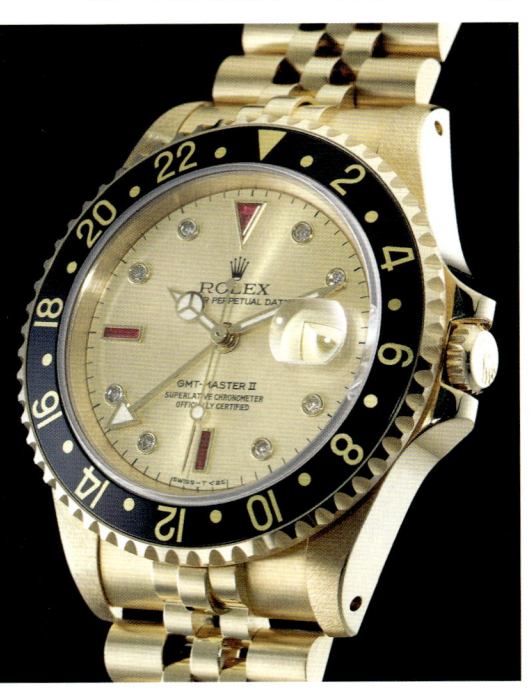
Also available: without gems, black or bronze dial and ring; bracelet: Oysterlock, Jubilé, Superjubilé.
Prices: on request.

OYSTER PERPETUAL DATE EXPLORER II — REF. 16570

Movement: mechanical, automatic winding, caliber Rolex 3185. Officially certified "chronometer" (C.O.S.C.).
Functions: hour, minute, center second, date, second time zone, 24-hour indication.
Case: stainless steel, three-piece case (Ø 40 mm, thickness 12.5 mm), polished and brushed finish; sapphire crystal with Cyclope magnifying glass on date; brushed bezel, fixed, with the 24 hours engraved, useful for displaying the time of a second time zone; screw-down crown with double safety device and case protection; screwed-on case back. Water-resistant to 10 atm. 
Dial: white enameled; luminescent applied black painted gold round and bâton markers; printed minute track; luminescent black painted gold Mercedes hands.
Indications: date at 3, second time-zone 24-hour display with arrow-pointed red center hand.
Bracelet: Oysterlock in brushed steel; fold-over clasp.
Price: on request.

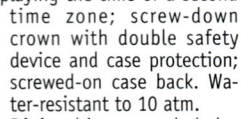

OYSTER PERPETUAL EXPLORER — REF. 14270

Movement: mechanical, automatic winding, caliber Rolex 3000. Officially certified "chronometer" (C.O.S.C.).
Functions: hour, minute, center second.
Case: stainless steel, three-piece brushed and polished case (Ø 36 mm, thickness 11.6 mm); sapphire crystal; screw-down crown, with double safety device; screwed-on case back. Water-resistant to 10 atm. 
Dial: black enameled; luminescent applied white gold Arabic numerals and bâton markers; printed minute track; luminescent white gold Mercedes hands.
Bracelet: Oysterlock in brushed steel; fold-over clasp.
Price: on request.

ROLEX

OYSTER PERPETUAL DATE — REF. 15210

Movement: mechanical, automatic winding, caliber Rolex 3135. Officially certified "chronometer" (C.O.S.C.).
Functions: hour, minute, center second, date.
Case: stainless steel, three-piece case (Ø 34 mm, thickness 11.5 mm); sapphire crystal with Cyclope magnifying glass on date; slightly knurled bezel with embossed polished hour markers; screw-down crown with double protection; screwed-on case back. Water-resistant to 10 atm.
Dial: white enameled; luminescent applied white gold bâton markers and Arabic numerals; printed minute track; luminescent white gold bâton hands.
Indications: date at 3.
Bracelet: Oyster in brushed steel; fold-over clasp.
Also available: steel and yellow gold, Oyster bracelet: smooth bezel Ref. 15203, knurled bezel Ref. 15223; yellow gold, knurled bezel Ref. 15238, Oyster bracelet, Jubilé.
Prices: on request.

OYSTER PERPETUAL DATEJUST — REF. 16234

Movement: mechanical, automatic winding, caliber Rolex 3135. Officially certified "chronometer" (C.O.S.C.).
Functions: hour, minute, center second, date.
Case: stainless steel, three-piece case (Ø 36 mm, thickness 12 mm), polished and brushed finish; sapphire crystal with Cyclope magnifying glass on date; knurled bezel in 18 kt white gold; screw-down crown with double safety device; screwed-on case back. Water-resistant to 10 atm.
Dial: in mellow pink mother-of-pearl; applied white gold Arabic numerals; white gold bâton hands.
Indications: date at 3.
Bracelet: Jubilé in brushed steel, with polished central links; fold-over clasp.
Also available: with various dial colors and bracelet types.
Prices: on request.

OYSTER PERPETUAL AIR-KING — REF. 14010

Movement: mechanical, automatic winding, caliber Rolex 3000.
Functions: hour, minute, center second.
Case: stainless steel, three-piece case (Ø 34 mm, thickness 11.5 mm), polished and brushed finish; sapphire crystal; slightly knurled bezel with embossed polished hour markers; screw-down crown with double protection; screwed-on case back. Water-resistant to 10 atm.
Dial: bright blue; applied white gold bâton markers; luminescent dots on the printed minute track; luminescent white gold bâton hands.
Bracelet: Oyster in brushed steel; fold-over clasp.
Also available: with white enameled dial and printed Roman numerals; silvered dial and smooth bezel Ref. 14000.
Prices: on request.

OYSTER PERPETUAL DATEJUST — REF. 78248

Movement: mechanical, automatic winding, caliber Rolex 2235. Officially certified "chronometer" (C.O.S.C.).
Functions: hour, minute, center second, date.
Case: 18 kt yellow gold, three-piece case (Ø 30 mm, thickness 10.5 mm), polished and brushed finish; sapphire crystal with Cyclope magnifying glass on date; screw down yellow gold crown, with double protection; screwed-on case back. Water-resistant to 10 atm.
Dial: champagne-color; applied yellow gold bâton markers; 2 applied yellow gold triangular markers set with rubies; printed minute track; yellow gold bâton hands.
Indications: date at 3.
Bracelet: Oyster in brushed yellow gold, with polished central links; fold-over clasp.
Also available: without rubies, steel with Oyster bracelet, pink dial and Roman numerals Ref. 78240.
Prices: on request.

ROLEX

OYSTER PERPETUAL — REF. 77513

Movement: mechanical, automatic winding, caliber Rolex 2230. Officially certified "chronometer" (C.O.S.C.).
Functions: hour, minute, center second.
Case: stainless steel and 18 kt yellow gold, three-piece case (Ø 30 mm, thickness 10 mm), polished and brushed finish; sapphire crystal; knurled bezel; screw-down crown in gold, with double safety device; screwed-on case back. Water-resistant to 10 atm.
Dial: white enameled; printed Roman numerals; yellow gold bâton markers and luminescent dots on the printed minute track; luminescent yellow gold bâton hands.
Bracelet: Oyster in brushed steel, with central links in polished gold; fold-over clasp.
Price: on request.

OYSTER PERPETUAL LADY DATEJUST — REF. 79136

Movement: mechanical, automatic winding, caliber Rolex 2235. Officially certified "chronometer" (C.O.S.C.).
Functions: hour, minute, center second, date.
Case: platinum, three-piece case (Ø 26 mm, thickness 10.5 mm), polished and brushed finish; sapphire crystal with Cyclope magnifying glass on date; bezel set with diamonds; screw-down crown in platinum, with double protection; screwed-on case back. Water-resistant to 10 atm.
Dial: silvered; applied white gold square markers set with diamonds; printed minute track; white gold bâton hands.
Indications: date at 3.
Bracelet: Superpresident in platinum, brushed finish, with polished central links; invisible fold-over clasp with embossed crown logo.
Price: on request.

OYSTER PERPETUAL LADY — REF. 76198

Movement: mechanical, automatic winding, caliber Rolex 2130. Officially certified "chronometer" (C.O.S.C.).
Functions: hour, minute, center second.
Case: 18 kt yellow gold, three-piece case (Ø 24 mm, thickness 9.5 mm), polished and brushed finish; sapphire crystal; knurled bezel; screw-down crown in gold, with double protection; screwed-on case back. Water-resistant to 10 atm.
Dial: black; applied yellow gold square markers set with diamonds; printed minute track; yellow gold bâton hands.
Bracelet: Oyster in brushed gold with polished central links; fold-over clasp.
Also available: with smooth bezel, silvered dial and applied bâton markers Ref. 76188.
Prices: on request.

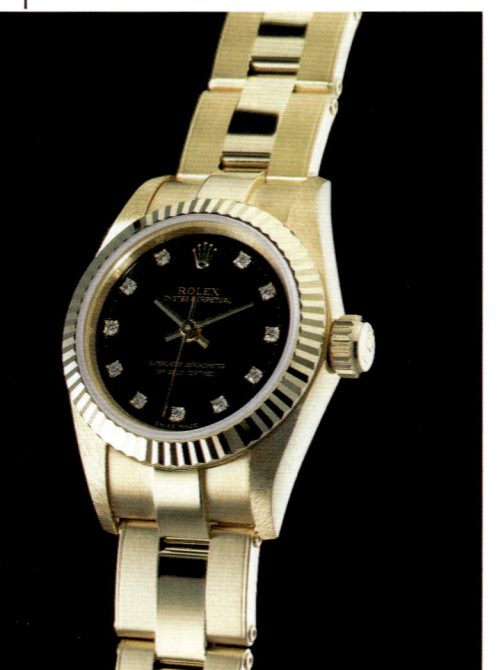

OYSTER PERPETUAL LADY DATEJUST — REF. 80298

Presented at the Basel Show in April 1999, this Oyster Perpetual Lady Datejust perfectly witnesses the new aesthetic evolutional trend chosen by Rolex: a vast collection of women gold models in various colors, adorned with precious stones and dials with colored gems, often to be combined with the same gems used in sets.
This photograph shows a model with 18 kt yellow gold case and bezel studded with 32 brilliants of heavy weighing into carats (1.45 kt appr.), while the bracelet is set with 174 brilliants (2.35 kt appr.). The dial, with 10 markers made of brilliants, is in white mother-of-pearl.
Price: on request.

ROLEX

CELLINI REF. 5330/5

Movement: mechanical, manual winding, by Rolex.
Functions: hour, minute.
Case: 18 kt pink gold, three-piece tonneau-shaped case (height 37 mm, width 36 mm, thickness 6.3 mm); jointed lugs; sapphire crystal; pink gold crown; snap-on back.
Dial: white; applied pink gold Arabic numerals and pointed markers; pink gold Dauphine hands.
Strap: crocodile leather; pink gold fold-over clasp.
Also available: with dial slate-grey; in the medium size Ref. 5320/5; in the small size Ref. 5310/5.
Prices: on request.

CELLINI REF. 5320/5

Benvenuto Cellini, a very great Italian artist, is considered the most important goldsmith of all times. Born in Florence in 1500, Cellini, a contemporary of Raphael's, Leonardo's and Michelangelo's, by his work contributed to make become goldsmith's art a fine art. Rolex intended to pay homage to this great artist by dedicating him their "classical" collection, which ranges from the most traditional extra-thin models to those which pay a tribute to contemporary aesthetic trends. This is the case of the new Cellini presented in 1999, which have a resolutely modern case design, where some themes loved by the Genevan House are clearly echoed, such as the horizontal link between the lugs, the tonneau-curved case side and emphasized circular bezel. These are all details typical of the Ovetto model of the Forties.
Proposed in three sizes - 26, 32, 37 millimeter diameters - the Cellini of this version is available with leather strap and white or slate-grey dial. The photograph shows the intermediate size (33,7x32x6 mm), with pink gold case and slate-grey dial.
Price: on request.

CELLINI REF. 4113/8

Movement: mechanical, manual winding, caliber Rolex 1602.
Functions: hour, minute.
Case: 18 kt yellow gold, two-piece rectangular case slightly curved on the four sides; sapphire crystal; waterproof gold crown; snap-on back.
Dial: champagne-color; applied yellow gold bâton markers; yellow gold bâton hands.
Strap: crocodile leather; yellow gold clasp.
Price: on request.

CELLINI REF. 4133/8

Ever since an elegant watch pretends a thin gold case, a well readable and rigorous dial, a pure and timeless design. All of these features are perfectly confirmed by the Rolex Cellini collection, using manufactured hand winding mechanical movements. The photograph shows a model with case in yellow gold with a particular design, an agreeable grey dial tone and a rigorous seamless black strap in crocodile leather.
Also available: lady's size with blue dial Ref. 4129/8.
Prices: on request.

263

Scatola del Tempo

Throughout the world, those who would dress elegantly, dress in Italian styles. Italy has won the status of being a point of reference, a parameter, a touchstone of that certain, inimitable "nonsocché" that stays firmly within the grasp of the "Bel Paese". And even Switzerland, home to all that is great in watchmaking, looks to Italy when it comes to "dressing" its most exclusive products. Watches, in fact, from being cult objects have become objects of culture, now also dress in Italian styles. And "Scatola del Tempo" came about in Barzanò on Lake Como, as the first of a new trend. The idea was to create cases for special watches that were not the usual sausage-like envelopes nor the boxes they came in from the shop. The evolution of watch collecting, the collecting of top quality watches, calls for something exclusive where these pieces can be kept. This was not to be a child's game of treasure chests. It is instead a question of taste, and not only: travelling, for example, and the desire to have some solid protection together with soft, perfectly sized wrapping for one's carefully chosen collection. And so those splendid leather and silk cases we all know were made.

The core of its production and the philosophy of Scatola del Tempo are tangible in the very functional cases designed precisely for the complicated watches with automatic winding mechanical movements. As the owner of a perpetual calendar well knows: if the watch stops because it hasn't been wound regularly, then the calendar must be brought up to date. Since calendars can be updated only by going forward and according to a very precise procedure, possible errors in the setting can even make it necessary to ask the House for assistance. The series of mechanical cases, the "Rotors", made by Scatola del Tempo was designed precisely to keep these watches wound. There is a rotating mechanism inside each case that substitutes the natural movement of the wrist. Each of these, from the simplest boxes to the more voluminous cases, is entirely made by hand in the old craft traditions of Italy. The best leathers and most precious briar-woods are used for the exterior, and the interior is lined in exclusive silk materials. The silk has a Paisley design that is woven into the cloth, it can be seen and it can be felt by a caressing hand. Scatola del Tempo has also remembered the lovers of fine writing implements, and there are fine cases in which to keep fountain pens. And cases that can hold and protect men's accessories - for cuff links, or even rings, as well as the tiny instruments needed for tiny operations, mechanical or otherwise. Scatola del Tempo has certainly not forgotten women, and offers them cases for smaller sized watches as well as boxes and cases for jewellery.

On this page:
The latest offers have a new two-directional winding system with microprocessor electronic control of the action. These are thoroughly tested mechanisms made in Switzerland, identical to the new Pendulette's mechanism (on the left page).

7RTA *-This very luxurious briar-wood model with two little doors is divided in two parts. The upper part holds and can wind three watches; the lower hold four watches that do not need winding or it can hold other accessories (top).*

2RT *-This model allows two watches to be wound at the same time. In the upper section there is a tray where watches, jewellery and other accessories can be placed. Natural leather and Black (bottom).*

1RT Pendulette

The 1RT Pendulette is the newest creation from Scatola del Tempo. Slightly smaller than the original 1RT, the Pendulette has several big innovations. The first of these innovations is a completely new electronic system, which controls the rotation. After it is turned ON, the Pendulette will rotate for exactly 1.300 revolution per day, stopping in exactly the same position it was when it began. (If the unit is turned OFF before the 1.300 revolution cycle is complete, it will still stop in exactly the same position as when it was first started). Another innovation is the cylinder housing, with a precisely engineered groove which holds the spring-loaded watch holder. The spring-loading mechanism makes it easy to put virtually any size watch on the holder. Powered by standard LR-20 alkaline batteries, which last at least one year under normal use.

The 1RT Pendulette is available in two models: gold-colored brass with tan leather or silver-colored brass with black leather.

The "SdT" Watch

The name of this chronograph alludes to the name of the Italian company that is a leader in the production of precious leather cases for watches, considering taste and quality that is particularly modern as well as formal and functional choices of definite class.

Chronograph with automatic movement (Valjoux cal. 7750) with three counters and date. Steel case with screw-down crown and screwed-on case back, water-resistant to 10 atm. Dial with Arabic numerals and sword style hands with red/sky-blue "SdT" logo, counters and flange with tachymeter scale contrasting the black background. Calfskin strap and case with electronic rotational winding system programmed at 1200 revolutions in 24 hours, the basic piece of the company in Barzanò, an old hamlet in the Province of Lecco in the north west of Italy.

Scatola del Tempo

The boxes with Rotory Mechanism

These devices, designed for automatic movement wrist watches (particularly useful for perpetual calendars) substitute the wrist's movement for keeping the watches wound regularly. The S.C.S. & C. Scatola del Tempo has for several years produced special containers with one or more rotating supports run by an electronic micro-motor that supplies the movement for ideal winding. The traditional models offer ten different rewinding programs, in this way it is possible to simulate one's own activity level through a program selector placed inside the battery holder. Each program specifies a set schedule (considering the natural habits of people who wear the watches by day and set them down at night) of so many hours of rotations in both directions. Starting from the setting '0' there is a gradual lessening in the number of running hours but an increase in the number of rotations. The indications show, besides on-off, the state of the batteries (both automatic LED signal on the exterior, and a dial indicator on the back activated by a button) and the stand-by power. By using a 6 volt transformer in the jack, one can eliminate the batteries.However, rotors using alkaline batteries will work for about one year for all models.

Top, left:
6RTSP - Box for keeping six automatic watches wound plus two drawers for watches and jewellery (cuff links, rings, lighters, pens, etc.).
Black, natural leather, red.

Right:
1RT - Box for keeping one automatic watch wound. Black, natural leather, red.
In the one-watch box the selection of the rotation direction (clockwise, suitable for almost all automatics, or counter-clockwise as some need) can be made by using a selection-slide on the front of the rotor.

Trousse - Tool box with utensils produced by Bergeon, a Swiss company, for the care of one's watches.

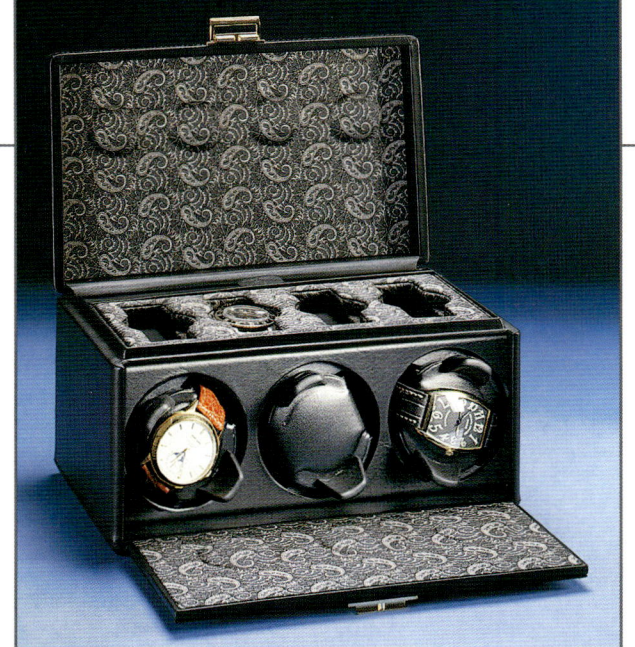

Scatola del Tempo

From the top:
7RT - Box for keeping three automatic watches wound plus four places for watches with leather straps or rigid bracelets. Black, natural leather, red.

1RTSL - Box for keeping one automatic watch wound, in black. Made in nylon and black leather with an opening with a gold colored metal ring making the watch visible, this article has a very good price.

3RT - Box for keeping three automatic watches wound, in black, leather, red. It is available in the Squelette version with briar wood base and the motor gears visible in black polished brass.

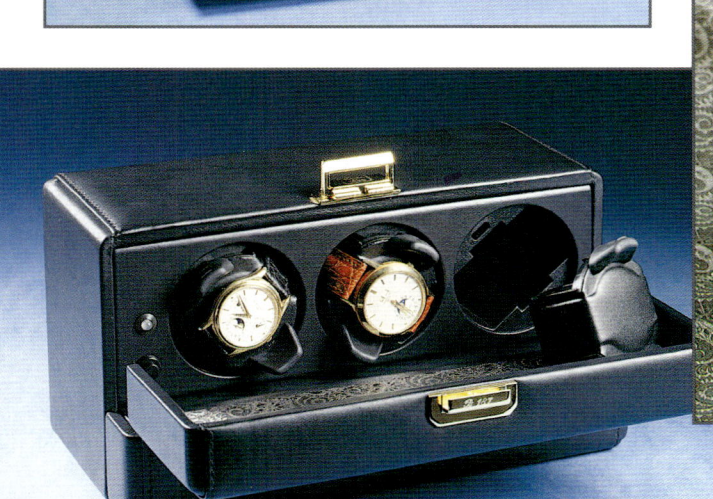

Bottom, from left:
2A - Box for two watches with leather straps or flexible bracelets. Black, natural leather, red.

1P - Men's jewellery box for travel, black with space for one watch and accessories (cuff links, rings, lighters, pens, etc.)

1A - Box for one watch with leather strap or flexible bracelet. Black, natural leather.

Bottom: 4B - Box for four watches with leather strap or flexible bracelet. Black, natural leather.

267

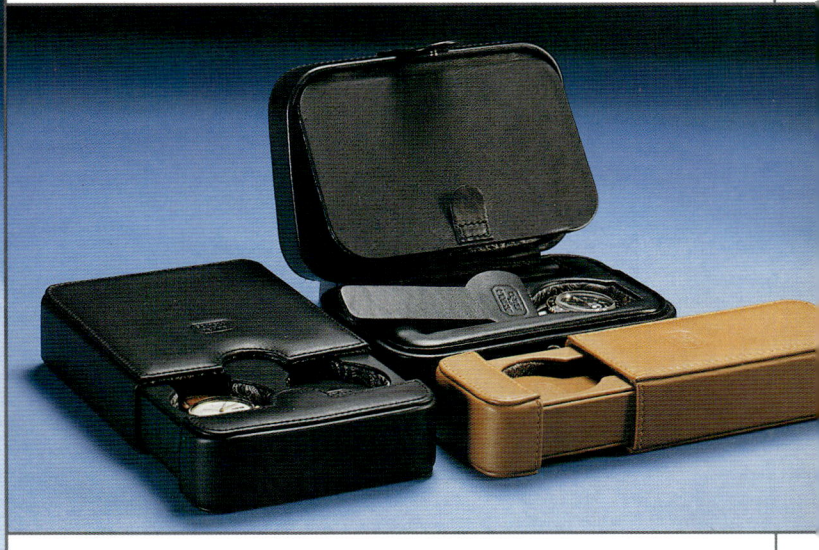

Scatola del Tempo

Technical specification

Exterior structure: Evaporated beech wood covered in natural organic tanned leather.
Interior: flexible polyurethane resin, differentiated density, covered in jacquard silk in paisley design or in leather. The internal structure can hold perfectly the specified number and size of watches. Each place provides the necessary space for the winding crown and any possible push-pieces for other functions.
Clasp: in gilded brass, marked and numbered by hand.
Each piece is entirely hand made by craftsmen; the hardware has received anti-magnetic treatment.

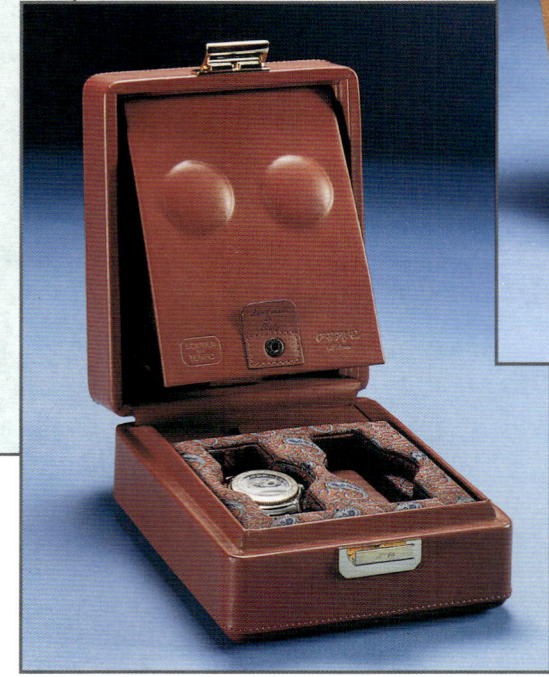

Bottom: 2+2 - Box for two watches with leather strap and two watches with rigid bracelet. Black, natural, red.

Above:
4+4SP -Travel box for eight watches with leather strap or flexible bracelet. Black, natural leather, red.

Bottom:
16B - Travelling case with places for sixteen watches with leather strap or rigid bracelet. Black, natural leather.

Bottom:
4+4 RA - Briar-wood box for four watches with leather strap plus four with rigid bracelet.

Scatola del Tempo

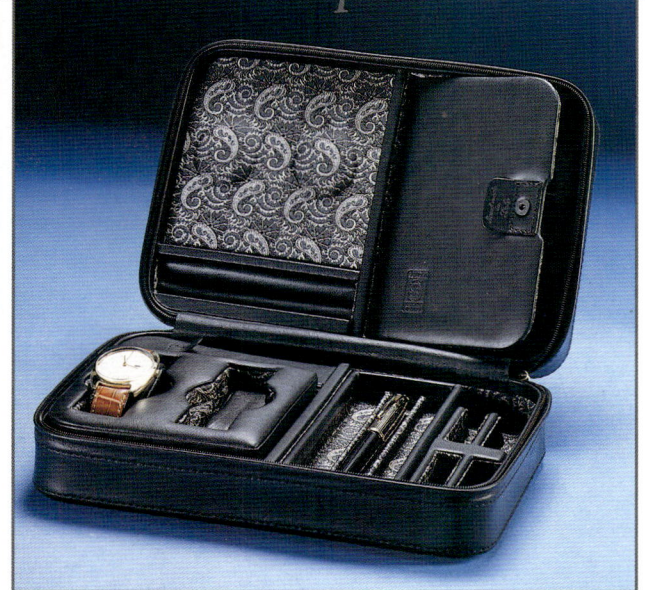

Left:
3P - Men's accessories case in travel version for three watches and various accessories (cuff links, rings, lighters, pens, etc.).
Black, natural leather, red.

Right:
4P - Men's accessories case for four watches with leather strap and accessories (cuff links, rings, lighters, pens, etc.).
Black, natural leather.

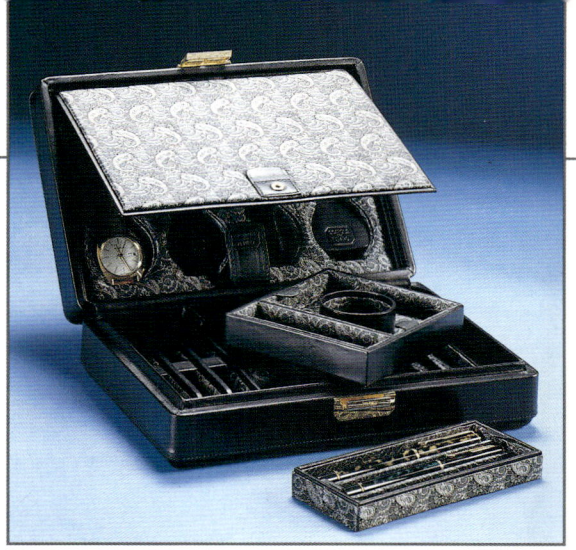

Right:
Treasure Box D - Travel jewellery box for women. Red, blue, green.

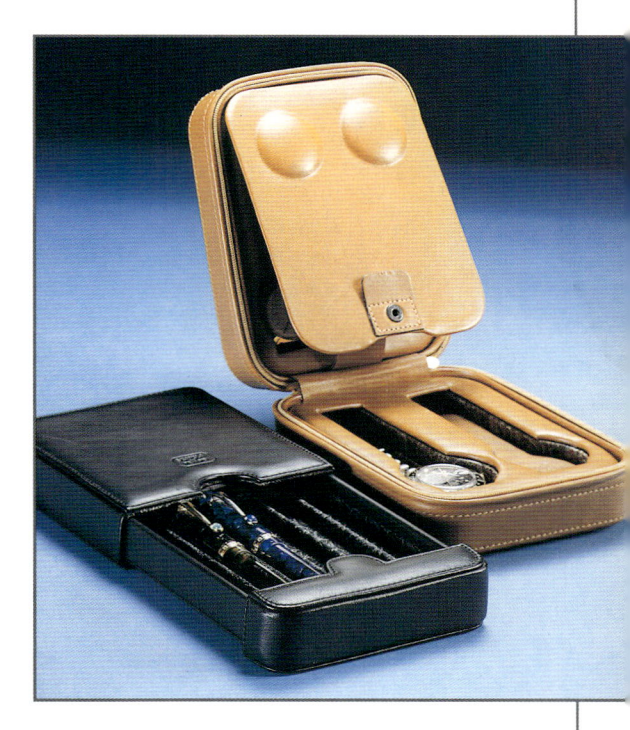

Top, from left:
Small pen case - Holds six pens and comes in black, natural leather and red.
4A - Travel box for four watches with leather strap or flexible bracelet. Black, natural leather, red.

Pen cases
Bottom: The medium size model carries 12 pens and comes in black, natural leather, red.
Right: The large size holds 24 pens and comes in red.

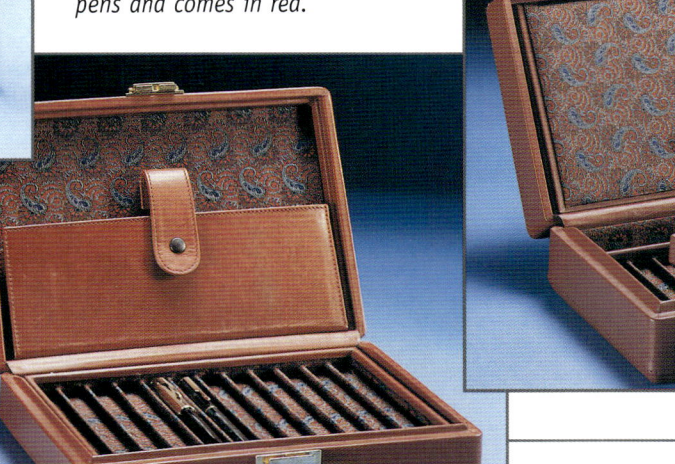

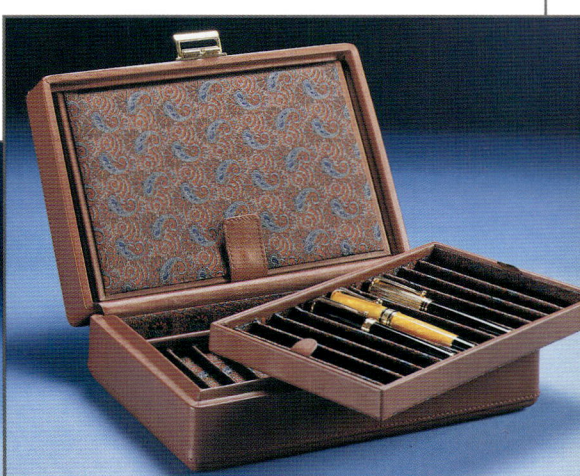

Above:
Treasure Box C - Large jewellery box for women. Red, blue, green. Medium size available in green.

269

TAG Heuer

What could possibly link five of the most famous stylists of the world with TAG Heuer? Its a question of the links of a bracelet. On one side we have fashion superstars such as Karl Lagerfeld, Thierry Mugler, Narciso Rodriguez, Alexander McQueen and Gianfranco Ferré. And on the other, a Company famous primarily for its production of high quality sports watches. The bracelet in question is the vigorous, sinuous model from the collection called Link, one of the latest at TAG Heuer. Its particular shape was a source of inspiration for the five stylists, who accepted eagerly the challenge of developing sculpture-clothing, on the edge of extravagance, by using the basic element of the bracelet, an "S" of steel, a remarkable expression of strength.

TAG has not abandoned its technological vocation as the latest Kirium collection shows, designed by Jorg Hysek. Among the new versions, the Automatic Chronograph, simple and essential in its elegant lines and the advanced technology of its construction. It is pure understatement: Kirium with a rubber strap uniting extreme sport with the natural suppleness of the strap; Kirium Ti5, the first watch in the world in Grade 5 polished titanium, carbon fibre dial and quartz movement with a lithium battery and 8 year power reserve.

The models of the Classic collection will satisfy collectors and fine watch enthusiasts and repropose some of the classics from Heuer's collections: the second edition of the chronograph, Monaco, that became famous when it was worn by Steve McQueen in the 1970 film, "LeMans"; a Carrera Automatic a GMT and a chronograph in "Racing" version. As for "contemporary" models, the Collection 2000 has been completed with the Exclusive models. Modern design, automatic movement, it has a style that is serious and distinct, decisive lines and balance in its use of steel. The special edition of the chronograph 6000 (only 500 pieces) is destined for collectors. It was made to celebrate the 50th anniversary of the Formula 1 World Championship.

The History

1860 - The Company was founded at Saint-Imier, Switzerland. **1869** - Heuer patents his first manual winding system. **1887** - Heuer patent for the oscillating pinion chronograph, still used in chronographs made by the best known houses. **1889** - The collection of Heuer chronographs is presented at the Paris World's Fair and is awarded a silver medal. **1908** - Invents and patents the dial with the pulse-meter, still used in medical situations. **1911** - Heuer presents the first clock for automobile dashboards, with "Time of Trip" indicator. **1916** - The Company experiments the first precision mechanism to measure time to one hundredth of a second, the Micrograph. **1920** - Heuer is appointed official timekeeper of the Olympic Games of Antwerp; in '24 the same will happen for Paris and in '28 at Amsterdam. **1930** - The use of the automobile is increasingly common, and Heuer builds the first dashboard clock with an hour counter and the first chronograph with several dials. **1933** - The first dashboard chronometer with hour counter: Autavia. **1949** - The House laboratory produces the extraordinary chronograph, Mareograph, that shows the tides. Patented the same year. **1964** - The Carrera, the first functional design chronograph. **1965** - The Microtimer is patented, the first miniaturized sports chronometer, with readings down to $1/1000$ of a second. **1971** - Heuer is the official time keeper for Ferrari up to 1979. **1972** - Another patent. This time for Microsplit, the first digital pocket chronometer. **1974** - Heuer is official chronometer for Ferrari. **1976** - The new Microsplit chronometer with LED (liquid crystal) display. **1980** - Heuer is the official time-keeper at the Moscow Olympics and the Lake Placid Winter Olympic Games. **1983** - The first quartz analogue chronograph with 12 hour, 1 hour and 30 second counters. **1985** - An important year in the history of contemporary watchmaking. Heuer joins TAG (Technologie d'Avant-Garde, which acquires a majority position in the company) and from now on the company becomes TAG Heuer. Thus the precision of Heuer mechanics is accompanied by the use of innovative materials which is TAG's specialization. The headquarters at Marin now has branches throughout the world. **1986** - TAG Heuer presents the sports watch model, Formula 1, in steel and fibre-glass. This year Alain Prost brings the Company back to the racing world with his world championship. **1987** - The TAG Heuer S/El (sport/elegance) collection is presented and at the same time by sponsoring Marc Girardelli, Helmut Hoeflehner and Harti Weirather, the Company enters the world of World Cup skiing. **1989** - Heuer becomes the official time-keeper of the World Cup trials for downhill skiing for F.I.S. **1992** - TAG Heuer official timekeeper of the World Championship of Formula 1 racing. **1994** - Model 6000 is chosen as "Watch of the Year" by more than 40,000 enthusiasts and 8,000 specialists in this sector. TAG Heuer is always the excellent result of a perfect combination: sports and precision. This explains the frequency with which the House has been chosen as official time-keeper in those sport specialities most closely tied to time, that is, where time is the real competitor. Over the years it has been able to propose a wide range of watches to satisfy even the most exacting professional with its guarantee of reliability and durability. **1997** - Kirium, a new collection of sports watches is presented in September. Created by the German designer, Jorg Hysek, the line presents a new case, bracelet and dial. **1998** - An aggressive publicity campaign, based on the competition experiences of the McLaren Mercedes team is the '99 season opener for the Company. Kirium has a full steel quartz chronograph. Futuristic conception for the S/El West McLaren Mercedes chronograph that measures up to a tenth of a second and has a silver, black and red dial, the McLaren colors. The new "6000" chronograph, the chronometer movement entirely hand assembled. The TAG Classic collection is a re-edition of Monaco, the square chronograph worn by Steve McQueen in "Le Mans", much sought by collectionists in the Seventies, it was the first watch to have the Chronomatic movement.

TAG HEUER

KIRIUM CHRONOGRAPH   REF. CL2112.BA.0701

Movement: mechanical, automatic winding, ETA caliber 2894/2.
Functions: hour, minute, center second, date, chronograph with 3 counters.
Case: stainless steel, three-piece brushed case (Ø 41.5 mm, thickness 13.6 mm); curved sapphire crystal; polished counter-clockwise turning bezel, with tritium marker and engraved minute track, useful for the calculation of diving times; screw-down crown with case protection, with microgasket preventing water and dust infiltrations; screwed-on case back. Water-resistant to 20 atm.
Dial: silvered; luminescent applied round markers; printed minute track on the beveled ring; luminescent skeletonized hands.
Indications: small second at 3, hour counter and date at 6, minute counter at 9, center second counter.
Bracelet: brushed steel, with polished central links; fold-over clasp with double safety device.
Also available: leather strap; brushed steel, blue or black dial. Lady's size, quartz movement, steel with polished and brushed finish, silvered, blue, black or bordeaux dial, leather strap or bracelet.
Prices: on request.

KIRIUM   REF. WL5110.BA.0700

Movement: mechanical, automatic winding, caliber 2892/A2. Officially certified "chronometer" (C.O.S.C.).
Functions: hour, minute, center second, date.
Case: stainless steel, three-piece brushed case (Ø 37 mm, thickness 11 mm); curved sapphire crystal; counter-clockwise turning bezel, with tritium marker and engraved minute track, useful for the calculation of diving times; screw-down crown with case protection, with microgasket preventing water and dust infiltrations; screwed-on case back. Water-resistant to 20 atm.
Dial: silvered; luminescent applied round markers and Arabic numerals 6, 9 and 12; printed minute track with 4 luminescent dots on the beveled ring; luminescent Mercedes hands.
Indications: date at 3.
Bracelet: brushed steel, with polished central links; fold-over clasp with double safety device.
Also available: black dial; case and bracelet polished-brushed, blue, green or copper dial; leather strap. Lady's size (Ø 28 mm, thickness 10) and quartz movement: polished steel, blue or white dial or steel with polished and brushed finish, silvered or black dial, strap or bracelet.
Prices: on request.

SERIES 6000 GOLD   REF. WH5143.FC.6059

Movement: mechanical, automatic winding, ETA caliber 2892/A2. Officially certified "chronometer" (C.O.S.C.).
Functions: hour, minute, center second, date.
Case: 18 kt yellow gold, three-piece case (Ø 38 mm, thickness 10 mm), polished and brushed finish; flat sapphire crystal with magnifying lens on date; matte finished counter-clockwise turning ring with polished embossments and engravings; yellow gold screw-down crown with case protection, with double gasket; screwed-on case back. Water-resistant to 20 atm.
Dial: white; luminescent applied markers; printed minute track on the beveled ring; luminescent Mercedes hands.
Indications: date at 3.
Strap: crocodile leather; fold-over gold clasp.
Also available: with gold bracelet, with double safety device, with interlaced links; anthracite or rhodium plated dial; in the medium size (Ø 36 mm, thickness 10 mm) white dial, leather strap or bracelet.
Prices: on request.

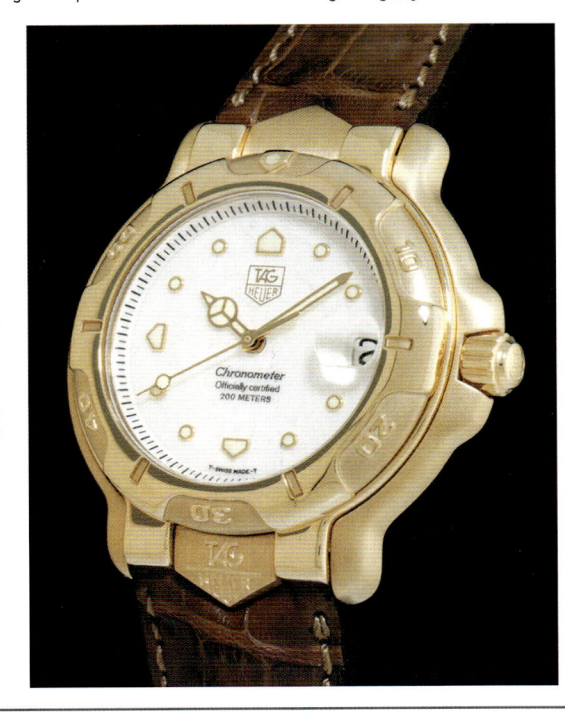

SERIES 6000 CHRONOGRAPH   REF. CH5112.BA.0675

Movement: mechanical, automatic winding, ETA caliber 2894/2. Officially certified "chronometer" (C.O.S.C.).
Functions: hour, minute, center second, date, chronograph with 3 counters.
Case: stainless steel, three-piece case (Ø 40 mm, thickness 12 mm), polished and brushed finish; flat sapphire crystal; matte finished counter-clockwise turning ring with polished embossments and engravings; screw-down crown with case protection, with double gasket; ogival pushers; screwed-on case back. Water-resistant to 20 atm.
Dial: anthracite; applied Arabic numerals; luminescent dots on the minute track; luminescent Mercedes hands.
Indications: small second at 3, hour counter and date at 6, minute counter at 9, center second counter, tachymeter scale on the beveled ring, minute track.
Bracelet: stainless steel, with interlaced links, polished and brushed finish; fold-over clasp with double safety device.
Also available: white, blue or copper dial; leather strap; steel and yellow gold, white dial, leather strap or bracelet.
Prices: on request.

271

TAG HEUER

LINK CHRONOGRAPH   REF. CT2111.BA.0550

Movement: mechanical, automatic winding, Valjoux caliber 7750.
Functions: hour, minute, small second, date, chronograph with 3 counters.
Case: stainless steel, three-piece brushed case (Ø 39.7 mm, thickness 15.8 mm); curved sapphire crystal; brushed counter-clockwise turning bezel, with engraved minute track, useful for the calculation of diving times; screw-down crown with case protection, with microgasket preventing water and dust infiltrations; screwed-on case back. Water-resistant to 20 atm. 
Dial: black; applied bâton markers with luminescent dots; luminescent sword style hands.
Indications: date at 3, hour counter at 6, small second at 9, minute counter at 12, center second counter, minute track with divisions for $1/5$ of a second, tachymeter scale on the beveled ring.
Bracelet: stainless steel, integrated with brushed links; recessed fold-over clasp with double safety device.
Also available: blue dial; steel with polished and brushed finish, white dial; quartz movement.
Prices: on request.

LINK CHRONOMETER   REF. WT5110.BA.0550

Movement: mechanical, automatic winding, ETA caliber 2892/2. Officially certified "chronometer" (C.O.S.C.).
Functions: hour, minute, center second, date.
Case: stainless steel, three-piece brushed case (Ø 39.7 mm, thickness 13.2 mm); curved sapphire crystal; brushed counter-clockwise turning bezel, with engraved minute track, useful for the calculation of diving times; screw-down crown with case protection, with microgasket preventing water and dust infiltrations; screwed-on case back. Water-resistant to 20 atm. 
Dial: black; applied Arabic numerals; applied bâton markers with luminescent dots; luminescent sword style hands.
Indications: date at 3.
Bracelet: stainless steel, integrated with brushed links; recessed fold-over clasp with double safety device.
Also available: white dial; steel with polished and brushed finish, blue dial.
Prices: on request.

2000 CLASSIC CHRONOGRAPH   REF. CK2110.BA.0330

Movement: mechanical, automatic winding, Valjoux caliber 7750.
Functions: hour, minute, small second, date, chronograph with 3 counters.
Case: stainless steel, three-piece case, matte finish (Ø 40 mm, thickness 13.5 mm); flat sapphire crystal; counter-clockwise turning dodecagonal bezel, with 6 polished hold riders, a tritium marker and engraved minute track, useful for the calculation of diving times; screw-down crown with case protection; screwed-on case back. Water-resistant to 20 atm. 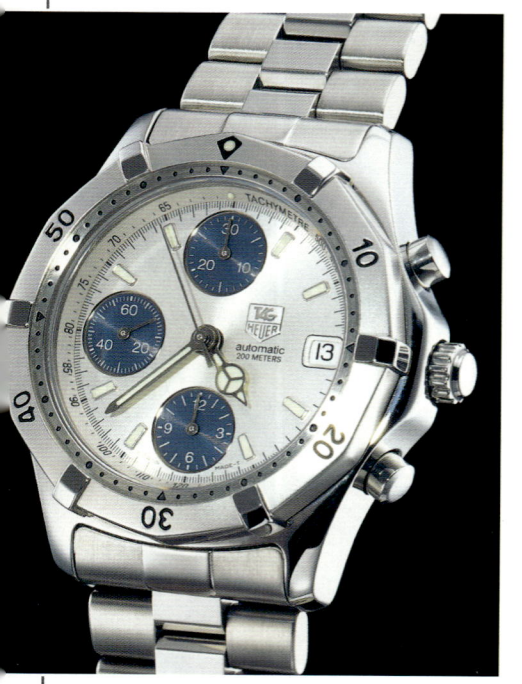
Dial: silvered; blue zones with concentric-circles pattern; luminescent applied bâton markers; luminescent Mercedes hands.
Indications: date at 3, hour counter at 6, small second at 9, minute counter at 12, center second counter, tachymeter scale on the beveled ring.
Bracelet: stainless steel, matte finish; extensible fold-over clasp with double safety device.
Also available: red or blue dial and silvered counters.
Prices: on request.

2000 EXCLUSIVE   REF. WN2111.BA.0311

Movement: mechanical, automatic winding, ETA caliber 2824/2.
Functions: hour, minute, center second, date.
Case: stainless steel, three-piece brushed case (Ø 39.6 mm, thickness 11.5 mm); flat sapphire crystal; counter-clockwise turning dodecagonal bezel, with 6 polished hold riders, a tritium marker and engraved minute track, useful for the calculation of diving times; screw-down crown with case protection; screwed-on case back. Water-resistant to 20 atm. 
Dial: black, Clous de Paris texture; applied polished bâton markers with luminescent dots; silvered railway minute track; applied polished Arabic numerals; luminescent bâton hands.
Indications: date at 3.
Bracelet: stainless steel, brushed finish with polished central links; fold-over clasp with double safety device.
Also available: silvered dial.
Prices: on request.

TAG HEUER

MONACO II CHRONOGRAPH   REF. CS2111.FC.8119

Movement: mechanical, automatic winding, caliber ETA 2894/2.
Functions: hour, minute, small second, date, chronograph with 3 counters.
Case: stainless steel, three-piece case, curved square, polished and brushed finish (size 38 mm, width 38 mm, thickness 13.5 mm); curved Plexiglas crystal; semi-recessed crown with case protection; elliptical faceted pushers; engraved case back, attached by 4 screws. Water-resistant to 3 atm.
Dial: black, with sun pattern finish; applied bâton markers; luminescent dots on the round minute track; luminescent bâton hands.
Indications: small second at 3, hour counter and date at 6, minute counter at 9, center second counter, minute track.
Strap: black leather; stainless steel clasp.
Price: on request. Numbered series.
Also available: brown leather strap.

CARRERA GMT   REF. WS2113.BC.0795

Movement: mechanical, automatic winding, Eta cal. 2893/2, power reserve of 42 hours, 28,800 vibrations per hour (vph), Incabloc shock-resistant system.
Functions: hour, minute, center second, date, second time zone, 24-hour indication.
Case: stainless steel (Ø 35.5 mm, thickness 11.3 mm); curved Plexiglas crystal; screwed-on case back. Water-resistant to 3 atm.
Dial: black; printed bâton markers and Arabic numerals; printed railway minute track; luminescent bâton hands.
Indications: date at 3, second time zone–24-hour with arrow-shaped red-pointed center hand.
Strap: brown leather; stainless steel clasp.
Also available: leather strap, smooth or punched, black leather; black crocodile leather strap.
Prices: on request.

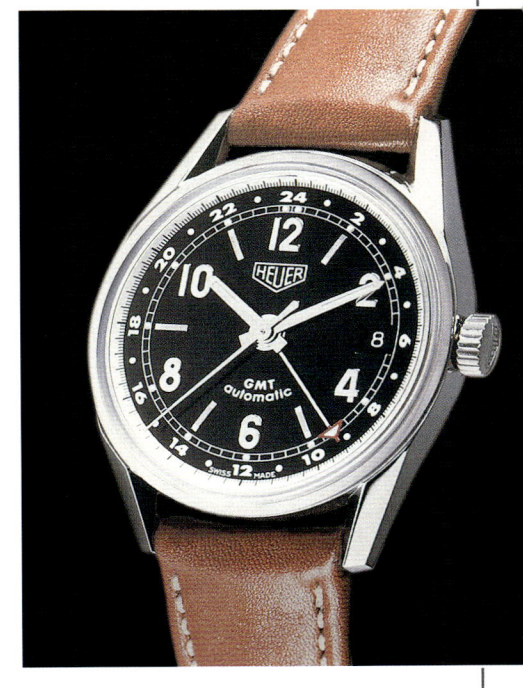

CARRERA CHRONOGRAPH   REF. CS3140.BC.0727

Movement: mechanical, manual winding, TAG Heuer caliber 1873 (Lemania base).
Functions: hour, minute, small second, chronograph with 3 counters.
Case: 18 kt yellow gold (Ø 35.5 mm, thickness 13 mm); curved Plexiglas crystal; yellow gold crown; screwed-on case back. Water-resistant to 3 atm.
Dial: silvered; zones with concentric-circles pattern; applied bâton markers with luminescent dots; luminescent bâton hands.
Indications: minute counter at 3, hour counter at 6, small second at 9, center second counter, hundredth scale, minute track with divisions for 1/5 of a second on the beveled ring.
Strap: crocodile leather; yellow gold clasp.
Also available: stainless steel, punched black leather strap. Carrera "Racing", stainless steel, copper dial and brown crocodile leather strap or black dial and punched black leather strap.
Prices: on request.
New edition of the original model realized in 1964.

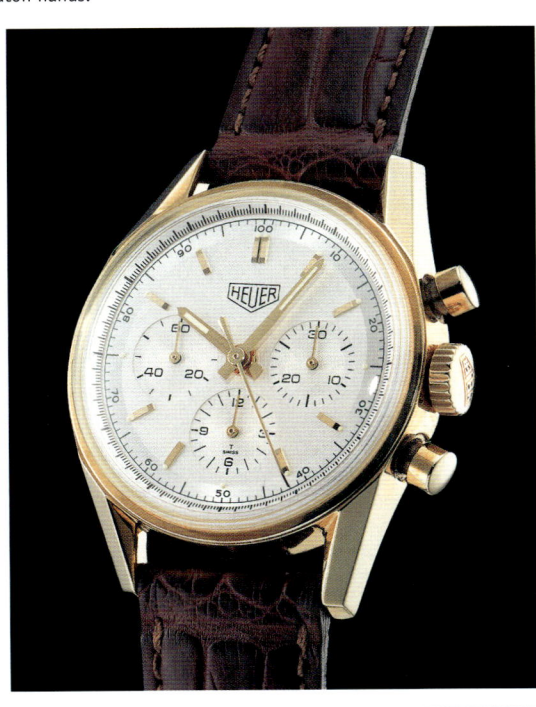

CARRERA   REF. WS2112.BC.0725

Movement: mechanical, automatic winding, Eta cal. 2824/2, power reserve 40 hours, 28,800 vibrations per hour (vph), Incabloc shock-resistant system.
Functions: hours, minutes, seconds, date.
Case: steel (Ø 35.5 mm, thickness 11.3 mm); domed Plexiglas; screwed-on back. water-resistant to 3 atm.
Dial: silvered; applied bâton markers and Arabic numerals; luminescent dots on the railway minute track; minute track with division for 1/5 second on the flange; luminescent bâton hands.
Indications: date at 3.
Strap: leather; steel clasp.
Also available: black dial; punched black or smooth brown strap.
Prices: on request.

Ulysse Nardin

This name is always a synonym for precision and reliability in marine chronometry. He has dedicated 1999 to the conquest of the most complicated mechanisms. The latest, ambitious marvel of technology is the GMT± perpetual calendar. This is the only one that, besides having an exclusive rapid time zone change system with permanent indication of the original date, allows up-dating the calendar both forward and back using only the crown. The mechanisms are extremely smooth and the GMT±, precisely because it is extremely functional and simple to use, is designed to be worn everyday even though it is among the most sophisticated watches ever created.

For world travellers, the GMT± Big Date is invaluable, it allows the regulation of various time zones at the same time and instantly without interfering with the working of the watch that always remembers what time it "really" is in the "Hometime" aperture. Permanent indication of the original time is also part of the San Marco Big Date, recently renewed with an exclusive rapid time zone change system and showing the Big Date in the double aperture at 2 o'clock. The aspect of Michelangelo is completely changed, particularly the shape of the case which, in the new model, that flanks but does not substitute the old, is no longer rectangular but instead tonneau.

A small but definite innovation for the famous marine chronograph, with the date between 4 and 5 o'clock and no longer at 12, considerably improving the graphic balance of the dial.

Ulysse Nardin has suggested a new version of Portobello with a platinum case. The characteristic Champlevé

The History

Certainly, the specialization chosen by Ulysse Nardin is unusual. This House, founded in the shadow of the Jura Massif, a thousand kilometers from the sea, is inextricably linked to marine chronometry, and in this sector has won almost all the 18 gold medals awarded at International Exhibitions. The story of this attraction has its roots as far back as the last part of the 18th Century, in the area near Le Locle. Here, the Nardin family was known for its skill in building marine chronometers that were precise to half a second and made it possible to fix the point of longitude. It was essential that these instruments be extremely precise, considering that only one second, at the Equator, corresponds to 463 meters.

1823 - Ulysse Nardin was born at Le Locle on the 22nd of January. After some training with his father, Leonard Frederic, he was sent to William Dubois, considered one of the most precise watch "builders" of the time.
1846 - At the age of 23, Ulysse Nardin was signing chronometers and complicated clocks thanks to the experience he had accumulated working with a watchmaker who was specialized in astronomical pendulum clocks. His shop became a small manufacture, increasingly specialized in marine chronometry, and the official supplier to many naval fleets.
1855 - Ulysse's only child, Paul David Nardin, is born.
1858 - Founding of Astronomical Observatory of Neuchâtel.
1860 - Ulysse acquires a high precision astronomical regulator to regulate his pocket chronometers (built in 1768 by Jacques-Frederic Houriet, it is now in the museum of Le Locle). The first exports to the United States, and mounting fame.
1861 - His chronometers won the gold medal at the London World's Fair.
1865 - The factory moves to its present address in Rue du Jardin, 3.
1876 - Ulysse Nardin dies at 53 on February 20th, probably of a heart attack. The Company is taken over by his son, Paul, then 21 years old. All the Marine Chronometers are tested by the Geneva and Neuchâtel Observatories.
1877 - The office in Geneva is opened for sales and some phases of production.
1878 - Gold Medal for the quality of his pocket model Marine Chronometers at the Paris World's Fair.
1893 - Gold medal and first prize at the Chicago World's Fair.
1900 - The wars of the century have made production fly. Ulysse Nardin can boast of 4,000 chronometry approvals warded by various Observatories and he is "recommended" by the navies of 48 countries that have adopted his product.
1908 - At the Tokyo World's Fair, Mikado and the Royal Prince purchase three Pocket Model Ulysse Nardin Chronometers.
1911 - Third Swiss patent for the perfect control of the chronographic wheel of time mechanism.
1960 - The technological revolution due to quartz forces Ulysse Nardin, like many other Swiss companies, to yield his place in the forefront. Rather than a crisis, it is a collapse: the manufacture closes at the end of the 1960's and is abandoned. Its archives are lost, hundreds of drawings and

plans are destroyed during the 20 year blackout.

1975 - The Neuchâtel Observatory publishes its last book on the efficiency of the chronometers. These in fact are no longer scientifically interesting in the age of electronics. This is, therefore, its last report, and shows that, starting from 1846 Ulysse Nardin had been awarded: 4,324 certificates of precision for marine chronometers (95% of those issued); 2,411 prizes of which 1.069 were firsts; the World's Fairs had brought him 14 Grand Prix and 10 Gold Medals.

1983 - The name is purchased by Rolf Schnyder, an ambitious manager who trained in marketing at Jaeger-LeCoultre, pioneer in the production of components for watchmaking in South East Asia, and owner of the Precima of Kuala Lampur in Malaysia. This is a model-company employing 2,000 people, and turns out millions of dial and quartz movements directed towards Swiss watch production. Schnyder is firmly convinced that mechanical watchmaking has a future, and plans a début for the "new" company that will immediately place it in the Olympus of the great names.

1985 - At the Basel Fair, the Astrolabium Galileo Galilei, and incredible wristwatch - created by Ludwig Oechslin, a young and brilliant engineer whom Schnyder discovered and convinced to work on the project - brings astral indications to the classic complications in great watches. Its immediate success indicates the road to be followed.

1988 - the Copernicus Planetario is presented.

1989 - Two important complication models: the San Marco with minute repeater, and the Split-Seconds Berlin.

1992 - The Tellurium Johannes Kepler completes the trilogy of the astro-complication masterpieces.

1993 - A new complication with the San Marco sonnerie. Beginning of the Great Ships in polychrome Cloisonné enamels.

1994 - The GMT± is the only double time zone with a patent for forward and reverse correction.

1996 - The 150th anniversary of the company name sees the birth of the Marine Chronometer. Its excellent reception convinces the House to create a collection (1997) around it. The Ludwig Perpetual has absolute synchronization between the date discs thanks to its sophisticated entirely train-based mechanism.

1998 - The Single Button Chrono is presented to commemorate 175 years since the birth of Ulysse Nardin. Among the "special" watches is the San Marco Jungle, with Cloisonné automatons (or Jaquemarts) in a tropical scene. The Portobello was also presented considering its case holding a wrist/pocket model chronometer inspired by the 1708 battle between Spanish galleons and the English fleet. The double aperture "big date" is also introduced, both on the San Marco GMT± and on the San Marco Big Date with new automatic UN 34 movement.

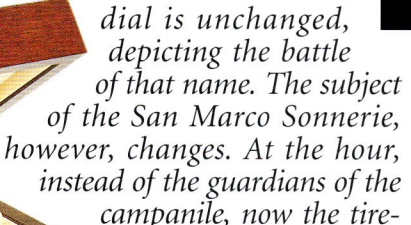

dial is unchanged, depicting the battle of that name. The subject of the San Marco Sonnerie, however, changes. At the hour, instead of the guardians of the campanile, now the tireless blacksmith are to remind us of the fleeing hours, hammering their anvils when it is time.

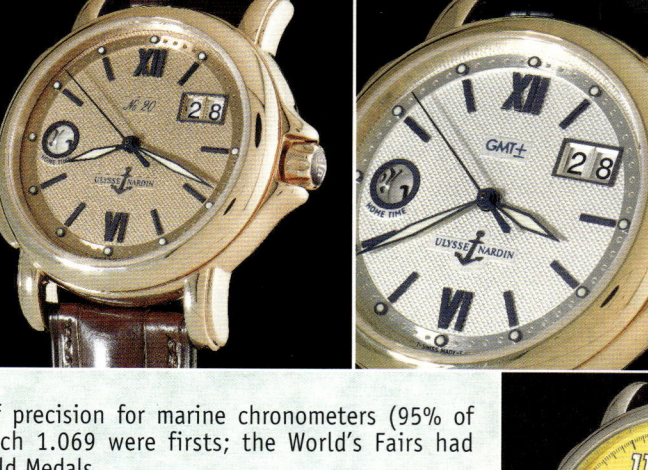

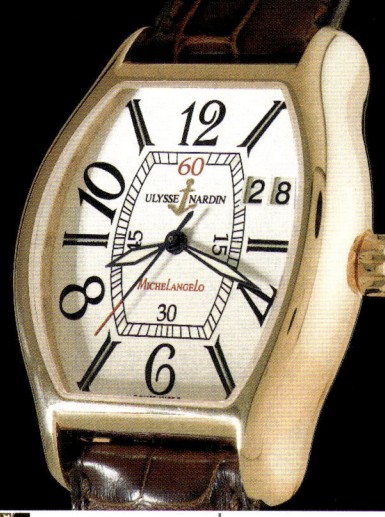

275

ULYSSE NARDIN

Ulysse Nardin's photographs were reduced by 6% with respect to the other pieces.

CHRONOGRAPH RATTRAPANTE — REF. 440.22

Movement: mechanical, manual winding, caliber Venus 179 of the Fourties.
Functions: hour, minute, small second, split-second chronograph with 2 counters.
Case: 18 kt white gold, three-piece case; curved sapphire crystal; white gold crown with pusher; white gold oval pushers; snap-on back displaying the movement through a sapphire crystal. Water-resistant to 3 atm.
Dial: black; zones with concentric-circle pattern; applied white gold Roman numerals; white gold Breguet hands. 
Indications: minute counter at 3, small second at 9, center second and split-second counters; minute track with divisions for 1/5 of a second; tachymeter scale on the beveled ring.
Strap: crocodile leather; white gold clasp.
Price: on request.
Realized in a limited edition of 10 pieces for each version, also in yellow or pink gold.
Also available: with ivory dial and silvered counters.

BERLIN II CHRONOGRAPH RATTRAPANTE — REF. 583.22/7

Movement: mechanical, automatic winding, caliber Ulysse Nardin 57, derived from the Valjoux 7750, to obtain the split-second function and the indication of a second time zone time.
Functions: hour, minute, small second, second time zone, 24-hour indication, split-second chronograph with 3 counters.
Case: stainless steel, three-piece case (Ø 40 mm, thickness 14.2 mm); curved sapphire crystal; screw-down crown with case protection; split-function pusher between 7 and 8; case back attached by 5 screws with an engraving reminding the 1936 Olympic Games of Berlin. Water-resistant to 3 atm. 
Dial: silvered, engine turned (guilloché) by hand; zones with concentric-circle pattern; applied bâton markers; blued stainless steel leaf style hands.
Indications: second time zone 24-hour display at 3, hour counter at 6, small second at 9, minute counter at 12, center second and split-second counters, minute track with divisions for 1/5 of a second, tachymeter scale on the beveled ring.
Bracelet: steel; double fold-over clasp, with safety pusher.
Price: USD 9,600.
Also available: leather strap USD 9,000; in yellow gold USD 15,000; only gold bracelet USD 22,600.

MARINE CHRONOMETER CHRONOGRAPH — REF. 353.22/7

Movement: mechanical, automatic winding, Ulysse Nardin caliber 35 (ETA caliber 2892 base + chronograph module), 28,800 vph, 57 jewels.
Functions: hour, minute, small second, date, chronograph with 3 counters.
Case: stainless steel, three-piece case (Ø 38 mm, thickness 12.9 mm); flat sapphire crystal with antireflective treatment on both sides; screwed-on knurled bezel; steel tag fixed on the case side by 2 screws with progressive number engraved; screw-down crown; screwed pushers; case back in anallergic titanium fastened by 4 screws, with engravings of the 18 medals won by Ulysse Nardin at international shows. Water-resistant to 20 atm. 
Dial: silvered; embossed blue painted Arabic numerals; luminescent blue painted Poire hands.
Indications: center second counter, small second at 3, date between 4 and 5, hour counter at 6, minute counter at 9, minute track with divisions for 1/5 of a second and luminescent dots, tachymeter scale on the beveled ring.
Bracelet: steel; stainless steel fold-over clasp.
Price: USD 3,900.
Also available: leather strap USD 3,300; black or blue dial.

MARINE CHRONOMETER — REF. 263.22/7

Movement: mechanical, automatic winding, Ulysse Nardin caliber 26. Officially certified "chronometer" (C.O.S.C.).
Functions: hour, minute, small second, date, power reserve.
Case: stainless steel, three-piece case (Ø 38 mm, thickness 10.85 mm); flat sapphire crystal with antireflective treatment on both sides; screwed-on knurled bezel; steel tag fixed on the case side by 2 screws and progressive number engraved; screw-down crown; case back in anallergic titanium fastened by six screws, with engraved list of the 18 gold medals awarded between 1862 and 1964. Water-resistant to 20 atm. 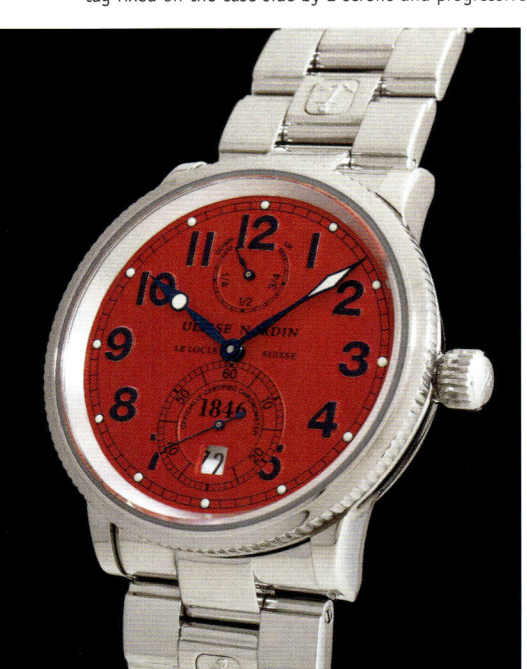
Dial: red; embossed blue painted Arabic numerals; luminescent dots on the blue painted railway minute track; luminescent blue painted Poire hands.
Indications: small second and date at 6, power reserve at 12.
Bracelet: steel; stainless steel fold-over clasp.
Price: USD 3,900.
Realized in 1996 to celebrate the 150th anniversary of the foundation of the House, in a numbered edition.
Also available: leather strap USD 3,300; silvered, blue, white lacquer or yellow dial, Arabic or Roman numerals; white dial, Roman numerals, or silvered dial, Arabic numerals.

ULYSSE NARDIN

GMT± PERPETUAL   REF. 321.22

Movement: mechanical, automatic winding, Ulysse Nardin caliber 32.
Functions: hour, minute, small second, perpetual calendar (date, day, month, year), second time zone, 24-hour indication.
Case: 18 kt yellow gold, three-piece case, numbered (Ø 38.5 mm, thickness 12.7 mm); curved sapphire crystal; yellow gold crown with blue enameled logo, for the correction of the whole calendar (clockwise and counter-clockwise); ellipsoidal pusher at 8 for the forward movement of the hour hand, at 4 for their backward movement; case back attached by 6 screws, displaying the movement through a sapphire crystal. Water-resistant to 3 atm.
Dial: silvered; applied yellow gold bâton markers; luminescent dots on the printed minute track; luminescent blued stainless steel leaf style hands.
Indications: date (with double disc) at 1, month between 3 and 4, two-digit year at 6, day and small second at 9, independently adjustable center hand indicating the 24 hours of the second time zone on the fixed beveled ring.
Strap: crocodile leather; yellow gold fold-over clasp.
Price: USD 27,800.
Also available: with diamond bezel USD 33.800; with bracelet USD 35,500; in pink gold USD 27,800, with diamond bezel USD 33,800, with bracelet $ 41,000.

ASTROLABIUM GALILEO GALILEI   REF. 991.22

Movement: mechanical, automatic winding, Ulysse Nardin caliber 97. Engraved and hand-skeletonized; skeletonized gold rotor. Mechanism for the astrolabe functions conceived and produced by Ulysse Nardin. **Functions:** hour, minute, 24-hour indication, analogue and perpetual representation of the Gregorian calendar (solar time, sunrise and sunset, dawn and dusk, month, day, date, sun position, equinox and solstice, cardinal points and time hours; rising and setting of the moon, moon phase, position of the moon and cardinal points; zodiac, solar and lunar eclipse). **Case:** 18 kt yellow gold, three-piece case (Ø 40, thickness 13 mm); curved sapphire crystal; bezel with engraved alternated Roman numerals and 24 hours; yellow gold crown; case back attached by 4 gold screws, displaying the movement through a sapphire crystal.
Dial: grey-white enameled; luminescent yellow gold bâton hands. **Indications:** three hands in sun, moon and dragon shape; turning disc (grid) made up by a perimeter and an of-center ring; day at 6.
Strap: crocodile leather; yellow gold clasp.
Price: USD 59,500. **Also available:** Astrolabium, Planetarium, Tellurium "Trilogy case" pink gold USD 210,00, limited edition of 20 pieces; with central attachment; platinum, with lugs, sapphire crystal case back (on request).

TELLURIUM JOHANNES KEPLER   REF. 889.99

Movement: mechanical, automatic winding, Ulysse Nardin caliber 97. Hand-finished, hand engraved. Perpetual calendar mechanism conceived and produced by Ulysse Nardin. **Functions:** hour, minute, perpetual calendar (moon phase, zodiac, sun and moon eclipse, second time zone, 24-hour indication). **Case:** platinum, three-piece case (Ø 43 mm, thickness 15 mm); flat sapphire crystal; bezel with engraved blue enameled Arabic numerals and four griffes at the quarters (Roman numerals, sun-shaped marker at 12); white gold crown; snap-on back displaying the movement through a sapphire crystal. Water-resistant to 5 atm.
Dial: cloisonné enameled and blue sapphire.
Indications from the center: white gold and polychrome enameled center disc representing the continents, white gold perimeter with the 24-hour world time engraved; month and zodiac (hands with moon, dragon head and dragon tail shapes), hour and minute indications by white enameled white gold markers on beveled rings.
Strap: crocodile leather; platinum clasp.
Price: USD 99,000.
Edition limited to 99 pieces.
Also available: yellow gold leather strap USD 69,000, bracelet USD 76,600; blue sapphire dial, gold plated globe USD 60,000; "Trilogy case" pink gold, leather strap, 20 pieces, on request.

PLANETARIUM COPERNICUS   REF. 800.22

Movement: mechanical, automatic winding, Ulysse Nardin caliber 80. Made up by 213 components, hand-engraved with skeletonized rotor in white gold. Super-mechanism for the planetarium features conceived and produced by Ulysse Nardin.
Functions: hour, minute, center second, perpetual calendar (analogue representation of the Copernican solar system). **Case:** 18 kt white and pink gold, three-piece case (Ø 40 mm, thickness 13); curved sapphire crystal, divided in 12 inside screen-printed sectors for an easier planetarium reading; Roman hours numerals engraved on the bezel; white gold crown; case back attached by 4 screws, displaying the movement through a sapphire crystal.
Dial: made up by 7 meteorite rings: Earth (fixed), the five main planets (turning), at the center of the bâton hands the Sun; the Moon rotating around the Earth; the external ring or equator, with months and constellations, makes one turn in a year.
Strap: crocodile leather; central attachment; gold clasp.
Price: USD 136,00. Edition limited to 65 pieces.
Also available: yellow gold with moving attaches USD 52,000; platinum, sapphire crystal case back (on request); only gold bracelet 12.500, "Trilogy case", pink gold, leather strap, 20 pieces, 295.000.

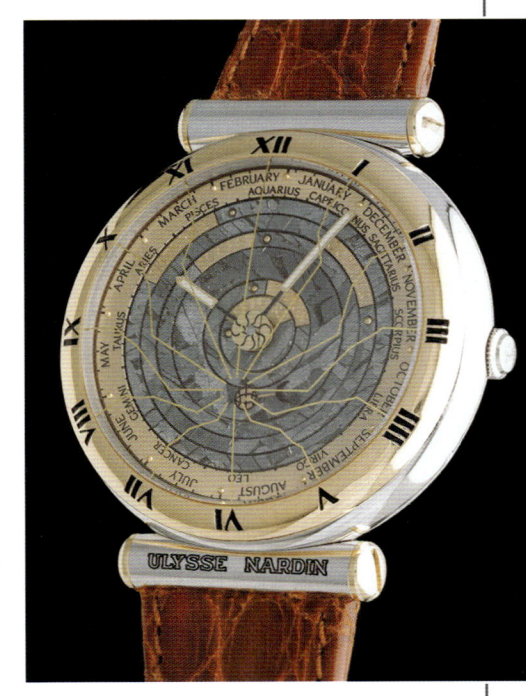

ULYSSE NARDIN

MONOPUSHER 175TH ANNIVERSARY — REF. 381.22

Movement: mechanical, manual winding, antique, Ulysse Nardin caliber UN-38 (Ø 24 mm, 10'''1/2, thickness 4.20 mm), 21 jewels, 21,600 vibrations per hour (vph), power reserve 40 hours. Beveled, Côtes de Genève and circular graining finished.
Functions: hour, minute, small second, chronograph with 2 counters.
Case: 18 kt yellow gold, three-piece case (Ø 37 mm, thickness 9.4 mm); curved crystal; yellow gold crown Louis XV type with coaxial chronograph pusher; case back attached by 4 screws, with embossed portrait of Ulysse Nardin. Water-resistant to 3 atm. 
Dial: white; printed Arabic numerals; Poire blued stainless steel hands.
Indications: minute counter at 3, small second at 9, center second counter, minute track with divisions for 1/5 of a second, pulsometer scale in red.
Strap: crocodile leather; yellow gold clasp.
Price: USD 13,800. New edition of a model of 1930, realized to celebrate the 175th anniversary of the foundation of the House, in a limited edition of 175 pieces in yellow, pink or white gold.
Also available: pink gold (same price); white gold USD 14,500.

MICHELANGELO II BIG DATE — REF. 233.48/52

Movement: mechanical, automatic winding, Ulysse Nardin caliber 22 (ETA 2892 base + date module), 23 jewels, 28,800 vibrations per hour (vph).
Functions: hour, minute, second, date.
Case: stainless steel, two-piece tonneau case (height 37 mm, width 35 mm, thickness 12.1 mm); curved sapphire crystal; screw-down crown with blue enameled logo, for date correction (clockwise and counter-clockwise); case back attached by 4 screws with personalizable tag "dedicated to:". Water-resistant to 10 atm. 
Dial: white; printed oversized Arabic numerals; luminescent dots on the railway minute track; luminescent lozenge hands.
Indications: big date at 2.
Strap: crocodile leather; stainless steel clasp.
Price: USD 3,450.
Also available: pink gold USD 9,900. Both versions are available with silvered, black or blue dial with markers and screen-printed Arabic numerals.

SAN MARCO GMT± BIG DATE — REF. 223.88/52/7

Movement: mechanical, automatic winding, UN caliber 22 (ETA cal. 2892-A2 base + module for the 2nd time zone jumping-hour indication), 23 jewels, 28,800 vph (Ø 25.6, thickness 5,.5 mm, 11'''1/2). **Functions:** hour, minute, center second, date, second time zone, 24-hour indication. **Case:** stainless steel, three-piece case (Ø 40, thickness 11.8 mm); curved sapphire crystal; screw-down crown with case protection, logo in blue enamel, useful for calendar correction (clockwise and counter-clockwise); rectangular pushers at 10 for the forward movement of the hour hand, at 8 for their backward movement; case back attached by 6 screws with an embossed Lion of St. Mark. Water-resistant to 10 atm. **Dial:** black; luminescent Arabic numerals; white printed minute track; luminescent lozenge hands. **Indications:** big date at 2, jumping 24-hour second time zone at 9. **Bracelet:** steel; double fold-over clasp. **Price:** USD 4,250. **Also available:** smooth copper or yellow dial, Arabic num., silvered or blue guilloché, markers; leather strap 3,650; PT, leather strap 17,900, limited edition to 50 pcs.; pink gold, leather strap 11,900, brac. 19,500, limited edition to 100 pieces; yellow gold, silvered dial guilloché, markers, leather strap 10,900 brac. 18,500. With caliber UN 20 (Ø 38 or 40, thick. 12 mm), blue or silvered dial: steel, leather strap 3,300, brac. 3,900.

SAN MARCO ALARM — REF. 603.77/7

Movement: mechanical, automatic winding, old manufacture, Ulysse Nardin caliber 60 (A. Schild 5008 base), 17 jewels, 28,800 vibrations per hour (vph) (Ø 30 mm, thickness 7.6 mm, 13''').
Functions: hour, minute, center second, day-date, alarm.
Case: stainless steel, three-piece case (Ø 38.5 mm, thickness 12.45 mm); curved sapphire crystal; crowns with logo in blue enamel, for winding and time setting at 2, for the sonnerie at 4; case back attached by 8 screws with an embossed Lion of St. Mark. Water-resistant to 3 atm. 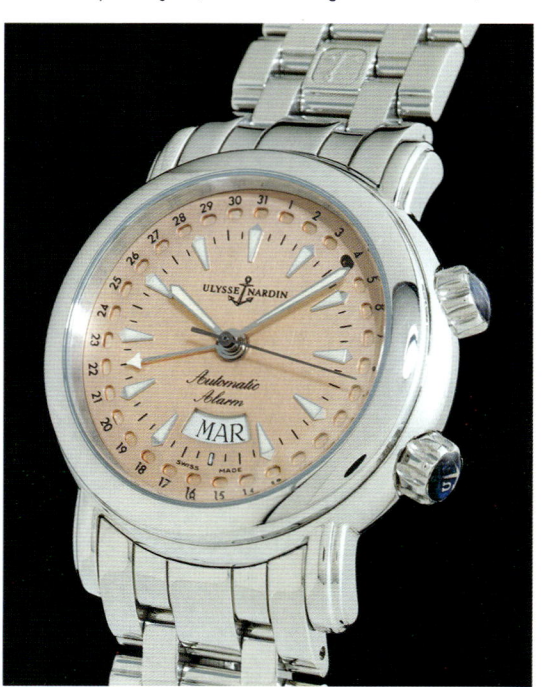
Dial: metallized, salmon; luminescent applied triangular markers; printed minute track; luminescent sword style hands. **Indications:** day at 6, turning disc date, indicated in two small windows on the peripheral dial ring; sonnerie with pointer like an arrow-shaped center hand.
Bracelet: steel; double fold-over clasp.
Price: USD 4,500.
Also available: silvered or black dial; leather strap USD 3,900; yellow gold, leather strap USD 9,500. Only gold bracelet USD 17,100.

ULYSSE NARDIN

SAN MARCO SONNERIE EN PASSANT   REF. 759.20/619

Movement: mechanical, automatic winding, Ulysse Nardin caliber 75 (ETA 2892 base + sonnerie module), 41 jewels (Ø 33 mm, thickness 8.3 mm, 11'''1/2). Bridges and pillar-plate decorated with Côtes de Genève and circular graining pattern and beveled.
Functions: hour, minute, sonnerie striking the hour and the half hour on demand and en passant. **Case:** platinum, three-piece case, numbered (Ø 40 mm, thickness 12.9 mm); curved sapphire crystal; white gold crown with blue enameled logo; pusher at 2 for en passant sonnerie setting, at 4 for the repeater; case back attached by 6 screws with an embossed Lion of St. Mark. Water-resistant to 3 atm.
Dial: solid silver and mother-of-pearl, engine turned (guilloché); applied white gold Arabic numerals; white gold leaf style hands; an automaton in white gold, reproducing one of the Jaquemarts of St. Mark's Tower in Venice, simulates the striking of time on a white gold bell. **Indications:** hand at 2 for en passant sonnerie setting (hours and half-hours, on one timbre) when it is on the cabochon marker.
Strap: crocodile leather; platinum clasp.
Price: USD 71,500. Limited edition.
Also available: yellow gold/pink gold USD 56,500; blue enameled dial: yellow gold/pink gold USD 59,000; platinum USD 74,000; only gold bracelet USD 64,100.

SAN MARCO BIG DATE   REF. 343.22

Movement: mechanical, automatic winding, Ulysse Nardin caliber 34 (ETA 2892 base + date module), 26 jewels, 28,800 vibrations per hour (vph).
Functions: hour, minute, small second, date.
Case: stainless steel, three-piece case (Ø 37 mm, thickness 9.7 mm); curved sapphire crystal; crown with blue enameled logo, for date correction (clockwise and counterclockwise); case back attached by 4 screws with embossed Lion of St. Mark. Water-resistant to 3 atm.
Dial: matte black, zones with concentric-circle pattern; applied bâton markers; luminescent dots on the printed minute track; luminescent leaf style hands.
Indications: small second at 6, big date at 12.
Strap: crocodile leather; stainless steel clasp.
Price: USD 2,950.
Also available: in yellow or pink gold, leather strap USD 5,950, bracelet USD 13,550. Each version is available with silvered, black or blue dial, applied markers.

FORGERONS MINUTE REPEATER   REF. 719.20

Movement: mechanical, manual winding, caliber UN-71 produced by the Laboratories Claret and modified by Ulysse Nardin (Ø 27.6 mm, thickness 6.6 mm, 12'''1/4), 31 jewels, 18,000 vibrations per hour (vph). Beveled pillar-plate, Côtes de Genève and circular graining finished bridges. **Functions:** hour, minute, minute repeater.
Case: platinum, three-piece case, numbered (Ø 39 mm, thickness 12.4 mm); curved sapphire crystal; repeater slide on case side; white gold crown; screwed-on case back displaying the movement through a sapphire crystal. Water-resistant to 3 atm.
Dial: solid gold, engine turned (guilloché), hand-enameled (each layer is applied with a goose pen and stove baked to give dials a characteristic translucent look which emphasizes the guilloché finish; applied white gold bâton markers and Roman numerals; white gold leaf style hands, white gold automatons; the automatons represent two working blacksmiths and simulate the striking of hours, quarters and minutes on an anvil.
Strap: crocodile leather; platinum clasp.
Price: USD 210,000.
Edition limited to 30 pieces per version.
Also available: pink gold USD 190,000. Jacquemarts, 30 pieces, (same prices); only gold bracelet on request.

SAN MARCO "TRAFALGAR" CHRONOMETER   REF. 131.77SP

Movement: mechanical, automatic winding, Ulysse Nardin caliber 13, 11'''1/2. Officially certified "chronometer" (C.O.S.C.).
Functions: hour, minute, center second.
Case: 18 kt yellow gold, three-piece case (Ø 37 mm, thickness 8.35 mm); curved sapphire crystal; yellow gold crown with enameled logo; case back attached by 4 screws with an embossed Lion of St. Mark. Water-resistant to 3 atm.
Dial: solid gold, cloisonné by hand, numbered, representing the battle of Trafalgar; cabochon applied yellow gold markers; yellow gold leaf style hands.
Strap: crocodile leather; yellow gold clasp.
Price: USD 20,000.
Edition limited to 25 pieces.
Also available: platinum USD 25,000, 5 pieces.
The refined San Marco chronometer collection with dial cloisonné in polychrome enamels includes different subjects: the reproductions of the Rialto bridge in Venice, the Chillon castle on the lake of Geneva, the Ulysse vessel, the sea battle of Halifax and the Spanish looking "Toreador".

Vacheron Constantin

One of Vacheron Constantin's newest offerings is the Overseas chronograph. It's an addition to the Overseas collection launched in 1996, which heralded the company's entry into the realm of sporty, tough-guy styling rendered in manly steel. The watch has a self-winding calibre, number 1137, a big, twin-window calendar at 12 o'clock, a center seconds chrono hand and a constantly running seconds subdial at 6 o'clock. The watch keeps track of elapsed time with two totalizers, one for the minutes, at 3 o'clock, and one for the hours, at 9 o'clock. The push-pieces and crown screw into the case. When they're locked in, the watch is water resistant to 150 meters. When they're unscrewed, it's water resistant to 20 meters. The watch has a glare-resistant sapphire crystal, triple safety clasp on the bracelet, silvered dial and black rhodium markings for easy reading in dim light. One more special feature: the caseback is engraved with a medallion showing the ship piloted by the Italian explorer Amerigo Vespucci, who, of course, lent his name to the continent he visited in the 15th century. The Overseas chrono is also available in 18k gold. This year the company is celebrating its 245th anniversary. It is trumpeting its longevity with the launch of a new model called 245. Part of the "Les Complications" collection, the 245 has a self-winding movement, a retrograde date indicator and a subdial at 6 o'clock showing the days of the week. The back is fitted with a transparent sapphire crystal. It comes in white or pink gold and is water resistant to 30 meters. In an entirely different mode: the 1972 model, harking back just 28 years. That's when Vacheron launched an elegant but eyecatching asymmetric dress watch with trapezoidal case. The updated version, part of the "Les Historiques" collection, comes in men's and women's models. It

The History

The very oldest watchmaking company has never stopped production. It was founded in 1755 by Jean Marc Vacheron, whose grandson is joined by François Constantin in 1819. From that year the Company bears the name famous throughout the world. For a long time, Vacheron Constantin has been the most prestigious name known to the general public, thanks to the great refinement of its watch product which, in the past. was particularly known for its extra-thin pocket model. The House is responsible, however, for some important technical innovations, for example the system of interchangeable part, fundamental for the growth of the Swiss industry, that was perfected by Georges-Auguste Leschot. Always at the top, the Vacheron Constantin reached the apex of design during the Art Déco period, and in the 30's and 40's when several models were made that have yet to be surpassed for beauty and originality. An outstanding example of this is the so-called "big chocolate candy", while of the round models the complete calendar with drop-shaped lugs from the 1940's must be mentioned.

1751 - He was only twenty years old when Jean-Marc Vacheron became an independent watchmaker.
1755 - He opens his first work shop in the "Cité" in Geneva and it will become the foundation of the Maison.
1785 - The watches carry the name Vacheron Girod. In 1810 Barthélémy Girod moves to Paris in order to organize the sales distribution of the watches to be sent there from Geneva.
1816 - The Company name becomes Vacheron-Chossat & Cie.
1819 - On the 1st of April, Vacheron is joined by François Constantin and creates the Vacheron & Constantin name. Great sales success on the Italian market as well as the Turkish, which was trendy and very rich at that time.
1833 - After Europe, commercial relations with the United States were begun.
1840 - One year after his arrival at Vacheron Constantin, George-Auguste Leschot perfects the tools for the production of a calibre whose components are interchangeable. The is the start of the "industrial era" of watchmaking, and the end forever of pure and simple handcrafted work.
1854 - The financial year closes with a profit of 175.000 Swiss francs for each of the partners.
1855 - A keyless winding system is introduced.
1880 - This year the Cross of Malta is registered as the company trademark.

1911 - The appearance of the first women's wristwatches, to be followed two years later by men's models produced in series.
1915 - Europe in at war. A special series of pocket chronograph is made for sappers from the U.S. expeditionary forces.
1919 - Vacheron Constantin makes its first marine chronometer.
1936 - The year of the tonneau minute repeater with retrograde perpetual calendar.
1939 - Anticipating the War, the Maison produces a series of models with aluminium cases.
1953 - The Chronomètre Royale is introduced and for the first time the hallmark of the "Geneva Seal" appears.
1955 - To celebrate the bicentenary, the thinnest movement in the world is created: 1.64 mm high.
1960 - 70's - Alongside its traditional production, the Maison introduces products with quartz movement.
1996 - Vacheron Constantin becomes part of the Vendôme Luxury Group. The current production grows with a range of models inspired by the past that are serious, extremely refined, as well a series of complication watches (minute repeaters, tourbillons, perpetual calendars). Besides these models, which we could call classic, there is now the Overseas line, the first real sports and diving watch ever produced by the Maison. It is characterized by a particular patent which ensures its water resistance even if the crown is not screwed completely down.
1997 - A round model in limited numbers, with automatic, extra-thin movement, is awarded the "Geneva Seal" hallmark. A tonneau cambré is reproposed with moving lugs, inspired by a 1912 model (and in fact 1,912 pieces were made), with manual movement. The Kalla Amalfi men's model, oval, white gold and 148 baguette and trapezoid cut diamonds, is a step toward the world of jewelled watches.
1998 - It's called Toledo, like the most precious swords in the world. In fact, the newjumping Vacheron Constantin, of which only 500 pieces were made, has high level technology and razor-sharp aesthetics: no superfluous details on the squared cambré case or beautiful dial. The "just time" comes in a new, larger size and new movement (cal. 1312) with date at 6 o'clock and sweep seconds. There are some interesting developments of this line already in the catalogue. The extra-thin, now called Patrimony, has been given a sapphire crystal back thus shedding light on the recently gained "Geneva Seal".

has a manual-wind movement (calibre 1055) and comes in 18k yellow gold. Vacheron has a plethora of other recent introductions. Among the most interesting: the Mercator, a platinum watch with an antique map of the world on its face - a tribute to 16th-century cartographer Gerardus Mercator; a new tourbillon skeleton model with twin barrels and power reserve indicator; the Patrimony, with an ultra-thin manual-wind movement; the COSC-certified Chronomètre Royal with self-winding movement and calendar at 3 o'clock, plus a sparkling array of women's jewellery watches such as the diamond-studded Kyushu, with round, oval or tonneau cases; and new square or round Fiorenza models, each set with nearly 200 diamonds.

VACHERON CONSTANTIN

PERPETUAL CALENDAR MINUTE REPEATER — REF. 30020

Movement: mechanical, manual winding, caliber 1775 QP, 30 jewels, 18,000 vibrations per hour (vph). Realized together with caliber 1775, in a limited edition of 200 numbered pieces.
Functions: hour, minute, perpetual calendar (date, day, month, year, moon phase), minute repeater.
Case: platinum, three-piece case (Ø 37 mm, thickness 9.5); drop-shaped lugs; curved sapphire crystal; 4 correctors and repeater slide on case side; white gold crown; snap-on back displaying the movement through a sapphire crystal.
Dial: in gold, silvered; bâton and faceted square markers, applied white gold logo; white gold bâton hands, burnished steel leaf style hands in zones.
Indications: date at 3, moon phase at 6, day at 9, month and four year cycle at 12.
Strap: crocodile leather; platinum clasp.
Price: 462'000 CHF.
Also available: yellow gold 426'700 CHF.

CHRONOGRAPH PERPETUAL CALENDAR — REF. 49005

Movement: mechanical, automatic winding, caliber 1136 QP, 38 jewels, 21,600 vibrations per hour (vph).
Functions: hour, minute, small second, perpetual calendar (date, day, month, year, moon phase), chronograph with 3 counters.
Case: platinum, three-piece case (Ø 38 mm, thickness 12.5 mm); curved sapphire crystal; 4 correctors on case side; white gold rectangular crown and pushers; case back attached by 8 screws.
Dial: in gold, rosé, engine turned (guilloché) with small waves pattern; applied white gold bâton markers and logo; white gold bâton hands; printed minute track.
Indications: date and minute counter at 3, moon phase and small second at 6, hour counter and day at 9, month and four year cycle at 12, center second counter, minute track with divisions for $1/5$ of a second.
Strap: crocodile leather; platinum clasp.
Price: 77'500 CHF.
Also available: with solid gold white lacquered dial 77'000 CHF; pink gold with solid gold white lacquered dial or with solid gold black guilloché dial 62'600 CHF.

TOURBILLON — REF. 30050

Movement: mechanical, manual winding, with double barrel and tourbillon device caliber 1760 (set up in cooperation with Nouvelle Lemania), 29 jewels; balance with adjusting screws, 18,000 vibrations per hour (vph).
Functions: hour, minute, small second, power reserve.
Case: platinum, three-piece case (Ø 38 mm, thickness 6.6 mm); curved sapphire crystal; white gold crown; snap-on back displaying the movement through a sapphire crystal. Water-resistant to 3 atm.
Dial: silvered, engine turned (guilloché), aperture on the tourbillon; applied white gold pointed markers, Roman numerals and logo; white gold Dauphine hands.
Indications: small second at 6 integrated in the tourbillon carriage, power reserve at 12.
Strap: crocodile leather; platinum clasp.
Price: 154'300 CHF.
Also available: yellow gold 135'600 CHF; Squelette Ref. 30051, pink gold 186'400 CHF.

JUMPING HOUR CARRE — REF. 43041

Movement: mechanical, automatic winding, caliber 1120 MR; gold rotor personalized, skeletonized and hand-chased. Hallmarked with the "Geneva Seal" (watchmaking's highest distinction of quality).
Functions: Jumping hour, retrograde minute.
Case: 18 kt yellow gold, three-piece "cushion-shaped" case (height 36 mm, width 36 mm, thickness 8.5 mm); flat sapphire crystal; pink gold crown; progressive numbering (up to 100 pcs) engraved on the side opposite to the crown; case back attached by 4 screws, displaying the movement through a sapphire crystal. Water-resistant to 3 atm.
Dial: silvered, engine turned (guilloché Soleil); jumping hour window at 12; circle sector retrograde minute ring, applied yellow gold Arabic numerals and lozenge markers; yellow gold Dauphine hand.
Strap: crocodile leather, hand stitched; yellow gold clasp.
Price: 33'900 CHF. Edition limited to 500 pieces, 200 of which in pink gold, 100 in yellow gold and 200 in white gold.
Also available: pink gold with pink dial (same price); white gold silvered dial 35'200 CHF.

VACHERON CONSTANTIN

OVERSEAS CHRONOGRAPH — REF. 49140/423

Movement: mechanical, automatic winding (Frédéric Piguet base).
Functions: hour, minute, small second, date, chronograph with 3 counters.
Case: 18 kt yellow gold, three-piece case (Ø 40 mm, thickness 12.5 mm), polished and brushed finish; flat sapphire crystal; shaped bezel, fixed inside by 8 screws; screw-down crown in gold, with triple gasket, case protection; yellow gold screw down pushers; case back attached by 8 screws with "Overseas" windjammer embossed medallion. Water-resistant to 15 atm.
Dial: silvered; applied yellow gold faceted polished bâton markers and logo; luminescent dots on the printed minute track; luminescent faceted polished yellow gold bâton hands.
Indications: minute counter at 3, small second at 6, hour counter at 9, big date at 12, center second counter.
Bracelet: gold, integrated in the case, polished and brushed finish; double fold-over safety clasp in gold.
Price: 36'600 CHF.
Also available: stainless steel, silvered dial 14'200 CHF.

OVERSEAS — REF. 42042/423J

Movement: mechanical, automatic winding, caliber 1310. 21 kt gold rotor. Officially certified "chronometer" (C.O.S.C.).
Functions: hour, minute, center second, date.
Case: 18 kt yellow gold, three-piece case (Ø 37 mm, thickness 8.5 mm), polished and brushed finish; flat sapphire crystal; shaped bezel, fixed inside by 8 screws; yellow gold screw-down crown with case protection and triple gasket; case back attached by 8 screws with "Overseas" windjammer embossed medallion. Water-resistant to 15 atm.
Dial: anthracite; applied polished yellow gold faceted bâton markers and logo; luminescent dots on the printed minute track; luminescent yellow gold faceted bâton hands.
Indications: date at 3.
Bracelet: in gold, integrated in the case, polished and brushed finish; double fold-over safety clasp in gold.
Price: 26'300 CHF. The model in the photograph is out of stock. Only available with silvered dial.
Also available: stainless steel, silvered dial 8'400 CHF; steel with quartz movement Ref. 72040, 6'300 CHF.

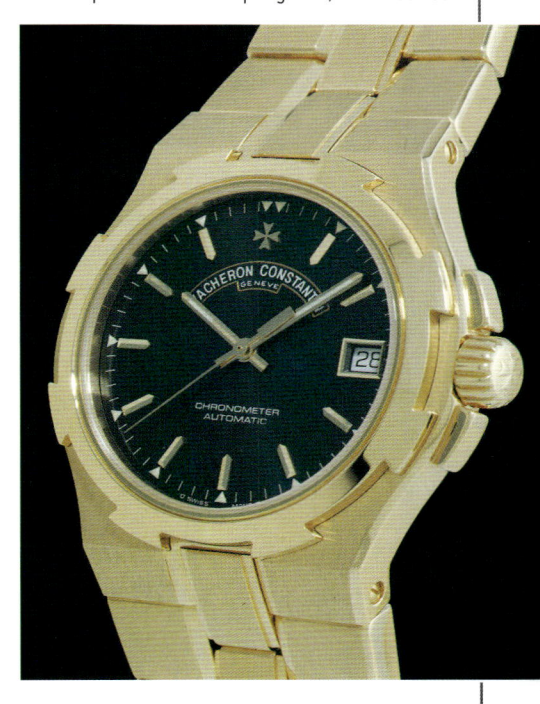

LES COMPLICATIONS "245" — REF. 47245

Movement: mechanical, automatic winding, caliber 1126 (Jaeger-Le Coultre caliber 889 base), rotor with 21 kt gold peripheral mass.
Functions: hour, minute, day-date.
Case: platinum, three-piece case (Ø 36.7 mm, thickness 10.5 mm); curved sapphire crystal; date pusher on case side at 10; white gold crown; case back attached by 4 screws, displaying the movement through a sapphire crystal. Water-resistant to 3 atm.
Dial: black, engine turned (guilloché) with graining pattern; applied white gold logo, Roman numerals and hemisphere; bâton hands in white gold.
Indications: day at 6, fan-shaped date at 12 with retrograde center hand.
Strap: crocodile leather; white gold clasp.
Price: 33'300 CHF.
Also available: pink gold, silvered dial guilloché 22'600 CHF; white gold, silvered dial guilloché 23'400 CHF.

FULL CALENDAR — REF. 47051

Movement: mechanical, automatic winding, caliber 1126 QG, 33 jewels, 21,600 vibrations per hour (vph).
Functions: hour, minute, full calendar (date, day, month).
Case: 18 kt white gold, three-piece case (Ø 36 mm, thickness 9.8 mm); curved sapphire crystal; bow-shaped small lugs; 4 correctors on case side, recessed; white gold crown; snap-on back. Water-resistant to 3 atm.
Dial: silvered, matte finish; applied white gold Roman numerals and logo; white gold bâton hands.
Indications: day and month below 12, date with half-moon center hand.
Strap: crocodile leather; white gold clasp.
Price: 21'100 CHF.
Also available: in yellow gold 18'700 CHF.

283

VACHERON CONSTANTIN

LES HISTORIQUES "POINÇON DE GENEVE" — REF. 43039

Movement: mechanical, automatic winding, caliber 1120 MSQ. 18 kt gold rotor yellow and white, personalized, skeletonized and hand-chased. Hallmarked with the "Geneva Seal" (watchmaking's highest distinction of quality).
Functions: hour, minute.
Case: 18 kt yellow gold, three-piece case (Ø 35 mm, thickness 7 mm); curved sapphire crystal; yellow gold crown; snap-on back displaying the movement through a sapphire crystal. Water-resistant to 3 atm.
Dial: ivory; applied yellow gold Roman numerals and logo; printed minute track; yellow gold leaf style hands.
Strap: crocodile leather, hand stitched; yellow gold clasp.
Price: 19'900 CHF.
Also available: white gold 20'500 CHF.

CHRONOMETRE ROYAL — REF. 47022

Movement: mechanical, automatic winding, caliber 1126/1. Officially certified "chronometer" (C.O.S.C.).
Functions: hour, minute, center second, date.
Case: 18 kt yellow gold, two-piece case (Ø 34 mm, thickness 8.4 mm) polished and brushed finish; curved sapphire crystal; yellow gold crown; snap-on back. Water-resistant to 3 atm.
Dial: silvered, matte finish; applied yellow gold faceted bâton markers, Roman numerals and logo; printed minute track; yellow gold Dauphine hands.
Indications: date at 3, bordered in yellow gold.
Strap: crocodile leather, hand stitched; white gold clasp.
Price: 15'000 CHF.
Also available: white gold 16'700 CHF.

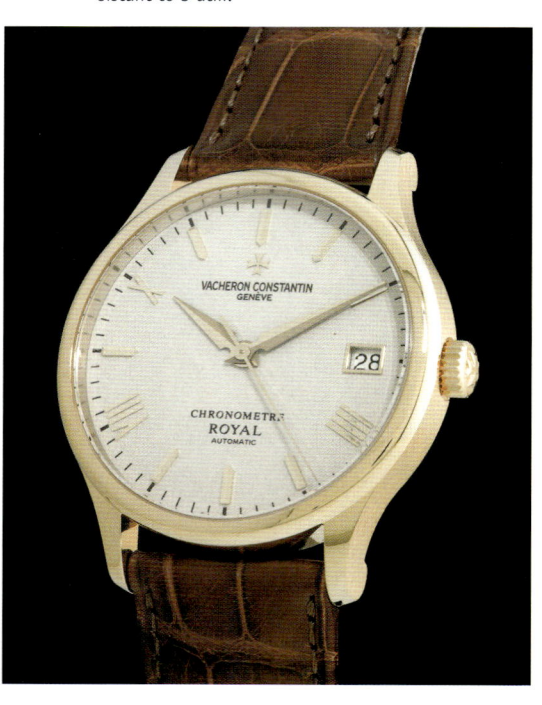

SMALL SECOND — REF. 91060

Movement: mechanical, manual winding, caliber 1017, 21 jewels, 21,600 vibrations per hour (vph).
Functions: hour, minute, small second.
Case: 18 kt white gold, two-piece case (Ø 32.2 mm, thickness 7.3 mm); curved sapphire crystal; white gold crown; snap-on back. Water-resistant to 3 atm.
Dial: silvered; applied white gold pointed markers, Arabic numerals and logo; gold, grey, sword style hands.
Indications: small second at 6.
Strap: crocodile leather; white gold clasp.
Price: 9'400 CHF.
Also available: in yellow gold 8'300 CHF.

LES HISTORIQUES SMALL SECOND — REF. 92239

Movement: mechanical, manual winding, caliber 1014, 17 jewels, 18,000 vibrations per hour (vph).
Functions: hour, minute, small second.
Case: 18 kt yellow gold, three-piece case (Ø 33 mm, thickness 6.8 mm); curved sapphire crystal; yellow gold crown; snap-on back. Water-resistant to 3 atm.
Dial: silvered, slightly bombé; applied yellow gold pointed markers, Arabic numerals, logo and cabochon minute track; yellow gold bâton hands.
Indications: small second at 6.
Strap: crocodile leather; yellow gold clasp.
Price: 11'200 CHF.
Also available: platinum 16'300 CHF.

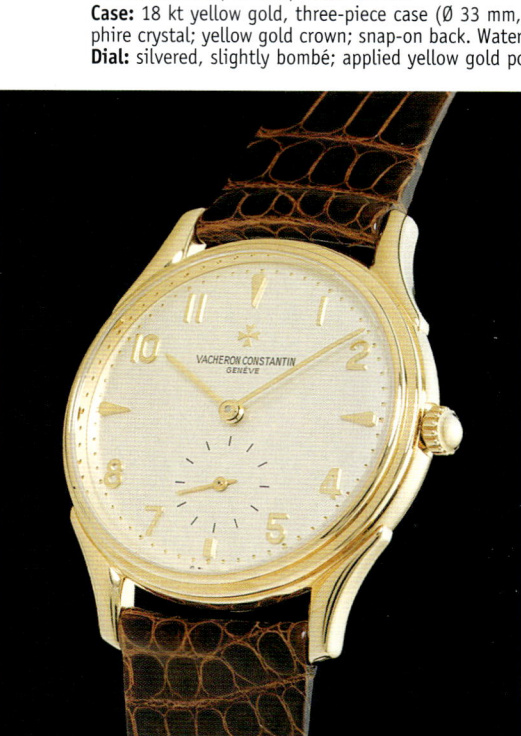

VACHERON CONSTANTIN

PATRIMONY — REF. 33593

Movement: mechanical, manual winding, extra-thin caliber 1003, 18 jewels, 18,000 vibrations per hour (vph). Hallmarked with the "Geneva Seal" (watchmaking's highest distinction of quality).
Functions: hour, minute.
Case: 18 kt white gold, two-piece case (Ø 31.5 mm, thickness 5.8 mm); curved sapphire crystal; bezel with a row of set brilliants (68 stones, 0.35 kt); white gold crown; snap-on back displaying the movement through a sapphire crystal. Water-resistant to 3 atm.
Dial: white; printed Roman numerals; applied white gold logo; burnished gold leaf style hands.
Strap: crocodile leather; white gold clasp.
Price: 17'500 CHF.

LES HISTORIQUES "1972-MCMLXXII" — REF. 37010

Movement: mechanical, manual winding, caliber 1055 (Frédéric Piguet caliber 6.10 base), 21 jewels, 21,600 vibrations per hour (vph).
Functions: hour, minute.
Case: 18 kt yellow gold, two-piece case, asymmetric trapezoidal slightly anatomic shape (height max. 36.5 mm, width 26 mm, thickness 7 mm); curved sapphire crystal; recessed yellow gold crown; case back attached by 4 screws. Water-resistant to 3 atm.
Dial: silvered, vertically brushed; printed bâton markers and 4 stylized Roman numerals; burnished yellow gold sword style hands.
Strap: crocodile leather; yellow gold clasp in an asymmetric trapezoidal shape matching the case design.
Price: 12'800 CHF.
Also available: pink gold 13'100 CHF; white gold, silvered or grey blued dial 13'700 CHF.

LES HISTORIQUES "1912" — REF. 37001

Movement: mechanical, manual winding, caliber 1132, 20 jewels, 21,600 vibrations per hour (vph).
Functions: hour, minute.
Case: 18 kt pink gold, two-piece tonneau-curved case (height 35 mm, width 30 mm, thickness 6.5 mm); curved sapphire crystal; pink gold crown; case back attached by 8 screws, with the date "1912" engraved together with the progressive number of the limited edition. Water-resistant to 3 atm.
Dial: silvered, matte finish, curved; printed Arabic numerals and minute track; black anodized pink gold leaf style hands.
Strap: crocodile leather, padded; removable lugs with screw connection; pink gold clasp.
Price: 12'500 CHF.
New edition of the original model realized in 1912, in a limited edition of 1162 numbered pieces; furnished with an elegant leather wallet-type case.
Also available: white gold 13'600 CHF, 750 pieces.

LES HISTORIQUES TOLEDO — REF. 42100

Movement: mechanical, automatic winding, caliber 1310.
Functions: hour, minute, center second, date.
Case: 18 kt yellow gold, two-piece case, square praline-shaped (height max. 38 mm, width 32.2 mm, thickness 8 mm); flat sapphire crystal; yellow gold crown; case back attached by 4 screws. Water-resistant to 3 atm.
Dial: silvered opaline, "old basket pattern" engraved at the center; applied yellow gold square markers, Roman numerals and logo; printed railway minute track; yellow gold leaf style hands.
Indications: date at 6.
Strap: crocodile leather; yellow gold clasp.
Price: 13'600 CHF.
Also available: with bracelet 22'700 CHF; white gold, blue dial, leather strap 15'200 CHF, bracelet 25'100 CHF.

Van Cleef & Arpels

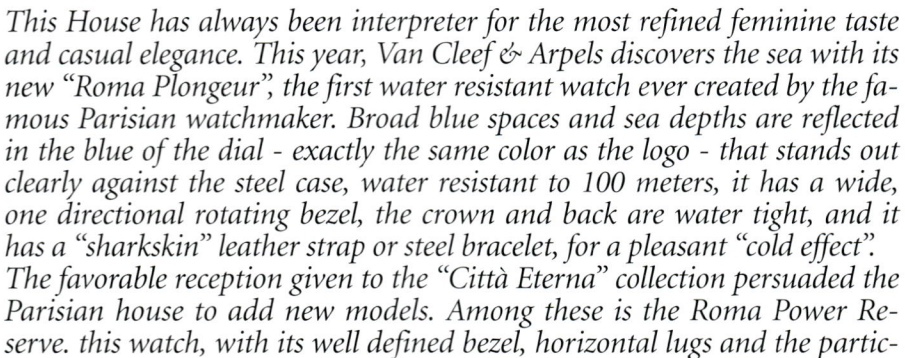

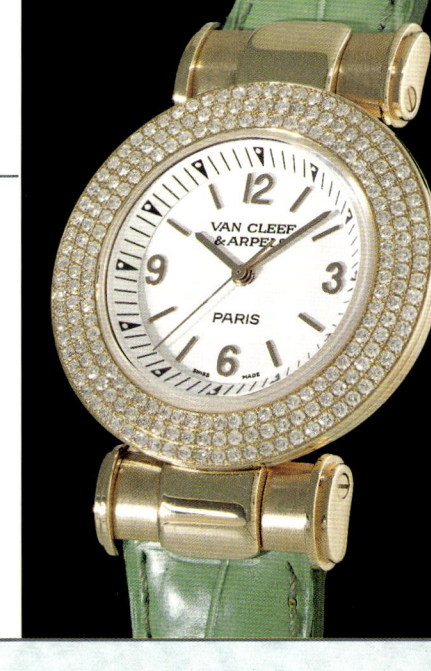

This House has always been interpreter for the most refined feminine taste and casual elegance. This year, Van Cleef & Arpels discovers the sea with its new "Roma Plongeur", the first water resistant watch ever created by the famous Parisian watchmaker. Broad blue spaces and sea depths are reflected in the blue of the dial - exactly the same color as the logo - that stands out clearly against the steel case, water resistant to 100 meters, it has a wide, one directional rotating bezel, the crown and back are water tight, and it has a "sharkskin" leather strap or steel bracelet, for a pleasant "cold effect".
The favorable reception given to the "Città Eterna" collection persuaded the Parisian house to add new models. Among these is the Roma Power Reserve. this watch, with its well defined bezel, horizontal lugs and the particular center attachment that dominate the entire structure, perfectly represent the sporting but "distinguished" style typical of the Van Cleef & Arpels tradition.
The modern version of the 1930's timepieces - a very crucial moment for watchmaking - is the easily transformed, chameleon-like "Domino 39", an original creation with which the Company has confirmed its real spirit of sophisticated jeweller-watchmaker. Dusting off an idea from the far-off 1939, the House introduces this watch with "shutters", that can become, a second and according to taste and to the moment, a jewel. Thanks to two little windows that open or close, either the watch dial is revealed or the very discreet monogram, VC&A. Just a delicate touch on the clasps (at 6 and at 12 o'clock) to turn the white dial back up. It is made in yellow gold or grey, with a croco strap or gold bracelet, in either the simple or the richly jewel-set version, the ingenious mechanism, after a full seventy years, is still a success. Satisfying, if it does, the desire of every woman to wear on her wrist a versatile object that can adapt to the moment and, especially, to the mood ...

The History

Van Cleef & Arpels - a life lived among fabulous gems and the gleaming lights of gold and platinum.

1906 - Julien and Charles Arpels, the youngest members of a family of expert jewellers and experts in their own right, join a distant cousin, Alfred Van Cleef who has been married to their sister, Estelle, for ten years. On June 16th of that year, the first Van Cleef & Arpels salon opens at no. 22 on Place Vendôme. Subsequently, the third brother, Louis will join them.

1910/20 - The four young men begin to become famous, but at the outbreak of the war the Arpels brothers leave for the front, including Estelle as a Red Cross nurse. Alfred is left to run the Company by himself Estelle had taken care of Lieutenant Emile Puissant who will later marry her daughter Renée and become the administrator of the Company.

1921 – Van Cleef and Arpels is the first great jewellery company to open at Cannes.

1922 - The arrival of the designer René-Sim Lacaze means that the lovely inspirations of Renée Van Cleef-Puissant can be created (she in the meantime has become the artistic director) and a new style can be brought to the French company.. In these years, the wristwatch has become a fundamental accessory, and VC&A work hard at turning simple timepieces into luxurious jewels.

1925 - The Grand Prix was awarded to VC&A at the Paris Exposition of the Decorative Arts for a matching jewellery set made in the form of roses, with diamonds, rubies and emeralds. By the end of the 1920's, "pendentif" watches yield to the more practical wristwatches. Among the most admired models, inlaid with enamels and precious stones, are the watch with violets - to become famous during the '30's - or the "daisy", whose dial is hidden in a sapphire heart, or even the one whose design was inspired by the radiator of the Limousine, with little flaps that open on the dial.

1927 - The dial of one pocket model shows a Chinese magician who indicates hours and minutes with his hands upon command.

1930 – The men's watch made of a twenty dollar gold piece becomes a classic.

1933 - Invention of the "serti mystérieux", a particular way of setting stones, that gives necklaces and bracelets a lightness and flexibility previously impossible.

1935 - A branch is opened at Montecarlo.

1937 - The wedding jewellery for the duchess of Windsor.
1939 - Julien and Louis set out for New York and open new sales space on Fifth Avenue.
1940 - A new shop is opened in Palm Beach.
1949 - The year of the "PA 49", designed by Pierre Arpels, and destined to become the most famous watch of the Parisian house. The strap is held by horizontal bars tangential to the round case and connected to it by a small sphere.
1954 - The "Boutique Van Cleef & Arpels" is created: a new conception of commerce, where the jeweller's creativity meets the clients' imagination.
1960 - Branch opens in Geneva.
1967 - Creation of the crown for the consecration of the Persian Empress Farah Diba.
1972 - In Place Vendôme a new sector dedicated entirely to watches is opened: the Boutique des Heures.
1974 - The conquest of Japan with the opening, other than Tokyo, of about twenty sales points.
1980's - VC&A opens shops in the most important cities, including Rome, Milan and Naples.
1990's - The collections, for men and women, are almost all renewed. They are all inspired by a vivacious luxury, they are light and effervescent, typical of the Van Cleef and Arpels creativity. Very "Parisian", but internationally efficacious from Sydney to Bahrain.

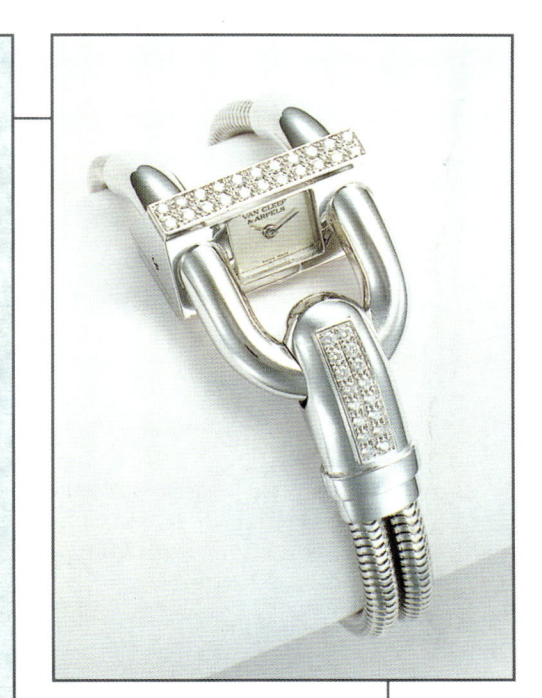

VAN CLEEF & ARPELS

ROMA CHRONOGRAPH — REF. 134072/1201BD

Movement: mechanical, automatic winding, ETA 2892/A2 base + Dubois Dépraz DD 2020 chronograph module.
Functions: hour, minute, small second, chronograph with 3 counters.
Case: 18 kt yellow gold, three-piece case (Ø 39 mm, thickness 12 mm); bezel with engraved tachymeter scale; antireflective flat sapphire crystal; case back attached by 6 screws. Water-resistant to 3 atm. 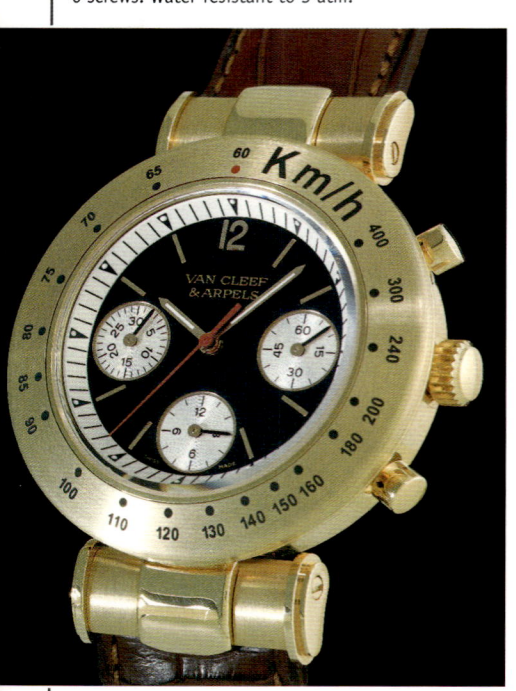
Dial: black enameled; silvered zones decorated with concentric-circle pattern; applied bâton markers (Arabic numeral 12); luminescent bâton hands.
Indications: small second at 3, hour counter at 6, minute counter at 9, center second counter, minute track on the beveled ring.
Strap: crocodile leather; central attachment, polished and brushed finish; fold-over safety clasp, in gold.
Price: 16'040 CHF.
Also available: simple clasp 14'740 CHF; bracelet 24'950 CHF; steel leather strap and fold-over clasp 5'630 CHF, bracelet 6'730 CHF. All available with black enameled dial and silvered counters or white enameled dial and black counters.

ROMA CHRONOGRAPH — REF. 534072/122005

As a natural evolution of the Roma collection whose look is typically sportsmanlike, this chronograph maintains all of its aesthetic values with respect to both case design and dial proportions. The part which was of course modified is the movement - a traditional mechanical caliber, automatic winding, with its chronograph feature with three counters implemented by the additional Dubois Dépraz module. The bezel design is resolutely original, with its engraved tachymeter scale and the outsize writing "km/h" positioned at 12. The "all steel" version shown in the photograph is the one which nears the spirit of this model to the utmost, adapting itself without any problem also for heavy duty purposes and enjoying the unmistakable fascination offered by the black dial.
Price: 6'730 CHF.

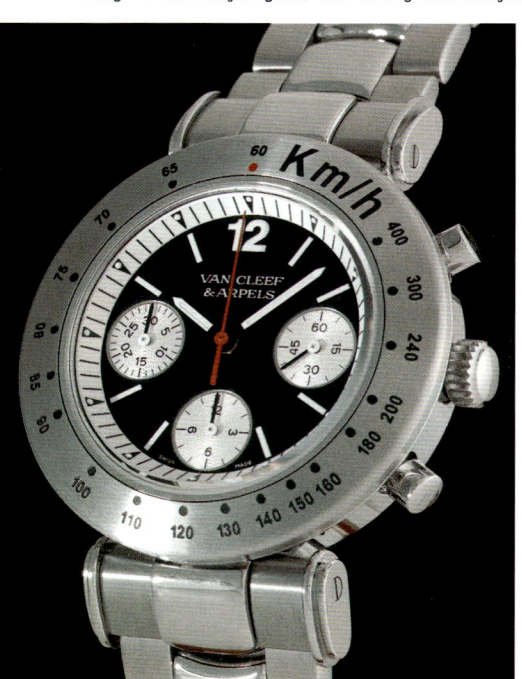

ROMA DIVER — REF. 533070/126005

Movement: mechanical, automatic winding, Eta 2824-2.
Functions: hour, minute, center second.
Case: stainless steel, three-piece case (Ø 38.5 mm, thickness 11.6 mm); antireflective flat sapphire crystal; counter-clockwise turning bezel, knurled, with engraved minute track; screw-down crown with case protection; case back attached by 6 screws. Water-resistant to 10 atm. 
Dial: Pantone blue; luminescent printed bâton markers and Arabic numerals; printed minute track with luminescent triangular markers on the beveled ring; luminescent stainless steel sword style hands.
Bracelet: stainless steel, with central attachment, polished and brushed finish; fold-over safety clasp.
Price: 5'350 CHF.
Also available: shark-skin strap 4'270 CHF.

ROMA AUTOMATIC — REF. 532054/117005

Movement: mechanical, automatic winding, Eta 2824-2.
Functions: hour, minute, center second.
Case: stainless steel, three-piece case (Ø 36.5 mm, thickness 8.5 mm); antireflective flat sapphire crystal; case back attached by 6 screws, water-resistant to 3 atm.
Dial: black enameled; luminescent bâton markers and Arabic numerals; printed minute track with luminescent triangular markers on the beveled ring; stainless steel white painted bâton hands. 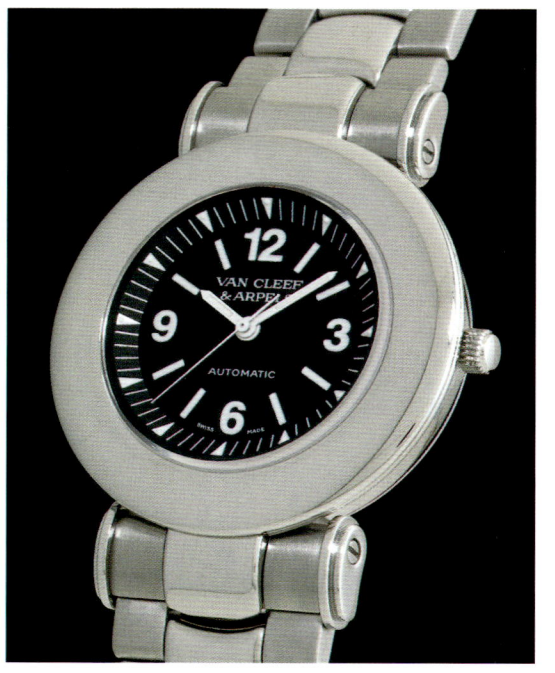
Bracelet: stainless steel, with central attachment, polished and brushed finish; fold-over safety clasp.
Price: 4'360 CHF.
Also available: leather strap 3'280 CHF; yellow gold leather strap and clasp 8'510 CHF, fold-over clasp 9'790 CHF, bracelet 18'700 CHF; white gold with 2 rows of brilliants on bezel, leather strap and 26'620 CHF, fold-over clasp 28'120 CHF, bracelet 38'300 CHF. All available with black or white dial and Arabic or Roman numerals.

VAN CLEEF & ARPELS

ROMA POWER RESERVE — REF. 535073/137005

Movement: mechanical, automatic winding, Eta 2892/A2 + Dubois Dépraz DD9040 power reserve module.
Functions: hour, minute, center second, power reserve.
Case: stainless steel, three-piece case (Ø 36.5 mm, thickness 8.5 mm); antireflective curved sapphire crystal; screw-down crown; case back attached by 6 screws; water-resistant to 3 atm.
Dial: white lacquered; skeletonized luminescent bâton markers and Arabic numerals; printed minute track with triangular markers on the beveled ring; luminescent stainless steel black painted bâton hands.
Indications: power reserve at 6.
Bracelet: stainless steel, with central attachment, polished and brushed finish; fold-over safety clasp.
Price: 5'940 CHF.
Also available: leather strap 4'840 CHF; rosé dial and luminescent markers; yellow gold, white dial and applied markers, leather strap 13'070 CHF, bracelet 21'980 CHF.

ROMA POWER RESERVE — REF. 135073/1391BD

The Roma collection, intended as a homage paid to the "eternal" town and its manifold artistic and cultural suggestions, materializes without compromises the vision of a sportsmanlike watch, typical for Van Cleef & Arpels. In this model nothing is left to hazard and everything respects the constructive and aesthetic canons of the Parisian House. Volumes are important. The bezel mightily frames the dial and the large horizontal lugs which match the traditional design of the central attachment. The whole, together elegant and attractive, since its first appearance met the favor of the public, for which reason this collection was recently enlarged by the new Plongeur and this Power Reserve. The photograph shows the version with 18 kt yellow gold case, white dial with applied markers, and crocodile leather strap with yellow gold fold-over clasp.
Price: 13'070 CHF.

LES CLASSIQUES "P.A. 49" — REF. 12101/051BN

Movement: mechanical, manual winding, extra-thin, Jaeger-LeCoultre caliber 839.
Functions: hour, minute.
Case: 18 kt yellow gold, two-piece case (Ø 30.5 mm, thickness 4.5 mm); flat sapphire crystal; central attachment; yellow gold crown; snap-on back.
Dial: white lacquered; printed bâton markers, Roman numerals and railway minute track; bâton hands stainless steel, black enameled.
Strap: crocodile leather; yellow gold clasp.
Price: 6'820 CHF.
Also available: lady's size (Ø 24.2, thickness 5.2 mm), with quartz movement, yellow gold: without brilliants: leather strap 3'760 CHF, bracelet 11'200 CHF; with a row of brilliants on bezel and bracelet 16'630 CHF; with 2 rows of brilliants on bezel and bracelet 22'090 CHF; with dial and bracelet in pavé brilliants 54'950 CHF.

LES CLASSIQUES "P.A. 49" — REF. 53101/069FF5

A consolidated style is still distinguishing the watch production signed by Van Cleef & Arpels who propose evolutions of classical themes, such as circle and straight line, that underline cases or the two segments from which bracelet or leather strap originate with the three characteristic "boules" which entered history "under the name of Van Cleef" attachment. As is compulsory for those who experience a watch as a "creation" to seize in each individual detail, Van Cleef & Arpels dedicate an extraordinary accuracy to bracelets, even in this full steel version (Ø 31, thickness 5.5 mm) with black dial and quartz movement. More precious versions with invisibly set diamonds are not lacking (such as the famous "Serti Mystérieux").
Price: 2'770 CHF.
Also available: leather strap 1'490 CHF; white dial; yellow gold, white dial, leather strap 4'070 CHF, bracelet 13'750 CHF.
With mechanical movement, manual winding, sapphire case back, steel, leather strap, white dial Ref. 51136/055BN, 1'670 CHF.

Zannetti

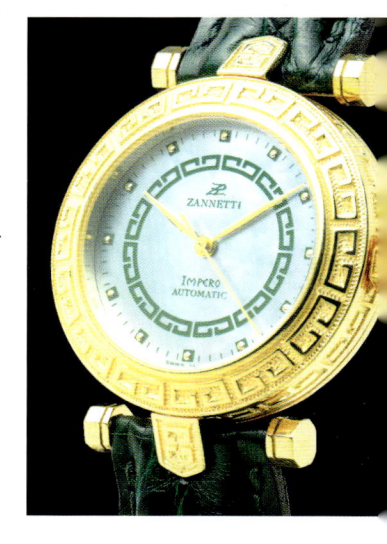

Step out of the crowd to build a new watch, where form seems to materialize as function, and originality, no longer an end to itself, becomes the discovery of a new aesthetic dimension. This, synthetically, is Zannetti's philosophy, one of the few independent master watchmakers left.

His research is essentially stylistic and remarkably blends the taste and the imagination of this erudite artist, who searches through the past for the potential to live better in the present with the manual craft and the tradition of the "classic" artisan. It becomes understandable, then, why each of his creations starts with a hand-drawn sketch (without the help of powerful CAD, so dear to today's builders) and that then turns into a colored drawing to become final diagrams to be used in production.

But his job hardly ends here: the case that is the result of the initial work is then finished, engraved and polished all by hand, and will then be enamelled and polished again. The movements, in turn, are carefully finished and made precious with hand-made components, as for example in the new Montgolfier whose gold rotor is the result of completely hand done engraving. We find the same is true of the dials, where mother of pears, gold, opals and enamels create unique visual experiences.

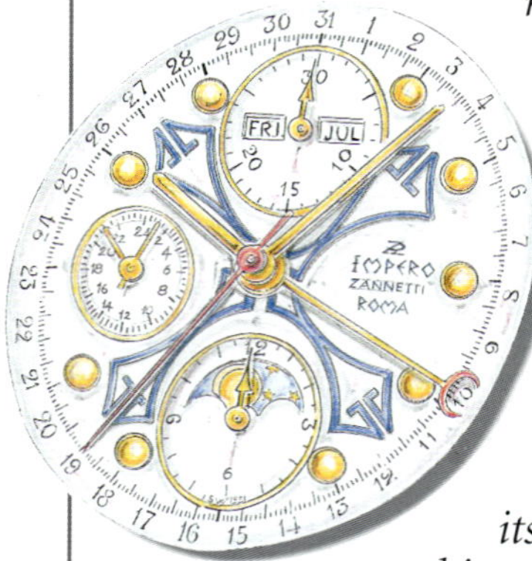

The result of all this research of line and material is the creation of a watch neither static nor cold in its formal beauty, but pleasantly warm and easy to wear. In his most famous collection, Impero, the inspirational motifs were drawn from the classic lines of the Roman Empire, with elements recalling columns, helmets, lances, to be made more evident by colored enamels or by the clever play of light and shadow that is created by the engraving.

Decidedly different but no less interesting is the "Rana Scrigno collection", derived from the artist's interest in that little beast that has become a symbol of distinction for him, or a charm, or simply the emblem of his production.

291

Modello Dafne Versione gioiello

Zannetti n° 711

Whatever the reason, this "frog" is successful among the feminine public throughout the world. Essential and innovative, Dafne is also dedicated to the feminine public, simple in the palladium version, sumptuous in gold and precious stones. Artistic inspiration becomes important again in La Montgolfier, a classic GMT as far as its functions go but absolutely new in its dial graphics. It is decidedly beautiful and balanced, and the dramatization of the terrestrial globe is its greatest strength. The last note regards the future. It should be rich in innovation; a new five-minute repeater is being prepared as well as a collection dedicated to the most famous racing car drivers.

Enameling has always been one among the most difficult but very impressive arts of classical jewellery. Yet technical difficulty and working time are always compensated by results exerting a great visual impact and intrinsically agreeable at touch. Thus, the Impero di Zannetti model, once it receives its enameled Greek fret, turns into a new watch that lives among color contrasts - between the purity of palladium, the richness of gold and the chromatic effects of blue, red or green enamels. The source of inspiration is clearly the world of ancient Rome, and the Greek fret characterizing this model acts like a frame on the case side and bezel. The same motif is met, though differently stylized, on the dial whose background is in mother-of-pearl or opal, according to the different versions. Thus background and decorations are, obviously, kept in accordance with the enamel color chosen.

Prices: Yellow gold with dial in blue mother-of-pearl and blue screen-prints; with dial in red mother-of-pearl and red screen-prints; with dial in green mother-of-pearl and green screen-prints; with dial in white mother-of-pearl and red or blue screen-prints; with opaline dial and blue mosaic (10,000 USD). Palladium with dial in white, blue, red, green mother-of-pearl and screen-prints of the same color as the dial; with dial in white mother-of-pearl and red or blue screen-prints; with dial in opal blue mosaic (4,600 USD); with white/blue or blue enameled case (5,000 USD).

292

The History

Riccardo Zannetti, designer, "fantasist", master watchmaker, lives and works in the heart of Rome. His is the story of a great passion for fine jewellery and watchmaking conceived at the start of the century when his grandfather, Carmine, master goldsmith and ardently interested in fine mechanics, began that extraordinary adventure in technical perfection and design that is today Zannetti. He was succeeded by Mario Zannetti, Riccardo's father, who was a professor of drawing and a world famous artist in his own right. The geometry that influences today's production is his, as is his love for the mechanical Great Complications.
Riccardo Zannetti inherits an artistic committment of a very high level and he adds to it his talent and the perfection of a great watchmaker. His workshop is a real artist's workshop, one of the few that has survived among those that for the last five hundred years spread the tradition of fine Italian watchmaking throughout the world.

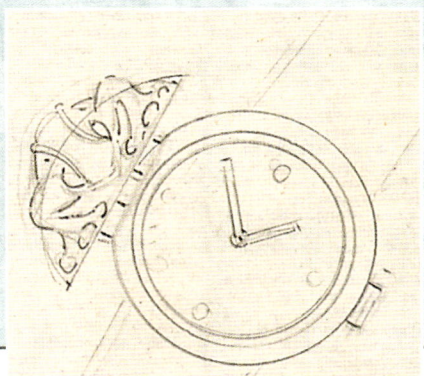

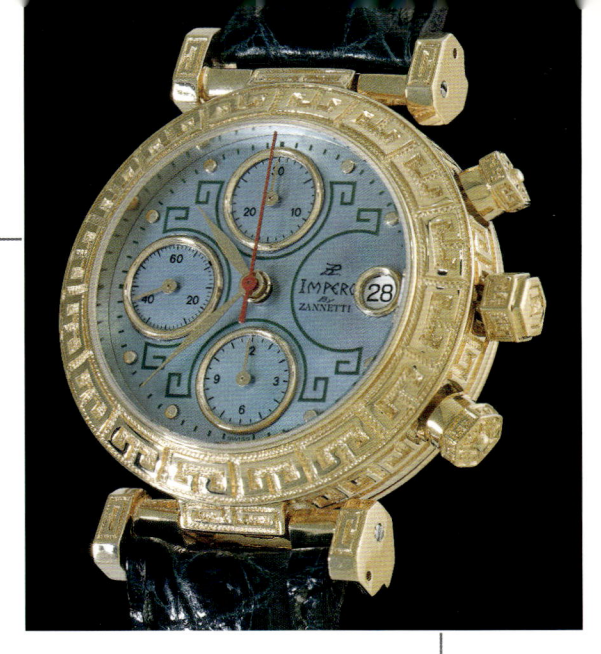

The Impero chronograph is an absolutely unique and matchless watch of its kind. Inspiration is drawn from the fascination of the art of ancient Rome, such as the symbol of the Greek fret framing the case side, the bezel and all the details, or the plumed helmet engraved on the bottom. This sumptuous watch combines the technical features typical of a chronograph with the characteristic values of jewels, where no element, even the smallest, is neglected. Its construction, entirely based on handicraftwork, allows only an absolutely limited edition (at most 150 pieces for each color); the production number is engraved at the center of the case bottom. Also the winding rotor is wholly hand-engraved, and this precious element is totally concealed by the case back, according to a use typical for the high Horlogerie. The photograph shows the solid gold version, sumptuous and appearing, with an entirely hand-engraved and hand-finished case, jointed lugs, dial in mother-of-pearl and secret logo engraved inside the sapphire crystal.
Prices: yellow gold with blue dial, matching green screen-print; with blue dial, matching red screen-print; white mother-of-pearl dial and red or blue screen-print; opaline blue mosaic dial (9,000 USD).

The last creation of Zannetti's is the Montgolfier model, a "traditional" GMT with arrow hand, whose resetting is done by using the crown, combined with a ring of raised 24 hours (soon also a version with engraved bezel will be available). All the constructive and aesthetic details refer to the specific function: on the blue or silvered enameled dial the globe is raised, while on the crown it is engraved; the wind rose is enameled at 6, while two large gold plated arrows (as the markers) give the sense of the rotating Earth. A touch of high craftsmanship is shown by the solid gold rotor, completely hand-engraved, representing a balloon suspended in the sky. Realized with a gold or palladium case, it will be produced in a limited series of 150 numbered pieces for each version.
Prices: yellow gold, blue dial (6,000 USD); palladium with silvered dial; with engraved bezel (3,400 USD). Edition limited to 150 pieces for each version.

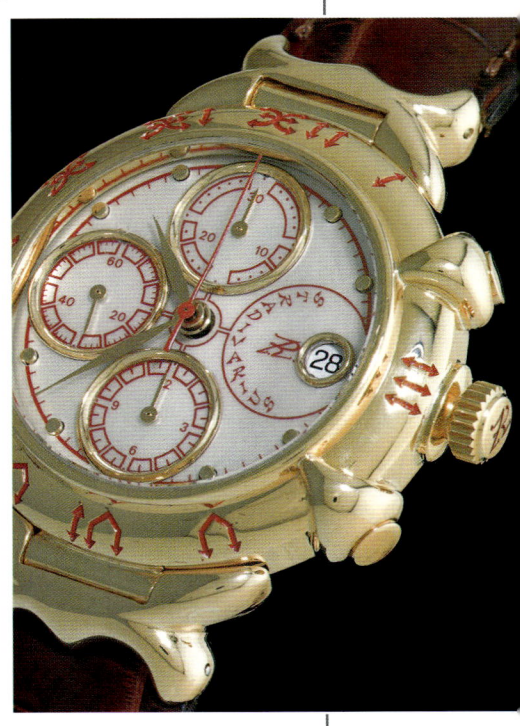

293

Zenith

The company that in 1969 produced the world's first automatic chronograph, the El Primero, is still improving on that technical triumph. It has launched three new watches incorporating the El Primero movement. One is called the Rainbow Fly-back. The fly-back function allows the wearer to time two events simultaneously or to time discrete events such as laps in a race. When the first event finishes, the wearer presses a button to stop the seconds hand and records the time. When he presses the button again, the hand "flies back" to where it would have been if it hadn't been stopped. He then presses the button again when the second event is finished. The 13-ligne, 31-jewel movement has a balance that vibrates 36,000 times per hour. The watch has a power reserve of more than 50 hours and complete date indicators. The case and bracelet are in steel and the watch has an integrated double folding clasp. It's water resistant to 100 meters. The second new El Primero model is a steel and black-dial, moonphase version of the Chronomaster, with a COSC-certified movement. The watch has a tachymeter scale and a transparent sapphire case back and is water resistant to 30 meters. It comes with an international five-year guarantee. The third is called the Class El Primero, a steel manual-wind model with power reserve of more than 50 hours. It has a cambered crystal, a tachymeter scale and see-through back and is water-resistant to 100 meters. Also new from Zenith is the rectangular-cased Port-Royal V Elite. It has a 11'''1/2, ultra thin (just 3.28 millimeters high) automatic movement that contains 26 jewels. The face is decorated with exaggerated Arabic numerals and has a date window at 6 o'clock and a seconds subdial at 9 o'clock. The watch has a power reserve of 50 hours and is water resistant to 30 meters. It's made of steel and comes with steel bracelet with integrated double-folding clasp or leather strap. In addition, there's the new Class Elite model, in ultra-thin automatic or manual-wind versions, with a 50-hour power serve. It comes in steel and has a domed dial, date window and small seconds hand.

The History

It was at Le Locle, one of the most famous centers of Swiss watchmaking, in the heart of the Canton of Neuchâtel that, in 1865 when he was only 22 years old, George Favre-Jacot founded the Manufacture. His already considerable experience plus his young age - and pioneering instinct - made him one of the first to understand the importance of the interchangeable quality of the components. This was a demonstration of his racing ahead which was to characterize his entire career and production. In his hands, the concept of watchmaking became less old fashioned, and he began to gather the good news carried in by the industrial age without losing the irreplaceable qualities lent by the human mind. And of course by able hands!

1875 - Many innovations at Zenith contribute to the evolution of the Maison and of the entire watchmaking sector. And in fact, after just ten years of its founding, Zenith gives work to 10% of the Le Locle population. **1900** - Each year there is a new success, up to winning the first prize at the Grand Prix of Paris. **1911** –The time has come for Favre-Jacot to take another leap ahead, and now is when the definitive name "Zenith" first appears on the important Le Locle plant that has its own foundry. From this moment on there is a continual series of awards and recognitions: 1,565 if not more from all over the world and up to the present, from the World's Fairs of Paris, Milan, Barcelona and Montreal, to the Diamond International of New York and the Golden Mercury of Rome, placing the Company in first place among the Houses awarded prizes by the chronometry Observatories. The "real" manufactures are few and far between, that is, those that are able to plan projects that can revolutionize their entire production. as instead Zenith has accustomed us to see. Introducing a new movement is an unusual occurrence, and yet many of the Manufacture's creations, taken one by one, could easily have represented a prestigious "una tantum" achievement in the entire history of many Houses. At this time, Zenith has three top of the line mechanical movements: El Primero, mechanical chronograph available with automatic or with manual winding; Elite, ultra-thin movement, and this too has either manual or automatic winding; the 5011K, manual winding movement for marine chronometers or precious pocket watches. In any case, however, from 1996 all its mechanical watches, even the simplest, have Zenith calibers .No mean trick, considering that at the present time the majority of watches depend upon a small number of specialized factories for their movements, and that almost all of these factories are owned by big watchmaking concerns that could, if they wanted to, practically control production. **1997** - Two important new watches: the sports chronograph Rainbow Fly-back and the Chronomaster Elite with power reserve. **1998** - Zenith is on the Internet (www.zenith-watches.ch). At the top of the new production are the Skeletons, result of the collaboration with Kurt Schaffo, the world's best interpreter of skeletonization of movements. The pink gold collection of the Chronomaster is introduced; Port Royal V is modernized and its aggressive design encloses the Manufacture's famous movements El Primero (chronograph) and the ultra-thin Elite. Zenith presents the ladies with Caprice, with round or square forms marked by Roman numerals engraved on the bezel. **1999** - Zenith ownership passes to the LVMH (Louis Vuitton Moët Hennessy) Group together with Chaumet, Ebel and TAG Heuer, creating one of the most important powers in world watchmaking.

ZENITH

PORT ROYAL V EL PRIMERO   REF. FLX 402.0450.400/21

Movement: mechanical, automatic winding, caliber Zenith El Primero 40.0.
Functions: hour, minute, small second, date, chronograph with 3 counters with a precision of 1/10 of a second.
Case: stainless steel, three-piece case (Ø 40 mm, thickness 13 mm); antireflective curved sapphire crystal; rectangular pushers; case back attached by 6 screws, displaying the movement through a sapphire crystal. Water-resistant to 5 atm.
Dial: black, tone on tone; counters decorated with concentric-circle pattern; applied faceted triangular markers; embossed white painted Arabic numerals; luminescent dots on the printed minute track; luminescent Modernes hands.
Indications: minute counter at 3, date between 4 and 5, hour counter at 6, small second at 9, center second counter, minute track with divisions for $1/5$ of a second.
Bracelet: stainless steel, polished and brushed finish; double fold-over safety clasp.
Price: 4'200 CHF.
Also available: silvered dial; leather strap 4'000 CHF.

PORT ROYAL V ELITE DUAL TIME   REF. FND 401.0450.682/21

Movement: mechanical, automatic winding, extra-thin caliber Zenith Elite 682.
Functions: hour, minute, small second, date, second time zone, 24-hour indication.
Case: stainless steel, three-piece case (Ø 38.5 mm, thickness 9.8 mm); antireflective curved sapphire crystal; rectangular pusher at 10 for the setting of a second time zone; case back attached by 6 screws, displaying the movement through a sapphire crystal. Water-resistant to 5 atm.
Dial: black, tone on tone; luminescent square markers on the printed minute track; applied faceted triangular 24-hour markers and printed Arabic 24-hour numerals; luminescent sword style hands.
Indications: date at 3, small second at 9, second time zone 24-hour display with arrow-point center hand.
Strap: crocodile leather; stainless steel clasp.
Price: 2'900 CHF.
Also available: silvered dial; with bracelet 3'100 CHF.

PORT ROYAL V ELITE   REF. FMC 401.0450.680/01

Movement: mechanical, automatic winding, caliber Zenith Elite 680.
Functions: hour, minute, small second, date.
Case: stainless steel, three-piece case (Ø 37 mm, thickness 8.50 mm); antireflective curved sapphire crystal; case back attached by 6 screws, displaying the movement through a sapphire crystal. Water-resistant to 5 atm.
Dial: silvered, tone on tone; zones decorated with concentric-circle pattern; applied faceted triangular markers; printed Arabic numerals; luminescent dots on the printed minute track; luminescent black painted Modernes hands.
Indications: date at 3, small second at 9.
Strap: crocodile leather; stainless steel clasp.
Price: 2'600 CHF.
Also available: black dial; with bracelet 2'800 CHF.

PORT ROYAL V ELITE CARRE   REF. FMH 402.0250.684/21

Movement: mechanical, automatic winding, caliber Zenith Elite 684.
Functions: hour, minute, small second, date.
Case: stainless steel, three-piece rectangular case (height 35 mm, width 31.1 mm, thickness 8.3 mm); antireflective curved sapphire crystal; case back attached by 4 screws, displaying the movement through a sapphire crystal. Water-resistant to 5 atm.
Dial: black, tone on tone; zones decorated with concentric-circle pattern; applied faceted triangular markers and printed Arabic numerals; luminescent dots on the printed minute track; luminescent Modernes hands.
Indications: date at 3, small second at 9.
Bracelet: stainless steel, polished and brushed finish; double fold-over safety clasp.
Price: 3'150 CHF.
Also available: silvered dial; leather strap 2'950 CHF.

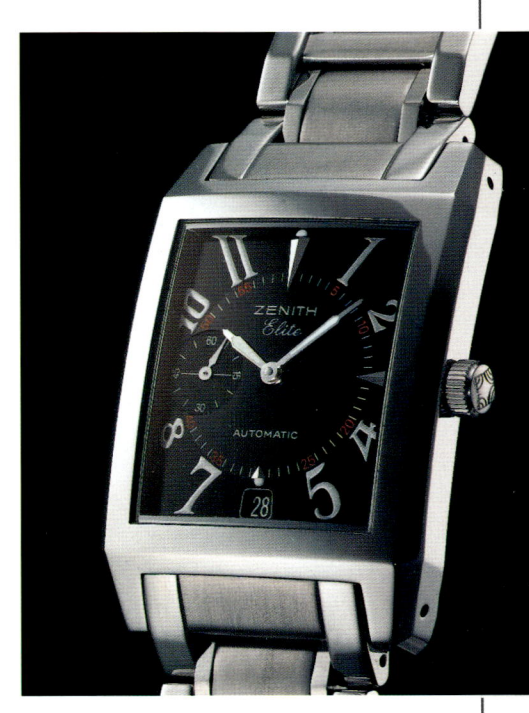

ZENITH

CHRONOMASTER EL PRIMERO   REF. FMY 402.0250.410

Movement: mechanical, automatic winding, caliber Zenith El Primero 41.0. Officially certified "chronometer" (C.O.S.C.). **Functions:** hour, minute, small second, full calendar (date, day, month, moon phase), chronograph with 3 counters with a precision of 1/10 of a second. **Case:** stainless steel, three-piece case (Ø 40, thickness 13.5 mm); curved sapphire crystal; 2 correctors on case side; crown and oval pushers steel; case back attached by 6 screws, displaying the movement through a sapphire crystal. Water-resistant to 3 atm. **Dial:** silvered; zones decorated with concentric-circle pattern; applied triangular markers and Roman numerals; printed minute track; Régate hands. **Indications:** month at 2, minute counter at 3, date between 4 and 5, hour counter and moon phase at 6, small second at 9, day at 10, center second counter, tachymeter scale, minute track with divisions for 1/5 of a second. **Bracelet:** stainless steel, polished and brushed finish; double fold-over safety clasp. **Price:** 6'400 CHF.
Also available: leather strap 6'100 CHF; steel, black dial, leather strap 6'100 CHF; yellow gold, white dial, leather strap 11'000 CHF; pink gold, silvered dial, leather strap 11'000 CHF; limited series, 18 kt gold rotor hand-chased, yellow gold, dial white lacquered, leather strap (produced on request).

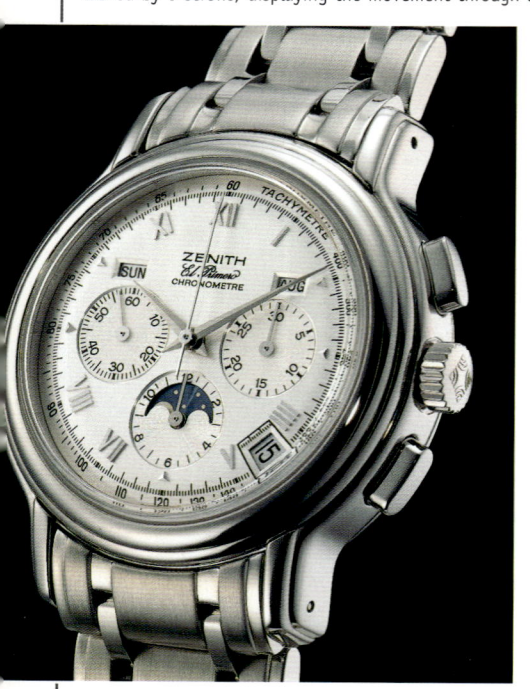

CHRONOMASTER EL PRIMERO   REF. LAZ 330.0240.400

Movement: mechanical, automatic winding, caliber Zenith El Primero 40.0. Officially certified "chronometer" (C.O.S.C.). **Functions:** hour, minute, small second, date, chronograph with 3 counters with precision a 1/10 of a second. **Case:** 18 kt yellow gold, three-piece case (Ø 40 mm, thickness 13.5 mm); curved sapphire crystal; gold crown and oval pushers; case back attached by 6 screws, displaying the movement through a sapphire crystal. Water-resistant to 3 atm. **Dial:** silvered, engine turned (guilloché) in the central part and brushed finish on the hour ring, bombé; zones engine turned (guilloché) in the central part and brushed finish on the ring; applied yellow gold Arabic numerals; printed minute track; gold leaf style hands (coloring by galvanization). **Indications:** minute counter at 3, date between 4 and 5, hour counter at 6, small second at 9, center second counter, tachymeter scale, minute track with divisions for 1/5 of a second. **Strap:** crocodile leather; yellow gold clasp. **Price:** 9'050 CHF.
Also available: with gold dial 9'250 CHF; stainless steel, smooth dial blue or white or silvered engine turned (guilloché) 4'750 CHF.

CHRONOMASTER ELITE "HW"   REF. LAX 317.0240.655

Movement: mechanical, manual winding, extra-thin caliber Zenith Elite 655. Officially certified "chronometer" (C.O.S.C.). **Functions:** hour, minute, small second, date, power reserve. **Case:** 18 kt pink gold, three-piece case (Ø 36 mm, thickness 8 mm); curved sapphire crystal; pink gold crown; snap-on back. Water-resistant to 3 atm. **Dial:** silvered, engine turned (guilloché) in the central part and brushed finish on the hour ring; applied pink gold triangular markers and Arabic numerals; pink gold leaf style hands. **Indications:** power reserve between 1 and 2, date between 4 and 5, small second at 9. **Strap:** crocodile leather; pink gold clasp. **Price:** 6'350 CHF. International five-year guarantee.
Also available: in yellow gold (same price); platinum 9'750 CHF.

CHRONOMASTER ELITE   REF. BYX 30.0240.670/31

Movement: mechanical, automatic winding, extra-thin caliber Zenith Elite 670. 18 kt gold rotor. Officially certified "chronometer" (C.O.S.C.). **Functions:** hour, minute, center second, date. **Case:** 18 kt yellow gold, three-piece case (Ø 36 mm, thickness 8 mm), numbered; curved sapphire crystal; yellow gold crown; snap-on back displaying the movement through a sapphire crystal. Water-resistant to 3 atm. **Dial:** white; applied yellow gold Roman numerals; printed minute track; bâton gold hands. **Indications:** date between 4 and 5. **Strap:** crocodile leather; yellow gold clasp. **Price:** 5'550 CHF.

ZENITH

RAINBOW EL PRIMERO "FLY-BACK"   REF. FMZ 402.0470.405/25

Movement: mechanical, automatic winding, caliber Zenith El Primero 40.5.
Functions: hour, minute, small second, date, chronograph with 3 counters with a precision of 1/10 of a second and "fly-back" feature.
Case: stainless steel, three-piece brushed case (Ø 40, thickness 12.5 mm); flat sapphire crystal with antireflective treatment on both sides; bi-directional turning bezel (60 clicks), black enameled with complete scale useful as additional minute counter (both traditional and count-back) and luminescent pointer; crown with case protection; graduated screwed-on case back. Water-resistant to 10 atm.
Dial: black; luminescent Arabic numerals; printed minute track; luminescent white painted sword style hands.
Indications: oversized minute counter at 3, date between 4 and 5, hour counter at 6, small second at 9, center second counter, minute track with divisions for 1/5 of a second, telemeter scale on the beveled ring.
Bracelet: stainless steel, brushed finish; double fold-over safety clasp
Price: 4'300 CHF.
Also available: stainless steel, black dial with colored minute counter, leather strap, fold-over clasp 4'050 CHF, bracelet 4'300 CHF.

RAINBOW ELITE   REF. FKD 402.0471.670/74

Movement: mechanical, automatic winding, extra-thin caliber Zenith Elite 670. Officially certified "chronometer" (C.O.S.C.).
Functions: hour, minute, center second, date.
Case: stainless steel, three-piece case (Ø 39 mm, thickness 10 mm); flat sapphire crystal; counter-clockwise turning bezel, with black aluminum ring, marker with a luminescent dot and graduated scale, useful for the calculation of diving times; screw-down crown with case protection; screwed-on case back. Water-resistant to 20 atm.
Dial: mustard yellow; luminescent Arabic numerals; printed minute track; luminescent black painted sword style hands.
Indications: date between 4 and 5, perimeter minute track and 5 minute numerals on the beveled ring.
Bracelet: steel; double fold-over safety clasp.
Price: 2'750 CHF.
Also available: stainless steel, white or black dial, applied markers, bezel with black aluminum ring (same price); yellow gold & stainless steel, white or blue dial, applied markers, bezel with blue aluminum ring 4'100 CHF.

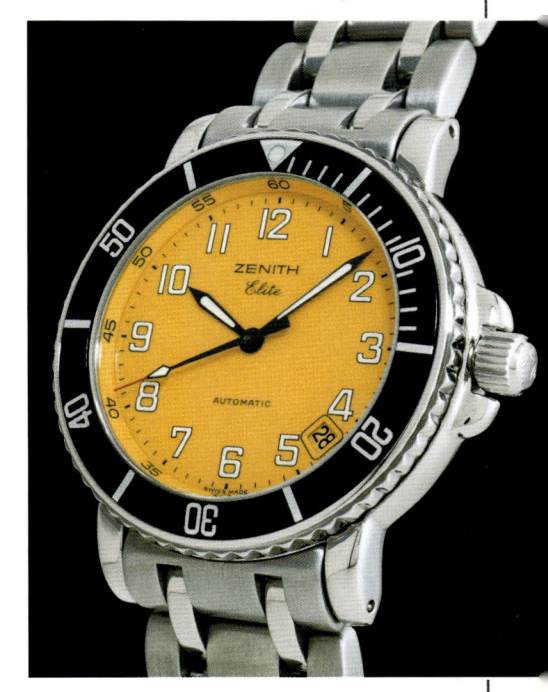

CLASS EL PRIMERO   REF. FHR 402.0500.400/01

Movement: mechanical, automatic winding, caliber Zenith El Primero 40.0.
Functions: hour, minute, small second, date, chronograph with 3 counters with a precision of 1/10 of a second.
Case: stainless steel, three-piece case (Ø 38 mm, thickness 12 mm); brushed lugs; curved sapphire crystal; oval pushers; snap-on back displaying the movement through a sapphire crystal. Water-resistant to 10 atm.
Dial: silvered, slightly bombé; additional zones decorated with concentric-circle pattern; applied bâton markers; printed minute track; luminescent bâton hands. **Indications:** minute counter at 3, date between 4 and 5, hour counter at 6, small second at 9, center second counter, tachymeter scale, minute track with divisions for 1/5 of a second.
Bracelet: stainless steel, polished and brushed finish; double fold-over safety clasp.
Price: 3'650 CHF.
Also available: black dial; leather strap 3'300 CHF.

CLASS EL PRIMERO CARRE   REF. FGI 401.0425.400/51

Movement: mechanical, automatic winding, caliber Zenith El Primero 40.0.
Functions: hour, minute, small second, date, chronograph with 3 counters with a precision of 1/10 of a second.
Case: stainless steel, three-piece case, square shape (height 35 mm, width 36.5 mm, thickness 12.2 mm); curved sapphire crystal; olive pushers; case back attached by 4 screws. Water-resistant to 3 atm.
Dial: bright blue; applied pointed markers (Roman numeral 12); printed minute track; bâton hands.
Indications: minute counter at 3, date between 4 and 5, hour counter at 6, small second at 9, center second counter, tachymeter scale, minute track with divisions for 1/5 of a second.
Strap: crocodile leather; jointed coupling with removable lugs; stainless steel clasp.
Price: 4'100 CHF.
Also available: with white, black or coppered dial.

297

Addresses

AHCI, Académie Horlogère
des Créateurs Indépendants
36, Quai du Seujet
1201 Geneva, Switzerland
Tel: +41 (22) 732 43 74

A. LANGE & SÖHNE
Lange Uhren GmbH
Altenberger Strasse, 15, Postfach 45
01768 Glashütte in Sachsen, Germany
Tel: +49 (35053) 48541

AUDEMARS PIGUET
Audemars Piguet & Cie SA
1348 Le Brassus, Switzerland
Tel: +41 (21) 845 14 00

BAUME & MERCIER
Baume & Mercier
61, Route de Chêne
1211 Geneva 29, Switzerland
Tel: +41 (22) 707 31 31

BEDAT
Bedat & Co.
41a, Route de Chêne
1208 Geneva, Switzerland
Tel: +41 (22) 718 01 88

BLANCPAIN
Blancpain SA
Chemin de l'Etang, 6
1094 Paudex, Switzerland
Tel: +41 (21) 796 36 36

BOUCHERON
Les Montres Boucheron SA
15, Rue de la Confédération
1204 Geneva, Switzerland
Tel: +41 (22) 818 45 10

BREGUET
Montres Breguet SA
1344 L'Abbaye, Switzerland
Tel: 41 (21) 841 90 90

BREITLING
Breitling SA
Case Postale 1132
2540 Grenchen, Switzerland
Tel: +41 (32) 654 54 54

BULGARI
Bulgari Time SA
34, Rue de Monruz
2008 Neuchâtel, Switzerland
Tel: +41 (32) 722 78 78

CARTIER
Cartier International
51, Rue Pierre Charron
75008 Paris, France
Tel: +33 (1) 40 74 62 07

CASA DAMIANI
Casa Damiani S.p.A.
Viale Santuario, 46
15048 Valenza, Italy
Tel: +39 (0131) 92 96 11

CEDRIC JOHNER
Cédric Johner SA
13, Chemin de la Montagne
1224 Chêne-Bougeries, Geneva, Switzerland

CHAUMET
Chaumet International SA
12, Place Vendôme
75001 Paris, France
Tel: +33 (1) 44 77 24 00

CHOPARD
Chopard & Cie SA
8, Rue de Veyrot
1217 Meyrin-Geneva 2, Switzerland
Tel: 41 (22) 719 31 31

CONCORD
Concord Watch Company SA
35, Rue de Nidau
2501 Bienne, Switzerland
Tel: 41 (32) 329 34 00

DANIEL JEANRICHARD
Daniel JeanRichard
Cernil-Antoine, 14
2301 La Chaux-de-Fonds, Switzerland
Tel: +41 (32) 925 70 50

DANIEL ROTH
Daniel Roth SA
18/20, Rue Plantamour
1201 Geneva, Switzerland
Tel: +41 (22) 716 09 06

DE GRISOGONO
de Grisogono Genève
106, Rue du Rhône
1204 Geneva, Switzerland
Tel: +41 (22) 317 10 80

EBEL
Ebel SA
113, Rue de la Paix
2300 La Chaux-de-Fonds, Switzerland
Tel: +41 (32) 912 31 23

EBERHARD & CO.
Eberhard & Co. SA
Rue du Jura, 34
2500 Bienne, Switzerland
Tel: +41 (32) 342 51 41

EUROPEAN COMPANY WATCH
R.C. Time S.r.l.
Via Fatebenefratelli, 30
20121 Milan, Italy
Tel. +39 (02) 659 22 88

FRANCK MULLER
Franck Muller Genève SA
22, Rue de Malagny
1294 Genthod, Switzerland
Tel: 41 (22) 959 88 88

FRED
Fred Joaillier SA
6, Rue Royale
75008 Paris, France
Tel: +33 (1) 53 45 15 36

GERALD GENTA
Gérald Genta SA
18/20, Rue Plantamour
1201 Geneva, Switzerland
Tel: +41 (22) 716 09 06

GIRARD-PERREGAUX
Girard-Perregaux SA
1, Place Girardet
2301 La Chaux-de-Fonds, Switzerland
Tel: +41 (32) 911 33 33

GLASHÜTTE ORIGINAL
Glashütte Uhrenbetrieb GmbH
Altenbergerstrasse, 1
01768 Glashütte in Sachsen, Germany
Tel: +49 (35053) 460

HUBLOT
Montres MDM Fabrication SA
Route de Divonne, 44
1260 Nyon 2, Switzerland
Tel: +41 (22) 362 19 70

I.W.C.
International Watch Co. Ltd.
Baumgertenstrasse, 15
8201 Schaffhausen, Switzerland
Tel: +41 (52) 635 65 65

JAEGER-LECOULTRE
Jaeger-leCoultre SA
Rue de la Golisse, 8
1347 Le Sentier, Switzerland
Tel: +41 (21) 845 02 02

OFFICINE PANERAI
Vendôme Italia S.p.A.
Via Ludovico di Breme, 45
20156 Milan, Italy
Tel: +39 (02) 302 61

OMEGA
Omega SA
Rue Stampfli, 96
2500 Bienne 4, Switzerland
Tel: +41 (32) 343 90 23

PARMIGIANI FLEURIER
Parmigiani Fleurier SA
Rue du Temple, 11
2114 Fleurier, Switzerland
Tel: +41 (32) 862 66 30

PATEK PHILIPPE
Patek Philippe SA
Chemin du Pont du Centenaire, 141
1211 Geneva 2, Switzerland
Tel: +41 (22) 884 20 20

PAUL PICOT
Paul Picot SA
6, Rue du Doubs
2340 Le Noirmont, Switzerland
Tel: +41 (32) 953 15 31

PIAGET INTERNATIONAL SA
61, Route de Chêne
1208 Geneva, Switzerland
Tel: +41 (22) 707 32 32

RAYMOND WEIL
Raymond Weil SA
36/38, Av. Eugène-Lance, P.O.Box 1569
1211 Geneva, Switzerland
Tel: +41 (22) 884 00 55

ROGER DUBUIS
Sogem SA
12, Avenue Industrielle
1227 Geneva, Switzerland
Tel: +41 (22) 827 49 49

ROLEX
Montres Rolex SA
3/7, Rue François Dussaud
1211 Geneva, Switzerland
Tel: +41 (22) 308 22 00

SCATOLA DEL TEMPO
SCS & Co. S.r.l.
Via dei Mille, 17
23891 Barzanò, Italy
Tel: +39 (039) 921 14 81

TAG HEUER
TAG Heuer SA
14a, Avenue des Champs-Montants
2074 Marin, Switzerland
Tel: 41 (32) 755 60 00

ULYSSE NARDIN
Ulysse Nardin SA
3, Rue du Jardin
2400 Le Locle, Switzerland
Tel: +41 (32)) 931 56 77

VACHERON CONSTANTIN
Vacheron Constantin SA
1, Rue des Moulins
1204 Geneva, Switzerland
Tel: +41 (22) 310 32 27

VAN CLEEF & ARPELS
Start, Style & Art SA
50, Avenue de la Praille
1211 Geneva, Switzerland
Tel: +41 (22) 343 95 20

VERSACE PRECIUS ITEMS
G.V. Gioielli SA
86 bis, Route de Frontenex
1208 Geneva, Switzerland
Tel: +41 (22) 737 07 77

VINCENT CALABRESE
Vica SARL
19a, Boulevard de Grancy
1006 Lausanne, Switzerland
Tel: +41 (21) 617 08 34

ZANNETTI
Zannetti
Via Monte d'Oro, 19
00186 Rome, Italy
Tel: +39 (06) 687 66 51

ZENITH
Zenith International SA
34, Rue des Billodes
2400 Le Locle, Switzerland
Tel: +41 (32) 930 62 62